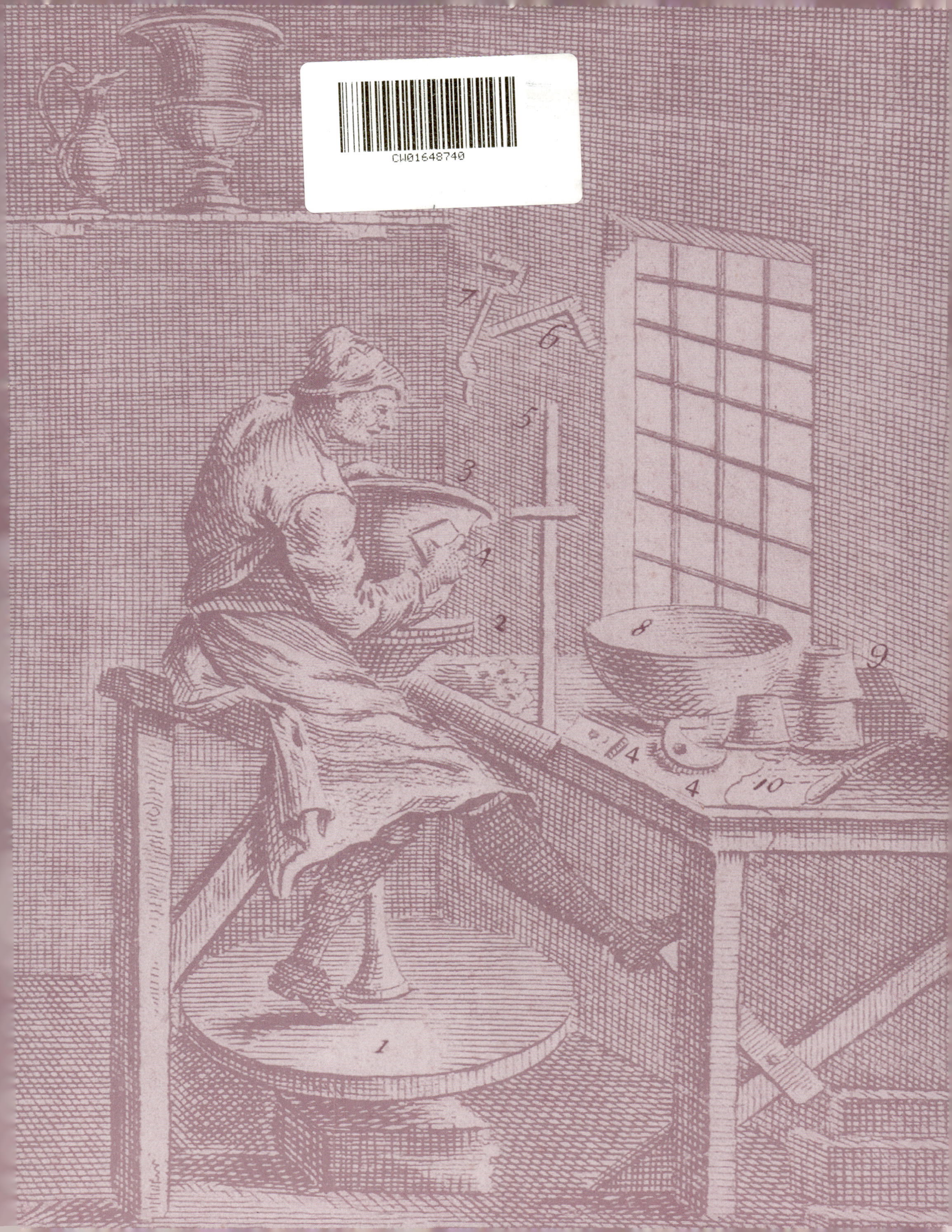
7
6
5
3
4
2
8
9
4
4
10
1

Irish
DELFTWARE
an illustrated history

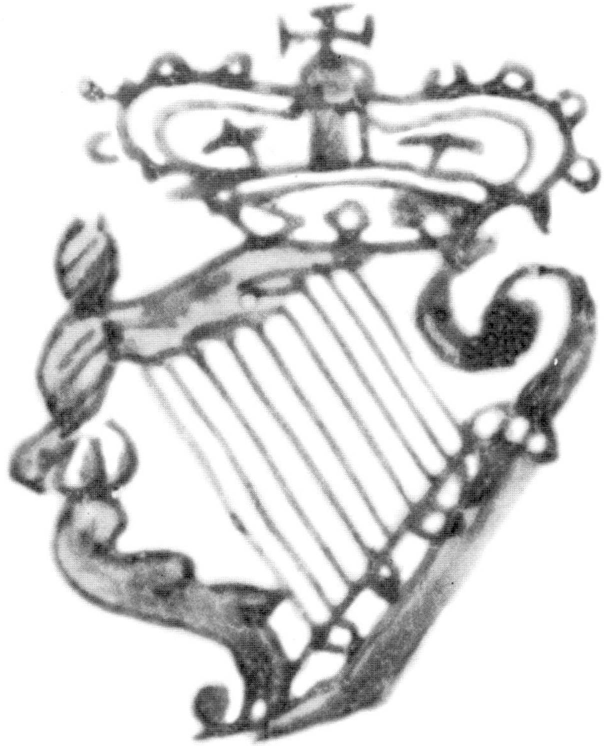

by Peter Francis

JHP

First Produced in 2000 by

Jonathan Horne Publications
66c Kensington Church Street
London W8 4BY

ISBN 0 9533112 2 8

Produced and designed by Jonathan Horne
Created and printed by David Hewitt

CONTENTS

PREFACE AND ACKNOWLEDGEMENTS

> *'We can record no history of Pottery in Ireland: for beyond the manufacture of coarse-glazed brown ware, garden pots, &c., no manufacture of earthenware or porcelain deserving the name has ever been carried on in this country'*
>
> Catalogue of the Irish Industrial Exhibition, 1853 [1]

This remark, written just eighty years or so after Ireland's delftware industry ceased, shows there was a time when some of the best of the early Irish potters were almost entirely forgotten. When we contrast this statement with the evidence presented in this book, we gain a clear indication of just how much has been learned in over a century of study.

As late as 1874, the pioneering ceramic historian William Chaffers could find *'no history of the manufactories of pottery in Ireland ... even during the 18th-century we have been unable to find scarcely any record of them'*.[2] Nonetheless, some important evidence was beginning to emerge. Hugh Owen published Henry Delamain's letters in 1873, (Appendix II), and the Belfast delftware shoe dated *'1724'* **(Fig.7)** was illustrated for the first time by George Benn in 1877.[3]

As in so many areas of Irish decorative arts, it fell to M.S. Dudley Westropp of the National Museum of Ireland to make the most outstanding early contributions. The two monographs that Westropp produced on Irish ceramics in 1913 and 1935 still represent the essential core of our documentary information on the Irish potteries.[4] Some of Westropp's manuscripts survive, and it is interesting to discover the role played by two of his principal correspondents at this time; Aubrey Toppin in England, (who had worked at the National Museum during the early 1900s), and the distinguished London dealer, Louis Gautier.[5]

Following a lull of several decades, our understanding of Irish delftwares improved dramatically in 1971, when Rosc Teoranta and the Irish Georgian Society collaborated in organising the first exhibition of Irish Delftware at Castletown House near Dublin.[6] The purpose of this exhibition was *'to bring together examples of all of the known documentary pieces,* [to provide] *an opportunity for comparisons to be made'*. As it turned out, the organisers succeeded in gathering a wonderful range of outstanding pieces from private and public collections in Ireland, England and America. The exhibition was equally successful in achieving its stated aim of *'stimulating further research on what is a comparatively neglected subject'*. However, it was to be the exhibition catalogue, written by Michael Archer and Patrick Hickey, that came to represent its most lasting and tangible contribution. Archer supplemented this work a few years later with a slim volume entitled *'Irish Pottery and Porcelain'*, and together these two publications have served as the standard texts on Irish delftware. There have been other notable contributions in recent years, particularly those of Ada Longfield, (Leask), and Mairead Dunlevy of the National Museum.[6]

The present book grew out of a request from Jonathan Horne for a catalogue to accompany his exhibition of Irish delftware, to be shown on his premises in London from October - December 2000, and at the Hunt Museum in Limerick from January - March 2001. Until now, my own publications on Irish ceramics have focussed on the recent discoveries in Belfast, and so the original intention was simply to graft the new information concerning the Belfast potteries onto previous, published accounts of

Dublin delftware. Once started, however, it soon became evident that a substantial quantity of new information has come to light in recent years. My first and most heartfelt debt of gratitude is therefore owed to Jonathan Horne, for continuing to support this study, even as the catalogue inexorably grew into a book, and finally into quite a large book. The work would have been impossible without Jonathan's absolutely solid support, encouragement and editorial skills.

I am also particularly grateful to Michael Archer, both for sharing his exceptional understanding of the subtleties of Irish delftware, and for so generously making available all of his own research material for this book. Without his vital contribution, it would have been impossible to even contemplate such a comprehensive study, and many of the most valuable illustrations would quite simply have been unobtainable. David Halliday's assistance is also gratefully acknowledged. His interest in the subject acted as the initial spark that first prompted the exhibition, and his continued support throughout has come to represent a significant contribution.

Other individuals have been similarly generous with their research. John Austin very kindly allowed me to study his detailed notes and photographs of the *'coarsely-painted'* excavated wares from Colonial Williamsburg, which proved crucial in evaluating this new and intriguing group. The Knight of Glin not only discovered the Michael Stritch letter concerning the Limerick pottery, but also brought the first known painting by Peter Shee to my attention. The Knight has been entirely supportive of every aspect of this project since the very beginning, and I am particularly appreciative of the various efforts that he has made on my behalf. Madame Noël Sauzey, Professor Louis Cullen and Monsieur Alain Braastad were also generous in providing the portraits of James Delamain and Marie Ranson. Dr. Jean Agnew, who discovered the Belfast Potthouse letter of 1706, came to adopt a role comparable to that of a Samaritan, enduring many long telephone calls as we tried to disentangle the family relationships of David Smith and John Chambers. I am happy, at long last, to be in a position to acknowledge the help that Dr. Agnew has given on many occasions, both in the past and within the last few weeks.

Some of the research that appears in this book, relating to the Belfast Potthouse particularly, is now several years old, but I would feel remiss if I did not express my gratitude to those who were involved at that time. Dr. Tom McNeill, Maura Mulholland and Tom McErlean all shared in the excitement of those early discoveries, and the assistance of Nick Brannon and Dr. Chris Lynn of the Environment and Heritage Service was invaluable. Much of the documentary research that followed could not have been carried out without the support of Professor Brian Walker, Linda Canning and many others at the Institute of Irish Studies, Queen's University, where the *'Belfast Potteries Project'*, as it became known, was subsequently conducted.

Many staff in the various Irish museums have also given generously of their time and knowledge to assist in this publication, particularly Kim Mawhinney, Elizabeth McCrum, Trevor Parkhill and Mike Robinson of the Ulster Museum in Belfast; Ciaran Macgonigal, Fiona Davern and John McCormack of the Hunt Museum in Limerick; and Deirdre Power and Mairead Dunlevy of the National Museum in Dublin. It is a particularly pleasant duty to acknowledge the help that Mairead has given me during the past eighteen years, since my work on Irish ceramics first began.

Other individuals have provided assistance of various kinds and at various times, for which I am also grateful. These include George Stacpoole in Limerick, Dr. Nessa Roche and Yvonne Healey in Dublin, Evelyne Miller and Jim Cullen in Wexford, Garry Atkins, John Sandon, Anton Gabszewicz, Tim Holdaway and Simon Westman in London, Margaret Macfarlane and Neil Hyman of the Hampshire County Museum Service, Julia Poole of the Fitzwilliam Museum in Cambridge and George Haggarty in Edinburgh. David Hewitt has spent many long hours, with great patience, transforming my disjointed manuscripts into a presentable tome, and the financial contribution made towards the publication costs by Mr. M. Stern, General Manager of Klinge Pharma & Co., Killorglin, Co. Kerry is gratefully acknowledged. In reality, the work would have been impossible without the help of many other individual contributors, and I am grateful to every one of them, but I would like to direct particular thanks towards the various private collectors in Ireland and overseas who prefer to remain anonymous.

I have saved the last paragraph for four individuals whose support has meant most in a personal sense. Nicholas and Susan Mosse have helped since this project began, whether in explaining how a pot might have been made, or in driving about the country to look at Dublin delftware. Their involvement has turned many tasks that could so easily have been chores into fun. My mentor in antiques, Professor Mike Baillie, made a gallant and valuable contribution by casting his informed eye over my manuscripts as they rolled off the press, but my friend and partner, Rosie Agar, drew the shortest straw. Not the least of Rosie's contributions was in keeping our shop open, week after week without a break, as I continued to work on the text. For this, and for much more besides, my thanks are not enough.

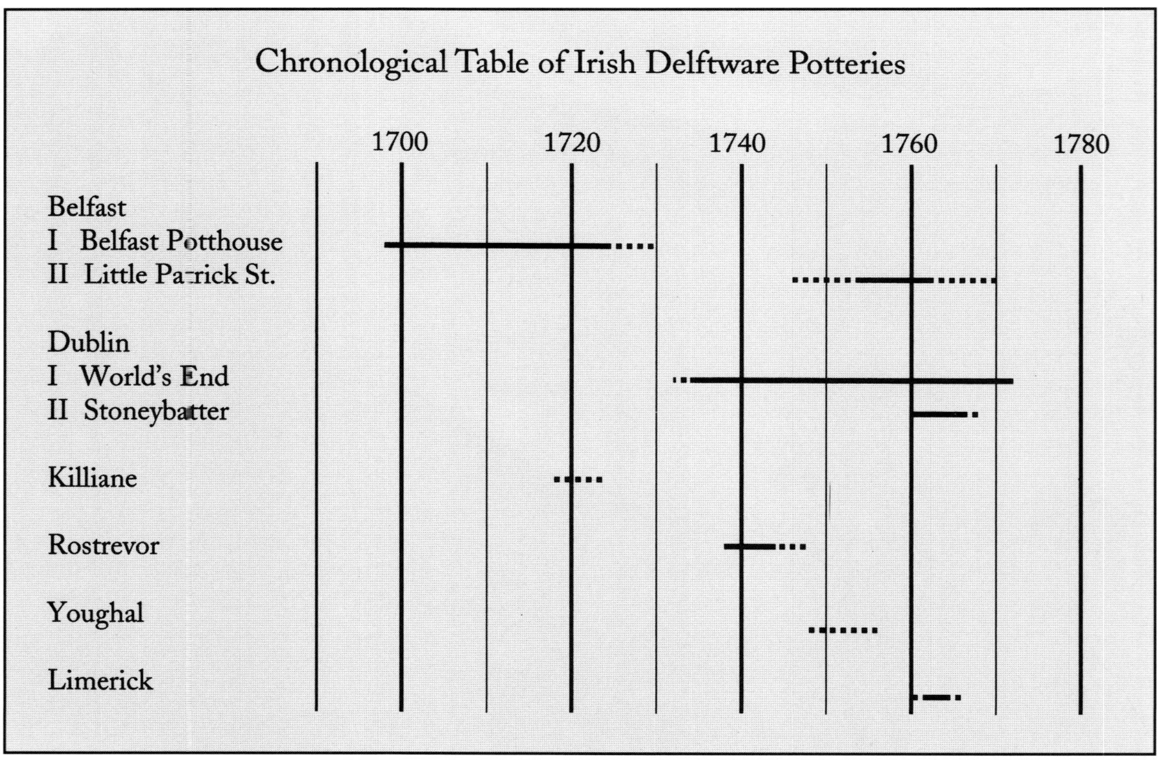

INTRODUCTION

The word *'delf'* is still occasionally heard in Ireland, describing the common crockery employed in most households for everyday use. Tradition holds that such wares were considered inferior to the fine-quality *'china'* that was reserved for special occasions.

Both of these terms, *'delf'* and *'china'*, date from the seventeenth and eighteenth centuries, when true, translucent porcelains were only made in China and Japan, and hence were prohibitively expensive for most families. From 1697 onwards, the one locally produced alternative to *'china'* in Ireland was *'delft'* or *'delftware'*, which although frequently decorated to imitate *'china'*, was in reality an altogether different material. Delftware was not translucent. It was also heavier, thicker and less durable than *'china'*, but because it was clean, affordable and easily available, delftware became the most popular whiteware of the early eighteenth century. Henry Delamain's achievements of the 1750s probably mark the high point of delftware manufacture in Ireland, but just a few years later, by about 1762, there were already signs that delftware's popularity would not endure'.[7] With the development of new and improved white ceramics in England, most notably the *'creamwares'* marketed with great success by Josiah Wedgwood, delftware manufacture ultimately ceased in Ireland towards the end of 1771.

Although the word *'delf'* describes all manner of crockery, the term *'delftware'* is in fact a specific, local term, describing one particular type of pottery known technically as a *'tin-glazed earthenware'*. During the eight hundred years or so since it was first introduced to Europe from the Near East, tin-glazed earthenware has come to assume many guises. In Italy, for example, it is called *'maiolica'*, in France *'faience'*, in Spain *'faenza'*, in Holland *'delft'* and in England and Ireland *'delftware'*. Even within the British Isles, tin-glazed earthenware has had many names - the terms *'Gallyware'*, *'White Ware'*, *'Painted Ware'*, *'Holland Ware'* and (in Scotland) *'Lame Porcelain'* were all employed during the seventeenth-century. These were gradually displaced by the more familiar *'Blue and White Earthen Ware'* or *'Delft Ware'* during the first half of the eighteenth-century, as the town of Delft in Holland grew in reputation as a distinguished centre of tin-glaze manufacture. Yet it is important to remember, especially when confronted with this confusing array of terminology, that the pottery itself - tin-glazed earthenware - remained essentially the same everywhere. A delftware potter in Dublin used the same technology and ingredients as his counterparts making faience in France or maiolica in Italy. There were of course local variations in the materials available, but most of the differences in character and style derive principally from regional tastes, and from the skills of the potters themselves.

The techniques of delftware manufacture arrived in the British Isles with Huguenot refugees from Flanders during the 1560s, who initially settled at Norwich, close to the clay deposits in East Anglia.[8] By 1571, the first delftware pottery had been established in London, where most of the industry was to remain for the next century or more. London was by far the largest marketplace for delftware in the country, so it is perhaps natural that most of the potters should have settled there.[9] Another crucial consideration, however, was the fact that sources of delftware clay also lay nearby, in Norfolk, Suffolk and (from 1681) Kent.[10] By the middle of the seventeenth-century only one delftware pottery operated outside of London, at Brislington on the outskirts of Bristol - and even here the potters would almost certainly have relied on clays brought from East Anglia.

This comparatively small industry began to change dramatically during the 1670s and 1680s, with the growth of transatlantic trade.[11] In 1676, four delftware potteries were working in London. Less than a decade later, by 1684, the number of potteries had doubled to eight, with new ventures opening up for the first time towards the west of the city, at Lambeth and Putney. Coinciding with this rapid growth in London, Bristol's second pottery was established at Temple Back in 1683, and much farther afield, attempts were made to establish the first delftware pottery in North America, at Burlington, New Jersey in 1684.[12] Yet even during this period of rapid expansion there appears to have been no attempt to establish a delftware pottery in Ireland, (not even in Dublin, which then was the second largest city in the British Isles). Delftware potters were not to arrive in Ireland until a decade later, by which time the industry had changed again.

War with France disrupted many normal patterns of trade from 1689 onwards so that, by the early 1690s, London's delftware industry was experiencing recession for the first time.[13] In 1693, a number of potters seem to have been made redundant at the Montague Close delftware pottery in Southwark, as they took the unprecedented step of advertising their services to anyone possessing the funds necessary for building a delftware pottery;

> *'Any Gentlemen that are desirous to be Concerned in the Art of Pot making, and Painting of fine Earthen Ware, curiously imitating the Holland Ware, and are willing to set up a Pot-house, may hear of Artificers (that will perform the same on reasonable Terms) at Mr. Downings at the Plume of Feathers at St Mary Overies, Southwark.'*[14]

As we discover presently, (p.11), one of the Montague Close potters, Matthew Garner, seems to have been born in Belfast originally, but even he made no attempt to return home when he was put out of work. This advertisement seems to have failed to attract a financial backer, yet rather than move home, Garner instead remained in London to establish a different kind of pottery, for the manufacture of stoneware.[15] At that time, the stoneware trade was entirely dominated by just one individual, the celebrated potter John Dwight. Other potters clearly had the same idea as Garner, as he found himself in competition with two further stoneware potteries that also had designs on Dwight's share of the market.[16] As events transpired, Dwight fought his corner forcefully with heavy-handed and costly litigation. Within a few years, all three of these aspiring competitors were forced out of business, (and two of them moved subsequently to Ireland).[17]

From 1695, the problems experienced by English potters were made considerably worse by the *'Excise Act'*, imposed by Parliament as a temporary, tax-raising measure to help pay for the protracted Jacobite wars.[18] With recession already affecting the delftware industry in London, and other avenues of pottery manufacture closed, it is at about this time we begin to see the first attempts to establish delftware potteries in other parts of the British Isles. The principal difficulty for these more remote potteries, located hundred of miles from the known clay deposits in East Anglia and Kent, was that their success was contingent upon the discovery of new, independent sources of delftware clay. (The delftware pottery in New Jersey, for example, clearly failed because the potters there could *'finde noe Clay in the Country that* [would] *make white ware')*.[19]

Consequently, a number of attempts were made to establish delftware potteries in various parts of the British Isles, beginning in Edinburgh in 1695, then at Belfast and Whitehaven in Cumberland in 1697, at Liverpool in 1701 and again in Edinburgh in 1703-6.[20] All of these attempts were unsuccessful with just one, notable, exception - the Belfast Potthouse, the first of the Irish delftware potteries. Almost certainly, the reason for the solitary success of the Potthouse was that this was the only venture to discover its own, entirely new source of delftware clay at Carrickfergus, seven miles from Belfast. Ultimately, the clays that the Belfast potters discovered at Carrickfergus were to profoundly influence the distribution of delftware potteries throughout the north of England, Ireland and Scotland during the eighteenth-century, just as East Anglian clays had influenced their distribution during the seventeenth-century. Without Carrickfergus clay, it is by no means certain that the delftware industries that later became established in Liverpool, Dublin, Glasgow and elsewhere, could ever have developed at all.

When we examine the delftwares that were produced by the Belfast Potthouse in the early 1700s, (pp.18-33), they seem virtually indistinguishable from English delftwares of the same period. Yet for the potters who made them, the commercial environment in which they worked in Ireland was very different to that which they had previously experienced in England. From the late seventeenth-century onwards, Ireland's imports and exports were heavily constrained by a body of legislation known collectively as the *'Navigation Acts'*, which remained in force until 1780, (by which time delftware manufacture in Ireland had ceased).[21]

The impositions caused by these complex acts varied with time, but for delftware potters there were two principal consequences. The most serious was that all Irish manufacturers were prohibited from exporting goods to the American colonies directly - wares could only be shipped out via an English port, thus acquiring additional customs duties. The second constraint was that direct imports from overseas were similarly prohibited. All overseas imports, *'from America, Africa and Asia'* were first required to land *'at some port of England or Wales* [or Scotland from 1707] *and pay custom there or forfeit ship and goods'*.[22] These import tariffs would have affected most of the Irish potters who intended selling overseas, such as David and Patrick Smith in Belfast or the Delamains in Dublin, who would have sought to exchange the delftwares they sold abroad for other goods, such as rum or raw sugar, for the return journey to Ireland. The financial penalties imposed by the navigation acts did not entirely prohibit overseas trade - goods such as tobacco and sugar were imported regardless - but they certainly placed Irish potters at a distinct disadvantage when compared to their English counterparts.

Opportunities for selling abroad were further limited by England's protective import duties, which effectively ensured that it was impossible for an Irish manufacturer to sell delftware in England on a large scale. In 1762, for example, the duty imposed on Dublin delftware sent to England by William Delamain amounted to approximately 3½ pence per pound weight.[23] At about the same time, landscape-painted plates **(Fig.107)**, which weigh about one pound apiece, were costing between 3 and 6 pence each, so that their price in England would have been roughly doubled by the import duty.[24]

The delftware industry that developed in Ireland was therefore very small indeed compared to that which existed in England. In reality, this situation developed out of a combination of circumstances - it is a gross oversimplification to imply that there might have been a single cause - but in the case of delftware manufacture, the additional costs incurred by these various trade tariffs and duties probably represented a significant commercial obstacle. For example, when Carrickfergus clay became widely available in England from 1723 onwards, thirteen delftware potteries were established in Liverpool alone, compared to the one or two that worked in Ireland.[25] The eighteenth-century Irish glass industry tells a similar story, in that - for as long as export restrictions remained in place - a single Dublin glasshouse was usually sufficient to satisfy the entire home demand for fine table-glass. The legislation was removed in 1780, and by 1785, *five* fine glasshouses were working throughout the country, all exporting to foreign markets.[26]

Despite the adverse legislation, some Irish delftware was certainly exported.[27] Henry Delamain reported *'a great demand ... from Germany, Spain and Portugal'* in 1755, and exports to Jamaica and the West Indies were described during William Delamain's time in 1762.[28] It is also likely that some Irish delftware, perhaps a significant proportion, was sold by wholesale or retail in Ireland to traders who in turn resold these shipments overseas. Mrs Ann Day, for example, who worked at the Delamain's pottery in Dublin, informed the Dublin Society in 1762 that *'The great consumption of the ware is at home'* - a statement that was probably entirely accurate.[29] Mrs. Day then proceeded to explain, however, that three of their best customers were in Cork, which was the final port of call for many Irish and English ships bound for North America. Ideally, the Delamains would probably have preferred to exploit these overseas markets themselves, rather than selling - in effect - to intermediaries, but they do not appear to have possessed the necessary capital. Nonetheless, the recent discoveries of Dublin delftware on five archaeological sites in Virginia and New York suggest that the overseas trade was substantial, despite the apparent paucity of documentary records to this effect.[30]

When we review the seventy-five year history of delftware manufacture in Ireland, from 1697-1771, it is clear that just one pottery in Belfast or Dublin was sufficient to supply most of the country's modest needs for most of the time. As in England previously, (in Norwich and then London), the industry first became established close to the delftware clay deposits (close to Belfast), before moving on to the largest marketplace in the country (Dublin) during the 1730s. The first of the Irish potteries, the Belfast Potthouse, seems to have been a substantial venture, comparable in size to some London delftware potteries of the same date. John Chambers' original pottery at the World's End in Dublin was probably built on a similar scale, yet its steady decline during the late 1740s and early 1750s suggests that the small, Irish market was insufficient to sustain even this modest level of production. But if this was the case, then why did Henry Delamain invest so heavily in the Dublin pottery during the 1750s?

Delamain's expenditure seems to have been entirely directed towards improving the pottery, with new buildings, kilns and a glaze-mlll, and introducing new manufacturing techniques such as coal-fired kilns and transfer-printing. In theory at least, these investments should have enhanced both the pottery's efficiency and the quality of its wares. By showing that Irish delftware could equal foreign goods in quality but at lower cost, Delamain presumably hoped to corner a larger share of the home market, which was spending substantial sums of money on these imported wares. (His Irish delftware was reported to be *'30 per cent Cheaper than the French earthenware')*.[31] Delamain probably also believed that his cost savings would allow Irish delftware to be sold cheaply overseas, despite the additional duties they incurred from export tariffs. As we trace the subsequent decline of the Dublin pottery through the 1760s, however, it becomes obvious that these foreign markets were never developed to anything like the extent that Delamain had probably envisaged. In the event, the pottery he had built to accommodate a workforce of two to three hundred individuals more likely employed around fifty, falling to just twenty workers in 1762.[32] Delamain's premature death in 1757 meant that his heirs and successors were burdened with a pottery that was much too large to be sustained by the home market; they were also left without sufficient capital to adequately explore the alternatives.

In addition to the two main potteries in Belfast and Dublin, there were a number of other, concerted attempts to manufacture delftware in Ireland. The exports of Carrickfergus clay show there was a marked increase in delftware manufacture in England from 1739, a date which coincides with the establishment of a further Irish pottery at Rostrevor.[33] There even appears to have been a brief period, during the early 1760s, (a few years before delftware manufacture ceased completely), when as many as four delftware potteries worked in Ireland simultaneously - with one in Belfast, two in Dublin and a fourth in Limerick. Why this should have been the case remains a mystery. It is particularly curious that three of these potteries should have appeared during the Seven Years War, (1756-63), when Mary Delamain in Dublin apparently claimed that *'the export of the ware to foreign markets was prevented by the war'*.[34]

Another mystery that might well continue to perplex researchers for some years to come concerns Irish transfer-printed delftwares.[35] The techniques of transfer-printing were first patented by a Dublin engraver, John Brooks, who worked as an associate of Henry Delamain in London in 1753-4. (See p.48). Dublin textile manufacturers were also in the forefront of developing new printing techniques at this time.[36] A Dublin engraver, Michael Hanbury, even won an award for exhibiting transfer-printed *'china and earthenware'* that he produced in Dublin in 1758.[37] Yet despite Delamain's claims that he had *'purchased the art of printing earthenware'* in 1753, the technique was never mentioned again by his successors, and not one piece of transfer-printed Dublin delftware has ever come to light.[38] The only known Irish examples were produced by John Stritch in Limerick in 1761, who now appears to have resided in France for the three years immediately beforehand.[39]

When Dudley Westropp recorded some of this primary, documentary information in 1913 and 1935, he might well have been just as puzzled by the absence of transfer-printed Irish delftware as we are to this day. Even this brief introduction will hopefully have shown that progress has been made in understanding certain aspects of the history of delftware manufacture in Ireland, but clearly, a great deal more remains to be discovered. The harp-marked Dublin delftwares, first described more than a century ago, are now old acquaintances.[40] Some Dublin delftwares, on the other hand, such as the coloured and *'coarsely-painted'* wares, have only recently been recognised, and so new examples continue to come to light. Other types, such as the early Dublin wares, or the delftwares produced in Rostrevor, continue to elude us, just as they eluded Westropp.

The one feature that seems to remain constant is that the more we learn, the more we discover that Irish delftwares, like many things made in Ireland - such as glass or silver or furniture - possess a character that is entirely their own. This perception is very different to that which prevailed in 1853, when the Irish Industrial Exhibition could find little of merit among the products of its native craftsmen (p. 4). But perhaps the most encouraging development of all in recent years is the fact that Irish archaeologists now grant seventeenth and eighteenth-century sites some of the status that they have long enjoyed on the far side of the Atlantic. The modest excavations in Belfast and Virginia have clearly demonstrated the unique part that only archaeology can play in revealing more of Ireland's ceramic history. Now that attitudes are changing, it will be fascinating to learn of the further discoveries that the future undoubtedly holds in store.

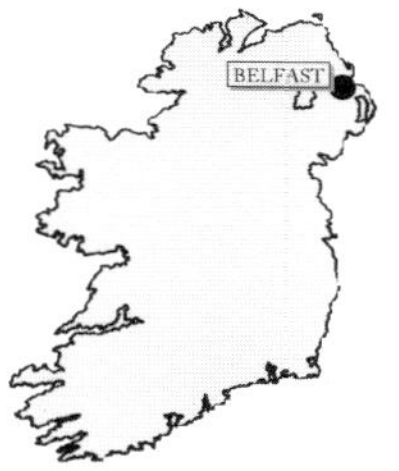

CHAPTER 1 : BELFAST

The Belfast Potthouse (1697 - c.1725)

Documentary evidence associated with the Belfast Potthouse mainly concerns the merchants who owned and financed the venture, and so it is difficult to identify the individual potters responsible for introducing the art of delftware manufacture to Ireland. Circumstantial evidence strongly suggests, however, that the key figure was an experienced delftware potter from London, Matthew Garner, who may originally have been born in Belfast in about the year 1666.

Garner's potting career commenced in London in April 1680 when he was apprenticed to Thomas Harper, the owner of the Montague Close delftware pottery in Southwark.[1] After leaving Harper's employment in 1693 or 94, Garner established a stoneware pottery in Gravel Lane, Southwark, with another delftware potter in London, Luke Talbot. They invested large sums of money in their new venture, but soon afterwards were taken to court by the renowned stoneware potter, John Dwight, facing charges of patent infringement. Garner and Talbot ultimately prevailed against Dwight, but their financial fortunes never recovered from the encounter. Short of money, they mortgaged their pottery in 1697 to one Nathaniel Oade in return for a loan of £100, but Oade, on learning the extent of their financial plight, promptly demanded immediate repayment. When the money was not forthcoming, Oade took possession of the pottery, their homes, and all their goods. Garner and Talbot were declared bankrupt and turned out of their houses with their wives and children in May 1697.

It was reported in London much later, in 1718, that Matthew Garner was forced by these unhappy circumstances to move to Ireland.[2] A Matthew Garner is known to have lived in Belfast in the early eighteenth-century, and if this was the same man, then clearly, he had simply returned to the family home to escape bankruptcy. The precise wording of the document in 1718 is that Garner was obliged '*to fly to Dublin in Ireland, where he has since kept a Pot-house*', but there is no evidence of any substantial '*Pot-house*' in Dublin at this time. Almost certainly, the pottery in Ireland that Garner had '*kept*' for the intervening twenty-one years was the Belfast Potthouse.

As we discover presently, one of the four merchants who founded the Belfast Potthouse was related by marriage to the Matthew Garner who lived in Belfast. So too was the pottery's landlord, who leased the site on which the Potthouse was built. The coincidental timing of Garner's arrival in Ireland in 1697 is a further reason for suspecting that he was the potter behind the Belfast Potthouse, but as his name is not specifically recorded on any documentation relating to the venture, it is impossible to be certain.[3] Matthew Garner is only mentioned in Belfast again much later, in 1725, when both he and his widow were buried. By further coincidence perhaps, this latter date also seems to correspond with the approximate date of closure of the Belfast Potthouse.

Although Garner's association cannot be proven, the merchants who owned this new pottery in Belfast possessed no knowledge whatever of delftware manufacture. They must therefore have brought in delftware potters from somewhere, and wares excavated on the pottery site confirm that London was the most likely source. (See pp. 18 - 33). Regardless of whether the potters arrived in Belfast by invitation or, as in Garner's case, they simply turned up on the doorstep, many other considerations would have influenced the merchants in their decision to support such a venture.

Above all, the establishment of a fine-quality pottery was well suited to the commercial climate prevailing in Belfast at that time. Unlike Dublin, which had been a large city for many centuries, (with a population of around 62,000 in 1706), Belfast had consisted of little more than a castle and a cluster of houses at the beginning of the seventeenth-century.[4] During the second half of the century, the town's rapid growth and prosperity were widely recognised as a phenomenon, impressing several contemporary commentators. **(Fig. 1)**. By 1700, although Belfast remained a small town with fewer than 5,000 inhabitants, (compared to Cork's population of 17,500, for example), the value of its port trade

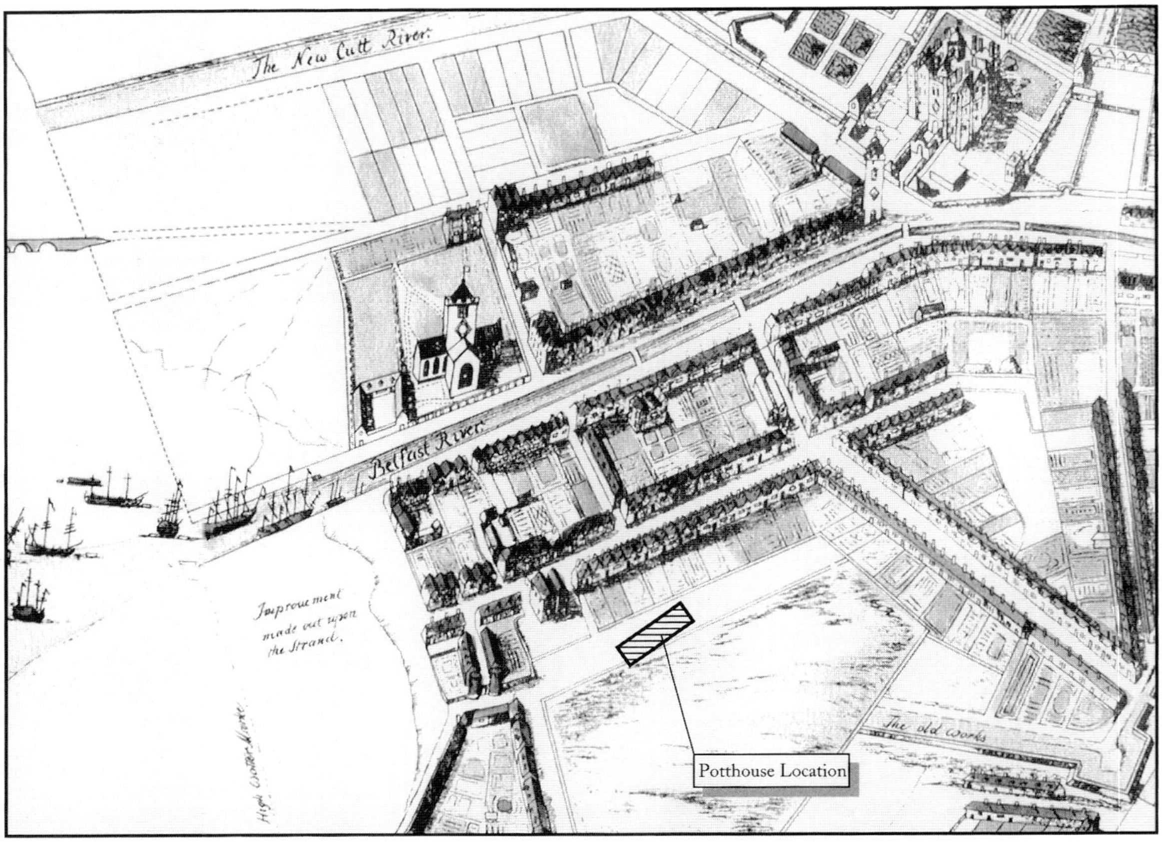

Figure 1. Thomas Phillips' map of Belfast, 1685.

ranked fourth in the country. This exceptional commercial activity generated unprecedented wealth, which in turn promoted a sizeable local market for luxury goods. By the time the Potthouse was established, Belfast had stationers and a printing press, a bookbinder, several goldsmiths, a watchmaker, a clockmaker, brass-makers and pewterers, gunsmiths and a confectioner.[5] Fine luxury glass, on sale in the High Street since the late 1670s, was imported from Dublin, London, France and Holland.[6] By around 1700, imports of French and Dutch earthenware were arriving routinely, supplemented by occasional cargoes from as far afield as Spain and Portugal, the Baltic States and Germany.[7]

The Garner family in Belfast were prestigious members of the small, tightly knit community of merchants that had transformed the town's fortunes since the 1650s.[8] Some, (including one Rev. Matthew Garner), were distinguished clerics. If Matthew Garner, the London-trained potter, was indeed one of their number, then to have been apprenticed into the delftware trade he must obviously have occupied one of the more inferior positions within the family's ranks. Nonetheless, his family would have been well known to all of the merchants who later became involved in the Potthouse.[9]

On a practical level, most of the essential raw materials for a delftware pottery were also available in the north of Ireland. Local forests existed at that time so that supplies of kiln fuel were assured.[10] The unusually diverse potting clays on the shores of Belfast Lough, perhaps the most important prerequisite for the pottery's success, were probably recognised as early as the thirteenth century.[11] Two different types of clay were necessary for delftware manufacture and both were available locally. The rarer, white-firing (lean) clays from Carrickfergus, later to become invaluable to delftware potteries all around the Irish Sea, were probably known by 1683, although their suitability for making delftware probably remained untested in 1697.[12] More common red-firing (fat) clays existed in much greater quantity near Belfast itself. These red clays had primarily been used in brick making, but they seem to have gained an outstanding reputation for quality. Shortly after the Potthouse was built, for example, the builders of St. Paul's Cathedral in London specifically ordered 5,500 bricks from a Belfast brick-maker, for the construction of the inner brick cupola of the dome (from which the great stone lantern is suspended).[13]

A further consideration at this particular time is that English manufacturers were paying exceptionally high duties on their delftwares, as a result of the Excise Act, (imposed in 1695 to help pay for the Jacobite wars).[14] The Excise Act did not extend to Ireland, which provided Irish manufacturers with a unique opportunity to undercut their English competitors. In 1697, the year in which the Belfast Potthouse was probably proposed, a fine-quality glasshouse was also established in Dublin - allegedly for the specific purpose of exploiting this tax loophole. The glasshouse apparently offered large financial incentives to entice English glass-workers to Ireland, much to the consternation of their employers.[15]

The earliest indication that the Potthouse existed was reported in July 1698 by Dr. William Sacheverell, then Governor of the Isle of Man. Forced into port by bad weather on his way to Scotland, Sacheverell described the town as follows;

'Bellfast is ... well built, full of People, and of great Trade. The quantities of Butter and Beef; which it sends into Foreign parts, are almost incredible: I have seen the Barrels pil'd up in the very Streets. The new Pottery is a pretty Curiosity, set up by Mr. Smith, the present Sovereign, and his Predecessor Captain Leathes, a Man of great Ingenuity ...'.[16]

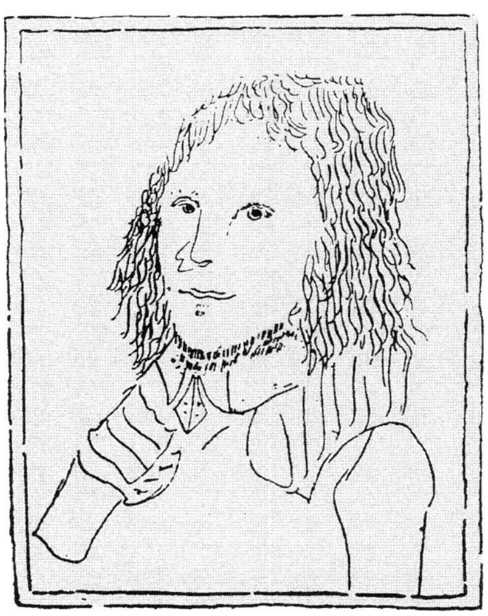

The two individuals mentioned by Sacheverell were prominent in Belfast society and are readily identified. Captain Robert Leathes, **(Fig.2)**, whose family originated in Whitehaven in Cumberland, had an exceptional career.[17] He was a burgess of Belfast for forty-eight years and served five terms as sovereign, (a post roughly equivalent to mayor). Much of his status derived from his various positions as comptroller to the earl of Donegall, as seneschal of the manor of Belfast and constable of Belfast castle, but he also had considerable personal prestige. When the first Potthouse lease was drawn up two years after Sacheverell's visit, in 1700, Robert Leathes was not listed amongst the merchants involved, but the assertion that he had helped to *'set up'* the pottery was probably accurate nonetheless. As agent for the estates and affairs of the earl of Donegall, it was essential that the owners at least gained his compliance in their endeavour, but the fact that Leathes personally escorted Sacheverell to the Potthouse suggests he took a more active interest in this novel and *'pretty Curiosity'*.

The second individual mentioned by Sacheverell, *'Mr. Smith'*, was Captain David Smith, who was then serving as the sovereign of Belfast. David Smith was the principal owner of the Potthouse, and so he and his relations will be examined in more detail shortly.

It seems safe to assume that the Potthouse was working when Sacheverell visited in 1698, although this is not specifically stated. It was certainly working by 1699, a date that is recorded on a piece of kiln furniture found on the site **(Fig. 3)**. Yet for some reason, the first lease agreement for the pottery was not signed until September 1700 - fully two years after Sacheverell's visit. There is no obvious explanation for the delay.

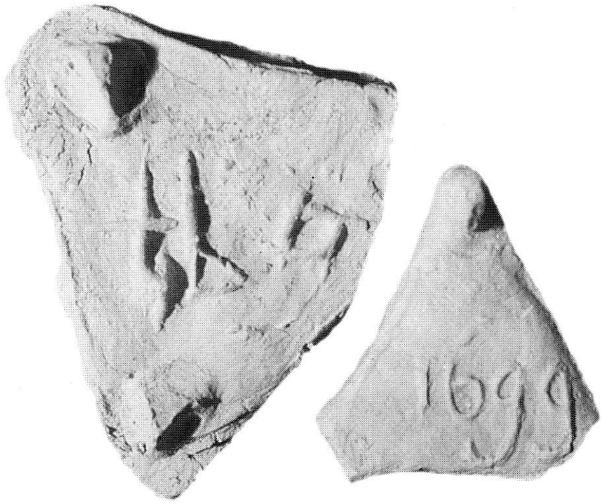

Above Centre : Figure 2. *Captain Robert Leathes, a contemporary sketch.*

Top Right : Figure 3. *Two trivets recovered near the Potthouse site, one dated 1699, the other with the initials of an unidentified potter, 'tb'.*

Possibly, the merchants involved did not wish to commit to an expensive, long-term lease, before the potters had adequately demonstrated that they were capable of producing delftware.

The 41-year lease on the Potthouse property, signed on the 26th September 1700, shows that the pottery was in fact owned by a consortium of four local merchants.[18]

David Smith Esq., sovereign
(Mentioned by Sacheverell in 1698)
Patrick Smith, merchant
(David Smith's younger brother)
Thomas Crawford, merchant
(Brother-in-law of David & Patrick Smith)
Henry Chads, merchant
(Unrelated to the Smiths & Crawfords, but probably related to Matthew Garner)

These four merchants, each one a burgess or from a burgess's family, clearly represent the businessmen who financed and managed the Potthouse, rather than the potters who actually worked there. The first three were closely related; Thomas Crawford was married to Janet Smith, the sister of David & Patrick.[19] The fourth individual on this list, Henry Chads, stands out, as he seems to have been entirely unrelated to either the Smiths or the Crawfords. Significantly, however, he was closely related by marriage to the Garner family of Belfast.[20] Both Chads and the Garners were in turn related to another Belfast family that we encounter presently, the Thetfords, who were later to acquire the '*Grand Lease*' in which the '*Potthouse Lease*' was situated. (The Thetfords, in effect, became the pottery's landlords). Henry Chads' name was also inscribed on the keystone of a Belfast bridge in 1696. This suggests he may have possessed civil engineering skills, which could have proven beneficial to the partnership when the pottery was being built.[21]

Regardless of the precise nature of Chads' involvement, the lease agreement proves that the Smith family of Belfast held the principal interest in the Potthouse. As we shall see, branches of this family later extended into other parts of the Irish delftware industry. One group of Smiths, for example, came to own the largest of the two delftware clay leases at Carrickfergus. (See p.169). Others intermarried with the family of John Chambers - probably the same John Chambers who founded the first delftware pottery in Dublin in the 1730s. (See p.35). From a documentary researcher's viewpoint, it is disappointing that the family possessed such an undistinguished surname, as it means the precise nature of these relationships are often difficult to establish. The confusion that arises will become more evident later, when we discover that two of the potters who worked in Belfast were also named Smith.

The brothers David and Patrick Smith, the principal partners in the Potthouse, were prominent Belfast merchants.[22] Their father William had moved to Belfast from his native Glasgow in 1656, and prospered greatly in trade. When he died in July 1684, the estate that David and Patrick inherited included £3,800 in cash alone - an exceptional sum of money for the time. (Some of the better-paid potters in Belfast, by way of comparison, earned c.£25 per annum).

All four of the Potthouse founders, as Protestants and supporters of William III, fled for a brief period to Scotland in 1689 when attainted by the '*Patriot Parliament*' of James II, but they resumed their normal mercantile activities upon their return. David and Patrick had been left shares in a number of ships, at least one of which, the 120 ton '*Adventure*', was of sufficient size to engage in transatlantic trade. (Their brother-in-law and partner in the pottery, Thomas Crawford, also owned ships in his own right). David served as supercargo, (buyer's agent), on a ship trading in Danzig in 1680, and was master of another ship, the '*Thomas*', during the 1680s. Following in his father's footsteps, David was made a burgess from 1690 onwards, and, as Sacheverell remarked, he was serving as Belfast's sovereign when the pottery was set up, (for two annual terms, from 1698-1700).

David and Patrick Smith were therefore well established within the upper echelons of Belfast society, yet the most distinguished feature of their commercial careers was neither their wealth nor their status, but the fact that they were amongst the only merchants in Belfast who earned their livelihood through manufacturing. Most Belfast merchants at this time simply bought and sold other peoples' goods, whereas the Smiths owned and operated Belfast's sugar refinery. (The family was also previously involved with a less successful ironworks).[23] After the Potthouse was opened, it seems that the sugar refinery was maintained by Captain David Smith's sons, John and William, whilst his brother Patrick - as we discover shortly - assumed management of the pottery.[24]

Given the family's background, it is possible to envisage several reasons why the Smiths should have contemplated investing in a comparatively high-risk venture such as delftware manufacture. (Bear in mind that by 1697, with the exception of Bristol, almost all attempts to set up an independent delftware pottery outside London had failed). As owners of the sugar refinery, they had practical experience of operating a moderately large-scale manufacturing enterprise. A further benefit for the Smiths in particular was that a pottery would have provided their sugar-house with a ready supply of earthenware sugar-moulds, in which the distinctive, conical, sugar-loaves of refined sugar were formed **(Fig.4)**. The need to acquire sugar-moulds was obviously insufficient justification for establishing a fine-quality, blue and white delftware pottery, but it was probably no coincidence that the first Scottish delftware manufacturer, Robert Douglas, was also a sugar-maker by profession. (Douglas was attempting to make delftware in Edinburgh at about the same time, from 1695 onwards).[25]

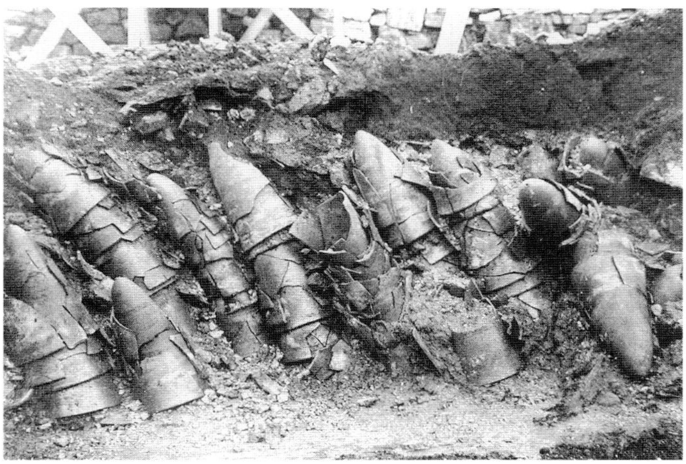

Figure 4. *Sugar-moulds excavated in Usher's Street, Dublin, 1934. This was probably the site of James Walker's coarse pottery from the mid-eighteenth century onwards.*

By far the most likely incentive for making delftware, however, for Douglas as much as for the Smiths, is that fine-quality blue and white pottery would have represented a high-value, non-perishable export for the transatlantic market. The fact that these merchants were refining sugar meant that they were already committed to transatlantic trade, bringing in raw sugar from the West Indies. Despite the constraints of the navigation acts, (See pp.8-9), delftware would have represented an ideal cargo for the outward voyage to the colonies and plantations, supplementing more standard exports of agricultural supplies and provisions. There was also strong local demand for fine-quality earthenware at that time, and a regular, extensive trade with Dublin. Duty would have been paid on exports to England and (from 1707) Scotland, but nonetheless, major cities such as Glasgow and Liverpool would probably have been regarded as good potential markets, as no other delftware potteries were then operating north of Bristol.

The leading figure in the enterprise, David Smith, died in 1705, less than five years after the lease agreement was signed.[26] David's demise seems to have caused difficulty for his younger brother Patrick, as we learn from a remarkable letter written in 1706, recently discovered by Belfast historian Dr. Jean Agnew.

A few comments are required to place this letter in context. By 1706, it would appear that Robert Douglas's early attempts to capitalise on the delftware monopoly for Scotland had failed. His successors were two Edinburgh & Leith merchants, George Linn and William Montgomerie, who were granted a new, fifteen-year monopoly in 1703.[27] Almost certainly, Linn and Montgomerie were the two individuals who entreated their friend, Andrew Skeen, to write to the Belfast merchant Isaac Macartney in 1706, persuading him to visit the Belfast Potthouse to make inquiries on their behalf. We do not have a copy of Skeen's letter from Edinburgh, but a transcript of Macartney's reply has survived, written in Belfast on 15th June 1706.[28]

'*...As for yr memorandum About our potthouse. I have speak to ye Men who are not Preintice to the house and find only two fitt for Engaging the works yr frind has to Doe in Directing the finishing* [of] *the Mill, Kill and Oven, and makeing up some works for tryall of yr wood and Clay. There is one J*[ohn] *Smith will undertake the Ordering* [and] *the building of the mill, kill and oven, as also to burn and Glase, for wch he Demands £26 p Annum. His son John Smith will Engadge to turn and paint at £24 p Annum. The*[y] *demand ten pound to bear there Charges over, and* [state] *that they will not Engage Longer than to finish the works, Except* [for whatever work] *you give them after you find ye Clay and every thing Else Answer.* [They demand] *the same wages those of there trade gett att London - which I think* [is an] *Unreasonable provision, being Cheaper wth you than att London. They have promised to wait an answer before they Leave* [Belfast, as they plan] *to go for Bristoll. They do not agree with your friends. As you desired, I designed not to Lett Mr. Pa*[trick] *Smith know of my speaking to these men, who Likewise promised me not to speak to any person about it, yett discovered it to him. Ye Excuse they make is that they were forced to do it, haveing hired to go some way. You desire to know Mr. Pa*[trick] *Smith's Character. Truely I never knew anything but justice by him & what every one takes him to be; he is reduced in his fortune In the world, but not by any outward Extravagance. What judgement he has in manadgeing a Pott House I know not further than that he was concerned in this house, & was frequently Looking after the work-men & the burning of ye ware, when I took any friends thither to See it, & he says he has good knowledge, & can by overseeing & directing make 3 or 4 men do as much as 10 men...* '.

Three months later, in September 1706, Macartney remarked to a correspondent that he had since, '*per* [Andrew Skeen's] *order, paid to a potter sent from hence to Edinburgh £2-4-8*', indicating that one of the Belfast potters had pursued the offer of work in Scotland.[29] This might well have been one of the two John Smiths mentioned, but if so, then other town records show that he subsequently returned to Belfast. (The attempt to establish a delftware pottery in Scotland also appears to have been unsuccessful).

On closer reading, this letter reveals a number of details concerning the situation at the Potthouse in 1706. Patrick Smith, not a potter by training, was working as the manager of the Potthouse. He was also '*reduced in his fortune In the world*', probably in consequence of his brother David's death the year before. Strangely, however, although Patrick was clearly in reduced circumstances in 1706, the Smith's sugar business appears to have been thriving - so much so that they opened a second sugar-house nearby at about this time.[30] (This was situated in '*Sugar House Entry*', just opposite '*Pot House Lane*' - **see Fig. 9**). Viewed with other documentation, this reference to Patrick Smith as the pottery's manager suggests that he may have been demised both shares in the Potthouse by his brother David's will, whereas David's two sons, John and William, seem only to have been interested in the sugar-house.

The letter also tells us something of the nature of the workforce in Belfast. Many of the potters were '*Preintice to the house*', that is, bound into serving their apprenticeships at the Potthouse and thus not free to work elsewhere. Others, such as the two John Smiths, were independent freemen, or journeymen potters. Although they worked in Belfast on long-term contracts, having been '*hired to go some way*', they were obviously free to travel largely as they pleased in search of work. John Smith and his son even indicate that they were prepared to delay their planned departure for Bristol until they heard word from Scotland. The reference to Bristol is noteworthy for another reason, for a third potter who turns up in Belfast shortly afterwards, James Margerum, is known to have established a pottery in Bristol at about this time. It is also interesting that the Belfast potters were fully informed of the rates of pay in London.

In view of their common surname, it is impossible to tell whether the two John Smiths mentioned as potters were related to David and Patrick, the Potthouse owners. One of David's two sons was certainly called John Smith, and as David's brother Patrick was working at the Potthouse by 1706, then it is equally possible that his son was also. Nevertheless, other town records suggest that

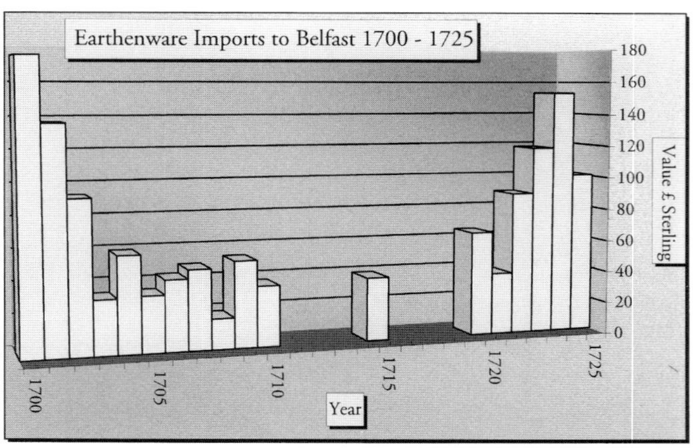

***Figure** 5. Customs records of earthenware imported into Belfast from England, Holland and France, 1700 - 1725.*

David's son John and these two potters were quite distinct individuals. His son, at the sugar-house, seems invariably to have been described as a '*merchant*', whereas the others were listed simply as '*potters*'.[31] The Smith surname was not as common in Ireland at this date as it was in England, and so a family relationship might well have existed. If so, however, then the two John Smith '*potters*' were more likely cousins or second cousins of David and Patrick, rather than more immediate family members.

Patrick's reduced personal circumstances give the impression that the Potthouse was not doing well in 1706, but another remark, written two years later, suggests quite the opposite. The distinguished Irish scholar Dr. Thomas Molyneux of Dublin visited the north of Ireland in August 1708, and in his brief description of Belfast he reported:

'Belfast is a very handsome, thriving, well-peopled town; a great many new houses and good shops in it...Here we saw a very good manuficture of earthenware, which comes nearest to Delft of any made in Ireland, and really is not much short of it; it is very clean and pretty, and universally used in the North, and, I think, not so much owing to any peculiar happiness in the clay, but rather to the manner of beating and mixing it up'.[32]

Molyneux's statement that Belfast delftware was '*universally used*' in the north of Ireland is corroborated by customs records, which show that the quantities of earthenware imported into Belfast dropped dramatically once the Potthouse had been operating for a few years.[33] **(Fig.5)**. In 1700, earthenware to the value of £175 was imported into Belfast from England, Holland and France, but by 1703 the value of these imports had decreased to just £34. They subsequently remained low whilst the Potthouse was working - averaging just £43 per annum during recorded years of the next two decades.

In May 1709, ownership of the Grand Lease for the area that contained the Potthouse was transferred to one Francis Thetford, another of Belfast's merchant elite (who, as mentioned previously, was also closely related to the Garner family).[34] The owners of this Grand Lease were probably not personally involved in running the Potthouse - they were simply the landlords - but the lease transfer documents are valuable nonetheless, for they list the names of various individuals who were then living in the adjoining '*Potthouse Tenements*'. **(Fig.6.** See also **Fig.9)**. Among these tenants, two names stand out; Thomas Wilson, and the more distinctively named James Margerum.

28 May 1709	**27 Oct 1722**
The Potthouse	**The Potthouse**
P. Smith & H. Chads	T. Banks
(D. Smith d. 1705)	(R. Hodgkinson d. by 1722)
(T. Crawford d. 1708)	
Tenants Recorded Once	Tenants Recorded Once
John Ambrose	Robert Armstrong
James Gembell (shop)	Robert Armstrong (shop)
James Hunter	John Brown
John Kane	George Carson
William Kinkade (cellar)	John Chalmers (Chambers)
William Kinkead	Patrick Fferguson
James Marjoram	John Gordon
Edward Wilson	George Guthery
Thomas Wilson	-- Jameson
Mrs Wilkison	Robert McGee
Robt. Woods	James Hamilton Maxwell
	William Moore
	William Rogers (cellar)
	Widow Stewart
Tenants Recorded Twice	Tenants Recorded Twice
Patrick Campbell	Patrick Campbell
John Gillmore	Widow Gilmore
Phillip Harding	Widow Harden
James McDowell	James McDowell
Alexander McKenny	Widow McKinney
	James McKinney

Figure 6. *Belfast Potthouse 'Tenement' Residents.*

Thomas Wilson, *may* have been the son of potter Richard Wilson, baptised in St. Saviour's parish in Southwark in 1682.[35] (Matthew Garner's stoneware pottery in London lay in the same parish). James Margerum, on the other hand, was *certainly* an English delftware potter. A James Margarinn, probably the same man, began his potting career in 1681 as an apprentice to John Campion, at the delftware pottery near Hermitage Dock, London.[36] By 1701, he was in Bristol, setting up his own delftware pottery at Redcliff Back.[37] This pottery continued to operate until well into the eighteenth-century, but there is no record of James Margerum in Bristol after 1705. He most likely came to Belfast between 1705 and 1707, when the Redcliff Back pottery seems to have changed hands.

In 1710, the Belfast potters appear to have faced competition from England for the first time, for in that year Liverpool's first delftware pottery was established in Lord Street. This new pottery's first advertisement in May 1710 stated that it was set up with the specific intention of making '... *all Sorts of fine White and Painted pots and other vessels and Tiles in imitation of China, both for Ireland and outward trade*...'.[38] In other words, the Liverpool potters had clear designs on selling to the Irish market. Ironically, they were only able to produce

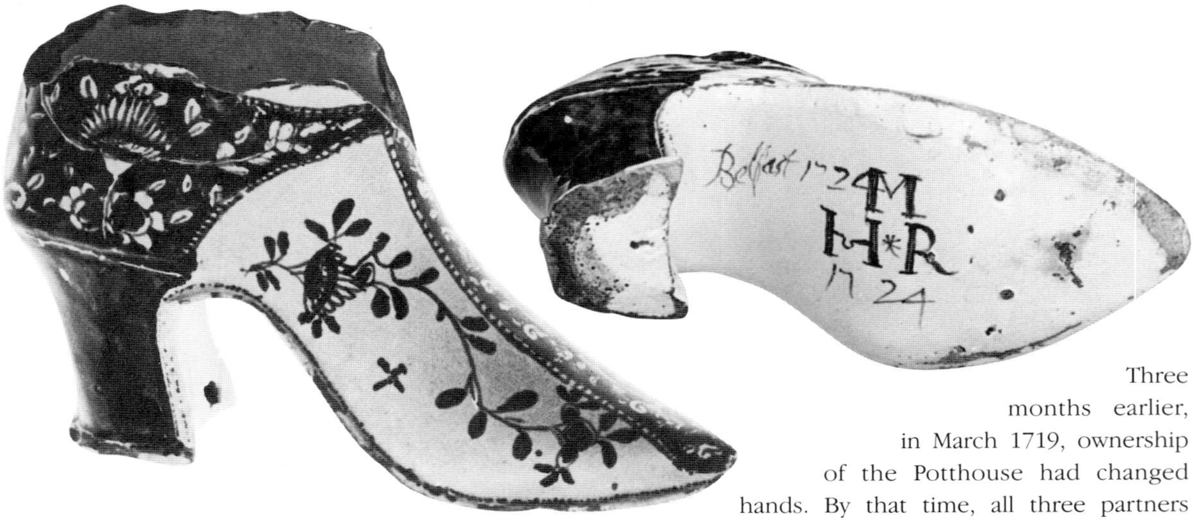

delftware by importing clays that had been discovered by the Belfast potters. The Liverpool venture was initially charged customs duty on '*the clay brought from Belfast*', but this money was soon returned. For reasons that are not yet clear, duty does not appear to have been routinely charged on Carrickfergus clay until large-scale exports began in 1723.[39]

Despite this growing competition from England, there is little evidence to suggest that any decline occurred at the Belfast Potthouse between 1710 and about 1720 - to all appearances, the pottery seems to have worked steadily throughout. Supplies of local timber seem to have ceased fairly abruptly around 1716, so that fuel costs must have increased thereafter, (thus removing one of the main reasons for siting a pottery in Belfast).[40] Some unhappy events are also recorded in a local burial register concerning the two John Smiths, the potters, who lived in two adjoining tenements in lower North Street, close to the Potthouse.[41] In February 1713, the wife of one the John Smiths died, followed in February 1716 by a child in the family. In June 1717 one Samuel Henney, described as a '*painter*', was buried, his funeral paid for by a John Smith (either one of the potters, or possibly David Smith's son). Finally, we learn that one of the two John Smiths (presumably the elder) was himself buried on the 4th June 1719.[42]

Three months earlier, in March 1719, ownership of the Potthouse had changed hands. By that time, all three partners associated with the Smith family had died. The deeds to the leasehold were thus sold on by the sole surviving partner, Henry Chads, to another Belfast merchant, Richard Hodgkinson, who may have been one of Chads' younger in-laws.[43] The nature of the transfer could suggest that the Potthouse was beginning to run into financial difficulty, for Chads agreed to sell the leasehold to Hodgkinson in return for a token payment of just 5 shillings, on the assurance that Hodgkinson would then settle debts that Chads had incurred of just over £87. On the other hand, it is equally possible that these debts were unrelated to the pottery - Chads may simply have used the deeds to secure a loan. Whatever the

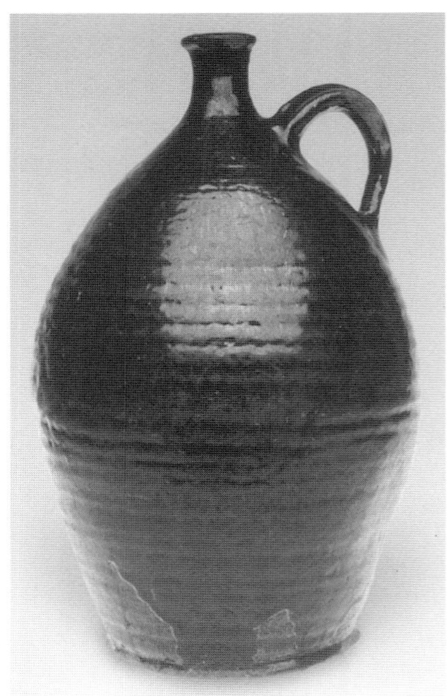

***Above* : *Figure* 7.** *Two views of the original 'Belfast Shoe', dated 1724, made for the marriage of 'HM' to his bride 'R'. Ht. 90 mm., L. 145 mm.*
***Right* : *Figure* 8.** *A black-glazed, high-fired earthenware flagon, probably produced at the Belfast Potthouse towards the end of its working life. Wasters found on the pottery site indicate that these black-wares and delftwares were sometimes fired together in the same kiln. Ht. 16⁷/₈ in., 428 mm.*

cause, the upshot of this exchange was that from March 1719, the Potthouse had a new owner, Richard Hodgkinson.

Further information can be gleaned from examining the fortunes of the pottery's landlord, Francis Thetford (who as we have seen, acquired the Grand Lease containing the Potthouse sub-lease in 1709). Thetford's health began to fail from 1719 onwards, and as time passed his debts steadily mounted. He was eventually forced to secure a series of loans against his Belfast properties, which in turn created a flurry of legal documentation that sheds a little more light on the Potthouse during its closing years. This information is most useful for establishing the location and the size of the pottery, but it also provides us with a second list of occupants at the *'Potthouse-Tenements'* **(Fig. 6)**.

When Thetford began to run into debt in August 1719, he first offered up just one portion of his Grand Lease as security on a loan of £100 - the sub-lease relating specifically to the Potthouse.[44] This clearly indicates that the pottery was still in a reasonably healthy state at that stage, and was probably valued at several times the amount borrowed. Sixteen months later, in November 1720, Thetford assigned a further portion of the Grand Lease to secure a second, independent loan of £40 from the Belfast merchant Thomas Banks, who had succeeded Robert Leathes as agent for the Donegall family's estates, (p.13).[45] The significance of Banks' association will become apparent shortly.

Francis Thetford died in 1722, and on 6th September of that year his executors sold the entire Grand Lease for £560.[46] The deeds of transfer record that, by this date, the new owner of the Potthouse sub-lease, Richard Hodgkinson, had also died, so that his executor, the aforementioned Thomas Banks, was then acting as the pottery's manager. Thomas Banks' name has special significance as he is identified later as co-owner of one of the two leases for Carrickfergus clay.[47] This suggests that Banks himself may have made a conscious decision to foster the trade in Carrickfergus clay at the expense of the Belfast Potthouse. Carrickfergus clay exports certainly increased dramatically soon after Banks assumed management.

The quantities of foreign earthenware imported into Belfast also began to climb in 1722, **(Fig. 5)**, which seems to confirm that the Potthouse was then in decline. One John Inglefield, the master of the *'Industry'* of Carrickfergus, delivered the first recorded shipment of 11 tons of Carrickfergus clay to Robert Fazackerly in Liverpool on the 10th April 1723.[48] (See Appendix I, Table Ib). By the end of that year, a total of 132 tons of Carrickfergus clay had been exported, all apparently arriving in Liverpool ready-prepared for use in delftware manufacture.[49] Most of these shipments went to a number of new delftware potteries that sprang up in Liverpool from 1723 onwards, as soon as Carrickfergus clay became readily available. (A total of thirteen delftware potteries were ultimately to open in Liverpool, all reliant upon Carrickfergus clay).[50] Although the £53 that was paid for the Carrickfergus clay exported during that first year was a relatively small sum, especially when compared to the income of a reasonably healthy pottery, most of this money was probably profit.

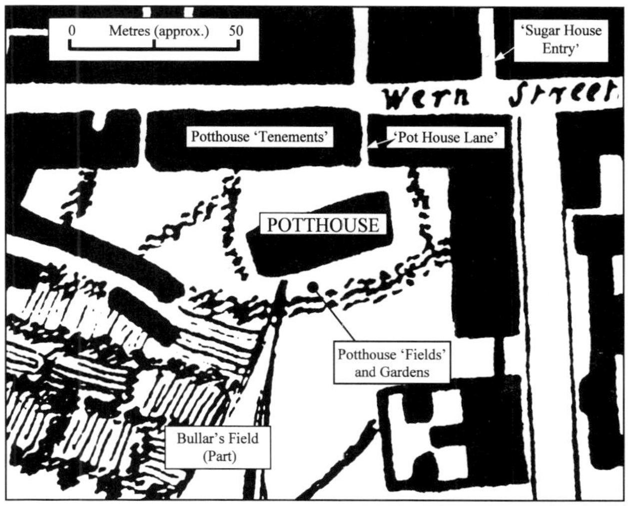

Figure 9. *Detail of the 1757 map of Belfast (see also Fig. 190), showing the Belfast Potthouse and its context. The entry 'Pot House Lane' is now known as Hill Street.*

The Belfast Potthouse obviously carried on for a few years more, however, as the only documentary example of Belfast delftware - the *'Belfast shoe'* - is dated 1724 **(Fig.7)**. In addition, shards recovered from the Potthouse site indicate that utilitarian, black-glazed coarse-wares and delftwares were occasionally fired together in the same kiln.

Presumably, this represented a deterioration in quality that occurred towards the end of the Potthouse's working life. **(Fig. 8)**.

Black-glazed wares were probably produced on the same site until the 1730s, and so the precise date of closure of the Belfast Potthouse is unclear. Delftware manufacture had probably ceased there by 1728, however, for in that year the surviving John Smith seems to have been working in Bristol, introducing Carrickfergus clay to the potters there.[51] (A house in Belfast that had belonged to John or his father was re-let in July 1723).[52] The most likely date for the pottery's closure is presently believed to have been some time around September 2nd 1725, when an '*old Matthew Garner*' was buried in Belfast by members of the Thetford family.[53] In the very same church, just two weeks earlier, an individual we have not yet encountered, John Chambers, also attended the funeral of his father.[54] Chambers, as we shall see, plays the principal role in the next chapter of Irish delftware history, when the industry moved south to Dublin during the 1730s.

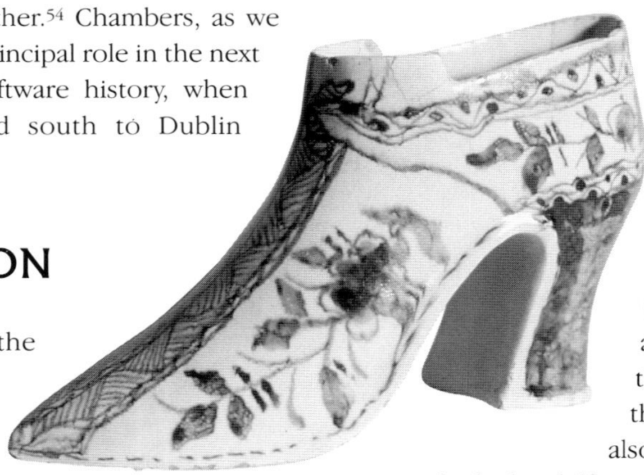

LOCATION

Although the original lease that was signed in 1700 no longer exists, some details of the pottery can be gleaned from later documents. Described as the '*Potthouse & Soaphouse*' in 1718, it was situated in an area of open ground in central Belfast known as Bullar's Field.[55] This was close to the main thoroughfare of '*Broad*' or Waring Street, and although the open situation allowed the kiln to be set slightly apart from neighbouring habitation, it is surprising that the fire risk and '*annoyance by smoak*' did not cause greater problems. Many of Belfast's more '*noisome and offensive*' trades, such as abattoirs and tan-pits, were already situated in this part of town, so perhaps kiln smoke was considered a comparatively minor irritation.

***Above** : **Figure 10**. A second 'Belfast Shoe', discovered by Shirley Tumelty in Belfast in 1995. Ht. 90 mm., L.145 mm. See also Colour Plate 1.*

The property was in two parts. One was a large parcel of ground and tenements '*with all the appurtenances thereunto belonging*', which had a frontage 133 feet wide onto Waring Street.[56] Adjoining this property were two tenements and gardens that had been demised to David Smith by a separate lease. There are no accurate maps of Belfast from the first half of the eighteenth-century, but the position of the main pottery building is apparent on a hand-drawn map produced in 1757, shortly before the building was demolished to make way for a new iron-foundry.[57] **(Fig. 9)**. The lane-way that led to the pottery from Waring Street has since grown into present-day Hill Street, although the name '*Pot House Lane*' survived until as late as 1788.[58] The Potthouse, its grounds and tenements occupied an area of about 300 square metres, which was larger even than some London delftware potteries of similar date.[59]

The references to the '*Potthouse & Soaphouse*' indicate that the waste wood-ash (potash) produced by the pottery kiln was employed to manufacture soap on site, providing the Smiths with yet another product to sell. The fact that this soap-house was set within the pottery grounds itself might also provide clues to the manner in which the delftware was manufactured.[60] Potash, an essential ingredient of soap manufacture, was produced in large quantities when the pottery kiln was fired, whilst '*soaper's-waste*' in turn represented a valuable constituent of certain delftware glazes. By conspicuous coincidence, the Montague Close pottery in Southwark, where Matthew Garner served his apprenticeship, is also known to have contained a '*soap-house*' within its grounds.[61]

The Potthouse must also have employed a local mill for grinding glaze ingredients and colouring materials, but its location is unknown.

ATTRIBUTED WARES

For many years only one piece of delftware was attributed to Belfast, a documentary delftware '*choppine*' or miniature ladies shoe, **(Fig. 7)**, which first appeared in print as long ago as 1877.[62] The inscription on the base indicates that the shoe was made in Belfast in 1724 as a wedding gift for the marriage of 'HM' to his bride 'R'. (There would originally have been a pair). In 1877, the shoe was recorded as being *'the property of a lady in Belfast, who states that it belonged to her grandmother'*, confirming that the shoe had probably remained in Belfast since it was made, and hence had been intended for the marriage of a local couple. Attempts to identify the individuals concerned have to date proven unsuccessful. The shoe was presented in 1935 to the National Museum in Dublin by a Mrs. Mai Beatrice Moorhead of Belfast.[63]

Although the painted floral sprays are similar in style to English and Dutch examples, some aspects of the decoration are unusual. On the upper part, for example, around the heel, the colouring of the decoration is inverted, so that the floral sprays stand out in white against a blue-painted background. The Belfast shoe is also shorter than most, just 90 mm. or 3½ in. high. (The majority are in excess of 4 inches high). Yet despite these distinguishing characteristics, the shoe did not lead to any new attributions of Belfast wares for more than a century.

In 1995, however, a second early delftware shoe turned up on a market stall in central Belfast. **(Fig. 10, Colour Plate 1)**.[64] This example is not documentary - it bears no inscription of any kind - and although similarly decorated in blue and white, the colour and painting style are quite unlike those of the original shoe. (The character of the second shoe is more in keeping with 'standard' English examples). Nonetheless, there can be little doubt that both were made in Belfast, as both were formed in the same mould **(Fig. 11)**. They are therefore identical in size and shape, allowing for slight differences due to warping in the firing, and hand trimming of the edges. Further confirmation that the second shoe was made in Belfast comes from a bowl shard recovered at the Potthouse site in 1994, which is painted with a floral motif that appears on the shoe's heel. **(Fig. 12)**. An additional bonus is that the second Belfast shoe is complete, whereas the upper part of the original shoe is missing.

English examples of these shoes, originally a Dutch invention, are not uncommon. A London provenance has been assigned to most although a few are thought to be of Bristol manufacture. Many, like the original Belfast shoe, **(Fig. 7)**, are inscribed with two or three initials, and bear dates ranging from the late-seventeenth century to the mid-eighteenth century. Twenty-five examples of closely similar form to the Belfast shoes are illustrated by Lipski and Archer, with a date range of 1703-68.

Despite the obvious differences in their decoration, both of the Belfast shoes exhibit a characteristic that appears to be unique, which should hopefully allow other examples to be recognised easily. Most shoes of this general form possess a moulded shoe-buckle on the front top edge, but the Belfast shoes are entirely plain. (A small, tied bow has been *painted* in this position on the second shoe). As this portion of the original Belfast shoe was lacking, the feature was not previously obvious.

Another notable characteristic shared by the two Belfast shoes is that the *'sole'* of the shoe stands proud, as a distinct ridge running around the bottom edge. On the majority of published delftware shoes,

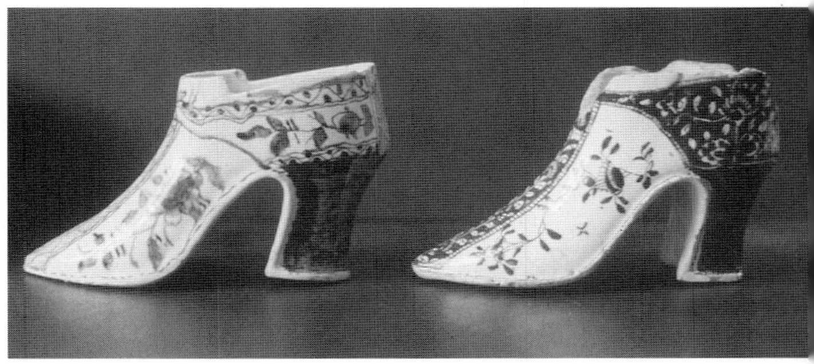

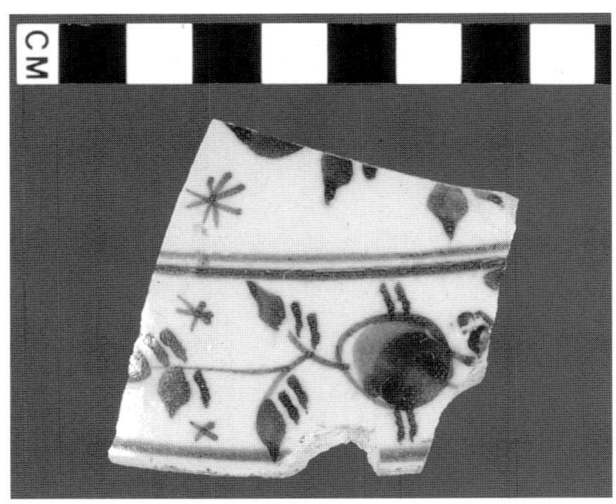

Top : ***Figure 11****. Comparison of the two 'Belfast Shoes'.*

Bottom : Figure 12. *Delftware bowl rim-shard recovered from the Belfast Potthouse site in 1994. The border motif also occurs on the heel of the second 'Belfast Shoe'. (Compare Figs.10 & 11).*

the '*sole*' instead meets the shoe's sides as a continuous, smooth curve. The painters of both of the Belfast shoes also appear to have paid particular attention to painting the top edge of this protruding sole with fine dots, simulating stitching.

There is a possibility that a third delftware shoe may have survived in Belfast until 1892, but its present whereabouts are unknown.[65] Although not documentary, this was reputed to have been in the possession of descendants of Robert Leathes, **(Fig. 2)**. Some of Leathes' other possessions (such as his *lignum vitae* 'wassail' or punch-bowl) have survived in the Ulster Museum. Unfortunately, Robert M. Young, the Belfast historian who recorded the shoe's existence, gave no details of its appearance except that it was '*blue and white*'. It is possible, therefore, that the shoe discovered in 1995 and the unmarked shoe described in 1892 are one and the same.[66]

EXCAVATIONS

Robert M. Young also appears to have been the first individual to locate and investigate the Potthouse site. In 1911, in response to a request for information on Belfast's early potteries in the magazine '*Notes and Queries*', he briefly mentioned that '*Some fragments* [of Belfast delftware] *were recently unearthed in Rosemary Street* [a continuation of Waring Street] *sufficient to show its affinity to Dutch or Rouen tin-glazed ware*'.[67] Young even published a small photograph of an otherwise unrecorded porringer handle, **(Fig. 31)**, indicating that he had found these fragments of Belfast delftware before 1909.[68]

More recently, during the 1980s, building work near the Potthouse site revealed an unusually diverse assemblage of post-mediaeval pottery. (The area had once been part of '*Bullar's Field*', in which the Potthouse was also situated. **See Fig. 9**). This prompted further investigation by two archaeologists from the Queen's University of Belfast, Dr. T. E. McNeill and Prof. M. G. L. Baillie.[69] Amongst the ceramics they encountered were a number of fragments of delftware biscuit, which clearly showed that the Potthouse site lay close by. At about the same time, the present author's documentary research had located the pottery's position, and so attention duly focussed towards an area about one hundred metres due west of these finds, on present-day Hill Street, (which in the eighteenth-century was known as '*Pot House Lane*').

To date, there has been no planned, formal excavation of any part of the Belfast Potthouse site. Nonetheless, on three occasions, delftware fragments have been collected during building work, showing that a layer of pottery waste occurs throughout this Hill Street area at a depth of c. 0.8 - 1.4 metres below surface. Confirmation that the Belfast Potthouse lay in Hill Street came in 1990, with the help of Dr. McNeill, Prof. Baillie and a third archaeologist from Queen's University, Maura Mulholland.[70] A very large quantity of material was recovered on that first occasion, including the dated '1699' trivet **(Fig. 3)** and the unique inkwell **(Fig. 44)**, but it was later discovered that the most valuable glazed and decorated delftware fragments constituted less than one percent of the total assemblage. Saggar and delftware biscuit fragments, **(Fig.13)**, which made up the bulk of this first assemblage, were collected more selectively on subsequent occasions.

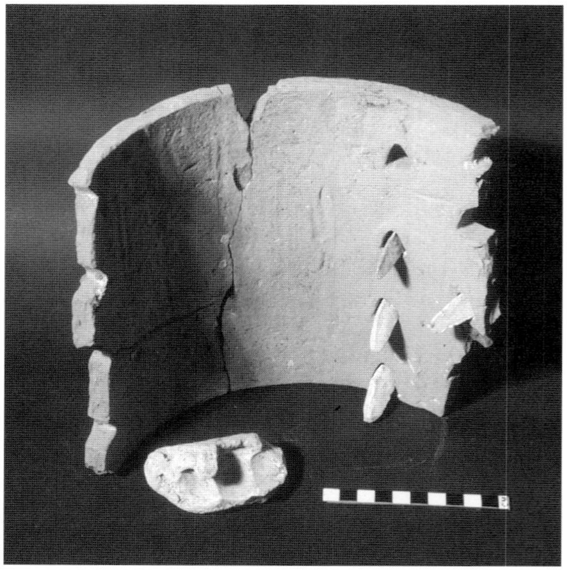

Figure 13. *A large portion of a typical delftware 'saggar', recovered in Hill Street in 1990. Delftware plates were stacked in these cylindrical containers during firing, each supported by three short, triangular pegs inserted around the circumference. This example would have accommodated eight delftware plates of 220-30 mm. diameter. Ht. 205 mm. The fired clay mass in the foreground, with potter's fingerprints deeply impressed, is a clay 'wad'. These were wedged between stacks of saggars ('bungs') in the kiln, to help stabilise the arrangement.*

Some very rare coloured delftware fragments were collected by the author in 1993,[71] but perhaps the most valuable assemblage found to date was encountered in 1994, during re-cobbling work at the junction of Hill Street and Exchange Place. **(Fig.14)**. This small deposit was first spotted by archaeologist Tom McErlean, who, with the support of the Environment and Heritage Service, negotiated a short interruption in the work. This investigation was conducted with the assistance of several archaeologists, kindly provided by the Environment and Heritage Service, and so the delftware collected on that occasion was in better condition than most recovered previously.[72] Later, it even proved possible to reconstruct a number of profiles, including the rare barrel-shaped biscuit-ware tankard illustrated in **Fig. 38**.

For the purposes of this summary, the finds recovered at these three locations in Hill Street in 1990-94, (which were all collected within an area of 35 metres radius) are described as a single, '*Belfast Potthouse*' assemblage.

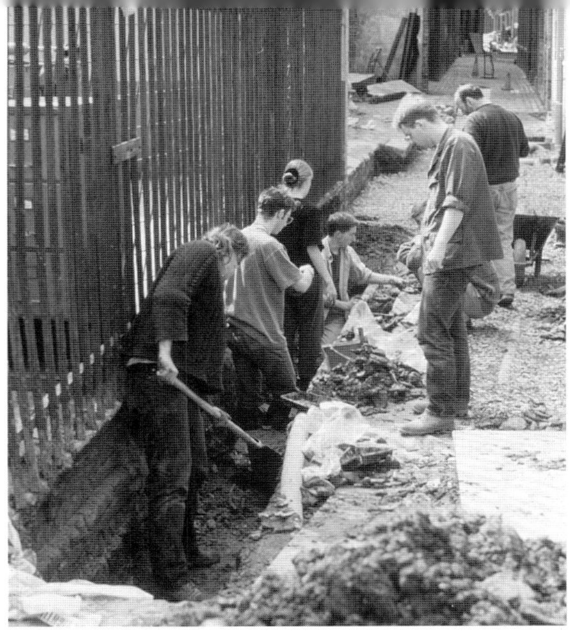

Figure 14*. Archaeologists from the Environment and Heritage Service excavating a small deposit of delftware wasters in 1994, at the junction of Hill Street and Exchange Place, Belfast.*

EXCAVATED WARES

As on most delftware pottery sites, the assemblage recovered from the Belfast Potthouse largely consists of clinker, kiln furniture such as saggar fragments **(Fig. 13)**, and anonymous body shards of unglazed delftware biscuit. The glazed and decorated shards, which give a more immediate indication of the quality of wares produced by the pottery, represent well under 5% of the total finds. One impression that was quickly dispelled by these investigations, however, was that the Potthouse might simply have been a small, local pottery, producing down-market goods for the provincial market. On the contrary, the wares recovered could probably bear comparison with the products of almost any delftware pottery that was then operating in England. The fact that Belfast delftwares are essentially indistinguishable from those of their English counterparts might well explain why they have not been identified in greater numbers in the past.

A common perception that the finds tend to disprove is the notion that the colour of delftware biscuit can serve as an indicator of origin. (A red body colour, for example, is sometimes considered indicative of continental, rather than English tin-glaze). The range of biscuit-ware fragments recovered from the Belfast Potthouse displayed every colour and texture imaginable, from extremely fine, deep red, to a coarse, pale straw-colour or almost pure white. There was certainly no indication that the visual appearance of the Carrickfergus clay body might help in identifying Belfast delftwares. The only correlation observed in this regard was that body colour often varied with the size and form of the object. Small vessels such as cups and porringers, with fine details, were generally produced using a very fine quality, red or pink-firing clay, whereas larger bowls and plates were usually made using the coarser, standard, straw-coloured delftware body.

Most of the glazed shards are undecorated, but around 30% were painted in cobalt-blue, more rarely in manganese purple. For the most part, the painting is undistinguished, consisting of rudimentary floral motifs, with a variety of simple border designs. **(Figs.15-18)**. The predominantly coarse character of the painting does not seem to have varied with the size of the object - most of the small tea-bowls were just as coarsely painted as the very large punch-bowls. **(Fig. 19)**. Some small objects, however, such as the small mug fragment illustrated **(Fig. 20)** and the '*Bird on a rock*' pattern tea-bowl **(Fig. 25**, top right) are more deftly executed. These painted delftware wasters obviously represent a useful starting point for attributions, but a serious obstacle to progress lies in the fact that many of these designs

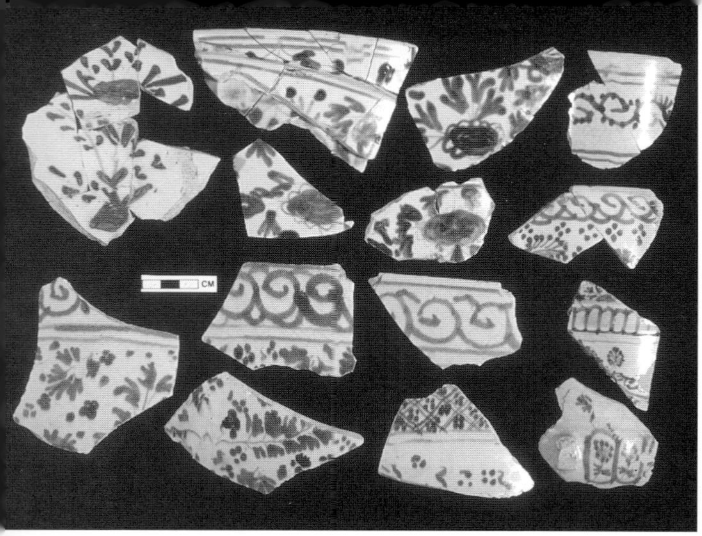

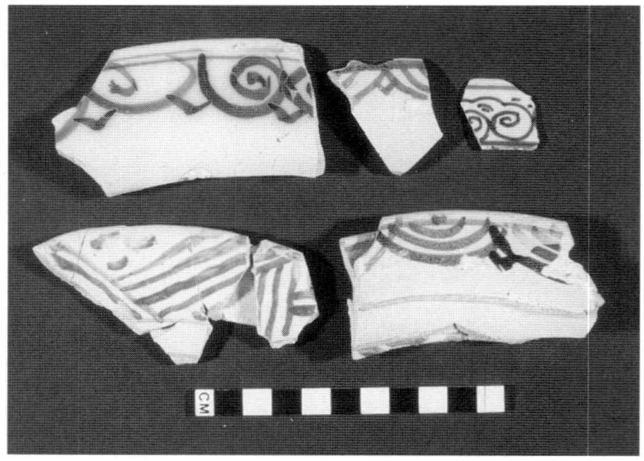

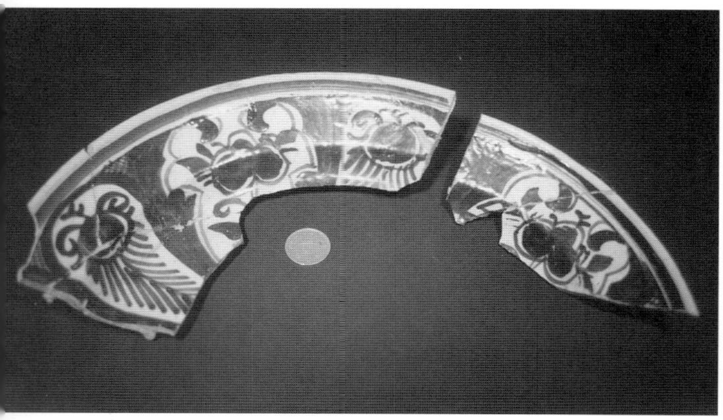

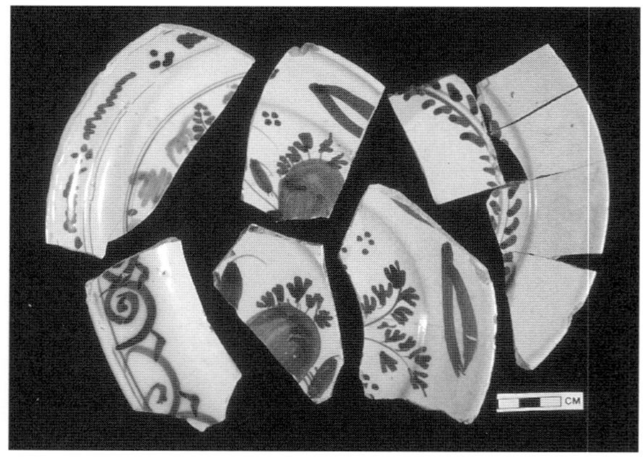

***Top left* : *Figure 15*.** *A selection of large fragments, mainly from bowls, showing the typically coarse character of the standard blue and white painted decoration. The shard on the top right is part of a jug spout. The two shards at bottom right are from a more complex vessel, probably a large, two-handled cup.*
***Top right* : *Figure 16*.** *A selection of plate-border designs.*
***Bottom left* : *Figure 17*.** *The rim portion of charger-sized dish, (Diam. c. 270 mm), with repeating panel-style decoration copying the Chinese. The dish was found during excavations close to the Potthouse in 1980, and was initially considered a continental import.*
***Bottom right* : *Figure 18*.** *Plate fragments. The example on the right, with a painted circular wreath, is of a type that often contains text in the centre - usually 'God Save King George', 'In Memory of Queen Anne' or a line from the 'Merry Man' verse. Unfortunately, no portion bearing the central text was recovered.*

were also produced by English potteries. It is therefore a simple matter to bring together a range of objects that are *comparable* to delftwares produced in Belfast, but positively identifying an individual piece of Belfast delftware is very much more difficult.

Two groups of shards illustrate some of these problems. The first group **(Fig.21)** are portions of a medium-sized, deep bowl, decorated with random dabs of cobalt blue. This style of decoration was so simply achieved that it was probably a common and widespread pattern originally, and several different types of object exhibiting this decoration are extant, albeit with slight colour variation.[73] It is certainly interesting to record that the pattern was produced in Ireland, but it is also highly unlikely that such a simple style of decoration, on its own, will lead to new attributions.

Brush-painted designs exhibit greater character, but even here, attribution remains difficult. **Fig. 22** (overleaf) illustrates a number of under-fired dish shards painted with a complex floral pattern, alongside an intact plate of identical design. From this evidence, there can be little doubt that this pattern was produced in Belfast, but as the intact plate was not painted by the same hand as the shards, it is impossible to confirm that this particular plate was made in Belfast. This highlights a serious obstacle to attribution that often is not apparent,

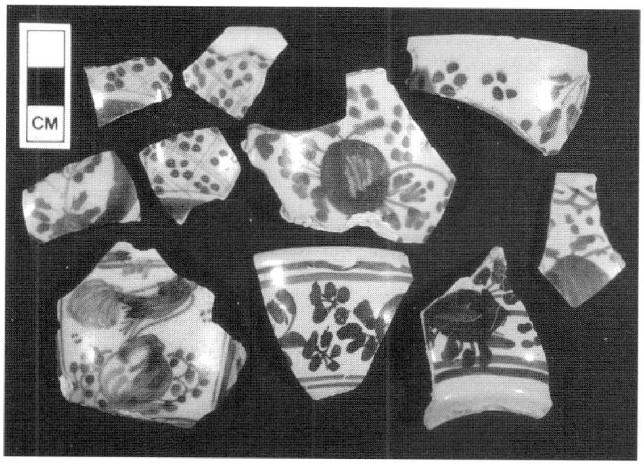

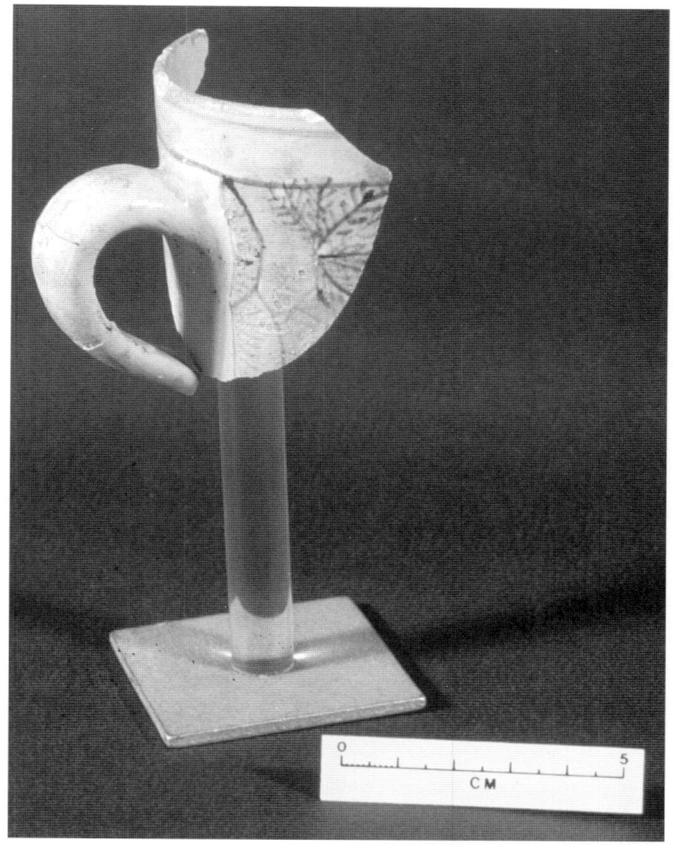

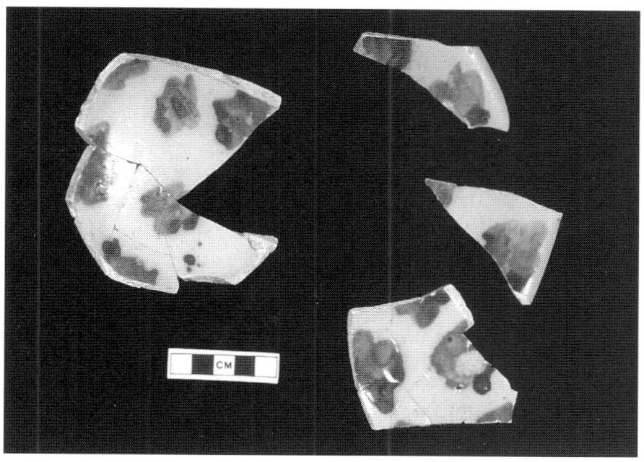

***Top left* : Figure 19.** *Fragments of tea-bowls. The majority are coarsely painted with rudimentary floral motifs.*
***Right* : Figure 20.** *Portion of a small, straight-sided tankard, with blue-dash handle. The cobalt-blue decoration has misfired to a light tan colour. Although the blue painted design can still be discerned, only the additional, manganese highlights are obvious.*
***Bottom left* : Figure 21.** *Fragments of a medium-sized deep bowl with turnover rim, c. 7 in. (180 mm.) diam., with dabbed cobalt blue decoration.*

namely, that unless one is fortunate enough to discover a piece of delftware that was obviously painted by the same hand, at about the same time, the attribution will probably remain weak.

More complex, figurative designs offer better hope for attributions based on painting alone, but unfortunately, such designs are also among the rarest of wasters. (Presumably, greater care was taken in producing finely painted wares. The same argument may explain the rarity of coloured delftware fragments). It was interesting to record a motif known as the '*Three-Brick*' pattern on one large dish fragment, **(Fig. 23)**, as this was previously considered diagnostic of Bristol delftwares.[74] The only true 'charger' fragment found (with a clear lead glaze on the reverse side) was also painted with a figurative design, in this case a Chinese landscape. **(Fig. 24)**. Although the roof of the building and the rocky outcrop appear distinctive, no examples with similar features have yet been encountered in the literature. Other figurative patterns included the '*Seated Chinaman*' pattern, **(Fig. 25 left)**, which was derived from Japanese porcelains. This pattern was popular throughout Europe for many years, and hence was probably produced by most delftware potteries in England during the late-seventeenth and early-eighteenth centuries. '*Leaping Bird*' designs were another common theme, but the painting styles of the two examples found in Belfast do seem to exhibit some degree of individuality. **(Fig. 25, centre and right)**.

Not all floral patterns were devoid of character, as three further excavated examples demonstrate. The first are fragments of a large punch-bowl, **(Fig.26)**,

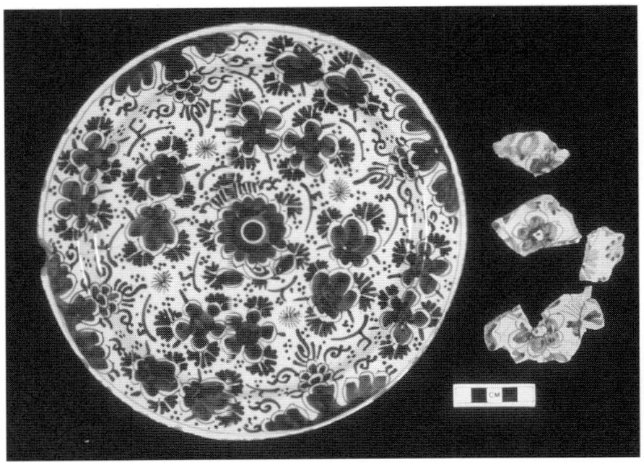

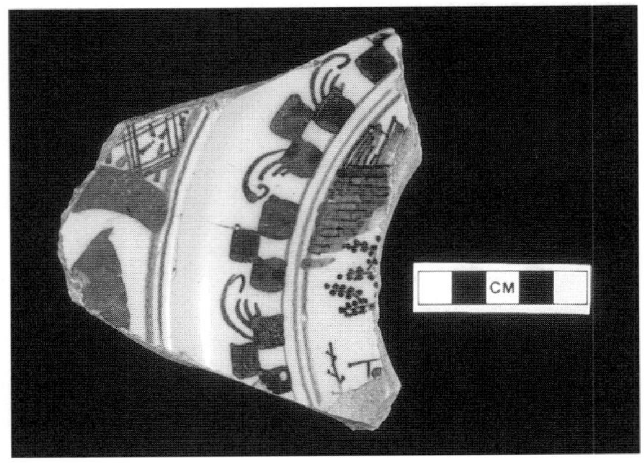

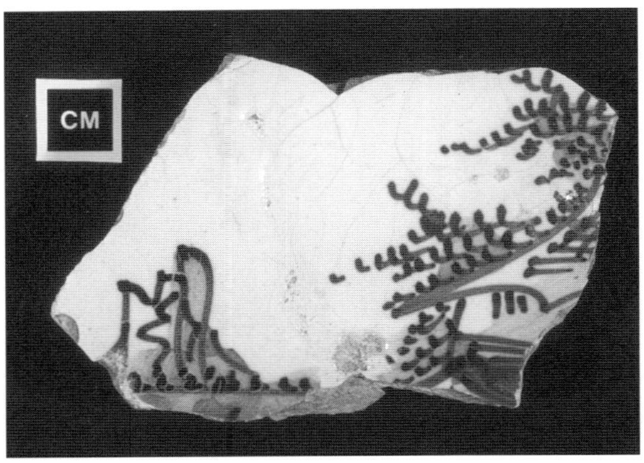

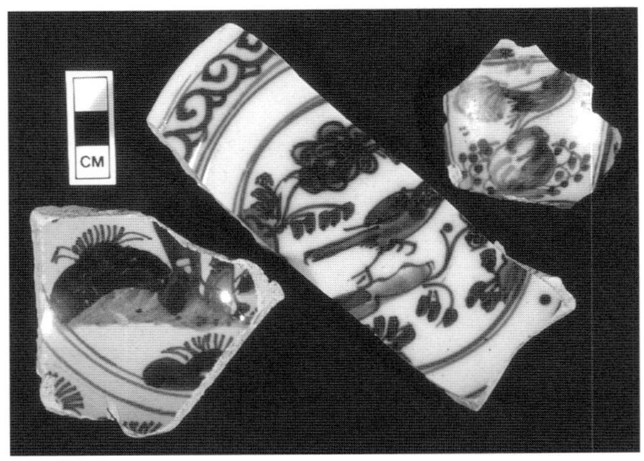

Top Left : Figure 22. *Flower-painted shards, shown alongside an intact English or Irish plate of similar design.*
Top Right : Figure 23. *Portion of a large, heavy dish (11 mm. thick), with a Chinese-style landscape in the central well. The 'Three Brick' motif was once considered exclusive to Bristol delftware.*
Bottom Left : Figure 24. *The only true 'charger' fragment recovered from the Belfast Potthouse site, (with a clear, lead-glazed underside). Surprisingly perhaps, it is rare to find Chinese landscape decoration on chargers.*
Bottom Right : Figure 25. *Three of the more distinctive figurative patterns recorded. The 'seated Chinaman' pattern on the left was an extremely common one at the time, but the two 'leaping bird' designs are more distinctive.*
The blue-painted central fragment, from a small-sized plate, was highlighted in yellow and/or green on the body and branch, but the colours have mis-fired. The fragment at top right is part of a tea-bowl.

painted in cobalt blue and manganese with six individual panels, each of which portray a different type of flower. Sufficient fragments of this bowl were found to allow a reasonably accurate reconstruction to be made. **(Fig. 27)**. Other wares were more finely painted. **Fig. 28** shows fragments of a small bowl and a saucer, delicately painted with fine brush strokes to replicate the Chinese, pencilled style of decoration. The pattern of the saucer, with its central insect, is almost identical to a known example.[75] Once again, however, as this saucer and the shard were not painted by the same hand, we can only be certain that saucers of this design were produced in Belfast.

A third floral-decorated fragment, in this case the central portion from a plate of standard size, (c. 8 in. diam.), is much more coarsely painted. **(Fig. 29)**. The pattern appears to show a rose and thistle, suggesting that it was produced to commemorate the Act of Union between Scotland and England in 1707. A comparable style of '*Union*' plate has been excavated in London, but this example from Belfast is very much more crudely executed.[76]

Before the shards were first recovered, it was expected that any coloured delftware shards found, **(Colour Plate 2)**, would probably represent the most distinctive and informative fragments of all, but this did not prove the case. As on English delftware sites,

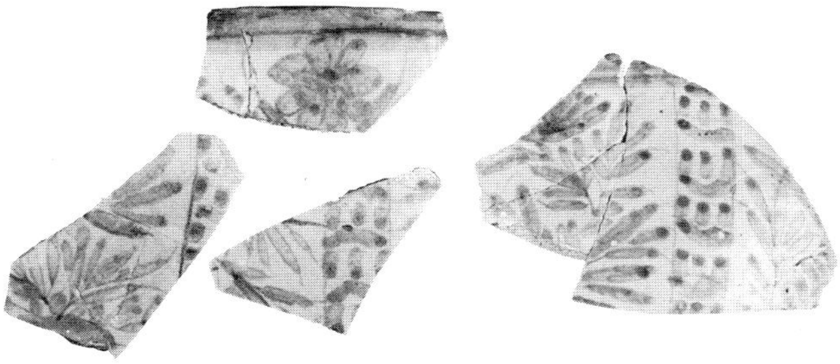

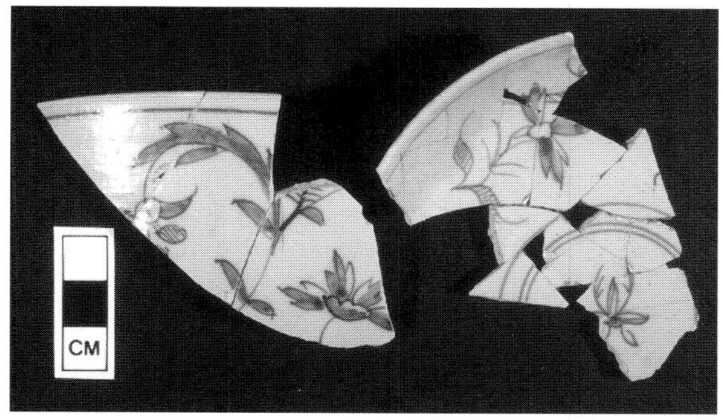

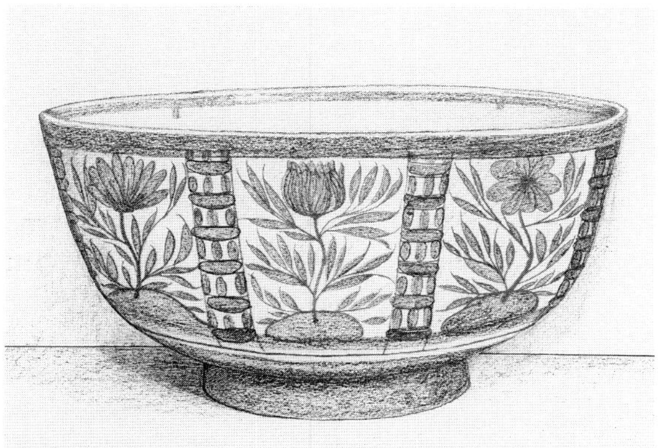

Top : **Figure 26**. *Fragments of a large punch-bowl, decorated in cobalt blue and manganese purple. Probable Diam. c. 300 mm..*
***Above* : Figure 27**. *A reconstruction of the bowl illustrated in Fig.26.*
***Top right* : Figure 28**. *'Pencilled' decoration on fragments of a bowl (left) and saucer (right).*
***Below right* : Figure 29**. *Plate fragment painted with a crude, 'Union' design of thistle and rose, commemorating the union of Scotland and England in 1707.*

coloured shards are exceptionally rare, and the very few that do survive are subject to precisely the same problem as blue and white shards, namely, that painted decoration alone is unlikely to lead to new attributions, unless the pieces were obviously painted by the same hand. These difficulties are again illustrated in **Colour Plate 3**. Here, the plate is painted with a design recorded amongst saucer shards from the Potthouse site, but as they were not painted by the same hand, the attribution cannot be confirmed. (A similar pattern was also produced in blue and white - see Fig. 17). The most that can be said is that this pattern was certainly produced in Belfast, probably in both blue and white and in polychrome. Dated examples of plates featuring this design range from 1721 to 1738, which indicates that other potteries continued to produce this design long after the Belfast Potthouse closed.[77]

Rather than painted designs, the features that are likely to prove the most reliable and diagnostic for attribution purposes are the small, moulded details. During the early eighteenth century, before mould making became a specialist trade in its own right, the moulds and formers for such details would have been produced by the potters themselves. A moulded feature, such as a porringer handle, for example, should therefore be a reliable and specific indicator of Belfast delftware. Six different styles of porringer handle have now been found in Belfast, **(Fig. 30)**, one of which was excavated in the early 1900s and has not been re-encountered since. **(Fig. 31)**. Despite this variety, no examples matching the Belfast designs have yet been discovered, with the possible exception of a plain white porringer sold in London in 1992.[78]

When we examine the Belfast wasters more closely, other, less obvious moulded details become apparent. The plain white cup fragments, for example, **(Fig. 32)**, all appear to have been produced with the aid of some kind of former, and hence possess an identical, thin ridge running around the body, about a third of the way up.

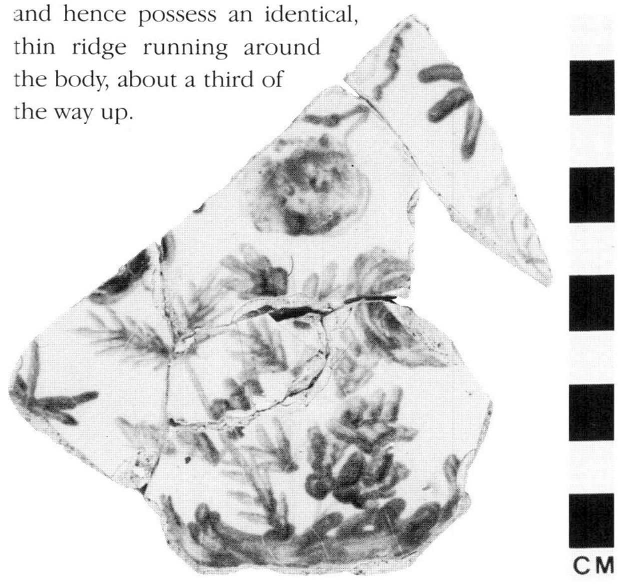

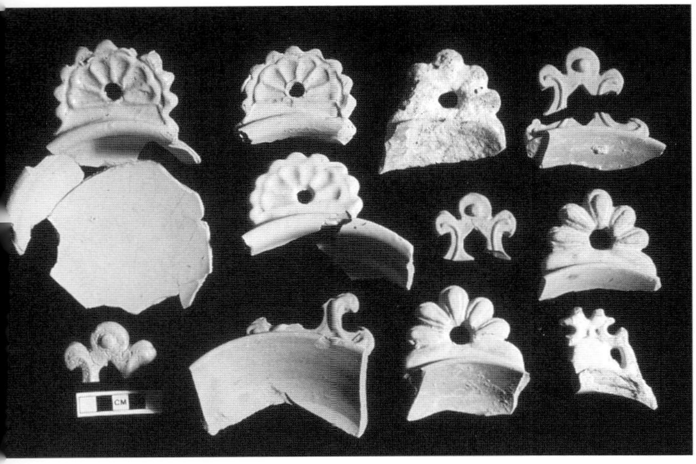

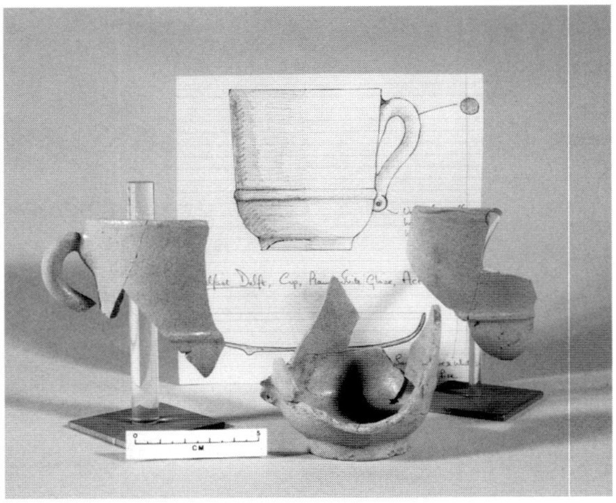

Fragments of a different style of small, waisted and flared cup, more properly termed a *capuchine*, have only been recorded amongst the Potthouse wasters in plain white delftware, but these too appear to have been thrown with the aid of a former. **(Fig. 33)**.[79] The same profile is evident on a cup of identical size in Colonial Williamsburg, which in addition has been decorated in blue and white with iron-red, on-glaze decoration. **(Fig. 34)**. Identical colours, and the same, painted scroll motif are found amongst the Belfast assemblage, suggesting that this intact cup at Williamsburg may have originated at the Belfast Potthouse. The shape was a common one, however, and so despite these similarities the attribution must remain 'English or possibly Irish'. A very similar capuchine or cup is illustrated by Archer, (Cat. H.2), which is attributed to London, probably Lambeth.[80]

Other possible attributions derive from similarly small, moulded features. For example, a large fragment of a flared, straight-sided tankard was excavated in Belfast, crudely painted with alternating vertical stripes of cobalt blue and copper green. **(Fig. 35. See also Colour Plate 2)**. The intact tankard shown **(Fig. 36)** is similarly decorated in stripes, but it is much smaller, and the cobalt blue stripes alternate with manganese-purple rather than copper-green. Despite these differences, these two tankards share a distinctive feature - two raised, moulded bands running around the body of the pot - one appearing about an inch below the rim, the other around the base. As these two tankards are of different sizes, the attribution is inconclusive, but the correspondence in these small, moulded details does significantly improve the possibility that the intact tankard was made in Belfast.

Tankard bases of all sizes were amongst the more common biscuit-ware vessels recovered. Most appear to have been wheel-thrown, and although many exhibit incised ridges about 1/2 in. to 1 1/2 in. above the base, each one was individual in character - the forms themselves were not diagnostic. Nonetheless, in recent years, one particular group of highly distinctive cylindrical tankards

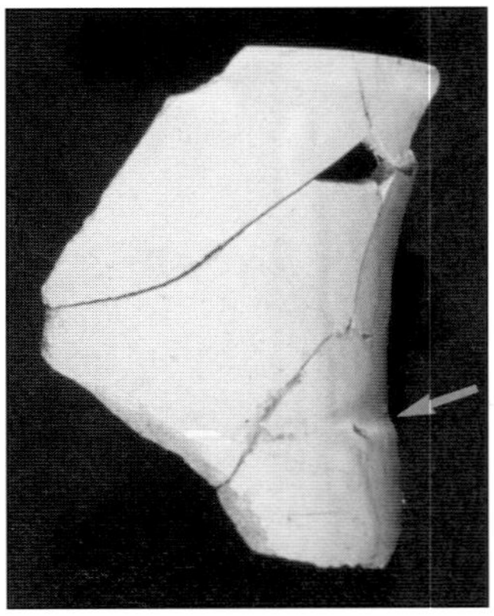

Top left : Figure 30. *Porringer handles recovered from the Belfast Potthouse site. (See also Fig. 31). An intact porringer, with a handle matching any of these designs, would almost certainly be attributable to Belfast.*
Lower left : Figure 31. *An extreme enlargement of a photograph published by R. M. Young in 1909, showing an otherwise unrecorded porringer handle from the Belfast Potthouse site. (See footnote 68 for ref.).*
Top right : Figure 32 *Plain white, broad-bodied cups, with a median ridge and a distinctive handle terminal.*
Bottom right : Figure 33. *Plain white, small, flared cup or capuchine, with a distinct, mould-formed 'waist'.*

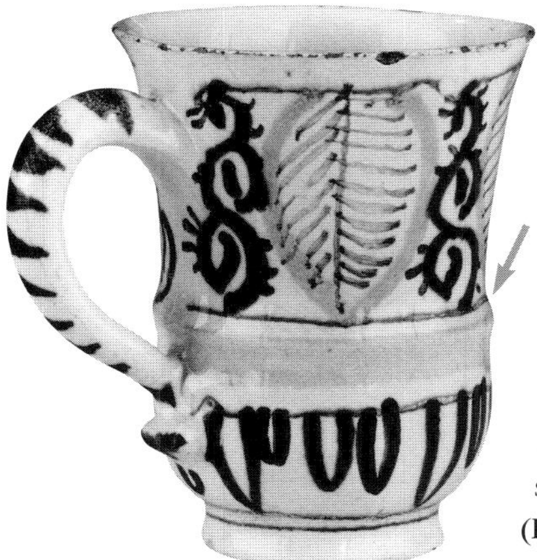

has come to be associated with Belfast, **(Figs.37, 37a, Colour Plate 4)**. These polychrome *'Union'* tankards, which commemorate the Act of Union between England and Scotland in 1707, occur in at least two sizes. The taller example **(Fig.37)** is painted with a six-banded lattice, the smaller type, **(Fig.37a)** has five lattice bands. The painted script *'union'* is similar in both cases, although there are slight variations in colour, and the top border pattern differs significantly.

Attention was drawn to these *'Union'* tankards by a well-known collector in Belfast, the late Robert Jackson, who discovered two examples, decorated in the same colours as the larger type of tankard, **(Fig. 37)** on a Belfast market-stall in 1970. Both tankards were sold into the London trade in about 1972, but their present whereabouts appear to be unknown. (The example in **Fig. 37** has been known since before 1948, and in **Fig. 37a** since 1954). The colours of the larger tankard are distinctive (the green bands especially), although they do seem to compare well with some of the colours recorded on the Belfast Potthouse site **(Colour Plate 2)**. The Smith family, the owners of the Potthouse, had many relatives living in Glasgow, and there was extensive trade in all manner of goods between Belfast and Glasgow at that date. For all of these reasons, there is good reason to believe that these *'Union'* tankards might well have been produced in Belfast - presumably for the Scottish market, perhaps for Scottish families in Ulster - but the attribution must remain tentative until more conclusive evidence is found. Delftwares commemorating the Scottish Act of Union have also been excavated on the site of the Vauxhall Pottery in London. (See Britton, *London*, p. 70).

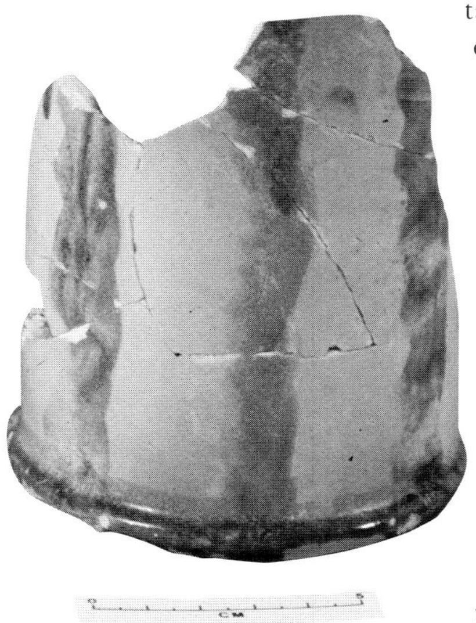

One of the only distinctive tankard forms from Belfast is a large, barrel-shaped tankard, recorded in delftware biscuit at the Potthouse site **(Fig.38)**. This form has been further enhanced with two series of concentric, incised bands, above and below a broad, plain central band. The barrel shaped profile and handle attachment can be clearly seen.

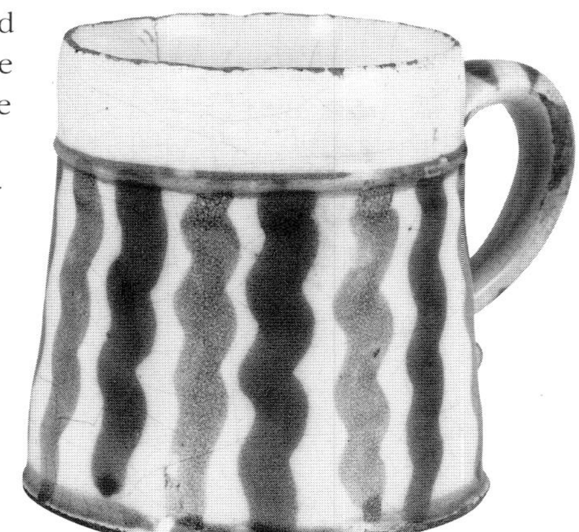

Barrel-shaped tankards of this date are extremely rare in delftware, and only one example analogous to the Belfast waster appears to be extant.[81] This is a fine, commemorative tankard inscribed *'To the Pious Memory of Queen Anne 1720'*. **(Fig.39, Colour Plate 5)**. The basic form, handle termination and size (basal diam. 3¼ in., 82 mm.), appear identical to the Belfast example, and the incised horizontal, concentric bands have been highlighted with painted blue lines. In addition to this close match of form, the Queen Anne tankard is also similar to the second Belfast shoe in colour and appearance **(Colour Plate 1)**. On balance, therefore, this important tankard is perhaps the firmest Belfast attribution to have come out of the excavated finds.

Top left : Figure 34. *A flared cup or capuchine from the Colonial Williamsburg collection, of identical form to the fragment illustrated in Fig. 33, decorated in cobalt-blue and iron-red. Ht. 76 mm., 3 in. (Illustrated in colour in Austin, p. 40, Pl. 8).*
Bottom left : Figure 35. *A tapered mug fragment, decorated with copper-green and cobalt-blue stripes. Ht. 100mm. Two thin moulded ridges are evident, at the very top edge of the fragment, and around the base. The upper ridge is not visible in this photograph.*
Middle right : Figure 36. *A small tapered mug, identical in form to the fragment shown in Fig, 35, but of much smaller size. Ht. 82 mm., 3¼ in. The two moulded ridges are evident at the top and bottom of the painted stripes.*

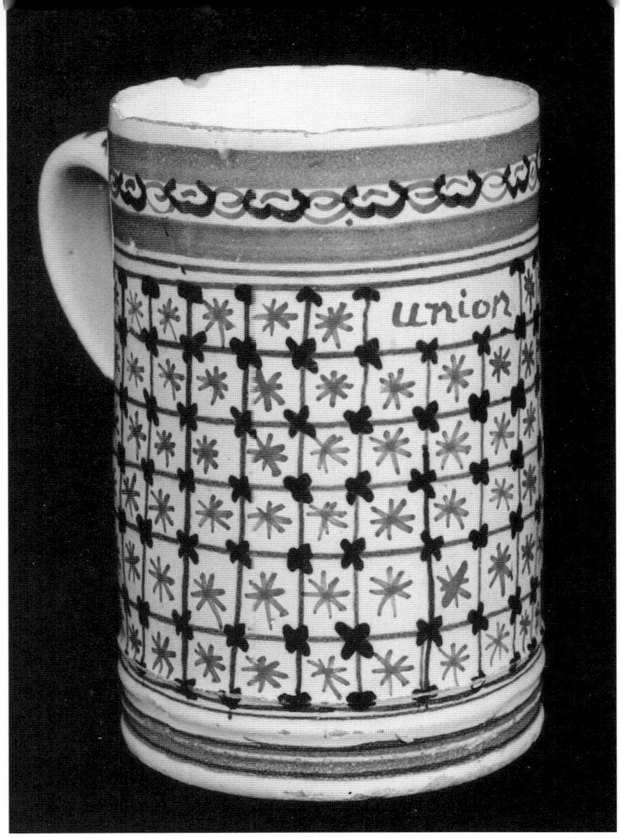

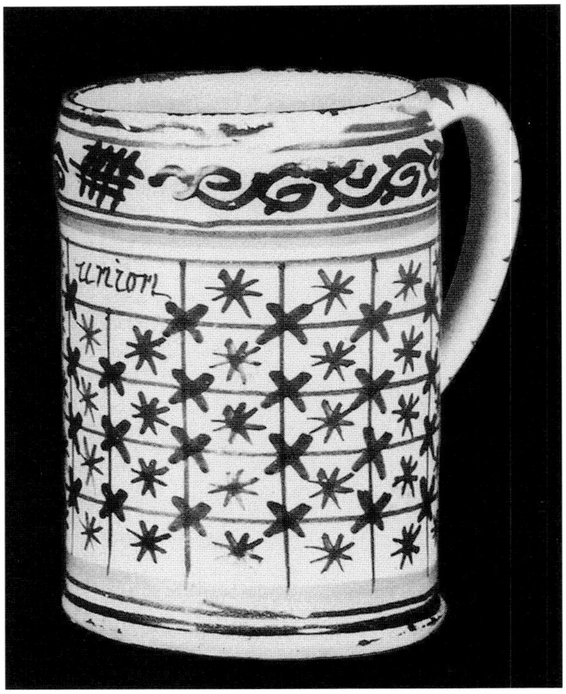

An interesting barrel-shaped flask was recently recorded in London, **(Fig. 40)**, which is also well worth considering in this context.[82] (The unusual shape is copied from K'ang Hsi period Chinese porcelain originals.[83] The 'lid' of the barrel is fixed - the flared 'bung' at the top is in fact the pouring spout). Like the biscuit-ware tankard fragment from Belfast, and the Queen Anne tankard, this flask bears incised, horizontal bands. (The bands that occur on the much larger barrel, attributed to Dublin, c.1748, **Fig. 51** are similarly spaced). Other motifs within the painted decoration consist of bands of *rui* heads, crosshatched diamonds and keyfret designs, but only the *rui* heads have been recorded amongst the Belfast shards. Once again, however, the character of the glaze and decoration is strongly reminiscent of the second Belfast shoe, and so a Belfast attribution is certainly possible. Had the biscuit-ware tankard fragment from Belfast not exhibited a handle terminal, this barrel-flask would have seemed a particularly convincing match.

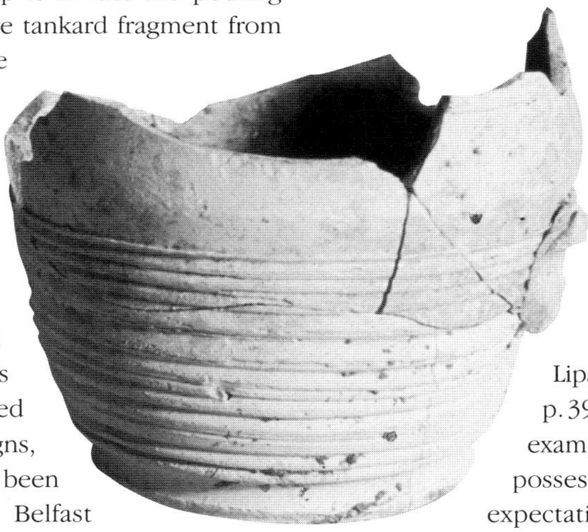

Flatware fragments made up the largest part of the excavated material from Belfast, but few of these forms were in any way distinctive. A very large quantity of biscuit-ware fragments were found of large, fluted and scalloped dishes, copying metal shapes, (see for example Lipski & Archer, Nos. 96 & 98, p.39). As on most English examples of these dishes, none possessed a footrim. Contrary to expectation, however, the great majority of these dishes were not press-moulded, as they appear. Instead, the Belfast potters

***Top left* : *Figure 37*.** *Tall tankard commemorating the Act of Union between Scotland and England in 1707. Two tankards of this type were discovered in Belfast in 1970. Ht.5½ in.,140 mm.*
***Top right* : *Figure 37a*.** *Short 'Union' tankard. Ht.4¾ in.,120 mm.*
***Bottom* : *Figure 38*.** *Excavated biscuit-ware waster of a barrel-shaped tankard, basal diam.3⅛ in.,80 mm.*

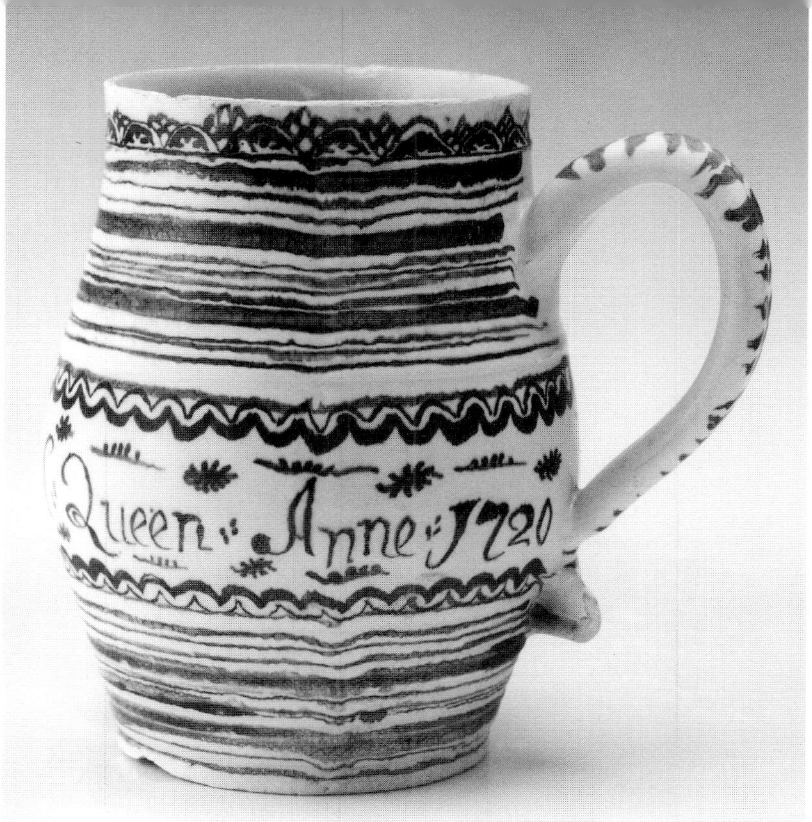

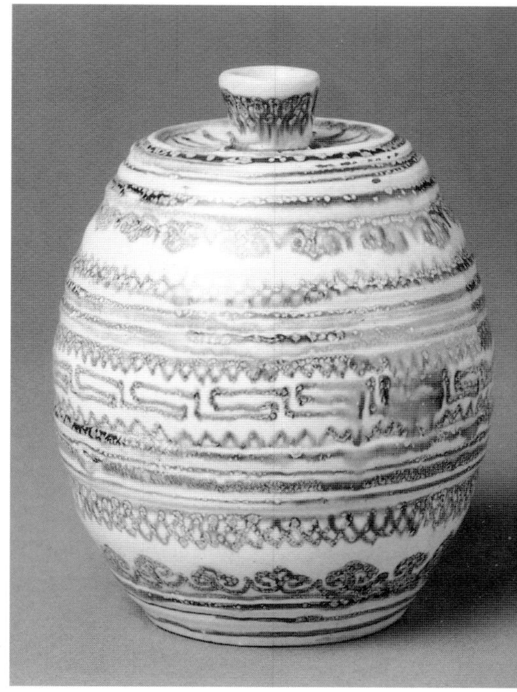

achieved the lobed border by simply running a finger outward across the damp clay. As they were not made in moulds, however, the forms are not diagnostic. A small number of more complex dish fragments were also found which seem to be analogous to forms produced at Brislington. (See for example, Lipski & Archer no. 124, p. 46). Some of these were certainly press moulded, but none of the fragments recovered was sufficiently large to aid in identifying an intact example.

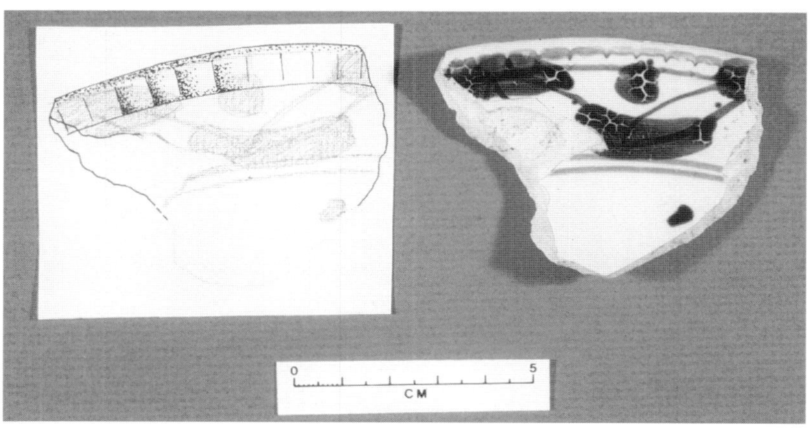

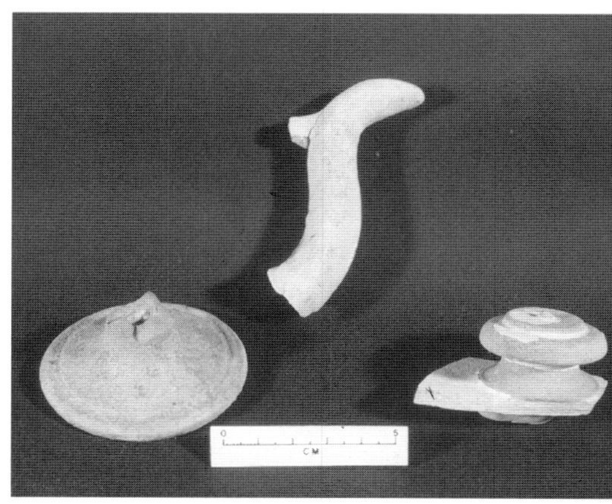

Top left : Figure 39. *Barrel-shaped tankard,probably made in Belfast, with incised bands inscribed 'To the Pious Memory of Queen Anne 1720'. The form matches the excavated biscuit-ware example (Fig. 38). Ht. 6 1/8 in., 156 mm. Basal diam. 3 1/4 in. 82 mm. See also Colour Plate 5.*

Top right : Figure 40. *Delftware barrel-shaped flask, possibly Belfast, with four bands of incised or moulded hoops, an integral top, and a short, flared pouring spout in the centre. Painted in blue with bands of concentric circles, rui heads, crosshatched diamonds and keyfret design. Ht. 4 7/8 in., 125 mm.*

Bottom left : Figure 41. *Plate rim fragment from the Belfast Potthouse site, with distinctive 'pie-crust' or dentate moulding around the rim, underneath the glaze.*

Bottom right : Figure 42. *Three of the more unusual objects recorded in Belfast. Left to right; Goblet base, Ewer spout and Posset-pot knop.*

Only one, very much smaller feature was observed on some of the more standard Belfast plates, which might prove useful. **(Fig. 41)**. The painted border pattern on the example shown is an extremely common one, but the fine, dentate moulding around the rim is an unusual and distinctive feature. (The faint moulding is largely disguised by glaze, and so might easily be overlooked).

In summary, the range of wares encountered on the Belfast Potthouse site seem to represent the typical repertoire of an early-eighteenth century delftware pottery. Many of the more standard wares found are not illustrated here, but they include all manner of plates and bowls, a barber's bowl, wet and dry drug jars, jug fragments, chamber pots and spittoons, porringers, posset pots, table salts and many other vessels. Some wall tile fragments were also recorded, although none were glazed or decorated. In contrast to the later Dublin pottery, no painted backmarks of any kind were observed, but one biscuit-ware bowl base did bear a large incised 'M' inside the footrim, c. 2 cm. in height.[84]

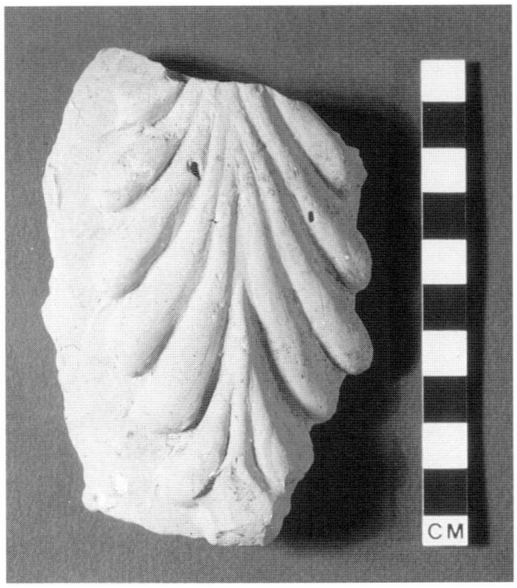

Several of the Belfast biscuit-ware shards were more unusual, however, and few comparable examples seem be recorded in delftware literature. The ewer-spout shown in **Figure 42**, for example, obviously copies Chinese and continental forms, but no English examples of such ewers seem to have been recorded.[85] The biscuit-ware base fragment, shown on the left of **Fig. 42**, seems to be part of a rare delftware wine-goblet. Most surviving goblets are much older than the Belfast Potthouse (c. 1650-60), although the bowl of one example, excavated by Prof. Garner in London, bears a comparable date (1715).[86] The very large pendant moulding **(Fig. 43)**, almost certainly comes from a large urn, as similar moulding is recorded on a massive, blue-splashed, late-seventeenth century urn, attributed to London.[87] Yet perhaps the most remarkable object excavated to date is a large, biscuit-ware, ink-well fragment. **(Fig. 44)**. No similar inkwells appear to have been recorded in English delftware, although a single example is known in Dutch delft. **(Fig. 45)**.[88] The small circular scar of a candle-sconce is still evident on the Belfast inkwell, (placed centrally, between the holes for the inkwell and sand pot). There are also remains of a shallow pen-tray along the front edge.

Many of the problems encountered in

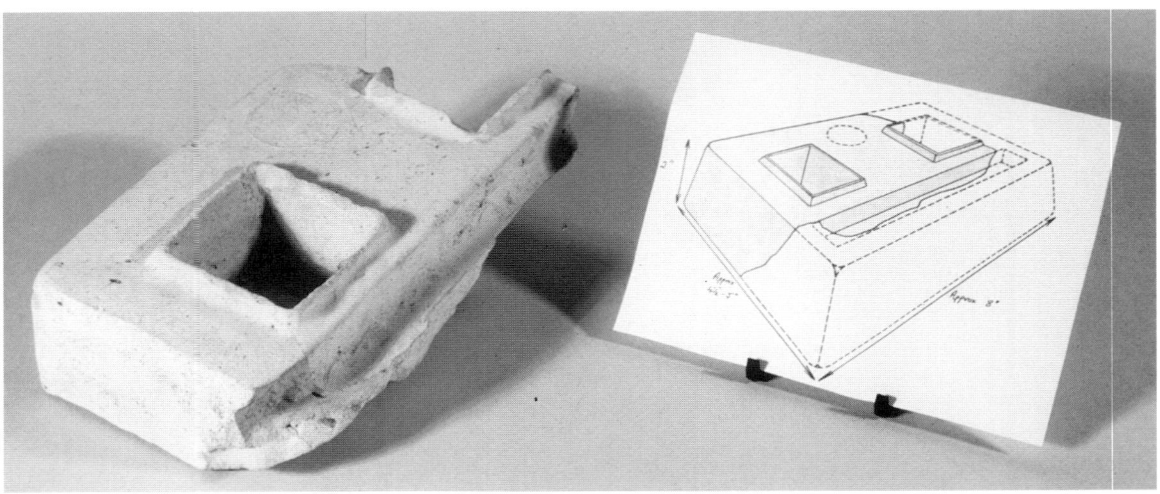

*Top : **Figure 43**. Large pendant moulding, probably from a large, glazed urn. (For indoor rather than outdoor use).*

***Bottom** : **Figure 44**. Biscuit-ware inkwell fragment from the Belfast Potthouse site. The form appears to be unrecorded in English delftware. A surface scar indicates that a candle-sconce was also present originally, placed centrally between the two, square wells.*

attributing wares to Belfast are summarised in one of the most impressive pieces of delftware of all - a previously unrecorded polychrome posset pot, dated 1724, which recently turned up in the Isle of Man. **(Fig. 46, Colour Plate 6)**. As we have already seen, this painted

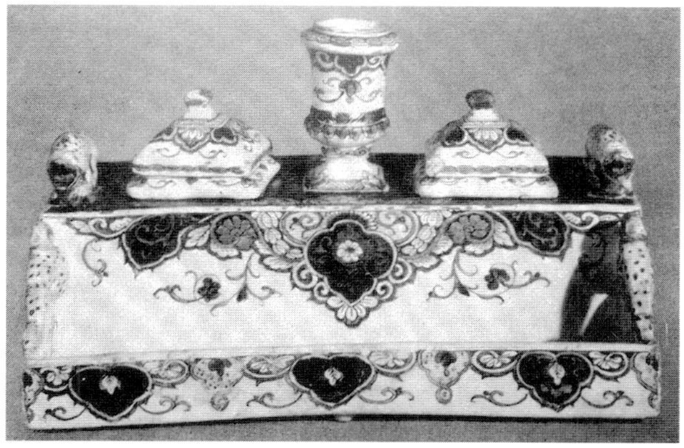

knops and spouts have been recorded, **(Fig. 42, left, Fig. 47 right)**. Even the date, 1724, is coincidental with the date of the original Belfast shoe. Yet despite all of this supporting evidence, the only safe course is to suggest that this posset-pot *may* have been made in Belfast.

design was one of the more common patterns produced in Belfast, **(Fig. 47)** and its colours also closely match the excavated shards. The green leaves, which have been drawn with a broad, italic brush or

Without moulded details or some other distinguishing, diagnostic feature, the attribution cannot be conclusively established.

Nonetheless, the very fact that such wonderful

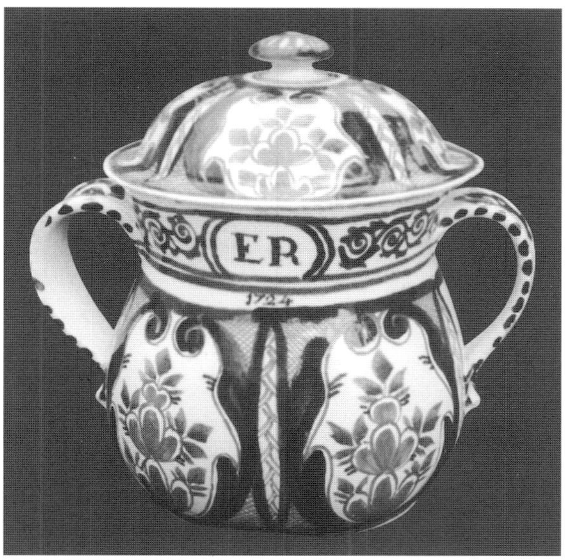

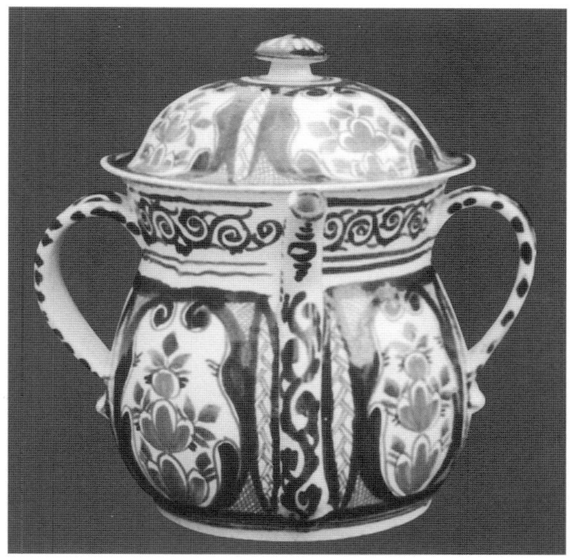

quill, are identical in style to leaves on the heel of the second Belfast shoe **(Figs. 10, 12)**. In addition, we know that posset pots of this approximate size were certainly produced in Belfast, as both

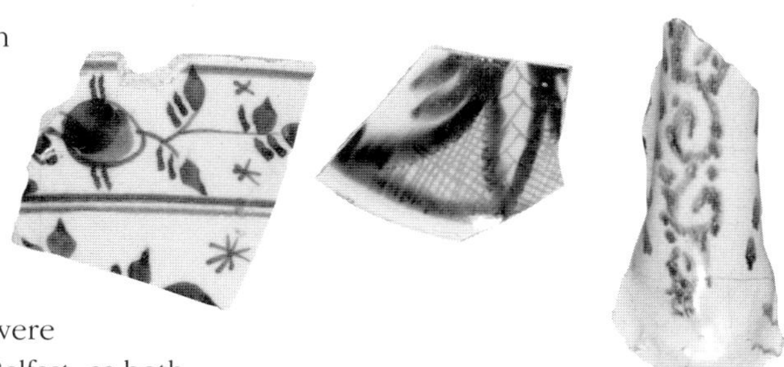

objects can be considered *potentially* Irish shows how far these researches have come in recent years. Hopefully, there will be many further surprises in the years ahead, as more Belfast delftware comes to light.

Top : ***Figure 45.*** *A Dutch delft inkwell of similar form to the example recorded in Belfast. (Size not recorded).*

Middle left and right : ***Figure 46.*** *A polychrome posset-pot, inscribed 'ER 1724', of similar form to examples recorded in Belfast. English or possibly Irish. Ht. 9 in., 229 mm. See also Colour Plate 6.*

Bottom : ***Figure 47.*** *Excavated shards from the Belfast Potthouse site, including a posset-pot spout (right).*

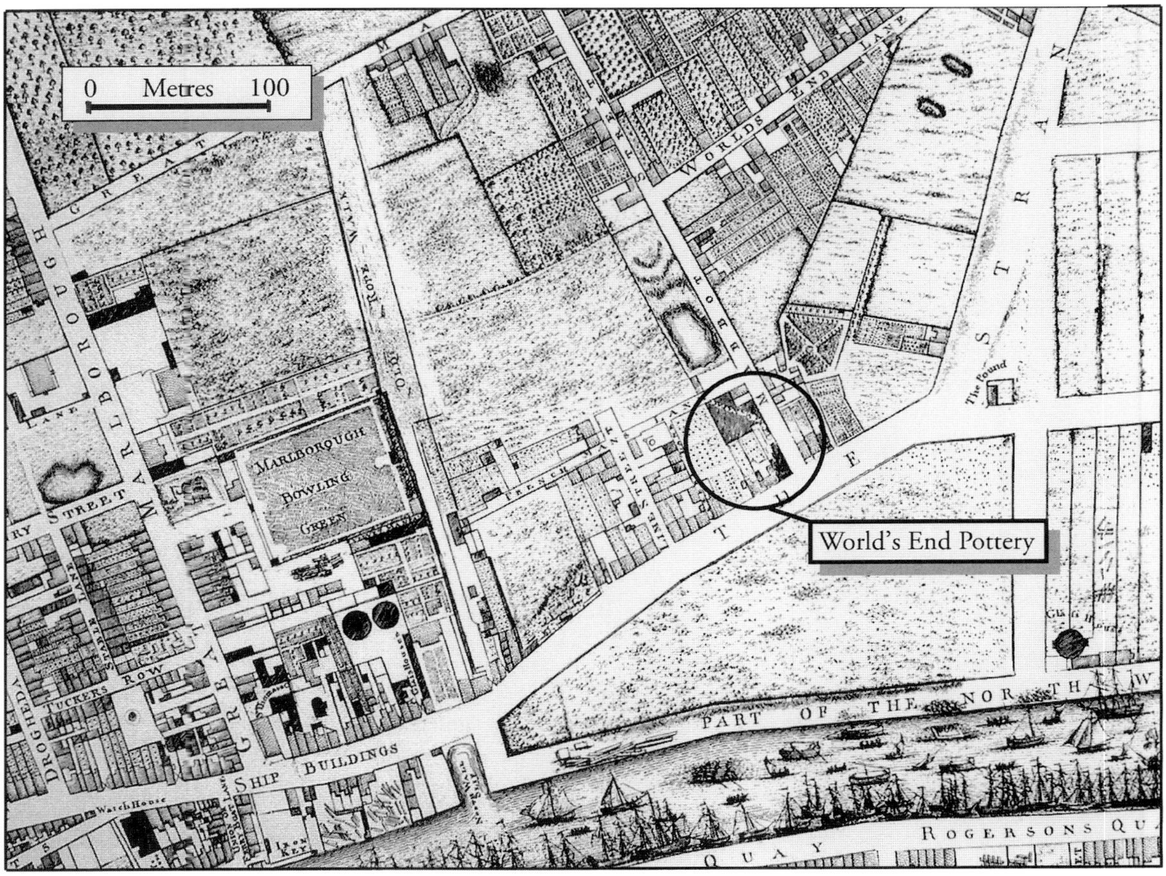

Figure 48. *The 'World's End' and the Strand, from John Rocque's map of Dublin, 1756.*

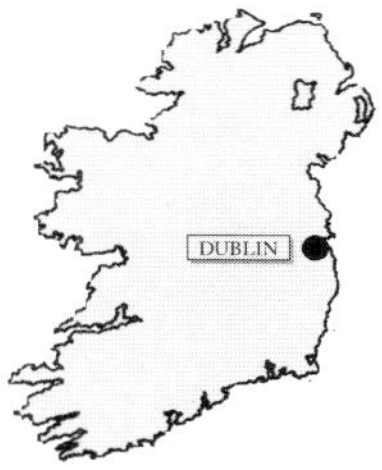

CHAPTER 2
DUBLIN; THE WORLD'S END POTTERY
PART 1; Documentary History
i : John Chambers (before 1735 - c.1747)

The first delftware pottery in Dublin was probably established between 1733 and 1735, although the earliest documentary confirmation of its existence dates from several years later, when an advertisement appeared in the *Dublin Daily Advertiser* of 5th February 1737;

'At the World's End, near the Ship Buildings on the North Strand, is a White Pothouse erected, where all manner of blue and white earthenware is made, equal in goodness in every respect to any imported from Delft or England, and will be sold 25 per cent. cheaper than any can be imported from abroad; as the goods are no way inferior to any foreign goods, it is humbly hoped the proprietors of said work will meet with encouragement. N. B. - There will be good encouragement to wholesale dealers, and apothecaries will be supplied with all manner of pots for their use by directing to Mr. John Chambers at said Pot House'

This is the earliest mention of the pottery at the '*World's End*' in Dublin, later known variously as the '*Irish Delft Manufactory*', the '*China Manufactory*' or simply '*the Pot House on the Strand*', which in its day was the largest and most successful fine-quality pottery in Ireland.[1] During the 1730s, the area known as the World's End represented the very eastern margin of Dublin's northern suburbs, **(Fig.48)**. The broad expanse of flat ground that lay farther east, between the true shoreline (The Strand) and the diverted course of the River Liffey, was prone to flood at high tides, but this problem gradually eased as land-reclamation progressed during the 1730s and 40s.

Although there were numerous vacant green-field sites nearby, John Chambers chose to erect his new '*White Pothouse*' on a plot of ground that was already built upon by 1728.[2] Unfortunately, there is no evidence on the 1728 map to indicate the nature of the business that existed there previously. A pottery probably operated in this general area from the late-seventeenth century onwards, for the death of one Thomas Grissold or Grizold, a '*potter on the Strand*', was recorded in c.1706, but the Strand was a large area, and the two potteries may have been unconnected.[3]

The distinguished Dutch potter, John Philip Elers, also moved to Dublin from London before 1701. (His tale is similar to that of Matthew Garner in Belfast, p.11. Both Elers and Garner produced stonewares before coming to Ireland, and both had legal encounters with John Dwight).[4] Elers was made a freeman merchant of the City of Dublin, '*gratis*', in Michaelmas 1702, having reputedly been established in trade there by the wife of John Shute, a London barrister, (later created 1st Baron and Viscount Barrington). There is little specific evidence of John Phillip Elers' activities following his arrival in Ireland. From 1714-22, he most likely earned his livelihood as a dealer in oriental porcelain, selling goods purchased by his brother David at the East India Company sales in London. The family also seem to have prospered in Ireland - Elers' son Paul, who trained as a barrister, went on to become the co-purchaser of land near Dublin in 1728 for £30,000.[5]

The origins of the delftware manufacturer, John Chambers, are similarly obscure. There is no mention of any individual of this surname working in the delftware industry in England, Scotland or Ireland, prior to his appearance in Dublin in the 1730s, which suggests that, like David and Patrick Smith in Belfast, Chambers came from a mercantile rather than a potting background. The most likely candidate, or rather, the *only* potential candidate identified so far, was a John Chambers from Belfast, who by exceptional coincidence was closely related to the Smith family, the owners of the Belfast Potthouse. Unfortunately, we face the same difficulties with Chambers as we encountered with Matthew Garner in Belfast, in that whilst there is strong circumstantial evidence to suggest the two John Chambers in Belfast and Dublin were the same individual, there is, as yet, no conclusive proof of the fact.

If we assume for now, however, that the connection is correct, then the John Chambers who established the first delftware pottery in Dublin was born in Belfast towards the end of the seventeenth-century. (The surname was variously recorded as '*Chambers*', '*Chalmers*' and '*De la Chambre*').[6] He was the second son of a Belfast merchant, also named John Chambers, who had served in 1706 as an executor of the will of David Smith, the founder of the Belfast Potthouse.[7] By the 1720s, the Smiths and the Chambers were merchant families in Belfast of roughly equivalent stature - both were involved in transatlantic trade with the West Indies, and both were reasonably wealthy. They were also very closely tied by marriage. One of John Chambers' sisters, Mary, was married to a Patrick Smith *junior* of Belfast, (who later moved to Waterford). A second sister, Elizabeth, was married to Dr. Andrew Smith, the son of Andrew Smith of Dublin, another distant relation of the Belfast Smiths.[8]

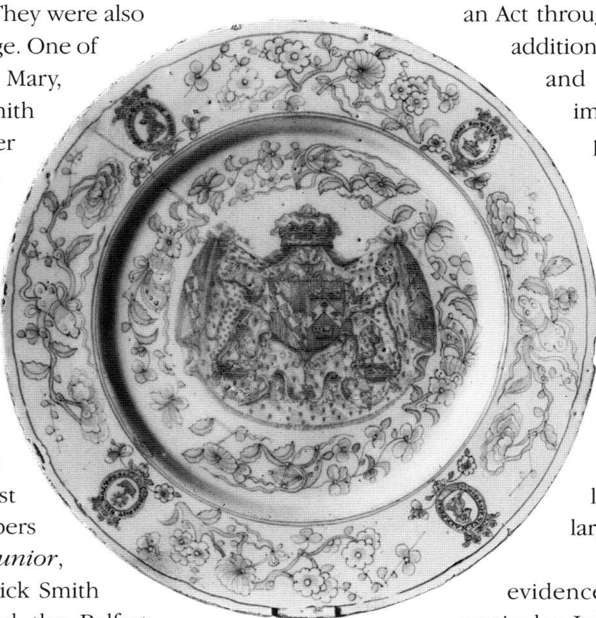

The individual who most clearly points to a link between the Belfast Potthouse and the Chambers family is Patrick Smith *junior*, possibly a nephew of Patrick Smith *senior*, who had managed the Belfast Potthouse in 1706. (See p. 16).[9] Patrick *junior* was also probably related to another Smith, '*Ann Smith, widow*', who in 1731 owned the larger of the two leases for Carrickfergus Clay (Appendix I, iii, p.170). Both put up £500 towards James Swift's proposal for a bank in Dublin in 1721.[10]

John Chambers' father was buried in Belfast in August 1725. Two years later, in October 1727, all of his six children, including John, jointly sold the Belfast properties they had inherited to their brother-in-law, Patrick Smith *junior*, for £520.[11] (These properties included one building - the '*Mansion House*' in High Street - which sounds as if it may have been the Chambers' family home). There are no subsequent references to John Chambers in Belfast, although other members of his family remained. John clearly did not move straight to Dublin in 1727, however, for in June 1731 he corresponded from Antigua in the West Indies with Arthur Dobbs Esq., then an MP for Carrickfergus, actively engaged in establishing the Dublin Society.[12]

After 1727, John Chambers' elder brother James, described as '*a mariner*', continued to reside close to the old Belfast Potthouse, where he died on January 15th, 1733.[13] From that date onwards, John was the senior member of the Chambers family, which perhaps gave him the independence and financial freedom that he needed to set up in business on his own. Later that same year, on 20th November 1733, the Irish Privy Council passed an Act through Parliament that applied additional duties on earthenware and oriental porcelain imported into Ireland, thus providing further incentive for establishing a delftware pottery in Ireland itself.[14] Unlike the first Irish delftware pottery in Belfast, which had been situated close to the sources of essential raw materials, the Dublin pottery was instead located amidst Ireland's largest marketplace.

Although the evidence is circumstantial, this particular John Chambers was better placed than most to set up the first delftware pottery in Dublin. He had lived less than 200 yards from the only previous delftware pottery in Ireland, the Belfast Potthouse, and he may even have worked there in some capacity, as a John Chambers is recorded in 1722 in the '*Potthouse tenements*', **(Fig.6)**[15]. Chambers was also related by marriage to the Smiths, the family that once owned the Belfast Potthouse, and which still owned the delftware clay deposits at Carrickfergus. (Patrick Smith *junior*, who might seem the Smith family's more natural successor in the pottery business, was more concerned with linen manufacture from an early age).[16] Chambers also had relations living in Dublin, where the new pottery was established, and from 1733 onwards, he was independent, well travelled and comparatively wealthy.

Assuming that he came from Belfast, it is tempting to believe that Chambers might simply have moved the Potthouse workforce south in the early 1730s to establish the Dublin pottery, but this probably did not happen. The dates at which Belfast closed and Dublin began are not clearly resolved, but there was almost certainly an interval of several years between the two ventures. Chambers himself testified in 1739 that he had been *'at great Expense in bringing Workmen from abroad'*, which tends to confirm that the Dublin potters had not come directly, (although some might obviously have worked in Belfast previously).

The earliest evidence to show that the Dublin pottery was working comes from delftware objects rather than documentary evidence. During the late 1920s, an impressive pair of delftware plates turned up in London, bearing the arms of Sackville impaling Colyear and clearly marked *'DUBLIN 1735'* on the reverse. **(Figs.49 a & b, Colour Plate 7)**. Lionel Sackville, for whom these plates were made, had married Elisabeth Colyear in 1709 and was created 1st Duke of Dorset in 1720. He served as Lord Lieutenant of Ireland from 1731-7, and was resident in Ireland for the parliamentary sessions of 1731, 1733 and 1735. He was also the President of the Dublin Society from its foundation in 1731, and was thus acquainted with Chambers' correspondent, Arthur Dobbs. Almost certainly, as Michael Archer has observed, *'both plates were made as part of an application for financial support'*, probably to the Irish Parliament.[17] If so, however, the effort seems to have gone unrewarded as no payments are recorded.

It is worth pointing out that Chambers' pottery was not necessarily in financial difficulty, simply because it petitioned for aid. The Irish Parliament and (from 1739/40) the Dublin Society (See box p.39) offered grants to encourage a wide variety of Irish manufactures, and there was little to be lost in making an application. At this early date, during the late 1730s and 40s, prestige was probably the main incentive, as the amounts awarded were usually comparatively small. (Crisp & Co. and the Rostrevor pottery, for example, proclaimed their Dublin Society awards with special newspaper advertisements, even though the value of the premiums they received was under £20). Only later, when the Irish Parliament awarded very much larger grants, did the money itself become the main focus of interest. (Delamain, for example, and some Dublin glassmakers, were to receive sums totalling several thousands of pounds during the 1750s).[18]

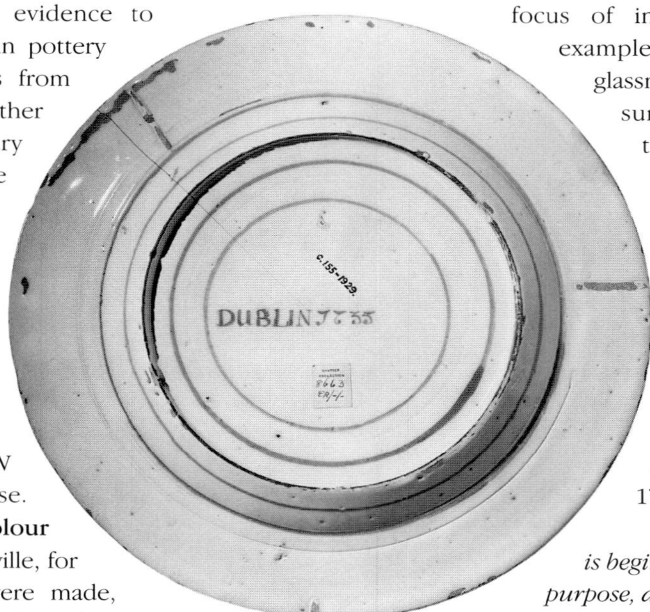

The Dublin Society's early philosophy towards the Irish earthenware potteries is explained by the Rev. Dr. Samuel Madden in his pamphlet entitled *'A letter to the Dublin Society ...'*, published in 1739. He records that;

'... our Earthen Ware, ... is beginning to be set up to good purpose, and with large advantage, both at Rosstrevor, [See p.146] *and near Dublin, and may by the Societies care, and with a moderate expence to carry it further, be carried on to much greater perfection. We may at least so far enlarge it, as to save the greatest part of our importations of that kind, and as this is a very practicable and useful undertaking, it will therefore deserve to be further'd and favour'd, by promoting new improvements in it, and employing more and abler hands to carry it on, so that possibly we may come in a few years to export it to others'*.[19]

In February 1739, even before premiums were awarded on a regular basis, John Chambers presented the Dublin Society with a petition requesting *'encouragement'* for his pottery.[20] Unexpectedly perhaps, in the light of Samuel

Figures 49 a & b. *A large, blue and white delftware plate or dish, bearing the arms of Sackville impaling Colyear, and inscribed on the reverse 'DUBLIN 1735' within four concentric circles. Diam. 306 mm., 12 in.*

Madden's remarks, this was unsuccessful, and so Chambers then applied to the Irish Parliament for aid, on 10th November 1739, stating that he had been *'at great Expence in bringing Workmen from abroad and erecting a Kiln in this Kingdom to bake and burn Earthen Ware'*.[21] This request was also denied, so that in January 1740 Chambers was constrained to present a third application, once again to the Dublin Society, but on this occasion in the hope of gaining a standard *'Premium'*, in line with the new award scheme that had just been introduced.[22] This third application was also unsuccessful, despite the Society's stated aim of supporting Irish potteries, which may explain the fact that no subsequent applications by Chambers are recorded. In Chambers' defence, his lack of success may not necessarily reflect unduly upon the quality of the wares he produced. In these early years, the Dublin Society seems to have placed greatest emphasis on promoting agricultural and industrial inventions, so that an established business such as Chambers' pottery might simply have been considered an unsuitable candidate. The Society failed to support other candidates that today might seem to have been eminently worthy. The Dublin engraver John Brooks, for example, credited with the invention of transfer-printing, also sought encouragement in February 1741 *'for having introduced the Art of* [Mezzotint] *Graving into this kingdom* [of Ireland]', but he too was refused.[23]

From the scant documentary evidence available, it is difficult to determine how long Chambers continued to operate the World's End pottery in Dublin after January 1740. (See also the remarks on p.163, concerning a William Lake). There is a very strong possibility that some of the Irish potters amongst his workforce had been involved in establishing the pottery in Rostrevor in 1739, (p.147). The most likely outcome seems to be that Chambers continued to operate the pottery as its proprietor until shortly before May 1747.[24] On this date, the Dublin Society finally approved aid, but the award went to the new partnership that succeeded Chambers as owners of the World's End works; John Crisp & Company (p. 41). John Chambers' final passing was recorded a few years later in the *Dublin Journal* of August 12th, 1751, with the briefest of epitaphs; *'Died John Chambers, formerly proprietor of the Pot House on the Strand'*.[25]

WARES

The identical pair of armorial plates with the inscription *'DUBLIN 1735'*, mentioned previously **(Figs. 49, 49a, Colour Plate 7)**, are the only two pieces of delftware that can be attributed with certainty to the World's End pottery during Chambers' period of ownership. The two plates are of unusually large size (306 mm., 12 in. diam.). The example illustrated now resides in the Victoria and Albert Museum in London, its companion is in the Metropolitan Museum of Art, New York.[26]

By far the most significant, even surprising, feature of the V & A plate is that the reverse is almost completely typical of Dublin delftware, even though it pre-dates more familiar, post-Delamain wares by 20 years or more. The 'Dublin' characteristics include distinctive small 'splits' in the body, bare areas of biscuit where glaze has 'pulled back', a white 'under-slip' beneath the tin-glaze, a ground-off foot-rim, and thick 'pools' of glaze towards the edge.[27] (See p.80 -2). In other words, the evidence of this plate suggests that manufacturing techniques, and the ingredients of the glaze, remained constant at the World's End pottery for as long as delftware was made there. The one characteristic on the reverse that is not typical of Dublin is the pattern of four concentric blue lines, which will be discussed presently.

The armorial design on the front of the plate, on the other hand, is quite unlike other known examples of post-Delamain Dublin delftware. The only similarity noted was the unusually white ground colour, which is comparable to that of some post-Delamain *monogrammed* wares, (see p. 80). Otherwise, the fine cobalt-blue painted decoration is rather light in colour, especially for Dublin, and there is no trace of the *'sunken-blue'* characteristic that is so often considered diagnostic (see p. 81). The design itself is also unusual for an armorial. The family arms are closely contained within a surround of four, finely painted Chinese-style flower-sprays, each of which contains a Buddhist emblem. The entire design has been shaded with fine blue lines, rather than a solid wash, to imitate the *'pencilled'* style of decoration that derives from certain Chinese blue and white porcelains. Around the outer border are four additional flower sprays containing Buddhist symbols, which alternate with badges of the Order of the Garter bearing crests of the Colyear and Sackville

The Dublin Society

The Dublin Society, later the Royal Dublin Society, was founded in 1731 by a small group of Irish philanthropists *'for improving Husbandry, Manufactures, and other useful Arts and Sciences'*. Although modelled loosely on the Royal Society of London, it differed from its English counterpart in placing greatest emphasis on the promotion of practical innovations, of immediate benefit to the inhabitants of Ireland and the economy, rather than on the pursuit of pure science.

In 1739, the Rev. Dr. Samuel Madden persuaded the Society to introduce a system of monetary rewards for exceptional achievement. These annual *'Premiums'* proved a popular innovation and were considered a prestigious award. Funds were initially provided by private individuals, and so the earliest premiums were comparatively small, usually under £30. From 1746, however, these private funds were supplemented with an annual grant of £500 from the public purse, in recognition of the valuable service that the Society rendered to Irish agriculture and industry.

At the same time, the Irish Parliament disbursed more substantial financial aid to manufacturers, with awards that often amounted to hundreds or even thousands of pounds. From the 1740s onwards, in judging the relative merits of applicants, Parliament deferred increasingly to the opinions of the Dublin Society committee. For petitioners like Henry Delamain, who sought to tap into these large parliamentary *'bounties'*, it was therefore essential to first gain the support of the Dublin Society, even though the value of their premiums was almost inconsequential compared to the parliamentary awards. (See p.50).

From 1761, growing criticism of the manner in which the Irish Parliament distributed its funds caused the system to be revised, granting greater powers to the Dublin Society. Parliament initially gave £10,000 to the Dublin Society, which in turn formed a large committee to decide how these funds were to be redistributed amongst individual petitioners. (It was to this Dublin Society committee that William Delamain and his employees applied in 1762. See pp.59 - 62). During the mid-1760s, further revisions resulted in the standardisation of parliamentary aid distribution through the Dublin Society. From about 1764 on, manufacturers were generally awarded premiums on a straightforward, proportional basis, equivalent to 15% of their annual production.[18]

families. (The Colyear crest of a unicorn's head appears to have been misrepresented as a ram's head). This peculiar combination - an armorial design closely intertwined with Chinese and Buddhist floral motifs - has not been observed on other examples of armorial delftware. Consequently, although the style of decoration is highly distinctive, these pieces have not led to new attributions. (The *'pencilled'* style of decoration, on its own, is certainly not diagnostic of Dublin - the style was commonly employed elsewhere until the 1740s or even later).

A less obvious feature of these plates is the very simple design of four concentric circles that appears on the reverse. Frank Britton, writing in 1982, seems to have been the first to recognise that such *'under-rim markings'*, as he described them, can sometimes be regionally distinctive.[28] Under-rim markings were never intended as distinctive, identifying marks - many were simply copied from Oriental or continental prototypes (*cf.* **Fig. 60b**). Nonetheless, as they were usually painted freehand, they appear to possess some of the characteristics of a signature. Used cautiously, they can assist in establishing a broad, regional classification - certain groups of marks, for example, are generally thought to be associated with the Bristol area, others with Liverpool. It is important to stress, however, that these markings are features that ideally should only be used to suggest or reinforce an attribution, in combination with other characteristics. Without additional, supporting evidence, they are by no means proof of the source of one particular piece of delftware.

Concentric circles, such as those that appear on these *'DUBLIN 1735'* plates, are among the simplest and rarest under-rim markings recorded on English and Irish delftware. (Most markings consist of more complex *'noughts and crosses'* motifs, or swiftly executed, sprig-like flourishes). In cataloguing the 800 pieces of delftware in Bristol City Art Gallery,

Britton found only five plates or shallow dishes bearing concentric circle markings of this kind. These, he considered, were all *'quite unmistakable as a group,* [with] *a soft blue in their decoration, and four of them having a very flat, wide rim'*.[29] Britton observed that the *'DUBLIN 1735'* plates also exhibit this soft blue colour and have a distinctively wide, flat rim, but his conviction that these light-blue oriental designs were all attributable to Liverpool, c. 1760, led him to conclude that the *'DUBLIN 1735'* plates must also have been made there. On balance, this seems highly unlikely.

An alternative possibility is raised by Britton's observations, however, which is that delftwares exhibiting these concentric circle markings might instead have originated in Dublin, during John Chambers' period of ownership. An investigation of such plates initially appeared promising, as dated examples seemed to span the years 1737 - 1744, (rather than c. 1760), and hence coincided very neatly with John Chambers' period of operation.[30] With further research, however, it was found that a shard belonging to this group has been excavated in Liverpool.[31] Ultimately, the only safe conclusion to be drawn from this study was that the majority of plates bearing concentric circles were probably made in Liverpool as Britton indicated, but a proportion of them - as yet undifferentiated - might well have been produced in Dublin. The Irish potters seem to have derived many of their designs directly from Liverpool, and so there is every reason to expect that their under-rim markings should also appear similar. The main distinguishing features of the *'DUBLIN 1735'* plate are its unusually white ground colour, and the obvious 'Dublin' glaze characteristics on the reverse. With further study, it may be possible to recognise other, potentially Irish examples, which exhibit similar features.

One example of this *'concentric circle'* group is illustrated here, **(Figs. 50, 50a)**, painted with the popular *'Mandarins'* pattern and dated 1737. This exhibits only two concentric circles on the reverse, compared to the four on the *'DUBLIN 1735'* plates. (The flat-rimmed profile also appears similar to the Chambers pieces, until we realise that many plates of this period exhibit the same profile, regardless of their source). The *'Mandarins'* seems to have been one of the more common Chinese patterns on delftware of the 1730s.[32] An unexpected coincidence, however, is that this precise pattern was also copied some fifteen years later in Bow porcelain.[33] Bow made comparatively few plates at this early period (c. 1750-55), but two other designs that they produced at the same time, the *'Broken Scroll'* and *'Sampan Lake'* patterns **(Fig. 116 & 117)**, also turn up as two of the most popular designs in Dublin delftware. It is therefore possible that the delftware plate illustrated was produced in Dublin, but the entire group requires further study before any firm conclusions can be drawn.

In summary, Frank Britton's observations concerning the under-rim markings represent a fresh approach to looking for early Dublin delftware, and they may lead to the discovery of an example in the future. It is clear, however, that wares with concentric circles on the reverse were produced both in Liverpool and Dublin. For now, the main advantage of studying wares that bear these markings is that they help us to focus our attention on delftwares made during John Chambers' time, in the late 1730s and early 40s. It is especially encouraging that many obvious 'Dublin' features are present on wares that were produced as early as 1735, for it suggests that other, early examples of Dublin delftware might also be distinguishable - if we could find them.

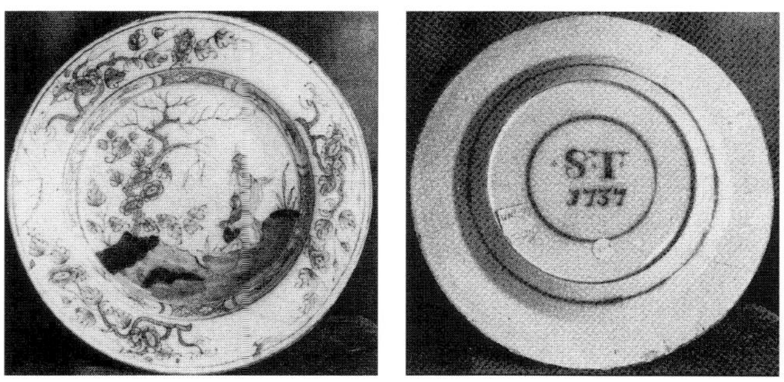

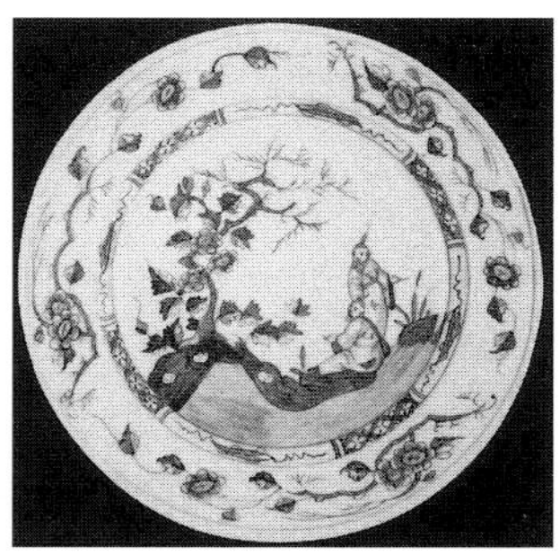

***Left and middle : Figures 50 & 50a.** Blue and white DELFTWARE plate painted with the 'Mandarins' pattern. On the reverse the inscription 'ST 1737' within two concentric circles. Diam. 8⁵/₈ in., 219mm.*
***Right : Figure 50b.** BOW PORCELAIN version of the 'Mandarins' pattern, c.1750-52. Diam. 8⁵/₈ in., 219mm.*

DUBLIN; THE WORLD'S END POTTERY

ii : John Crisp & Company (before May 1747 - early 1749)

John Crisp and Company are first mentioned as the owners of the World's End Pottery in May 1747, when the Dublin Society awarded;

'a premium of £10 for the best sets of dishes and plates of earthenware to John Crisp and Co., who carry on their delft ware at the World's End, on the Strand. Their ware seems to be as good as any imported, for colour, size and paint; all made of Carrickfergus clay, as those of Liverpool are.'[1]

The sets referred to in these Dublin Society awards (from 1747-51) were substantial, each consisting of '*12 Dishes and 3 Dozen of plates*' from the previous year's production. Three such sets were submitted, so that each application was ultimately judged on the basis of 144 pieces of delftware - a fairly rigorous examination.[2] The remark that Crisp's wares were '*all made of Carrickfergus clay, as those of Liverpool are*' suggests that Liverpool delftware potters were then setting the standards of quality against which Irish wares were being judged. Later, from the early 1750s, comparisons were more commonly drawn against French '*Rouen*' or '*Burgundy*' wares.

A similar premium of £8 was awarded in the following year, which Crisp & Co. duly pronounced to the public in the *Dublin Courant* of 4th June 1748;

'At the Irish Delft Warehouse on the North Strand, near the Ship Building, Dublin, are made and sold by wholesale and retail a variety of blue and white delft-ware, allowed by the Hon. the Dublin Society to be as good as any imported '[3]

This scant documentary evidence tells us little about John Crisp and his consortium, apart from the fact that they were awarded modest Dublin Society premiums during the brief period of their tenure. Some of Henry Delamain's later connections raise the possibility that John Crisp may have been a relation of the celebrated London jeweller and potter Nicholas Crisp, who owned a delftware and porcelain pottery in Lambeth with potter John Saunders (p.53).[4] The literature available concerning Nicholas Crisp and his porcelain manufacturing activities continues to grow, but to date, no *John* Crisp has appeared amongst his relations.[5]

A London court case in 1747 provides some incidental insight into the competition that Crisp and Co. faced in Dublin.[6] Litigation was brought by a delftware dealer in Dublin, one Richard Skadan, against Thomas Bodle of London, the proprietor of the Montague Close pottery at Southwark. It seems that after declining an offer of co-partnership in the pottery, Skadan lent Bodle £200 for five years, in return for the immediate delivery of £300 worth of delftware to Dublin, and with the promise of a further £300 worth to come in the succeeding twelve months. Skadan claimed that Bodle did not fulfil his part of the contract, prompting the court case and bankruptcy proceedings. Perhaps the most noteworthy feature of the case is the very large quantity of delftware involved. For Crisp's pottery in Dublin, £300 worth of delftware would probably have represented a very substantial portion of their annual production, perhaps even the greater part. The incident also confirms that the Montague House pottery seems to have had a particular association with Ireland over a long period of time. (From Matthew Garner in the 1680s through to Samuel Wilkinson in 1760. See p.11 and p.59).

WARES

A famous set of six plates, each bearing the inscription '*$I^{C}E$ 1748*', has long been attributed to John Crisp in Dublin.[7] At least one of these, now in the British Museum, was purchased at the sale of the Earl of Gosford's collection at Gosford Castle (County Armagh) in 1921. Other well-known examples of Dublin delftware first came to public attention at this same sale, most notably the dated, polychrome '*Verner*' bowl **(Colour Plate 31)**.

In addition to this exceptional Irish provenance, the inscription on the plates is said to commemorate the marriage of John and Elizabeth

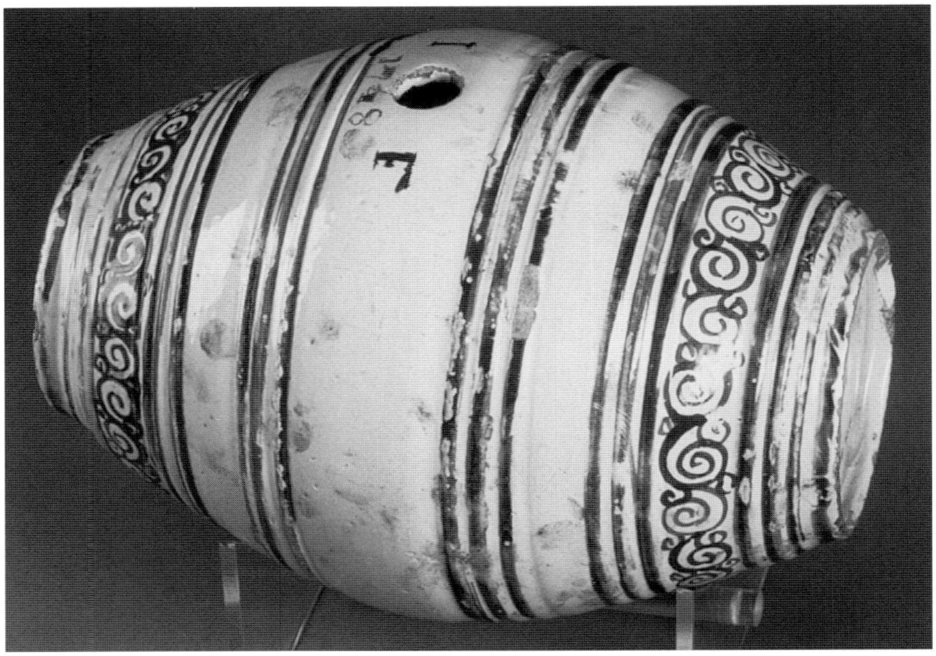

***Figure 51.** Large blue-painted delftware barrel, inscribed 'IF 1748', with bands of moulded or incised hoops. Probably for dispensing wine or brandy. Possibly made in Dublin during John Crisp's period of ownership.*
Ht. 10¾ in. 274 mm., Diam., min. 4¾ in. 121 mm., max. 8 in., 203 mm.

Crisp in 1748 - a date which coincides precisely with Crisp's period of ownership of the Dublin pottery.[8] Unfortunately, there is no corroborating evidence to confirm either that John Crisp's wife was called Elizabeth, or that they were married in 1748.

The known assemblage of Dublin delftware has grown significantly since 1921, and with time, these six plates have appeared increasingly incongruous. Should it by chance transpire that the initials indeed correspond accurately with those of John Crisp and his wife, the plates would still stand out as being unlike all other known examples of Dublin delftware in every respect - in colour, glaze, painting-style and form. Reviewing an example of these plates in the Victoria and Albert Museum, Michael Archer observed, '*Setting aside the source from which the plates came and the initials which appear on them, there are no grounds, stylistic or otherwise, for connecting these plates with Dublin*'.[9] We have already seen (p.38) that the wares produced by Crisp's predecessor, John Chambers, possessed many recognisable Dublin characteristics as early as 1735. These six plates are therefore unlike all other known examples of Dublin delftware, whether they were produced before 1748 or afterwards. It seems very much more likely that these '*I ^{C}E 1748*' plates are simply English, (possibly Bristol, as Archer suggests), and are entirely unconnected with either John Crisp or Dublin.

This means that no 'indisputable' examples of John Crisp's delftware are presently known, but a tentative attribution is suggested for a large wine or brandy barrel in the Hunt Museum, Limerick, inscribed and dated '*I F 1748*'.[10] **(Fig. 51)**. Only five, large-sized, delftware barrels are presently known. The other four were certainly or probably made in Dublin, albeit a few years later. (See '*Barrels*', p.107), and so there may be grounds for believing that large delftware barrels of this kind were unique to Ireland.

The barrel is unusual in many respects, but the general character of the glaze conforms well to known Irish delftware. The glaze is extremely uneven, having run or pooled in some areas, yet pulled away entirely in others to leave areas of biscuit exposed, (near the rims at either end especially). The painted blue decoration is slapdash - line thickness varies greatly, and there are many errant fingerprints and marks, just as we find on many monogrammed, post-Delamain wares. (*cf.* **Colour Plate 12. Top left of reverse side)**. The personal inscription suggests that the barrel was specially commissioned, yet this could not have been regarded as a particularly fine-quality object when it was made. The scrolled borders are also very similar to some that appeared on punch bowls produced in Belfast more then 20 years earlier. (*cf.* **Fig. 15**).

If this barrel was indeed produced in Dublin during the late 1740s, then it provides some insight into the improvements that Henry Delamain brought to the pottery when he purchased the works in 1752. In most respects the body and glaze appear identical to those that were employed in Delamain's time - the principal differences lie in the improved quality of the potting and painting of the later wares.

A more finely painted piece of delftware, which might conceivably be attributable to Dublin during Crisp's period, is an armorial plate dated 1747, bearing the arms and crest of the Hillary family.[11] **(Fig. 52)**. The family is recorded in Essex, Yorkshire and Warwickshire, but this particular plate seems to have been produced for a branch associated with Rigg House, Co. Cork. It was first recorded in the collection of the celebrated Cork antiquarian Robert Day in 1892,[12], who had been given the plate by a *'Miss Janes of Waterford'*.[13] (Day optimistically suggested that the plate was of Youghal manufacture, but this seems unlikely. See p. 150).

Apart from the Irish association of the coat of arms, there are few clues to indicate where the plate was made. The style of the armorial is uncommon, however. Armorial services were certainly offered for sale by Irish delftware potteries during the 1740s, (at Rostrevor, for example), and so although the evidence is extremely tenuous, the possibility that this plate could be Irish should not be entirely ruled out.

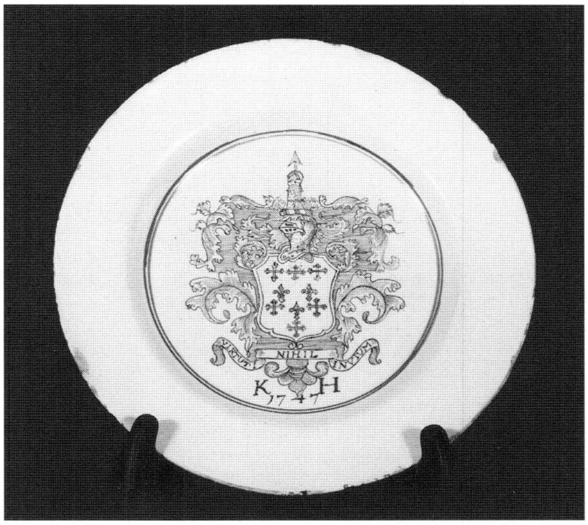

Figure 52. *Blue painted plate with coat of arms of Hillary and the motto VIRTUTI NIHIL INVIUM, inscribed 'KH 1747'. Formerly in the collection of Robert Day, Cork. Possibly Irish. Diam., 8 3/16 in., 206 mm.*

2 : 1

DUBLIN; THE WORLD'S END POTTERY

iii : David Davis & Company (before April 1749 - c. April 1752)

Like their predecessors John Crisp & Co., David Davis & Co. owned the World's End pottery for a brief period only. Most of our knowledge concerning these new proprietors comes, once again, from the pronouncements of the Dublin Society. In April 1749, the Society's premium was adjudged to '*David Davis on the Strand, near the Ship-buildings*', for his '*dishes, Plates and Fruit baskets*', (see Wares), which were said to '*excel any of the like imported, in the blue and white colour and the beauty of the work and cheapness*.'[1] The award for their exhibit was £8 - the same amount that John Crisp & Co. had received in the previous year, which tends to suggest that little had changed at the World's End pottery apart from the arrival of new management. Even their newspaper advertisements remained constant for in 1749 Davis & Co. re-ran the notice of the '*Irish Delft Warehouse*' that had been used by Crisp & Co. a year earlier (see p.41).[2]

Davis & Co. received two further Dublin Society premiums in succeeding years, in May 1750 and December 1751.[3] The latter application was supported by the production of six sets of earthenware, (twice the usual number), '*and for the Goodness and Painting thereof... an additional £4* [was] *granted by the Society*', bringing their total award to £12 rather than the usual £8. Despite this additional bonus, these awards were tiny in comparison to the *thousands* of pounds that Henry Delamain was to obtain a few years later.

A significant feature of Dublin Society awards made during the late 1740s and early 50s is that Davis & Co. seem to have been the only competitor for the premium, which suggests that they were the only delftware pottery working in Ireland at that time. This may have been the case, but it might instead reflect upon the small premiums that the Dublin Society was then offering. (£8 equated roughly to eight months' salary for one apprentice).[4] When we compare the premiums that were awarded for coarse earthenwares at that time, it is certainly conspicuous that almost all of these payments went to potteries close to Dublin, even though similar potteries were probably operating in other parts of the country.[5] Perhaps, if the delftware potteries recorded in Belfast (p.152) and Rostrevor (p.146) were working during the late 1740s and early 1750s, they may have been discouraged from applying for these small awards by the costs involved in shipping three sets (144 pieces) of delftware to Dublin.

Two documentary references suggest that delftware manufacture may have ceased entirely at the World's End pottery towards the end of Davis & Co.'s period of ownership. One is Henry Delamain's remark, in his 1753 petition to Parliament, in which he stated that he had purchased the works '*When the Delft manufacture failed in this city*'.[6] More conclusively, the Dublin Society altered the wording of its awards around Christmas 1751-2 to offer a new premium of £20 '*for erecting a Manufactory of earthenware in Imitation of Delft, Roan* [Rouen] *or Burgundy wares*'.[7] For a brief period, therefore, between Davis & Co.'s final Dublin Society award in December 1751, and Henry Delamain's purchase of the works in April 1752, delftware manufacture may actually have ceased. Even so, as Delamain paid the salaries of '*the most knowing persons ... to prevent their leaving the kingdom*', the works could scarcely have closed for long.[8] The £580 (and additional debts) that Delamain reputedly paid for the works also suggests they were far from derelict when he purchased them.

The coincidence in timing between the death of John Chambers in August 1751, and Henry Delamain's purchase of the pottery in April 1752, raises the further possibility that John Chambers may have been involved with the World's End pottery until Delamain took over. If this was the case, then perhaps the individuals named as Chambers' successors, John Crisp and David Davis, were simply invited into partnership to provide financial or other support, without fundamentally altering the pottery or its workforce. (In other words, the continued presence of John Chambers until August 1751 may have been represented within the '*and Company*' portion of the title). A similar situation is believed to have occurred between c.1768 and 1771, when Edward Stacey seems to have been the owner of the

World's End works, yet applications to the Dublin Society were presented in the name of James Roche, (see p. 66). Even so, the original pottery that existed on this site was a relatively modest affair, certainly when compared to the ambitious venture that Henry Delamain had in mind when he arrived in 1752.

WARES

No examples of delftware are presently attributed to the World's End pottery during Davis & Co.'s period of ownership. The practice of marking individual pieces with painter's monograms or numbers is generally presumed to have been introduced by Henry Delamain, but this is by no means proven. (It is even possible that painter's marks were not introduced until *after* Delamain's death, in January 1757).

The '*Fruit-baskets*' mentioned in the Dublin Society application in 1749 seem to have been a new introduction by Davis, and they were to remain a feature of Dublin's repertoire for the next decade at least. ('*Fruit-baskets*' were mentioned by Davis & Co. in 1749, '*Bread-baskets*' by Mary Delamain in 1759 - see pp.109-14). The celebrated Mrs. Delany, in a letter written from Delville to her sister Mrs. Dewes on 30th June 1750, remarked;

'Tuesday went to Dublin on business; first to a place called the World's End, where I spent an hour and a half in choosing out a set of earthenware for the Duchess of Portland, such as yours, and a dozen baskets for Mrs. Montagu, as she desired'.[9]

It is not entirely clear that the baskets to which Mrs. Delany referred were of earthenware, but to judge from the numbers that have survived, there is little doubt that delftware baskets were popular items. In *Faulkner's Dublin Journal* for 20th January 1752, the auctioned effects of the Archbishop of Tuam included '*a set of Irish Ware Dishes, Plates and Fruit Baskets*'.[10] This latter remark also confirms that Irish delftware had a recognisable and distinctive character, even before the arrival of Henry Delamain.

2 : 1
DUBLIN; THE WORLD'S END POTTERY
iv : Henry Delamain (c. April 1752 - January 10th 1757)

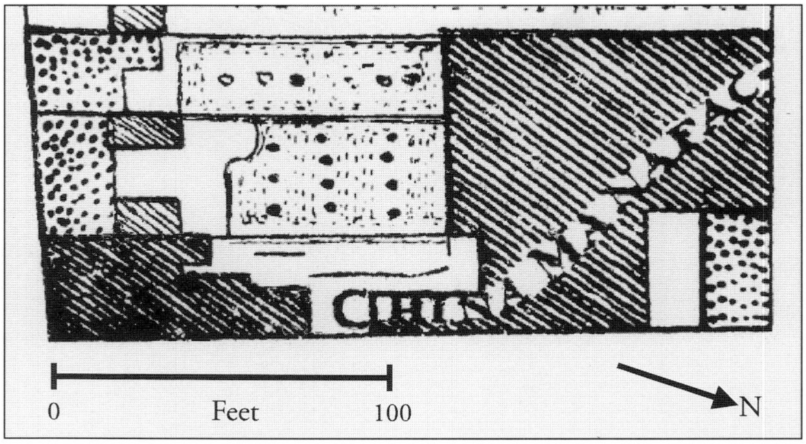

***Figure 53**. A detailed plan of Delamain's 'China Manufactory' in 1756, enlarged from John Rocque's map of Dublin.*

Henry Delamain was just 43 years old when he died in 1757, having owned the pottery at the World's End in Dublin for less than five years. Yet despite the brevity of his career, Henry Delamain was to exert a far greater influence upon Ireland's fine-ceramics industry than any other individual. For many, even today, his name remains synonymous with Irish delftware.

The Delamain family's association with Ireland began with Sir Nicholas Delamain, (Henry's great-great-grandfather) who arrived in England during the early seventeenth-century in the retinue of Henriette de France, the consort of Charles I.[1] Nicholas remained at the London court following the royal marriage, but in 1639 he was knighted and created a '*Farmer General of the Kingdom of Ireland*', whereupon he settled in Ireland with his wife, Ms. Lascelles, a Lady-in-waiting to the Queen. Although the family's titles were revoked under Cromwell, the Delamains remained in Ireland subsequently and prospered as landowners and merchants, intermarrying amongst the Anglo-Irish rather than Huguenot community, despite their French origins.

Henry Delamain himself was born in 1713, the eldest son of Henry senior and Sarah (*née* Steele) of Co. Kildare and Dublin. When he was forty years of age, he stated that he had lived abroad for more than 20 years, and had served for a time as a Captain in the Prince of Saxe Gotha's service in Flanders, probably during the war of the Austrian Succession, (1743-48). On 24th July 1745, when still in his early thirties, Henry was in London, where he was married for the *second* time to one Ziphorah Maitland, *née* Alvares, (described twelve years later as '*an old Jewish woman*').[2] Henry's subsequent business activities suggest he was well acquainted with London, and he might well have lived there for a time, but his wife Ziphorah did not accompany him to Ireland. The mother of Henry's two children, Mary Delamain *née* Bijar, who lived as Henry's wife and widow in Dublin and later inherited the pottery, was not in fact married to him.

As we have seen, (p.44), the World's End pottery was probably in a state of decline by 1751-2, when the Dublin Society offered their new premium '*for erecting a manufactory of earthenware*'. By that stage, Henry was already living in Dublin, having established himself in the fine-ceramics trade as a wholesale dealer in Chinese porcelain and tea, as we learn from an advertisement in *Faulkner's Dublin Journal* of 30 Nov. - 1 Dec. 1751;

'*The great China and tea wholesale Ware room, at Felster Warehouse, the corner of Marlborough-street near the Strand, will be opened every Monday, Wednesday and Saturday from 10 to 3 o'clock where all sorts of East India goods will be Sold to dealers. All orders from any part of the Kingdom shall be carefully executed by a letter directed to Henry Delamain at the said warehouse.*'[3]

(The warehouse was situated 400 yards or so from the pottery, towards the centre of Dublin).

'Account of money expended by Henry Delamain on earthenware manufacture from his commencement to the time of his first application to Parliament in 1753' [4]
[i.e. between April 1752 and November 1753] :

- *Paid former proprietor for purchase of manufactory*	*£ 580*	*00 0*
- *Paid for additional buildings and improvements*	*£1456*	*14 2 1/2*
- *Paid for building nine kilns of different construction to discover the method of burning with coal*	*£ 630*	*00 0*
- *Paid for building mills at Palmerstown for grinding colours*	*£ 287*	*00 0*
- *Paid for sundry utensils*	*£ 456*	*00 0*
- *Paid for sundry materials*	*£ 312*	*00 0*
- *Paid for bringing several workmen from England and other parts, maintaining and paying wages until works were perfected, several of whom deserted the works, having been bribed from abroad.*	*£ 730*	*00 0*
- *Paid expenses in making experiments to discover the art of burning with coal instead of wood in the course of nineteen months.*	*£1860*	*00 0*
total	*£6311*	*14 2 1/2*

Henry bought out the previous owners of the World's End pottery for £580, in April 1752 or thereabouts. There then followed a period of intense activity and correspondingly vast expenditure. During the next year and a half, Delamain reputedly spent over £6,000 of his own capital on an ambitious range of related projects, all centred upon transforming the World's End works into one of the most substantial and efficient delftware potteries in the British Isles. At the same time, in parallel with upgrading the pottery itself, he developed a new type of coal-fired delftware kiln, and he built a flint and glaze-grinding mill at Palmerstown, three miles west of Dublin. **(Fig. 54)**. In the midst of these projects in Ireland, during the third quarter of 1753, Henry also seems to have found time to engage in another innovative venture in London, the Battersea Enamel Works, (See Box, p.48), presumably with a view to pursuing the manufacture of transfer-printed delftwares in Dublin.

Although there are no contemporary documents from this early period, we can deduce much of the activity that took place in Dublin between c. April 1752 and October 1753 from accounts presented later to the Irish Parliament.[4] (See table above). Given that these accounts were presented in support of an application for financial aid, they should perhaps be judged with some caution. Nonetheless, it is clear that Delamain expended considerable effort and a great deal of his own money in upgrading the pottery. We can gain some impression of the scale of the new *'China Manufactory'* from a plan of the works, taken from John Rocque's 1756 map of Dublin, **(Fig. 53)**.

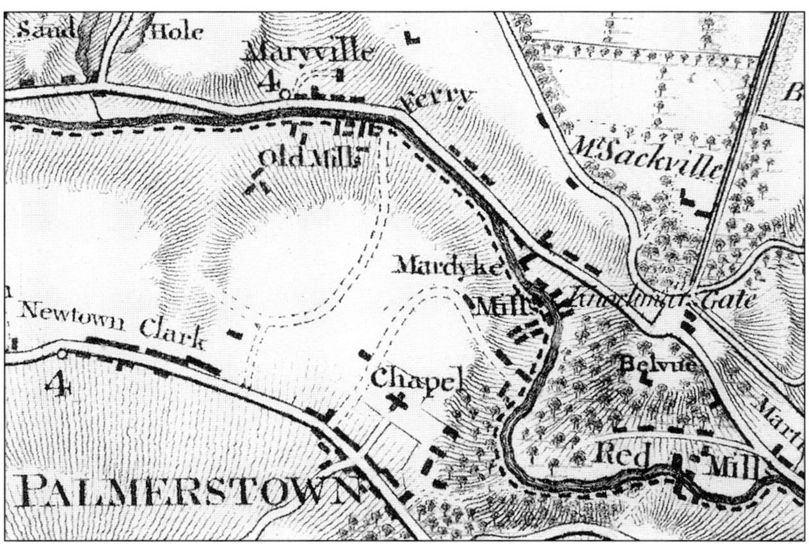

Figure 54. *Palmerstown c.1800, 3 miles west of Dublin, where Henry Delamain built his flint and glaze-grinding mill in 1752-3.*

In the course of these improvements, Delamain leased an additional plot of ground close to the pottery in

Battersea Enamel Works

Few names in the decorative arts achieved lasting fame in so short a period as the enamel works at York House, Battersea, which operated for less than three years between 1753 & 56. The venture was established with the aim of developing and exploiting a new decorative technique - the art of firing transfer-printed images directly onto enamels.

The Battersea works were founded during the third quarter of 1753 by a consortium of three individuals named as '*Messrs. Jansen* [sic], *Delamain & Brooks*'[5]. The principal partner was Stephen Theodore Janssen, a distinguished merchant, alderman and M.P. who served as Lord Mayor of London in 1754. Like Henry Delamain, Janssen was of French descent yet was an outspoken critic of French commercial interests, becoming the Grand President of the Anti-Gallican Society in 1754.[6] Janssen's son-in-law, Lorenzo Moore, was an Irishman and a graduate of Trinity College, resident at Merrion Square in Dublin during the 1750s.[7]

A second partner was John Brooks, the Dublin-born engraver, who is now generally accredited as the inventor of transfer-printing on '*Enamel, China, Glass, Delft and other Wares*'. Brooks had petitioned the Dublin Society as early as 1741 for '*encouragement for having introduced the Art of* [mezzotint] *Graving into this kingdom*', but he received no support in Ireland.[8] By 1746 he had moved to London with some of his most talented pupils, establishing a studio in the Strand, and he presented his first unsuccessful petition for the transfer-printing patent from Birmingham in Sept. 1751. (Two further applications were made in 1754 & 55 from Battersea). Brooks may have become acquainted with Janssen through the Anti-Gallican Society, as both were active members during the early 1750s.[9] Following the closure of the Battersea works Brooks continued to reside in London, in the company of James Gwin - an exceptionally gifted Irish artist, responsible for some of the finest Battersea designs **(Fig. 55)**.[10]

The third partner was a '*Messr. Delamain*', almost certainly Henry Delamain of Dublin, who presumably offered the partnership his expertise in delftware manufacture. In return, Delamain probably gained knowledge of the transfer-printing process, for in his petition to the Irish Parliament in November 1753 he specifically stated that he had '*purchased the art of printing earthenware with as much beauty, strong impression and despatch as can be done on paper*'. Clearly, therefore, Delamain had intended manufacturing transfer-printed delftwares in Dublin, yet to date no examples of transfer-printed Dublin delftware have been recorded. (The only known examples of transfer-printed Irish delftware were produced in Limerick several years later, in 1761. See p.162).

Despite the truly outstanding quality of its products, the Battersea enamel works were not a financial success. Trouble began within the first year, and records reveal that Brooks had left by the first quarter of 1754, only six months after the business started. By the third quarter of 1754, Delamain's name had also been removed. Janssen was made bankrupt in January 1756, but it would appear that production had ceased long before then, (making the span of actual manufacturing less than two years). An article written some years later firmly placed the blame on Brooks' shoulders, stating that this '*manufacture might have been very advantageous but through the bad management and dissipated conduct of Brooks it was in great measure the cause of the ruin of Janssen*'.[11] Brooks may have maintained an interest until the works were closed, as he was declared bankrupt only two weeks after Janssen. The unsold stock was disposed of by auction shortly afterwards.[12]

Given the number of Irish individuals connected with the Battersea works, it is perhaps to be expected that some of their products should exhibit strong Irish associations. The previously unpublished writing box or casket illustrated, **(Fig. 55)**, is one of the largest examples of Battersea enamel to have survived. The central transfer-print illustrates a continental subject in the style of Watteau, long attributed to the celebrated English engraver Robert Hancock, prior to his move to Worcester in c. 1756.[13] From an Irish perspective, however, the prints on either side of this central design are more significant, as they suggest that the box was produced for the Irish market. The allegorical image on the left represents '*Paris adjudging the apple to Hibernia in the presence of Britannia*', whilst that on the right portrays '*The warrior Britannia instructing Hibernia and the Linen Industry*'. An enamel plaque illustrating this second image is known, bearing the following contemporary inscription on the reverse;

> '*Drawn by Gwin, engraved by Ravenet for ye Battersea Manuf're under Sir S. Theodore Janssen.*
> *Ye design a Compt. for Linen Manufacturers of Ireland during ye Lieutenancy of ye Duke of Dorset*'[14]

The original drawings upon which these transfer-prints were based were therefore the work of the celebrated Irish artist James Gwin, who began his career as an engraver in Dublin in 1723, and remained John Brook's close colleague following the closure of the Battersea works. Lionel Sackville, the Duke of Dorset, was Lord Lieutenant of Ireland for the second time from Sept. 1751 - May 1755. (The Sackvilles probably received gifts of landscape-decorated Dublin delftware from Henry Delamain at about the same time. See p. 95). Other Battersea boxes bearing the '*Hibernia and the Linen Industry*' transfer-print are known, which bear additional printed portraits of the Duke of Dorset himself, and of the celebrated Irish beauty, Maria Gunning.[15]

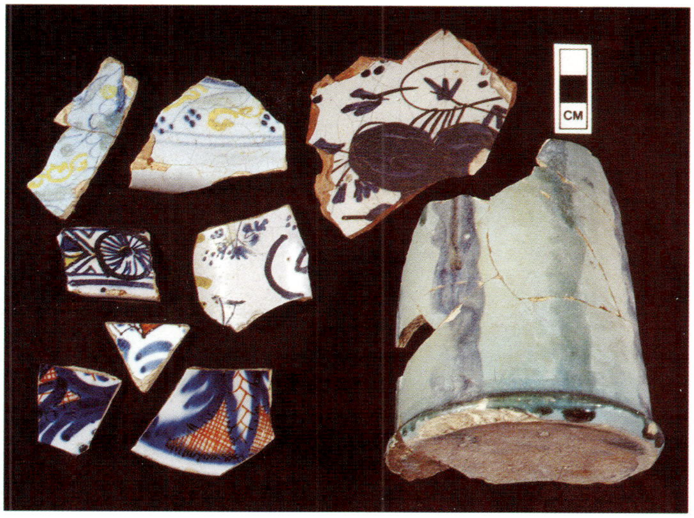

Below *: 1. A delftware 'choppine' or miniature ladies shoe, manufactured at the Belfast Potthouse, c.1720-25. This example was made in the same mould as the original 'Belfast Shoe' which is inscribed 'HMR Belfast 1724'. (See Figs. 7, 11 & 12). Ht. 90 mm., L. 145 mm.*

Above *: 2. Coloured delftware fragments were exceptionally rare at the Belfast Potthouse site, suggesting that greater care was taken in their manufacture. This small group represents almost 50% of the total coloured assemblage recorded. (See pp.26-9).*

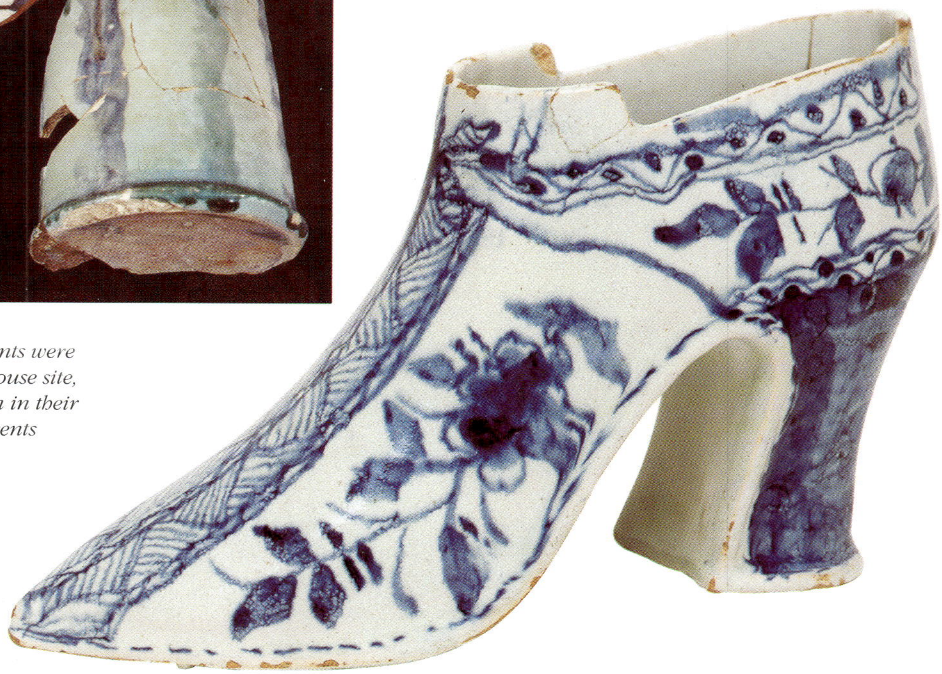

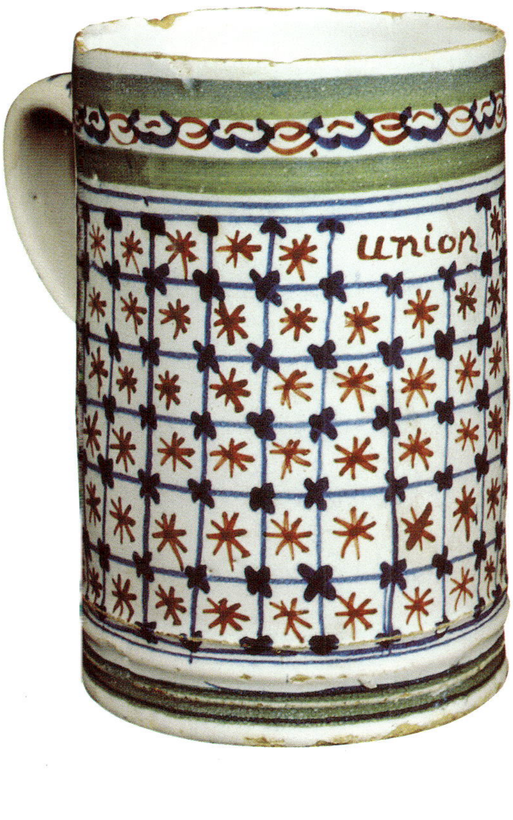

Below right *: 3. An English or Irish plate, matching a design recorded on saucer shards (bottom right) from the Belfast Potthouse. (See p.27). Diam. 9 1/5 in., 233 mm.*
Left *: 4. English or Irish tankard commemorating the Act of Union between Scotland and England in 1707. Two tankards of this type were discovered in Belfast in 1970. (See p. 29). Ht. 5 1/2 in., 140 mm.*

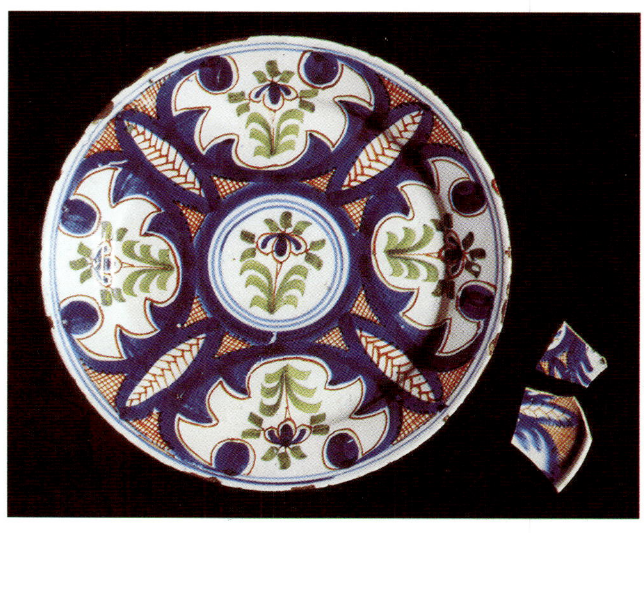

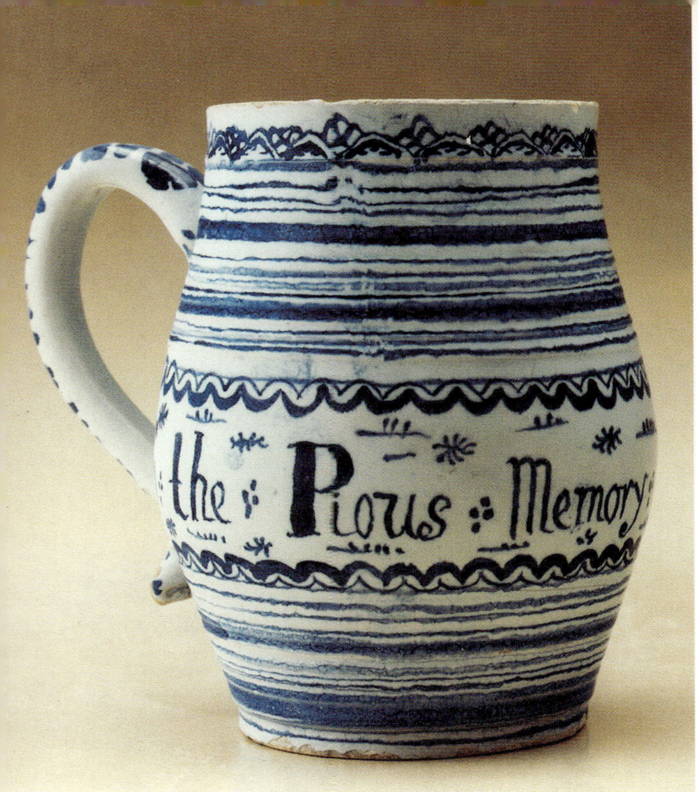

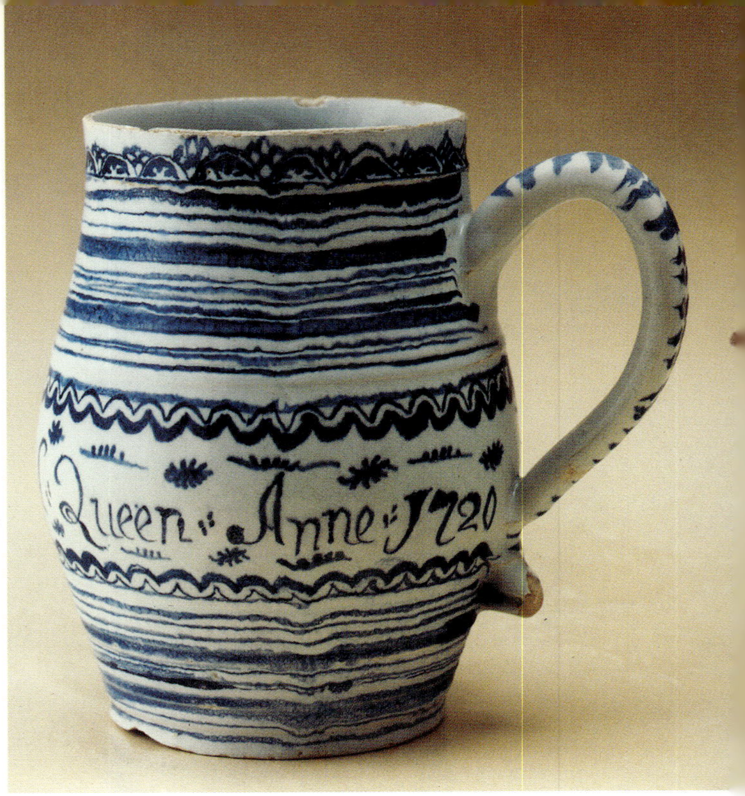

***Above* : 5.** *A commemorative barrel-shaped tankard, probably Belfast, bearing the inscription 'To the Pious Memory of Queen Anne 1720'. The form is identical to a waster from the Belfast Potthouse site. The colour and character of the glaze are also extremely similar to the delftware shoe illustrated in Colour Plate 1. (See pp.29-31). Ht. 6 1/8 in., 156 mm. Basal diam. 3 1/4 in. 82 mm.*

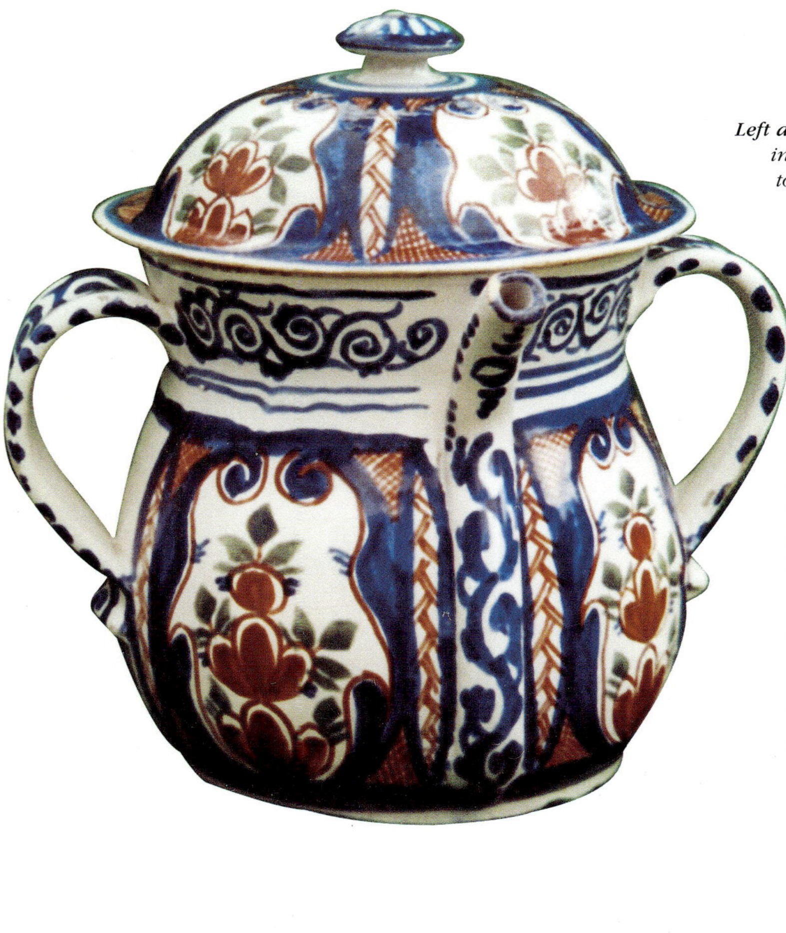

***Left and below* : 6.** *A previously unrecorded posset-pot, inscribed 'ER 1724', of similar form and decoration to delftware shards excavated in Belfast. English or possibly Belfast. (See p.33). Ht. 9 in., 229 mm.*

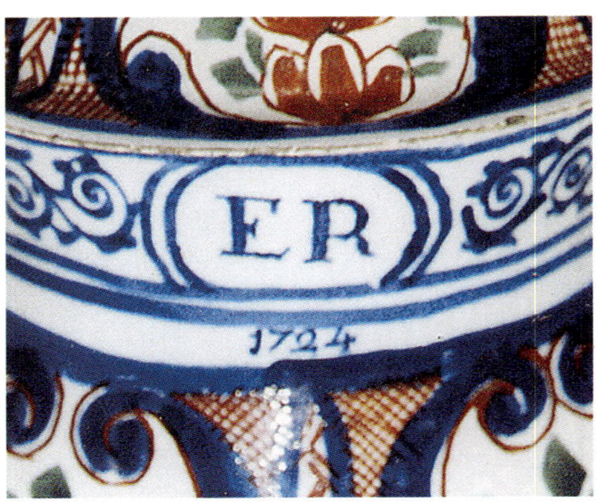

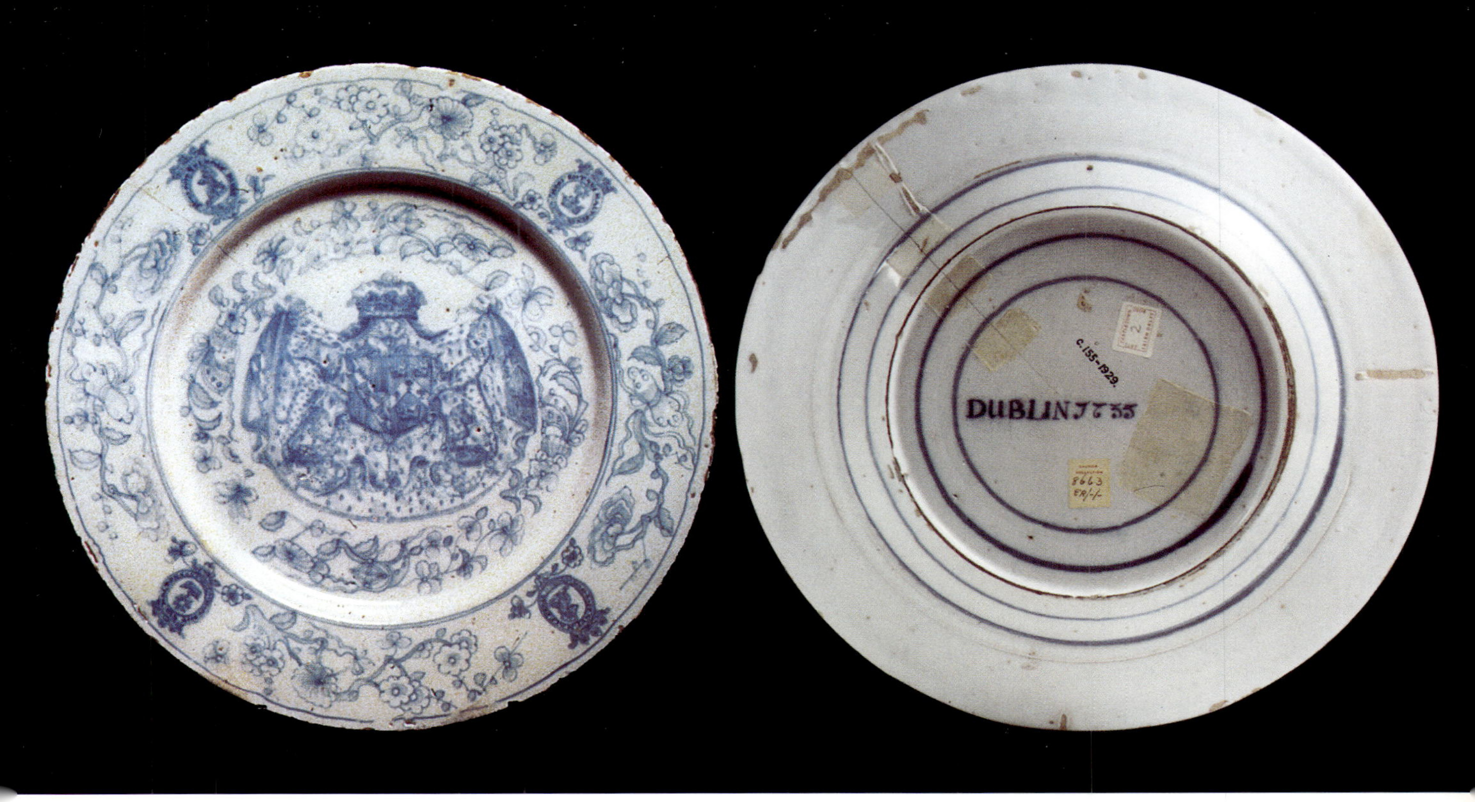

Above left *: 7. Large plate, one of a pair, bearing the arms of Sackville impaling Colyear, produced in Dublin in 1735 by John Chambers for Lionel Sackville, Lord Lieutenant of Ireland. These plates constitute the earliest evidence of delftware manufacture at the World's End Pottery in Dublin. Diam. 12 in., 306 mm. Note the presence of distinctive 'Dublin' characteristics on the reverse, and the four 'concentric circles'. (See pp.37-40).*

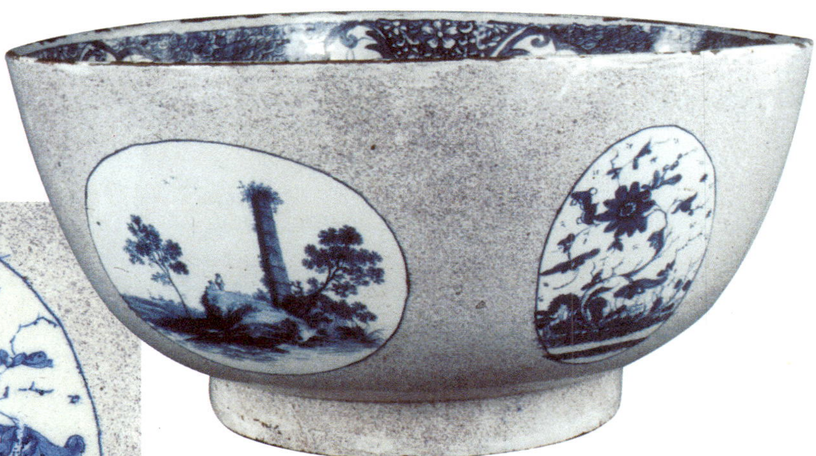

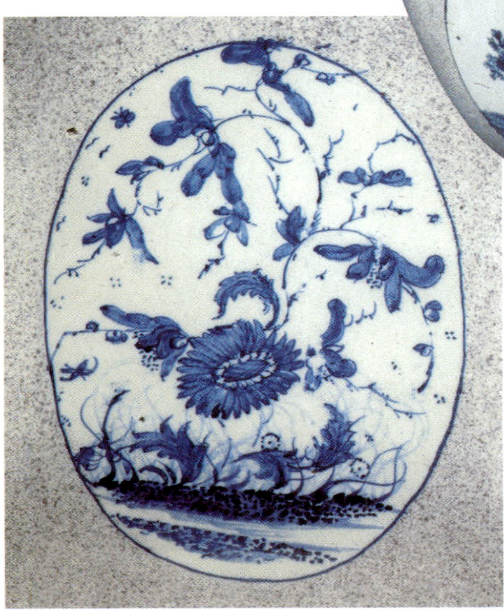

Above : 8. *The 'Primate's Coals' Bowl, produced by Henry Delamain in 1753 in support of his application for Dublin Society and parliamentary support. (See p.51-2). The features of this bowl that are most commonly illustrated are the landscape-decorated side-panels, (above), which show that this form of decoration was produced as early as 1753. The alternating flower-painted panels are more mundane and hence are rarely seen (left), but in complete contrast to the landscapes, these are unlike any other flower-painted decoration that is presently attributed to Dublin.*
Diam. 16 1/16 in., 408 mm., Ht. 8 1/8 in., 206 mm

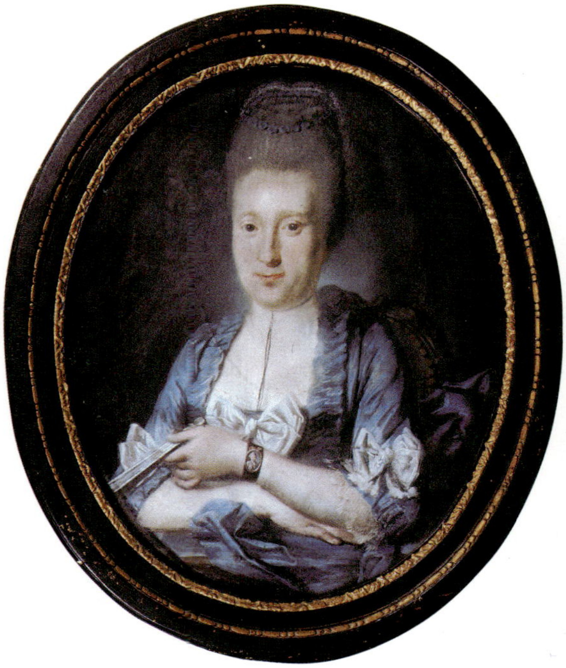

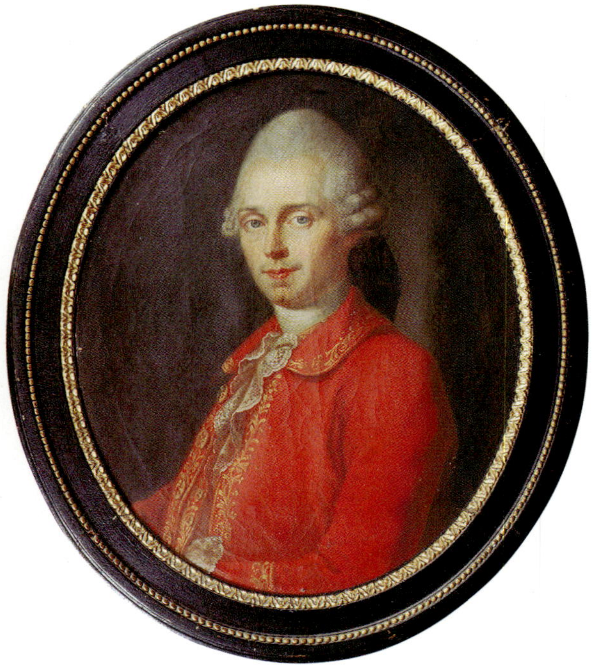

Above left* : *9. *Marie Ranson, daughter of Issac Ranson of Jarnac, and wife of James Delamain.*

Above right* : *10. *James Delamain, 1738-1800, son of William Delamain by his first wife Hannah O'Shaughnessy, who moved in 1760 to work in the brandy trade in Jarnac, near Cognac. (See p.59). The cognac business of Delamain & Co. continues in Jarnac to this day.*

Below left* : *11. *Delftware plate, bearing the arms of the Delamain and Ranson families, from a dinner service produced in Dublin by William Delamain for his son's marriage. The marriage contract was dated 1st November, and the ceremony took place on 24th November 1762. (See p. 71). Diam. 9 in., 230 mm., (side to side).*

Below right* : *11a. *The reverse of the Delamain/Ranson plate. Note the painter's mark 'NE', and the conjoined 'HD' monogram of Henry Delamain within the word 'Dublin', (even though the plates were produced more than five years after Henry's death).*

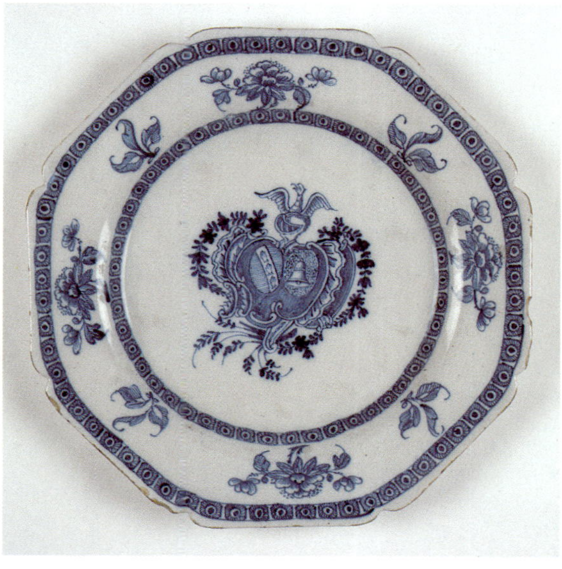

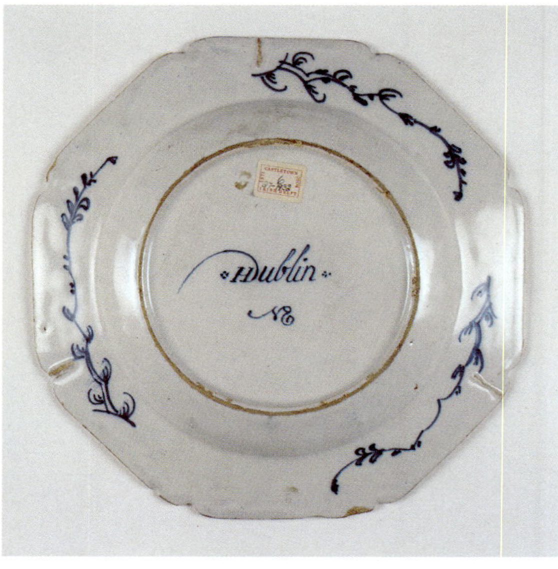

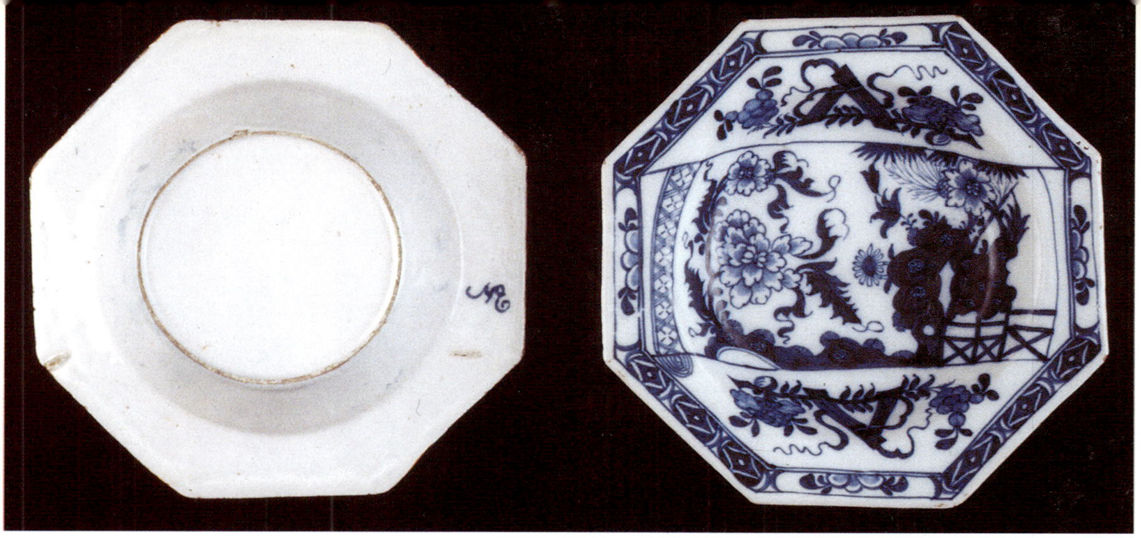

Above : 12. Front and reverse views of a Dublin delftware soup dish, painted with the 'Broken Scroll' pattern, bearing an under-rim painter's monogram, 'NE'. (Compare Colour Plate 11a). Diam. 9 in., 230 mm., (side to side).

Below : 13. Comparison of Dublin (left) and Liverpool (right) delftware plates, decorated with the common 'Chinese Flower-bowl' pattern. (See p.80). Diams. 9 3/10 in. and 8 9/10 in., 236 and 226 mm.
13a. The reverse of the Dublin (left) and Liverpool (right) delftware plates shown in Colour Plate 13.

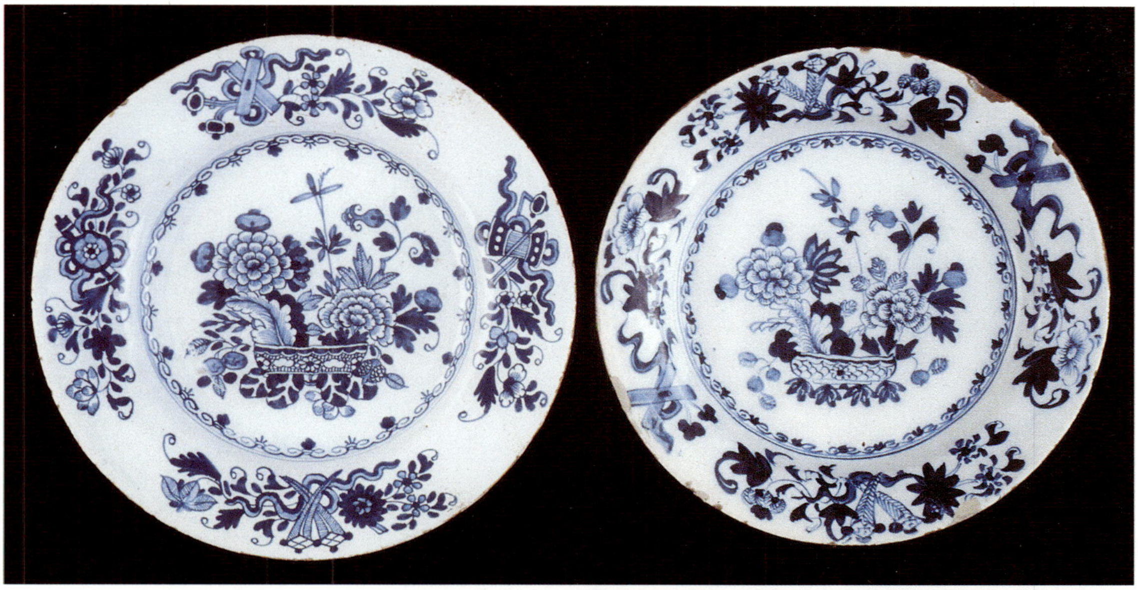

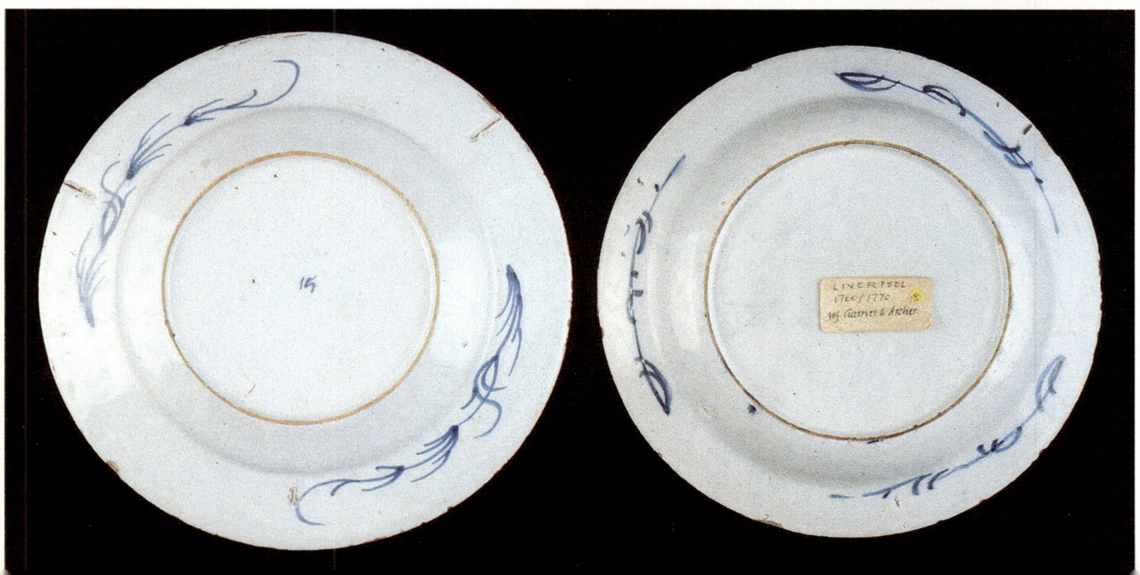

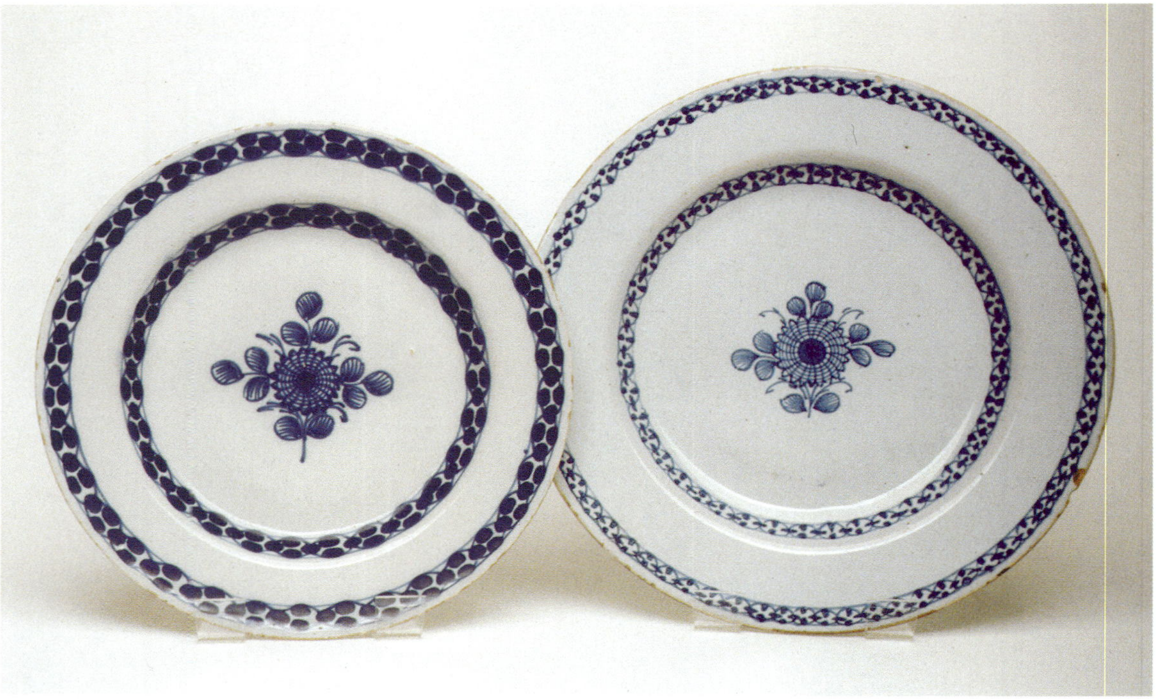

Above : 14. Two Dublin delftware plates, 'Radial Flower' pattern. The example on the left clearly exhibits 'sunken blue', especially around the border. The plate on the right exhibits no trace of this feature. Painter's marks '2' and '12' within the footrim. (See p.81). Diams. 9 1/5 in. and 10 3/5 in., 233 and 270 mm.

Below : 15. Dublin delftware bowl painted with the 'Three-window House' pattern, matching excavated examples recorded in Virginia, (p.84). Painter's number '2' on base. Ht. 3 7/8 in., 100 mm., Diam. 10 -10 1/4 in., 254 - 260 mm., footrim diam. 4 1/2 in., 115 mm.

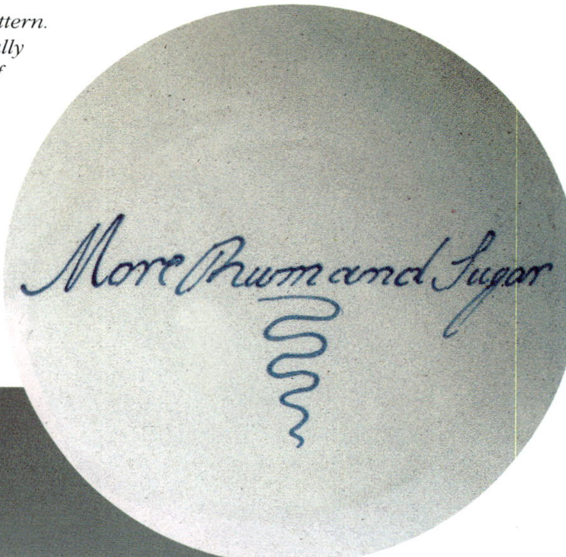

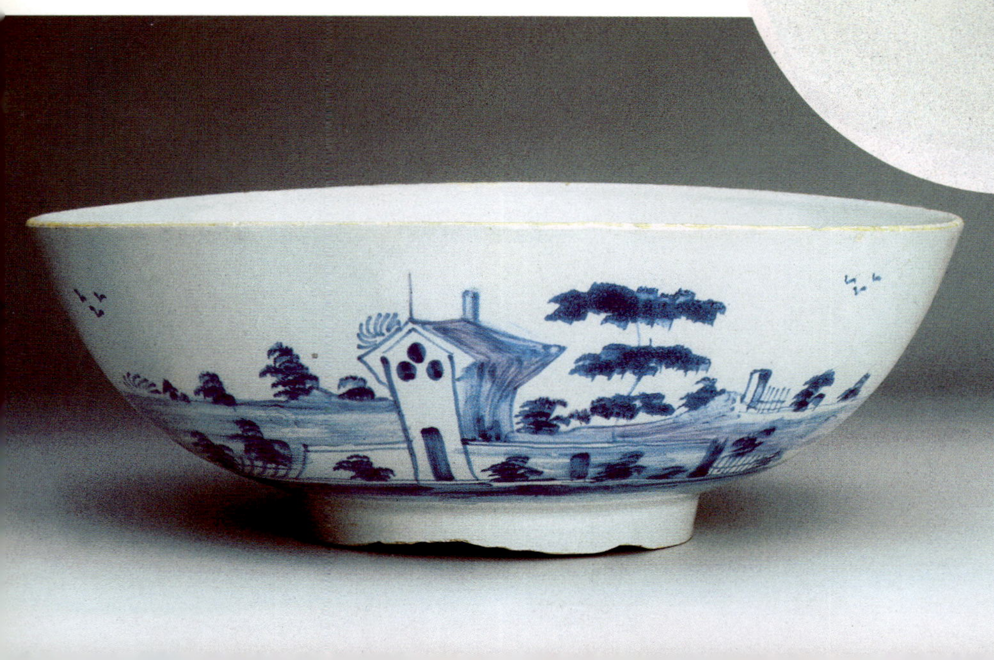

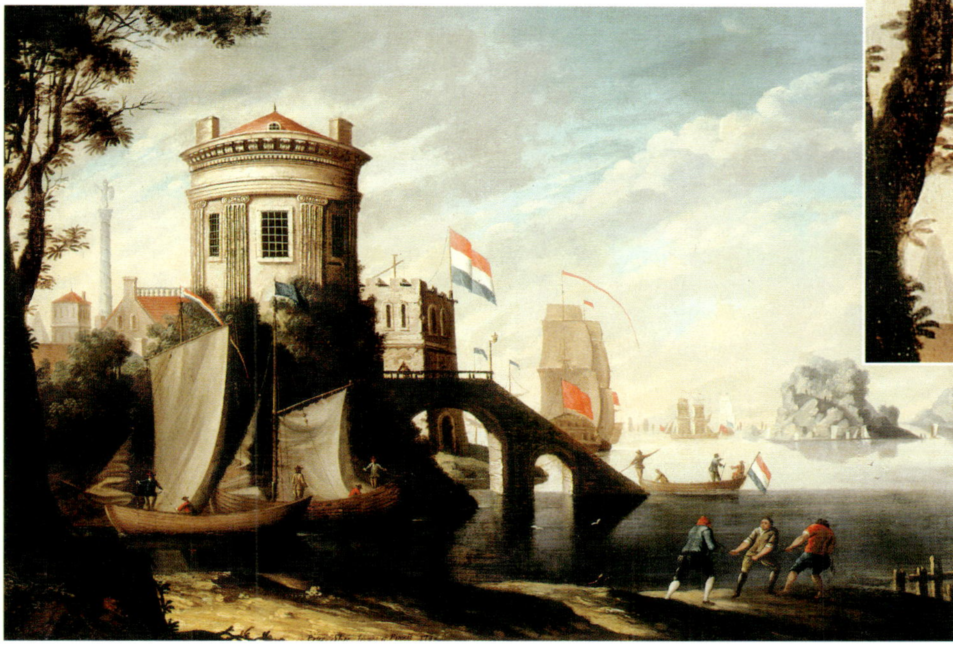

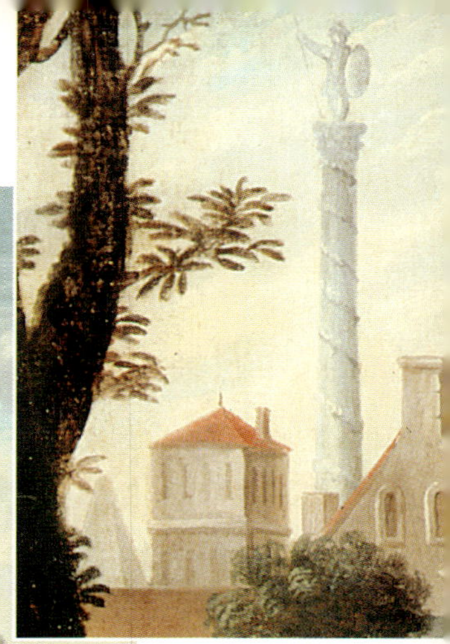

16. The first recorded oil painting by Peter Shee, (fl. 1748-67), an Irish artist employed at the World's End pottery during the 1750s and 60s. (See p. 97). Oil on canvas, signed l.c. : Peter Shee Invent. Et Pinxit 1748. 43 x 30 in., 109 x 76 cm.

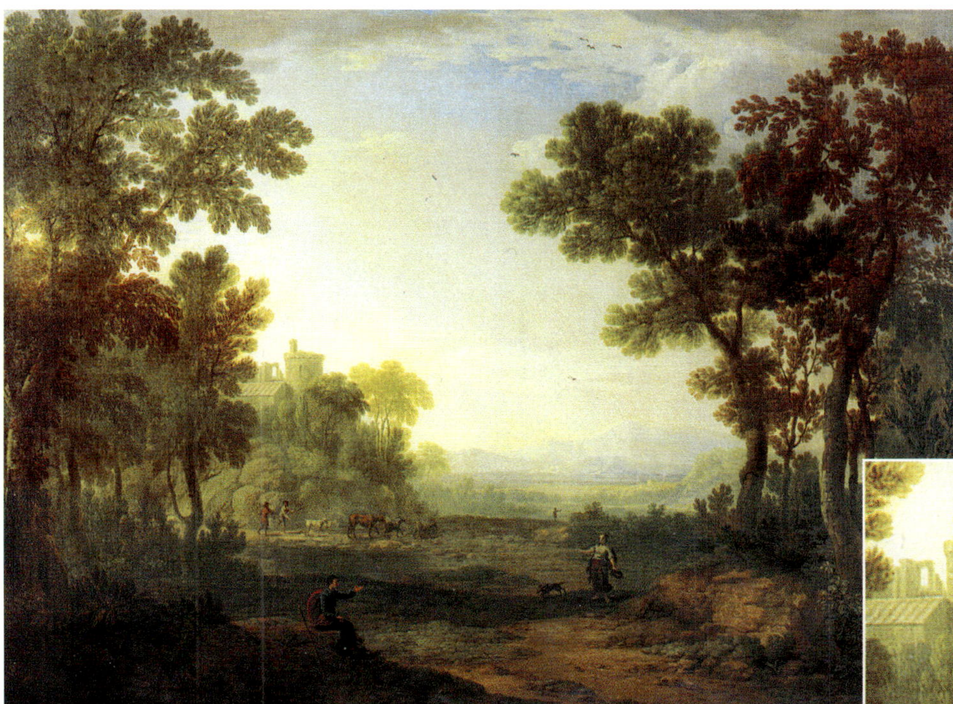

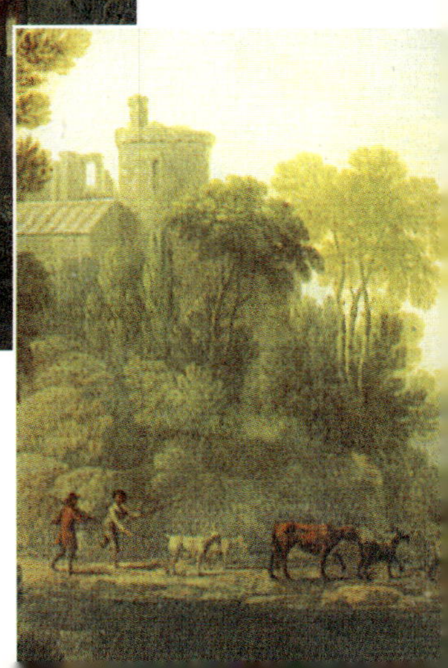

17. A fine-quality Arcadian landscape scene by the celebrated Dublin-born artist Robert Carver (c.1730-91), who may also have worked at the World's End pottery during the 1750s. (See p. 97). Oil on canvas, signed 'R.C. 1764', 48¼ in. x 37 in., 123 x 94 cm.

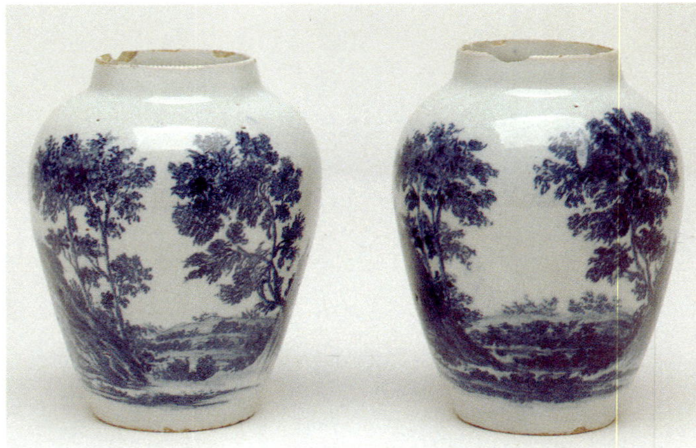

Above : **20**. *A pair of small jars, no marks. Dublin. Circa 1755-65. (See p.137). Ht. 4 in., 100 mm.*

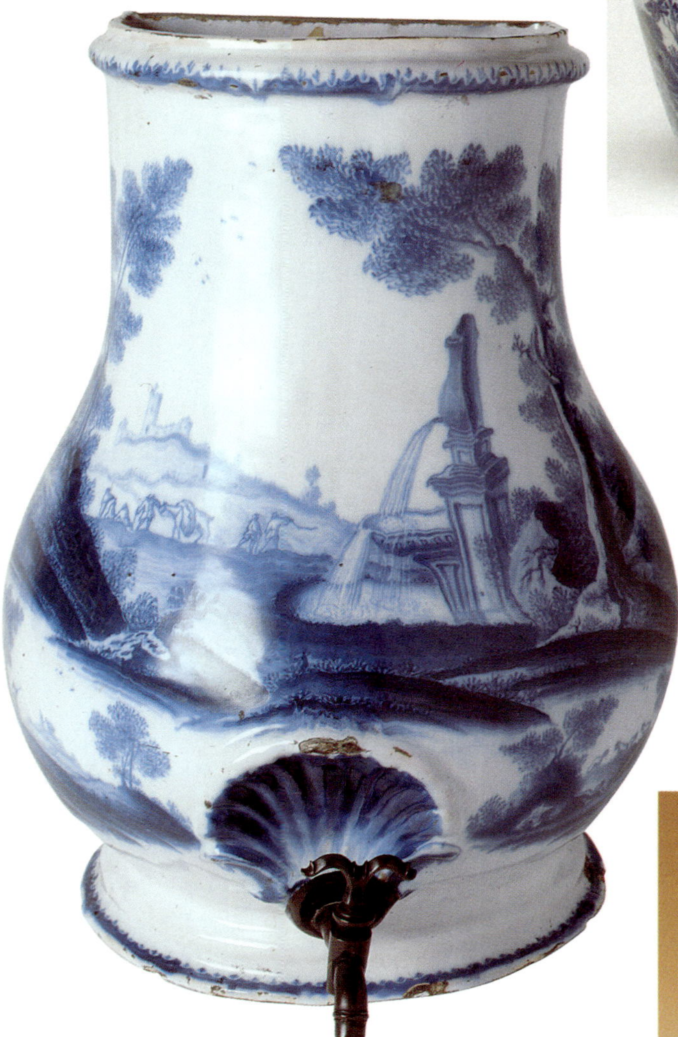

Above : **18**. *A Dublin wall cistern or water dispenser. Circa 1755-65, one of three examples known. The tap fitting may be original. The top back edge has been cut down. No marks. (See p.118). Ht. 15 in., 330 mm.*

Below : **19**. *A circular basket, harp and 'Dublin' mark on the reverse, (Fig. 59). Possibly one of three recorded in the possession of the Sackville family in 1913. (See 21 opposite and Fig.107). Diam. 8½ in., 215 mm*

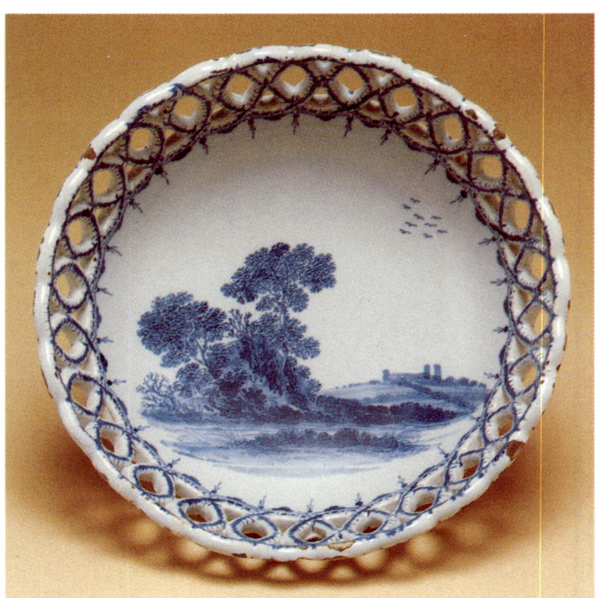

June 1753.[16] The names of the individuals who witnessed the signing of the lease are of considerable interest, for alongside the potter William Stringfellow, (the manager of the World's End pottery), are listed two *'Painters'*, Robert Carver and John Jolly. Jolly is unrecorded in relevant literature, but Robert Carver was a major Irish oil painter during the eighteenth-century, who specialised in creating romantic landscapes *'in the manner of Claude* [Lorraine]'.(See p.97). There is no direct evidence to show that Carver necessarily worked for Delamain, but this association may well represent more than simple coincidence.

Delamain's first recorded newspaper advertisement in the *Dublin Journal* of 16th October 1753 suggests that the improvements were then nearing completion:

'The new Delft Manufactory on the Strand is almost built, the proprietor of which to endeavour to establish the earthenware manufacture in this kingdom has provided the ablest masters for making earthenware, and instructing youth in all branches, and will take 25 Charter Schoolboy apprentices every year, and as they will be masters of the trade in three years, several manufactories can be supplied with workmen; and what it cost him large sums to discover, viz, inventing kilns to glaze delft with coals, grinding flint, glazing it, he will communicate all secrets of the trade to any person who will establish such works and will supply them with workmen to carry it on, so that large sums of money will be saved that goes out of it for French delft. I am sure no nation has better or cheaper materials for it.'

When this advertisement appeared, the Dublin Society had already decided to assist Delamain financially by recommending him *'to the bounty of Parliament'*, but the actual petition (requesting an unprecedented sum of money) was not submitted until a fortnight later (1st November 1753). The overtly altruistic tone of the advertisement, as much as its timing, suggests that this was perhaps a veiled attempt on Delamain's part to influence the generosity of the House. Delamain may also have persuaded a friend to write the rather

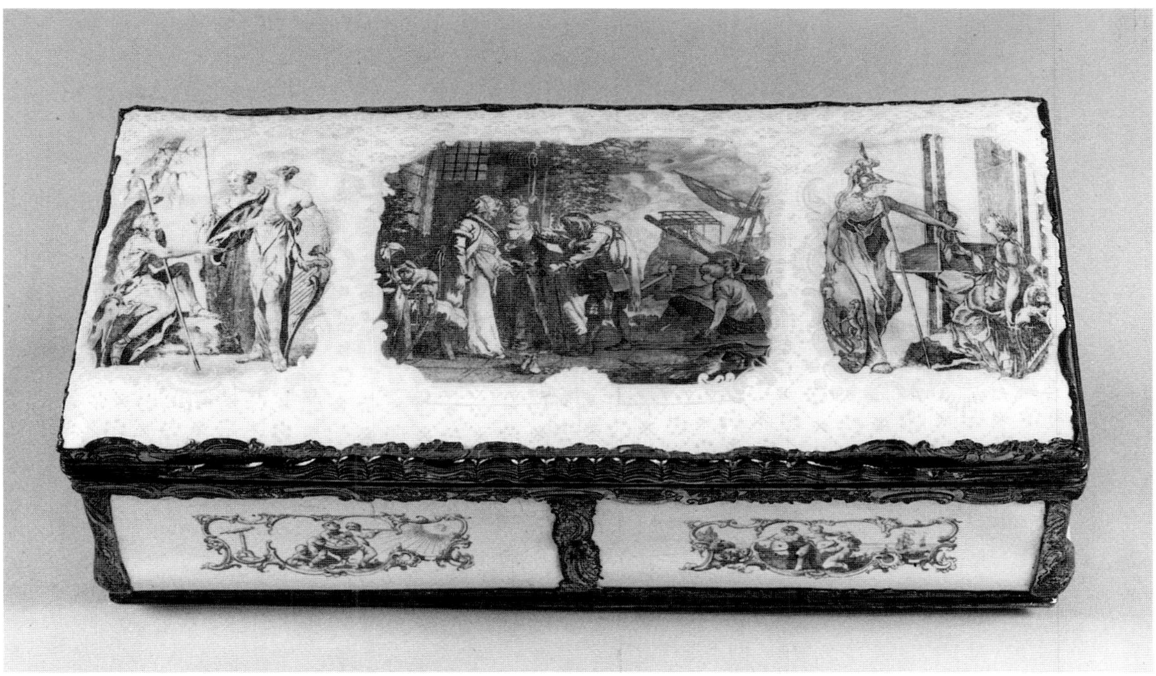

Figure 55. *A large, Battersea enamel writing casket or box, transfer-printed in purple, manufactured at Janssen, Delamain & Brooks' York House works, c.1753-56. Two of the transfer-prints on the lid, representing Hibernia and Britannia, were 'drawn' by the Irish artist James Gwin, and engraved by Simon Francois Ravenet, one of the most celebrated engravers associated with enamel manufacture in England. The mahogany interior is fitted for writing accessories.*
Gilt-metal mounts. 10 1/2 x 4 3/4 in., 260 x 120 mm., Ht. 3 1/4 in., 80 mm.

complimentary letter that appeared in the same issue of the *Dublin Journal*;

'I am surprised to see by an advertisement that Mr. Delamain has become potter, who I knew in Flanders, a captain in the Prince of Saxe Gotha's service, and who distinguished himself in the last war against the French. I am pleased that he has brought this beneficial branch of trade to such perfection as to be recommended by the Dublin Society to the bounty of Parliament; for I am assured by Mr. Duany and the Surgeons of the Infirmary on the Inns Quay that he was the first that introduced it for the benefit of their hospital. If this trade should miss after so large a sum already expended on it we shall lose a trade that will save large sums that go from us to France for earthenware'.[17]

As this letter states, the Dublin Society had already passed favourable judgement on Delamain's application, and their £20 premium was paid in due course.[18] Details of this decision were recorded a week or so later, in the Society's minutes for October 25th 1753;

'*We have examined several specimens of earthenware made of different clays of this Kingdom produced to us by Mr Henry Delamain of the City of Dublin, made at his manufactory on the Strand, and think most of them as good and some of them better than any imported into Ireland, and therefore recommend him and his undertaking to the consideration and bounty of Parliament, as the encouraging his work will be a means of establishing others which will employ and support numbers of industrious poor, will save considerable sums of money yearly at home, and bring money from foreign markets into this Kingdom. We have tried them with boiling water and they stood the heat of it without breaking or cracking.*'[19]

The remark that Delamain produced '*several specimens ... made of different clays of this Kingdom*' indicates that, in addition to all of his other activities at the pottery, he had gone to considerable lengths to discover and experiment with new sources of Irish clays. This would undoubtedly have impressed the members of the Dublin Society greatly - one of their principal aims, after all, was to find new ways of developing Ireland's own natural resources. Only one example of these experimental wares is now known - the exceptionally large and finely decorated punch-bowl, inscribed on the base '*Clay got over the Primate's Coals - Dublin 1753*', (opposite). If this impressive piece was truly representative of Delamain's application to the Dublin Society in 1753, then he had clearly gone to exceptional lengths to gain their support, (especially when we consider that it was probably made with an experimental Irish clay).

Shortly after achieving this success with the Dublin Society, Delamain submitted his petition for financial aid to the Irish House of Commons on November 1st 1753.[20]

Petition of Henry Delamain the younger of the City of Dublin, gentleman.

When the Delft manufacture failed in this city, the petitioner, convinced that it might be carried on greatly to the advantage of the nation, took said manufactory into his hands, built workhouses and kilns, erected a mill to grind flint and metals, and discharged debts affecting the old manufactory; and also supported the most knowing persons that were employed in the old manufactory whilst this new one was building, to prevent their leaving the kingdom; and purchased the art of printing earthenware with as much beauty, strong impression and despatch as can be done on paper. That the petitioner lived above twenty years abroad, where he acquired a knowledge of the manufacture of Delft and earthenware, and having taken a circuit through this Kingdom found that every province therein is furnished with the proper materials for making thereof. That the petitioner after many repeated experiments has discovered the secret of glazing delft wares with coals, and painting and glazing that ware. That the petitioner employs upwards of forty families in his manufactory, and proposes to take a number of charter-school boys, apprentice, by which means he will be able to supply new manufactories with artists. And the petitioner is willing not only to communicate all the secrets of his business to any persons setting them up, but also assist them in the construction of their kilns, etc. That the petitioner laid specimens of the ware made by him before the Dublin Society, who were of opinion that they were as good and some of them better than any imported into Ireland, and found on experiments made that they stood boiling water without breaking or cracking. And as it can be made near twenty per cent cheaper than it can be imported, he apprehends a great benefit will arise not only by preventing large sums from going out of the Kingdom for said manufacture, but also by exporting it to foreign markets, and prays for aid to enable him to carry on said manufacture.

A notable feature of Delamain's petition, and of his activities shortly afterwards, is the extraordinary effort he made to develop a coal-fired kiln. (See p.54). As Michael Archer has pointed out, Dublin seems to have been the only delftware pottery to have fuelled its kiln with coal - the technique does not appear to have been adopted by any English or Scottish delftware potters, despite Delamain's own efforts to promote its use.[21] The origins of this particular obsession were partly historical. By the eighteenth-century Ireland's forests, like those of most of the British Isles, were almost entirely depleted. Unlike England, Scotland or Wales, however, Ireland had no significant coal-deposits of its own to fuel its industry, and so, rightly or wrongly, this lack was widely perceived in the mid-eighteenth century as the cause of many of Ireland's economic ills. Consequently, large sums of money were expended by the Irish Parliament in trying to maximise the various small coal deposits that were known to exist in different parts of the country. By the early 1750s, explorations in County Tyrone, and the success of the Newry Canal, raised expectations in Dublin that the city might finally gain access to a dependable, local source of coal, ending the nation's total reliance upon imports.[22] Samuel Madden, one of the key figures in the Dublin Society, repeatedly stressed at this time that the exploitation of Ireland's coalfields was a matter of utmost priority for the country's economic development.[23]

The subtext to Delamain's interest in coal firing, therefore, was essentially patriotic. He was demonstrating to the Dublin Society and to Parliament that he was working towards utilising Ireland's own natural resources in new and innovative ways. By the same token, he was correspondingly improving his chances of gaining financial support. In this context, the earliest known example of Delamain's delftware, the large and impressive bowl inscribed *'Clay got over the Primate's Coals - Dublin 1753'* is of particular interest. **(Colour Plate 8, Figs. 56 a, b, c.)**.

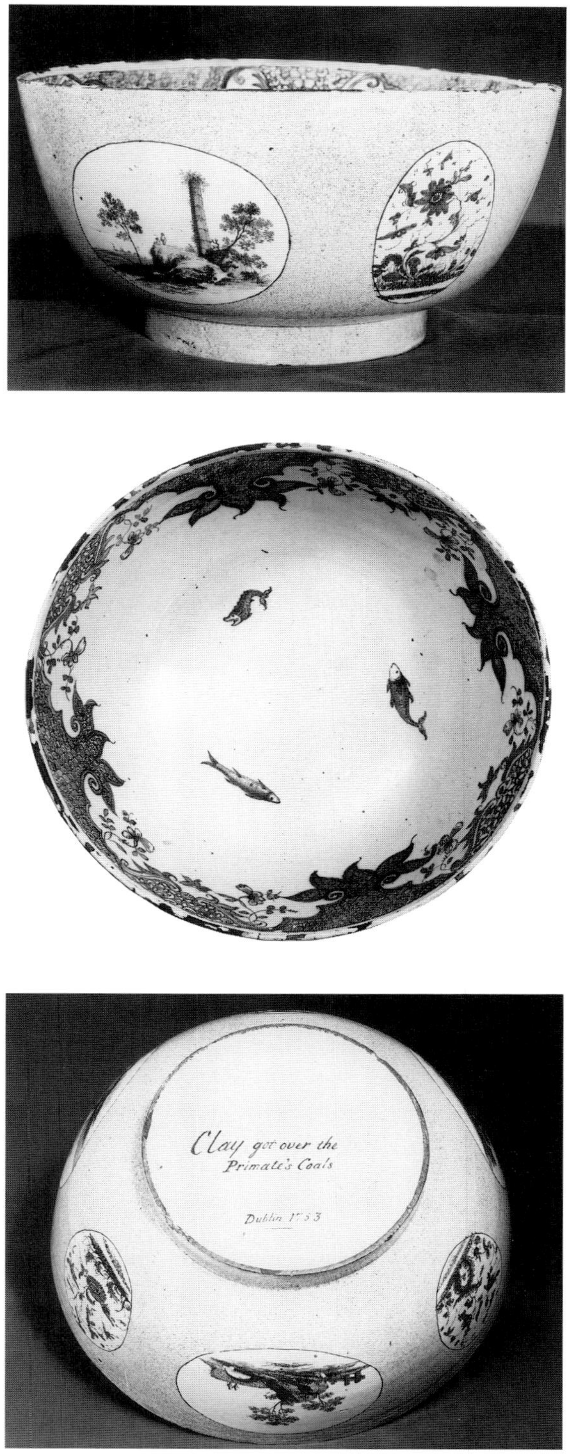

Figure 56 a, b, c. *The 'Primate's Coals' bowl (side, interior, base inscription), manufactured by Henry Delamain in 1753, probably in support of his application for Dublin Society and parliamentary support.*
See also Colour Plate 8.

When Delamain's delftware petition was submitted for consideration on 1st November 1753, Parliament was also judging a separate petition for aid from a powerful consortium of clerics and gentry that owned some promising exploratory coal mines in County Tyrone, known as the '*Primate's Pits*'.[24] (The owners included the Lord Archbishop of Armagh, the Archbishop of Tuam, Viscount Charlemont and others). The main coal seam of these pits, known today as the '*Derry Coal*', was overlain by a thick deposit of fireclays, of such exceptional quality that they later gave rise to a major coarse-ceramic industry in the nearby town of Coalisland.[25] (The clays were close to the surface, and hence could be extracted by open-cast quarrying). The inscription '*Clay got over the Primate's Coals...*' suggests that Delamain incorporated these Coalisland fireclays from the '*Primate's Pits*' in making this bowl, which would certainly have helped it to withstand the heat of boiling water as the Dublin Society reported.[26] If, as seems likely, he employed *both* Irish clays and Irish coals in its manufacture, then the bowl perfectly exemplified many of the ideals that the Dublin Society and Parliament were striving to promote.

The sum that Delamain received from the Irish Parliament a week later, £1000, may not appear generous in comparison with the £6,000 that he had reportedly spent in improving the pottery, but it was vastly greater than any sum awarded previously by the Dublin Society for earthenware manufacture in Ireland (£20). This very large grant was widely reported in the press, and may, to some extent, have been carried through on the coat-tails of an award of £4000 that was paid to the '*Primate's Pits*' consortium at the same time.

Almost as soon as he had won this exceptional award from the Irish Parliament, Delamain travelled to England to attempt to repeat his success, this time with a petition to the English Parliament. Specifically, he hoped to claim a bounty for his coal-fired kiln, which was just as eligible for an award as a commercially valuable innovation in England as it had been in Ireland. Shortly before leaving Ireland he also drew up his will.[27]

Unwisely perhaps, and indeed almost incredibly, Delamain committed many of his most secret instructions concerning the development of his invention to paper. These appear in a series of letters that he wrote from England to Mary Delamain, and to his pottery manager William Stringfellow, between 18th December 1753 and 9th January 1754, which are reprinted in full in Appendix II, (pp.171-5). The essence of the letters is that Delamain asked Stringfellow to confirm that the coal-fired '*large kiln*' in Dublin was a complete success, regardless of whether this was true or not. (He had obviously left Dublin before it was fully tested). Delamain needed the Liverpool potters to sign a petition endorsing his experimental coal-fired kiln, to strengthen his application to the English Parliament. A positive report from Stringfellow, who was a Liverpool potter himself, was therefore of paramount importance for the success of the application.[28] Apart from indicating to Stringfellow that providing this support would be to his financial benefit, Delamain also implied that the two of them might subsequently travel onwards together to Holland and Paris, '*on some extraordinary affairs to both our advantage*'. Curiously, Delamain instructed Stringfellow not to tell even their wives that they were going there.

Delamain submitted his application to the English House of Commons on the 21st January 1754, petitioning for a 'bounty' for his coal-fired kiln. (Appendix II, iv). The application was reported in the Irish press in very positive terms; '*Mr. Delamain... hath also petitioned our Parliament and offered to make a Discovery of his Art, upon giving him a Bounty; which it is thought, will be complied with*'.[29] Despite the problems that he was obviously experiencing with his large kiln, therefore, Delamain must have been optimistic that his petition would succeed.

Stringfellow seems to have complied with Delamain's wishes, and he reported favourably in person to the parliamentary committee charged with evaluating the petition. On his return to Liverpool, however, a John Hardman, (whom Delamain describes in one letter as '*my friend*') learned of the letters, and persuaded Stringfellow to turn them over to the committee. William Stringfellow also appears to have left Delamain's employment to work in Liverpool from that time onwards.[30]

Delamain's revelatory letters were posted to the committee by Hardman from Liverpool on February 12th 1754. (Appendix II, v). Considering their damaging content, it is perhaps unsurprising that nothing further is heard of the parliamentary petition, although Delamain himself does not appear to have been publicly disgraced by the affair.

A few years later, for example, he gained a second, very large grant from the Irish Parliament, which would have been impossible had he been shown to be an outright fraud. Coal-fired kilns also remained in use at the Dublin pottery for many years afterwards, and so the method itself appears to have been a genuine, practical innovation, just as Delamain claimed.

Delamain probably learned of these disclosures from Stringfellow, when he released him from his service shortly before 12th February 1754, but he seems to have pushed ahead with promoting the petition in London regardless. He was assisted in this by the delftware potter John Saunders, a co-partner in the Vauxhall porcelain works with Nicholas Crisp.[31] (Saunders may have become acquainted with Delamain through their common business interests in Battersea. Delamain was certainly involved in the Battersea enamel works at this time).

The following notice was duly published in the *London Public Advertiser* on February 16th 1754;

'We hear that Mr. Delamain the inventor of the kiln for burning white glazed earthenware with pit-coal instead of wood, has lodged a model of his kiln with the ingenious Mr. Saunders, Potter of Vauxhall in order (when he shall be directed to publish his invention) to enable any who desire it to build Kilns according to his plan. And that the public may the sooner reap the benefit of his invention, he will further undertake to give unquestionable security that whoever shall build kilns after his plan, and burn them with pit coal according to his direction shall be indemnified against any loss they may sustain by building or working such kilns and likewise that the glased earthenware, as also the Staffordshire kind, which shall be manufactured in his way, shall be better made and 10 per cent cheaper than by the methods now in use; which will enable them to undersell the French in all foreign markets, where they now annually vend above £100,000 worth, will employ members of our poor, and as 6s worth of coal in England will burn more ware for 24s worth of wood in France and fuel being the chieftest expense in this manufacture, no nation can rival us in this trade, if this plan is put in execution'.

A subsequent notice appeared in the *London Gazette* that ordered Delamain to publish his discovery *'for the good of the public'*, but there appears to have been no further interest amongst English potters in coal-fired kilns.[32] (See box p.54). Delamain seems to have returned to Dublin at some time after 19th March 1754, the date of this second advertisement. His departure from London may also coincide with the termination of his involvement in the Battersea enamel works.[33]

We hear nothing further from Henry Delamain until six months later, by which stage it seems that the World's End pottery had just reached completion, (having been in his possession for almost two and a half years).

Faulkner's Dublin Journal, 17-20th Sept. 1754;
'The earthenware manufactory on the Strand is now finished, and built to employ two or three hundred people. All Charter-School, parish or distressed tradesmen's children of either sex will be received and taught all the different branches of making all sorts of earthenware by the best masters. Each child during apprenticeship to get two shillings a week for the first year, three shillings for the second, three shillings and sixpence for the third, four shillings for the fourth, and four shillings and sixpence, for the last three years. - Henry Delamain.'

As Michael Archer has remarked, if Delamain's pottery ever worked to its full capacity, employing *'two or three hundred people'*, then it was a very large venture by the standards of the day.[37] The only evidence to corroborate the veracity of Delamain's estimates comes from the Downshire (creamware) pottery in Belfast, which was built in 1787 to accommodate a workforce of similar size.[38] On balance, however, both estimates were probably highly optimistic. Delamain's pottery might well have been able to *accommodate* a workforce of two to three hundred, had the orders been available to justify their employment, but there is no evidence to suggest that the World's End pottery ever worked to anything like its full capacity. Henry's brother and successor William Delamain similarly told Parliament in 1762 that *'three hundred people could be'* employed at the pottery, but when questioned further, he admitted that only *'Twenty hands were now employed'*. (p.62). The pottery's workforce seems to have been considerably larger during Henry Delamain's lifetime - Henry himself indicated that he employed *'upwards of forty families'* in

Coal - Fired Kilns

Henry Delamain's pottery in Dublin seems to have been unique in the British Isles, in firing its kiln with coal rather than wood. Delamain probably commenced experiments with coal-fired kilns as soon as he took over the works in 1752, and he claimed that he had *'perfected'* the method by the time of the pottery's first advertisement in October 1753.

There would have been considerable cost-savings in the use of coal, and the pursuit of such an invention was very much in line with the aims of the Dublin Society, but most delftware manufacturers did not favour its use for two reasons. Firstly, coal often burned at a higher temperature than wood, which caused over-firing. Secondly, coal smoke was thought to discolour the sensitive tin-glaze. Consequently, English potters seem to have been sceptical of Delamain's claims.[34]

To judge from his correspondence, Delamain had clearly fired delftware successfully in a small, experimental coal-fired kiln by the time of his petition to the English Parliament in January 1754, but he still encountered difficulties with the full-scale version. Delamain's experiments seem to have been entirely disregarded by English delftware potters subsequently, but there is little doubt that the Dublin pottery persisted with the method and succeeded in perfecting a full-size, coal-fired kiln. In 1761 & 62 for example, William Delamain applied for funds to purchase *'coal and other materials'*, and to lay in a *'sufficient stock of coals'* for their kiln. Yet despite their success, the method does not seem to have been adopted elsewhere. As late as 1767, Bristol delftware potters continued to remark that coal was *'unserviceable'* as kiln fuel.[35]

It is possible that some of the distinctive glaze characteristics observed on Dublin delftware might derive from the pottery's unique use of coal, but otherwise there seem to have been no obvious disadvantages in the method. There is certainly no indication amongst extant pieces that Dublin delftwares were routinely discoloured by coal smoke, as the English potters feared.[36]

November 1753 - but even so, hopes of employing two or three hundred seem to have represented little more than wishful thinking. The maximum number employed was probably closer to fifty, as William Delamain later mentioned that in addition to his twenty employees *'thirty men they had trained were in china factories in England'*, (p. 62).

In view of the great lengths that Delamain went to in order to produce fine-quality delftware in Ireland, and his apparently successful experiments with various Irish clays, it is surprising to find that he did not attempt to manufacture porcelain, a more valuable and prestigious product. The only indication that he was even interested in the subject comes indirectly, from an intriguing series of advertisements published in Waterford between May and September 1755, describing an alleged attempt to produce porcelain there.[39]

The individual at the centre of the Waterford porcelain venture seems to have been an unscrupulous Staffordshire potter, James Allen, of Lane Delph and Burslem, who gained financial support from a local merchant, Thomas Wyse, to undertake experiments. It would appear that some porcelain was indeed manufactured, to judge from an advertisement in the *Dublin Journal* on May 6th 1755, which began by stating *'Waterford, May 5th, 1755. This day was exhibited here some white transparent china ware made by a gentleman of this place...'*. There then followed an exchange of angry correspondence in the local press, with Allen claiming that spies from another pottery, specifically implying Delamain's in Dublin, had purposely been installed at Waterford in order to steal the secret of porcelain manufacture. These accusations were rebuffed with a string of counterclaims from the various accused, alleging that Allen had never made anything that was sufficiently like porcelain to be worth stealing, and that his claims were simply a smoke-screen to disguise his failure. Finally, in September 1755, five of the accused potters swore an affidavit stating that Allen was a known thief in Staffordshire, and that his aim was to deceive Mr. Wyse and Mr. Delamain with false promises, after which nothing further is heard of either Waterford porcelain or James Allen.

This interesting episode only bears passing relevance to Dublin, but two of the workmen at this new venture, one a turner, the other a sprig painter of earthenware, came *'well recommended'* from Henry Delamain's pottery in Dublin. The sprig painter mentioned is later identified as one Bryan McManus. Another individual who allegedly *'came from Delamain's work at Dublin'* was the ubiquitous John Smith, although there is no evidence to link him with the two John Smiths at the Belfast Potthouse (See p.16). John Smith himself stated that he was a workman of china-ware who had come *'from Chelsea at great cost to work'* in Waterford, but as there was no work for him there he *'was obliged to sell* [his] *clothes'* to get to Dublin afterwards. (No John Smith is recorded in Chelsea, although a potter of that name worked at Bow in 1748).[40] Other individuals - almost certainly all potters - were named in the final affidavit in Waterford; William Wright, John Simpson, Adam Jones and William Proctor (of Lesne Delft, Staffs). Some of these names appear to have been associated with the Pomona porcelain works at Newcastle under Lyme in Staffordshire.[41] The same individuals may also have worked for Delamain in Dublin at some stage - either before or after the Waterford venture.

The potters' statements are so conflicting that it is difficult to judge Henry Delamain's attitude to the porcelain experiments, but he was certainly aware of them, and he was no doubt cognisant of the fact that the Dublin Society would probably have offered a handsome premium to the first Irish porcelain manufacturer. Wyse in Waterford not only appears to have known of Delamain's interest, he even intended sending Allen *'to Dublin to make a piece of work for the said gentleman,* [Delamain], ... *and often declared he should be glad to have it in his power to render that gentleman any service..'*. For his part, Delamain replied that *'he* [was] *willing to serve Mr. Wyse or any other gentleman that would carry on or manufacture in his way, with workmen and everything he is capable of'*. Yet despite their obviously amicable relations, these Irish porcelain experiments appear to have ceased completely following Allen's departure, and nothing further is heard of the matter.

At about the same time, Delamain was beginning to experience a cash shortage for the first time. His personal finances had probably suffered in the previous few years, but this notice, in the *Dublin Journal* of 10th June 1755, contains the first ominous indication that the pottery was not doing well;

'The great efforts that is made by some people (whose interest it is) to hurt the earthenware manufactory in the Strand, obliges the proprietor thereof to inform the publick that the Hon. the Dublin Society has certified the earthenware made there is as good as any imported here, and is sold 30 per cent. cheaper than the French earthenware, to prevent the importation of which Delamain can prove that he has spent above £5,000 in building and furnishing one of the largest manufactories of the kind in Europe. As some of the clerks have sold some faulty ware that was ordered to be broken, to prevent which for the future, the ware will be sold at the India warehouse in Abbey Street, where all orders will be received and executed with expedition. The ware will be sold wholesale at the manufactory only.'

The *'India warehouse'*, which Delamain here indicates was to become the pottery's new retail outlet, was situated on the corner of Abbey Street and Jervis Street, closer to the centre of Dublin (and just over half a mile from the pottery). The address, later identified as *'1 Abbey Street'*, had been known as a *'china-shop'* long before it was taken over by Delamain. Catherine Davey, a china and glass retailer, sold a *'great variety of China toys & ornamented China'* on the site as early as 1743.[42]

The pottery's succeeding advertisement, which ran a few months later in several issues of the *Dublin Journal*, confirms that Delamain was running out of capital, (Aug. 30th - Sep. 9th 1755);

'To the merchants of the Kingdom of Ireland - I have brought my earthenware to such perfection that I have a great demand for it from Germany, Spain and Portugal, but for want of capital I am not able to export a quantity of it, which makes me have recourse to such gentlemen as trades in these Kingdoms to assist me by sending it abroad, and if they will pay the ready money for it, it will enable me to supply them with many thousand pounds worth of it annually; Since I have discovered the method of burning my ware with coal, and found out lately a good body and glaze, I can serve them on such reasonable terms that they can undersell the French in all the foreign markets. All losses on my ware that is sold abroad I will reimburse the exporters of it. The warehouse at the manufactory will be open Wednesdays and Saturdays only for wholesale.

N.B.- As complaint has justly been made of defective wares sold by the clerks at the manufactory, I am willing to exchange them (provided they are not abused by service) at the India warehouse in Abbey Street, where the ware is sold as usual by retail.'[43]

The excessive duty that was charged on delftware imported into England, (reported as 3½ d. per lb. weight in 1762), largely prohibited Delamain from selling there. Although this advertisement only records *'a great demand'* from continental Europe for Dublin goods, there can be little doubt that Delamain had expected that much of the pottery's income would have derived from foreign exports, as the scale of the improvements at the World's End pottery were such that the venture could never have been sustained by the comparatively small home market. One eighteenth-century Irish fine-glassmaker, working on a much more modest scale than Delamain, later stated that '*any one* [glass] *house in the Kingdom is more than sufficient to supply the whole internal demand.... should Export orders at any time fail, my Stores are* [soon] *overcharged with Goods*'.[44] Irish potters were probably just as dependent upon foreign orders as Irish glassmakers, and so Delamain's failure to fully develop these overseas markets may have been the main reason that his pottery never worked to full capacity.

Nonetheless, some overseas sales must have occurred. It therefore seems curious to find that the Irish customs books do not record a single export of Dublin delftware at any time during the eighteenth-century.[45] William Delamain and Ann Day in 1762 mentioned the export of consignments to the West Indies, and excavated evidence from Virginia and New York clearly shows that some Dublin delftware did make its way across the Atlantic. The complete absence of customs records is therefore difficult to understand. It is possible that Dublin delftware was occasionally smuggled out, in order to avoid export duty, but it seems highly unlikely that *all* exported Dublin delftware should have been dispatched in this fashion. Such omissions in the customs statistics are by no means confined to earthenware.[46] Whether by connivance with customs officers, or because the exports consisted of small quantities of miscellaneous goods, items such as delftware and glass simply do not seem to have been declared, and hence they do not appear in any Irish customs records, (prior to the advent of free trade in 1780).

The '*want of capital*' that Delamain described may have provided him with sufficient grounds to approach the Irish Parliament with a fresh petition for financial aid on the 6th November 1755.[47] In complete contrast to his earlier application, comparatively little is known of this second petition. Once again, however, the application was successful, and early in 1756 Delamain received the sum of £1,100, paid through the Dublin Society out of public funds allotted for such purposes. As on previous occasions, this was considered a generous award for the time, and was remarked upon in the Irish press.[48] For Delamain personally, however, these additional funds may have come at a cost, as we learn from news reported in London on March 13th 1756.

'*Dublin, March 13. We hear Delamaine's china and earthenware manufactory will be made a public work and trustees appointed for its government, and its generally thought it will employ more of our poor, and bring more specie into this kingdom, than any manufacture we can export, our linnen excepted.*'[49]

There is no evidence to suggest that Parliament's plans to make Delamain's pottery a publicly owned company were ever put into effect. Nonetheless, the very fact that these remarks were made suggests there was concern at the extent of the financial subsidies that Delamain required, and that Parliament sought to safeguard its substantial investments.

If Parliament had intended appointing '*trustees ... for* [the pottery's] *government*', then there may have been more specific concerns with Henry Delamain's management of the works, or perhaps there were signs, even then, that his health was failing. Regardless of how these affairs were finally resolved, all worries ceased for Henry Delamain nine months later, on 10th January 1757. His early death was widely reported in the Irish and English press, most notably in the *Dublin Journal* of 11th January;

'*Died Monday, universally lamented by all true Lovers of their Country, Captain Henry Delamain, formerly in the Duke of Saxe Gotha's service, Master of the Irish Delft Manufactory, who, by the expense of a large fortune and unwearied application, brought that ware to such perfection as to totally prevent the enemies of our Country the French from drawing large sums yearly from this country for Burgundy and Rouen wares. Mary Delamain, his widow, carries on the said manufactory*.[50]

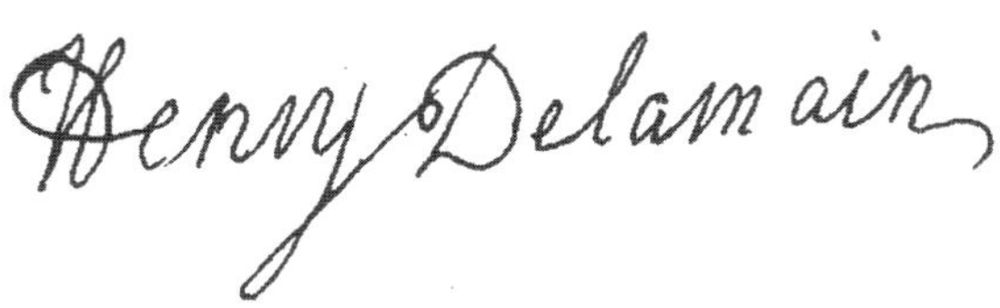

2 : 1
DUBLIN; THE WORLD'S END POTTERY
v : Mary Delamain (January 1757 - March 1760)

In his will, Henry Delamain bequeathed *'all his worldly substance ...to his dearly beloved friend Mary Bijar'* and their two children.[1] By coincidence, Henry's estranged wife Ziphorah died in London shortly after him.[2] To all intents and purposes, therefore, Mary was Henry's widow - in Dublin at least - and she assumed full title to the pottery. David Fitzgerald, a pottery dealer in Cork, was named as co-guardian of the two children.

Mary Bijar seems to have come from a Dublin family. Robert Bijar, probably Mary's father, bequeathed her the leasehold of his rented house in Abbey Street upon his death in 1751.[3] A Richard Bijar also witnessed the proving of Henry Delamain's will in December 1753, and this name continued to appear in Dublin directories (as a wine-cooper) until as late as 1807.[4] Mary seems to have placed no advertisements in the Dublin press, so that most of our information concerning her ownership of the pottery derives from an application for financial aid, presented to the Irish House of Commons almost three years later, on 9th November 1759.

It is unfortunate that so little is known of Mary Delamain's early years, as the late 1750s saw an unusual level of activity in the ceramics business in Dublin. The outbreak of the Seven Years War in 1756 disrupted many established patterns of trade, so that some London porcelain manufacturers seem to have experienced difficulty in transporting goods to their usual overseas markets. Consequently, a number of major auction events were organised in Dublin, possibly to help clear stockpiles. The Bow porcelain works were among the first English manufacturers to sell in Dublin by auction, (possibly guided by one of their founders, Thomas Frye, who was himself an Irishman).[5] Even though the factory had several good wholesale customers in Dublin, auction sales seem to have taken place as early as February 1755 [6]

In 1758, the scale of the auctions grew significantly, with major events offering an impressive range of wares from various English factories. Three of the largest porcelain sales took place at Young's Great Auction Rooms on Cork Hill, in April, July and December 1758. (The *wholesale* value of the Chelsea porcelain alone sold on these occasions amounted to £1932)[7]. John Bowcock, the agent for Bow, spent the early part of 1758 in Dublin arranging for these events. It may therefore be significant that two years later, the delftware potter Samuel Wilkinson, who might well have been Bowcock's brother or father-in-law, was to become a partner in the World's End pottery itself, from March 1760.[8]

In addition to experiencing this unprecedented level of competition from England, Mary Delamain was in the same position as her English competitors in *'finding that the export of the ware to foreign markets was prevented by the war'*. (See p.60). Having kept the pottery working without financial aid for almost three years, in what must have been difficult circumstances, Mary gradually ran short of capital. Her application to the Irish House of Commons on November 9th 1759 explains something of her situation;

'Petition of Mary Delamain, widow of Henry Delamain, late of the City of Dublin, earthenware manufacturer. *That the petitioner's late husband erected a manufactory for making earthenware, and brought it to such perfection as not only to excel anything of the kind ever attempted here before, but to equal the best foreign ware imported, on which he expended his entire fortune to the amount of £6,000 and upwards. That in the Session of 1753, the Parliament did grant him a sum of £1,000 as an encouragement for carrying on the said manufacture, and the Dublin Society upon inspection and having satisfaction received of his having expended said bounty in the improvement of said manufacture, did in the year 1755 confer on him a further sum of £1,100. That the said Delamain did with the best economy expend this latter sum also in finishing and improving his manufactory in the compleatest manner, but died on the 10th of January, 1757, leaving her destitute of a capital sufficient for carrying on the work extensively, as the sums granted were expended on completing the works, as* *well as his whole fortune, and some debts contracted which petitioner has since paid. That notwithstanding these difficulties the petitioner has since the death of her husband carried on said manufacture, which is allowed to be greatly improved, but for want of a capital to purchase materials at a prime cost is prevented from lowering the price of the ware, and giving the usual credit to merchants, shopkeepers, and retailers throughout the kingdom. If the petitioner receives assistance once more from Parliament she hopes it will enable her to give credit and lower the price of the ware so considerably to the wholesale dealers that they can afford to retail said wares 25 per cent. Under present prices, which there is no doubt would occasion such large demands at home and abroad as to increase the number of men to equal the apparatus which is sufficient to employ above two hundred of the poor natives, foreigners not now being necessary; keep and bring large sums of money into this kingdom, and be a lasting benefit to the Nation in general.*'[9]

Unfortunately for Mary Delamain, concerns of French invasion and anti-Union rioting in Dublin caused the Irish Parliamentary session to be cut short. No grants were disbursed to private petitioners in that year. (See petition, p.60).

Although Mary Delamain does not seem to have advertised in the press, one of her best customers, Mary Dorgan, placed the following advertisement in the *Cork Evening Post* on 26th November 1759;

'*Just imported from Dublin, by Mary Dorgan, all kinds of Delamain's Ware, large and small Dishes, a variety of Sallad Dishes and Plates, round and long Terenes* [Tureens], *scalloped and plain, Punch Bowls of different sizes, Bread Baskets, Sauce Boats and curious flower Pots of the same ware ... To be sold at the house in which Mr. Joshua Connor lived ... near North Gate, Cork.*'[10]

(A second advertisement on May 29th 1760 stated that Mary Dorgan continued to import goods '*from Delamain's Great Manufactory in Dublin*').

Mary Delamain was obviously a young woman when she died on March 4th 1760, as her two children were still minors. (Her daughter Mary was born before December 1753, her son, probably named Henry, arrived after that date).[11] Her death was recorded in *Sleator's Gazette* on 11th March 1760;

'*Tuesday last died Mrs. Mary Delamain, widow of the late Captain Henry Delamain who was the first that brought the earthenware manufactory to perfection in this Kingdom, and since his decease his said widow (endowed with all the virtues of a good christian, tender parent and sincere friend), continued with such advantage to the purchasers as to prevent the further importation of foreign wares*'.

An additional notice, which appeared in the *Dublin Journal* on March 8th 1760, recorded that the pottery was to be continued in as extensive a manner as formerly, for the benefit of the two children.[12] We learn more about Mary's period of management from accounts provided by her successors, but it is clear that her early death dealt a second, unexpected blow to the pottery.

2 : 1

DUBLIN; THE WORLD'S END POTTERY

vi : William Delamain & Samuel Wilkinson (March 1760 - c. February 1768)

William Delamain had probably never intended working in the pottery business, but the position was thrust upon him when both Henry and Mary Delamain died at a comparatively young age. He therefore assumed management of the pottery in trust for his orphaned niece and nephew.

William was the youngest of Henry Delamain's three brothers, born around 1720.[1] Like Henry, he was commonly referred to simply as '*the Captain*'. If anything, his early career seems to have been even more successful than Henry's. For many years prior to these events, William had apparently enjoyed '*gentle employ in Dublin Castle ... at his Majesty's service*', ultimately rising to the prestigious office of Marshall of the City of Dublin from about 1753 onwards. Even after he assumed management of the pottery, William Delamain seems to have maintained a number of additional business interests of his own. For example, when his son James, (for whom the Delamain/Ranson service was produced, Colour Plates 9-11), moved to live in France in September 1760, William used his influence and contacts to assist with the Dublin end of this brandy business.[2] William also owned a tea-importing business in 1761, with premises in Little Strand Street, near the Essex Bridge. This may have been the same tea-business that Henry had operated in 1751, (p.46), retailing at a new location.[3]

The second individual involved in the pottery, Samuel Wilkinson, is a new name, and his origins are more difficult to trace. The only likely candidate is a Samuel Wilkinson who had previously worked at the Montague Close delftware pottery in London. It was here that Matthew Garner was trained in the late-seventeenth century, (p. 11), and the same pottery also sold extensively in Dublin in 1746-7, (see p. 41). Evidence of Samuel Wilkinson's involvement is again circumstantial, resting primarily on the coincidence of *two* names. From 1708-35, the Montague Close pottery was owned and managed by an individual of the same name, Samuel *Wilkinson*.[4] He was succeeded there by another delftware potter, Richard *Day* (& son), who worked in London from 1735 until 1755, when the pottery closed. Both of these surnames reappear at the World's End pottery in Dublin from 1760 onwards - Samuel *Wilkinson* as the co-partner, and a Mrs Ann *Day*, as manager of the pottery's retail outlet in Abbey Street. Together, the two surnames make the coincidence more conspicuous. (There may also have been further connections through Mary Delamain's family).[5] The link is undoubtedly tenuous, but a further point to consider is that William probably had no practical experience whatever of running a pottery. Bringing in the retired manager of a large delftware pottery from London might therefore have been a practical and prudent move.

On 22nd April 1760, a month after assuming ownership, William Delamain and Samuel Wilkinson Esq. placed a long advertisement in the *Dublin Gazette*, explaining the changed circumstances to their customers. They also added that their prices were being lowered by 10%, they asked that debts should be paid and accounts presented speedily, and hoped '*that no person whatever will be offended that all goods must be paid for on delivery, as no books will be kept, nor will any material be bought for use of said manufactory, but with ready money*'.[6]

At about the same time, a second delftware pottery was being established in another Dublin suburb at Stoneybatter, (see p.157).[7] The second delftware pottery in Belfast was probably operating at that stage (p.152), and John Stritch also began producing his delftwares in Limerick from June 1761, (p.158). It seems, therefore, that the Irish pottery trade was in a reasonably healthy condition, despite - or perhaps even because of - the continuing Seven Years War.[8]

For whatever reason, the new proprietors of the World's End pottery do not appear to have petitioned for financial aid during their first eighteen months of ownership. Their application to the Irish Parliament was instead received at the end of the following year, on 6th November 1761;

'Petition of Samuel Wilkinson and William Delamain, executors of Mary Delamain, late of the

city of Dublin, earthenware manufacturer. That the late Henry Delamain erected a manufactory for earthenware, in which he discovered the art of burning with coal instead of wood, and brought it to such perfection as not only to excel anything of the kind ever attempted in this kingdom before, but to equal the best foreign ware imported, in which he expended his entire fortune of £6,000 and upwards. In 1753 Parliament granted him £1,000, and in 1755 the Dublin Society gave a further sum of £1,100. That on the decease of Henry Delamain, his late widow, Mary Delamain, carried on the business with great success, and declined troubling Parliament in 1757, assured that the manufacture would support itself; but finding that the export of the ware to foreign markets was prevented by war, Mary Delamain petitioned Parliament in 1759; but no further money was granted in that year to private petitioners. That the petitioners since the decease of Mary Delamain have carried on the manufacture for the advantage of the orphans of Henry and Mary Delamain in particular and of the nation in general with so much success as to prevent the import of foreign ware which annually carried out of the country above £10,000 to France, and have supplied dealers in every principal seaport of this kingdom. That petitioners, by commencing on a small stock are prevented from purchasing coals and other materials in the proper season, and lowering the price of the ware, or employing between two and three hundred of the poor natives, and, on a peace, of exporting to foreign markets above £20,000 worth every year, over and above the home consumption'.[9]

These claims that the Dublin pottery was so successful '*as to prevent the import of foreign ware which annually carried out of the country above £10,000 to France*' are reminiscent of similarly inflated remarks in the petitions of Henry and Mary Delamain. They imply that French imports were a major threat to Irish and English interests, but these claims are certainly not borne out by Irish customs records. **(Fig. 57)**. Imports from France did increase significantly around 1750, (rising to around £1200 p.a.), but they still represented just a small fraction of the value of imported English wares, and fell very far short of the figure of '*above £10,000*' quoted by William Delamain (See Appendix V).[10] During the Seven Years' War with France, between 1756 and 63, imports of French earthenware ceased completely. To have claimed that this was due solely to the success of the Dublin pottery, however, as William Delamain suggested, was obviously a gross exaggeration.

By the early 1760s, although Delamain and Wilkinson would have been unaware of the fact, the days of large parliamentary grants were waning, due to growing disquiet in the Irish Parliament concerning the manner in which such grants were distributed. This may explain why the pottery's applications were subjected to an unusual degree of enquiry in that year, with several individuals being called to present statements to a parliamentary committee. The committee reported favourably on the petition, on 12th November 1761, but as no grant was forthcoming William Delamain & Co. were required to make a fresh application, this time to a committee of the Dublin Society. Although this must have caused considerable inconvenience to those involved, the various depositions that were recorded during these hearings provide a more

Figure 57. Earthenware Imports To Ireland 1740-70

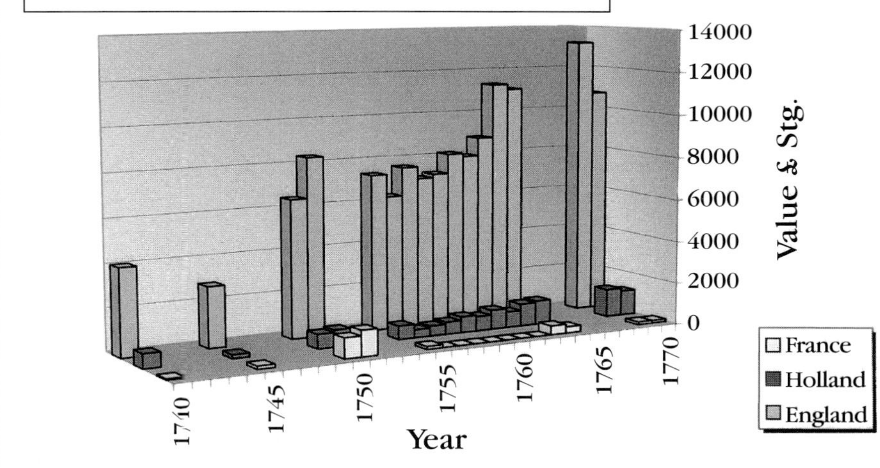

valuable and personal insight into the workings of Delamain's pottery than any petitions recorded previously. They also allow us to hear the words of two hitherto unknown individuals who worked at the pottery, in addition to those of the proprietor.

Beginning with the parliamentary committee hearings, which took place under oath on 10th November 1761, William Delamain was called first;

'***William Delamain,*** *being sworn, said that the late Henry Delamain expended £8,000 and upwards in building houses, mills, kilns and completing an apparatus for an earthenware manufactory sufficient to employ about three hundred people, in making experiments to discover the art of burning with coal instead of wood (which the many who attempted it in this kingdom and elsewhere have failed in), bringing artists from abroad at immense expense, in which he was opposed by the proprietors of different manufactures, and improving the earthenware manufacture. That the manufacture is brought to such perfection as to exclude the importation of Rouen and Burgundy ware these last five years, which annually carried out of this kingdom about £10,000, and is allowed equal to any earthenware in Europe. That the manufactory brought up a great number of apprentices, some of which are esteemed the first workmen in England, who, for want of a capital, the proprietors of this manufactory were obliged to discharge. That the proprietors entering on a small stock are disabled from purchasing coals, block-tin, lead, colours, clay raised in the North of Ireland, and other materials in the proper season, being all ready-money articles, the want of which subjects the manufacture to many losses. That a parliamentary aid would enable the executors to employ the entire apparatus which is sufficient to manufacture £40,000 worth of ware every year, half of which they could export to our islands in the West Indies, where some ware was sent by the late proprietor and was sold to advantage, and many orders have since come, which, for want of a capital, could not be complied with. That said aid would enable the executors to lower the price of the ware 20 per cent, and make it a lasting benefit to the nation without any further assistance from Parliament.* '[11]

The committee must then have requested corroboration of the pottery's financial expenditure during the time of Henry Delamain, and so they called to the stand one of the Dublin pottery's best known names, Peter Shee, in the company of a second individual, Mr. Edward Sankey. Shee was a landscape painter, and one consequence of this brief committee appearance is that he has often been considered responsible for decorating Dublin's celebrated landscape-painted delftwares, (p.95-99).[12] The testimony indicates that Shee wore a second hat, acting as the pottery's accountant (with Edward Sankey).

The financial statement that Shee supplied to the parliamentary committee concerning Henry Delamain's early expenditure is a valuable document (see p.47), but the remainder of his testimony simply reiterated statements made previously by William Delamain.

'***Peter Shee,*** *being sworn, said he was employed by Henry Delamain in the year 1752, and continued until 1757 as painter and clerk and that the said Henry Delamain was the first that discovered the art of burning with coal, instead of wood, by which the earthenware can be sold 30 per cent cheaper; that the manufactory is carried on since March 1760, by Samuel Wilkinson and William Delamain for the benefit of the children of the late Henry and Mary Delamain; that great quantities of the ware are sold in every principal city of this kingdom; that the late Henry Delamain expended £6311 14s 2½d of his own family fortune before his first application to Parliament in 1753 in bringing said manufacture to perfection.*'

The parliamentary committee reported favourably in response to Delamain and Wilkinson's application just two days later, on 12th November 1761. Perhaps as a result of changes in the manner in which grants were disbursed, however, no grant was forthcoming, and so yet another application was presented to the Dublin Society four months later, on 22nd March 1762.[13] The Dublin Society's application procedure, like that of the Irish Parliament, seems to have been more rigorous than in previous years. Once again, therefore, two individuals from the pottery were called to make depositions.

William Delamain, testifying for the second time, largely repeated his previous statement to the parliamentary committee. The early expenditure of the pottery, during Henry Delamain's years, seems to have been a topic of particular concern. Unlike the previous petition, however, which was a straightforward, prepared statement, William Delamain on this second occasion replied *ad lib* to specific questions from the Society committee The questions were not recorded, but the committee members did manage to draw from him some additional details;

'*Mr.* **[William]** ***Delamain****, being sworn, deposed that they have an account of every kiln that has been burnt since his brother's death in 1757. They have been very cramped all along, and particularly since his sister's death, by want of money, but have never stopped for one week since the first beginning. There are twenty hands employed in the house, and three hundred might be employed if they had the stock. They get their clay from Carrickfergus. The manufacture was first begun by his brother in 1753, when he got £1,000 from Parliament. He has been concerned as executor to his brother since March, 1760; and his sister* [in-law] *carried it on from her husband's death to her own. About thirty men brought up in this manufacture are now employed in the china manufacture in England. If they had £1,000, they could lay in a sufficient stock of coal, clay, and other materials to carry on the work effectually. The clay should be three years old before it is used; there is not a coal in Dublin for their use, and though three different sets of ware are bespoke by Mr. Secretary Hamilton*[14]*, they can't fire a kiln for that reason.* '

As was also the case with the parliamentary committee, a second witness was then called to corroborate William Delamain's testimony - on this occasion Mrs. Ann Day, the manager of the pottery's retail outlet in Abbey Street. Her transcribed answers, (to questions which again are not recorded), describe practical matters concerning the pottery's running, so that this is probably the most interesting testimony of all.

'***Mrs. Ann Day****, being sworn, said she can't say what the quantity of goods made yearly is. She keeps an account of the ware they sell, but the accounts are not cast up. The last account amounted to £1,000 for between the year and eighteen months, but that was only the cash amount; other goods being sold on credit that were not set down in that ... She thinks she can say with great justice that £50 worth a week might be made with the hands they have now. They have but twenty hands, and she thinks she can safely say the kiln they have now will produce that sum. They have a good demand, and would have more if the ware could be sold cheaper. They have reason to expect that their ware would meet with great success in the American islands, but the insurance is so high. They have sent some to Jamaica, and it returned in rum; but as they have not a capital, they can't give credit for the length of time necessary for the foreign trade; it is by the retail trade that they support the manufacture. The great consumption of the ware is at home; they have three established customers in Cork who would take a great quantity if they had a stock to supply them.* [Probably the dealers Patrick Sarsfield, Mary Dorgan and David Fitzgerald]. *The great demand is from the city of Dublin and the province of Munster. They don't supply the shops with their best ware, but some of the poorer sort of shops buy the second and third ware, and they have made a good deal of goods for Mr. Newton for about two years back.* [George Newton was one of the largest china-dealers in Dublin[15]]. *They might go upon making the flint ware, but are not acquainted with the method; theirs is not of that kind, but near the Burgundy ware and to imitate china. There is no ware in England of the same kind as theirs; and if they could send it there, they would find a greater call for it than they have here. The duty on their ware to England is threepence half-penny the pound weight, so that a set made for the Lord Lieutenant* [the Earl of Halifax] *and sent by him to England, amounted to £7 duty.*'

The remark that the pottery '*might go upon making the flint ware, but are not acquainted with the method*' is especially interesting. The mention of '*Flint ware*' at this date generally refers to creamware. By this stage, March 1762, even Josiah Wedgwood was not entirely confident of his ability to produce a perfected creamware, although the presentation service for Queen Charlotte was produced later that same year. The Dublin Society was obviously aware of new developments that were taking place in England, and they ultimately offered a premium for the manufacture of an Irish creamware from 1769.[16]

William Delamain's remark *'If they had £1000'* suggests he was seeking a premium comparable to the sums paid previously to Henry Delamain - especially after the efforts made in presenting these various applications. Instead, the pottery was awarded £300 in March 1762, which still proved generous in comparison with subsequent grants. (Ultimately they only received about £280, as awards made by Dublin Society in that year amounted to £500 more than the £10,000 allotted by Parliament and were reduced accordingly).[17]

During 1763, debates were raised in the Irish House of Commons questioning the effectiveness of large parliamentary and Dublin Society grants in supporting Irish industries. The MP for Limerick, Edmund Sexton Pery, who may recently have received a petition regarding the manufacture of delftware in Limerick, (see p.160), recommended that many small premiums would be more effective support to industry than a few large ones, and that payments should be made *'in proportion to their Quantity and Excellence'*.[18] In the same debate, Dr. Charles Lucas derided some of the very large payments that had been paid previously, and specifically cited the example of *'One Delamain* [who] *got money for making Rhone* [Rouen] *Ware, and the Work has been discontinued from that Time to this'*. As Michael Archer has observed, Lucas's remarks should perhaps be judged cautiously, but they do confirm William Delamain's assertion that the pottery had shed many employees after Henry Delamain's death, (down to a staff of just *'twenty hands'*).

A wedding notice that appeared in the *Dublin Freeman's Journal* on May 18th 1765 presents us with a surprise, as a previously unknown individual, Edward Stacey, described himself as a *'Partner of the Delft Manufactory at World's End Lane'*.[19] Although the address is slightly at variance with the correct address of the World's End pottery, there is little doubt that this is where he was working. Edward Stacey did not formally purchase any portion of the pottery lease until three years later, in February 1768, but the fact that he publicly declared himself a partner suggests that he was deeply involved in the pottery by 1765, if not before. Stacey's new wife, *'Widow Roscoe of Mecklenburg Street'*, may well have been related to a John and James Roscoe, who owned a delftware pottery on Shaw's Brow in Liverpool during the early 1760s.[20]

In August 1766 Ambrose Hanley and James Murphy, the owners of the second delftware pottery in Dublin at Stoneybatter, were found to have made false claims in their application for a Dublin Society premium.[21] (See p.157). James Roche or Roach, who discovered the fraud, was subsequently employed at the World's End pottery, where he is recorded in 1770. The Dublin Society also briefly mentioned the name of William Waldron on November 6th 1766. Waldron was probably a delftware painter, who had apparently been apprenticed to the World's End pottery, *'but his sight* [became] *so impaired'* that he had to leave.[22]

The principal effect of the parliamentary debates in 1763 was that from c.1764-5 onwards, payments to Irish manufacturers were awarded on a proportional basis, the payment equating to 15% of each applicant's annual production. The pottery had successfully petitioned for aid in 1762, but their applications in 1763 and 1764 had come to nothing. Once the new scheme was in place, however, (from June 1765) they received small, annual premiums in each of the subsequent years.

Year	Value of Annual Production
1761-2	>£1,000 [23]
1764-5	£1,000
1765-6	£762
1766-7	£568
1767-8	£300

As we might expect, these figures reveal that the World's End pottery did not thrive under Delamain and Wilkinson's management, but instead fell into a long, gradual decline. The premiums provide us with a precise indication of the steady fall in production during the latter part of the 1760s. One means of attempting to arrest these declining sales was to reduce prices in the Abbey Street shop. Shortly after receiving their premium of £114 from the Dublin Society in 1766, the pottery placed one of its most enlightening advertisements in *Faulkner's Dublin Journal* on 6 - 12th August 1766;

*'**Delamain's Earthen-ware Manufactory,** (1 Abbey Street): From the great encouragement given to said manufacture by the Right Hon. and Hon. the Dublin Society, the directors thereof take this public opportunity of returning their most grateful thanks to that most respectable body, and also the nobility and gentry who have been pleased to countenance and encourage this national undertaking. The executors of the late Henry Delamain beg to acquaint the Society and the public that they have lowered the price of earthenware, 15 per cent. The fine painted Landscape plates from 9s per dozen to 7s English, the second sort from 6s to 4s 6d; Dishes, Tureens, Epergnes, Boats, Bowls, Fruit and Salad Dishes and all other articles lowered 15 per cent. There is now a large assortment of the finest ware ever made, ready for sale, far superior to any imported. All commands to be directed to Mrs. Ann Day, at the ware-house in Abbey Street.'*[24]

Although the production figures clearly show that the pottery was slowly failing, this does not necessarily mean that the quality dropped in line with the fall in output. A significant statement in this advertisement is the remark that those involved with the pottery believed the wares they were then making were '*the finest ware ever made*'. Most of the Dublin wares copying Chinese porcelain designs were probably produced at about this time, during the 1760s (see p.89). The advertisement also indicates that they were offering a wide range of '*Landscape plates*' for sale, which many today consider to be amongst the finest of the Dublin products.

On 24th February 1768, Edward Stacey, who had described himself as a '*Partner of the Delft Manufactory*' as early as May 1765, purchased the lease for part of the pottery from the Delamain's executors. By that stage, the pottery was reduced to a small-scale business, with fewer than twenty workers and a total output of around £300 per annum. There are no subsequent references to Samuel Wilkinson or Ann Day, nor to Henry and Mary Delamain's two children, and so we know nothing of their fate. Captain William Delamain, however, continued to reside in Dublin until 1788, when he went to France to live with his son James.[25] It is recorded in 1790 that William '*carried the new French flag at the 14th July celebrations in Jarnac*', ostensibly in his official capacity as the '*Marshall of Dublin*'. He died at his son's home in Jarnac in 1793.[26]

2 : 1
DUBLIN; THE WORLD'S END POTTERY
vii : Edward Stacey, James Roche & Partners (February 1768 - December 1771)

Edward Stacey's acquisition of the World's End pottery seems to have taken place gradually, over a period of several years. He was first recorded in Dublin as early as May 1765, when in his wedding notice he described himself as a *'Partner of the Delft Manufactory at the World's End Lane'*.[1] (See p.63). At this stage, his partnership was probably agreed on an informal basis, as all other evidence suggests that William Delamain and Samuel Wilkinson remained in charge.

A more formal transfer of ownership was probably concluded three or four years later, in 1768 or 1769. On 24th February 1768, Delamain and Wilkinson sold Stacey the lease to a portion of the pottery (with its *'Houses, Buildings and Appurtenances'*), and also to Mary Delamain's former dwelling house.[2] The pottery continued to claim its Dublin Society premiums in the name of Delamain and Wilkinson, however, until as late as June 1768, (when they received £45 for an annual production valued at £300).[3]

The lease transfer in February 1768 clearly implies that Edward Stacey was actively involved in acquiring the World's End pottery, but he seems to have made no attempt to proclaim his ownership. (For example, later applications for Dublin Society premiums were sought in the name of *'James Roche and Partners'*, even though Roche's name appears nowhere on the lease document). A later newspaper advertisement helps to clarify this rather confusing situation. From this, it becomes obvious that the potters at the World's End pottery had formed a consortium, to take over the running of the works, in an attempt to turn the fortunes of the ailing pottery around. As later events confirm, Edward Stacey was probably the senior figure in this potter's co-operative.

Although many details of the ownership transfer remain unclear, the consortium had fully acquired the pottery by August 1769, at the very latest. Their first advertisement appeared in the *Dublin Journal* on February 22nd, 1770;

'This is to acquaint the nobility, gentry, and the public in general, that the workmen of the delft manufactory on the North Strand have rented said concerns from the executors of Mr. Henry Delamain for to carry on said works as usual, but in a far better and more extensive manner; and as they have been carrying it on these six months, they have now got a large assortment of ware, such as table-sets of India patterns, ornamental ware, etc, of the newest fashions; coats of arms, crests, views of gentlemen's country seats etc, done in the most elegant manner, far superior and cheaper than any of the kind can be imported, and will engage them to stand hot water. As they are new beginners they mean to sell their goods at the lowest profit for ready money only, and will give the greatest encouragement to those who buy to sell again. They likewise make all kinds of pots for apothecaries and perfumers. Country dealers will have their orders executed with punctuality, care and expedition at the most reasonable rates.'

There is no mention in this advertisement of the Delamain's shop in Abbey Street, which presumably the potters were unable to acquire. They therefore took steps to furnish themselves with a new retail outlet, as their next advertisement explained;

Dublin Journal, July 14th 1770.

'Whereas the workmen of the delft manufactory on the North Strand, formerly Delamain's, a few months ago rented said concerns from the executors of said Delamain, they take this opportunity of returning thanks to their friends and the public for the great encouragement since commencement in business, and acquaint the nobility, gentry, and public that they have opened a commodious shop in front of said concerns where they intend selling their goods and nowhere else, and have now a considerable assortment of excellent ware, such as plates, dishes, etc, far superior and cheaper than any of the kind imported. They likewise do landscapes, coats of arms, crests, and views of gentlemen's country seats, in the most elegant manner, and as they now have had the honour of receiving a bounty from the Dublin Society, they intend going on in a very extensive manner. They also make pots for grocers, apothecaries, and perfumers.'

James Roche is usually perceived as the workmens' manager, as their Dublin Society applications were submitted in the name of *'James Roche and Partners'*. Edward Stacey's signature is the only one to appear on the 1768 lease agreement, however, indicating that he was more likely the principal owner. One possible explanation could be that the consortium put James Roche forward as their representative because he was already regarded favourably by the Dublin Society committee, having exposed the Stoneybatter pottery's fraudulent application in 1765, (p.157).

The evident optimism of these two advertisements clearly indicates that the new owners started out with high hopes, and initially their sales did improve. Between August 1769 and April 1770, a period of less than nine months, they produced delftwares to the value of £340, (compared to £300 for a full year's production under Delamain and Wilkinson).[4] Unfortunately for the Dublin potters, ceramic technology had been developing rapidly in England during the previous decade, and the Dublin Society were no longer impressed with delftware. The Society's delftware premiums actually ceased entirely in 1769, to be replaced with a new award for the more innovative creamware, or in their own words, *'Earthen Ware in Imitation of that which is generally called Flint or Paris Ware'*.[5]

By pure ill timing, the World's End consortium made its first application for Dublin Society aid in the very year that awards were first offered for creamware, rather than delftware manufacture. In April 1770, the Society decided that the claim *'by James Roche and his Partners for manufacture of Earthenware ... tho' good in its kind, was not of the Sort for the making of which the Premium was offered'*.[6] As a special concession, however, they decided to award them a bounty of £50, as an encouragement *'in consideration of excellent Earthenware, of the same sort with delftware manufactured by them since the first of August last to the Amount in Value of £340.6.6'*.[7] From this it is clear that the World's End pottery was still producing delftware in April 1770, quite possibly of *'excellent'* quality.

In July 1770, the Dublin Society again offered their creamware premium, specifically seeking an *'Earthenware in Imitation of Staffordshire Ware, or that which is commonly called Yellow-Stone Ware'*, but the award was not claimed.[8] This suggests that the World's End pottery continued to produce delftware throughout 1770 and 1771, despite the fact that it was now perceived as old-fashioned. By the end of 1771, however, the pottery was obviously experiencing financial difficulty. On 12th December of that year the partnership presented the Dublin Society with a petition for aid *'to carry on the manufacture on the Strand'*.[9]

On the very same day, 12th December 1771, the Dublin Society received a second, more unexpected petition from two newly arrived creamware potters from Staffordshire - Edward Ackers and Thomas Shelly.[10] Ackers and Shelly initially seem to have attempted to establish their own, independent creamware pottery in Dublin, but the desired Dublin Society aid was not forthcoming. Consequently, they joined forces with the potters at the World's End, presumably by offering their knowledge of creamware manufacture in return for a partnership in the consortium. Thereafter, all of the World's End pottery's Dublin Society applications were entered in the names of *'Edward Stacey, Edward Ackers and Thomas Shelly ... manufacturers from Staffordshire, but now of the City of Dublin, for flint ware, commonly called Queen's ware, manufactured by them in Ireland, and chiefly of Irish materials...'*.[11] Their first premium for creamware was paid from March 1772, which suggests that the World's End pottery was converted from a delftware to a creamware pottery in the period between December 1771 and March 1772.[12]

Although the wares produced in 1771 marked the end of delftware manufacture in Ireland, the World's End pottery managed to carry on for a few years more. The change to creamware must initially have seemed a wise and promising move, for in the first year of production, the value of the pottery's output increased four-fold, to £1334.4.3.[13] By June 1773, Delamain's old pottery had become known as the *'new Paris or Queen's Ware manufactory'*, but sadly, the success was to be short-lived. At about the same time, Josiah Wedgwood opened an extensive shop in Dublin which seems to have represented overwhelming competition for the new venture. By November 1773, Edward Stacey was selling some of his Dublin property, probably in an effort to support the pottery, and by 1774 Thomas Shelly had returned to England.[14]

This first attempt to manufacture creamware at the World's End pottery seems to have ceased after just two years, during the summer of 1774. One or two failed attempts to revive the works followed, but production seems to have finally ended in June 1784, when one Edward Chetham, (another Longport potter), sold off the World's End pottery with *'all that and these the several Earthen Goods'* that it contained.[15] Ironically perhaps, it was at this point that the Irish creamware industry returned to Belfast, where Irish delftware had first been made almost a century before.

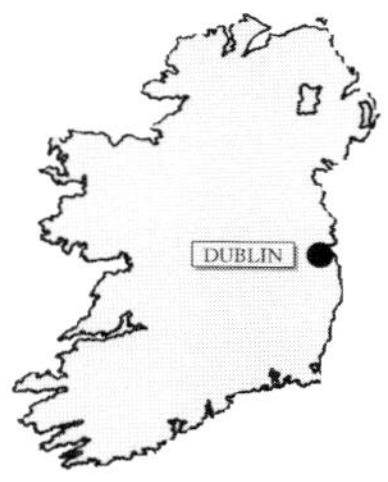

CHAPTER 2 • PART 2
DUBLIN DELFTWARE
i : Characteristics

INTRODUCTION

Delftware was made at the World's End pottery in Dublin for about thirty-six years, from c.1735 (or slightly earlier) until late 1771. The wares fall into two convenient date categories:

Pre-Delamain Wares	:	c.1735 - April 1752
Delamain and Post-Delamain Wares	:	April 1752 - late 1771

As we have seen, comparatively little is known of the *'pre-Delamain'* delftwares, made before Henry Delamain's arrival. To avoid confusion, objects dating from this early period have been described separately in the first part of Chapter 2, alongside the documented history of the pottery's early proprietors; John Chambers, John Crisp and David Davis. Almost all of the Irish delftware recognised today was produced after Henry Delamain began to improve and expand the pottery from April 1752 onwards. It is sometimes possible to differentiate delftwares made during the 1750s from those produced during the 1760s, but overall the dating is far from precise. These later, *'Delamain & post Delamain'* wares, (subsequently referred to simply as *'post-Delamain'* wares for convenience), have therefore been grouped together in the catalogue that follows.

The only previous exhibition of Irish delftware, which took place at Castletown House near Dublin in 1971, was undertaken with the express purpose of bringing together *'examples of all the known documentary pieces of Irish delftware, as well as accepted and disputed pieces,* [to provide an] *opportunity for comparisons to be made'*.[1] The well-illustrated catalogue produced for this exhibition, written by Michael Archer, has since served as the standard text on the subject.

The Castletown exhibition was intended primarily as a research exercise, and so it is remarkable to find that the great majority of these early attributions - more than 80% - have withstood the test of time. The exhibition catalogue thus remains a valuable guide for the identification of Irish delftware, illustrating a number of patterns that are not recorded here. With Michael Archer's kind assistance a list has been compiled of the Castletown attributions that are now considered questionable. (Appendix III, p.176). This will hopefully ensure that the catalogue remains a valuable reference work for many years to come.

There have been several major developments since the Castletown exhibition, the most important of which was the discovery of a range of polychrome Dublin delftwares. These too were first recognised by Archer towards the end of the 1970s, and although they remain rare, coloured wares represent some of the most attractive and intriguing Dublin delftwares of all. Another, more recent development has been the discovery of an entirely new range of comparatively primitive, *'coarsely painted'* wares. Research in this area has been greatly aided by John Austin's recent account of the delftware collections and excavations at Colonial Williamsburg.[2] These are still early days in the study of *coarsely-painted wares*, but a number of intact examples have already been found, and many more attributions are likely to follow.

The range of known Dublin delftwares has therefore grown since the Castletown exhibition, to the extent that it has become impossible to include an illustration of every recorded design. The following account therefore focuses on describing the main features of Dublin delftwares, with particular emphasis on differentiating them from English wares.

MARKS

More pieces of delftware can now be attributed to the World's End pottery in Dublin than to any other individual pottery in the British Isles. Alas, this is not because all Dublin delftwares are instantly recognisable. Some pieces, such as the landscape-

PAINTERS' NUMBERS AND MONOGRAMS RECORDED ON DUBLIN DELFTWARE

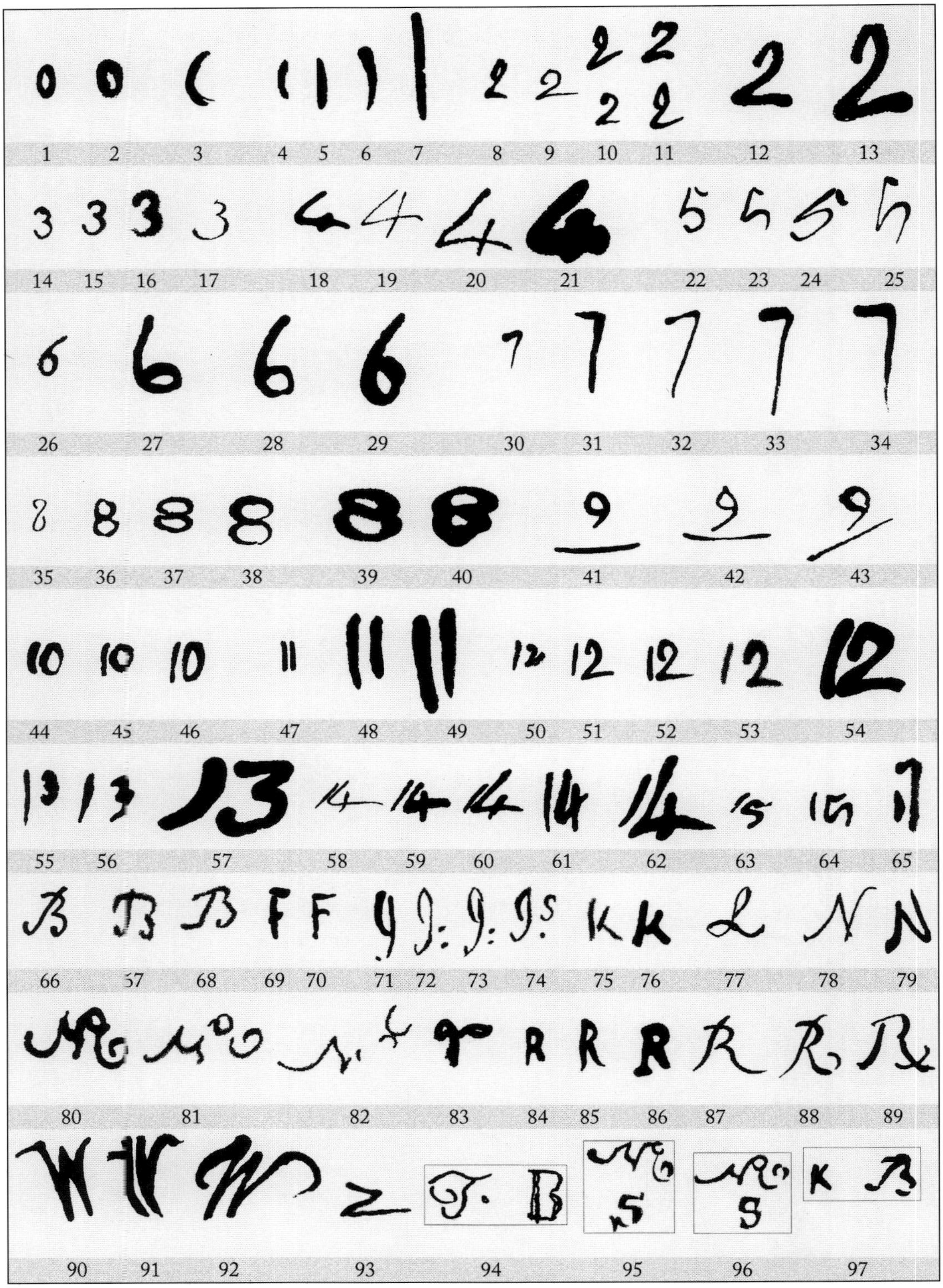

Figure 58. *See p. 196 for key. For further marks see Figs. 59 to 65.*

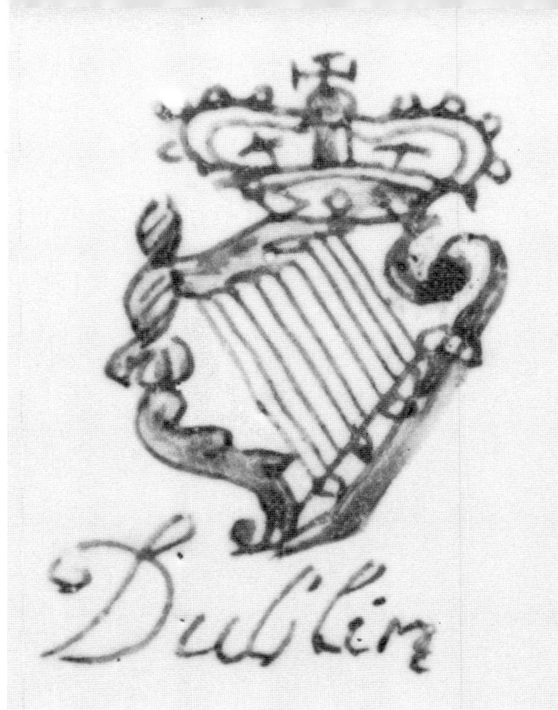

Figure 59. Harp and Dublin mark, on the reverse of the delftware basket illustrated in Colour Plate 19.

decorated wares, are indeed unique and conspicuous, but many standard blue and white Dublin delftwares are easily confused with their English counterparts, and with Liverpool wares especially.

Most Irish delftwares can be identified because of a small idiosyncrasy in Dublin's manufacturing practice, in that its painters often marked the reverse of the pieces they worked on with an identifying number, letter or monogram. **(Fig. 58)**. Letters and numbers sometimes occur on English delftwares too. Numbers are particularly common on Liverpool tiles, for example, but otherwise they are significantly rarer on English delftwares. In addition, Dublin seems to have been the only pottery to produce delftwares that were sometimes marked *under the rim*, (rather than within the footrim), whilst certain types of backmark, such as the painter's monograms, were virtually unique to Dublin. All of these distinctive characteristics aid in attribution.

On the basis of these backmarks, Dublin delftwares fall into five basic categories, each of which may be attributed to Dublin with varying degrees of certainty;

Documentary Wares	-	'*Dublin*' or Crowned Harp backmark
Monogrammed Wares	-	Painters' monogram backmark
Numbered Wares	-	Painters' number backmark
Other marks	-	Pseudo-oriental backmarks
Unmarked Wares	-	No distinguishing backmarks

The only backmarks that represent true factory marks are the crowned harp and '*Dublin*' marks **(Fig. 59)**. These are also among the rarest marks of all, being restricted to a small number of very fine-quality, presentation pieces. The most commonly encountered marks - the numbers and monograms - were purely intended for internal factory use, their presence indicating that the Dublin painters were sometimes paid on a piece-work basis. Documentary evidence suggests that similar schemes operated in English delftware (and porcelain) potteries, but the practice of *marking* individual pieces in this fashion seems to have been a more common feature of continental delftware potteries than most English ones.[3] The painted numbers on Dublin delftware do not relate in any way to patterns, sizes or forms, as they do on some later English porcelains, (such as New Hall for example). Instead, identical numbers can be found on a wide range of objects and designs.

The clearest indication that the various numbers and monograms relate to individual painters comes from the additional '*under-rim markings*' that occur on the reverse of some of the Dublin designs, such as the '*Chinese Flower-bowl*' pattern. **(Figs. 60a, 60b)**. The main pattern itself, on the front of the plate, was created by first '*pouncing*' the outline of the design in carbon or cobalt powder through a pierced stencil. The use of a stencil ensured that the pattern remained uniform throughout the entire dinner-service, regardless of who might have painted it, but unfortunately, this technique also served to disguise each individual painter's style. On the reverse side, however, the '*under-rim flourishes*' around the margin were painted swiftly in freehand, and we can readily see that each of the different painter's numbers corresponds to a different style of under-rim flourish - in other words, the numbers clearly relate to different individuals. (There has, as yet, been no systematic study of these *under-rim markings* on

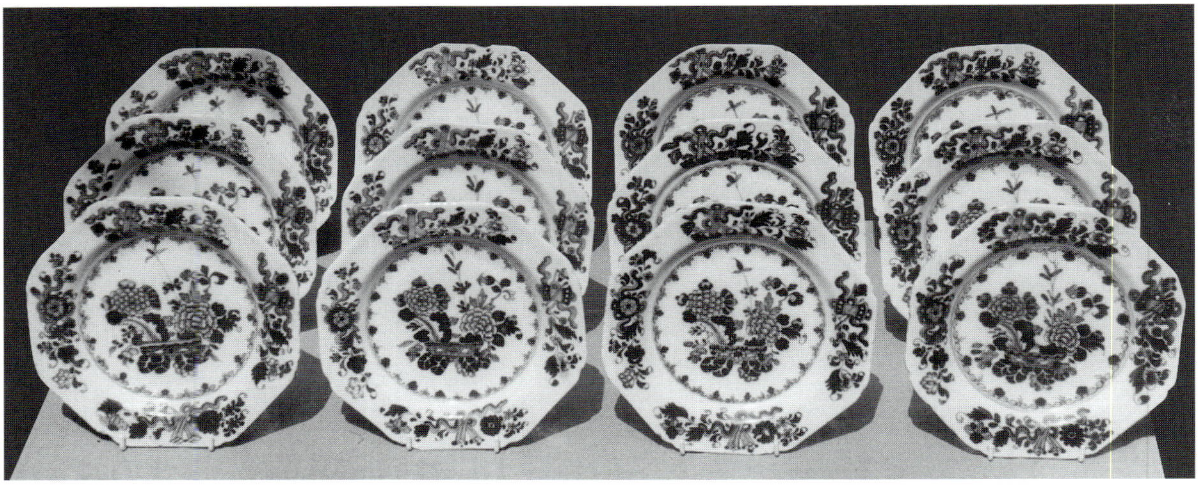

Irish delftware, of the kind undertaken by Frank Britton in his catalogue of the Bristol Museum collection - see p.39).

As the World's End pottery site has not been excavated, all attributions ultimately rest upon the very small number of pieces marked *'Dublin'*. The attributions are therefore hierarchical in nature; *'Documentary'* wares and the closely affiliated *'Monogrammed'* wares can be attributed to Dublin with a high degree of confidence, whereas *'Numbered'* and *'Unmarked'* wares - which can often be confused with English wares - are attributed more tentatively. The identification of Dublin delftware is not based on backmarks alone, but considering their importance in attribution, they are worth examining in more detail.

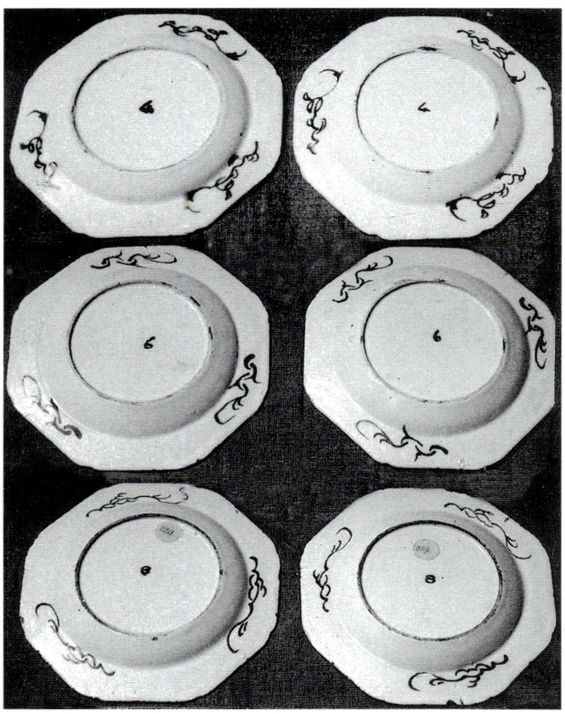

DOCUMENTARY WARES

There are essentially three different styles of documentary Dublin mark. The earliest occurs on the famous *'Primates Coals'* bowl, dated 1753 **(Fig. 56, Colour Plate 8)**, which was produced less than eighteen months after Henry Delamain took over the World's End works. The painted decoration usefully reveals many early Dublin characteristics, but the style of the inscription is unique, and so the mark itself is of limited value for attribution purposes. The painted floral panels on this bowl raise some interesting questions, however, **(Colour Plate 8, inset)**, in that the style of painting is unlike any other that is presently attributed to Dublin. It is possible, therefore, that the earliest flower-painted Dublin delftwares have not yet been fully recognised.

A second group of documentary Dublin delftwares are clearly marked with a crowned Hibernian harp, sometimes accompanied by the word *'Dublin'* painted in lowercase lettering. **(Fig. 59)**. All of the pieces thus marked, (mainly dinner plates and baskets), are very finely decorated with blue and white European

Top : Figure 60a. *A set of 12 Dublin delftware plates, painted with the 'Chinese Flower-bowl' pattern - one of the most common Dublin designs.*

Bottom : Figure 60b. *A selection of plates from the above group, marked with painters' numbers 4, 6 and 8. Note that each of the painters' numbers corresponds with a different style of 'under-rim flourish' around the margin.*

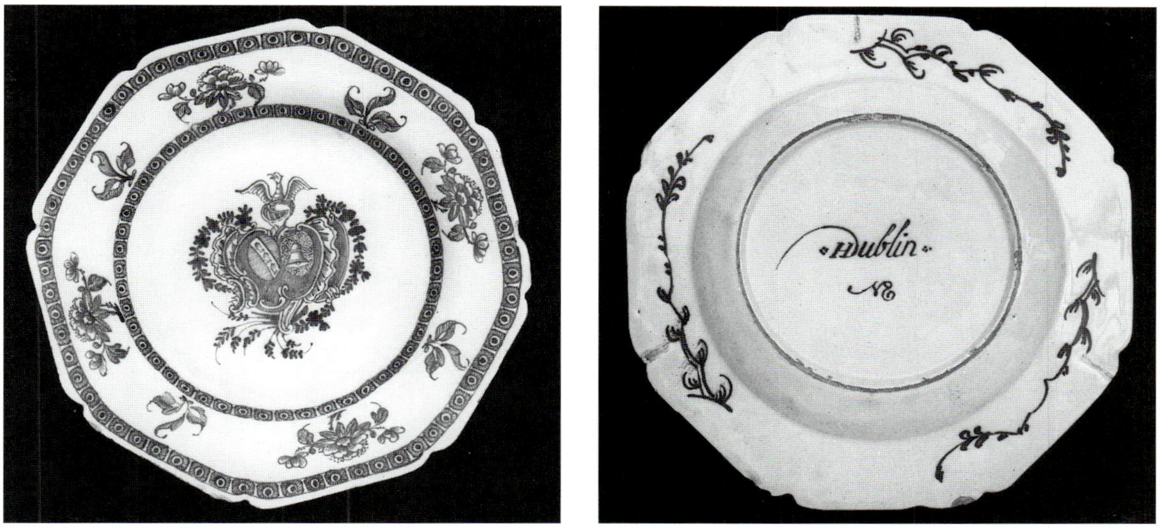

Figures 61. *Dish from a dinner-service made for the marriage of James Delamain and Marie Ranson in 1762. (See Colour Plates 9 - 11).*
Note the 'HD' monogram within the word 'Dublin', and the 'NE' monogram below. Width 230 mm., (side to side).

landscapes. Many are decorated with cobalt blue of the very finest quality. As a further mark of distinction, they were all given a final coating of clear, lead glaze, which imparted an unusually glossy, lustrous finish. (See Colour Plate 21).

There is a strong possibility that many, if not all of the pieces exhibiting this harp mark originally constituted part of a single service. **(See Fig.107)**. At least six examples - three plates and three circular baskets - marked with a harp and '*Dublin*' were in the possession of Mr. S. G. Stopford Sackville of Drayton House, Northamptonshire in 1913, and were recorded by Chaffers in 1874.[4] The overtly 'Irish' harp mark implies they were made for a special occasion or presentation - their owner in 1913 stated they had either been presented to the Duke of Dorset (Lord Lieutenant of Ireland in 1751-55) or to Lord George Sackville about 1753. Once again, however, even though these are textbook examples of Dublin delftware, harp marks are exceptionally rare. They are therefore of little assistance in recognising Dublin's more ordinary products.

For the purposes of attribution, by far the most useful documentary group is a single dinner service, made during William Delamain's time for his son's wedding in France in 1762 - the '*Delamain/Ranson*' service. **(Fig. 61, Colour Plates 9-11)**. The inscription on the reverse of these plates clearly contains the conjoined monogram '*HD*' (for Henry Delamain) within the word '*Dublin*'. This feature was long interpreted as an indication that the set was made during Henry Delamain's lifetime (Apr. 1752 - Jan. 1757), but it now appears that the wedding did not take place until almost six years after Henry's death, in November 1762.[5]

Regardless of their precise date however, these plates exhibit one exceptionally valuable feature - the painters monogram, '*NE*', which appears below the '*HDublin*' inscription. The identity of the '*NE*' painter is unknown, but fortunately this same monogram appears on many other pieces of delftware. Using this mark as our starting point, we discover that the very much larger group of '*Monogrammed*' delftwares can also be firmly attributed to Dublin.

MONOGRAMMED WARES

The '*NE*' painter's highly distinctive mark occurs on many kinds of objects, painted in a wide variety of styles. The individual concerned was obviously one of the more accomplished Dublin decorators, for although he or she was often constrained to produce standard designs, (such as the '*Broken Scroll*' pattern, **Fig. 62**, lower left), this monogram is also associated with a number of pieces that exhibit painting of exceptional quality. (For example, the armorials of the Delamain-Ranson service, the finely-detailed flower painting on the plates shown in **Fig. 160**, and the freehand landscape painting on the Armstrong jug, **Fig. 153**.).

When we look more closely at delftwares

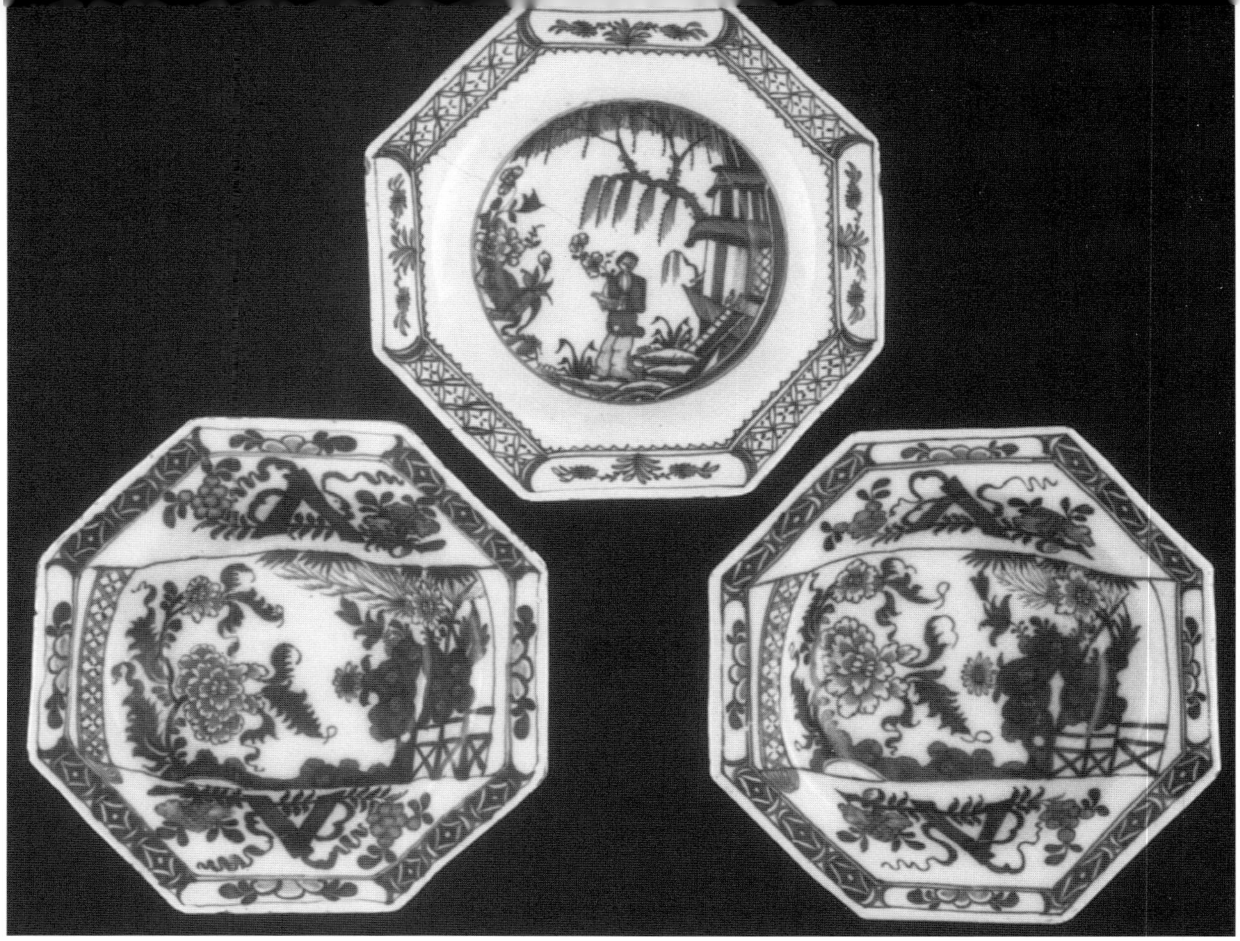

Figure 62. *Three Dublin delftware soup-dishes, two of 'Broken Scroll', one of 'Flower Lady' pattern. Under-rim monogram painters' marks. Widths c.9¹/₈ in., 230-233 mm., (side to side).*

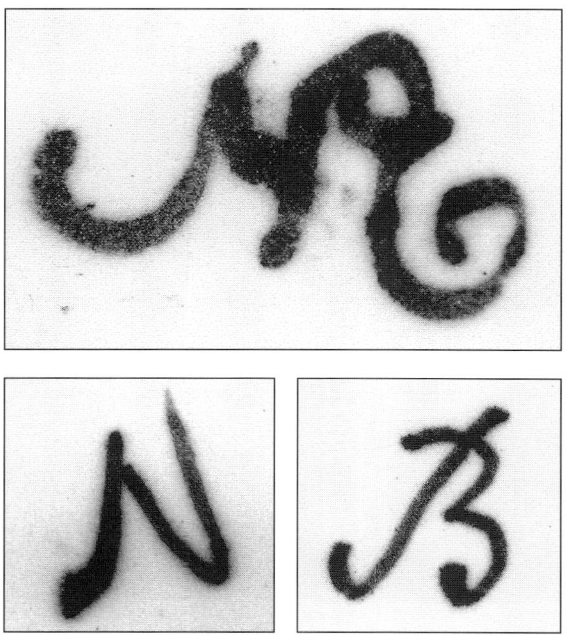

Top, 62a *: NE mark*
Bottom Left, 62b *: N mark* ***Bottom Right, 62c*** *: B or JB mark*

bearing the '*NE*' mark, however, it quickly becomes obvious that many other, similar monograms exist. (The '*NE*' monogram, in reality, turns out to be one of the rarer Dublin marks). For example, **Fig. 62** shows three octagonal soup dishes that have all been produced using the same mould or former, and must therefore have originated at the same pottery. (They all possess a distinctive, 4 cm. wide, shallow circular depression at the centre of the well). On the reverse, one is marked with the '*NE*' monogram under the rim, indicating that it was painted in Dublin by the decorator of the Delamain/Ranson service, whereas the other two possess quite different '*N*' and conjoined '*JB*' monograms, in exactly the same position. **(Figs. 62 a-c. See also Colour Plate 12)**. Clearly, therefore, '*NE*' was only one of several painters at work in Dublin, each of whom marked his or her work with a monogram.

Such monograms are extremely rare on delftwares made elsewhere in the British Isles, but it should be borne in mind that they do occasionally occur. George Haggarty in Edinburgh, for example, has recorded an uppercase '*G*' mark on several small bowl bases recovered from the site of the Delftfield pottery in Glasgow, and Garry Atkins in London has noted the monogram '*ED*' on a delftware basket that was probably made in London.[6] (This is similar to the basket illustrated in **Fig. 132**).

The range of recognised Dublin monograms expands rapidly when we examine surviving dinner services. Considerable efforts were made during the 1930s by Dudley Westropp of the National Museum of Ireland and Aubrey Toppin in England, (who worked in the National Museum during the early 1900s), to record monograms on services that came up for sale in Ireland and in London.[7] On the Revelstoke Service, (examples of which now are in the National Museum of Ireland), painted with the '*Broken Scroll*' pattern **(see Fig. 62, lower)**, Westropp recorded the following monograms;

Monogram	Occurrences
NE	1
B or JB	10
J or 9	13
K	9
L	1
R	10

Another '*Broken Scroll*' service, of 72 pieces, was sold in Waterford in 1936. This exhibited a total of 9 monograms, including the six listed above, together with '*N*', '*J:*' and '*J B*'. A further six pieces were entirely unmarked.[8] Gradually, Westropp and Toppin recorded a wide range of Dublin monograms, some with one letter, such as '*L*', '*N*' or '*Z*', others with two, such as '*NE*', 'J^S' and '*JB*'. Occasionally, two monograms seem to occur together on one object, for example '*K JB*' and '*NE S*' (or '*NE 5*'), presumably indicating that two decorators worked on the same piece. Some marks also seem to be exceptionally rare, and are only recorded on a limited range of objects; the monogram '*W*' for example, appears to be confined to one specific type of pierced and moulded dish. **(Fig. 123, left)**. The names of painters that are known to have worked in Dublin are discussed in more detail elsewhere (see p.97), but to date, it has not been possible to attribute any of these monograms to specific individuals.

On flatwares, monogram marks tend to occur in association with a rather restricted range of patterns. The two designs illustrated in **Figure 62** - the '*Broken Scroll*' and '*Flower-Lady*' patterns - are probably the two most common, although another design that often bears monogram marks, the '*Sampan Lake*' pattern, **(Fig. 90)**, also survives in some numbers. Most other examples of monogrammed wares tend to be unusual, 'one-off' designs, such as the moulded-edge plates in **Fig. 160**, landscape-painted plates, or the large apothecary jars **(Figs 144-5)**. In addition, monogrammed Dublin delftwares often exhibit a distinctive character, which can be quite different from the later *numbered* wares. **(See Colour Plate 12)**. These characteristics are discussed in greater detail presently, (p.80-1).

Because of the '*HDublin*' mark of the Delamain/Ranson service it was formerly presumed, as a rule of thumb, that monogrammed wares had been made during Henry Delamain's lifetime, (before Jan. 1757), and that numbered wares were produced subsequently. Now that the Delamain/Ranson marriage is known to have occurred in November 1762, this dating is offset by almost six years. Nonetheless, there can be little doubt that the monogrammed wares preceded numbered wares, as their designs are patently earlier. Furthermore, platters and tureen-stands with monograms tend to possess the early style of flat base, with no footrim, whereas most examples bearing painter's numbers are made in the later style, with a clearly defined or proud footrim. (The same range of footrims are evident in Chinese porcelains of this period). Although the precise date-ranges of the two styles of mark are difficult to establish, it is unlikely that monogram marks were used much beyond 1762, as their designs were becoming very old-fashioned by that time. The Bow porcelain works, for example, produced their versions of the '*Broken-Scroll*' pattern in c. 1749-52 and the '*Sampan Lake*' pattern in c. 1750-60.[9] Dated delftware plates painted with Dublin's '*Flower-Lady*' pattern **(Fig. 62, top)** are even recorded as early as 1744.[10]

There are several reasons for the imprecision in dating these two styles of mark. The main difficulty is that there are comparatively few dated examples of Dublin delftware, to help establish a clear chronology. (See p.78). Another cause of confusion is that there seems to have been a long period of overlap, when both numbers and monograms were employed. Often, it can be difficult to tell whether the mark represents a monogram or a number - a '*2*' or a '*7*' can look like an '*N*' or '*Z*', a '*B*' like '*13*', an '*S*' like a '*5*' and a lower case '*b*' like a '*6*'. There is ample evidence to show, however, that the position of the mark changed with time. On earlier, monogrammed flatwares, the mark is usually painted *under the rim,* and only occasionally within the footrim. On later, numbered wares, this situation is reversed - the number is usually painted *within the footrim* and only rarely appears under the rim.

Not all of the Dublin wares marked under the rim exhibit a painter's monogram, therefore - some instead exhibit a painter's number in the same position. As we have seen, recording the various monograms present has greatly increased our knowledge of Dublin wares, and so exploring these numbers, in turn, expands the range still further. An important point to stress, however, is that the presence of a mark *under the rim* - whether a monogram or a number - seems to be one of the most distinctive Dublin characteristics of all. No English delftware pottery is known to have routinely painted any kind of mark - decorator's mark, factory mark or otherwise - in this position.

NUMBERED WARES

Most delftwares presently attributed to Dublin fall into the category of '*numbered*' wares. (See, for example, **Fig. 60b**). A higher proportion of Dublin delftwares bear painters' numbers than English wares, but this by no means implies that English wares bearing numbers do not exist. Painters' numbers occur commonly on the reverse of Liverpool delftware wall tiles, for example. Unlike the very distinctive documentary and monogram marks, which on their own are often sufficient to establish a Dublin attribution, painters' numbers are therefore more ambiguous. Their presence (on objects other than tiles) is certainly an indication that a piece *may* be Irish, but on its own, a number seldom constitutes sufficient evidence to support a Dublin attribution. Deciding whether a piece of delftware is English or Irish usually rests on several criteria, only one of which is the presence - or absence - of a number.

Just one small group of numbered wares, in which the number appears (like Dublin monograms) *under the rim*, can reasonably be attributed to Dublin on the basis of the backmark alone. In practice, such marks are often confined to wares decorated with European landscape scenes, which would be readily recognisable as Dublin delftware regardless of the mark. Some of the painter's numbers that occur *under the rim* on this group are identical in character to those that occur *within the footrim* on the majority of Dublin numbered wares.

With closer study, many of the painter's numbers on Dublin delftware do seem to possess characteristics that are distinctive, and some can become more recognisable with practice. Most Irish numbers are small and neat compared to those that appear on English examples, but this is by no means a universal law. (The numbers illustrated in Fig. 60, for example, are exceptions to this rule). Nonetheless, some Dublin numbers can be reasonably constant in character, exhibiting the same, distinctive features wherever they occur. Painter number 14, for example, often painted the figure '*1*' at an odd angle, parallel to the upstroke of the '*4*'; Painter 3 generally signed his pieces with a very small and neat, well-formed '*3*', Painter 9 clearly underlined his mark (to distinguish it from 6) and Painter 11 usually drew two neat, closely spaced strokes of equal length, to produce a mark that looks more like a symbol of some kind than the number 11. The fact that such individual idiosyncrasies exist means that, in a few cases, the style of the painter's number alone can significantly increase confidence in an attribution.

The range of previously unrecorded punch-bowl designs excavated in Virginia, **(Figs. 72-80)**, provide a good example of how painters' numbers can be used to establish new attributions. If only one or two painters numbers had been recorded, then the attribution would probably have been unsustainable, but as eight different numbers were found, and each corresponded in style with numbers recorded on known examples of Dublin delftware, confidence in the attribution was correspondingly increased. **(Fig. 71)**.

The highest painter's number yet observed on Dublin delftwares is 17, and the only number missing from the sequence to date is number 16. There seems to be no obvious reason why 16 should not exist, but examples are certainly rare. The rarest number otherwise is 0, which has so far been recorded on only two pieces. **(Figs. 124** and **151)**.

The Dublin delftwares that bear a painter's number are likely to represent only a portion of the pottery's total range. For a variety of reasons, many other wares that were produced at the same time seem to have been unmarked. Viewed as a whole, numbered Dublin wares are restricted in their variety, with patterns copying Chinese porcelain predominating to an unusual degree. Some types of delftware are also suspiciously absent. For example, only two pieces of Dublin delftware decorated with a powder-blue or manganese ground have been recorded.[11] Many more powder-ground wares might well exist, but without painter's numbers on the reverse to draw attention to them, they have not yet been recognised.

Although painters' marks are comparatively rare on delftwares other than tiles, a number of English porcelain factories, such as Bow and Worcester, employed similar systems of numbers and symbols during the 1750s and early 60s.[12] The marks that come closest to the Dublin numbers, however, seem to be those that appear on porcelains produced by William Reid & Co., at Brownlow Hill in Liverpool, between 1756 and 61.[13] Unlike Bow and Worcester, where painter's *symbols* were the most common form of individual mark, almost all of the marks employed by William Reid's painters were simply numbers, from 1 through to 8, just as we find at Dublin (but from 0 - 17). Reid's numbers were sometimes very similar in character and appearance to those used in Dublin, and it is even possible that the number system could have been introduced to Ireland by potters arriving from Liverpool in the early 1760s.[14] At the very least, the presence of these marks on Liverpool porcelain does sound a strong cautionary note, in that it suggests that very similar painters' numbers almost certainly occur on Liverpool delftwares also.

UNMARKED WARES

As we have already seen, not all Dublin delftware was marked. Numbered and monogrammed dinner-services usually contain a few unmarked pieces, and even the finest quality landscape-painted plates often possess no mark. Unmarked Dublin delftware is therefore fairly common, but nonetheless, establishing a clear-cut Irish attribution without marks is extremely difficult. There are very many more unmarked English and Scottish delftwares than Irish.

The only sizeable unmarked assemblage that has been identified to date is the range of polychrome Dublin delftwares, first recognised by Michael Archer during the 1970s, and growing steadily into one of the most attractive and varied Dublin groups of all. The initial attribution came about from a large oval platter in the Morgan collection, the form of which - with its distinctive wavy edge - is identical to known Dublin landscape-painted platters. (Compare for example **Colour Plates 25** and **28**). On closer inspection, some features of the painting style are similar to known Dublin pieces, but the attribution would have remained highly speculative without the precise match of forms to provide confirmation. (In reality, the backs of these platters look much more alike than the fronts).

Since the first coloured platter was found, a dozen or more new examples have come to light, firming up the attribution still further. These include the Verner bowl, **(Colour Plate 31)**, purchased in Co. Armagh in 1921, and a range of wavy-edged plate fragments excavated at Dublin Castle, **(Colour Plate 29)**. The same style of painting occurs on several shell-shaped epergnes, **(Colour Plate 35)**, which correspond closely with blue and white examples that sometimes bear a typical Dublin painter's number or monogram, **(Colour Plate 36)**. More recently, a circular coloured platter was discovered in Dublin by Mairead Dunlevy of the National Museum **(Colour Plate 30)**. This bears a typical Dublin painter's number '*6*' in manganese, *under the rim*, which neatly confirms the attribution of the group as a whole. The colour and painting style of this coloured group is now so recognisable that it is even possible to attribute previously unrecorded forms to Dublin, such as the bough pots or candlesticks, **(Colour Plates 33** and **34)**, without relying on either the form itself or a painter's mark to provide confirmation.

Unfortunately, this method of attribution is not so conclusive when the style of decoration is less distinctive. For example, the Dublin polychrome wares found to date are mainly decorated with sparse flower sprigs, painted in a soft palette that imitates French or continental originals. It seems unusual to find that a more standard form of '*Fazackerly-type*' polychrome decoration is not recorded, copying English rather than French exemplars. Such wares might well exist, (possibly in larger numbers than French-style coloured Dublin wares), but if they do then presumably they are unmarked.

The bowls excavated in Virginia **(Figs. 81 - 86)** also provide us with a clear example of the uncertainty that can accompany the attribution of unmarked Dublin wares. As we have seen, there can be little doubt that the bowls bearing painter's numbers were made in Dublin. **(Figs. 71 - 80)**. On present evidence, however, it is impossible to express the same degree of confidence in the unmarked bowls that were excavated from the very same trench. **(Figs. 81 - 86)**. We can suggest that they *may* be attributable to Dublin, in view of this close association, but we cannot, as yet, demonstrate the fact. Perhaps, as the assemblage grows, other characteristics will become evident, that will help to tie the group to Dublin more firmly

In summary, unmarked Dublin delftwares certainly exist, probably in considerable numbers. Recognising that a piece of unmarked delftware was made in Dublin however, demands that some alternative means of attribution must be present - either a distinctive form or a unique painting style.

OTHER MARKS

Other backmarks certainly occur on Dublin delftware, but in practical terms they are unlikely to help in establishing new attributions. Two basic types of 'non-standard' mark are recorded.

Mock-Chinese Character marks

These distinctive marks seem to have been unique to the Dublin pottery but they are

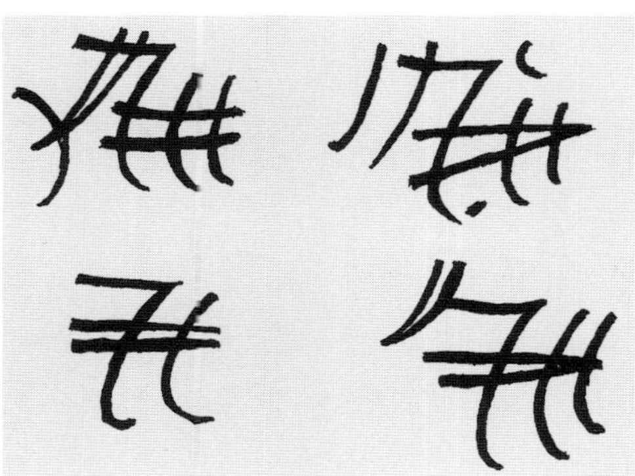

exceptionally rare. They have only been recorded on the very finest quality landscapes plates, which would obviously be attributable to Dublin even if they were unmarked. The majority, if not all, appear to be associated with the fine-quality set of documentary plates described earlier, (p. 71), some of which are also marked with Crowned Harps and '*Dublin*'.

The closest comparators to these mock-Chinese characters seem to be some rare marks that occur on blue and white Bow porcelains of the early 1750s, although the Dublin marks are very much larger in size.[15]

'Chinese Sprig' marks

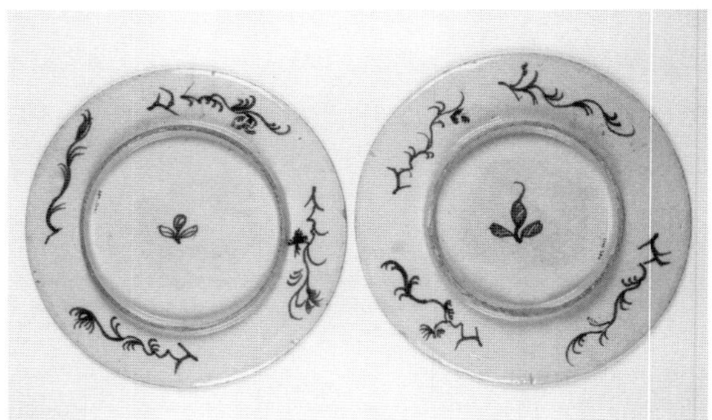

These leaf-like marks obviously derive from good fortune symbols that occur on many K'ang Hsi period Chinese porcelains. Two good examples occur on the reverse of a pair of landscape-painted table stands in the National Museum, **(Fig. 64)** and so there can be little argument that such marks do occur on Dublin delftware. Another example was recorded in the Castletown exhibition, (No. 74), the mark of which is illustrated below **(Fig. 65, left)**.

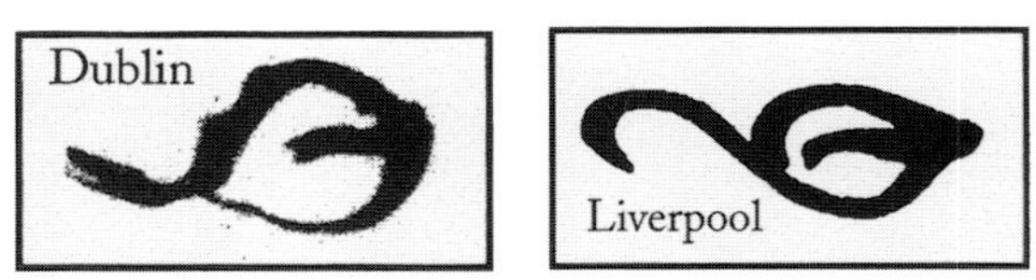

Speaking purely from personal experience, however, such sprig marks are rare on unequivocal examples of Dublin delftware. It is especially confusing that the sprig marks on English and Irish

Above Left : Figure 63. *Pseudo-Chinese marks on fine quality, blue-painted Dublin landscape plates, recorded by M.S.D. Westropp during the 1930s. A mark of this type is present on the plate illustrated in Colour Plate 21.*
Top Right : Figure 64. *Floral sprig marks on Dublin delftware, landscape-painted table stands, (see Colour Plate 22).*
Bottom Right : Figure 65. *Floral sprig marks recorded on an octagonal Dublin delftware platter (Castletown No. 74), and an octagonal Liverpool platter, (author's collection).*

delftware can sometimes be virtually identical. **(Fig. 65)**.[16] To add to the confusion, sprig marks also seem to occur most commonly on English wares that are generally similar in appearance to Dublin delftwares - on octagonal dishes for example, or services decorated with the *'Chinese Flower-bowl'* pattern. The English and Irish potters were obviously copying the same Chinese originals, including the floral sprig marks on the reverse.

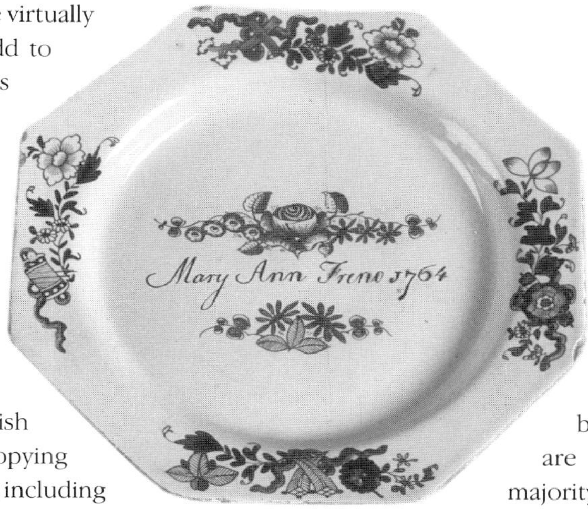

Most Irish wares on which these sprigs occur also possess two or three *'under-rim flourishes'* around the margin, which can help to some extent. (See, for example **Fig. 131**). On balance, however, the presence of a sprig mark is confusing, and if possible, it is best disregarded when deciding whether a piece of delftware was made in Dublin or Liverpool. There are other, more reliable indications than these marks to support an attribution. If these other indications are not obvious, then perhaps the piece is best left unattributed.

PERSONAL INSCRIPTIONS

Amongst English delftwares, personal inscriptions frequently provide a firm basis for attributions to specific potteries.[17] The same is not true for Dublin delftwares, principally because personal inscriptions are extremely rare. The great majority of Dublin delftwares that can be associated with specific families or individuals bear armorials or crests (see p.100), and even these are not common.

Only two personal names are recorded on Dublin delftware. The first, *'M:Walling'*, appears on the reverse of an octagonal soup dish, probably dating from the 1760s, which is painted with the *'Two Deer and Pagoda'* pattern, (p.92), and bears the painters' number *'2'* within the footrim. **(Fig. 66)**. Presumably, this plate once formed part of a dinner service, but no other inscribed examples are recorded. The surname is highly unusual, especially

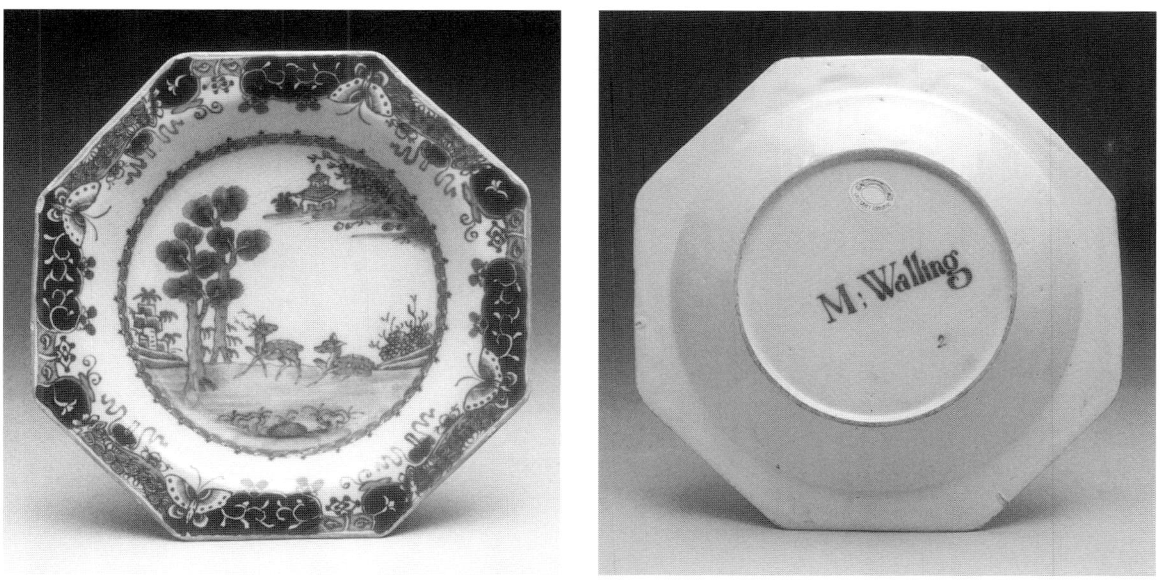

Top : ***Figure*** *67. Delftware plate, probably Dublin, decorated in cobalt blue, inscribed 'Mary Ann Freno 1764' in overglaze black, three under-rim markings' on reverse, no painter's mark. Width 9 in., 227 mm., (side to side).*
Below : Figures ***66a, & b.*** *Front and Reverse views of a Dublin delftware soup dish, c. 1760, 'Two Deer and Pagoda' pattern, painter's number 2, Width 8 3/8 in., 213 mm.*

in an Irish context, but a scan of mid-eighteenth century Dublin trade directories has found no occurrences of the name.

The second inscription, *'Mary Ann Freno 1764'*, appears on a pair of small, octagonal plates, one of which is illustrated. **(Fig. 67)** The border pattern, which also occurs on many *'Chinese Flower bowl'* pattern plates **(Colour Plate 13)**, is painted in typical cobalt blue, but it is extremely unusual to find the name painted in overglaze *black* (manganese?). This plate bears three *'under-rim flourishes'* but no painters' mark on the reverse, and because of its unusual character it is difficult to be certain that it is Irish. On balance, however, characteristics such as *'sunken blue'*, the uneven glaze on the reverse, and details of the central flower-painting suggest that it was probably made in Dublin. The surname *'Freno'* is an extremely unusual one, which appears to be a slightly Anglicised version of the Huguenot surnames *'Frenot'*, *'Fresnau'* or *'Freigneaux'*. Mary Ann Freno may have been descended from an Andrew *Freigneaux*, who was made a freeman Glover in Dublin in Christmas 1710.[18] A branch of the family, which used the *Freno'* spelling by 1720, are also recorded in Plymouth.[19]

Clearly, to judge from these two examples, the personal inscriptions on Irish delftware are of little assistance in attribution.[20] Perhaps the most poignant observation in this context is the complete absence of names that are patently Irish, (O'Brien or Murphy, for example, are two that spring readily to mind), which tends to suggest that Dublin delftware was beyond the means of many Irish people in the eighteenth-century. This is borne out by the documentary evidence. In 1853, for example, it was recorded that *'long after the invention of English earthen ware... the poorest of the* [Irish] *peasantry were still obliged to drink from coarsely formed wooden cups, and their plates, when they possessed any at all, were wooden trenchers...'*.[21]

DATE

Henry Delamain purchased the World's End pottery in April or May 1752, and delftware production continued there until the end of 1771 or so. Present evidence suggests that painter's marks were only employed at the pottery following Delamain's arrival, so that the maximum date range of marked pieces is believed to be c. April 1752 - c. Dec. 1771; a spread of almost twenty years. It should be stressed, however, that there is no clear evidence to indicate the year in which painters' marks were introduced. They may have been employed a few years before Henry's arrival in 1752, or they may only have become necessary after his death in 1757, when the workforce seems to have been reduced in size.[22]

The Delamain/Ranson service indicates that the earliest style of monograms marks were still in use as late as November 1762, (when the marriage took place), but they probably did not continue much beyond this date (see p.71 & 73). Dublin delftwares are therefore divided into two approximate date categories, on the basis of their marks alone;

c.1752 - early 1760s:	Monogram and under-rim marks
early 1760s - c.1772:	Numbered marks, within foot-rim

These date ranges are intended purely as a rough guide, as in practice it is often difficult to tell whether a piece was made during the 1750s or the 1760s. European landscapes, for example, were obviously one of Dublin's more popular and enduring

Dated Examples of Dublin Delftware

***'Primate's Coal's'* Bowl**	Manganese Ground, blue landscapes	1753	(Fig. 56, Col. Pl. 8)
***'Verner'* Bowl**	Polychrome Flowers	1756	(Col. Pl. 31)
Delamain/Ranson Service	Blue & white, octagonal, NE mark	1762	(Fig. 61, Col. Pl. 11)
Landscape plate	Manganese painted, wavy-edge	176_	(Fig. 68)
***'Mary Ann Freno'* Plate**	Blue-painted, black overglaze inscription	1764	(Fig. 67)

designs. They occur on the *'Primate's Coals'* bowl, dated 1753, and thus were in production within eighteen months of Delamain's arrival, yet they were still offered for sale by Edward Stacey as late as July 1770, less than two years before delftware manufacture ceased.

Dated examples of Dublin delftware can occasionally provide additional assistance in attempting to narrow down the date of manufacture of a piece, but only five dated pieces/groups are recorded. (See table opposite). Descriptions of each of these individual pieces appear elsewhere in the text.

The most unusual style of date is that which appears on the previously unrecorded landscape plate **(Fig. 68)**, where it is written in very tiny script on the plinth of the obelisk, (detail, below). The date is so small that it might easily be overlooked, and so it is possible that other, similar examples exist.

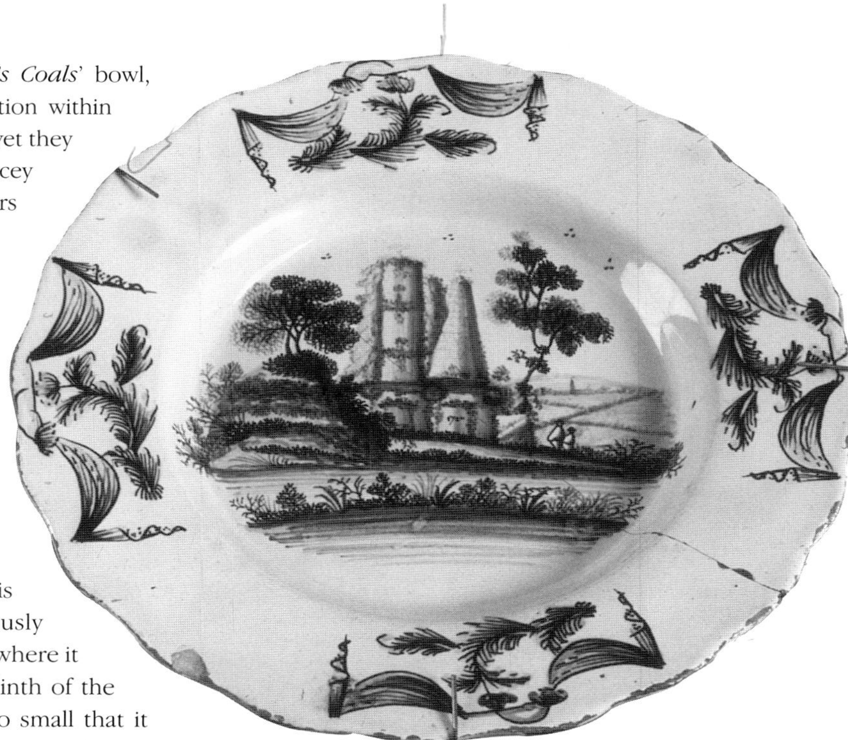

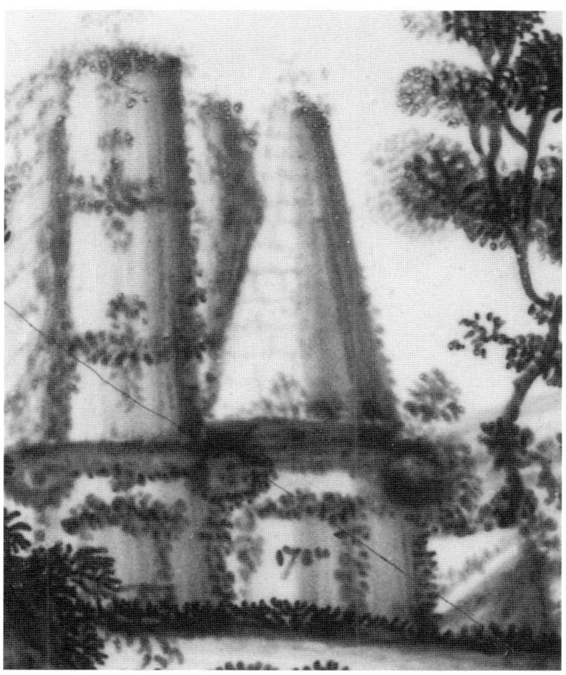

Figures 68a & b. Dublin delftware manganese-painted landscape, showing an indistinct, incomplete date on the plinth, '176_'. (This plate may originally have formed part of a nine-piece service recorded in 1976, some of which bore under-rim painters' numbers - See Austin, Cat. 290, p.168). No mark. Diam 10¼ in., 260 mm.

OTHER CHARACTERISTICS

Although marks are not the only features that distinguish Dublin delftware, they are certainly the most widely recognisable. Other characteristics are more subjective and open to a greater range of interpretations by different individuals. There are very few universal constants - most of the features described below are similar to painters' marks in one respect only, in that they are evident on some pieces, but entirely absent on others.

As we have seen, English and Irish potters employed identical materials and techniques to produce their wares, and delftwares produced in Liverpool can sometimes be exceptionally similar to Dublin products. Both Dublin and Liverpool used Carrickfergus clays, and both probably obtained many of their essential ingredients - such as cobalt - from the same suppliers. There also appears to have been a comparatively free flow of workmen between England and Ireland. Some probably came from London, but the majority of potters that have been identified in Dublin can be traced to Liverpool. William Stringfellow, Delamain's manager in 1753, was a Liverpool delftware potter originally.[23] So too was Edward Ackers, who arrived in 1771.[24] Edward Stacey, the owner of the Dublin pottery from c. 1765, was married to a '*Widow Roscoe*', who was probably related to John & James Roscoe, delftware potters on Shaw's Brow in Liverpool.[25] It should therefore not come as a surprise to find that Dublin and Liverpool wares often look confusingly similar, but it does mean, as Michael Archer has remarked, that '*There is an Irish-Liverpool category that will probably never be completely disentangled*'.[26]

Nonetheless, a number of characteristics are more typical of Dublin than other centres of manufacture. Usually, no single characteristic is sufficient to establish an attribution, but the presence of several in combination can be more convincing. Describing the physical appearance of a piece of Irish delftware is somewhat akin to describing the taste of an orange, in that reams of lengthy description convey little compared to practical experience. Anyone hoping to recognise Dublin delftware must, at some stage, handle some pieces, and preferably keep a few Irish and English examples for reference. Nonetheless, the plates illustrated in **Colour Plates 12-14** will hopefully give some impression of many of the features described here.[27] These include front and back views of;

- An early, '*NE*' monogrammed soup dish, painted with the '*Broken Scroll*' pattern **(Col. Pl. 12)**
- A numbered Dublin plate, and a Liverpool plate, both painted with the '*Chinese Flower-bowl*' pattern. These are shown side by side for comparison. **(Col. Pl. 13, 13a)**. also made by Lancaster & more evidence for that than other two.
- Two numbered Dublin plates, painted with the '*Radial Flower*' pattern, demonstrating the variation in appearance that occurs within Dublin delftwares. **(Col. Pl. 14)**. One of Lancaster's most popular designs — literally 100s of shards

The characteristics now described relate primarily to flatwares, such as plates, platters and soup dishes, as these are the most commonly encountered objects.

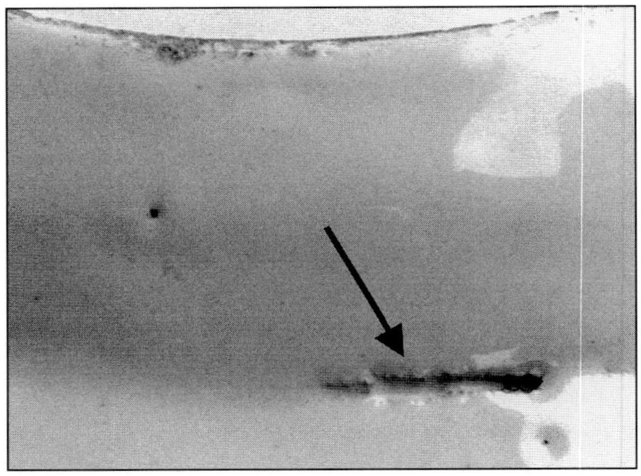

***Figure 69**. Detail of body 'split' or scar, on reverse of Colour Plate 14, left. 19 mm. in length.*

Body

As Dublin, Liverpool and Bristol all employed Carrickfergus clay, the Dublin delftware body is indistinguishable from that of English wares. Often, however, the body of Dublin delftware exhibits deep scars or 'splits', on the reverse of plates especially. **(Fig. 69)**. These appear to have been caused by a small piece of grit or hard clay, dragged over the surface when the plate was being thrown on the former. They are sometimes quite large features, perhaps two or three inches in length, but they are more usually about an inch long. Such 'splits' are a comparatively common and distinctive feature of Dublin delftware, but they can also be found on English wares occasionally.

Glaze

As with most delftwares, the front and back of a Dublin plate are entirely different in character. They are therefore described separately below.

The two sides share just a few features in common, the most obvious of which is colour. Little significance can be attached to glaze colour, as the cobalt and other pigments were probably imported from England. The only exceptions to this rule are some of the early, monogrammed wares, such as the '*Broken Scroll*' pattern, **(Colour Plate 12)**, which often exhibit a distinctive, very white ground colour. The glaze seems to have been produced using white, tin oxide in a neat, unadulterated form, without any hint of cobalt to soften its harshness. On the reverse, these plates and dishes are frequently disfigured by light dustings of stray cobalt powder, perhaps caused by finger marks. **(Colour Plate 12, left)**. The same, pure white ground colour is also evident on the John Chambers plates, inscribed *'DUBLIN 1735'*. **(Colour Plate 7)**.

A more occasional characteristic of Dublin delftwares is that the glaze sometimes contains many small, light coloured spots, which creates the impression that the glaze ingredients have been inadequately ground. Once again, this feature is most obvious on the very white, monogrammed wares.

Front: The painted designs on the front of most Dublin plates were produced by *'pouncing'* the design in carbon or cobalt powder through a perforated stencil, so that features of the painting are not usually individual or distinctive. The only wares that appear to have been painted freehand are the European landscapes, polychrome floral sprays and some of the *'coarsely-painted'* bowls excavated in Virginia. Recognising a distinctive, *freehand* painted detail can often help to establish or confirm an attribution.

Perhaps the most distinctive Dublin glaze characteristic of all is the phenomenon known as *'sunken blue'*, a term that describes the slight depressions that occur in the glaze surface in areas where cobalt blue has been applied.[28] (The feature is best seen by holding the plate close to a raking light). Usually, the more intense the blue colour, the deeper the depression. Occasionally a pale grey 'halo' is also present, around the individual blue brushstrokes.

The *'sunken blue'* effect was probably caused by the fact that the cobalt pigment contained more *'frit'* than the white-coloured ground, and hence had lower viscosity during firing. In some cases, where the blue has been applied thickly, the colour not only sinks into the white glaze but spreads slightly, and has a tendency to form large, rounded dots of intense blue colour. A clear example of this is evident on the borders of the *'Radial Flower'* pattern plate, **(Colour Plate 14, left)**. It is also obvious in the windows of the *'Three-window House'* pattern, **(Fig. 15)**.

As Dudley Westropp and others have remarked, *'sunken blue'* is one of the most widely recognised characteristics of Irish delftware, and it certainly occurs on the majority of blue-painted Dublin wares.[28] Unfortunately, *'sunken blue'* is a common feature of Liverpool delftware also, although it is rarely developed to the same extent. Generally speaking, if the effect is very obvious, as on the example illustrated in **Colour Plate 14**, then this can be a sign that the piece *might* be Irish. Like so many individual features, however, the presence of *'sunken blue'* is by no means sufficient to sustain an attribution on its own.

To complicate matters further, not all Dublin delftwares exhibit the phenomenon - the *'Radial Flower'* pattern plate shown in **Colour Plate 14 right**, displays no trace whatever of *'sunken blue'*. These two plates in **Colour Plate 14** do allow for interesting comparison, however, in that they clearly demonstrate the extent to which the presence or absence of this one feature, *'sunken blue'*, can dramatically alter the overall appearance.

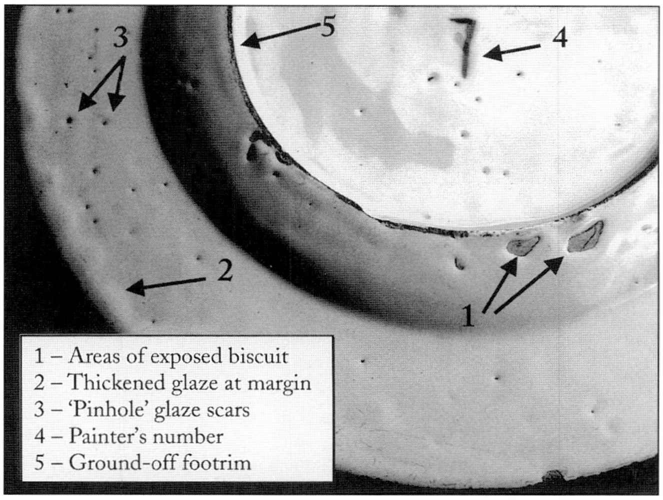

***Figure** 70. The reverse of a Dublin delftware plate, (Fig. 91a right) showing typical glaze characteristics. (see Glaze; Back)*

Back: Most Dublin delftwares seem to have been dipped twice in glaze. The first 'glaze' was an extremely thin, cream-coloured slip, applied directly onto the biscuit, presumably to lighten the biscuit-ware body and provide a uniform base-colour. This *'under-slip'* is usually only evident in areas where the overlying tin-glaze is thin, such as around the footrim. It seems to be present on almost all Dublin delftwares, but a similar *'under-slip'* does occur widely amongst English wares.

The second glaze to be applied was the true

Dublin Flatwares – checklist of features

	Certain	Probably	Possibly
Front			
Recognised 'distinctive' Dublin pattern (e.g. landscape)	*	*	
Recognised 'standard' Dublin pattern (e.g. 'Chinese Flower-bowl') ?Lancaster			*
Distinctive 'bleached white' ground colour (usually monogrammed) ? Dutch as well			*
Identical to distinctive Dublin forms (e.g. scallop-edged platters)		*	
'Sunken' Blue – everybody			*
Back			
Mark:			
Documentary or 'other' mark (Harp &c.)	*		
Monogram Under-rim	*		
Number Under-rim – everybody	*		
Number Recognised style, within foot-rim – everybody		*	
Number No. 1-17, but not identical to known examples – which are not proven to be Dublin			*
Floral Sprig (More usually English)			*
No Mark			*
Glaze/Body: (applies to all factories.)			
Uneven glaze			*
Glaze 'pools' or 'drips' towards edge			*
Bare areas of biscuit/white under-slip			*
'Splits' or tears in body			*
Ground-off footrim – generally worn off by usage			*

'*tin-glaze*', primarily a lead-glaze coloured white with tin-oxide. This glaze tends to be more uneven on the reverse of Dublin delftwares than on comparable English wares, which might reflect different manufacturing or firing practices. The unevenness of the highly mobile glaze results in a number of features that, in combination, can help to distinguish Dublin wares. Some of these features are illustrated in **Fig 70**.

As the glaze moved around on the underside of the plate during firing, (blown upwards and outwards by the kiln draft), some areas lost their glaze entirely, leaving areas of the biscuit-ware body or under-slip exposed. **(Fig. 70-1)**. This glaze loss chiefly occurs near the footrim or on the plate margins. There was a corresponding thickening in other areas, around the margins especially, and so there often appear to be thicker drips or pools of glaze under the rim. **(Fig. 70-2)**.

In some cases, the glaze on the reverse is peppered with small, pinhole glaze scars, possibly induced by escaping steam from the damp biscuit-ware body. Usually just a few are present, but as in the case illustrated, **(Fig. 70-3)**, pinhole scars sometimes occur in profusion. These are misleading, however, in that they are often interpreted as a distinctive, 'Dublin', characteristic. In fact they occur sporadically on all types of tin-glazed earthenware, regardless of its origin.

Footrim

The footrim of Dublin flatwares varies considerably; most have a recessed footrim, others a deep, applied or proud footrim, and some have none at all. When footrims are present, they almost invariably show signs of manual polishing, perhaps on a grinding wheel or flat surface, to ensure that the plate sat flat on the table. **(Fig. 70-5)**. As the glaze on the back of Dublin plates was obviously prone to run onto and over the footrims, then presumably it was prudent to ensure that grinding-off was a standard procedure.

In summary, Dublin delftware exhibits a wide range of features that are reasonably distinctive - the '*sunken blue*' glaze, or the highly uneven glaze characteristics on the reverse for example. No single feature was unique to Dublin, however. Precisely the same features can be observed on English wares, and on Liverpool wares especially. But viewed together with other characteristics, such as the presence of a painters' number, or a distinctive form, Dublin delftware is often more easily recognised than this rather cautious overview might suggest. The Dublin and Liverpool plates shown side by side in **Colour Plate 13 & 13a**, despite their obvious similarities, are visibly different, even though describing the precise nature of these subtle differences can be long-winded and difficult. In some cases, a checklist of the features that are present on a particular piece can help to quantify its 'possible' or 'probable' Dublin characteristics. (See table above). As was stated at the outset, however, the only way to become familiar with Dublin delftware is to handle some pieces. As in all things, there is no substitute for practical experience.

CHAPTER 2 • PART 2
DUBLIN DELFTWARE
ii : Decorative Styles

Dublin delftware falls into six, broad categories, each reflecting a different design source.

* *'Coarsely-painted'* wares
* Designs copying Chinese Porcelain
* European Landscapes
* Coloured Wares
* Armorials
* Other Sources (primarily English porcelain)

COARSELY-PAINTED WARES

This group of wares was only recognised for the first time within the last year. The Dublin attribution is based entirely upon archeological evidence discovered three thousand miles from Ireland, on the East Coast of North America.

The cornerstone of the attributions is an assemblage of thirty-five delftware punch-bowls, excavated from an eighteenth-century tavern site close to the courthouse in Chesterfield County, Virginia.[1] Only two other delftware shards were recorded, suggesting that the bowls may all have been broken as a result of a single, catastrophic event. Of the thirty-five bowls, at least seventeen - an unusually high proportion - bear a painter's number within the footrim. The numbers recorded were as follows;

Painter's Number	Recorded Examples
2	8
3	1
5	1
9	2
10	1
13	2
14	1
17	1

None of the excavated designs had previously been recorded on Dublin delftware. If only one or two painter's numbers had been present, then although we might have suspected that some of these bowls *might* have been Irish, it would have been impossible to prove the case one way or the other. As eight different numbers were recorded, however, and in every case the character of the number corresponded with examples on known Dublin delftware, confidence in the attribution was significantly increased. A selection of the painters' numbers found are illustrated in **Fig. 71**.

The highest number recorded on the excavated bowls, '*17*', also corresponds with the highest number previously recorded on Dublin delftware.[2] Once these numbers drew attention to the fact that the bowls might be Irish, similarities in the style of painting were also noted, even though the patterns themselves were unknown. The glaze characteristics of these bowls also conform with known Dublin wares, exhibiting a number of typical features. Had the numbers not been present, however, (and published), then it is doubtful that the assemblage would ever have been recognised as potentially Irish in the first place.

A wide range of patterns were recorded, all of them painted in a coarser, more rudimentary fashion than delftwares previously attributed to Dublin.

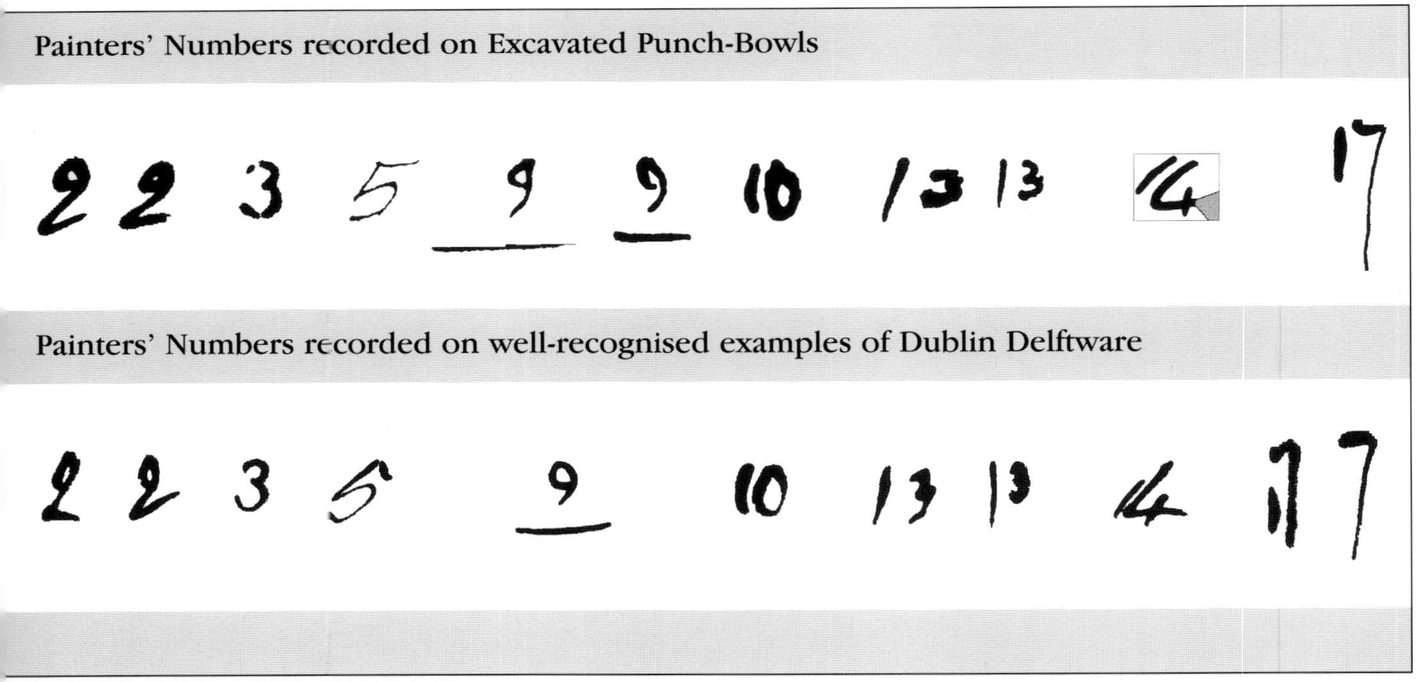

Figure 71.

'*Three-window House*' pattern (Figs. 72 - 74, Colour Plate 15).

Although only two are illustrated, fragments of at least eight bowls painted with this design were recovered **(Fig. 72)**. Six of these, with the painter's number '*2*' on the base, bore the inscription '*One Bowl More Will*' on the interior, **(Fig. 73)**, all painted by the same hand. (An identical bowl, with painter's number '*2*', has also been found on a separate excavation in New York State. Further examples are known from other parts of Virginia, closer to Williamsburg).[3]

Since these finds were made, an intact example of a '*Three-window House*' bowl has been discovered by Jonathan Horne in London. **(Colour Plate 15)**. The painter's number '*2*' on the base is similar in style to the excavated examples, and although the inscription on the interior, '*More Rum and Sugar*', was not recorded in Virginia, the handwriting style seems to be identical.

Not all of the '*Three-window House*' pattern bowls excavated in Virginia bore the painter's number '*2*'. One example was found with a '*3*' mark on the base, **(Fig. 74)**, which bears a different inscription on the interior, '*The Other Bowl and Then*'. The painted house also seems to face in the opposite direction to bowls bearing a painters' number '*2*'. The writing style of the text confirms that a different painter decorated this bowl.

'*Bamboo Fence*' pattern (Figs. 75 - 77).

This pattern was recorded on two punch bowl fragments in Virginia, both of which bear the painter's number '*13*'. The example illustrated is the more complete of the two. **(Fig. 75)**.

The coarsely painted pattern on these excavated bowl fragments is similar to, but not identical to, a '*Bamboo and Fence*' pattern that occurs on a large, Dublin delftware platter, recently purchased in England. **(Fig. 76)**. This platter, like the excavated bowls, is marked '*13*' on the reverse, although a dinner-plate is also known bearing the painter's number '*3*'.[4]

These '*Bamboo Fence*' patterns are commonly recorded on Chinese porcelain, **(Fig.77)**, demonstrating that there is no clear distinction between this group of '*coarsely-painted*' designs

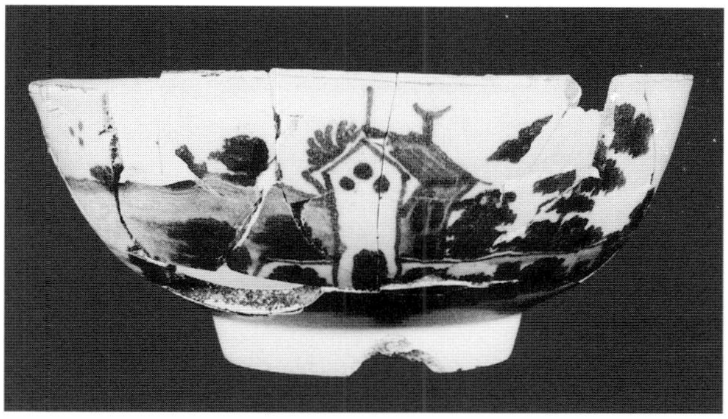

***Figure** 72. Excavated Dublin delftware punch-bowl of 'Three-window House' pattern, painter's number '2' on base. The sizes of the six bowls found of this pattern & number were : Ht. 3in.-4in., Diams. $6\frac{7}{8}$in.- 8in., footrim diams. $2\frac{7}{8}$ in.-$3\frac{7}{8}$ in.*

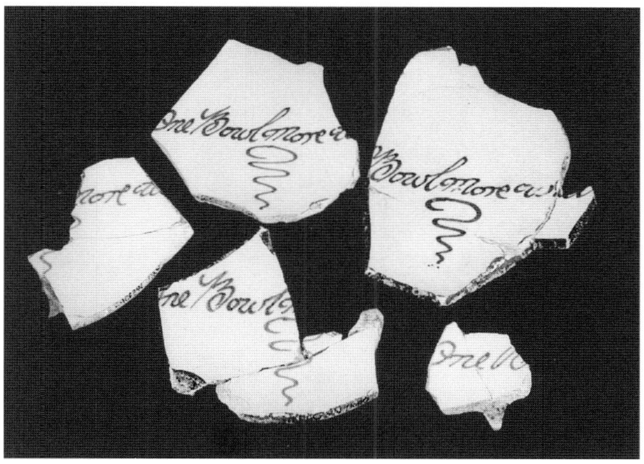

***Figure** 73. Interiors of excavated 'Three-window House' pattern bowls, each bearing painter's number '2'.*

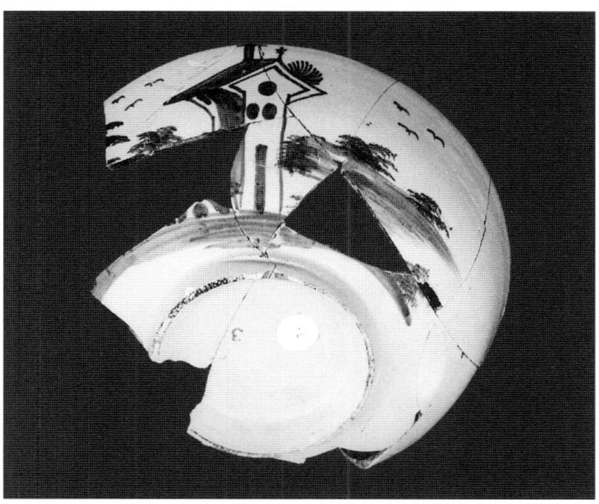

***Figure** 74. Excavated Dublin delftware punch-bowl of 'Three-window House' pattern, painter's number '3' on base. Inscribed on the interior 'The Other Bowl and Then'. Note that the house faces the opposite direction. (Compare Fig. 72). Ht. $3\frac{1}{4}$in., Diam. $7\frac{3}{4}$in., footrim diam. $3\frac{1}{4}$in.*

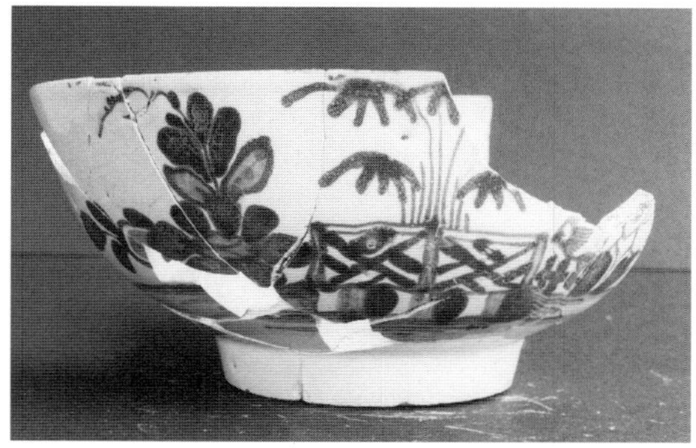

***Figure** 75. Excavated Dublin delftware punch-bowl of 'Bamboo Fence' pattern, painter's number '13' on base. Ht. $3\frac{1}{8}$in., Diam. $6\frac{3}{4}$ in., footrim diam. $3\frac{1}{8}$ in.*

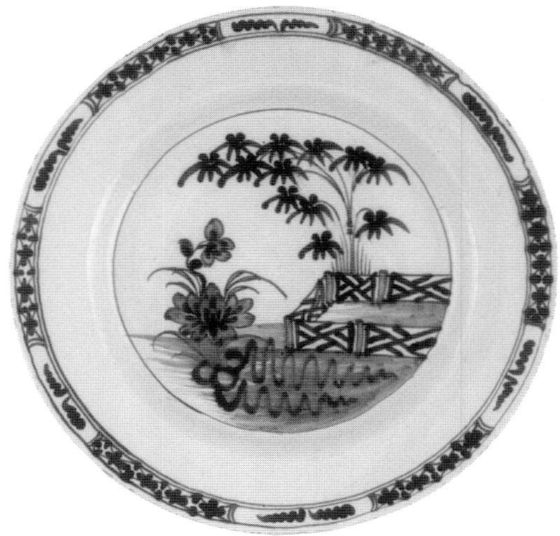

***Figure** 76. Dublin delftware platter featuring a 'Bamboo Fence' pattern, similar to - but not identical to - the excavated bowl shown in Fig.75. Painter's no.'13' within footrim. Diam. 14 in., 355mm.*

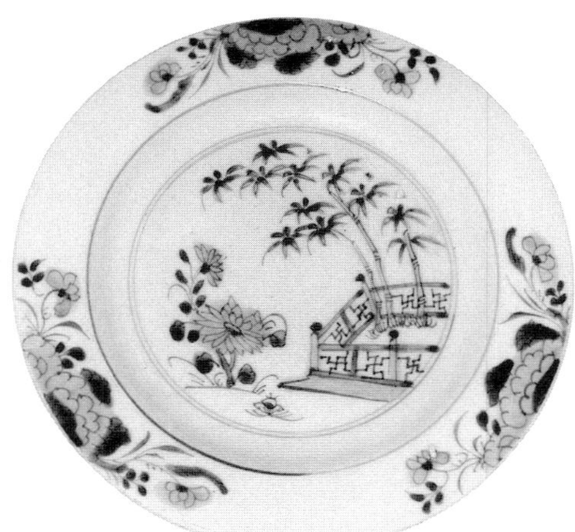

***Figure** 77. Chinese export porcelain plate featuring a similar type of 'Bamboo Fence' design. Diam. $9\frac{1}{4}$ in., 233 mm.*

and finer-quality Dublin wares that were more obviously copied directly from Chinese porcelain (See p. 89).

'*Large Flower*' patterns (Figs. 78 - 79).

Two of the excavated bowls are painted with an unusually large flower-head, flanked by buds and leaves, and interspersed with small dots of blue. **(Figs. 78, 79)**. One bears the painter's number '*5*', the other '*14*'. (Another example of a similar '*Large Flower*' pattern bowl, with the same painter's number '*14*' has been recorded on a separate excavation at Williamsburg).[5]

To date, no intact examples featuring these '*Large Flower*' patterns have been recorded.

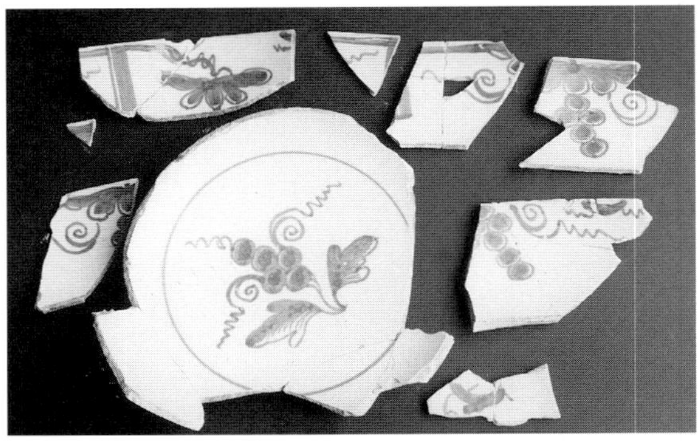

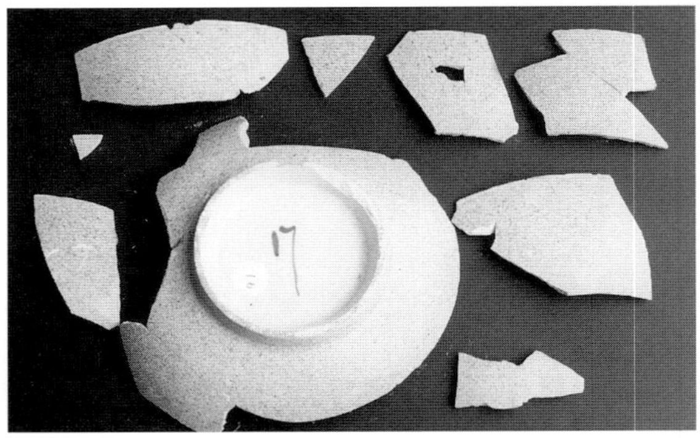

Top and Bottom : ***Figure 80***. *Excavated Dublin delftware bowl (possibly more than one). Decorated externally with uniform powdered manganese ground, internally in blue with 'Grapes & Vines'. Painter's number '17' on base. Ht.& Diam. - cannot determine. Footrim diam. 3¼ in.*

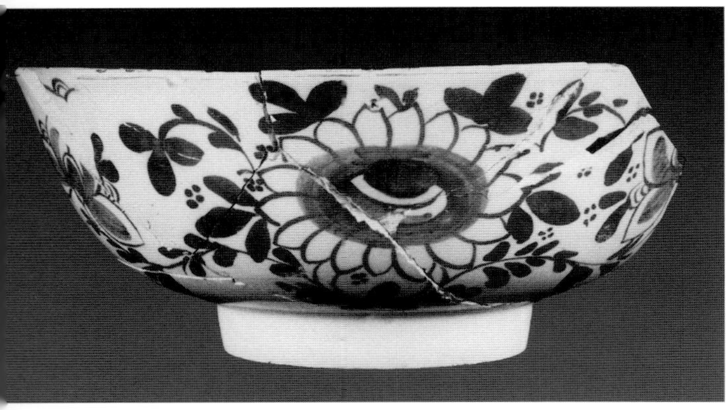

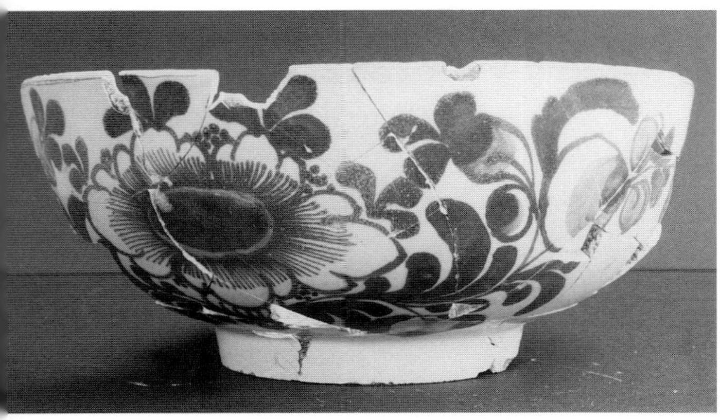

Top : ***Figure 78***. *Excavated Dublin delftware punch-bowl painted in blue with a 'Large Flower' pattern, painter's number '5' (in manganese). Ht. 3¼ in., Diam. 7¾ in., footrim diam. 3⅜ in*
Bottom : ***Figure 79***. *Excavated Dublin delftware punch-bowl painted in blue with a 'Large Flower' pattern, painter's number '14' on base. Ht. 3⅞ in., Diam. not recorded., footrim diam. 4 in.*

'*Grape & Vine*' pattern (Fig. 80).

One excavated bowl was recorded bearing the painter's number '*17*' on the base, and decorated on the exterior with a uniform, powdered-manganese ground. **(Fig. 80)**. A grape and vine motif appears on the interior, which is similar to, but by no means identical to, a grape and vine design recorded on one of the Dublin barrels. **(Fig. 122)**. Only one other example of Dublin delftware is known with powdered-manganese decoration, the celebrated '*Primate's Coals*' bowl **(Colour Plate 8)**.

Other Patterns (Figs. 81 - 86).

Various other punch bowl patterns were excavated in Virginia. None bears a painter's number on the base, yet the character of the delftware seems identical to other excavated bowls described above. There is a strong probability that many, if not all, of these unmarked bowls were also produced in

Dublin, but without the confirming presence of a painter's number, some doubt necessarily remains.

Overall, the unmarked bowls are painted in an even more fluid and cursory fashion than those described previously. The designs consist primarily of a large, swiftly painted floral sprig or spray. One of these bowls, (like the '*Three-window House*' pattern bowls), is inscribed on the interior '*One Bowl More*', which lends weight to the Dublin attribution of this unmarked group as a whole. **(Fig. 81)**. An intact example of a bowl painted with the same exterior design is recorded at Colonial Williamsburg, but this bears no inscription on the interior. **(Fig. 82)**.

Other floral designs **(Figs. 83, 84)** are similarly painted in a loose, fluid style. Although the match is not precise, this style of flower painting is strongly reminiscent of a delftware bowl recently discovered by Garry Atkins in London, now in a private collection. **(Figs. 85, 85a)**. Michael Archer first drew attention to the fact that this bowl exhibited a number of Dublin characteristics, (even before the excavated wares in Virginia were recognised).[6] The mark **(Fig. 85b)** is also very similar to the '*N*' monogram that occurs on Dublin delftwares, or it may even represent a variant of the well-known '*NE*' monogram. The fact that similar floral designs are recorded in Virginia strengthens the Irish attribution of the group as a whole. Some aspects of the floral painting are also extremely similar to those found on polychrome Dublin delftwares, such as the 'Verner Bowl' **(Colour Plate 31)**. (See also the flower painting on the border of the unusual, manganese-painted, scalloped dish, **Fig. 143a**).

Another distinctive motif recorded among these unmarked bowls is an unusual '*Trumpet flower*', reminiscent of a rose hip. **(Fig. 86)**. A few shards of similar design have also been found which are decorated in more unusual colour combinations, such as blue and manganese, for example, or even copper green and manganese.[7] Unfortunately, the fragments painted with these colour combinations are small, and

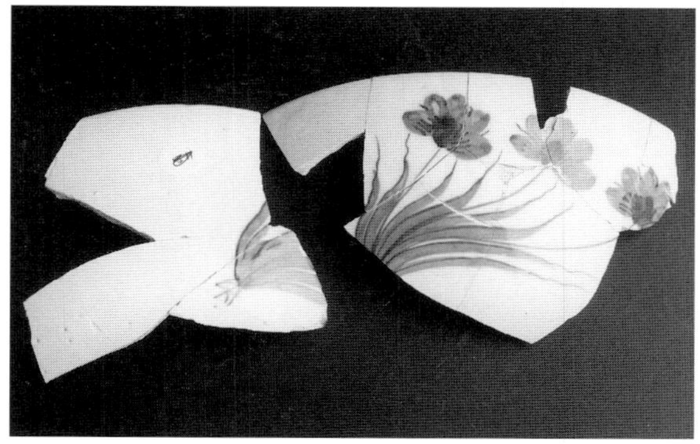

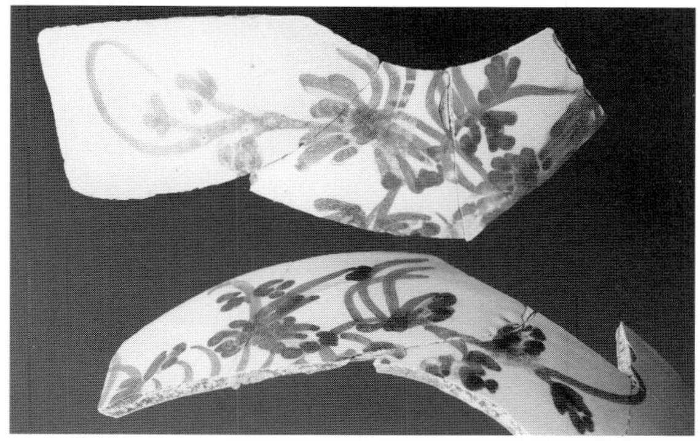

Top : ***Figure 83.*** *Excavated delftware punch-bowl fragment, floral design with elongated leaves, possibly Dublin. Size not recorded.*
Bottom : ***Figure 84.*** *Excavated delftware punch-bowl fragment with floral design, possibly Dublin. Size not recorded.*

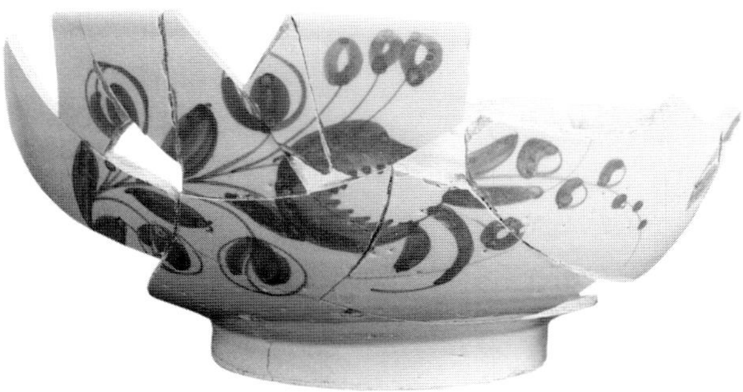

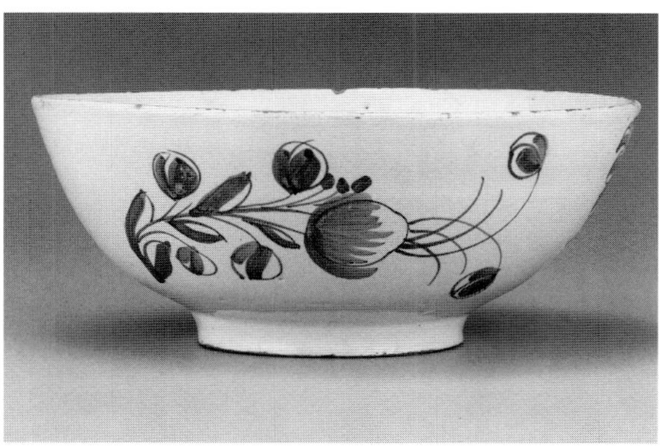

Top : ***Figure 81.*** *Excavated delftware bowl, probably Dublin, painted in blue, inscribed on the interior 'One Bowl More', (compare Fig.73). No mark. Similar designs were excavated, painted in blue and manganese. Ht. 4 in., Diam. unknown, footrim diam. 3¾ in.*
Bottom : ***Figure 82.*** *Delftware bowl, possibly Dublin. Ht. 3¾ in., Diam. 8¾ in.*

hence the individual designs are unclear. (No examples are illustrated here).

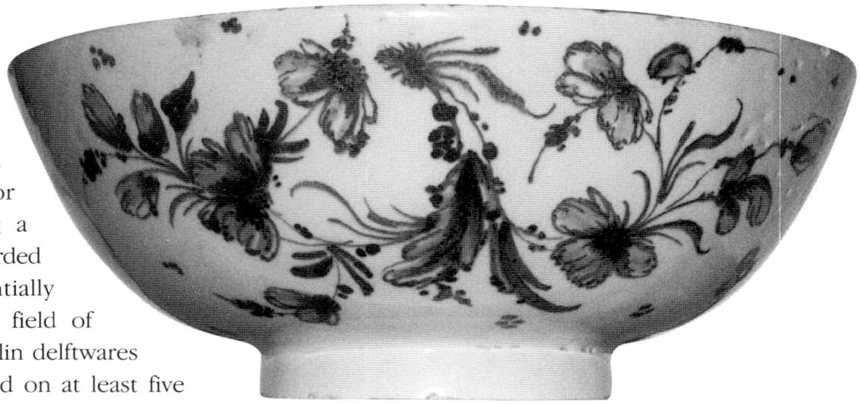

In summary, these excavated finds represent an important starting point for future research, highlighting a wide range of previously unrecorded Dublin designs, and potentially opening up an entirely new field of study. The fact that these Dublin delftwares appear to have been excavated on at least five sites in the states of Virginia and New York strongly suggests that Dublin delftware was exported in some quantity during the eighteenth-century, despite the absence of documentary records to this effect. It would also appear that the Irish potters produced different designs for the home and overseas markets - it would certainly be interesting to know whether more of the 'standard' Dublin designs, such as the typical '*Chinese porcelain*' patterns, have also been recorded on excavations in America.

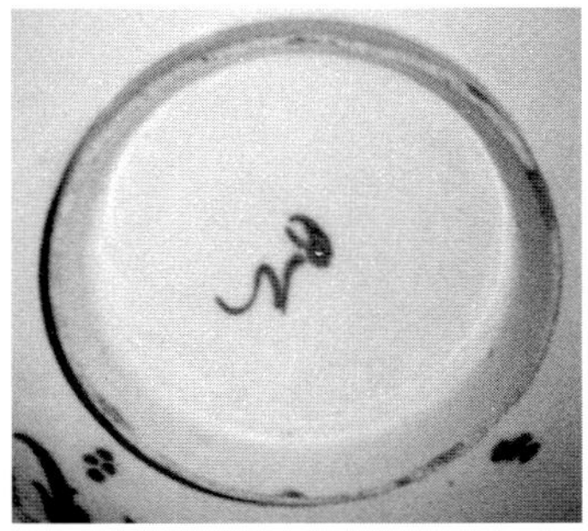

The realisation that Dublin was responsible for producing this wide range of '*coarsely painted*' wares in America is also beginning to lead to the discovery of similar wares closer to home. The '*Bamboo Fence*' pattern platter **(Fig. 76)**, for example, recently found in England, was only recognised as Dublin at first because of its similarity to the excavated patterns from Virginia. The design is so simple in comparison to most Dublin wares known previously, that it might easily have been considered English in the past, despite the presence of a painter's number '*13*' on the reverse. Another design purchased locally, painted with a '*Radial Flower*' pattern, **(Colour Plate 14)**, is perhaps one of the simplest and most 'coarsely-painted' Dublin designs that has yet been recorded, but it is a striking and distinctive pattern nonetheless.

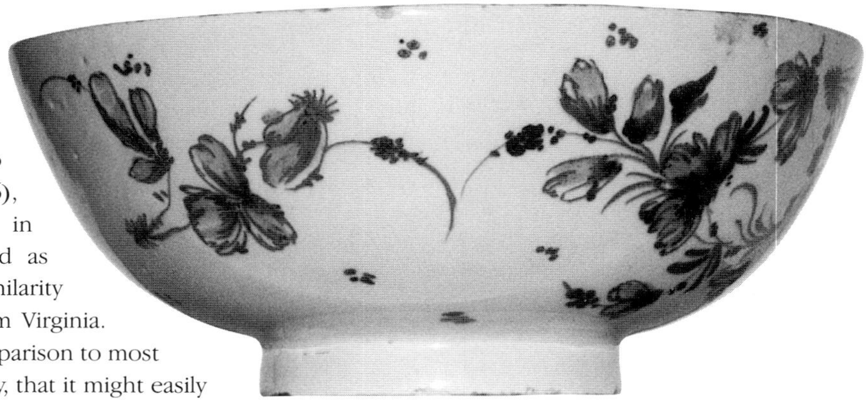

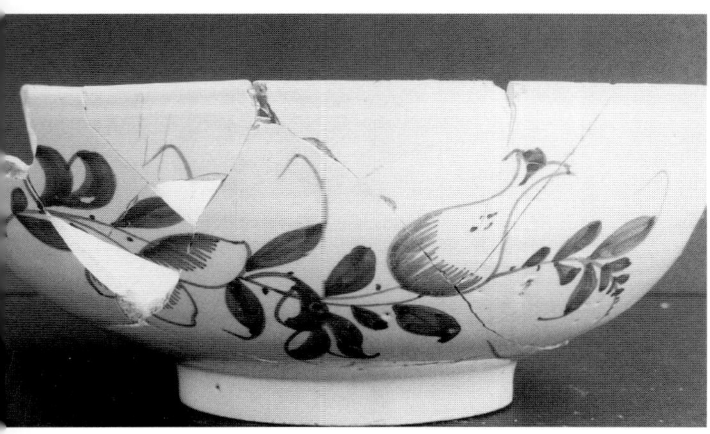

Above* : *Figures 85a, b, c. *Blue painted delftware punch-bowl, probably Dublin, with indistinct 'N' or 'NE' monogram mark on base. Diam. 230 mm., 9 1/10 in.*

Left* : *Figure 86. *Excavated delftware punch-bowl fragment with the 'Trumpet flower' design, possibly Dublin. No marks. Ht. 3 3/4 in.,Diam. 230 mm., 9 1/10 in., footrim diam. 3 3/4 in.*

CHINESE PORCELAIN DESIGNS

Most of the Dublin delftware designs presently known were copied directly from blue and white Chinese export porcelains. Chinese wares obviously represented a major influence on all manner of European ceramics at this time, but no other delftware pottery in the British Isles seems to have produced such a wide range of meticulous, precise replicas of Chinese originals. These wares may have been the Dublin delftwares that Mrs. Ann Day was referring to in 1762, when she stated that their wares *'imitate china'*. (See p.62). Stacey, Roche & Partners also advertised *'table-sets of India patterns'* in 1770. (See p.65. *'India china'* or *'East India china'* were contemporary terms for Chinese export porcelain).

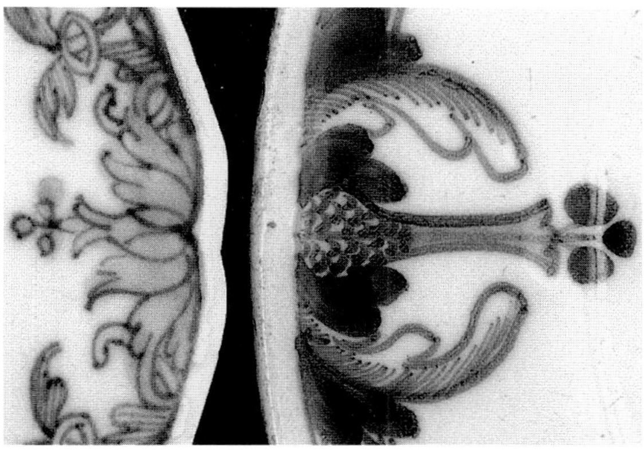

Henry Delamain himself, before he began making delftware, was a dealer in Chinese porcelain, and so he was probably well informed of contemporary fashions and prices, (p.46). Dublin's particular fondness for this type of delftware may have derived from the fact that true, Chinese porcelain was even more expensive in Ireland than in England. Ireland had been excluded from direct trade with the Far East since the seventeenth-century, and in 1721 the British Parliament passed an act forbidding Irish dealers to import East India goods from any country except by way of Great Britain.[8] The cost of Chinese porcelain in Ireland was therefore subject to additional customs duties, which were increased further from 1733 onwards.[9] This did not entirely preclude the sale of Chinese porcelain in Ireland, as a hundred or more armorial services were produced for Irish families between c. 1720 and 1820, but this was certainly a costly, luxury item.[10]

There is also evidence to suggest that the Chinese porcelains that were offered for sale in Ireland were often poor-quality, damaged goods — the tail end of the East India Company's auctions in London. As one authority recently noted, a *'curious feature of the "Nanking" that survived in Irish country houses ... was the general absence of complete, matching dinner services...* [This] *suggests that the Irish gentry must have bought piecemeal, and simply used the unmatching articles together, in a way they certainly did not do with the Mason's Ironstone . . .'.*[11] Another major advantage of Dublin delftware, therefore, was that it was readily available in complete, matching sets.

Five different Dublin designs are illustrated here **(Figs. 89-106)**, alongside the Chinese porcelain originals from which they were copied, allowing comparisons to be drawn. The main feature that immediately stands out is just how closely the Chinese patterns were replicated. Allowing for the fact that delftware does not lend itself so readily to fine brushwork, the copies are often precise. We can also see the origins of some features that have become recognised as distinctive, Dublin characteristics. The long, trumpet-like *'honeysuckle'* flower, for example, which occurs as a large and distinctive feature on some Dublin borders **(e.g. Fig. 102)**, is very much less pronounced on Chinese originals.[12] **(Fig. 87)**.

Although the main, central designs and the various border patterns were usually copied precisely, it seems that the different borders on the

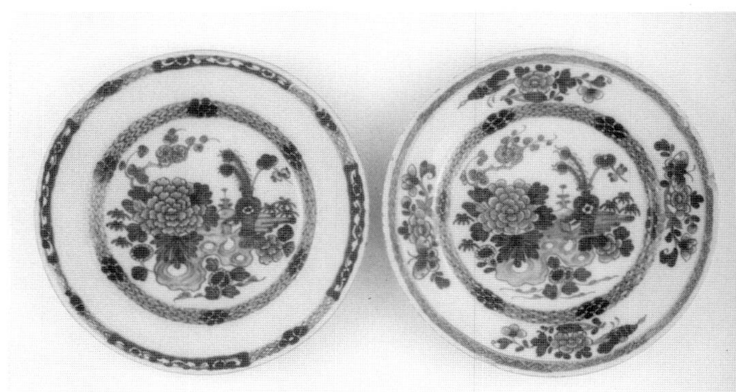

***Above** : **Figure 87**. 'Honeysuckle' border motif on Chinese porcelain (left) and Dublin delftware (right).*

***Right** : **Figure 88**. Two Dublin delftware 'Feathers in a Vase' pattern plates, of different border design. Diams. 233mm., Painters Nos. 5 (left) and 11 (right), within footrim.*

Chinese

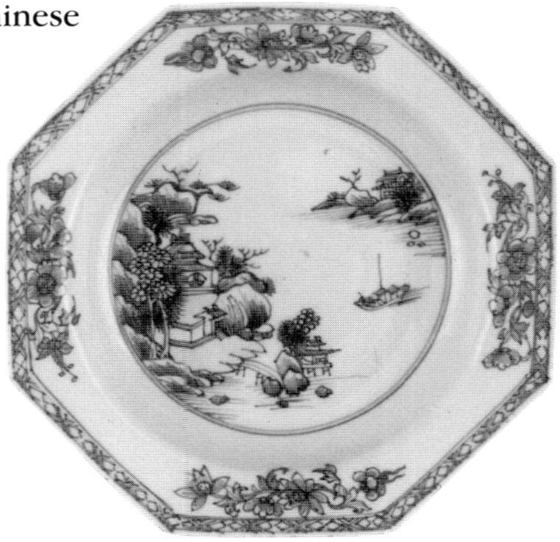

Dublin

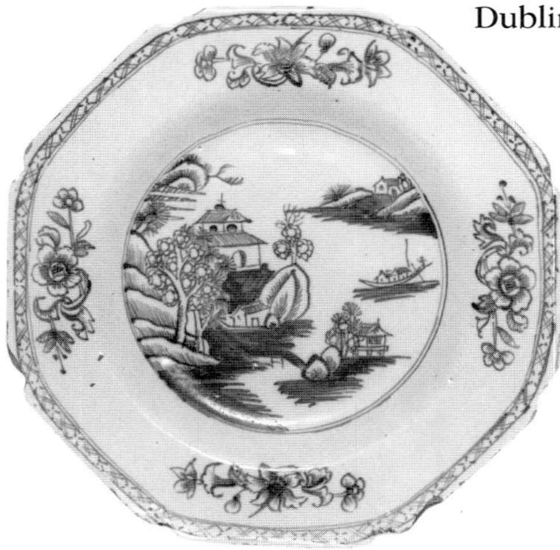

Chinese porcelains were used interchangeably. This is clear from the two Dublin delftware *'Feathers in a Vase'* pattern plates illustrated, which are identical in every respect apart from the border. **(Fig. 88)**. The *'Feathers in a Vase'* pattern is one of the most frequently recorded Dublin designs of all, second only in popularity perhaps to the *'Chinese Flower-bowl'* pattern **(Fig. 60a)**. Yet for some reason, the Chinese porcelain originals of both of these designs seem to be extremely rare.[13]

The *'Sampan Lake'* pattern **(Figs. 89 & 90)** was probably produced in Dublin over a period of several years. Many examples are marked with the earlier style of *monogram* mark, placed under the rim, whereas some (often more sparsely painted) exhibit the later type of *numbered* mark, painted centrally within the footrim. The same pattern was produced in porcelain at Bow during the 1750s, (see **Fig.117**), which raises the possibility that this particular design may have been copied from English rather than Chinese porcelain.

Most of the Dublin delftware copies of Chinese porcelain illustrated here bear a painter's number, within the footrim, suggesting that the majority were made during the 1760s. Geoffrey Godden records that Chinese examples of the *'Stag Pattern'* (probably one of the *'Two Deer'* patterns described below) were sold at auction in London in 1766.[14]

'Sampan Lake' and other Chinese Landscapes (Figs. 89 - 92).

The *'Sampan Lake'* pattern **(Figs. 89, 90)** was one of the most popular Chinese landscapes produced in Dublin. It is interesting to find that even the four floral motifs on the borders were copied from the Chinese, as on the Dublin examples they look more like a European addition.

Many other Chinese landscape views are known in Dublin delftware. (See, for example, Castletown Nos. 77, 92, 98). Usually, it is fairly obvious that the design has been lifted directly from a Chinese original, **(Figs. 91, 91a)**. In other cases, however, the source is less clear. The scene that appears on the

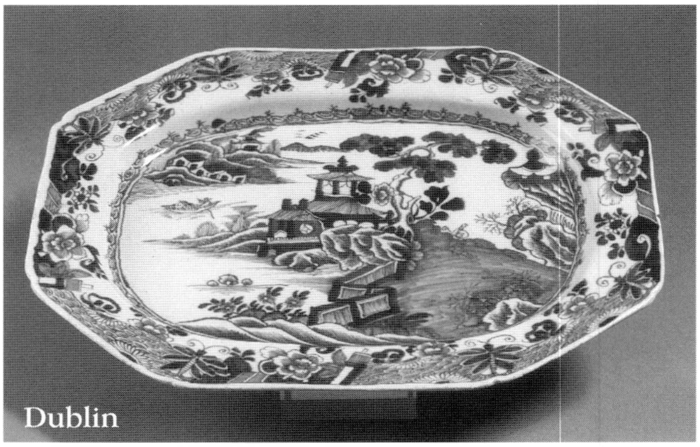

Top Left : Figure 89. *Chinese porcelain soup dish, of 'Sampan Lake' pattern, c. 1750. Width 220 mm., (side to side).*
Top Right : Figure 90. *Dublin delftware 'Sampan Lake' pattern soup dish, under-rim 'J' : monogram. Width 223 mm. (side to side). See also Fig. 117.*
Bottom Right : Figure 91. *Dublin delftware, large platter copying Chinese porcelain, featuring a 'Large Pagoda & Tree' pattern. Painter's number 11 in centre of base, no footrim. Length 19½ in., 493 mm.*

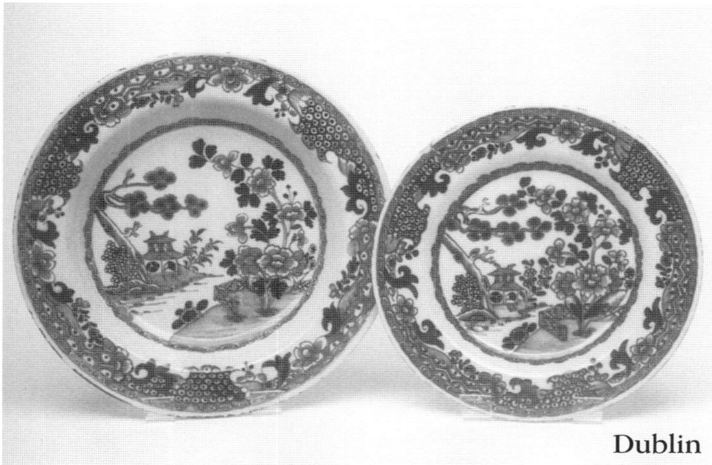

'Peony and Bamboo' pattern (Figs. *93 - 95)*.

Two slightly different versions of this pattern are known. On one, the border pattern is identical to the Chinese original illustrated, **(Figs. 93, 95)**. The other border is simpler, and features large, exaggerated 'honeysuckle' flowers — a typical Dublin feature, **(Fig. 94**. See also **Fig. 102)**. The central *'Peony and Bamboo'* design of each is identical.

wavy-edged platter in **Fig. 92**, for example, seems to be a hybrid. The foreground flower, tree and pagoda obviously derive from a Chinese source, but the hills and fields in the distance are identical to some that appear on Dublin's typical European landscapes, **(e.g. Colour Plate 19)**. It is quite possible therefore that some of the most attractive 'Chinese' scenes of all were simply invented by the Dublin painters.

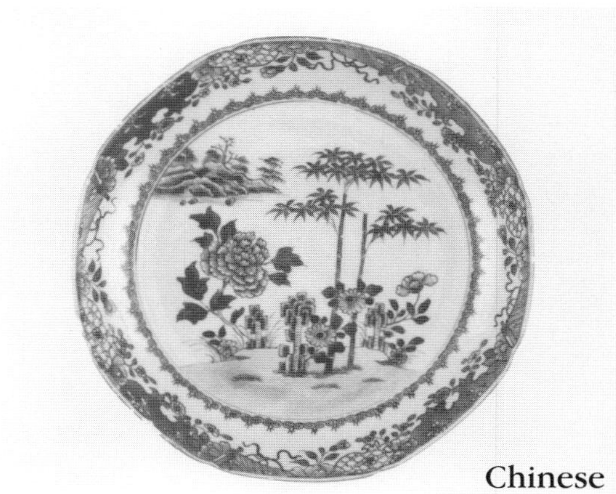

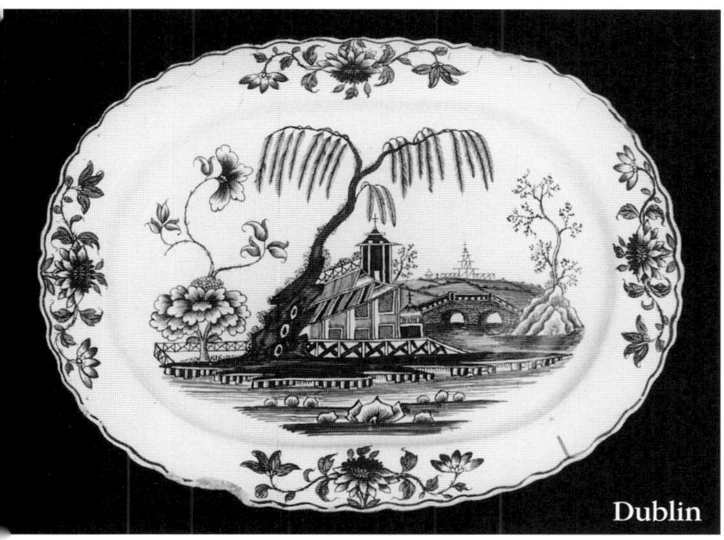

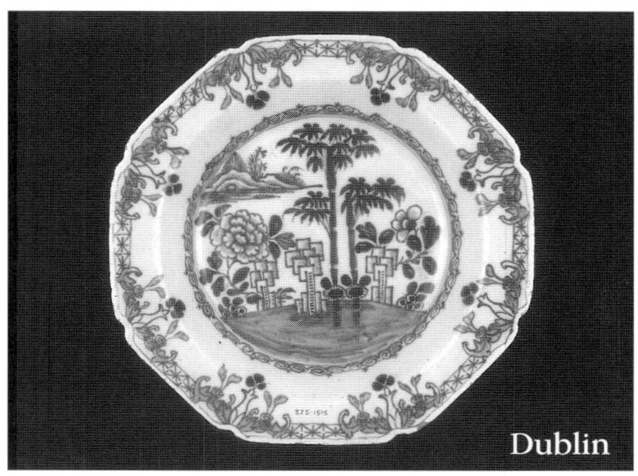

Top Left : Figure 91a. *Dublin delftware. Large, deep dish and a dinner plate, copying Chinese porcelain, featuring a 'Small Pagoda & large Flower' pattern. Painter's Nos. 12 (left) and 7 (right), within footrim. The reverse of the small plate is illustrated in Fig. 70. Diams. 280 and 235 mm.*

Bottom Left : Figure 92. *Dublin delftware hybrid landscape platter, showing features of both Chinese and European landscapes in combination. No footrim, under-rim 'IS' monogram, 537 x 405 mm.*

Top Right : Figure 93. *Chinese porcelain saucer-dish, 'Peony and Bamboo' pattern. c. 1750 -70. Rounded, octagonal edge. Width 253 mm., (side to side).*

Bottom Right : Figure 94. *Dublin delftware, 'Peony and Bamboo' pattern soup dish. Painter's number 6 within footrim. Width 222 mm., (side to side).*

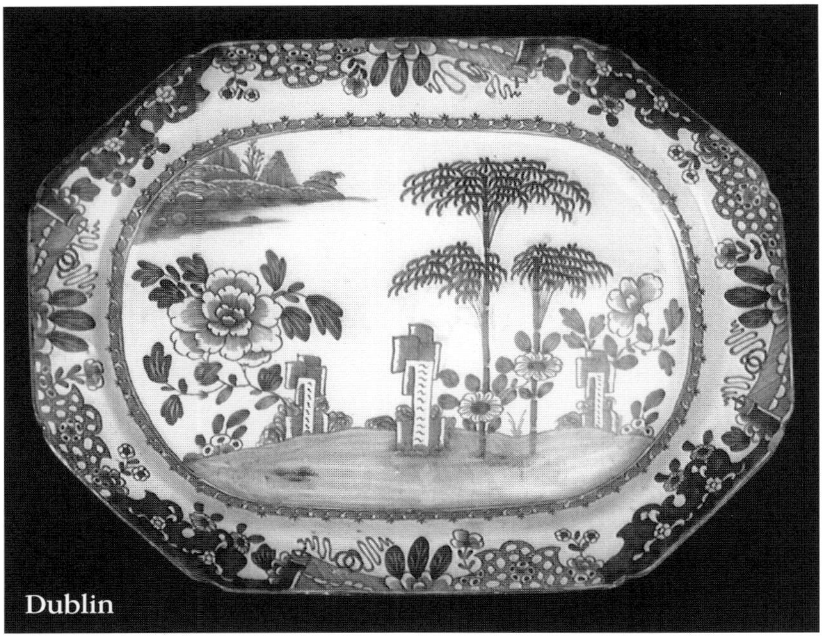

amongst the Dublin wares.

This group of *'Two Deer'* designs demonstrates very clearly that Dublin border patterns were used interchangeably. The border on the Chinese version of the *'Two Deer and Pagoda'* **(Fig. 96)** does not occur on any of the known Dublin *'Two Deer'* patterns, but it does occur on the *'Peony and Bamboo'* service described above **(Fig. 94)**. Most Dublin *'Two Deer'* services were instead painted with the border design that only appears on the second Chinese porcelain example shown, the *'Two Deer and Fence'* pattern **(Fig. 98)**.

'Two Deer' patterns (Figs. 96 - 100).

Two slightly different patterns featuring *'Two* Deer' are recorded in Dublin delftware, known for simplicity as *'Two Deer & Pagoda'* **(Fig. 97)**, and *'Two Deer & Fence'.* **(Fig. 100)**. Each was copied from a different original, **(Figs. 96, 98)**. Other variations in shape and border pattern create even greater variety

To confuse the issue further, Chinese porcelain plates and dishes seem to have been available in three different shapes - circular, octagonal or scallop-edged. Precisely the same three shapes were available in Dublin delftware **(Figs. 97, 99, 100)**. Note also that some of the Dublin octagonal plates have notched corners, **(Fig. 97)**, whereas others are plain-edged **(Fig. 66)**.

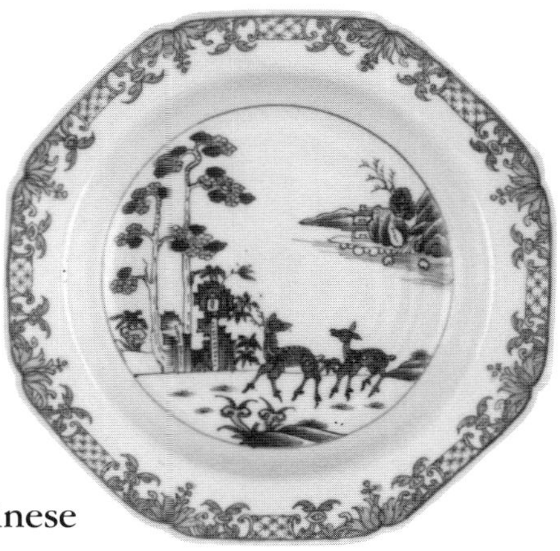

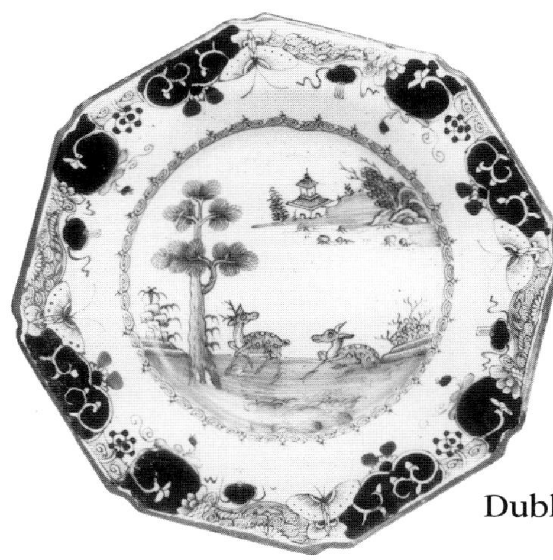

***Top : Figure** 95. Dublin delftware. 'Peony and Bamboo' pattern platter. Painter's number 6 within footrim. 505 x 385 mm.*

***Bottom Left : Figure** 96. Chinese porcelain 'Two Deer & Pagoda' pattern soup dish, Width 220 mm. (side to side).*

***Bottom Right : Figure** 97. Dublin delftware 'Two Deer & Pagoda' pattern small dish, with yellow-edge and notched corners. Painters' number 12 within footrim. (Compare the plain edge of the octagonal plate in Fig. 66). Width 8 in., 205 mm. (side to side).*

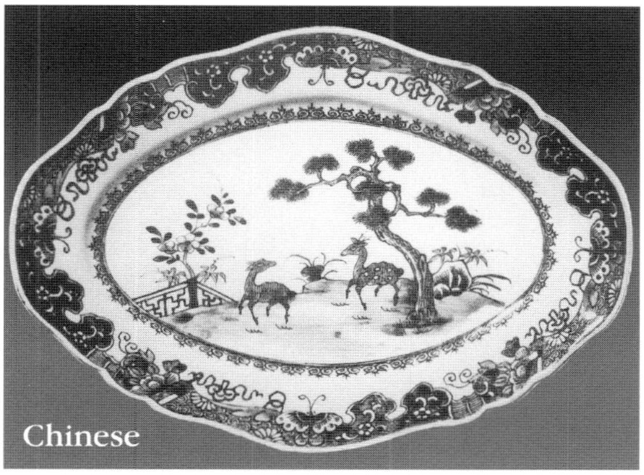

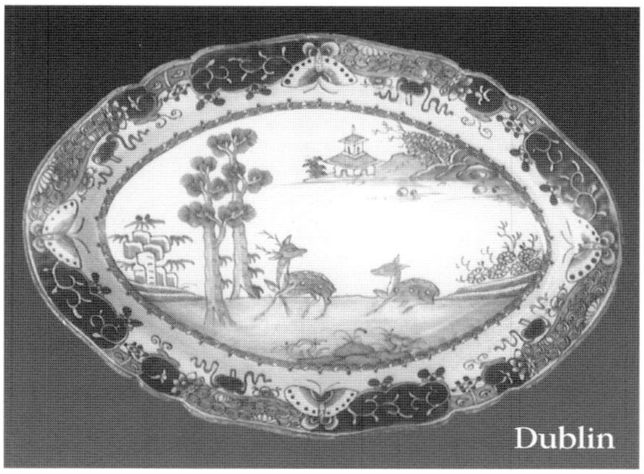

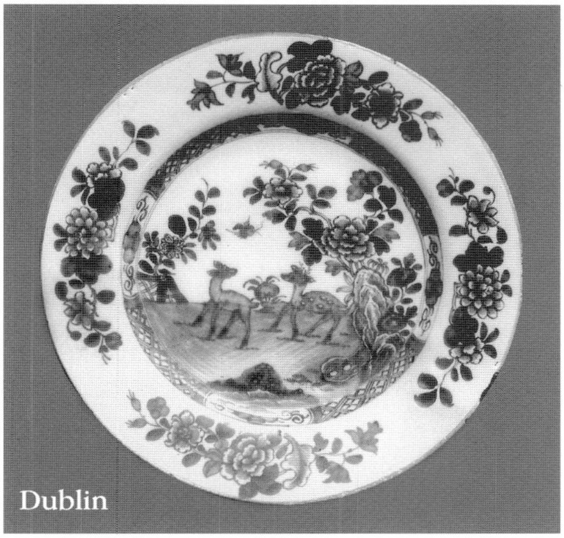

'Bird' patterns (Figs. 101 - 106).

Only one Dublin pattern featuring *'One Bird'* is recorded, but this is also one of the most recognisable Dublin patterns of all. **(Fig. 102)**. The Chinese porcelain example shown is not a precise match, but is very clearly in a similar vein. **(Fig. 101)**. The most notable feature of the Dublin plate is its border, which has been reduced to eight, greatly enlarged *'honeysuckle'* flower-heads and little else. **(Fig. 102)**.

As was the case with the *'Two Deer'* pattern, there are at least two Dublin versions featuring *'Two Birds'*. **(Figs. 103-106)**. The first, more crowded design, contains a fence, **(Figs. 104, 105)** the second features a distinctive bulrush on the right hand side. **(Fig. 106)**

It is particularly interesting to be able to compare the Dublin versions of the *'Two bird & fence'* pattern with the Chinese original, as it brings out the variations in quality that occur within Dublin delftware. The large octagonal platter **(Fig. 105)**, is well painted, with a typically bold and crowded border. (Circular plates and platters of this design are also recorded). The small, octagonal plate is poorly painted by comparison. **(Fig. 104)** This has a different border pattern to the previous example and is more loosely painted throughout. The two birds, which are meant to represent cranes or storks, look more like crows.

The second Dublin design, featuring *'Two Birds & Bulrush'* is altogether different in character, **(Fig. 106)**, and much more sparsely decorated. A Chinese porcelain original has not been located, but circular and octagonal versions are recorded, all with the same, very simple border. A third Chinese porcelain design featuring two long-tailed birds is recorded on a platter in the National Museum. A vase of this pattern is illustrated in **Fig. 173**.

Many more Dublin designs were copied from Chinese porcelain, the majority painted with floral rather than figurative subjects, sometimes with vases and *'Precious Objects'*. Many of these designs appear elsewhere in this book, while others are recorded in the Castletown catalogue.

Top Left : Figure 98. *Chinese porcelain 'Two Deer & Fence' pattern scalloped platter, c. 1760-70. Width 305 mm.*
Top Right : Figure 99. *Dublin delftware 'Two Deer & Pagoda' pattern scalloped platter, yellow edge. Painters' number 2 within footrim. 300 x 211 mm.*
Bottom Left, Figure 100. *Dublin delftware 'Two Deer & Fence' pattern plate, yellow edge. Painter's number 7 within footrim. Diam. 233 mm.*

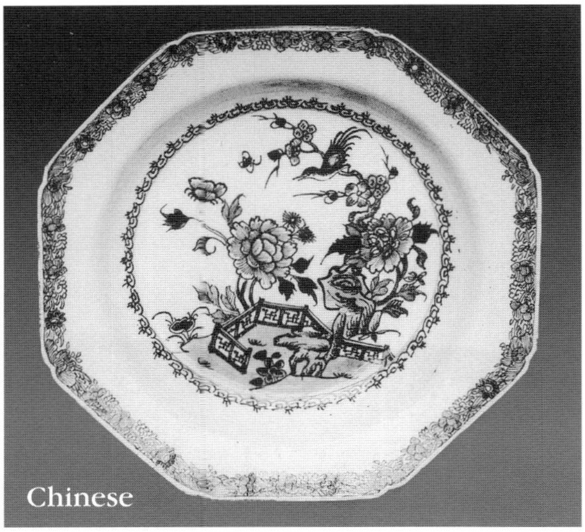

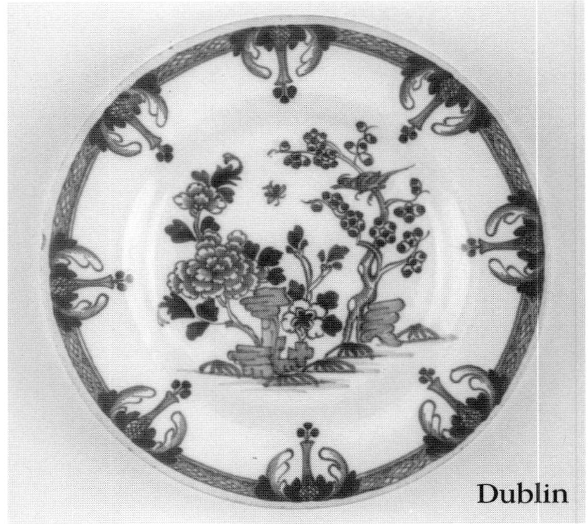

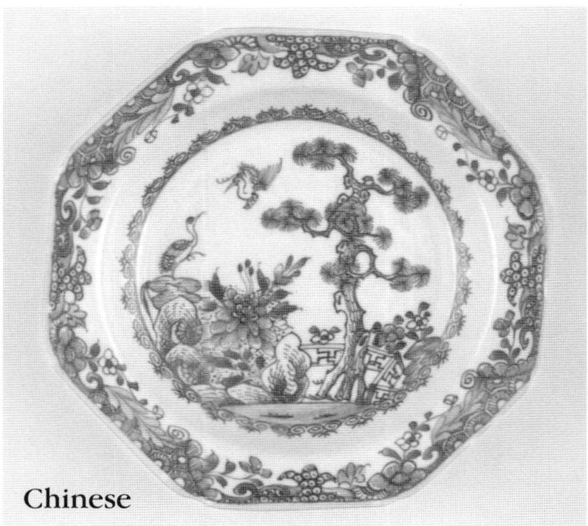

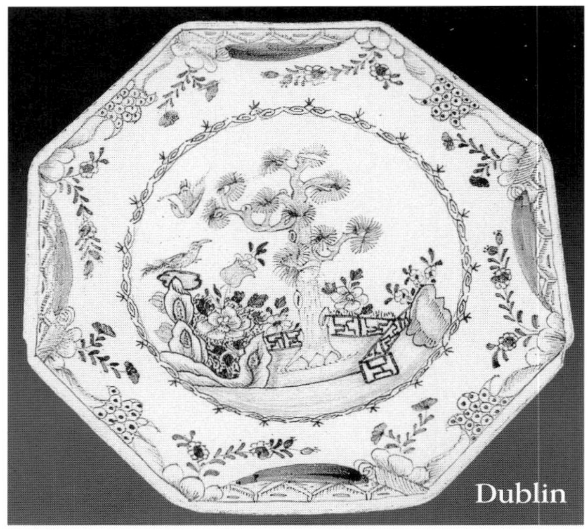

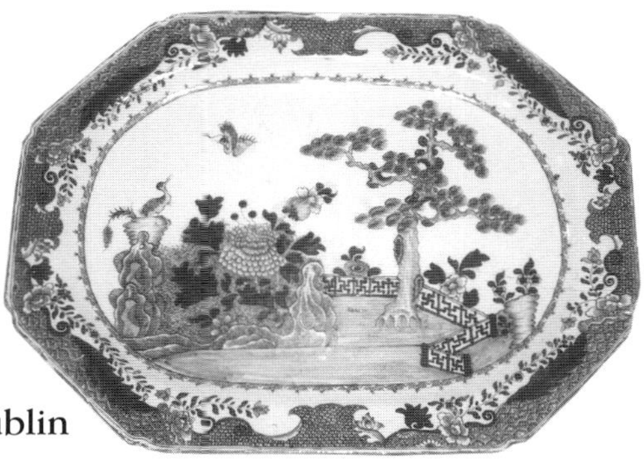

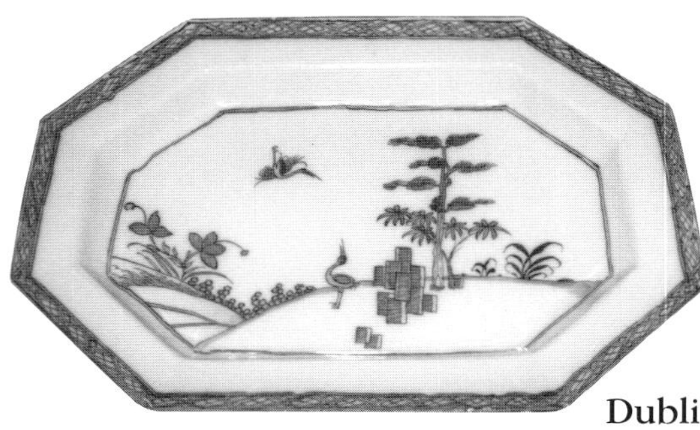

Top Left : ***Figure 101*** *Chinese porcelain 'One Bird & Insect' pattern soup dish, Width 219 mm. (side to side).*
Top Right : ***Figure 102.*** *Dublin delftware 'One Bird & Insect' pattern plate. Painter's number 14 within footrim. Diam 232 mm.*
Middle Left : ***Figure 103.*** *Chinese porcelain 'Two Bird & Fence' pattern soup dish, Width 221 mm. (side to side).*
Middle Right : ***Figure 104.*** *Dublin delftware 'Two Bird & Fence' pattern octagonal soup dish. Painter's Number 11 within footrim. Width 225 mm (side to side). Circular plates of this pattern are also recorded, some as small as 7 in., 178 mm. diameter.*
Bottom Left : ***Figure 105.*** *Dublin delftware 'Two Bird & Fence' pattern platter, Length 21 3/4 in., 550 mm., painter's number 4.*
Bottom Right : ***Figure 106.*** *Dublin delftware 'Two Bird & Bulrush' pattern platter. Painter's number 9 within footrim. 423 x 300 mm.*

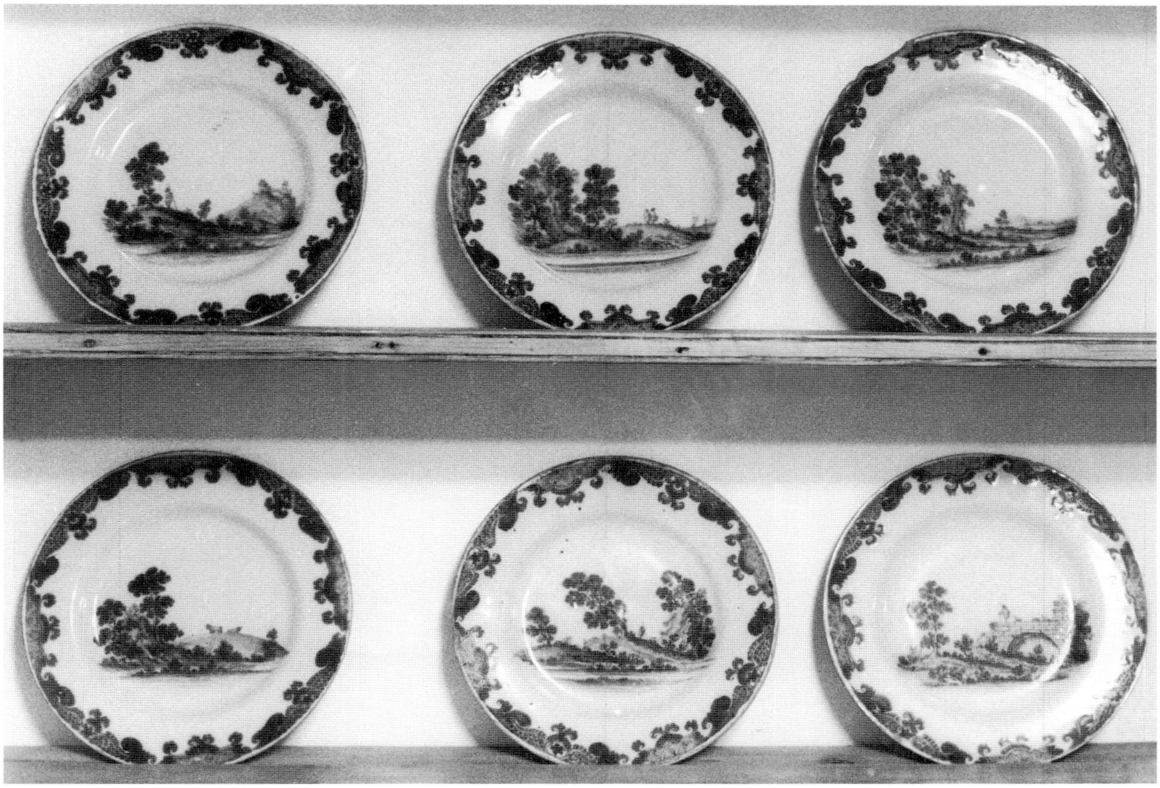

Figure 107. *A set of six, very fine quality Dublin landscape-painted plates, bearing crowned harp, 'Dublin' and mock-Chinese marks. Possibly part of a set of plates and baskets recorded in the collection of Mr. S. G. Stopford Sackville of Drayton House, Northamptonshire in 1913 and 1874, now dispersed. It is possible that this set was made by Henry Delamain for the Lord Lieutenant of Ireland, Lionel Sackville, in c. 1752-55. (See p.71). One example appears as Colour Plate 21. Photographed on the premises of Jellinek & Sampson, London, in 1977.*

EUROPEAN LANDSCAPES

(Colour Plates 16-27)

Dublin delftwares painted with European romantic landscapes probably represent the high point of ceramic manufacture in Ireland during the eighteenth-century. At their best, the Dublin landscapes possess an individuality and charm that is quite unmistakable. Possibly these were the wares that Mrs. Ann Day was referring to, when she remarked in 1762 that *'There is no ware in England of the same kind as* [ours]'. (See p.62).

Unlike most of the designs produced in Dublin, the landscape scenes seem to have been painted freehand, without the use of a stencil. **(Fig. 107)**. Although each one is individual, many elements reappear frequently in slightly different contexts. There are usually some finely painted, feathery trees set amongst rolling hills and fields, one or two figures silhouetted against the skyline, and often some ruins, houses or boats in the distance. The advertisements in 1770 indicate that Dublin also produced some actual, rather than imaginary, *'views of gentlemen's country seats'*, but none have yet been identified.

Attention has been drawn to the similarity that exists between these Dublin landscapes and some outstanding Dutch delftwares, painted by Frederik van Frijtom during the third quarter of the seventeenth-century, but it is unlikely that any direct connection exists.[15] The prevailing taste in Irish art at the time was for precisely this type of romantic, continental landscape, influenced and inspired by the work of seventeenth-century landscape painters such as Claude Lorraine.

Ireland was not alone in its appreciation of romantic landscape painting - the fashion seems to have embraced Europe at that time. The genre is therefore well represented in European ceramics of

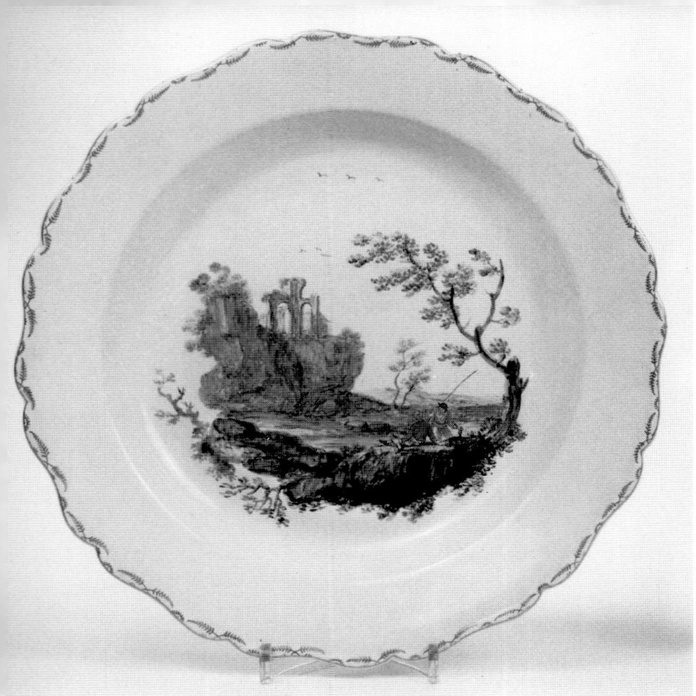

Figure 108. *Marseilles (Bonnefoy), wavy-edged circular dish, c. 1760-70, painted in colours, with distant blue hills & ruins. Gilt-edge rim. Diam. 325 mm.*

every description, on porcelains especially. The closest contemporary parallels in tin-glaze to the Dublin landscape wares seem to have been produced in France, particularly the southern part, and if Dublin landscapes were indeed based on continental prototypes, then these seem to represent a plausible source of inspiration. The colours employed by the Dublin potters were entirely different to those used by their continental counterparts, but the overall style of the design can sometimes seem very similar indeed. **(Fig. 108)**. Given Dublin's repeated claims that its wares were equal to imported '*Rouen or Burgundy*' wares, and the evident influence of French or even Italian designs in their polychrome wares, then a French origin for this style of delftware landscape does not seem out of the question.

The finely-painted landscapes on the '*Primate's Coals*' bowl, dated 1753, suggest that the range was introduced by Henry Delamain himself, and was in production less than eighteen months after he assumed ownership. This ties in with documentary evidence, which suggests that Delamain's principal philosophy was to dramatically improve the quality of the wares produced by the World's End pottery. At some stage in 1752 or 53, Delamain must have brought in one or more skilled painters to undertake the decoration of these exceptional wares. Once introduced, however, European landscapes were to remain a standard item for as long as delftware was made in Dublin. They were advertised for sale in 1766 by Delamain's successors, William Delamain and Samuel Wilkinson, and again by Edward Stacey & Co. in 1770, shortly before delftware manufacture ceased, (pp.64-5).

Looking more closely at the landscape-decorated wares illustrated in Colour plates 18-27, there is considerable diversity in the quality of painting - some are highly competent and of a professional standard, whilst others are more amateur. This diversity initially seems to correspond with the documentary evidence, as the pottery's advertisement in 1766 indicates that two basic qualities of landscape-decorated wares were available;

'*Fine painted landscape plates* [reduced]
from nine shillings to . .seven shillings [per dozen]'.

'*the second sort* [reduced] *from six shillings
to four shillings and sixpence* [per dozen]'.

When we examine the landscape-decorated wares more closely, it often appears that these first-quality and second-quality pieces can be easily distinguished - most first-quality wares were painted in cobalt blue, the second-quality in manganese purple, with a few notable exceptions (such as the Armstrong jug, **Colour Plate 26**). This perception is probably erroneous, however, in that the difference in quality we see today does not necessarily correspond with the variations described in 1766. On closer inspection, the majority of the 'first-quality' blue-painted pieces seem to date from the 1750s. Some possess the crowned harp, '*Dublin*' or mock-Chinese marks that are associated with the set that was probably produced during Henry Delamain's lifetime. **(Fig. 107)**. The manganese-painted 'second-quality' plates, on the other hand, are either unmarked, or else bear monograms or numbers on the reverse, suggesting they were made a little later - during the late 1750s or 1760s.[16] These evident differences in quality may therefore reflect a more general, gradual, decline that occurred during the years following the death of Henry or Mary Delamain.[17]

In the past, most Dublin landscape-decorated wares were attributed to just one Irish painter, Peter Shee, presumably because he was the only landscape artist that was known to have worked at the pottery.[18] The range of recorded styles clearly shows, however, that no single artist was responsible - there were at least five different individuals, to judge from the recorded painter's marks alone. (See footnote 16).

In recent years, the names of several additional Dublin painters have come to light;

John Jolly

Two individuals of this name are mentioned on a lease document of June 1753.[19] One John Jolly, (presumably the father?), leased a garden adjoining the pottery to Henry Delamain. A second John Jolly, (his son?), witnessed the signing, and was described as *'a painter',* alongside Robert Carver (see below). In view of the context in which his name appears, Jolly might well have had some association with the pottery.

Robert Carver

Described as *'a painter',* and a second witness to the 1753 lease agreement described above.[20] Robert Carver *(c. 1730-91)* was a major Irish artist.[21] Like his father Richard, he specialised in painting romantic landscapes in the manner of Claude, Poussin and Lambert, sometimes signing his works with the initials R.C. He was employed as scene painter at Smock Alley Theatre in Dublin from 1754, and moved later to the new theatre at Crow Street. Between 1765 and 1768, from his home on Lazar's Hill, *'he sent twenty pictures mostly depicting romantic landscapes with figures and ruins to the Society of Artists in Ireland'.* He also exhibited in London with the Society of Artists, becoming its President in 1777, and at the Royal Academy. Several examples of his work are known, **(Colour Plate 17)**, all apparently depicting Arcadian landscape scenes in the style of seventeenth-century French and Dutch artists.

Peter Shee

(fl. 1748 - 67). Shee was obviously involved in the Dublin pottery in December 1753, when he was mentioned in a letter by Delamain, and in 1761, when he was called to present the pottery's accounts for inspection. Strickland's *'Dictionary of Irish Artists'* records that Shee's career began in Dublin as a house painter, but he took to painting romantic landscapes *'in the manner of Claude'.* Landscapes remained his specialty, but he accepted other commissions. A group of allegorical paintings that Shee produced for the occasion of the King's marriage celebrations in Dublin in 1761 were put up to line the streets, and were highly praised.[22] He exhibited with the Society of Artists of Ireland from their first year (1765), and died at his home in New Street, Dublin in September 1767.[23]

Despite Shee's clear association with the Dublin pottery, the absence of any authenticated work by him has meant that, in the past, it was impossible to judge whether he may have been responsible for any of the landscape-decorated delftwares. In 1997, the first recorded painting by Peter Shee surfaced in San Francisco and made its way onto the London art market.[24] **(Colour Plate 16)**. As Strickland remarked, Shee's style, like Robert Carver's, was heavily derivative of continental prototypes. Shee's painting will be discussed at greater length presently.

'Mr. Hornby'

Mentioned by Henry Delamain alongside Peter Shee in his letter of December 1753, *('my respects to Mr. Hornby, Mr. Shee &c.').* His occupation is unknown.

Bryan McManus

Mentioned in Waterford in July 1755, where he is recorded as a *'sprig painter of earthenware'*, of the City of Dublin.[25] He was almost certainly employed by Delamain before this date, and perhaps afterwards also.

William Waldron

Mentioned in the minutes of the Dublin Society on 6th November 1766. He had been apprenticed to Delamain, *'but his eyesight got bad and he had to leave'.*[26]

William Stringfellow

Served his apprenticeship as a *'delft painter'* in Liverpool in c.1733-40, and acted as the Dublin pottery's manager in Delamain's absence in 1753.[27] His early release from Delamain's service in January 1754 suggests he had little connection with the landscape-decorated wares.

In attempting to identify the painters responsible for some of the finest quality landscapes, there seem to be two principal candidates; Peter Shee and Robert Carver, both accomplished painters in oils.

It is particularly interesting, at long last, to see an example of Peter Shee's work **(Colour Plate 16)**.

The composition is unlike any known delftware landscape, but Shee remains a strong candidate nonetheless. Some of the details in the painting, in particular, the Roman column, house and obelisk in the distance, (inset), are comparable to features that occur on Dublin delftware, as are the rather stocky figures and tree. On the other hand, several distinctive features in the painting do not occur anywhere in delftware. Flags are especially prominent on the fort and ships, yet no such flags appear on any delftware landscape. The circular building, and the manner in which the ships are painted, also differ significantly from similar features in delftware.

On balance, the entire composition is so unlike the delftware landscapes that it is impossible to draw any firm conclusions from the comparison. The features that are most similar - the trees, obelisk and column, appear a convincing match, until we realise that many Irish artists were painting similar imaginary landscapes using precisely these same compositional elements. The example of Robert Carver's work illustrated exemplifies this point. **(Colour Plate 17)**. Here, the trees and rounded hill in the middle distance also seem strongly reminiscent of some Dublin delftware landscapes. Once again, there are ruins on a hilltop, and below these, two goat-herders walk with their goats and horses, (inset). Similar herdsmen with their flocks appear on some of the delftware landscapes. **(e.g. Fig. 164, Colour Plate 24)**.

The discovery of paintings by *two* landscape artists mentioned in connection with the Dublin pottery represents a significant advance, but determining the artists responsible for the delftware landscapes remains next to impossible. The delftware artists obviously created their imagined landscapes using a set formula of compositional elements. Many oil paintings were produced in precisely the same way at this time, so that identifying the work of any one particular individual is fraught with uncertainty, especially when comparing work in two, very different media.

Perhaps the most serious inconsistency is the fact that neither artist's name corresponds with any of the monograms recorded on Dublin delftware. (It is difficult to imagine that either Shee or Carver would have signed his work with the initials *'NE'* or *'JB'* for example, yet these monograms appear on some fine delftware landscapes). If we instead use the monograms as a starting point for identification, then another Irish artist's name that is certainly worth considering is the highly accomplished Cork-born artist John Butts, *(c.1728-64)*. Butts is known to have moved to Dublin in 1757, where he worked variously as a scene and sign painter, and became acquainted with Robert Carver. A simple but splendid pen and wash study of trees survives in the National Gallery of Ireland **(Fig. 109)**. The Knight of Glin was the first to observe that the character of these trees is highly reminiscent of those that appear on Dublin delftware.[28] It is especially regrettable that no further drawings by Butts are known, as of all the artists mentioned here, the delicacy of his style shows greatest affinity with the delftware landscapes. Without further evidence it is impossible to do more than suggest - very tentatively indeed - that John Butts *may* have been associated with the Dublin pottery. Even if he was responsible for

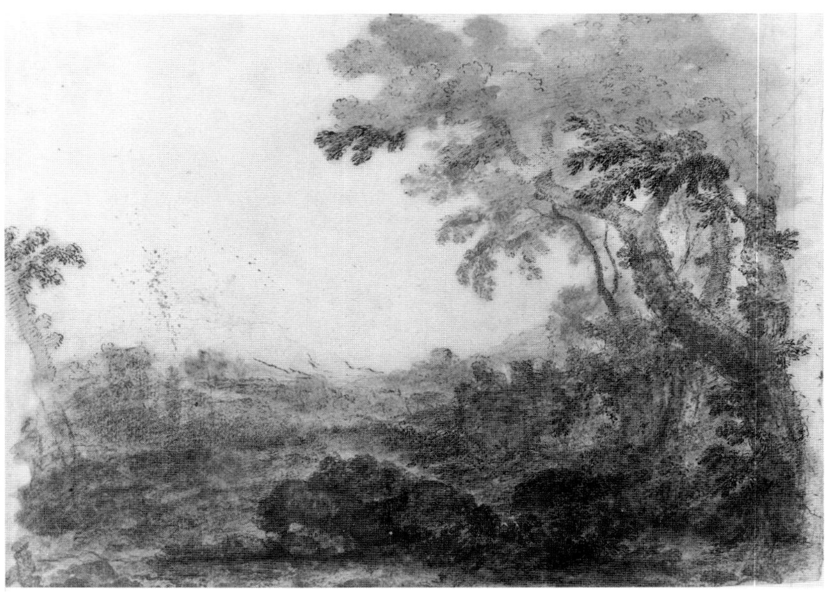

Figure 109. *'Trees above a Valley'. A pencil, crayon and ink study by the Cork-born artist John Butts (c. 1728-64).*

decorating the wares marked *'JB'*, however, the identity of *'NE'* - the best known Dublin painter of all - remains a complete mystery.

In summary, we are certainly beginning to make some headway in discovering more about the artists associated with the Dublin pottery, and locating a signed oil by Peter Shee is an important development. In reality, however, identifying the artists responsible for creating the delftware landscapes is still a long way off, and conclusive answers may simply not exist.

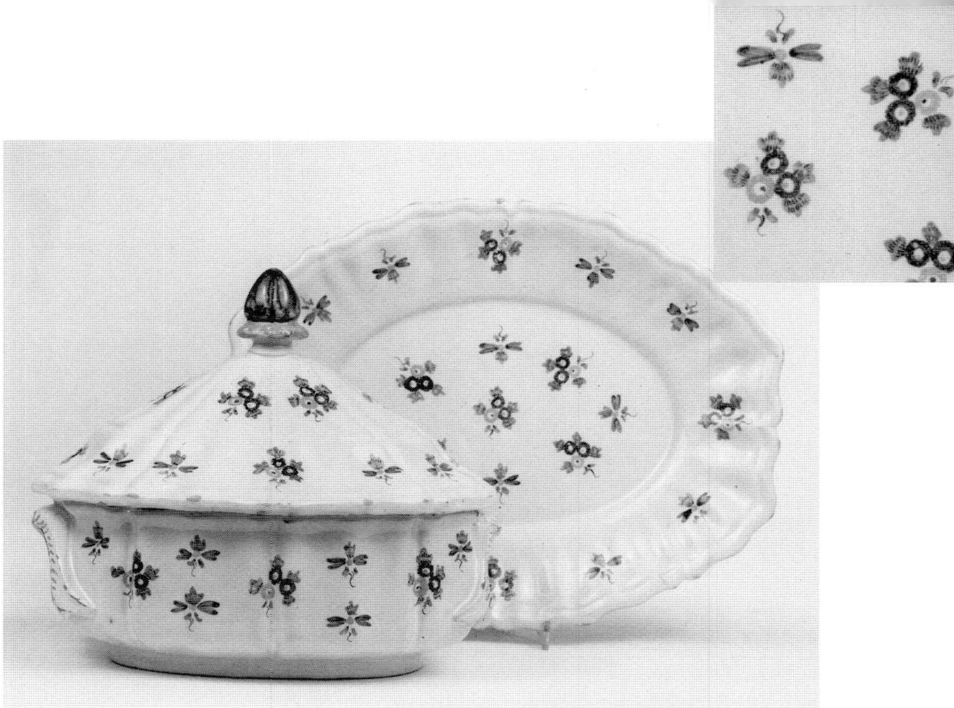

Figure 110. *A lobed oval Tureen, Cover and Stand, perhaps Bassano (northern Italy), decorated with painted floral sprigs in green, blue and yellow, c. 1770. (Compare Colour Plate 29, centre). The stand is 305 mm. wide.*

COLOURED WARES

(Colour Plates 28 - 35)

At the time of the Castletown exhibition in 1971, no examples of coloured Dublin delftware were known. Later in the 1970s, however, Michael Archer and Brian Morgan identified the first example, a large, wavy-edged oval platter, decorated with finely painted floral sprays around the border.[29] **(Colour Plate 28)**. The form of this dish (with 26 'scallops' around the edge) is essentially identical to other, more typical examples of Dublin delftware, decorated with European landscape scenes. (*cf.* **Colour Plate 25**). In reality, the similarity between the two platters is much more obvious on the reverse side - neither platter possesses a footrim, and the irregular glaze surface is highly distinctive. Despite the absence of painters' marks, both of these platters can be attributed to Dublin with some confidence.

The distinctive colouring and flower painting led Morgan and Archer to realise that a celebrated polychrome bowl in the Glaisher collection, at the Fitzwilliam Museum in Cambridge, **(Colour Plate 31)** was probably a Dublin product also.[30] The provenance of this exceptional piece of Irish delftware links it directly to Thomas Verner (d. 1788), of Verner's Bridge in Co. Armagh.[31] This association is further supported by the presence of the crest of the Verner family on the outside, (a boar's head couped), and the initials *'T. V.'* on the interior. On the bottom of the bowl is the inscription,

'DRINK DRINK WHILST YE HAVE BREATH
FOR THERE IS NO DRINKING AFTER DEATH.
T. V.
1756'

As Glaisher noted, these lines appear in the first verse of the eighteenth-century song 'Here's a Health to the Queen'.[32] The bowl was in fact attributed to Dublin by Glaisher and Bernard Rackham as long ago as the 1920s and 30s, on the evidence of its crest, initials, and provenance. Yet for fifty years or more, as the only known example of polychrome delftware with a (tentative) Irish attribution, the Verner bowl represented more of an anomaly than a starting point for new attributions.[33] Once the evident similarities between this bowl and the Morgan platter were recognised, however, the Dublin attributions of both pieces were mutually strengthened.

The colours employed on these two pieces are extremely unusual when compared with English delftwares, but strikingly similar to wares produced in France and even Italy during the third quarter of the eighteenth century. (The closest comparators in the literature seem to have been made in the southern part of France, from Bordeaux across to Marseilles, and into northern Italy). The tureen and stand illustrated in **Fig. 110**, for example, are attributed to Bassano (near Venice).[34] The similarity in colours are obviously not evident in this black and white illustration, (the only photograph available), but the strange, 'doughnut' like flower-heads within the floral sprays (inset) are virtually identical to some that appear on Dublin delftware. (compare **Colour Plates 28** and **29 centre**). Comparison with French faience clearly suggests that the overall designs of this group of polychrome Dublin wares were copied from continental rather than English tin-glaze, which fits well with the documentary evidence.[35] (Mrs. Ann Day in 1762, for example, specifically remarked that some Dublin delftware was like *'Burgundy ware'*. (See p. 62).

These two polychrome Dublin pieces were first published in 1979, since when a number of other examples have been found. An important development was the discovery of a small selection of polychrome shards during the excavation of Dublin Castle, (a mile or so from the pottery), once more identified by Michael Archer, and described by Roseann Meenan.[36] **(Colour Plate 29)** Most of these shards consist of fragments of wavy-edged plates of various sizes and patterns. Although there is considerable variation in the style of flower painting, the colours employed are distinctive throughout and readily recognisable. On one shard, the flower sprig includes a *'tied ribbon'*, **(Colour Plate 29, right)** and this same, distinctive feature appears on a large, circular platter that has since been discovered in Dublin by Mairead Dunlevy of the National Museum. **(Colour Plate 30)**. Perhaps the most important feature of this circular platter is the fact that it bears a small, painter's number '6' under the rim, which firmly ties this entire group of polychrome floral designs to the Dublin pottery.

The highly distinctive character of these polychrome wares means that other, more unusual objects are also readily recognisable as Dublin products. Two polychrome *'epergnes'* or table-centres have now been found, one of which is illustrated in **Colour Plate 35**. (For some reason, only blue and white or manganese examples of these epergnes exhibit painters' marks).[37] Three polychrome candlesticks are also known. The first example recorded was a single candlestick in a private collection **(Colour Plate 34)**, recognised as Dublin by Michael Archer in 1996. Since then, Jonathan Horne has brought to light a matching pair, now in the Minneapolis Institute of Arts. **(Fig. 136)**. The pair of bough pots in the Knight of Glin's collection are equally rare objects, which very clearly demonstrate a French influence. **(Colour Plate 33)**. Viewed together, the coloured Dublin delftwares that have been identified to date add an entirely new aspect to the Dublin pottery. The delicacy of the painting and the soft, understated colours have few parallels in English delftware.

Almost all of these polychrome wares are very simply painted, with freehand, scattered floral sprays. The one exception is a small jar or vase, of extremely unusual form and decoration. **(Colour Plate 32)**. A number of features point to a Dublin attribution. Firstly the fountain, which is similar to one that appears on a Dublin cistern, **(Fig. 140)** and a Dublin vase, **(Fig. 178)**. Below this hangs a garland of flowers, which is similar to other polychrome flower sprigs. The column and hanging roots also match features that are found on some landscape-decorated wares, whilst the peculiar 'shell-edge' motif below the fountain is comparable to the surround on Dublin armorials. Presumably this wide-mouthed jar once possessed a lid, but its actual function remains unclear.[38]

It would be surprising to find that these polychrome designs, based on continental originals, were the only type of coloured wares produced in Dublin. Blue and white Liverpool delftware was widely copied in Dublin, yet Irish versions of Liverpool's polychrome *'Fazackerly-type'* wares seem to be entirely absent.

ARMORIALS

Armorial wares were first produced in Dublin by John Chambers in 1735, and as late as 1770 the Dublin potters continued to advertise delftwares decorated with *'coats of arms, crests, ... done in the most elegant manner'*. (See p.38 and p.65). It seems safe to assume, therefore, that armorial wares represented a standard item of production for as long as delftware was made in Dublin.

Identifying Dublin armorial delftwares is more difficult than might be expected, however, as it seems that such wares rarely bear a painter's mark. (Perhaps, if they were known to be the work of one, particular skilled individual, then the painter's

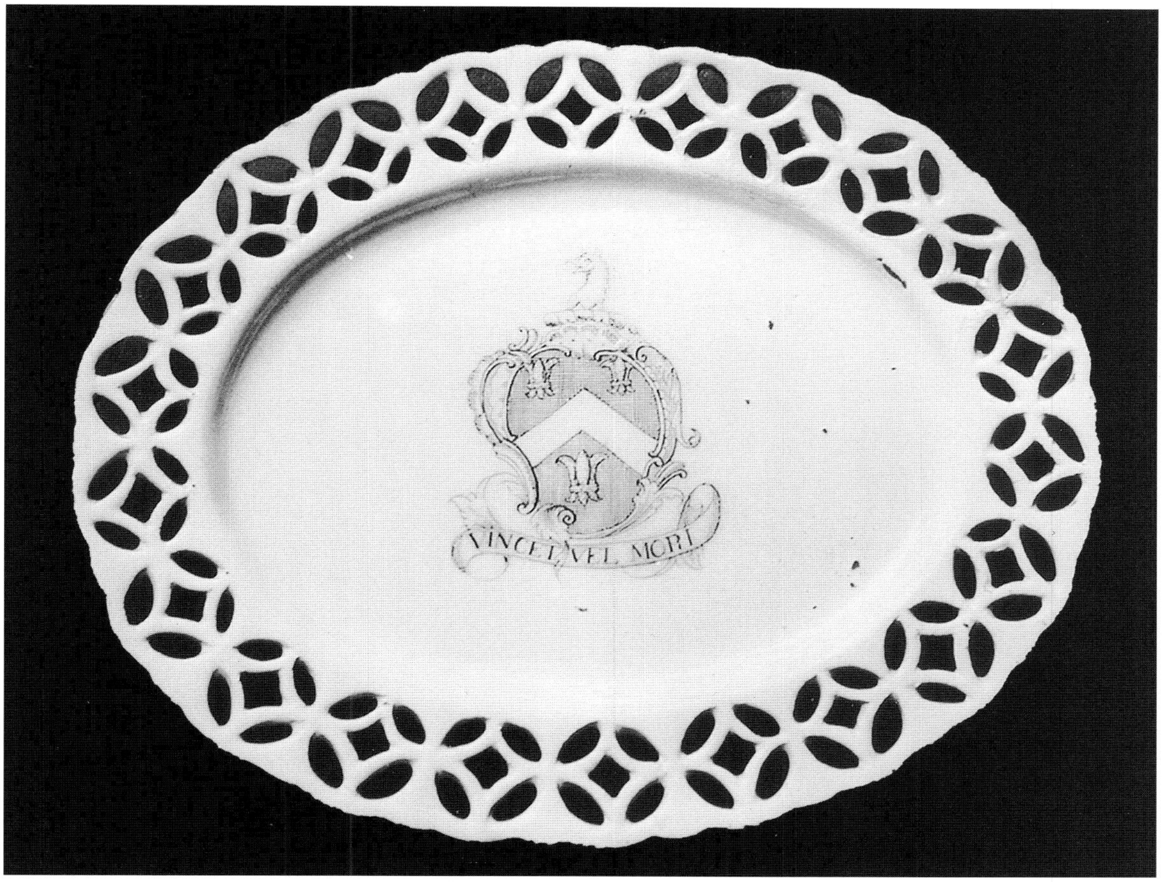

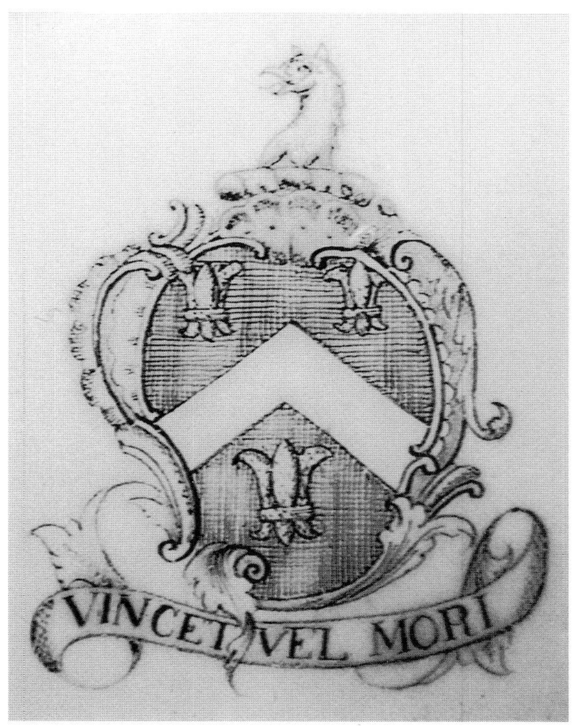

Above : Figure 111*. Dublin delftware armorial dish with pierced edges, of distinctive form. (See Figs. 124-5), bearing the arms of the Richards family, probably of Co. Wexford. 11 3/8 x 9 1/4 in., no mark.*

Right : Figure 111a*. Detail of Figure 111, showing coat of arms, painted entirely in blue.*

number or monogram was superfluous). We are aided by two examples that were indisputably made in Dublin; a pierced-edge plate of typical Dublin form, made for the Richards family, (probably of Co. Wexford, **Figs. 111, 111a**) and by the Delamain / Ranson service produced in 1762, **(Fig. 61, Colour Plate 11)**.[39]

One of the difficulties of identifying armorials is that many features are copied directly from other sources, such as bookplates. For example, both of these Dublin coats of arms are asymmetric, but this simply reflects prevailing rococo tastes, rather than representing a distinctive Dublin feature. The only conclusion that can be safely drawn from these armorials is that both are painted in the same, finely detailed and precise manner. They might well have

motto- incorrect latin
should read vincere vel mori - Victory or death

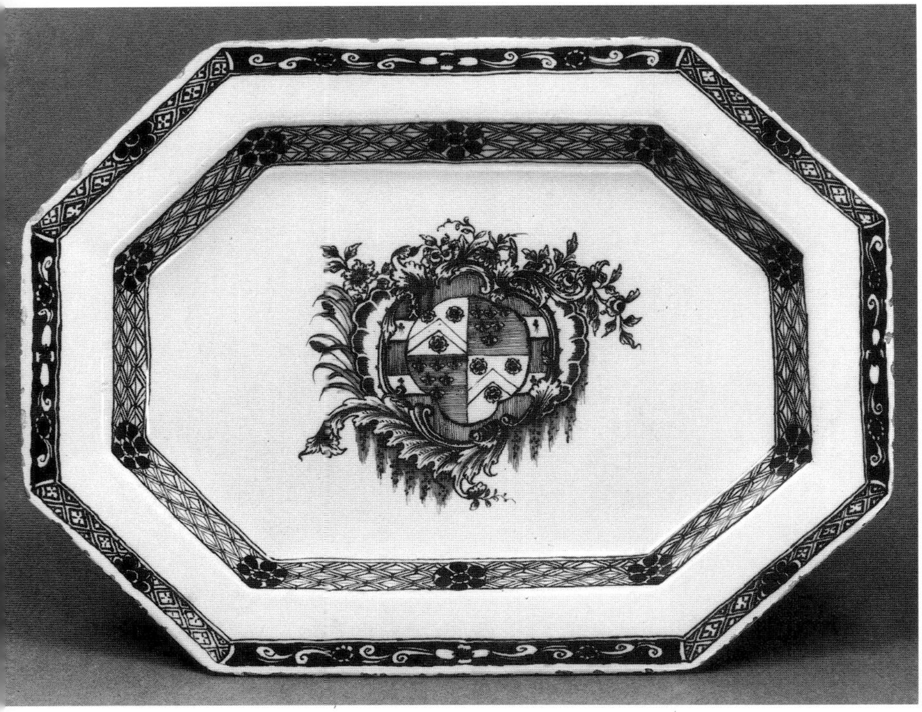

Figure 112. Delftware platter, probably Dublin, bearing arms of the Panton, Edwards and Wynne families, all of North Wales. Compare the border pattern on the plate illustrated in Fig. 88 left. L. 508 mm. No painter's mark.

been painted by the same hand, but there is no evidence to prove that this was the case. A wavy-edged surround occurs to the left side of each of the armorials, (reminiscent of the margin of a *'shell-edged'* creamware plate). These too are similarly painted, but otherwise there are few points of comparison.

Another armorial design that is probably attributable to Dublin occurs on an incomplete dinner service in the Colonial Williamsburg collection. **(Colour Plate 37, Figs. 112 & 112a)**.[40] The crest seems to represent the Panton, Edwards and Wynne families, all of Denbighshire in North Wales (just across the Irish Sea from Dublin). This same, distinctive, two-part border pattern is recorded on other, more obvious examples of Dublin delftware of the same form, most commonly on the *'Feathers in a Vase'* pattern **(Fig. 88, left)**. The finely detailed and precise armorial painting is very similar in style to the two Dublin armorials described previously, with the same 'shell-edge' surround again present to either side of an asymmetric crest. Other details within the rococo devices and flower garlands also correspond with known examples of Dublin delftware. No part of the surviving service seems to be marked with a painter's number or monogram, but otherwise they correspond with known Dublin delftwares in every respect.

The armorial tankard in Colonial Williamsburg, **(Figs. 113 & 113a)**, is a more unusual object, but there are grounds for believing that this too is Irish. The arms are interpreted as those of Lamb impaling Eyles of Coleshill, Co. Fermanagh.[41] A similar handle fragment is recorded in delftware biscuit from the site of the Thomas Greg's mid-eighteenth century pottery in Belfast **(Fig.196, p.155)**, but the armorial painting indicates that Dublin was the more likely source. The finely painted, asymmetric crest is again similar to those described previously, and the same 'shell-edge' surround is present. In addition, the small budded twig that appears out of

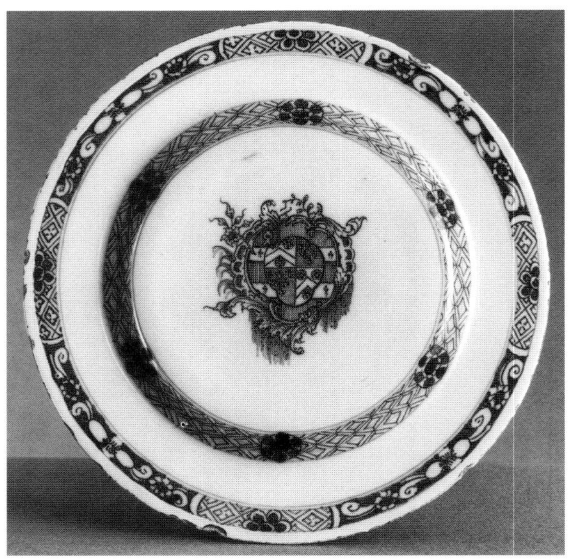

Figure 112a. A plate from the same part-service as the platter illustrated above. Six plates are recorded at Colonial Williamsburg, another example is in the National Museum of Wales in Cardiff. Diam. 235 mm. No painters' marks.

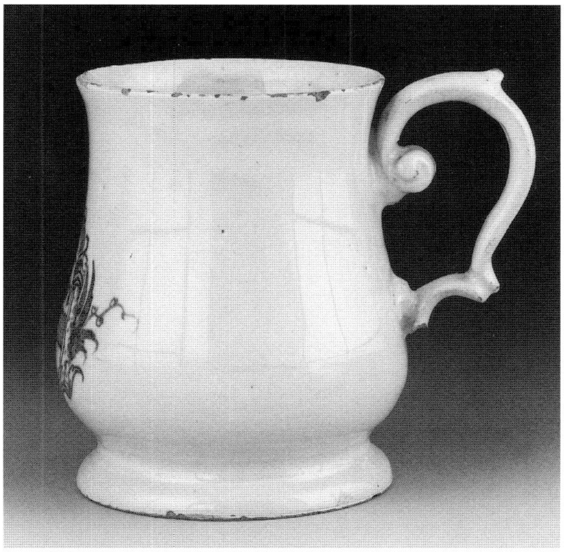

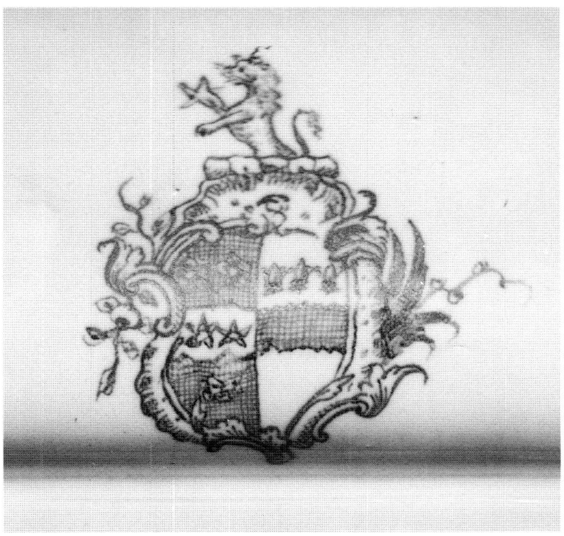

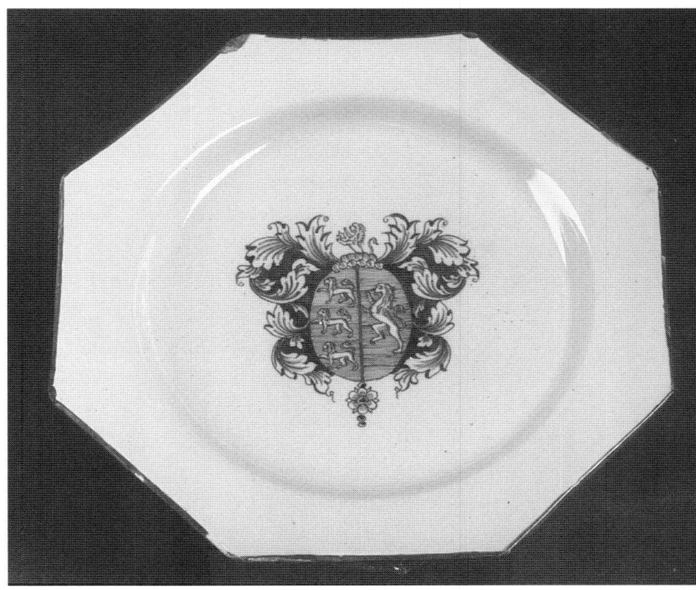

Above : Figures 113, 113a. *Baluster-bodied delftware mug or tankard of silver or pewter shape, painted with the arms of Lamb impaling Eyles of Coleshill, Co. Fermanagh. Probably Dublin. Ht. 95 mm. No painter's mark.*
Right : Figure 114. *Armorial delftware plate, probably English, possibly Irish, the arms perhaps for Ludlow of Shropshire/impaling Kynaston, or possibly of the O'Brien family, brown edged rim.*
Width 215, (side to side). No painter's mark.

the right hand side of the crest is a detail that occurs on other Dublin patterns (for example, amongst the shards recovered from Dublin Castle, **Fig. 154e, right**). not from a pottery context

There are therefore reasonable grounds for believing that all four of these armorials can be attributed to Dublin. Each one is different, but when viewed together they do seem to possess a coherent, common character. They all exhibit a high standard of draftsmanship, and the rococo devices, flower sprays, and 'shell-edge' surrounds are all painted in a similar, meticulous manner. All four feature an asymmetric crest, but this was obviously a prevailing fashion, not a characteristic that was unique to Dublin armorials.

It is useful to be able to compare four different Dublin armorials, but extending the range to embrace other armorial designs remains difficult, (especially as only one example - the Delamain/Ranson service - appears to bear the distinctive Dublin monograms). A number of armorial plates have been tentatively attributed to Dublin or Limerick in the past, but the principal difficulty in attributing these wares is that their designs were precisely copied from other sources. Armorial wares therefore possess comparatively few characteristics upon which an attribution can be reliably based. Two further examples serve to illustrate some of the problems.

The octagonal plate in **Fig. 114** originally appeared in the Castletown exhibition (No 10) as *'possibly Limerick'*, the tentative attribution being suggested on the basis of the Irish crest, brown edge, form, and the general similarity to the transfer-printed Limerick armorials **(Colour Plates 43-45)**. Since the Castletown exhibition, the arms have been re-interpreted as those of Ludlow of

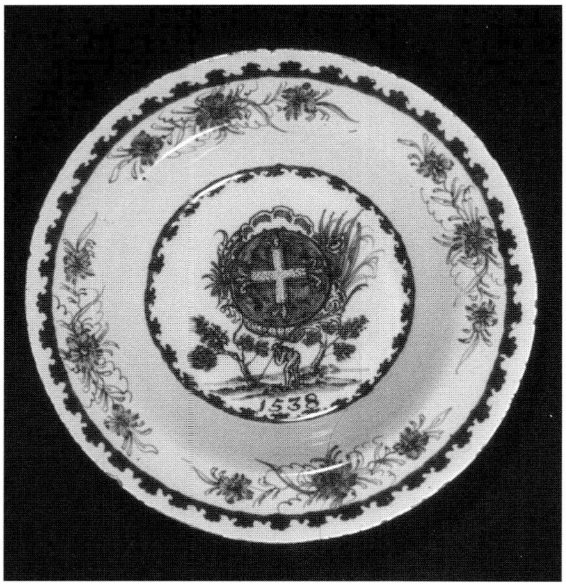

Figure 115. Delftware soup dish from a large service, decorated with arms identified as those of the Order of St. Cuthbert. English or Irish. Diam. 9¼ in., 235 mm. No painters' marks.

Shropshire/impaling Kynaston.[42] As we have already seen **(Fig. 112)**, at least one Dublin service was made for the Welsh market, and so the association with Shropshire (on the Welsh borders) does not necessarily preclude an Irish attribution. Apart from the fact that the arms are symmetrical, the overall painting style is comparable to the Dublin armorials described above, and certain details of the exuberant foliate mantling are very similar indeed. Yet there is no single detail of the painting or form that stands out as being unique. There is nothing in the plate's character or design to indicate that it is certainly English, but equally, if the coat-of-arms are not Irish, then there is no reason to postulate a Dublin origin. On balance, a probably English, *possibly* Irish attribution now seems reasonable for this piece.

The second, more unusual armorial **(Fig. 115)**, also appeared in the Castletown exhibition (No. 50). This is decorated with arms identified as those of the Order of St. Cuthbert.[43] (The style of cross is known as '*St Cuthbert's cross*'. The date '*1538*' presumably commemorates the destruction of St. Cuthbert's tomb during the dissolution of the monasteries). This large service has traditionally been associated with Dublin, and the character of the delftware itself is certainly compatible with known examples. Certain features of the decoration argue against a Dublin attribution, particularly the unusual central design and the style of flower painting in the borders, neither of which have been observed amongst other examples of Dublin delftware. On the other hand, now that several reliable examples of Dublin armorials have been recognised, we can see that several features of the central design compare well - particularly the 'shell-edge' surround above the arms, the foliate mantling below, and the grassy foliage to either side. (Compare, for example, the curved rushes that appear on the left side of the Panton/Edwards/Wynne armorial, **Fig. 112**). Despite these similarities, there is still insufficient evidence to positively establish a Dublin attribution - *'English or Irish'* remains the safest conclusion, but if more could be discovered about the Order of St. Cuthbert, then a more definitive attribution might still be possible. There is certainly a greater likelihood that this plate is Irish than the preceeding example **(Fig. 114)**.

OTHER INFLUENCES

We have seen that Dublin delftware designs were derived from a wide range of sources. Chinese export porcelains exerted by far the greatest influence, as was the case with most European potteries. It is sometimes difficult to tell, however, whether this influence came directly from Chinese porcelain, or indirectly, from Chinese designs that appeared on English ceramics.

French or continental tin-glaze seems have represented the primary inspiration behind Dublin's range of polychrome wares, and may have influenced their landscape-painted wares also. Dublin was probably more open to French trade and influence than any other city in the British Isles at this time, and Paris certainly appears to have been regarded as superior to London in matters of fashion.[44] As Henry Delamain indicated in some of his statements in 1753 (p. 55), Dublin may also have represented a significant marketplace for French ceramics, during the late 1740s and early 1750s especially. In 1750-52, for example, the French porcelain factory at Mennecy near Paris sold 3.6% of its entire output to a single dealer in Dublin named Irvin.[45] It is also worth recalling that William Delamain's son James was resident near Bordeaux throughout the 1760s, and was regularly sending consignments of brandy to Dublin.[46] Remarkably, some Dublin delftwares (painted with the *'Sampan Lake'* pattern) have also found their way into a small, local museum in the southern part of central France, where they are regarded as early examples of Limoges faience.[47] This could even suggest that some Dublin delftware was sold in France, perhaps sent by William Delamain with cargoes returning to his son in Bordeaux.

Amongst English ceramic manufacturers, associations with the Bow porcelain works in London seem to recur repeatedly. As we have seen (p. 57), Bow was founded by an Irish engraver, Thomas Frye, and the factory had several good wholesale customers in the city. Bow wares were obviously popular in Dublin, so it is perhaps to be expected that some Dublin delftware designs should be similar, but it is also possible that more direct, family connections existed. John Bowcock, a marketing agent for Bow, spent much of 1758 in Dublin arranging auctions, (p. 57). His wife, Ann Wilkinson, may have been the sister or daughter of Samuel Wilkinson, who became the co-manager of the World's End pottery from 1760.[48]

When we look beyond the documentary evidence, the influence of Bow can similarly be found repeatedly amongst Dublin delftwares. For example, Bow appears to have been the only English porcelain

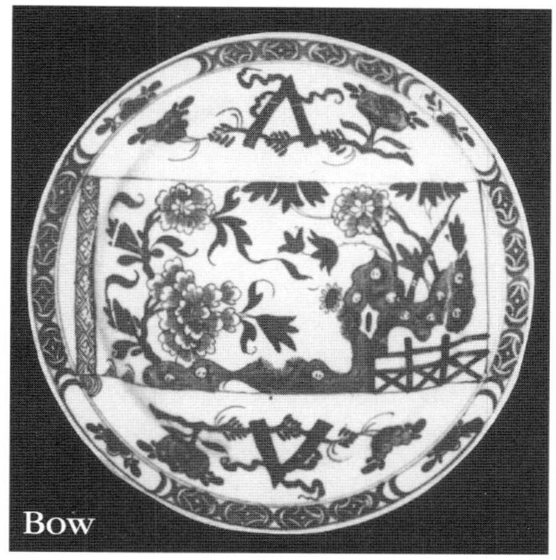

Figure 116. *'Broken Scroll' pattern Bow porcelain plate, c.1750-52. Diam. 223 mm.*

manufacturer to produce the *'Broken Scroll'* pattern, **(Fig. 116)**, one of the most popular Dublin delftware designs.[49] (*cf.* **Fig. 62.**). Bow also produced porcelain services of the *'Sampan Lake'* pattern, **(Fig. 117)**, which again was popular in Dublin delftware.[50] (Compare **Fig. 90**). More surprisingly perhaps, Dublin even copied some of Bow's more extravagant designs. When we compare the complex shell-form epergnes, for example, **(Figs. 146-148)**, Bow again

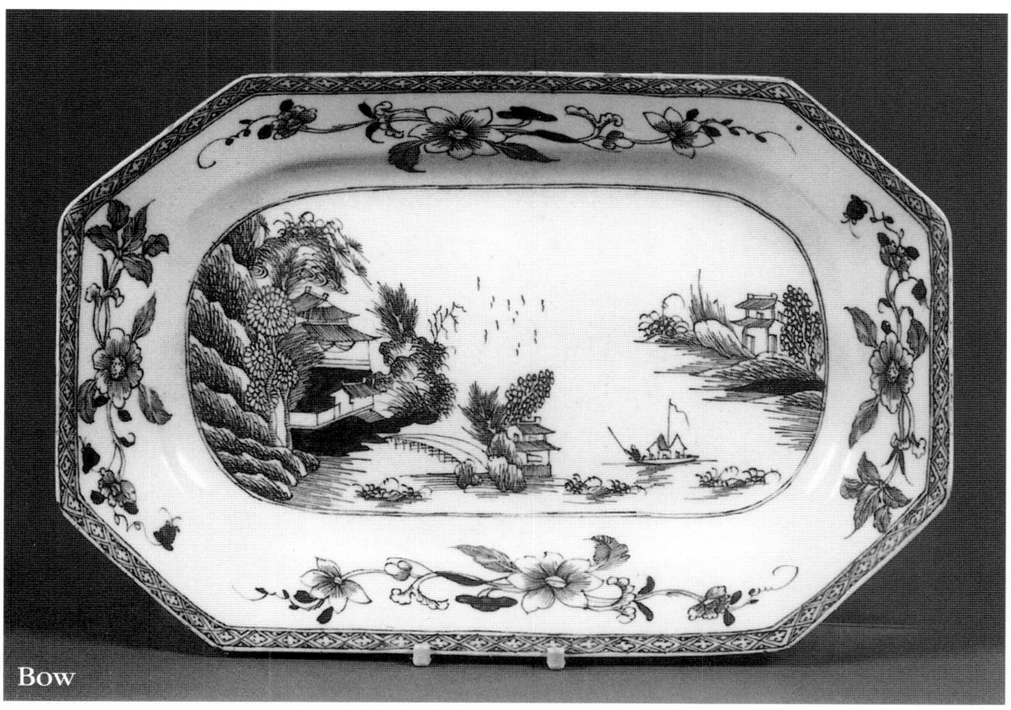

Figure 117. *'Sampan Lake' pattern Bow porcelain platter, c. 1755-60. L. 280 mm. Painter's number 20 in blue.*

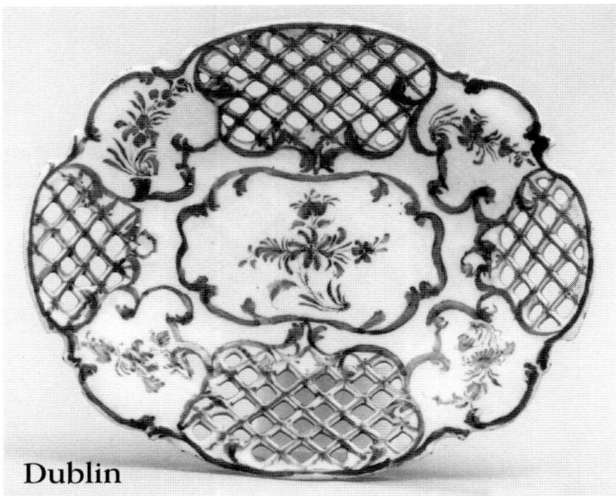

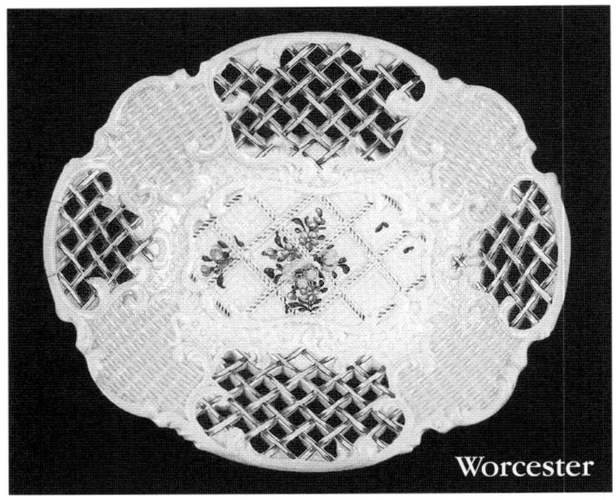

Left* : *Figure 118. *Dublin delftware moulded and pierced basket dish, painted in blue. L. 255 mm., no mark. Slightly different sizes are recorded. (See Fig. 123). The sides of this dish are more fully pierced than most Dublin examples.*

Right* : *Figure 119. *Worcester porcelain moulded and pierced basket dish. L. 258 mm. A dish of this type probably served as the original from which the Dublin mould was taken.*

appears to have represented the primary influence.[51] Many other, less significant coincidences exist.

Bow was by no means the only English porcelain manufacturer to sell in Dublin, but only one other instance of a direct influence has been observed. Moulded and pierced basket dishes, of the type illustrated in **Fig. 118**, are recognised as a distinctive Dublin form, but on closer inspection it is clear that the Dublin potters have simply lifted their mould for these baskets directly from a Worcester original, or possibly from one of Worcester's plaster moulds.[52] **(Fig. 119)**. Worcester porcelains were certainly on sale in Ireland at this time, and Henry Delamain may also have visited the Worcester factory in person in 1753 (Appendix II, Letter 1, 18th Dec. 1753).[53]

The most unusual design source in Dublin delftware, however, is represented by the three polychrome candlesticks **(Colour Plate 34**. See also **Figs. 136 & 137)**. These all appear to have been made in a two-part mould, lifted directly from a white, Staffordshire glass original. (See p.116). No other delftware factory is known to have produced wares imitating glass. The technique of using two-part moulds was not unique to Dublin, however. As Jonathan Horne has observed, a very fine pair of candlesticks decorated in *'Fazackerly'* colours was produced in Liverpool at about the same date. These also were made using a two-part mould, but in this case the mould was lifted directly from an original brass or silver candlestick.[54]

CHAPTER 2 • PART 2
DUBLIN DELFTWARE
iii : Forms

As the shards from the Belfast Potthouse have shown, the form of an object can sometimes provide the most reliable means of establishing an attribution. The following compilation of Dublin delftware objects does not pretend to be comprehensive. Many of the pieces illustrated are so widely dispersed throughout Europe and North America that it has been impossible to view more than a small selection at first hand, and the present whereabouts of several are unknown. Much can be gained from photographs, but some of the more problematic types of object, such as vases for example, will require more detailed study, if we are to clearly differentiate the Irish and English forms. Other types of object, such as plates and dishes, are now so numerous and varied that it has proven impractical to describe their entire range. The following list is therefore a preliminary study only, but one that hopefully will continue to grow.

For all its shortcomings, the list does tell us something new about the delftwares that were produced in Dublin. It is useful, for example, to be able to compare and contrast the full repertoire of Dublin delftware, to gain a broader understanding of the general quality of the wares. Certain types of object, such as the cisterns, wine barrels and epergnes, stand out as particularly distinctive, and might well have been unique to Irish delftware, (within the British Isles at least). An unexpected and perhaps more useful feature of this compilation is that it also allows us to understand something of the Dublin delftwares that have not yet been recognised. For example, only one form of Dublin delftware tureen has so far been recorded, but Mary Dorgan's advertisement of 1759 lists *'round and long Terenes scalloped and plain'*, (p.58). The known tureens are all *'long'* and *'plain'*, but we can gain some impression of the other forms we might expect to find from studying the shapes of the *'scalloped'* platters, painted with Chinese porcelain designs **(Fig.99)**, or the *'scalloped'* butter tubs **(Fig.134)**. In other words, the list provides a framework that helps us to understand both the Dublin delftware we know, and the Dublin delftware we have not yet met.

Larger works of this kind generally arrange the objects in broad categories according to their function, but this comparatively small range of forms is listed more simply in alphabetic order.[1]

BARRELS

As Michael Archer has observed, there has been a tendency in the past to attribute all barrels to Dublin.[2] The unusual, early-eighteenth century, barrel-shaped flask has already been discussed separately in the section concerning wares from the Belfast Potthouse (p.31, **Fig.40**), but amongst later eighteenth-century barrels, there appear to be two distinct types:

Small Barrels; under six inches in length, usually with a monochrome or powdered ground. These barrels possess a single hole on the side, often with a rectangular fitting around the aperture. This type of small, portable barrel appears to be exclusively English.[3]

Large Barrels; These range from 8½ to 11¾ inches (216 - 300 mm.), and are sometimes decorated with typical Dublin landscapes. Each possesses two holes - one on the side and another at one end, and there are no applied fittings around the aperture for tying on a cork. In total, only five of these large barrels appear to be recorded, at least three of which were certainly made in Dublin. There are grounds for believing that large barrels of this type may have been exclusively Irish.

The large barrels appear to be the only group that has associations with Ireland. The two most impressive are a manganese-painted pair, (11⅞ in., 300 mm. in length), which on each end bear the crest of the Molyneux family of Castle Dillon, near Armagh.[4] **(Fig. 120, Colour Plate 27)**, A similar but much smaller barrel, with no family crest or inscription, (L. 8½ in., 216 mm.), is painted in cobalt blue with a total of four different landscape scenes - two on either side of the body and one at each end.

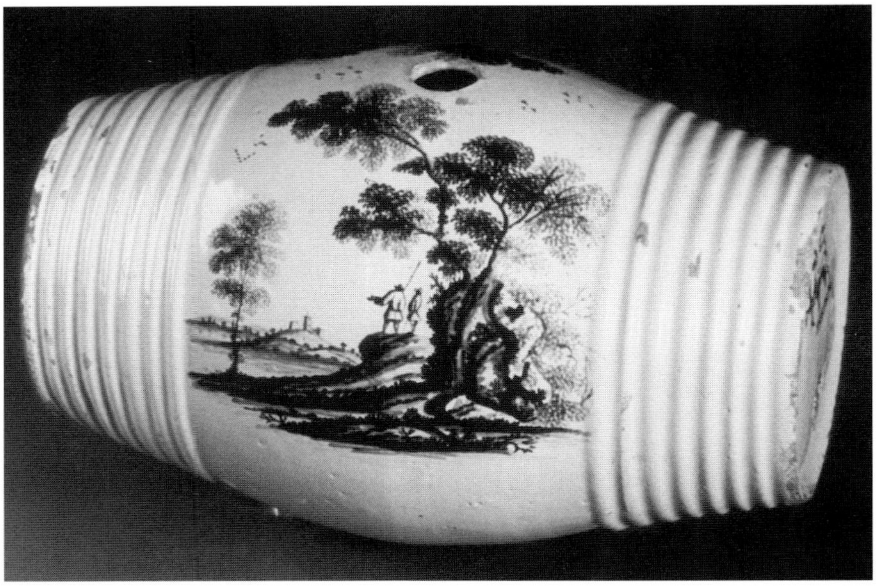

(**Figs. 121, 121a**).[5] No painter's mark is present on any of the five known large barrels, but the highly distinctive landscape painting indicates that these three, at least, were assuredly made in Dublin.

A fourth large-sized barrel (L. 9¼ in., 235 mm.) is more simply painted with a bunch of grapes on either end, and with flower sprigs to each side of the body. (**Figs. 122, 122a**).[6] Again, there is no mark, but otherwise the character of the painting and the glaze strongly suggest a Dublin attribution. (Compare, for example, the painting on some Dublin flower-bricks, **Fig. 150a**). The fifth example (L. 10¾ in., 274 mm.) is dated 1748, and thus has been tentatively attributed to Dublin during John Crisp's period of ownership. (See p. 42, **Fig. 51**). Four of these large barrels have a broad, plain, central band, with a series of 8 - 10 rounded, incised ridges at each end. (The spacing of the ridges is different on the earliest example, dated 1748). It is difficult to tell whether the barrels were formed using moulds, or were individually hand-thrown and incised. On the smallest, landscape-painted example (**Figs. 121, 121a**), the ridges have been highlighted with painted blue lines. This same feature occurs on the barrel dated 1748, and indeed, on both of the barrel-shaped objects that have been discussed in connection with the Belfast Potthouse (p.30, **Figs. 39 & 40**).

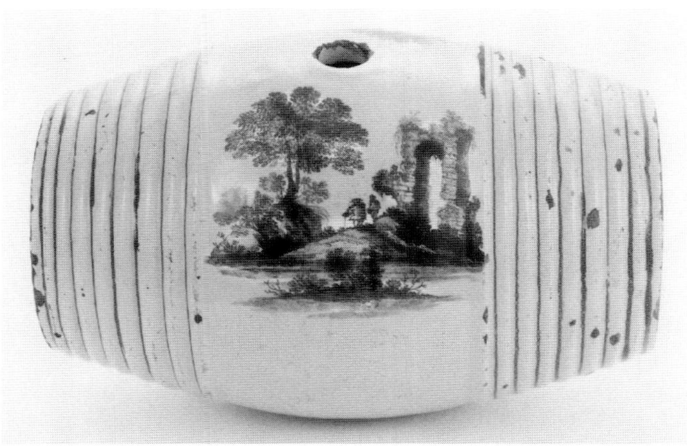

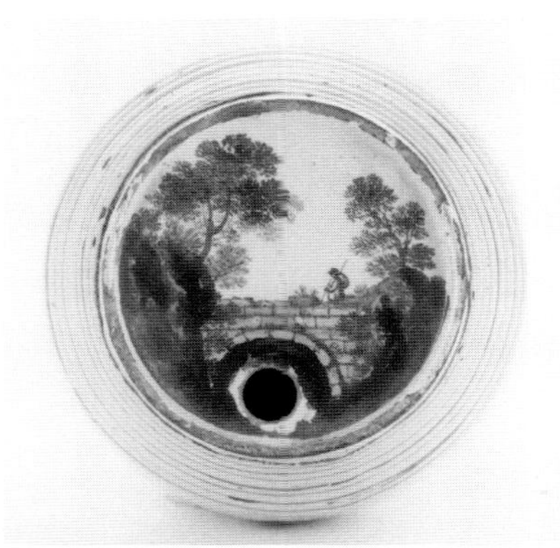

Unlike the small barrels noted above with a single aperture, the larger barrels were not intended as portable objects. They probably sat at table level on a wooden or metal cradle, with the side-hole to the top, allowing the contents to be dispensed by a tap inserted into the hole at one end. The three

*Top : **Figure 120**. Dublin delftware wine or brandy barrel, painted in manganese. One of a pair, each painted with European landscapes, and featuring the Molyneux crest on each end. L. 11⅞ in., 300 mm., girth 7⅝ in., 195 mm.*
***Middle : Figure 121**. Dublin delftware wine or brandy barrel, painted in cobalt blue, formerly Lipski coll. (Note the thin blue lines, highlighting the ridges at either end). Length 8½ in., 216 mm.*
***Bottom : Figure 121a**. End view of Fig. 121.*

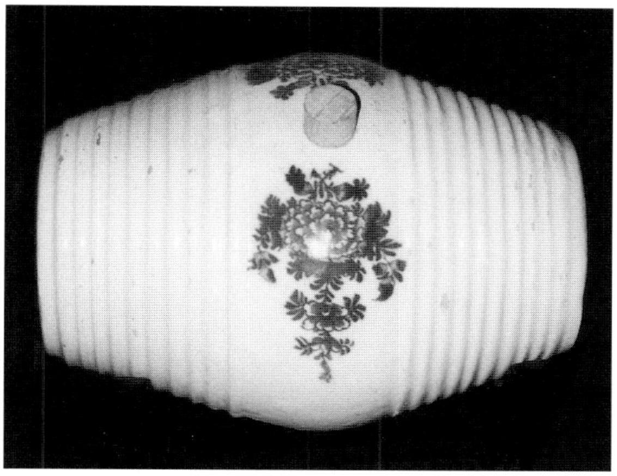

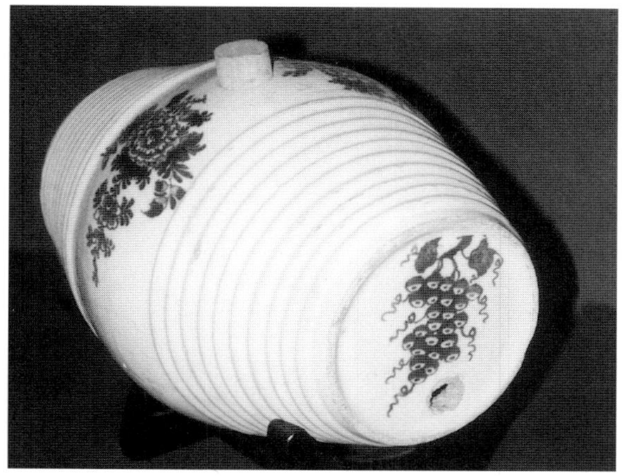

Left* : *Figure 122. *Delftware wine or brandy barrel, probably Dublin, painted in cobalt blue. Length 9¼ in., 235 mm. The very white, uneven glaze and details of the flower painting correspond with known Dublin wares.*
Right* : *Figure 122a. *End view of Fig. 122.*

fine quality landscape-painted barrels and the example with floral painting and grapes were almost certainly intended for use in private dining rooms. The other barrel, made during John Crisp's time **(Fig. 51)**, is more utilitarian in character, and hence may have been intended for use in an inn perhaps, rather than a private home.[7]

If all five of these pieces were made in Dublin, which seems possible, then it would appear that these large barrels, like wall cisterns (p. 118), were not produced elsewhere in the British Isles. There seems to be no obvious reason why such barrels should have been unique to Ireland. Dudley Westropp initially described such vessels as '*wine*' barrels in 1935, but he later corrected this to '*gin barrels*'.[8] Other authors have suggested they were used for dispensing beer, but the presence of painted grapes on one example suggests that wine remains the most likely answer. Another possible alternative is that they were intended for brandy, corresponding with the Delamain family's connections in that trade. Brandy and wine were just as popular in London as they were in Dublin, however, and comparable tin-glazed barrels seem to have been produced throughout Europe at about this time.[9] One possible explanation might be that the Irish market became familiar with this continental form through French faience, which seems to have been much more readily available in Ireland than in England. The apparent absence of obvious, English examples of large barrels is certainly puzzling.

BASKETS & PIERCED DISHES

Several types of Irish baskets and pierced-edge dishes are now recognised, although the attributions of this group of wares have been revised considerably in recent years, the Circular Baskets especially.

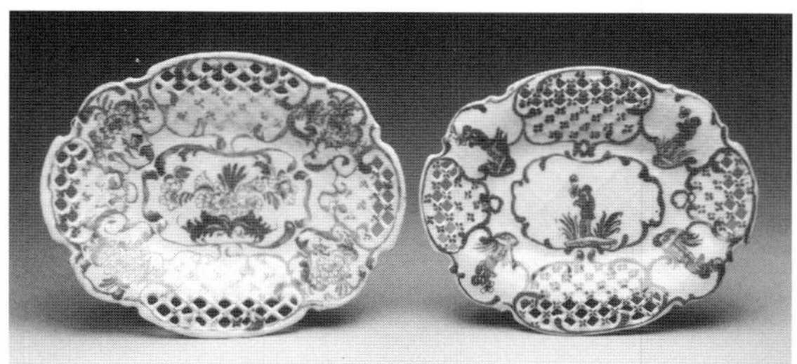

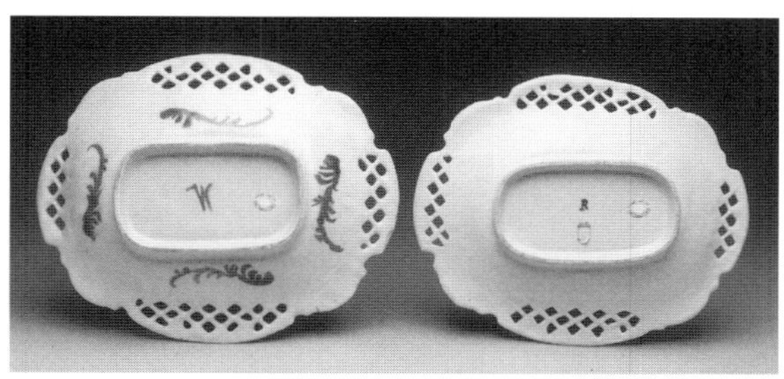

Top* : *Figure 123. *Two Dublin delftware Pierced Basket Dishes of identical form, demonstrating the size difference. Left Width 10in., 260mm. Right Width 9⅝ in., 245 mm.*
Bottom* : *Figure 123a. *The reverse of the dishes shown in Fig. 123. The footrim may have been applied separately. All known examples of these Pierced Basket Dishes are either unmarked, or bear a painter's monogram within the footrim.*

Documentary references exist for two different types of Dublin delftware basket. *'Fruit baskets'* were made by David Davis & Co. in 1749, (p.44), and were also listed among the Archbishop of Tuam's effects in 1752, (p.45). *'Bread Baskets'* were advertised for sale during Mary Delamain's time, in 1759, (p.58). It is difficult to be certain which of the various forms were referred to in these advertisements. The Circular Baskets described below are generally considered *'Fruit Baskets'*, whereas Deep Oval baskets are perhaps the most likely candidate for *'Bread Baskets'*.[10] Archer, pp. 334-6, also quotes late-eighteenth/early-nineteenth century references to sweetmeat and chestnut baskets in creamware catalogues.[11]

i. Pierced Basket Dishes

As noted previously (p.106), this style of pierced, basket dish was press-moulded, and appears to have been lifted directly from a Worcester porcelain dish, or possibly from one of Worcester's original plaster moulds. The sides of the Dublin delftware example illustrated in **Fig. 118** have been fully pierced, whereas the holes on the two illustrated here **(Figs. 123, 123a)** remain partly filled, but otherwise the form is identical throughout.

On all three of the dishes illustrated, the tall, well-formed footrim has probably been applied separately. The painted decoration on the example illustrated in **Fig. 123, right**, represents a detail from the *'Flower Lady'* pattern, one of the commonest of the earlier, 'monogrammed' Dublin patterns, which sometimes occurs with an *'NE'* monogram. The floral decoration on the remaining two baskets is more unusual, comparing more closely with floral decoration on Dublin polychrome wares than with most blue and white designs.**(Figs. 118, 123 left)**.

The considerable variation in size suggests that these baskets were produced for a number of years. (Size reductions occurred when additional biscuit-ware moulds were taken from the original, master mould). All of the marked examples recorded to date bear monograms within the footrim, which suggests they were not produced after the early 1760s.

ii. Pierced Oval Dishes

These shallow dishes also appear to have been press-moulded, and they are therefore of identical form throughout, although (as we have seen with the Pierced Basket Dishes above), the size is not necessarily constant. (Widths vary from 10⁵/₈ in,

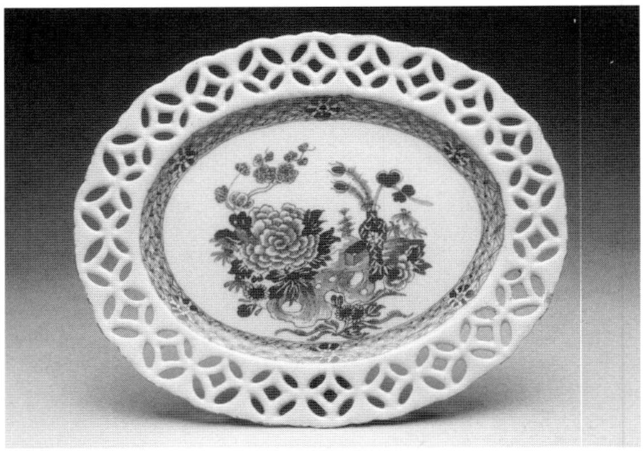

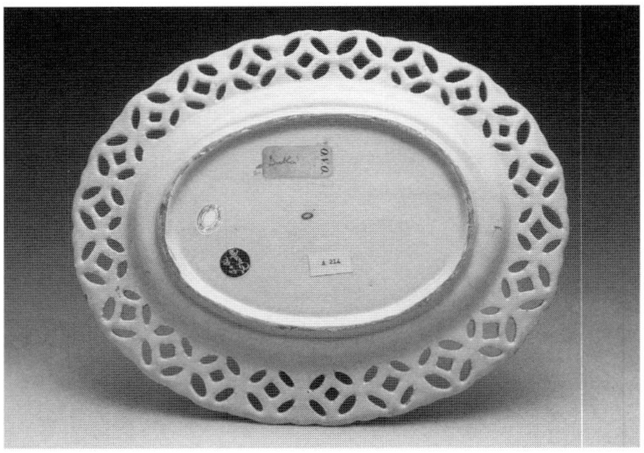

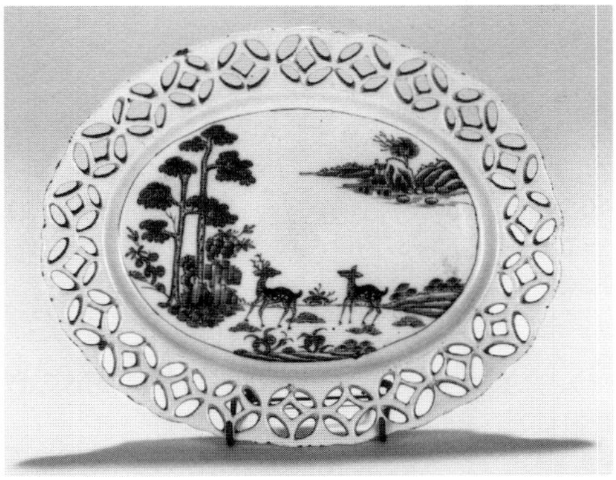

*Top : **Figure 124**. Dublin delftware Pierced Oval Dish, 'Feathers in a Vase' pattern, of typical form with 22 pierced 'cash' symbols around the margin. The dish also clearly indicates that painter's number '0' occurs on Dublin delftware. Width 11½ in., 290 mm.*

***Middle : Figure 124a**. Reverse of Fig. 124.*

***Bottom : Figure 125**. Dublin delftware Pierced Oval Dish, 'Two Deer & Pagoda' pattern, painter's number '8' within footrim on reverse. Width 10⁵/₈ in., 270 mm.*

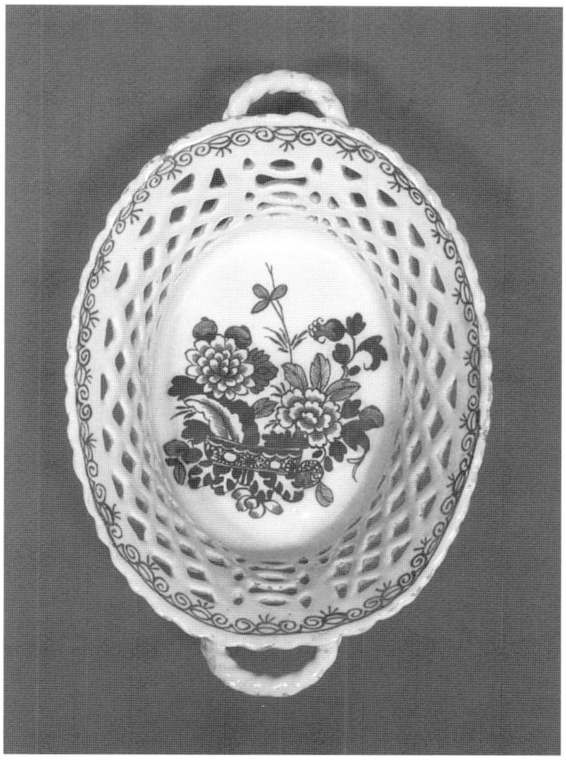

270mm. to 11½ in., 290 mm.). The slightly wavy edge is pierced with 22 circular motifs in the form of Chinese '*cash*' symbols. There is a small, well-formed oval footrim on the reverse, but otherwise the profile is almost flat, with a shallow central well.

The two examples illustrated in **Figs. 124 & 125** are typical of this readily recognisable Dublin form. (An armorial example is shown in **Fig. 111**). Both are painted with designs derived from Chinese porcelain - the '*Feathers in a Vase*' and '*Two Deer & Pagoda*' patterns, bearing the painter's number '0' and '8' respectively within the footrim. (A further example, painted with the '*One Bird*' pattern, **Fig. 102**, is recorded in a private collection, which bears painter's number '1' within the footrim). No monogrammed examples are recorded, suggesting that all of these Pierced Oval Dishes probably date from the 1760s. (They thus post-date the more complex, monogrammed, Pierced Basket Dishes described above in section i).

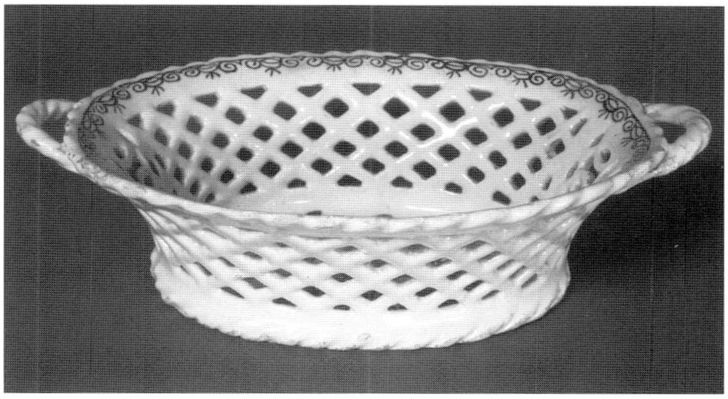

There appear to be few English delftware dishes of comparable form, although Worcester porcelain and white salt-glazed examples are recorded.[12] Creamware dishes of similar form in Wedgwood's 1774 catalogue suggest they may originally have been intended as stands for oval baskets, (possibly the Deep Oval Baskets described below).[13] The painted patterns on these pierced oval dishes mainly copy Chinese porcelain designs, which would tend to suggest that each one originally formed part of a dinner service.

iii. Deep Oval Baskets

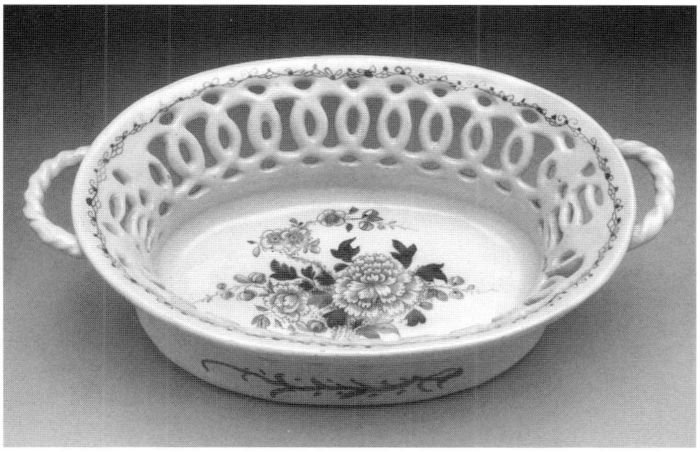

Only two of these Deep Oval Baskets have been recorded. It is impossible to conclusively establish that they are Irish, but details of the painted decoration, the character of the glaze, and the unusually white ground colour, all strongly suggest that both examples were probably made in Dublin. The two baskets initially appear identical, but the

Top : ***Figure 126***. *Delftware Deep Oval Basket, probably Dublin, cross-hatched piercing, 'Chinese Flower-bowl' pattern, no mark. L. 10⅝ in., 270 mm., W. 7 in., 180 mm., Ht. 2¾ in., 70 mm.*

Middle : ***Figure 126a***. *Side view of Fig. 126*

Bottom : ***Figure 127***. *Delftware Deep Oval Basket, probably Dublin, pierced 'intersecting' circles, no mark. L. 12 in., 305 mm., W. 7½ in., 190 mm., Ht. 3⅜ in., 80 mm.*

pierced patterns of their sides are entirely different. The first **(Figs. 126, 126a)** is pierced with a cross-hatched pattern, has a wavy top edge, and a rope-twist basal edge. The other, slightly smaller basket, **(Fig. 127)** is pierced with a pattern of *'intersecting circles'*, (see p.113), and has plain top and basal edges. Despite these differences, there are a number of common features. Both are very similar in their overall form, both have looped, rope-twist handles, and their flat, unglazed bases are virtually identical. Neither basket bears a painter's mark.

The example illustrated in **Fig. 126**, painted with the *'Chinese Flower-bowl'* pattern, was first recorded at auction in London in 1986 and was published shortly afterwards by Dennis Cockell.[14] The attribution in the auction catalogue, *'probably Dublin'*, was considered plausible by Cockell, and is further supported by at least one authority on delftware.[15] The *'Chinese Flower-bowl'* pattern, as we have seen in **Colour Plate 13**, can as often be English as Irish, but details in the flower painting and some of the other characteristics mentioned above, reinforce the Dublin attribution of this example.

The second basket, in a private collection in England, is more anomalous. The pierced pattern of *'intersecting circles'* on the sides is unlike the majority of known Irish circular baskets, (see below) which are pierced with a pattern of *'touching circles'*. In addition, the painted floral design on the interior is not a well-recognised Dublin pattern. On closer examination, however, different elements of the composition correspond closely to painting on known pieces of Dublin delftware. The most convincing match lies in the three distinctive, five-petalled *'plum tree'* flowers at the top of the design, which are identical to flowers on the spout of the *'Armstrong jug'*, **(Colour Plate 26)**.[16] A *'probably Dublin'* attribution therefore seems reasonable for this basket also.

It is possible that these Deep Oval Baskets were intended as *'bread baskets'* originally, although this is purely conjecture. It is also possible that they would have sat on flat, oval stands, similar to the Pierced Oval Dishes described in section ii above. This would be a more convincing possibility, however, if the patterns of the piercing also matched.

iv. Circular Baskets

Circular baskets of approximately this form were popular in a variety of ceramics over a long period of time. The earliest seem to occur in Japanese Arita porcelains of the late-seventeenth century, and the same shape was still produced by Worcester in the 1770s.[17]

For reasons that will presently become obvious, these Circular Baskets are most easily classified on the basis of the pierced design on the sides. The two basic patterns will be discussed in turn;

a. Baskets with *'touching circle'* sides
b. Baskets with *'intersecting circle'* sides

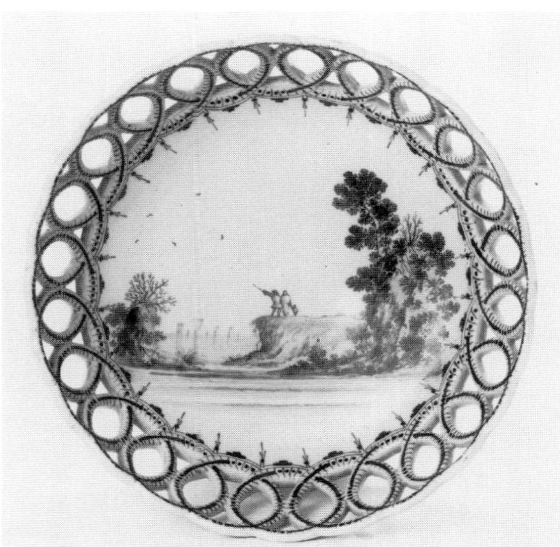

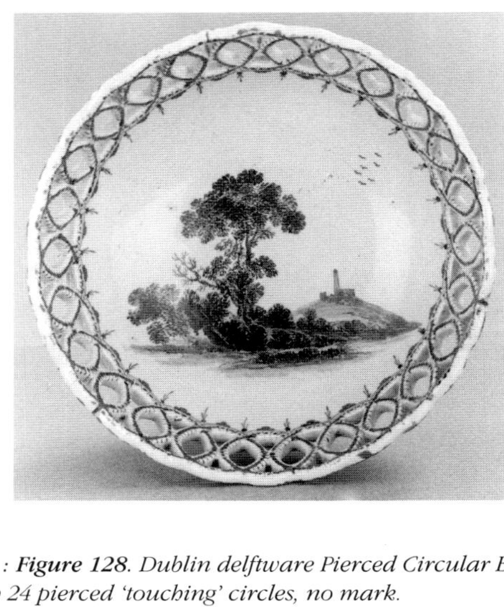

Left : Figure 128. *Dublin delftware Pierced Circular Basket, with 24 pierced 'touching' circles, no mark. Diam. 8½ in., 215 mm.*

Above Right : Figure 129. *Dublin delftware Pierced Circular Basket, with 26 pierced 'touching' circles, no mark. Diam. 6½ in., 165 mm.*

iv, a. Baskets with *'touching circle'* sides

Figs. 128 and 129 illustrate one of the most familiar Dublin delftware forms, the pierced Circular Basket. All but one of the Dublin baskets identified to date exhibit the same pattern of pierced circles around the sides, with the circles spaced so that each one touches its neighbour in the middle of the adjoining circle. Most are unmarked, but at least two examples are painted on the base with a crowned harp and *'Dublin'*. (One of these is illustrated in **Colour Plate 19, and Fig. 59**). The second marked example, illustrated by Westropp in 1935, was one of three in the possession of the Stopford Sackville family in 1913, which may have been made during Henry Delamain's lifetime for the Lord Lieutenant of Ireland, Lionel Sackville, or for Lord George Sackville. Three further unmarked examples are illustrated in the Castletown catalogue, (Castletown 25, 26 and 27). The only style of decoration recorded on baskets of this type seems to be fine quality, European romantic landscapes.

Although the pattern of the piercing is identical throughout, the actual number of *'touching circles'* varies. One basket in the National Museum of Ireland, (Castletown 27) bears 23 *'touching circles'*, the two examples illustrated in **Figs. 128 & 129** have 24 and 26 respectively, and the Stopford Sackville basket illustrated by Westropp possesses 27. A preliminary scan of published examples also suggests that there is no direct correlation between the number of circles and the diameter of the dish.

Circles	Diameter
23	160mm.
24	215mm., 215mm.
26	165mm., 165mm., 212mm.
27	160mm.

Porcelain baskets of identical form are made in Japan to this day, where the potter usually begins by impressing the pattern of the pierced circles lightly around the bowl's exterior.[18] Each pierced section is then individually cut and removed with a long, straight scalpel blade. Presumably, Dublin baskets were produced in the same manner, in which case the variation that we see in the number of circles has no useful, diagnostic significance.

iv, b. Baskets with *'intersecting circle'* sides

The presence of Dublin marks on some baskets meant that the majority of Circular Baskets were once considered Irish. Research by Dennis Cockell and others during the 1980s led to a re-evaluation, however, one consequence of which was that three of the baskets in the Castletown catalogue are now considered English.[19] It therefore appeared, until very recently, that the only baskets that were attributable to Dublin were those of *'touching circles'* type, even though this meant there was a peculiar lack of Dublin baskets decorated with more standard designs, based on Chinese porcelains.

Recently, Garry Atkins discovered a basket in London that was probably made in Dublin, but pierced with a pattern of *'intersecting'* rather than *'touching'* circles. **(Fig. 130)**.[20] This is decorated internally with the *'Chinese Flower-bowl'* pattern, a pattern that is common on both English and Irish wares. On the underside, within the footrim, is the painter's number '14', and around the outside are three further *'under-rim flourishes'*. The first clue that this bowl may have been made in Dublin comes from the painter's number, which is painted in a well-recognised and distinctive style. (The '1' lies at an unusual angle, parallel to the upstroke of the '4'. The same feature was noted on the excavated bowls from Virginia, **Fig. 71**). The

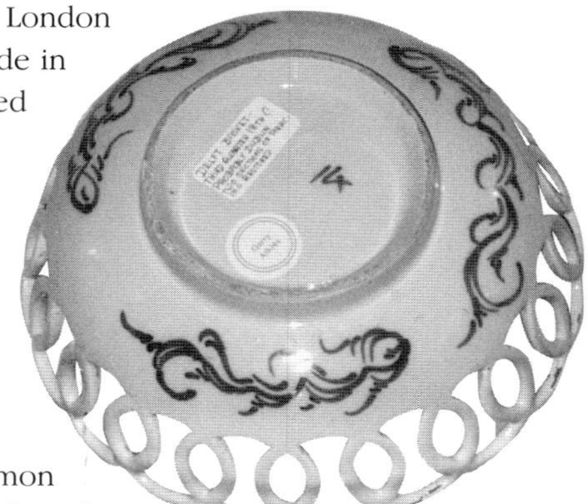

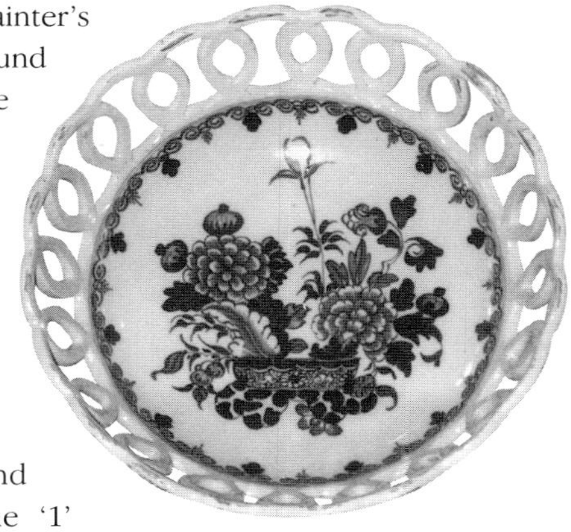

Above Right : Figure 130, 130a. *Delftware Pierced Circular Basket, probably Dublin, with 20 pierced 'intersecting' circles.. Approx. Diam. 7¹/₄ in., 185 mm.*

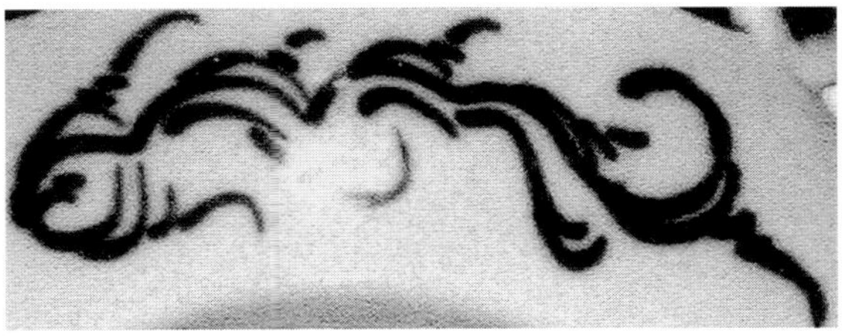

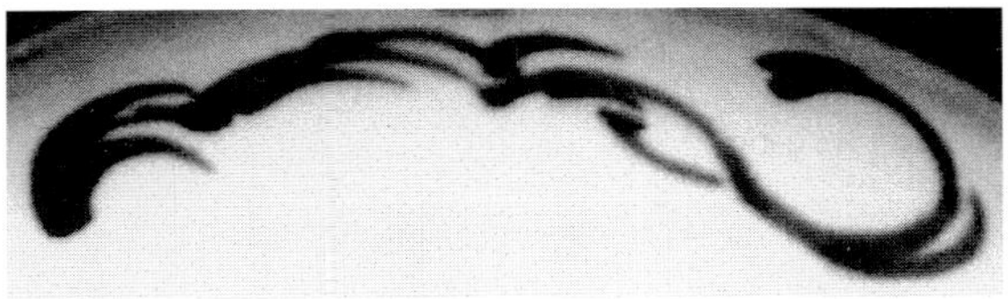

Figure 131. Comparison of 'Under-rim markings' on the Circular Pierced Basket (Fig. 130) and a Dublin delftware saucer-dish bearing painter's number 14, (bottom).

additional under-rim flourishes around the edge also compare closely with flourishes that appear on the underside of a large, Dublin delftware saucer-dish, in a private collection, **(Fig. 131)**, which similarly bears the painter's number '14', suggesting they might well have been painted by the same hand. Other features, such as the enlarged trefoil motif on the internal painted border, add to the probability that this basket was produced in Dublin.

Unfortunately, only comparatively poor quality photographs are available, and the dimensions are not recorded. There are 20 intersecting circles around the side, but as we have seen with the '*touching circles*' group, this number was probably not a constant feature. Nonetheless, it is significant that this new form has been recorded, as it allows many other baskets that were previously dismissed out of hand as English to now be considered more closely.

v. Other Basket Forms

Other designs of delftware basket are known which bear pierced patterns around the sides that are neither '*touching*' nor '*intersecting*' circles. None of the examples presently known appears to be Irish. One example is illustrated, however, to demonstrate just how similar English and Irish delftwares can sometimes be.

The basket illustrated, **(Fig. 132)**, in a private collection in London, bears the painter's number '8' on the underside **(Fig. 132a)**. A similar dish, painted with the same scene, is recorded with the painter's monogram '*ED*'.[21] The wavy edge and piercing of this example are identical to a slightly smaller basket illustrated in the Castletown catalogue, (Castletown 29), marked with a painter's number '4'. Both of the painted patterns resemble designs that appear on Dublin delftware, although it is significant that they are not recorded on more obvious Dublin forms, such as plates or platters for example. A much more complex form of basket is recorded by Archer, (G. 17), which is painted with a virtually identical scene, quite possibly by the same hand.

The presence of a painter's numbers on the reverse is usually a good indication that a piece might be Irish, but on closer inspection, the numbers that appear on these baskets are unlike examples recorded on Dublin delftware. The painted scene, although very reminiscent of Dublin landscapes, has a softer, more atmospheric style, and the tone of the cobalt blue would be unusually light for Dublin. This basket was therefore more probably made in England, possibly in Bristol, as Archer has suggested for the similar basket in the Victoria and Albert Museum.[22]

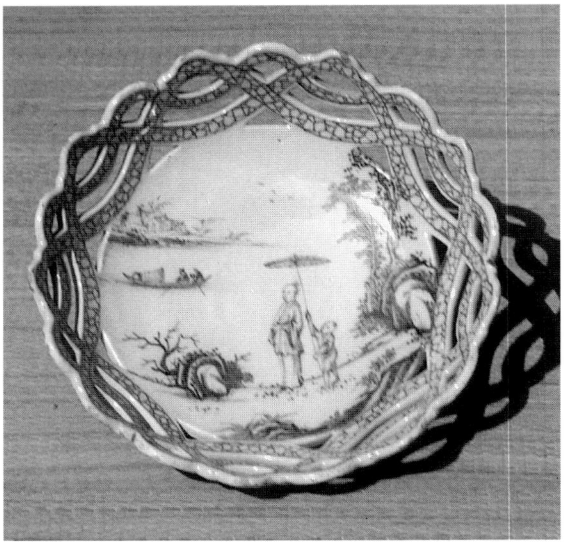

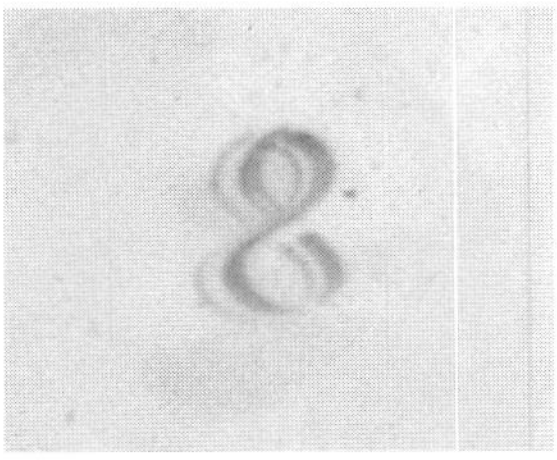

Figures 132, 132a. Delftware basket, probably Bristol, c.1760, with painter's number 8 on reverse. Another dish belonging to this group bears the painter's monogram 'ED'. Diam. c. 9½ in., 242 mm.

BOUGH POTS

Flat-backed bough pots were produced in large quantities by continental tin-glaze potteries, but they seem to be rare in English delftware. A few blue and white Liverpool examples have been recorded, but the form seems to have been more common in porcelain.[23] A wavy-edged bough pot produced at Chelsea in c.1753-55 is very similar in overall appearance to the Dublin pair.[24] **(Colour Plate 33)**. Mary Dorgan's description in 1759 of '*curious flower pots ... in Delamain's ware*', (see p. 58), may refer either to bough pots or to flower bricks.

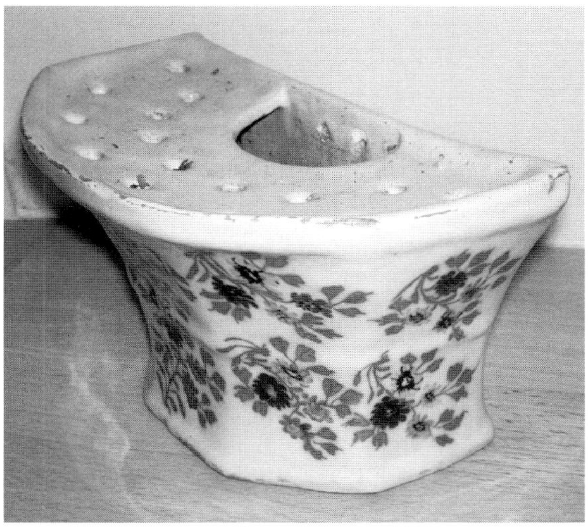

Each of the Dublin examples **(Fig. 133, Colour Plate 33)** has five facets on the convex front, a flat back pierced with two holes for suspension and 15 pierced holes on top, all formed before the biscuit firing. Both pots seem to have been slab-built, the front side (at least) having been press-moulded into a shaped former. There is a pronounced ridge around the waist of each pot. (A similar feature on the Chelsea example is painted to simulate a tied ribbon). On the base, the broad footrim around the thickened edge has been wiped free of glaze.

Above : Figure 133*. One of a pair of Dublin delftware Bough Pots, the only examples yet recorded. Ht. 4³/₄ in., 120 mm., W. 7³/₄ in., 195 mm., No marks. (See Colour Plate 33).*

Right : Figures 134, 134a*. Dublin delftware butter-tub and stand, blue painted 'parasol flower' pattern. Painters' marks 4 (on tub) and 9 within footrim (on stand). The pair to this tub and stand bears painter's number 2 throughout. L. Tub 5³/₄ in. 143mm., Stand 7¹/₄ in., 181 mm., Ht. Tub & Cover 3³/₄ in., 95 mm.*

The glaze on the reverse side of both examples is extremely uneven, and on the underside has pulled away entirely from the footrim to leave large areas of biscuit and under-slip exposed. On one example, there is a slight dusting of errant cobalt blue on the reverse, perhaps caused by finger-marks.

The attribution of these bough pots is based solely on their polychrome decoration, but the character of the glaze also conforms well to known Dublin delftware. As they were made in a mould or former, the form itself should also be diagnostic of Dublin, irrespective of the painted decoration.

BUTTER TUBS (AND STANDS)

Only one basic form of covered butter tub has so far been attributed to Dublin, although two different sizes are known and there are some minor variations in the applied details. **(Figs. 134 & 135)**. The body and cover of each tub has been press-moulded, with cylindrical, vertical flutes on the exterior. This vertical fluting is clearly defined on the lower part, and carries through onto the conical lid, where it gradually fades towards the knop. As

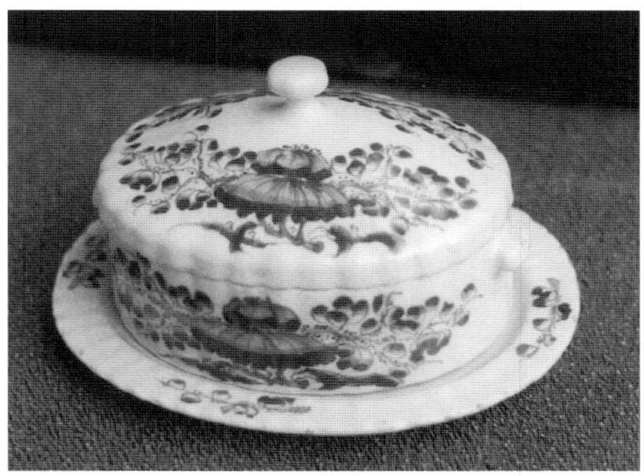

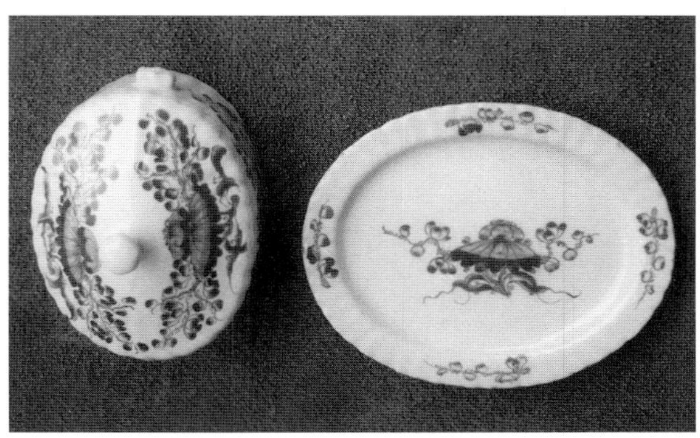

Michael Archer observed in 1971, this particular fluted form does *'not appear to have been used outside Ireland'*. (Castletown, p. 31).

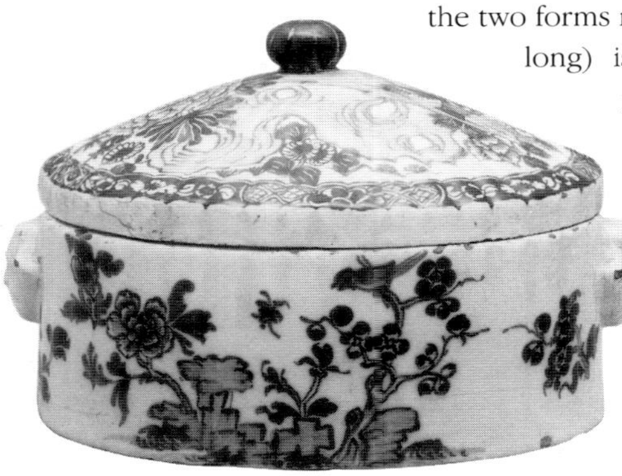

The first example, the smaller of the two forms recorded, ($5\frac{3}{4}$ in. long) is one of a pair painted with a pattern featuring the familiar *'parasol flower'*.[25] The crude handles on either end are little more than raised rectangular knobs, and on the lid, the rounded hexagonal knop is set on a short stalk. The underside is glazed and flat, with the painter's number '4' in the centre.

The original stand for this tub has also survived. This has moulded, wavy edges, mirroring the fluting on the tub, a well-defined oval footrim, and the painter's number '9' within the footrim. (The pair to this tub and stand, at Colonial Williamsburg, is marked with painter's number '2' throughout).

This particular pair of butter tubs are an important Dublin attribution, as they convincingly demonstrate that delftwares painted with this distinctive *'parasol flower'* were produced in Ireland. (In the past, the pattern was generally attributed to Glasgow, because of the profusion of small dots around the foliage. This is a noticeable characteristic of some delftwares with Scottish inscriptions and crests, which were undoubtedly produced at Delftfield).[26]

The second, larger type of butter tub, ($7\frac{1}{10}$ in long), in a private collection, is of very similar form. This possesses the same, vertically fluted body, but the handles are quite different, representing small, moulded face-masks, (similar to the large, open-mouthed face masks that occur on full-sized Dublin tureens - **see Fig. 171**). The knop is also shorter and more rounded than on the smaller tubs. The painted *'One Bird'* pattern occurs on a wide variety of Dublin wares of the 1760s, **(e.g. Fig. 102)**. This example also bears the painter's number '11' on the base and inside the lid.

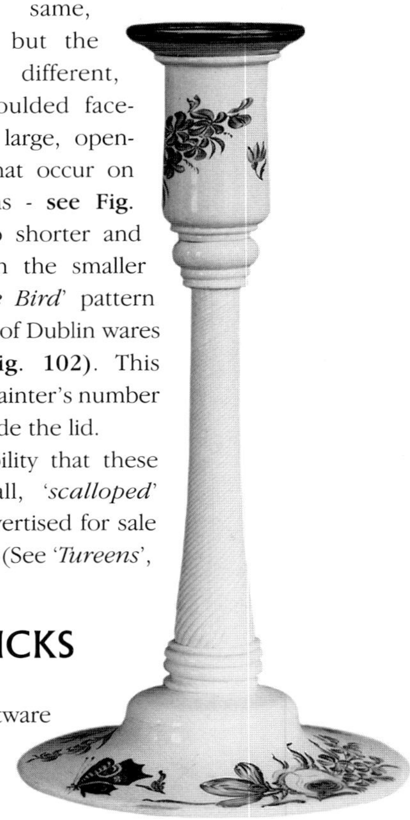

There is a possibility that these objects represent small, *'scalloped'* tureens, which were advertised for sale by Mary Dorgan in 1759. (See *'Tureens'*, p.133).

CANDLESTICKS

Three Dublin delftware candlesticks are presently known, (a pair and a single), all similar in size and decorated in polychrome with painted floral sprigs. **(Fig. 136, Colour Plate 34)**. Certain features, particularly the

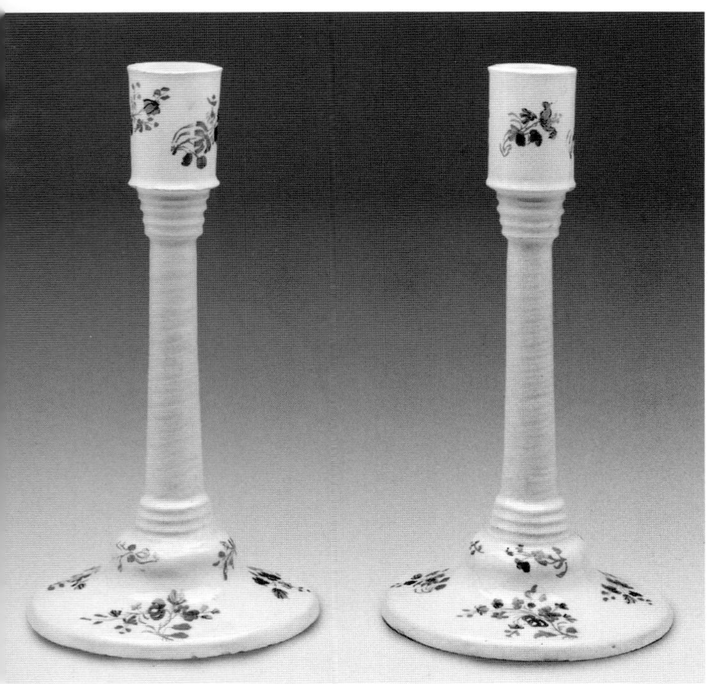

Top Left : Figure 135. *Dublin delftware butter-tub, or small tureen, blue painted 'One Bird' pattern. Painter's number 11 on flat, glazed base and inside lid.*
L. $7\frac{1}{10}$ in., 180 mm., Ht. 5 in., 125 mm.

Left : Figure 136. *The only recorded pair of polychrome Dublin delftware candlesticks, no marks, (See also Colour Plate 34). Ht. $9\frac{5}{16}$ in., 236 mm.*

Above Right : Figure 137. *White glass candlestick (one of a pair), with incised spiral-twist stem, probably made in South Staffordshire, c.1755-60. Painted floral sprigs in polychrome enamel. The sconce is fitted with a detachable metal liner. Ht. $9\frac{3}{8}$ in., 238 mm., Diam. $4\frac{7}{8}$ in., 123 mm.*

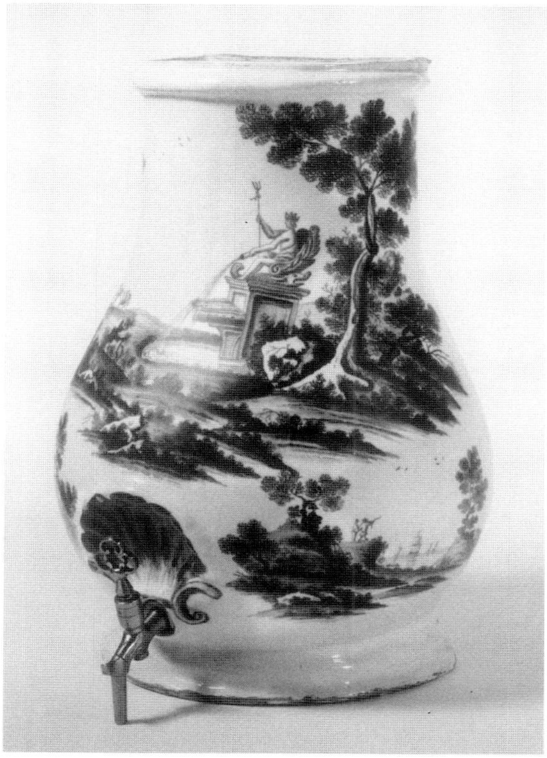

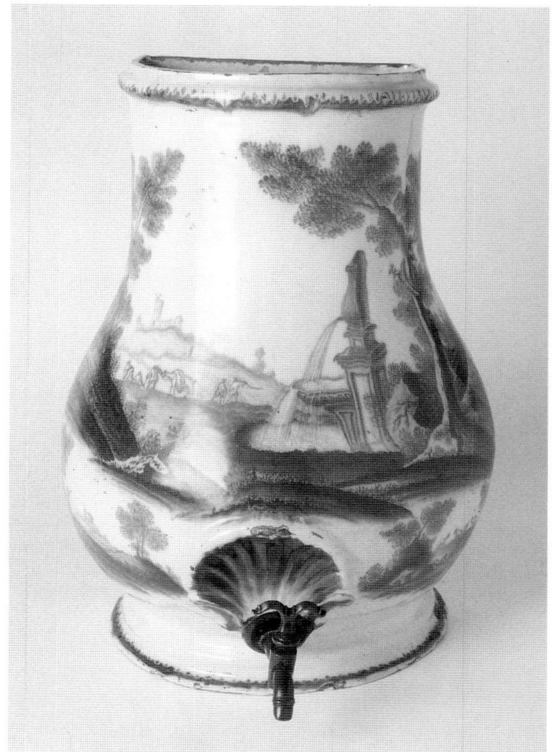

incised, spiral-twist moulding on the stem, are identical to a well known group of opaque white *glass* candlesticks produced in South Staffordshire c.1755 - 60.[27] **(Fig. 137)**. The stems of the delftware candlesticks are hollow, with a seam running throughout, which suggests that they were probably formed in a two-part mould taken directly from a glass original.[28] The very slight lip also suggests that the sconces were originally fitted with metal liners, as on the glass originals.

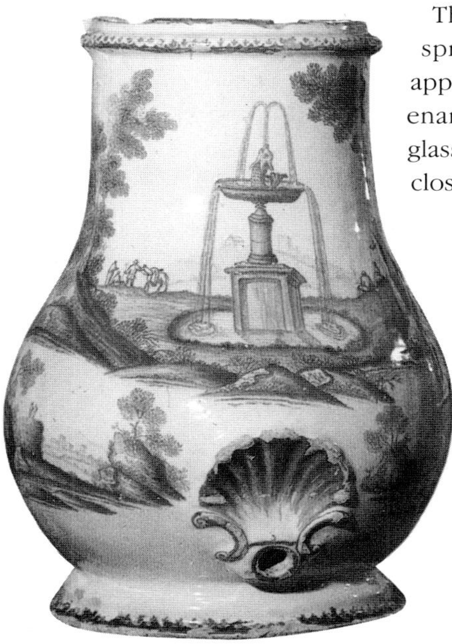

The painted floral sprigs superficially appear similar to the enameled sprays on glass examples, but on closer inspection they tie more closely with other polychrome examples of Dublin delftware. (It is possible that they were originally sold *en suite* with some of the polychrome Dublin tablewares). The style of flower painting most closely matches the circular platter **(Colour Plate 30)**, and some of the Dublin Castle shards **(Colour Plate 29)**.

Jonathan Horne has recorded a pair of Liverpool candlesticks, painted in *'Fazackerly'* colours, which were made in a two-part mould taken from brass or silver originals, but no other delftware pottery is known to have made copies of glass.[29] It is possible that white Staffordshire glass candlesticks were unobtainable or prohibitively expensive in Ireland, presenting the Irish potters with an opportunity to produce their own version.

Above Left : Figure 138. *Dublin delftware water cistern, with 'Neptune' fountain design. No marks. Ht. 15 in, 38 mm., max. width 11 in., 280 mm.*

Above Right : Figure 139. *Dublin delftware water cistern, with 'Cistern' fountain design. No marks. Ht. 15 in, 380 mm., max. width 11 in., 280 mm.*

Left : Figure 140. *Dublin delftware water cistern, with 'Dolphin' fountain design. No marks. Ht. 15¼ in, 385 mm., max. width 11 in., 280 mm.*

CISTERNS

Dublin seems to have been the only delftware pottery in the British Isle to produce these large and impressive objects, although continental examples are comparatively common. Only three Irish cisterns are known, all painted in cobalt blue. One (formerly Lipski collection) is in the Victoria and Albert Museum, **(Fig. 138)**, a second is in the National Museum of Ireland, **(Fig. 139 and Colour Plate 18)**, and the third (formerly Sybil Connolly collection) remains in private hands, **(Fig. 140)**.

Each cistern is decorated in a similar manner with three romantic landscape scenes; a large view across the top, and two smaller vignettes to either side of the faucet. The main view in each case portrays a different style of fountain, (reflecting their function), whereas the two smaller scenes are more typical Dublin landscapes, of the type found on plates, baskets and so on. The trefoil border that occurs on the top and bottom edge of two examples is one of the more distinctive of Dublin borders designs, occurring, for example on the Armstrong jug, **(Fig. 153)**, and on a number of Dublin landscape plates. **(Fig. 155)**.

Cisterns were originally intended as water containers, and the highly decorative character of the three Irish examples suggests they were used as dining-room fixtures, (like the large, landscape-decorated barrels used for wine or brandy, **Figs. 120-121**). The fact that two examples have the same trefoil border raises the slight possibility that they were once a pair. **(Figs. 139 & 140)**. The raised flange around the lip also confirms that they once possessed lids, which are now missing.[30]

All three cisterns appear to have been press-moulded using the same former and painted by the same hand. The flared base suggests they were designed to sit on a table-top or shelf, although each one has been broken off across the top back edge, indicating that the backs once continued higher. (There are two triangular notches at this position on one example, **(Fig.140)**, suggesting that the cisterns were originally fastened against a wall. These holes represent an obvious weak point in the design). Fortunately, the fountain that is painted on one example **(Fig. 139, Colour Plate 18)**, illustrates a cistern of this type in use. This clearly shows that the top back edges of all three were originally arched, and a few inches taller.

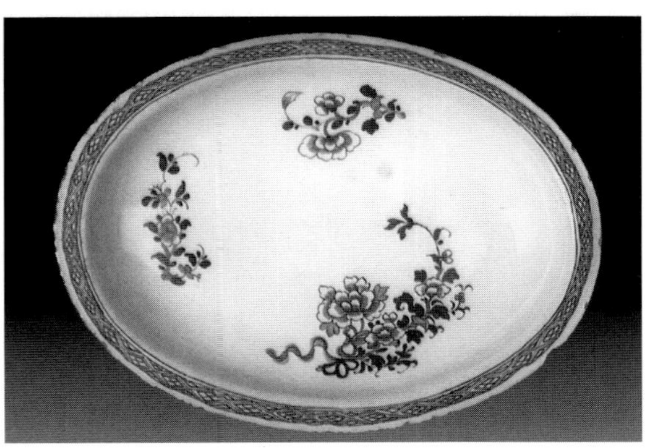

DISHES AND BOWLS

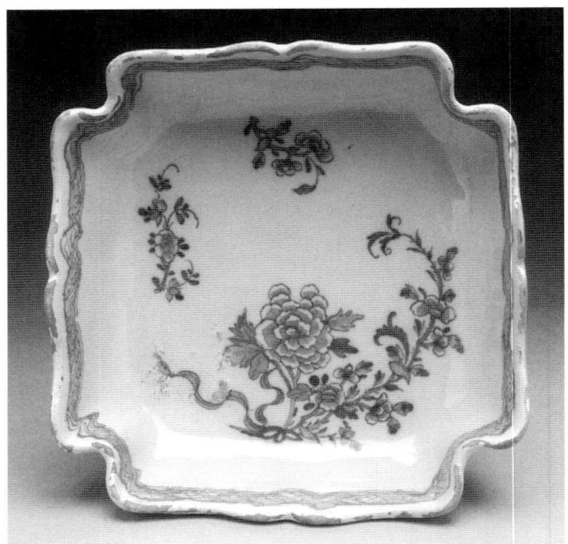

Dublin delftware dishes and bowls occur in a wide variety of forms and sizes. Mary Delamain produced '*large and small Dishes,* [and] *a variety of Salad Dishes*' together with '*Punch Bowls of different sizes*' in 1759, and William Delamain made '*Dishes...Boats, Bowls, Fruit and Salad Dishes*' in 1766. Many different dishes and bowls are illustrated throughout this book - amongst the '*coarsely-*

Left : Figure 141. *Dublin delftware, deep oval dish, with blue painted 'Flower spray & ribbon' design. Painter's number '2' within footrim. 9 x 4¾ in., 230 x 120 mm., Ht. c. 2¼ in., 57 mm.*
Above : Figure 142. *Dublin delftware cruciform dish, with blue painted 'Flower spray & ribbon' design. No mark. (Painters' numbers '3' and '7' are recorded on other examples). Circular footrim. L. 9 in. X 8½ in., 230 X 215 mm.*

painted' wares for example, (pp.83-88), but no attempt has been made to classify or describe them by form. Instead, the intention of this very brief section is simply to draw attention to three distinctive Dublin delftware dishes that might otherwise be overlooked.

The first is a rather plain, oval dish, **(Fig. 141)**, painted with a well-known Dublin design of a Chinese-style '*Flower spray & ribbon*'. (The same pattern occurs on two octagonal platters in the Castletown exhibition, Cat. Nos. 70 & 71). This dish has a broad (7 mm.), glaze-free footrim, within which is the painter's number '2'. There are also two large and two small '*under-rim flourishes*' around the edge of the underside. This dish must originally have formed part of a standard dinner service, but to date, no other examples of this shape have been recorded.

The shallow cruciform bowl illustrated in **Fig. 142** is painted with the same '*Flower spray & ribbon*' pattern. The form of this bowl, with its circular footrim, appears to be a distinctive, Dublin shape, although closely similar cruciform bowls do occur in Chinese export porcelain.[31] (Note especially the ogee curves on the rim). The example illustrated is unmarked, but two others are known, each painted with the '*Feathers in a Vase*' pattern, and bearing the painters' numbers '3' and '7'. (One is illustrated in the Castletown catalogue, No. 30). All three bowls are further enhanced on the outside with small floral sprigs.

The eight-lobed dish illustrated in **Fig. 143** is perhaps the most distinctive Dublin dish shape of all, but this example appears to be unique. The manganese-painted landscape, and the large drapes and feathers around the border are also highly distinctive Dublin motifs. Two further, floral swags in the border, **(Fig. 143a)**, with an abundance of small flowers, are unusual and useful details, which aid in the attribution of other, more problematic pieces of Dublin delftware. The closest comparable flower painting is found among the polychrome wares (p.99-100) and the bowls excavated at Colonial Williamsburg (p. 83-88).

DRAINERS

Michael Archer has tentatively suggested that an octagonal drainer in the Victoria and Albert Museum may have been produced in Dublin. (Archer F.61). This elongated octagonal drainer (not illustrated here), is pierced with forty-four small holes, arranged concentrically around a larger, central hole. A sunburst design is painted around this central hole, whereas the smaller holes are each ornamented with a six-petalled, daisy-like flower. On the underside, near the central hole, is the painter's number '3'.

Octagonal dishes of an appropriate shape for this type of drainer were certainly made in Dublin, and the presence of a painter's number on the reverse lends further weight to the Irish attribution. As Archer remarks, however, '*small numbers are* [also] *occasionally found on Liverpool products,*

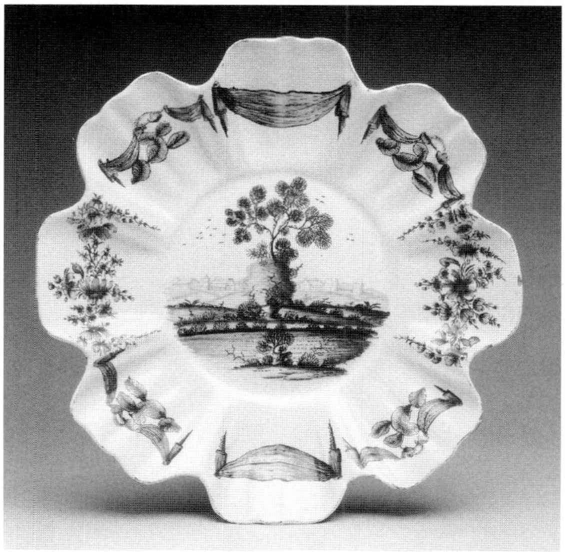

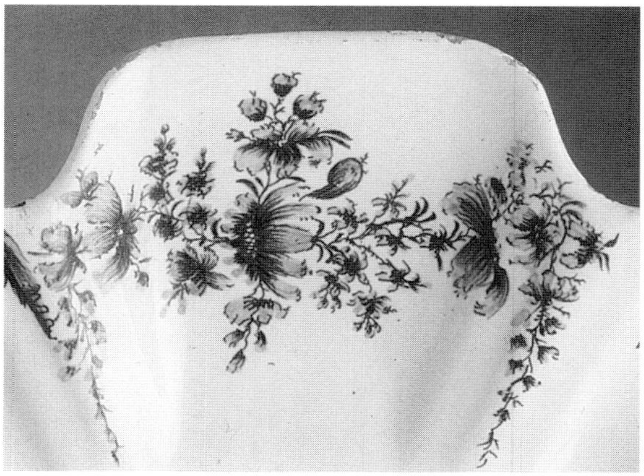

***Left** : **Figure 143**. Dublin delftware eight-lobed dish, painted in manganese (see Colour Plate 23),c.1755-65. No mark. Diam. 11¾ in., 300 mm.*
***Right** : **Figure 143a**. Detail of flower-painting on Fig. 143*

and the lack of evidence supplied by this drainer must make an attribution uncertain'. Considering the large number of dinner-service designs that are now recorded from Dublin, however, it seems surprising to find that more examples of Dublin drainers have not yet been recognised.

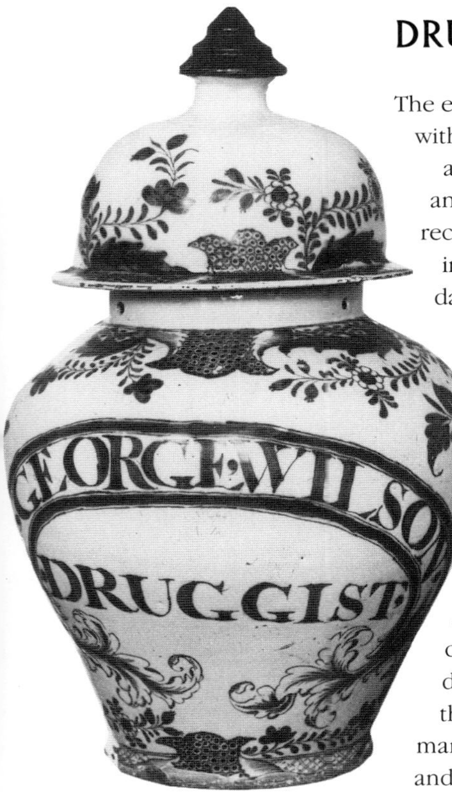

DRUG JARS

The earliest known drug jars with a Dublin provenance are a group of eight wet and dry drug jars recorded by G. E. Howard in 1931, which bear the date 1684 and the initials 'MH'.[32] According to Howard, '*These were traditionally made for Michael Hastings of Dublin and remained for generations in the chemist's shop of Messrs. Evans of that city*'. If the jars were contemporary with the date, however, then they pre-date delftware manufacture in Ireland and must have been imported.

Until recently, only one, impressive pair of Dublin drug jars was recorded, one, of which is illustrated. **(Figs. 144, a, b)**. These bear the name '*George Wilson*' in a banner above the legend '*Druggist*', and are decorated on the reverse with a Chinese-style tree amongst flowers. **(Fig. 144a)**. The example illustrated, which also appeared in the Castletown catalogue, (Cat No. 14), is now in the National Museum of Ireland. Both jars are marked inside the lid and on the base with a painter's monogram 'NE', below which is an additional 'S' or '5'. **(Fig. 144 b)**. The upper portion of the mark obviously indicates that the 'NE' painter decorated these jars, but the significance of the lower 'S' or '5' mark is unclear - possibly a second painter was involved in their manufacture.

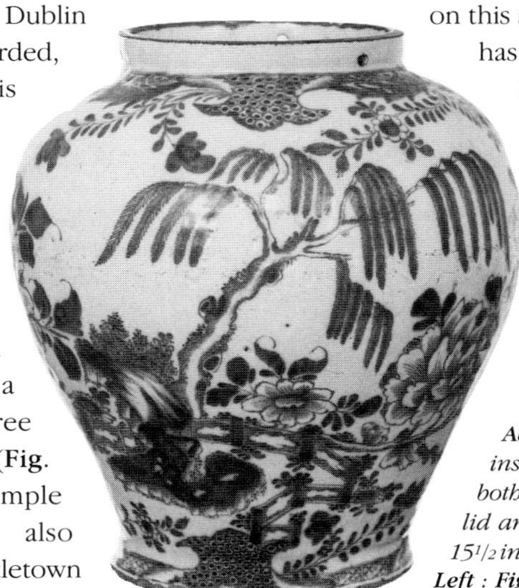

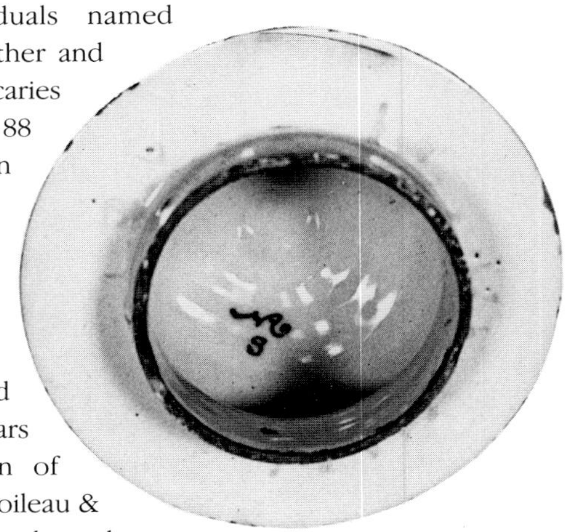

Two individuals named George Wilson, father and son, were apothecaries or druggists at No. 88 Bride Street in Dublin, and were active from 1714-54 and 1754-86 respectively. Their shop sign, dated 1753, remained with these drug jars in the possession of their successors, Boileau & Boyd, until 1982, when these and other apothecary's wares were formally presented to the National Museum.[33]

Recently, a second pair of these large, Dublin drug jars came to light. These were discovered in Northern Ireland by the late John Lewis-Crosby, formerly of Sotheby's, who forwarded a snapshot of one example to the author in 1994. **(Fig. 145)**. Although the lids of this second pair seem to be missing, the form is virtually identical to the '*George Wilson*' jars described above. The individual named on this second pair of jars, '*Ja*^{S}. *Stanley, Apothecary*', has not yet been found in eighteenth-century Dublin Directories, although he may well have been related to one Arthur Stanley, a '*druggist*' at No. 40 Bride Street during the late-eighteenth century.[34] (Coincidentally, the premises of George Wilson, for whom the other surviving pair were made, were also located in Bride Street). A '*John Stanley and Co., Drug, Oil and Colour-*

Above Left : Figure 144. *Dublin delftware drug jar, inscribed 'GEORGE WILSON DRUGGIST'. One of a pair, both marked with identical* $^{N}{}_{5}{}^{E}$ *monograms, inside the lid and on the base. Ht. of jar, 10 in., 255 mm., with lid 15½ in., 395 mm., width 9¼ in., 235 mm.*
Left : Figure 144a. *Reverse of Fig. 144*
Above Right : Figure 144b. *Lid interior of Fig. 144*

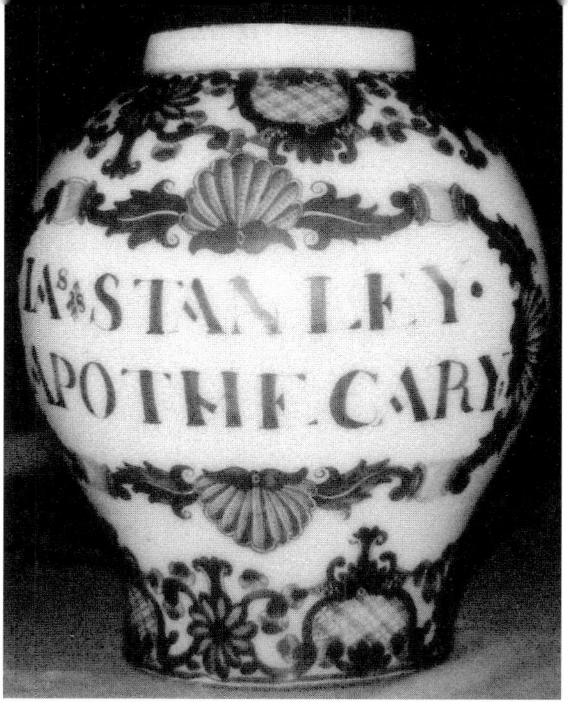

Figure 145. A previously unrecorded delftware drug jar, almost certainly made in Dublin, inscribed 'JAS STANLEY. APOTHECARY'. Marks and dimensions unrecorded, present whereabouts unknown.

merchants' were listed much later at No. 72 Dame Street (in 1807).

The present whereabouts of this second pair of drug jars are unknown, and so they have not been examined at first hand, but background details in the original photograph, (not shown), suggest they are similar in size to the pair made for George Wilson. A painter's mark may exist on the base, but this is not recorded. Even so, the Dublin association and the style of the painting suggest that these jars were almost certainly made in Dublin. (The large '*honeysuckle*' flower, for example, a typical Dublin feature, is evident a few inches below the letter 'C' of apothecary).

John Chambers first advertised apothecary wares in Dublin in 1737, shortly after the pottery opened, and '*pots for grocers, apothecaries and perfumers*' were still being produced by Delamain's successors in 1770, (p. 65). In 1753, Henry Delamain also appears to have introduced delftwares to '*Mr. Duany and the Surgeons of the Infirmary on the Inns Quay ... for the benefit of their hospital*'. (See p.50). It is therefore difficult to understand why more ordinary types of Dublin drug jar have not turned up. The only Dublin drug jars that have been identified to date are these large, impressive display pieces. Presumably, the majority of Dublin drug jars were unmarked, and hence they are not readily differentiated from English examples.

EPERGNES (CENTREPIECES)

The Oxford Dictionary records that the word '*epergne*' was first used to describe a table centre-dish or stand in 1761, quoting a contemporary remark that such '*Grand Epergnes* [were] *filled with fine pickles*'. Five years later, in August 1766, '*epergnes*' were listed amongst the wares manufactured by William Delamain and Samuel Wilkinson in Dublin, (p. 64). It seems likely, therefore, that these shell-form table centrepieces are the '*epergnes*' to which Delamain and Wilkinson referred.[35]

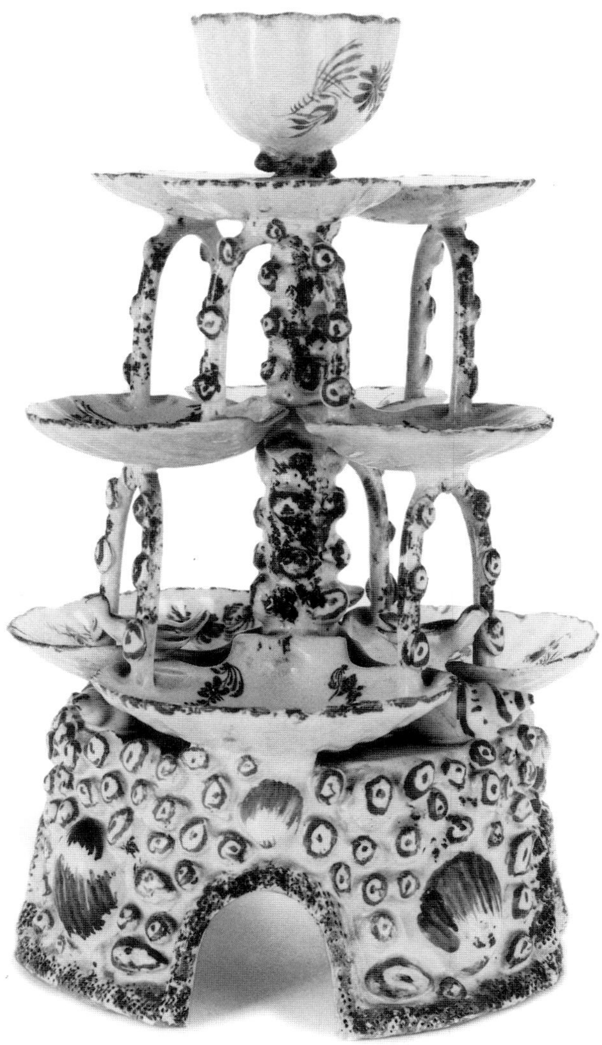

Figure 146. Dublin delftware blue-painted 'epergne on stand', the largest presently recorded. No mark. Ht. 16 1/4 in., 412 mm.

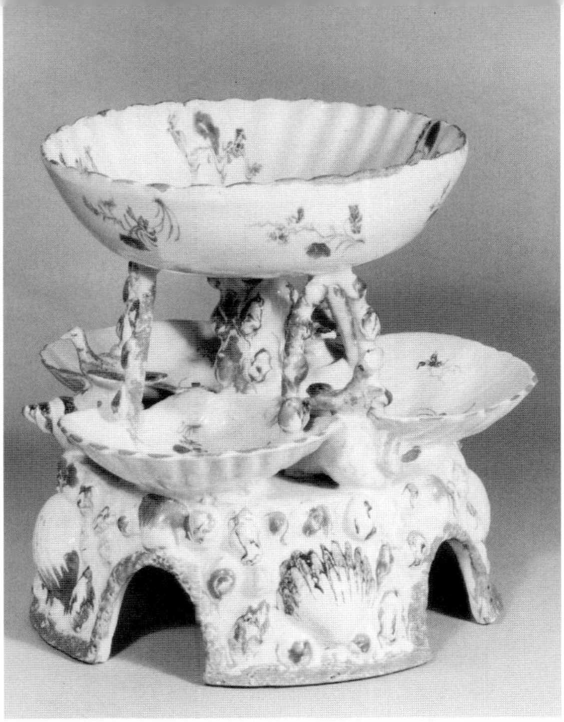

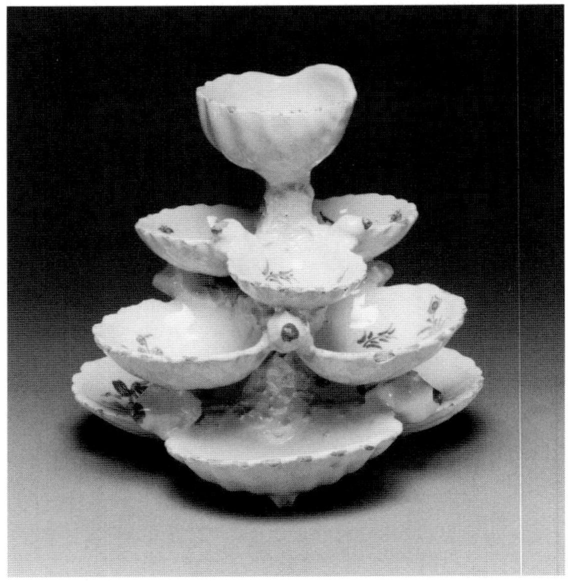

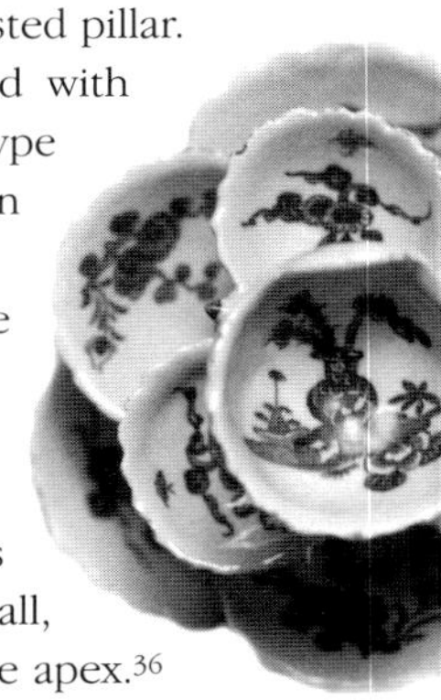

Above : Figure 147. *Dublin delftware polychrome 'epergne on stand', (Painted in similar colours to a second example, shown in Colour Plate 35). No mark. Ht. 10¾ in., 273 mm.*
Above Right : Figure 148. *Dublin delftware 'epergne without stand'. Painted in blue with elements from the 'Feathers in a Vase' pattern, painter's number '4' on base.*
Ht. 6¾ in., 175 mm.
Right : Figure 148a. *Top view of Fig. 148*
Below : Figure 148b. *Base of Fig. 148*

A total of seven Dublin delftware epergnes are now recorded, of two basic types;

i. *Epergnes on stands.*
(Figs. 146 & 147, Colour Plates 35 & 36).

ii. *Epergnes without stands.*
(Figs. 148, a & b)

i. Epergnes on stands

Five examples of this type are recorded, two of which are polychrome, two blue and white, and one manganese. Each one rests on a large, cylindrical stand or plinth with three arched apertures and moulded encrustations of cockleshells and pebbles. There is considerable variation in the tiers above this plinth, but there are also a number of features that are common to all five examples. Each tier of shell-dishes rests on, wishbone-shaped supports, three moulded birds are present on the bottom layer, and they each possess a central, shell-encrusted pillar. All five examples are painted with simple, floral sprigs, (of the type mainly recorded on polychrome wares).

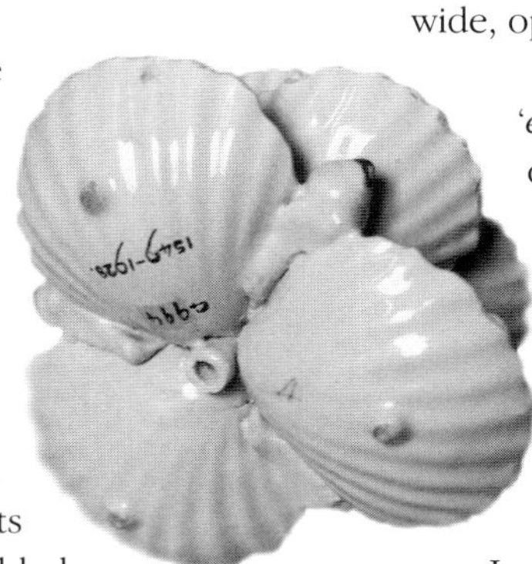

The tallest example recorded to date **(Fig. 146)**, is a blue and white epergne from the Lipski collection with 9, scallop-shaped dishes arranged in 3 tiers, and a small, fluted, teabowl-like dish at the apex.[36] Two polychrome examples are recorded; one in the Victoria & Albert Museum, **(Colour Plate 35)**, the other in Glasgow Museum **(Fig. 147)**.[37] These two coloured epergnes are virtually identical, and much smaller than the previous example. Each has only one tier of 3 scallop-shaped dishes, below a wide, open, fluted dish at the apex.

Perhaps the most unusual '*epergnes on stands*' recorded to date are two examples that bear a large, circular ring-support at the apex, which presumably held a large, detachable bowl. The first example (not illustrated), which is painted entirely in manganese, was discovered and described by Jonathan Horne in 1981.[38] This manganese epergne also bears a typical Dublin painter's monogram, 'B', on the top, in the centre of the dish support. The second example, from the Lipski collection, is decorated entirely in cobalt blue **(Colour Plate 36)**. Although the form is identical to the manganese epergne, there is no indication of a painter's mark. The painted floral sprigs are similar, however, to those that appear on Dublin's polychrome wares.

The presence of a painter's monogram on one example of the '*epergnes on stands*' suggests that they date from the 1750s or early 1760s, and hence pre-date the smaller '*epergnes without stands*', (which exhibit a painter's *number*).

ii. Epergnes without stands

Just two examples of this type are recorded. The shapes of the individual shell-formed dishes are not always the same as those that occur on '*epergnes on stands*', and so these are not simply smaller versions of the same type. The taller of the two known examples, in the Glaisher collection, **(Fig. 148)**, has 9 scallop-shaped dishes arranged in three tiers, with a different, more enclosed shell-form dish at the apex.[39] Two further features contribute to the Dublin attribution for this second group. Firstly, the topmost, central dish is painted in blue on the interior with motifs from the typical Dublin '*Feathers in a Vase*' pattern, **(compare Figs. 148a and 88)**. Secondly, the underside bears a typical Dublin painter's number '4'. **(Fig. 148b)**.

A second blue and white example, in a private collection, (not illustrated), has 6 scallop-shaped dishes in two tiers, with the same enclosed, shell-form dish at the apex. This is painted with floral sprigs (comparable to those on the bowl at the apex of **Fig. 146**), and bears no painters' marks.

In summary, the colouring of the polychrome examples, the style of the painting, and the painters marks indicate that both styles of epergne were made in Dublin, probably during the late 1750s and 1760s when such items were in vogue in porcelain also. The marks suggest that the imposing '*epergnes on stands*' slightly pre-date the smaller '*epergnes without stands*', although the comparable style of floral sprig painting on some examples suggests there was probably overlap. The forms were obviously copied from similar, shell-form, encrusted epergnes that were produced by many English porcelain manufacturers during the 1750s and 60s - at Chelsea/Derby, Liverpool, Vauxhall and Worcester, for example. Some of the smaller moulded details, however, (such as the enclosed shell-form dish at the apex of '*epergnes without stands*') indicate once again that Bow porcelains probably represented the main source of inspiration for the Dublin potters.[40]

FLOWER - BRICKS

A contemporary painting, illustrated by Archer, shows that the great majority of these unusual objects were flower containers, (rather than ink and quill-holders, as was once speculated).[41] Although their original name is not recorded, Mary Dorgan's advertisement in the *Cork Evening Post* for 26th November 1759 mentioned '*curious flowerpots ... in Delamain's ware*', which was

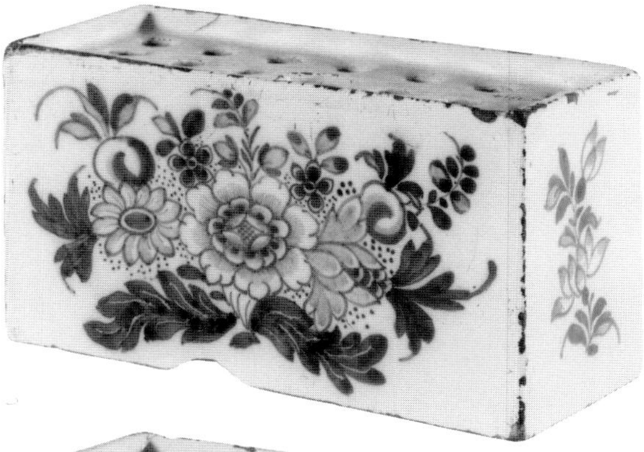

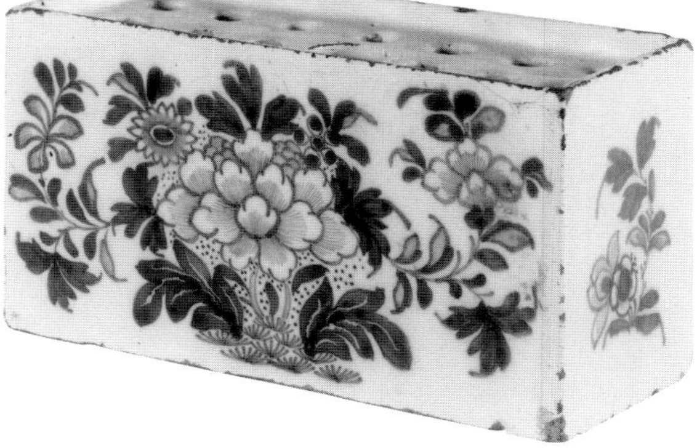

Top Right : Figure 149. *Dublin delftware flower-brick, the pair to the brick shown in Fig. 150. Painter's number '7' on base. L. 6 in., 152 mm.*
Note that the flower painting is different on all four sides of this pair of flower-bricks, but the form, size and painter's number are constant.
Bottom Right : Figure 149a. *Reverse of Fig. 149*

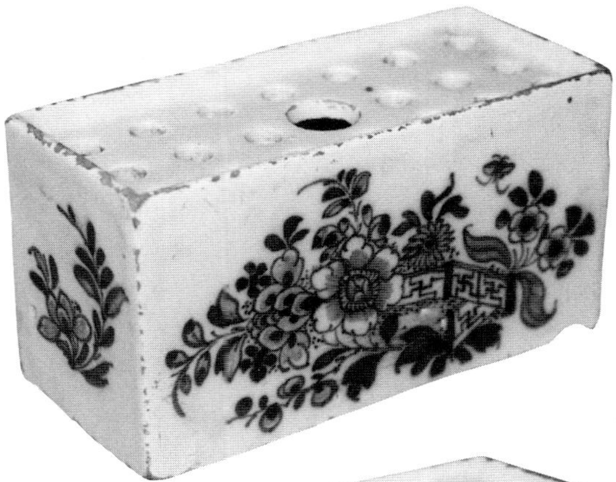

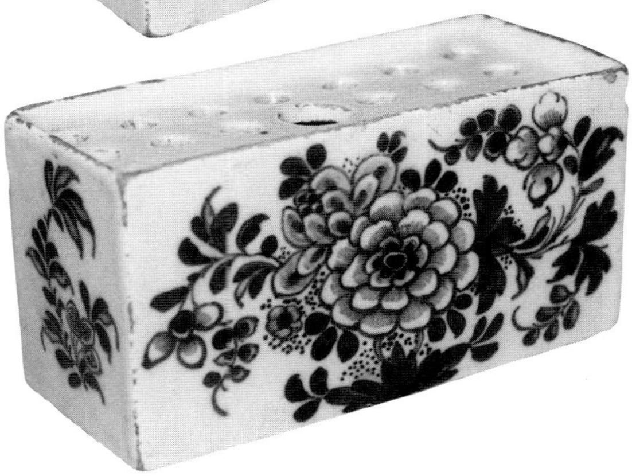

Above Top : ***Figure 150.*** *Dublin delftware flower-brick, the pair to the brick shown in Fig. 149. Painter's number '7' on base. L 6 in., 152 mm.*
Above : Figure 150a. *Reverse of Fig. 150*

probably a reference either to flower-bricks or to bough pots, **(Fig. 133)**.

Amongst the literature and various museum collections, only six Dublin flower bricks appear to have been recognised, (two pairs and two singles). Most are simply unadorned, rectangular forms with pierced tops and a recessed base, of the type shown in **Figs. 149 & 150)**.[42] Another example is slightly taller, with a narrow 'skirt' carved away around the base, creating a scalloped or ogee-shaped basal edge. **(Fig. 151)**.[43] An unexpected feature is that the basic arrangement of pierced holes is fairly constant in all recorded examples, consisting essentially of two sets of 9 holes on either side of a larger, circular, central aperture. **(Fig. 152)**. Two or four extra holes were sometimes added to either side of the central aperture, but otherwise the basic pattern is constant throughout.

Published flower-bricks show an exceptional diversity of hole shapes, spacings and patterns, so that the fact that all of these Dublin examples share the same basic pattern is significant.[44] This arrangement is not necessarily diagnostic of Dublin, however. Other flower-bricks, which seem to have been made in Liverpool, exhibit precisely the same pattern.[45] It would also be surprising to discover that other Dublin patterns did not exist.

The recorded painted decoration consists almost entirely of blue-painted, Chinese-style floral sprays, as illustrated, although it is interesting to observe that the two bricks of a single pair were not necessarily painted with identical patterns. **(Figs. 149, 150)**. A single flower brick, sold at Sotheby's in New York in 1994, (not illustrated), is painted with designs incorporating Buddhist emblems, which copy the border motifs that appear on *'Chinese Flower-bowl'* patterned plates, **(e.g. Colour Plate 13, left)**.[46] The most interesting pair, and the only

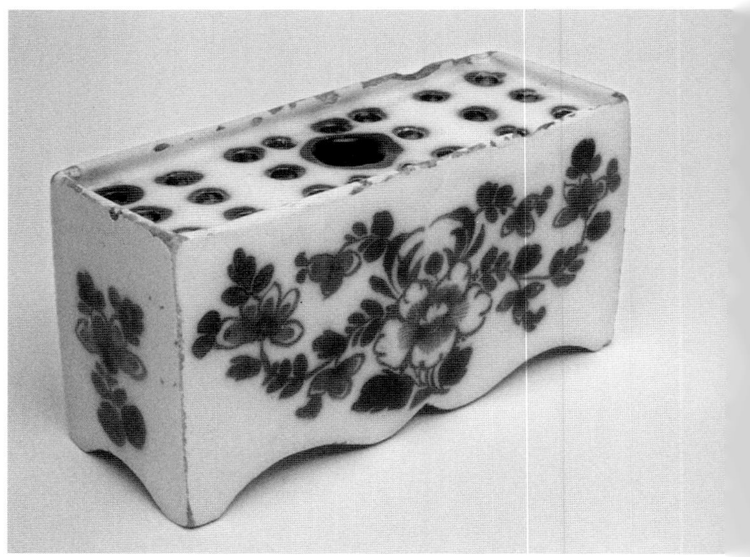

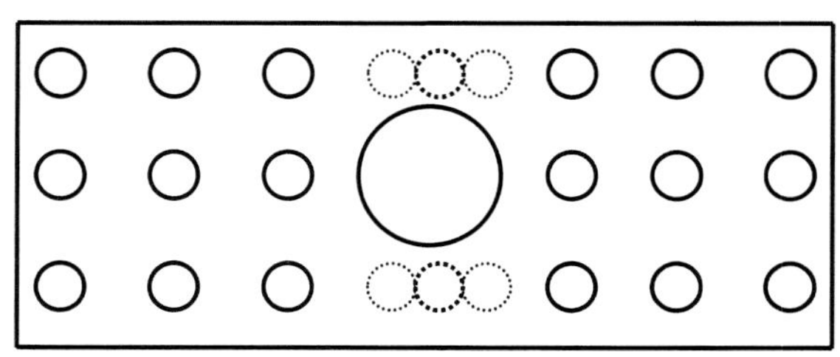

Above Top* : *Figure 151. *Dublin delftware flower brick, ogee-shaped basal edge. Painter's number '0' on base. L. $6^{1}/_{10}$ in., 155 mm., W. $2^{5}/_{16}$ in., 59 mm., Ht. $3^{1}/_{4}$ in., 83 mm.*
Above : Figure 152. *The basic arrangement of holes recorded to date on Dublin flower bricks. 2 or 4 extra holes are sometimes added to either side of the central aperture.*

'polychrome' pair yet recorded, are painted in blue and manganese with the distinctive *'parasol flower'*. (Not illustrated. The design is similar to that illustrated in **Fig.** ~~133~~ 134).[47] Like the previous example, this pattern also matches the border design of known Dublin flatwares, suggesting that some flower-bricks may originally have been intended for use as part of a dinner table arrangement.

JUGS

The great majority of eighteenth-century delftware jugs that have survived are puzzle-jugs, presumably because such vessels were not subjected to the wear and tear of everyday use. It is significant, therefore, that no Irish puzzle-jugs seem to have been identified, (either in delftware or in country pottery). This does not necessarily mean they do not exist, but their absence is surprising nonetheless. Perhaps the drinking games with which puzzle-jugs were associated were not commonly played in Ireland?

More utilitarian delftware jugs are now rare objects, as the form is fragile and the thin handles prone to breakage. The only jug presently attributed to Dublin is an impressive, highly decorative, large-sized beer or punch jug, painted with manganese-purple landscape views on each side, and bearing a crest of the Armstrong family below the spout. **(Fig. 153, Colour Plate 26)**. The landscape decoration is unmistakably Irish, but the Dublin attribution is further reinforced in this case by the presence of an 'NE' painter's monogram on the glazed base. The *'trefoil'* border motif, which lines the top and bottom edges, is another distinctive Dublin feature. (Compare the Dublin cisterns, **Figs. 139** and **140**). Perhaps the most unusual feature of the painting is the small *'plum tree'* flower spray on either side of the spout, which is closer in style to *'pencil-decorated'* flower painting on the Chambers-period plates, c.1735, **(Fig. 49)**, than to the floral decoration of most post-Delamain wares. In form, however, the Dublin jug is directly comparable to English examples dated 1757 and 1763, suggesting a probable date range for the piece of c.1755 - 65.

A second jug was attributed to Dublin in the Castletown catalogue, (Cat. 123). This is a medium-sized milk or hot-water jug, inscribed *'Mr. White 1750'*, and painted with the Chinese Lotus pattern. As a result of new archaeological evidence, this is now attributed to London.

Figures 153, 153a. *Dublin delftware tall jug, painted in manganese with landscape views, and bearing the crest of the Armstrong family. (The specific branch of the Armstrong family has not been identified). Painter's monogram 'NE' on base. Ht. 9¹/₁₀ in., 230 mm., Diam. 5¹/₂ in., 140 mm.*

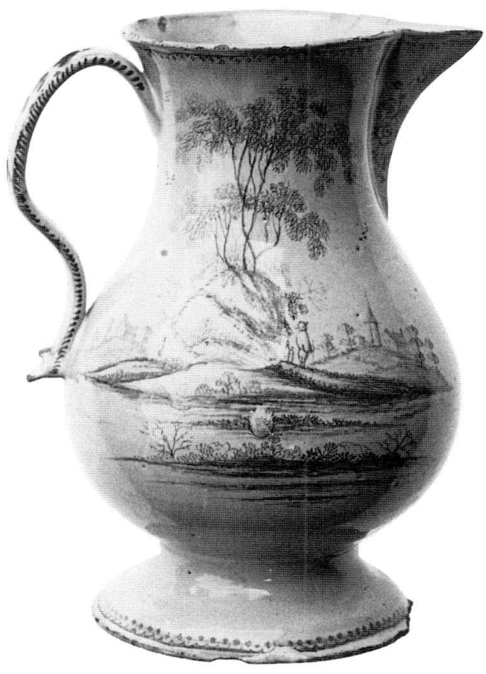

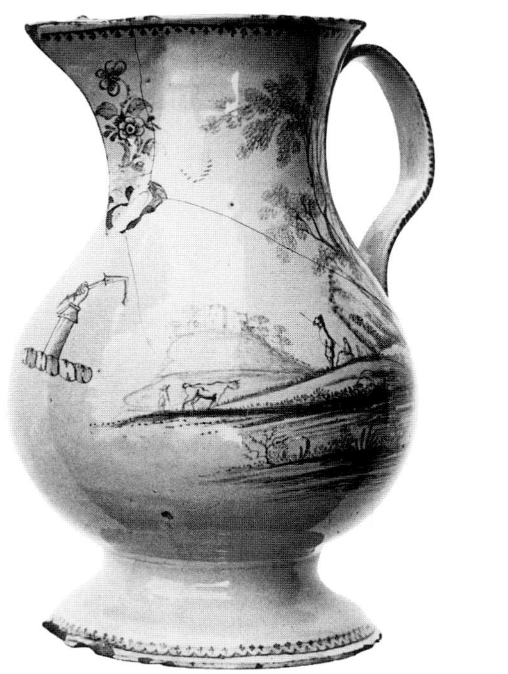

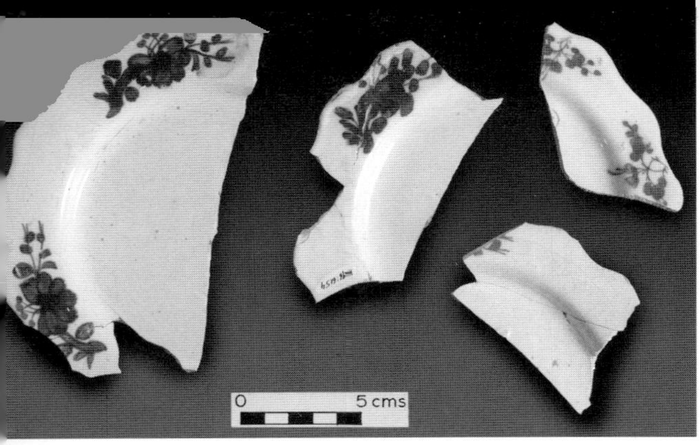

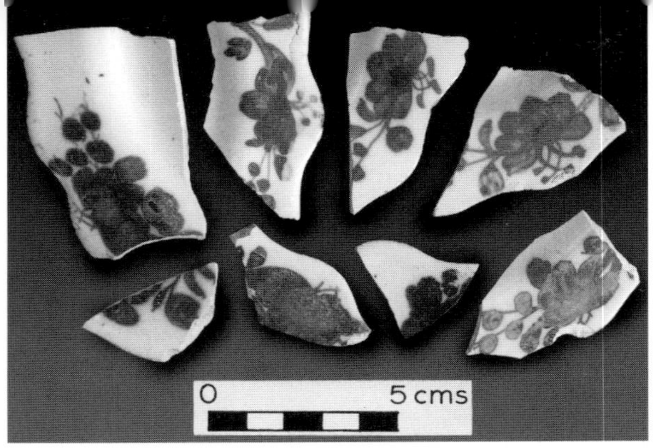

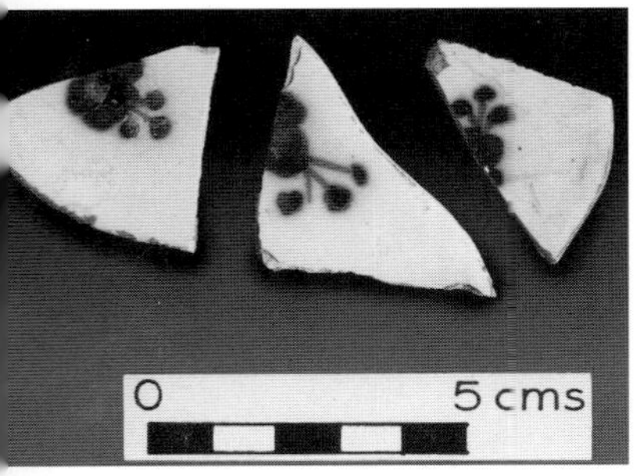

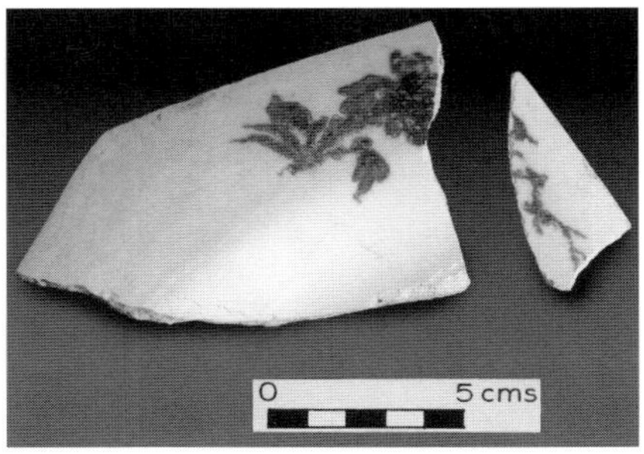

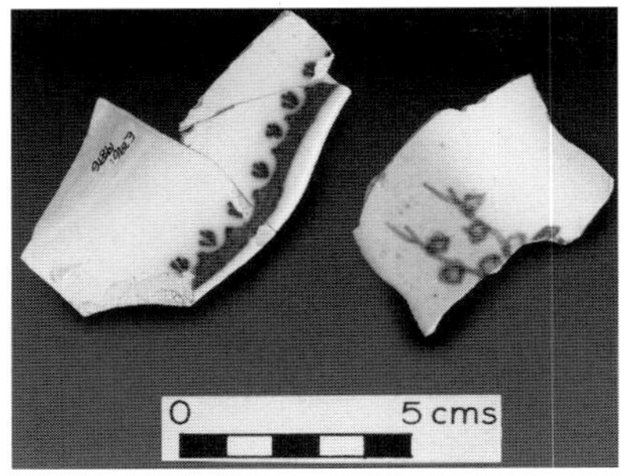

*Top Left : **Figure 154a.**, Top Right : **Figure 154b.**,*
*Bottom Left : **Figure 154c.**, Bottom Middle : **Figure 154d.**, Bottom Right : **Figure 154e.***

Dublin delftware fragments excavated at Dublin Castle in 1985-7. (See also Colour Plates 29 & 29a). All painted in blue with the exception of Fig. 154e, right, (manganese). Sizes as indicated by scale. No marks.

PLATES, PLATTERS AND OTHER FLATWARES

As was also the case with Dishes and Bowls, so many different forms of Dublin flatwares are now known that it is impractical to catalogue and describe each individual type. Many plates and platters of widely differing shapes and sizes are illustrated throughout his book. The primary purpose of this brief section is simply to introduce some unusual, distinctive forms that might otherwise be overlooked.

One of the more interesting developments of recent years was the discovery of a number of shards of Dublin delftware amongst a mixed assemblage excavated from a pre-1803 context at Dublin Castle, about a mile from the World's End Pottery site. (There has, as yet, been no investigation of the pottery site itself). Amongst this material was a group of twenty-four rim and body shards of wavy-edged and octagonal Dublin delftware plates, mostly painted in cobalt blue, but sometimes in manganese or polychrome. The Dublin characteristics of these shards were recognised by Michael Archer, and described by archaeologist Rosanne Meenan in 1991.[48]

The polychrome shards found have already been described, (p.100, **Colour Plate 29**). Like the coloured fragments, the blue-painted fragments recovered (**Figs.154 a-e**) were predominantly from small-sized, wavy-edged plates, and were simply painted with floral sprigs of various kinds. The most complete example, illustrated as **Colour Plate 29a**, seems to bear a stronger resemblance to French faience of the period

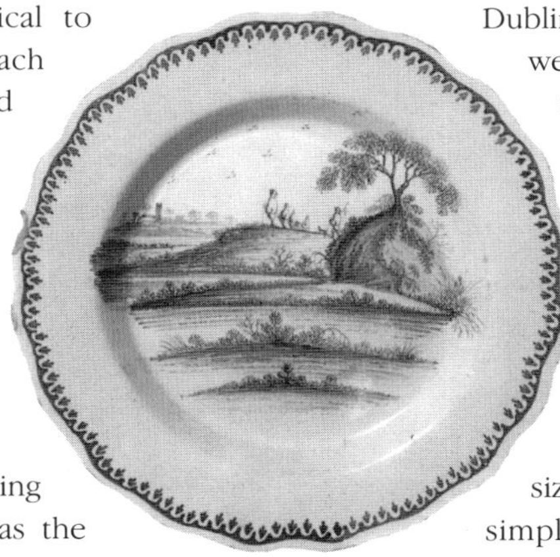

***Figure 155.** Dublin delftware, wavy-edged landscape plate, decorated in manganese, featuring a distinctive 'trefoil' border. (Compare Fig. 154e, left). Mark 'NE' under rim. Diam. 9³/₄ in, 250 mm. Manganese-painted landscapes featuring this border usually occur on plates with 20 lobes around the wavy-edge, whereas those painted in blue are usually on plates with 16 lobes. (Compare also the plates illustrated in Castletown, Nos. 40-47a).*

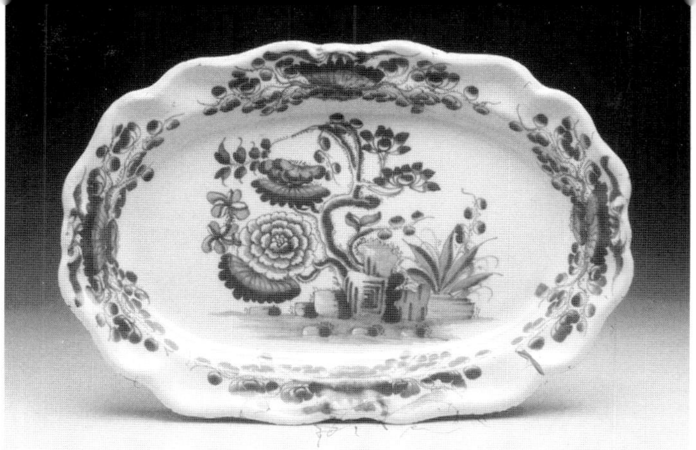

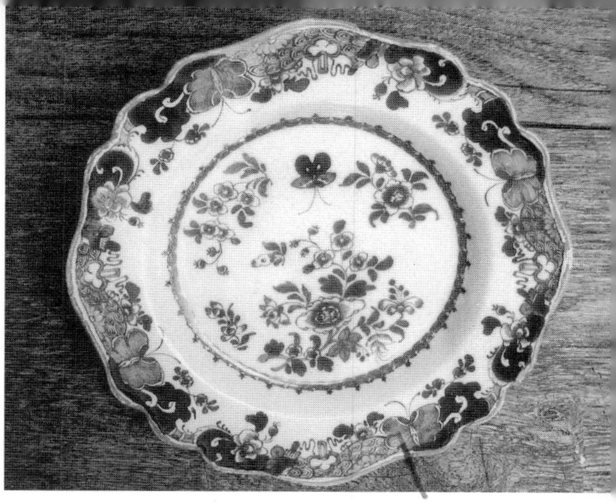

***Left* : *Figure 156*.** *Dublin delftware. Small wavy-edged platter featuring a version of the distinctive 'parasol flower' pattern. (Compare Fig. 154a & b, 134 and 179b). Painter's number '4' in centre of base, no footrim. Compare the border pattern with the butter-tub illustrated in Fig.134. Size 14 x 9½ in., 355 x 242 mm.*

***Right* : *Figure 157*.** *Dublin delftware wavy-edged plate copying a Chinese porcelain shape, 'Floral Sprays & Butterfly' pattern. (Also recorded on a large, circular platter; Castletown, No. 76). One of a set of eight, all bearing painter's number '2' within footrim. Max. diam., 9 in., 230 mm.*

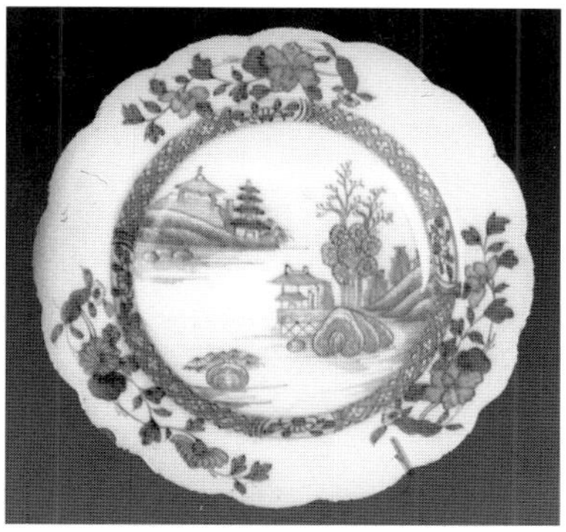

than to most English delftwares.[49] Two rim fragments were also found of a fine, blue-painted octagonal plate, **(Fig. 154d)**. One rim fragment is entirely decorated in manganese, **(Fig. 154e, right)**, whilst another plate fragment, of different wavy-edge form to the rest, bears the distinctive, Dublin *'trefoil'* border motif, **(Fig. 154 e, left)**.

Some of the patterns on these excavated fragments are readily recognised among extant pieces. The trefoil border, for example, **(Fig. 154e, left)**, is identical to that which appears on a well-known group of wavy-edged landscape plates, finely-painted in cobalt blue or manganese purple. **(Fig. 155)**. The floral sprigs on the margins of the plates illustrated in **Figs. 154a & 154b**, are clearly related to those that appear on the margins of wavy-edged flatwares painted with the distinctive *'parasol flower'*, **(Fig. 156)**, although the painting is much coarser. On closer inspection, however, many small features of the painting on these shards correlate with details found on other examples of Dublin delftware, (e.g. compare the sprigs in **Fig. 154e**, right, and **Fig. 113a**). Other flatwares featuring this same *'parasol flower'* are recorded, although there are several versions of the pattern, and the quality of the painting also varies. (Compare **Fig. 156** and **Fig. 134**). Other known examples include a standard dinner plate with a *'floral sprig'* mark, (Archer & Morgan, p.114) and a large, octagonal platter bearing the painter's monogram 'F', (Archer, G.24, p. 341). An illustration of an unmarked circular platter has also been published, and a fine-quality vase of this pattern is illustrated here in **Fig. 179**.[50]

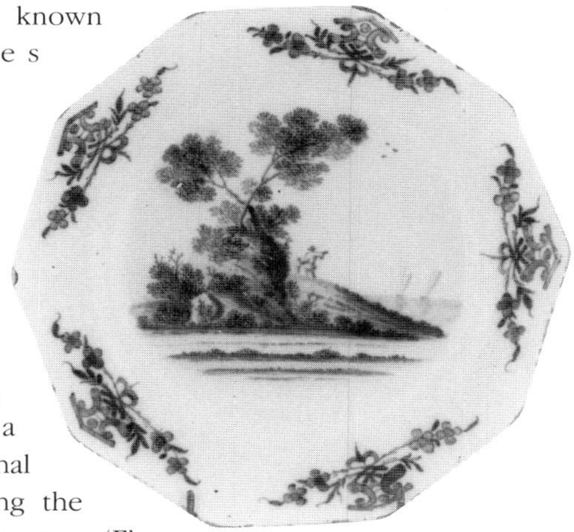

***Above Left* : *Figure 158*.** *Dublin delftware wavy-edged plate painted with 'Three Pagodas', copying Chinese export porcelain. Painter's Number 9. Diam. 8⅞ in., 225 mm.*
***Right* : *Figure 159*.** *Dublin delftware ten-sided plate. No other examples of ten-sided Dublin plates are recorded.The border pattern on this example also appears to be unique. No footrim or mark. Diam. 9⅜ in., 238 mm. (point to point).*

Although the shapes of many Dublin delftware wavy-edged plates seem broadly similar to French faience of the period, some - often with a yellow edge - were instead derived from Chinese porcelain. The plate illustrated in **Fig. 157**, decorated with a *'Floral Sprays & Butterfly'*, is one of a set of eight recorded

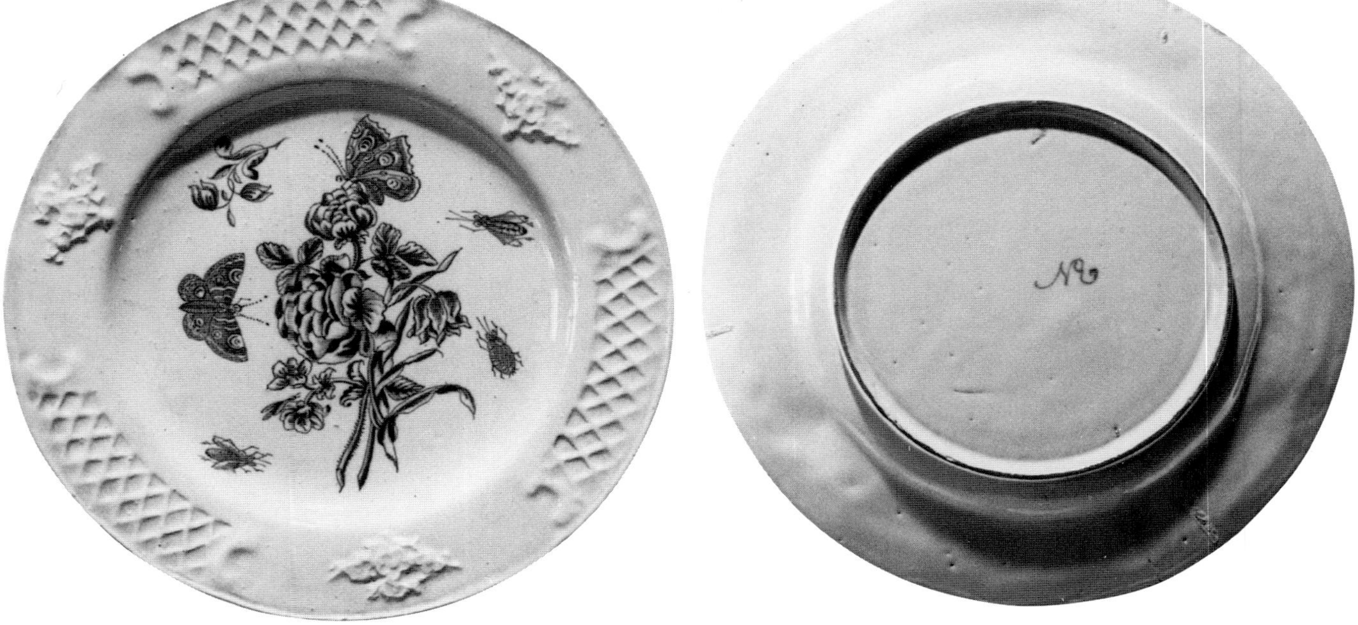

Figures 160, 160a. *Dublin delftware plate, moulded trellis and prunus panels on rim, finely painted with naturalistic floral sprays and insects. (One of a set of five recorded in 1971). Mark 'NE' monogram within footrim. Diam. 8⅝ in., 220 mm.*

recently by Garry Atkins in London, all of which bear the painter's number '2' within the footrim. The form of these plates seems to match the scalloped *'Two Deer'* platter illustrated in **Fig. 99**. (Both are also painted with a yellow-edge). Another style of wavy-edge is evident on a Dublin delftware plate in a private collection, painted with a previously unrecorded Chinese-style pattern featuring *'Three Pagodas'* **(Fig. 158)**. Although there is no yellow-edge in this case plates of precisely this form also occur in mid-eighteenth century Chinese export porcelain.

Most of the polygonal plates produced in Dublin, as we have seen in examining the *'Chinese porcelain'* designs (p.90) were simply octagonal, sometimes with notched corners. The finely decorated Dublin plate illustrated in **Fig.159** is unusual in being ten-sided. Although this was first recorded some thirty-five years ago, in the sale of the Garner collection in 1965, no other examples of ten-sided Dublin plates have yet been discovered.[51] The border pattern, which consists of five, repeating floral motifs with Buddhist emblems, also seems to be unique.

One of the most striking and distinctive Dublin delftware plate forms of all is also, sadly, among the rarest. **(Figs. 160, 160a)**. Five of these plates were recorded together in an Irish private collection in 1971, but no other examples have yet come to light.[52] The source of this unusual design has not been precisely identified. The moulded prunus flowers on the rim are similar in style to some white, moulded porcelain plates produced at Bow, c.1753, but these do not exhibit the trellis moulding that occurs on the Dublin plates.[53] The very finely painted, rather intense floral design in the centre, with insects and butterflies, initially seems to copy English transfer-printed porcelain, and some early transfer-printed wares of the late 1760s were indeed similar.[54] Amongst Bow and Worcester porcelains, however, there are two slightly earlier groups of *painted* floral designs, dating from c.1760-65, which are more strongly reminiscent of this Dublin pattern.[55] (These patterns are described at Worcester as the *'Heavy Naturalistic Floral'* group). The likely source of this design therefore seems to have been Bow or Worcester, but without finding a precise match for the moulding it is impossible to be certain. Once again, the monogram on the reverse confirms that the *'NE'* painter was among Dublin's most skilled decorators.

POTTED MEAT DISHES

Two examples of these small dishes are known, in a private collection. Both are octagonal, (with four long and four short sides), but they vary slightly in form and size.

The first example has a flared profile, and is 4¼ in. (107 mm.) wide at the lip. The painted deer on

Below : 21. *Fine-quality Dublin plate, one of a set that may have been produced for Lionel Sackville, Lord Lieutenant of Ireland, c.1753-55. Mock-Chinese script mark. (See Fig.63). Diam. 9 1/4 in., 235 mm.*

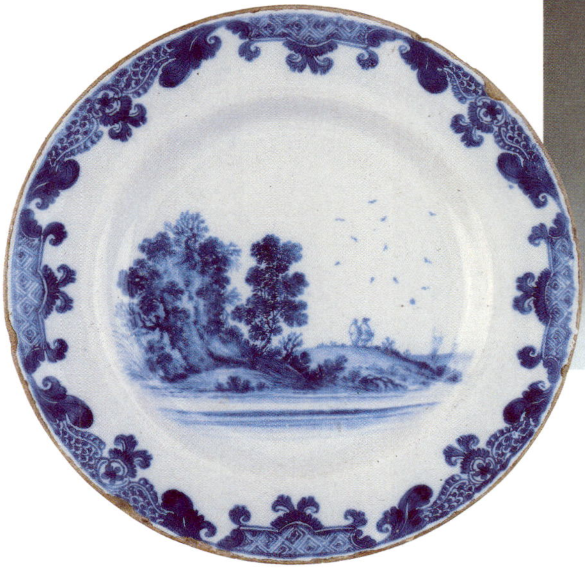

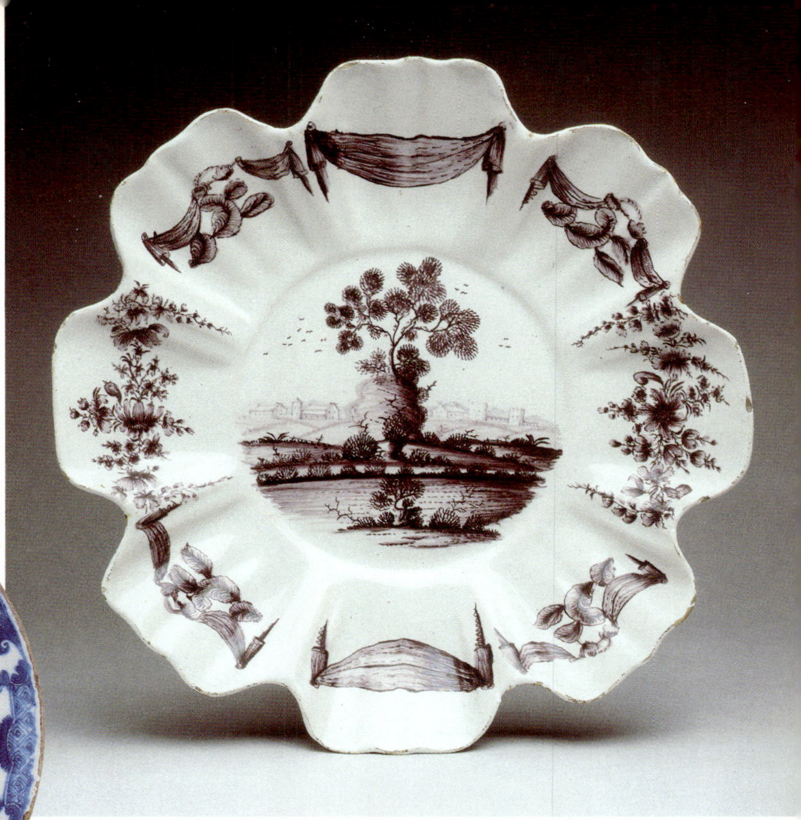

Above : 23. *A Dublin delftware dish of unusual eight-lobed form, circa 1755-65. No mark. (See p.119). Diam. approx. 11 3/4 in., 300 mm.*

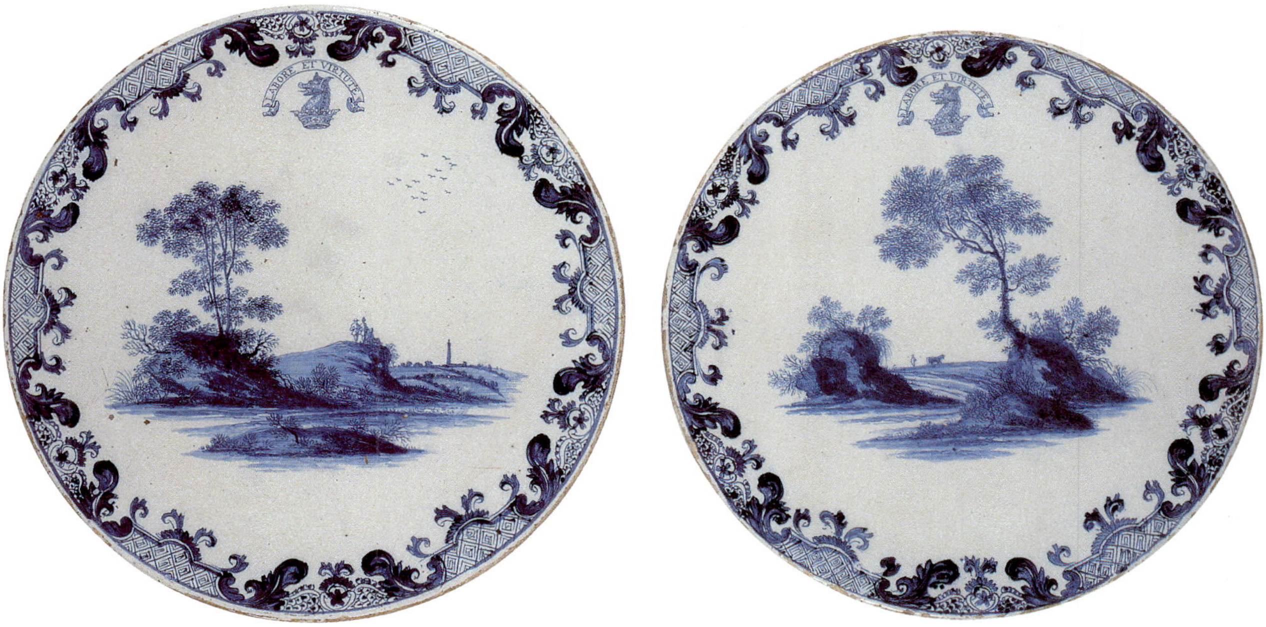

Above : 22. *A pair of fine-quality Dublin table stands, of slightly differing sizes, bearing a ducal crest and the motto 'LABORE ET VIRTUTE'. (Possibly of the Wilson family). Floral Sprig marks. (See Fig.64 and p.131). Diams. 10 3/5 - 11 in., 270 - 280 mm.*

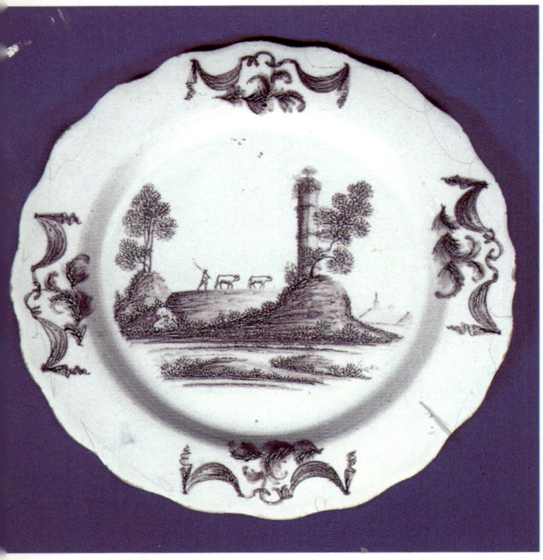

Top left : 24. A Dublin wavy-edge plate. No mark. 10 1/4 in., 260 mm.

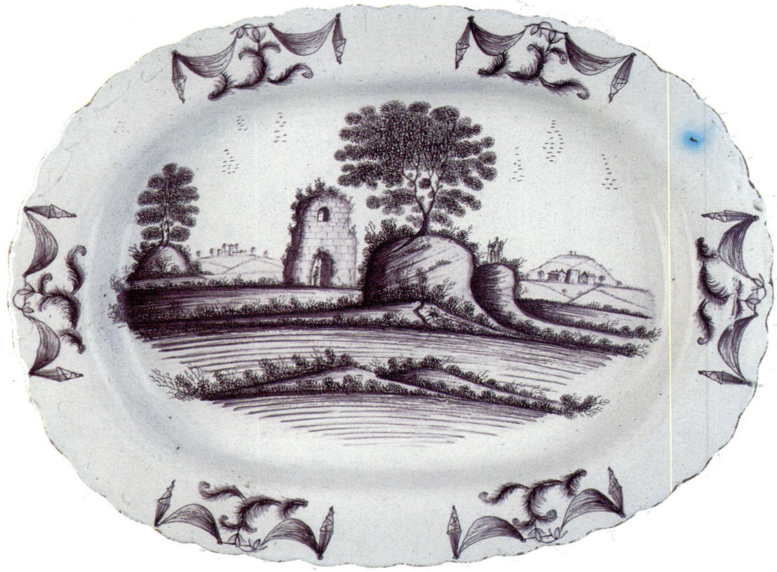

Above : 25. Large Dublin wavy-edge platter. Note the spot of errant copper-green pigment, top right. Under-rim painter's number '2'. 21 x 16 in., 535 x 405 mm.

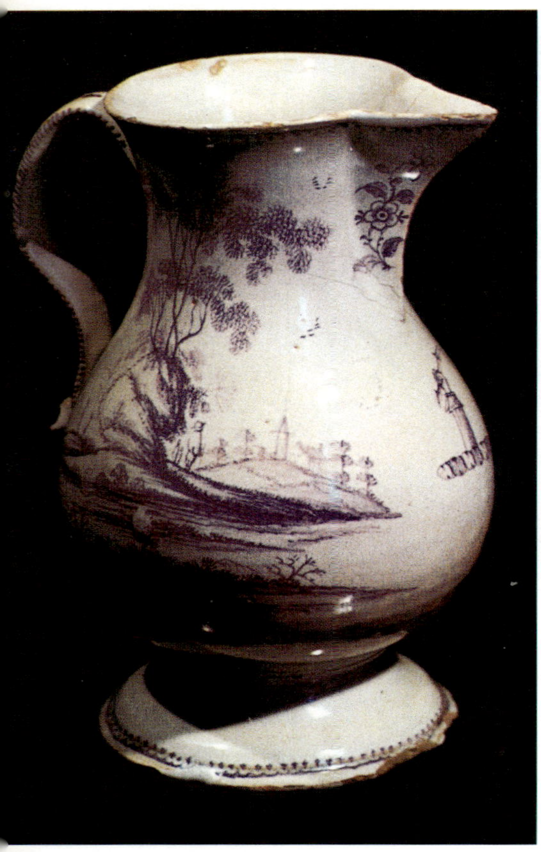

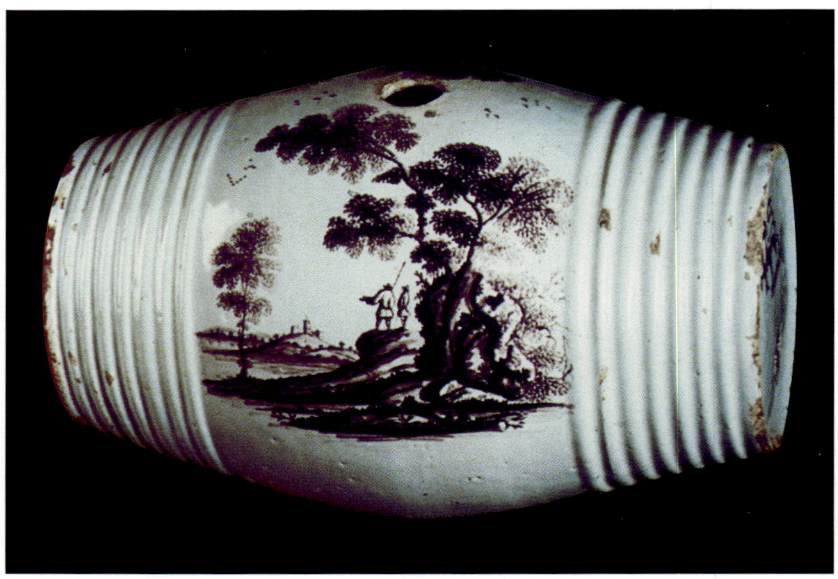

Above : 26. A Dublin jug, bearing the crest of the Armstrong family below the spout. Painter's 'NE' monogram mark on base. (See p.125, Fig.153). Ht. 9 in., 230 mm., diam. 5 1/2 in., 140 mm.

Left : 27. A Dublin wine or brandy barrel, one of a pair, bearing on each end the crest of the Molyneux family. No mark (See p.107). Length 11 3/4 in., 300 mm.

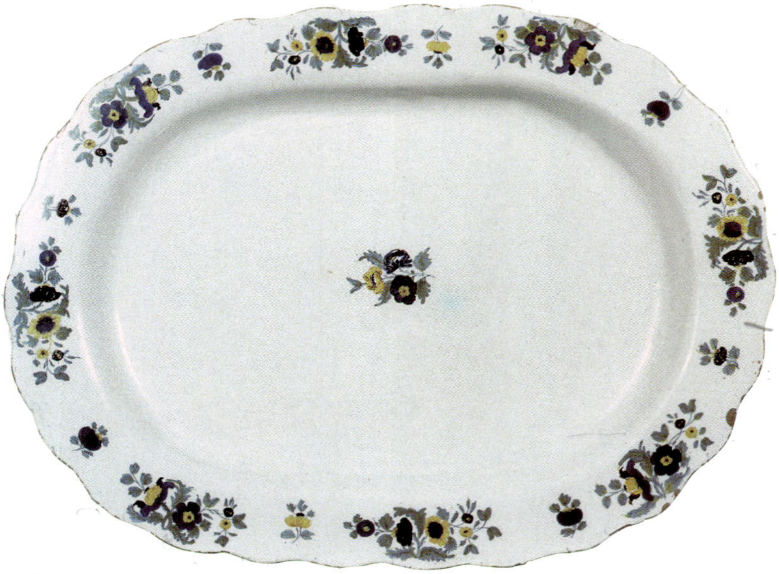

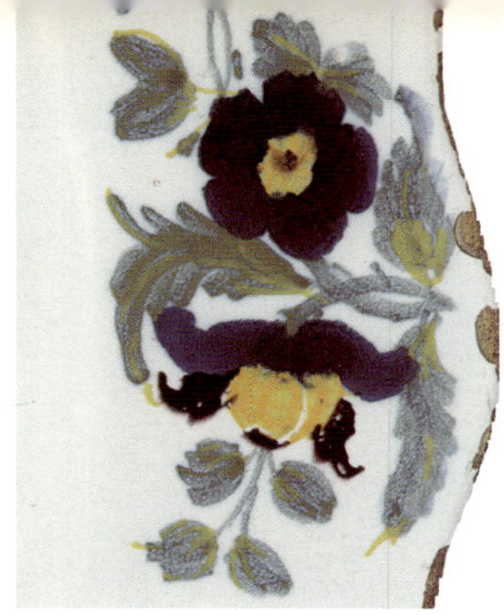

Left & above : 28. The 'Morgan' platter. This was the first example of coloured Dublin delftware to be recognised. (See p.99). The wavy-edged form is identical to examples that are decorated with typical Dublin landscapes. Note the trace of copper-green in the centre. (Cf. Colour plate 25, opposite). No mark. Length 22in., 560 mm.

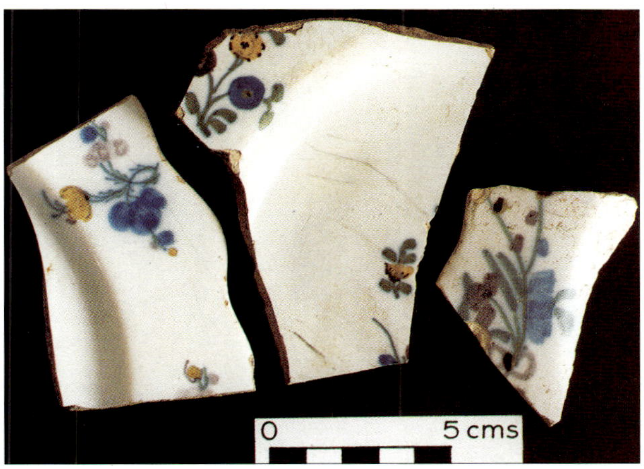

Centre left : 29. Polychrome Dublin delftware shards recovered in 1985-7 during excavations at Dublin Castle, (c. 1 mile from the pottery site). Note the 'tied ribbon' feature on one example, (right). See p.100. Compare Colour Plate 30.

Bottom left : 29a. Dublin delftware wavy-edge small plate, excavated at Dublin Castle. No mark. See p.126. Diam. $7^{1}/_{10}$ in., 180 mm.

Bottom right : 30. Circular platter. This is the only polychrome example recorded that exhibits a typical Dublin painter's number '6' under the rim. Note also the 'tied ribbon' on some of the floral sprays. See p.100. Diam. $15^{3}/_{4}$ in., 400 mm.

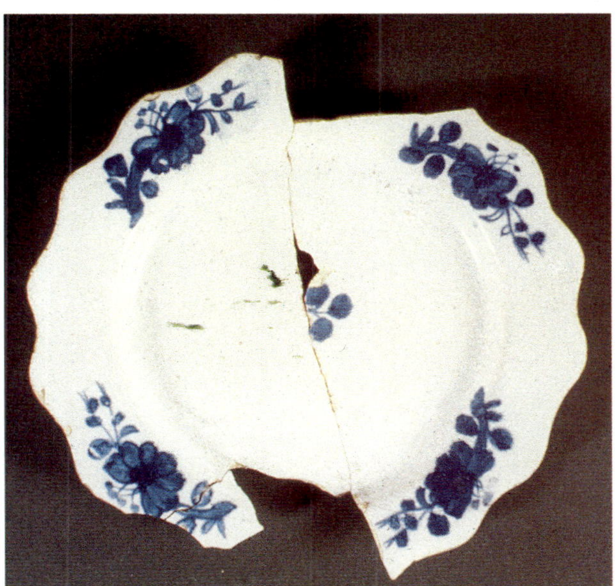

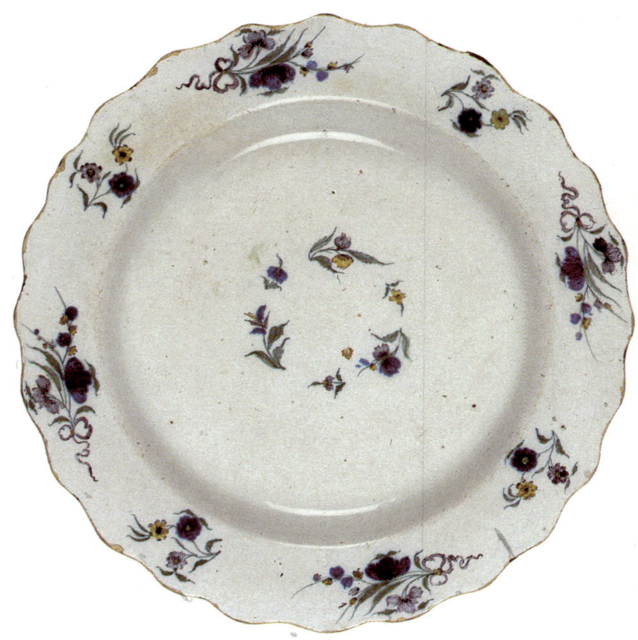

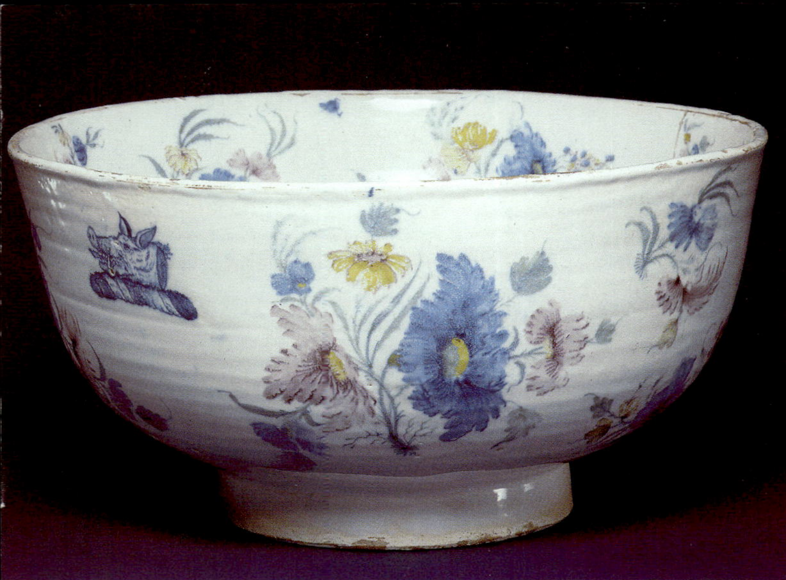

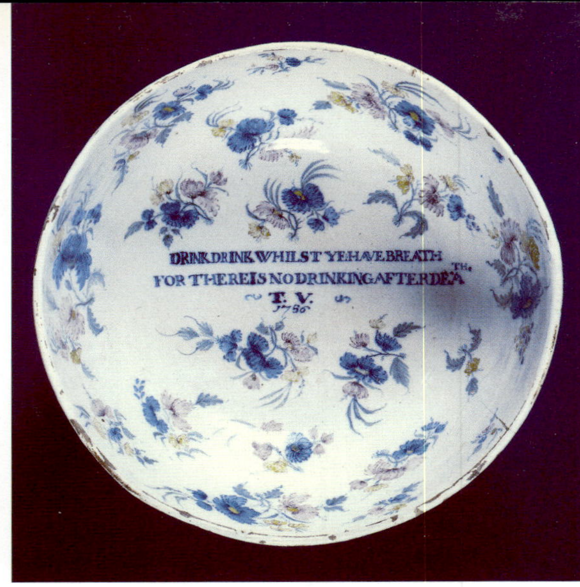

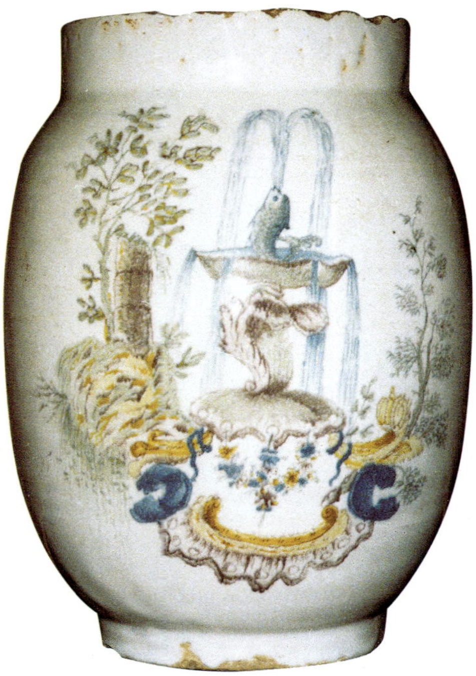

***Above left** : 31. Dublin delftware punch bowl, inscribed 'T.V. 1756', with the crest of the Verner family. The bowl is believed to have been made for Thomas Verner (d. 1788) of Verner's Bridge, Co. Armagh. The significance of the verse is explained on p. 99. No mark. Diam. 13 7/8 in., 352 mm., foot diam. 6 1/2 in., 165 mm., Ht. 7 in., 178 mm.*

***Above right** : 31a. The interior of the 'Verner Bowl'*

***Centre left** : 32. Wide-mouthed jar or vase. The painted design is the most complex yet recorded on coloured Dublin delftware. (See p. 137). No mark. Ht. 9 5/8 in., 245 mm.*

***Below** : 33. A pair of Dublin bough pots, possibly 'curious flower pots .. of Delamain's Ware', of the type sold in Cork in 1759. (See p. 115). No mark. Ht. 4 3/4 in., 120 mm. W. 7 3/4 in., 195 mm*

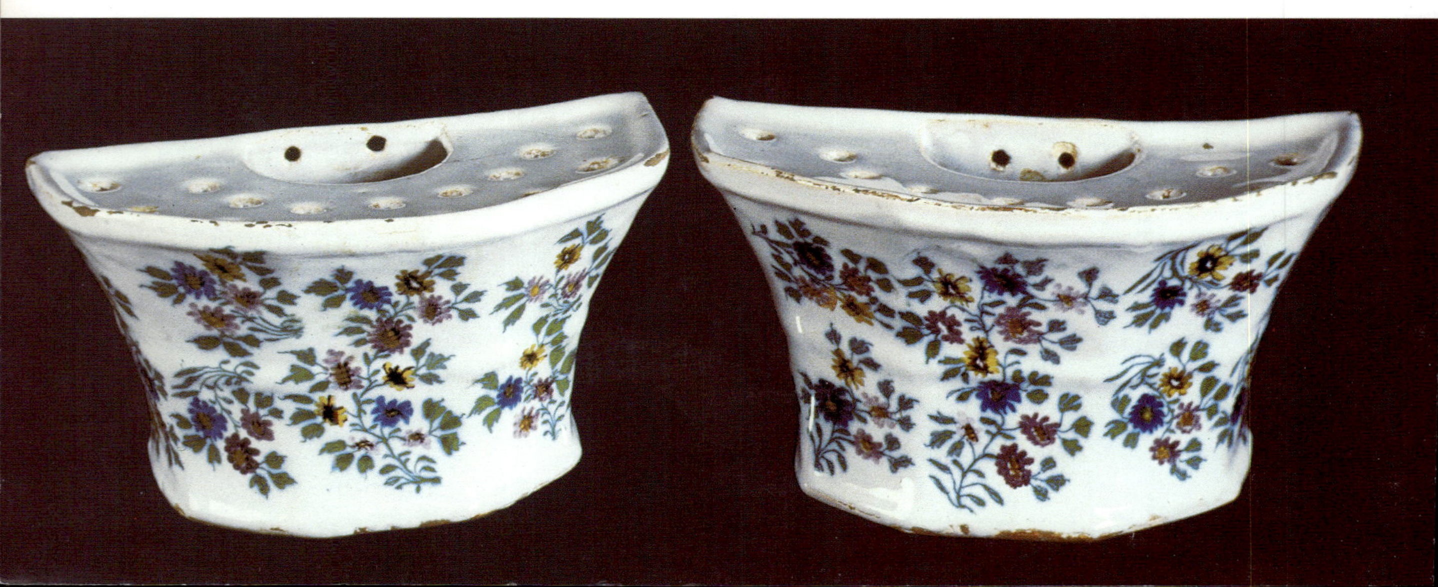

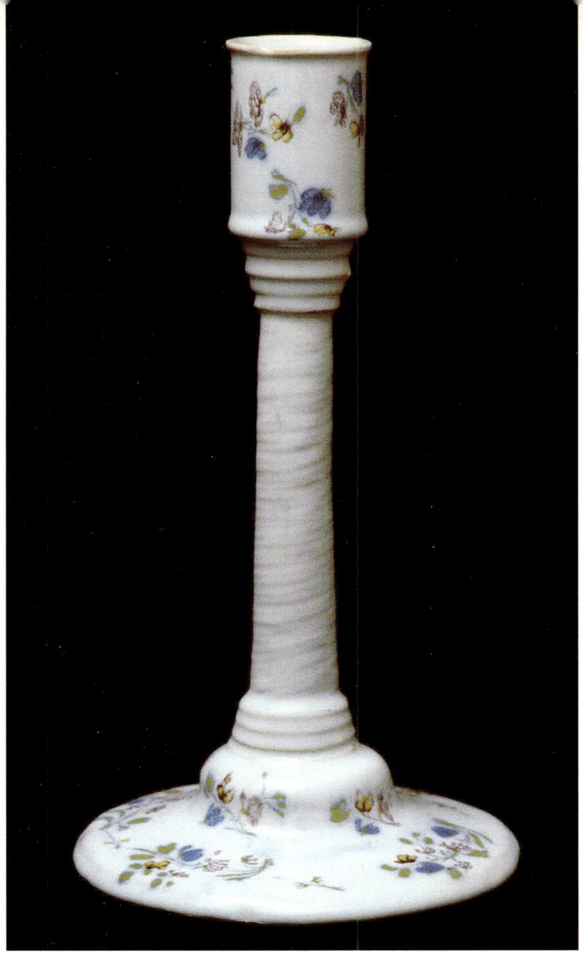

34. *Dublin delftware candlestick, copied from a South Staffordshire white glass original. (See p. 116). One of three examples known. No mark. Ht. $9\frac{5}{16}$ in., 235 mm.*

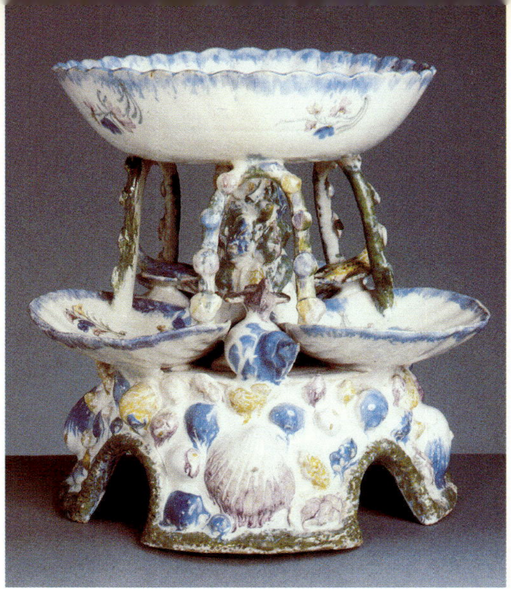

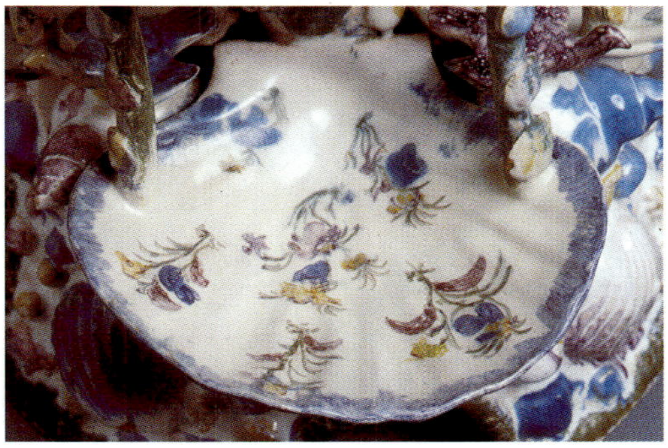

Above : 35 & 35a (detail). *Dublin delftware epergne on stand, decorated with typical coloured floral sprigs. No mark. Ht. $10\frac{3}{4}$ in., 273 mm. W. $10\frac{7}{16}$ in., 265 mm*

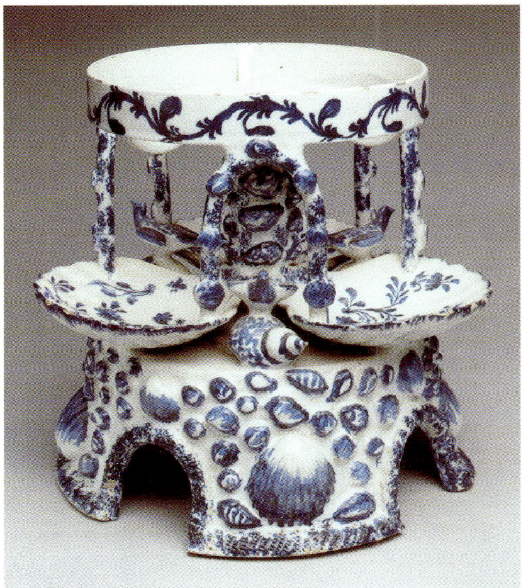

36. *Dublin delftware epergne on stand, with ring fitting to support a large, detachable bowl. Ht. $10\frac{1}{4}$ in., 260 mm. Internal diameter of ring $7\frac{1}{4}$ in., 185 mm. A second example is known, painted entirely in manganese, bearing the painter's monogram 'B'. (See p. 123).*

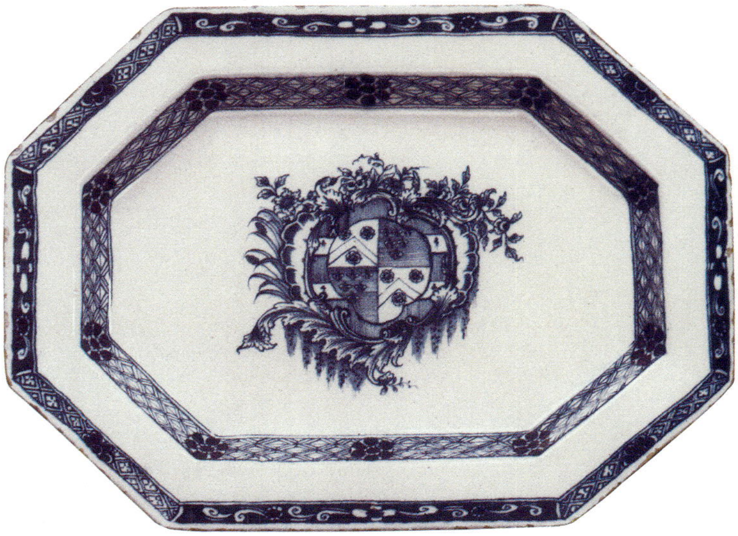

37. *Dublin delftware octagonal 'long' platter. Part of a dinner-service decorated with the arms of the Panton, Edwards and Wynne families, all of Denbeighshire in North Wales. There are no painters' marks on any portion of the surviving service. (See p. 102). Length 20 in., 508 mm.*

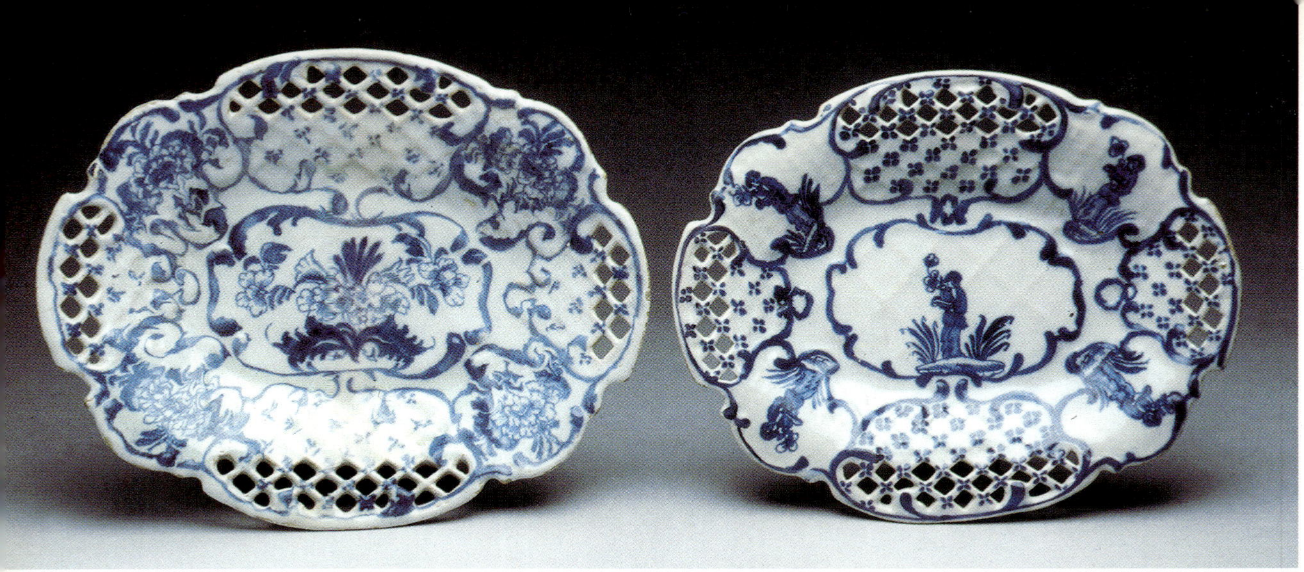

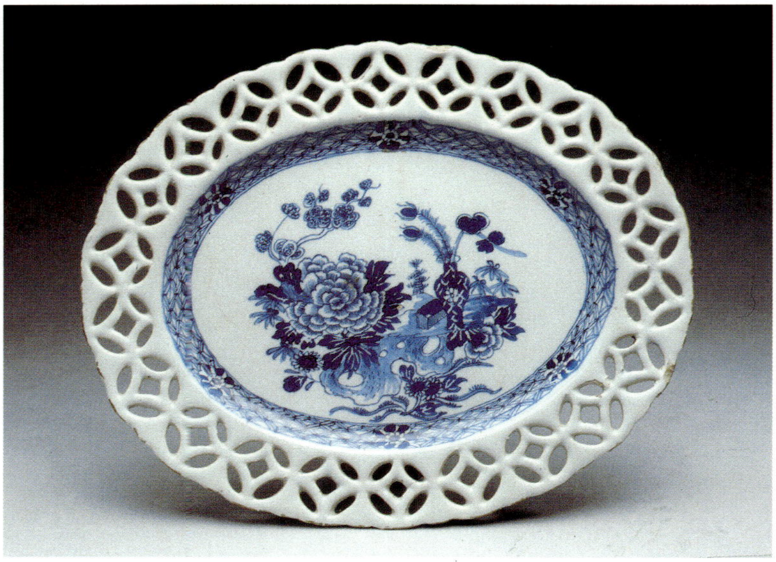

Above* : *38. *Two Dublin delftware moulded and pierced basket-dishes. Although both dishes have been copied from a Worcester porcelain original, there is significant variation in size. (See pp.106, 109, 110). For marks see Fig.123a. Left marked 'W', width 10 in., 260 mm. Right marked 'R', width 9⅝ in., 245 mm.*

Left* : *39. *Dublin delftware pierced-edge oval basket plate, 'Feathers in a Vase' pattern, painter's number '0' within footrim. (See Figs.111, 124-5). Length. 11½ in., 290 mm.*

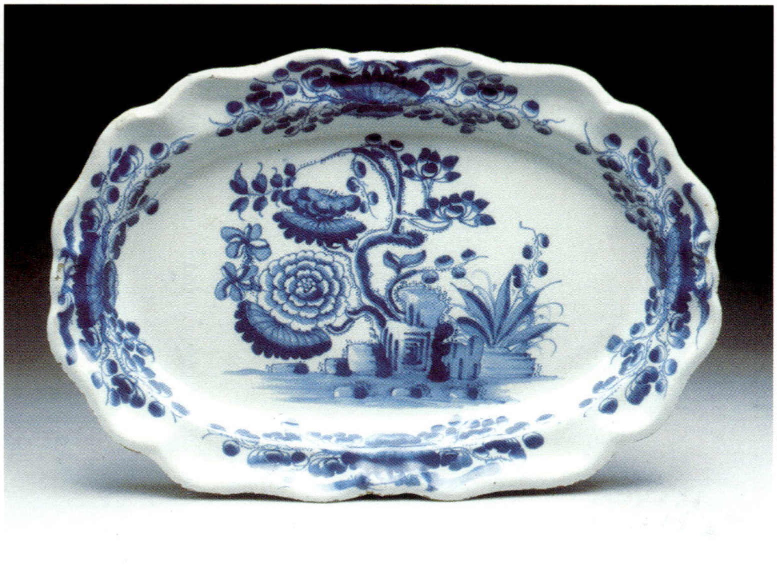

Left* : *40. *Dublin delftware wavy-edge small platter, painted with a version of the 'parasol flower' pattern. The same distinctive flower is recorded on various plates and platters, butter tubs and flower bricks, sometimes marked with floral sprigs or painter's numbers on the reverse. (See p. 126). Painter's number '4'. Length 14 in., 356 mm.*

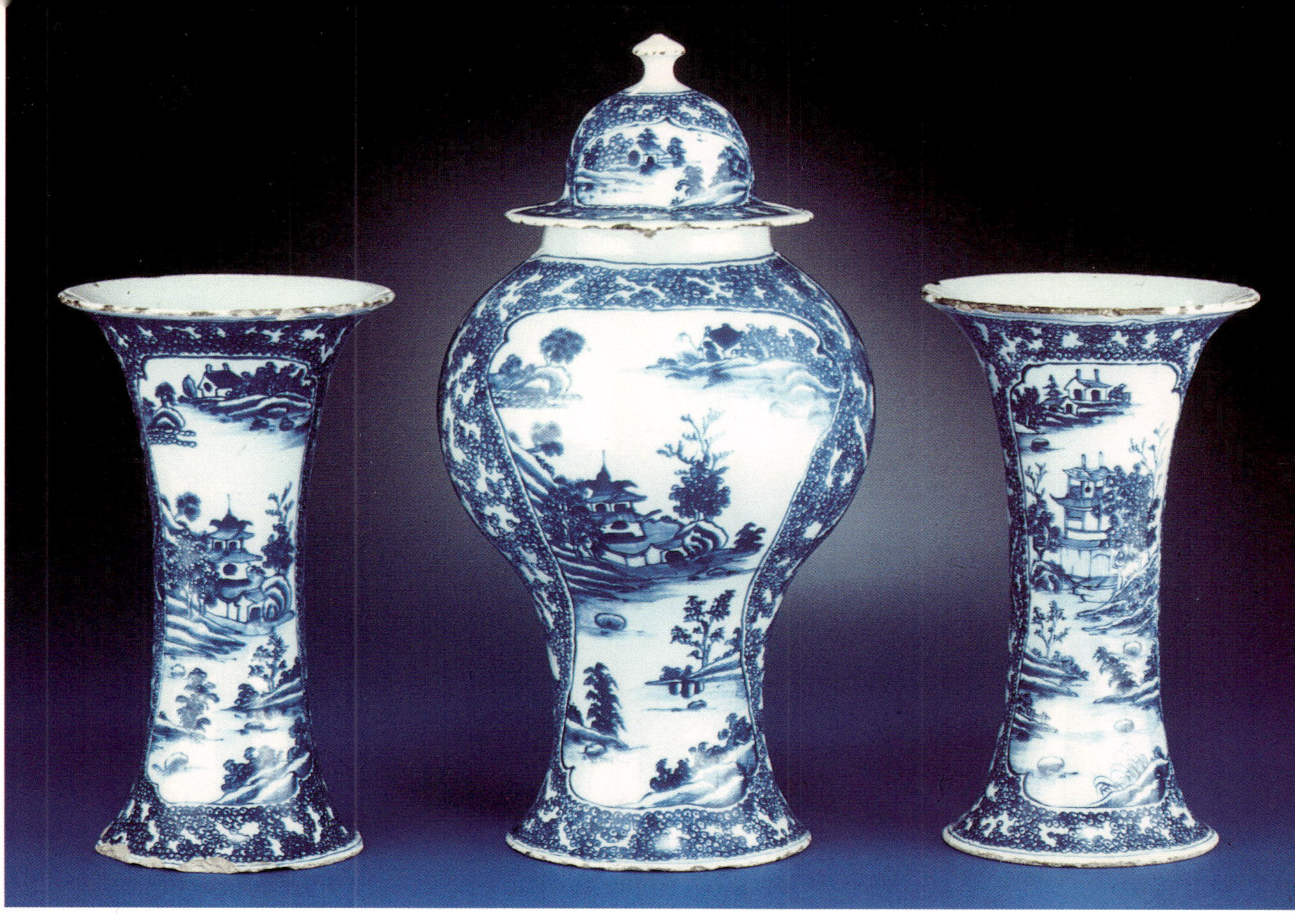

41. Dublin delftware, part-garniture of three vases painted with a compressed version of the 'Sampan Lake' pattern. Painter's number '4' on base of all three pieces. (See p.135). Ht.of baluster vase 11$\frac{1}{2}$ in., 292 mm. Flared vases Ht.. 8 in., 203 mm.

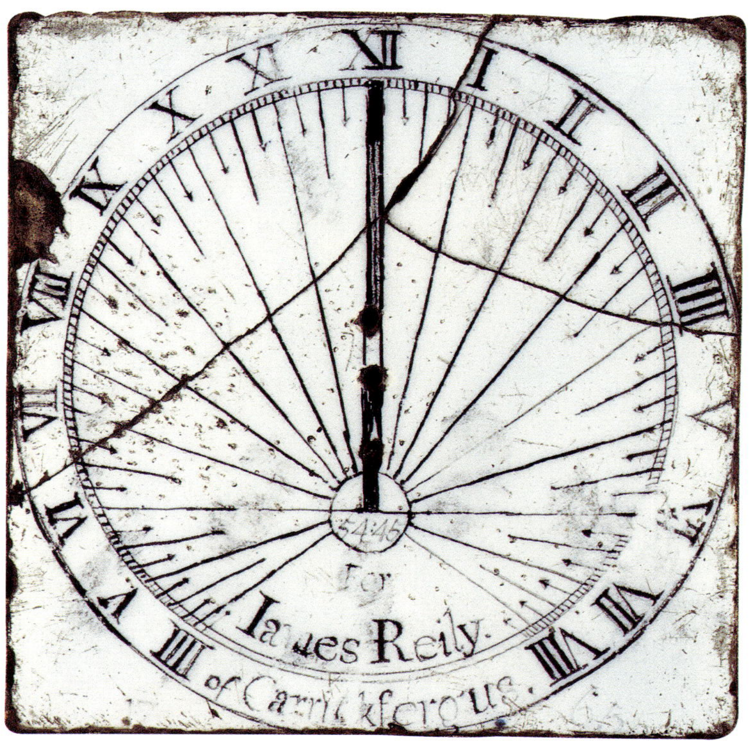

42. A unique, manganese-painted delftware sundial tile, attributed to the Little Patrick Street pottery, Belfast (<1754 - >1763), inscribed 'For James Reily of Carrickfergus 17 65'. (The date, on the bottom edge, is faint. No mark. (See p. 156).4$\frac{3}{4}$ in., 120 mm. square.

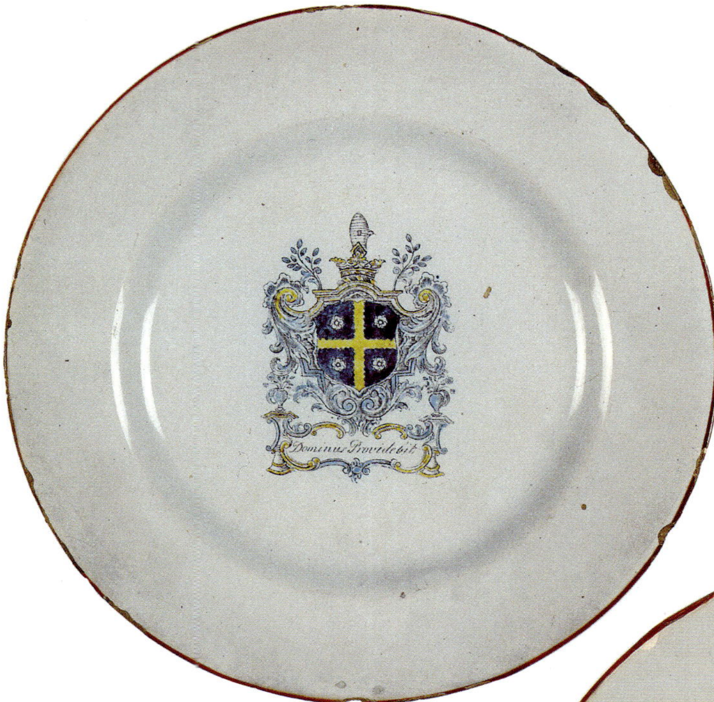

43, left. *Limerick delftware plate, bearing the transfer-printed arms of Francis Pierpoint Burton, MP for County Clare, highlighted with overglaze enamel colours. (See pp.160-2). Inscribed and dated on the back (45, below). Diam.* $8\frac{7}{10}$ *in., 221 mm.*

44, right. *Limerick delftware plate, bearing the transfer-printed arms of Edmond Sexton Pery, MP for Limerick, highlighted with overglaze enamel colours. (See pp.160-2). Inscribed on the back, Made by John Stritch Limerick 1761'. Diam.* $8\frac{3}{4}$ *in., 225 mm.*

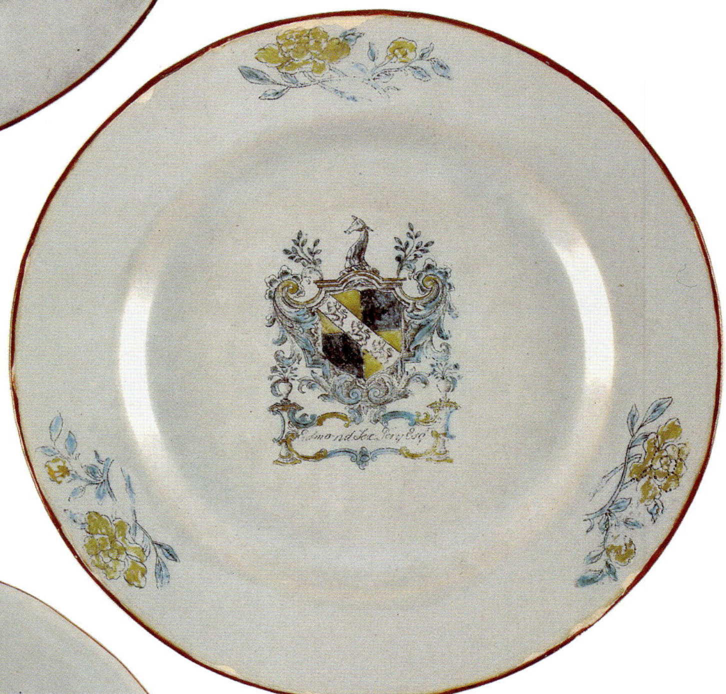

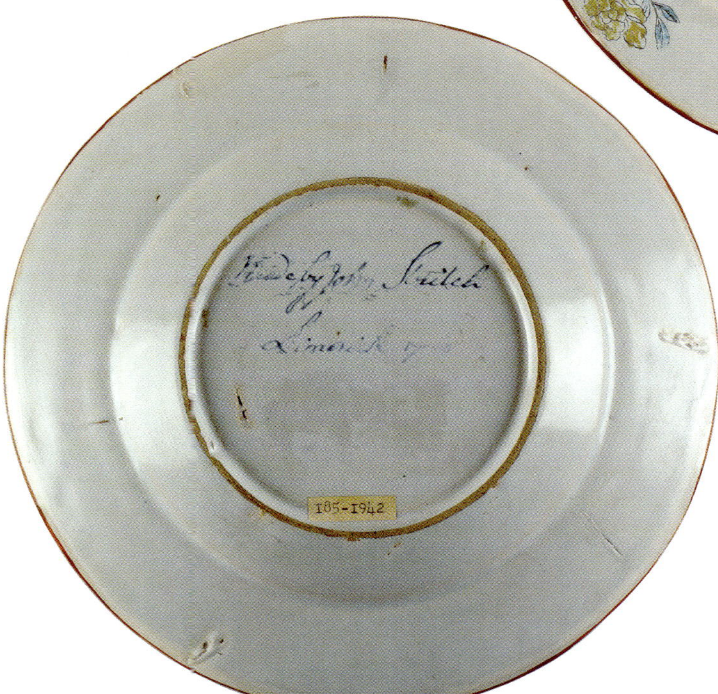

45, left. *Reverse view of the transfer-printed 'Burton' plate (Colour plate 43). Showing inscription 'Made by John Stritch Limerick 1761'. Note the* <u>*two*</u> *sets of three support scars around the rim (See pp.160-2).*

two sides and the trees on the reverse are details from the *'Two Deer and Pagoda'* pattern, **(Fig. 161)**. As on *'Two deer'* flatwares, the edge is lined in yellow ochre.

The second, smaller example **(Fig. 162)** has a vertical profile and is just 3¹/₈ in. (80 mm.) wide. The painted floral sprigs and crosshatched border are details from the *'Flower Spray & Ribbon'* pattern **(Figs. 141 & 142)**.

The undersides of these small pots are virtually identical, with a narrow footrim around the edge, and a slightly domed base. The first bears painter's number '4' in the centre, the second a painter's number '2'. The fact that both patterns also appear on flatwares suggests that these small dishes or tubs originally formed part of a dinner service. Both appear to haave been copied directly from Chinese porcelain. (A Chinese export porcelain potted meat dish in the author's collection is of identical size and form to **Fig. 161**).

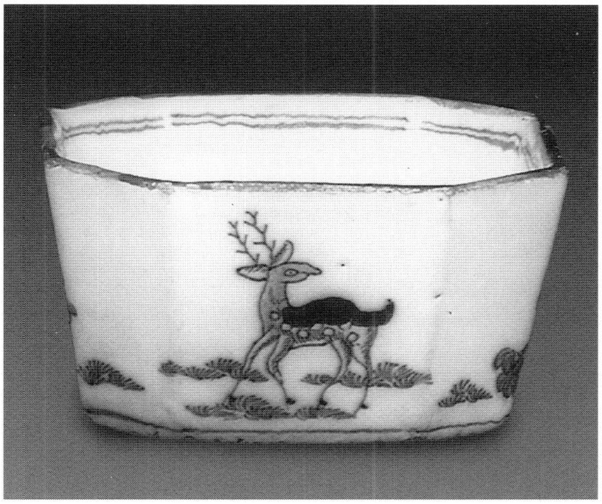

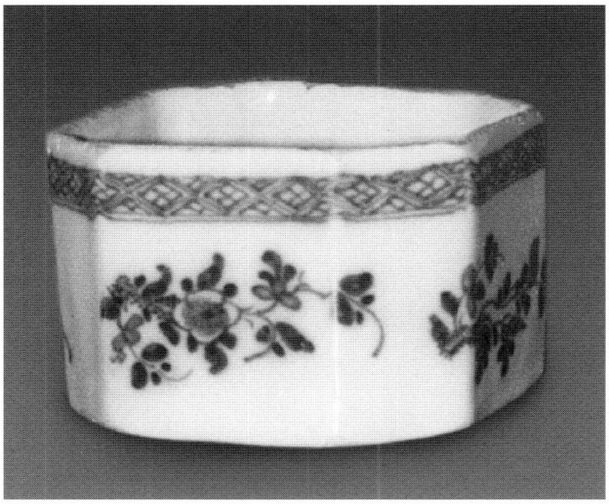

Top* : *Figure 161. *Dublin delftware octagonal potted meat dish, flared profile, 'Two Deer & pagoda' pattern, yellow edge. Painter's number '4' within footrim. Width (lip) 4¼ in., 107 mm.*
Bottom* : *Figure 162. *Dublin delftware octagonal potted meat dish, vertical profile, 'Flower Spray & Ribbon' pattern. Painter's number '2' within footrim. Width 3¹/₈ in., 80 mm.*

SAUCE BOATS

Mary Dorgan in Cork advertised Dublin delftware *'Sauce Boats'* during Mary Delamain's period of ownership in 1759, and so these items were certainly made. To date, however, no examples have been identified. One type of double-lipped sauceboat, with two handles modelled in the shape of foxes, is sometimes attributed to *'Dublin or Liverpool'*, when the painted decoration features European landscapes. (e. g. Ray, p. 173, pl. 48). Other examples are recorded, however, (e.g. Austin, p. 193, nos. 381-2), which are decorated with patterns that are not recorded among other Dublin delftware forms, which suggests that this group is probably not Irish.

SWEETMEAT SETS

These sets of small dishes, sometimes known as hors d'oeuvre sets, were probably used at the dinner table to serve pickles, condiments or small confectioneries. Only one type of Irish sweetmeat set is known; the full set comprises one relatively large tray, into which are placed five interlocking smaller dishes. Several complete sets are known in Dublin delftware, most of them decorated with patterns derived from Chinese porcelains, although a single example with a landscape scene is also recorded.

Other designs of sweetmeat sets exist, but these are readily distinguished from Irish examples, (e.g. Archer, G.10). The principal difficulty in recognising Irish examples is that one particular six-part sweetmeat set of almost identical design was also produced in England, probably in Liverpool, which seems to cause particular confusion. The main dish of one of these English examples is illustrated alongside the Dublin sweetmeat sets, to highlight the slight differences that exist.

The basic forms of the Irish sweetmeat sets are evident in **Figs. 163a-c**. Each individual dish in the set has a clearly defined footrim, and (in this case) is

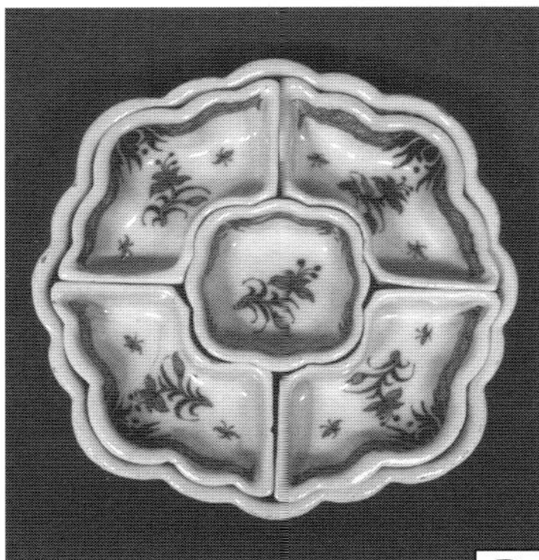

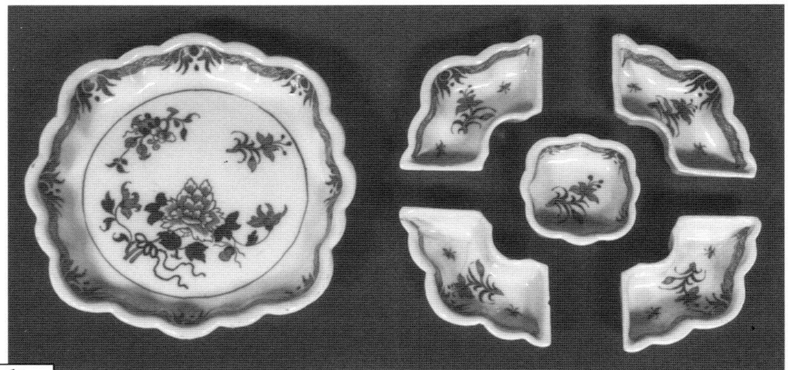

Dublin

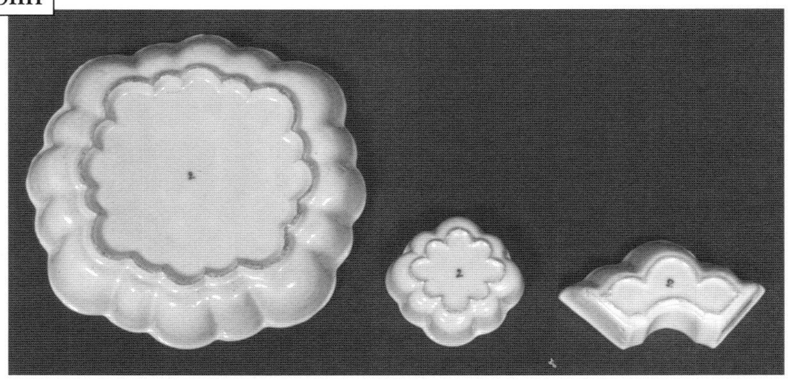

Figures 163 a - c. *Dublin delftware six-part set of sweetmeat or pickle trays. This example is unusual in bearing an otherwise unrecorded version of the 'Floral Spray & Ribbon' pattern (Type II). The border pattern is also unrecorded. Max. width of largest dish 8¾ in., 220 mm.*

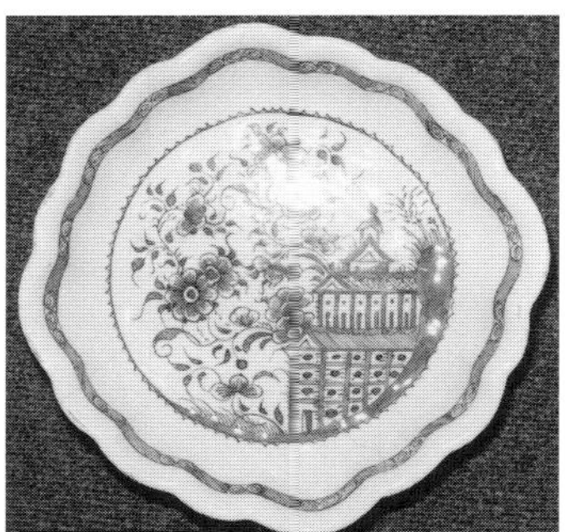

Liverpool

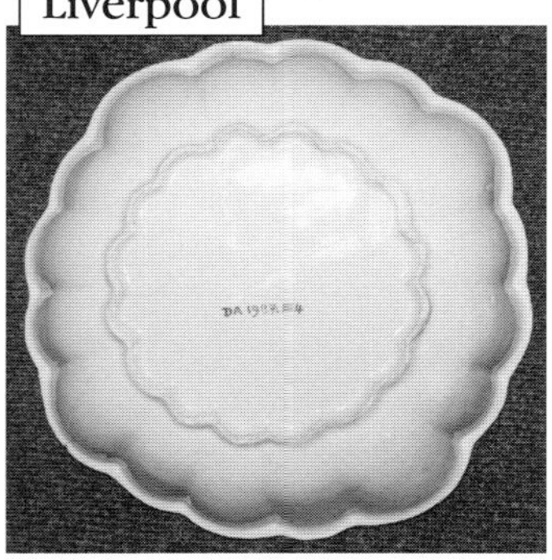

Top : ***Figure 165a.*** *Liverpool delftware sweetmeat tray, from a six-part set. No mark. Max. width 8¾ in., 223 mm.*
Bottom : ***Figure 165b.*** *Reverse of Liverpool sweetmeat tray*

Dublin

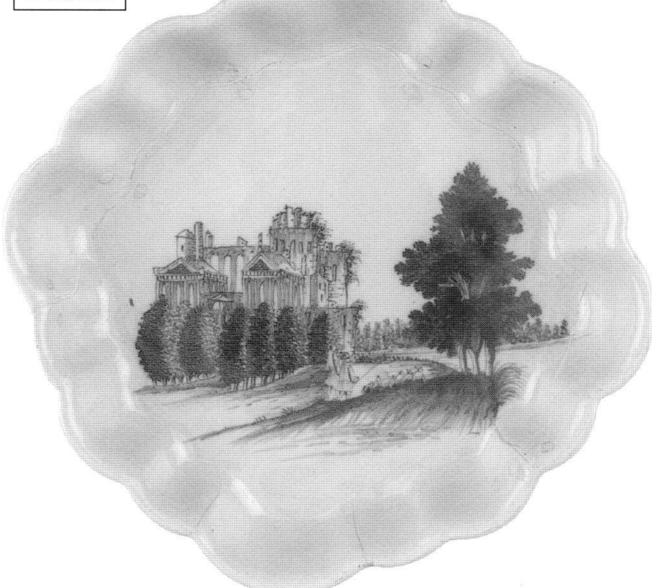

Figure 164. *Dublin delftware tray from a six-part sweetmeat or pickle set. The European landscape scene features a ruined classical building or cathedral in the distance, with a herdsman driving his flock in the foreground. No mark. Max. width 8¾ in., 220 mm.*

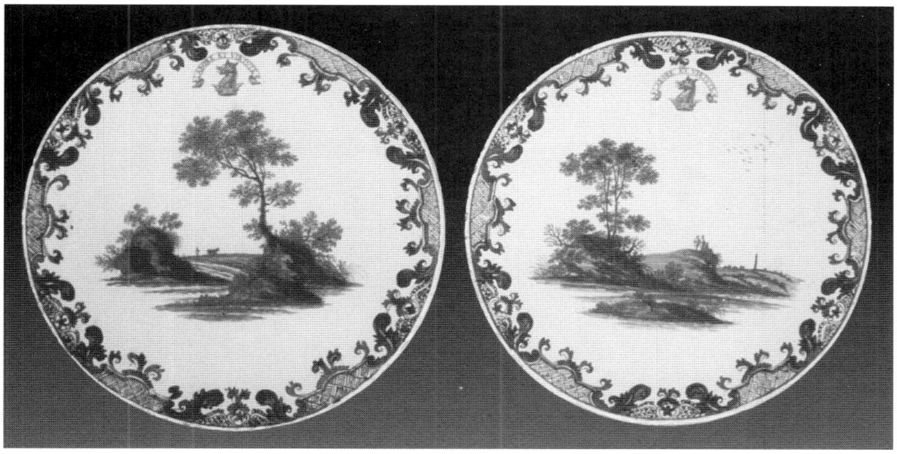

marked with a painter's number '2'. (Others are known that are unmarked, or bear painters' numbers '2', '3', '4' and 'S' or '8', both within the footrim and under the rim).[56] The only European landscape decorated example recorded is also illustrated. **(Fig. 164)**.

Each component of these sets was press-moulded, so that the forms are distinctive, but the English example **(Figs. 165a & 165b)** clearly demonstrates just how similar these Irish and English sweetmeat sets can be. The very slight differences in form are easiest to see in the shape of the press-moulded, scalloped footrims. **(Compare 163c, left and 165b)**. Both the English and Irish footrims exhibit 16 'scallops' or lobes, but overall, the footrim on the English example is roughly circular, whereas that on the Irish dish is closer to a square.

In this particular instance the painted design on the English set is not especially close to known Dublin patterns. Nonetheless, these sweetmeat sets do provide a clear illustration of just how closely the Irish delftware potters copied their competitors.

TABLE STANDS AND TRAYS

There is little to differentiate these two categories. Stands are usually entirely flat, allowing other vessels such as hot-water kettles or jelly-glasses to be placed on them. Trays or salvers have raised edges, and were used to carry objects to the table. Dated delftware examples of stands and trays have a comparatively wide date range, from 1669 - 1743, and so these Dublin examples, produced during the 1750s and 60s, might seem comparatively late.[57] The forms continued through into the nineteenth-century however, and are well represented in English blue and white transfer-printed earthenwares.

An impressive pair of large, circular table stands, bearing very finely painted landscape scenes, are the only Dublin table stands yet recorded. **(Fig. 166, Colour Plate 22)**. The same painted border design is present on the very fine plates that possess a provenance linking them to Lord George Sackville, the Lord Lieutenant of Ireland from 1751-55. (See **Fig. 107**). Unlike the plates, however, these stands bear a ducal crest above the motto 'Labore et Virtute'. The family has not been positively identified, but to the best of present knowledge, there appears to be no obvious connection with the Sackvilles.[58] It is probable, therefore, that these two stands were not made as part of this set, despite the identical border.

In illustrations, the painted border of these stands creates the impression that they are simply standard plates, with a raised rim, but in reality the upper surface is entirely flat, and altogether unlike a standard plate. The footrim on the reverse is also taller than a normal plate footrim, thus raising the stands about half an inch above the table surface. The distinctive markings on the reverse of these stands are discussed elsewhere **(Fig. 64)**. The rather crude

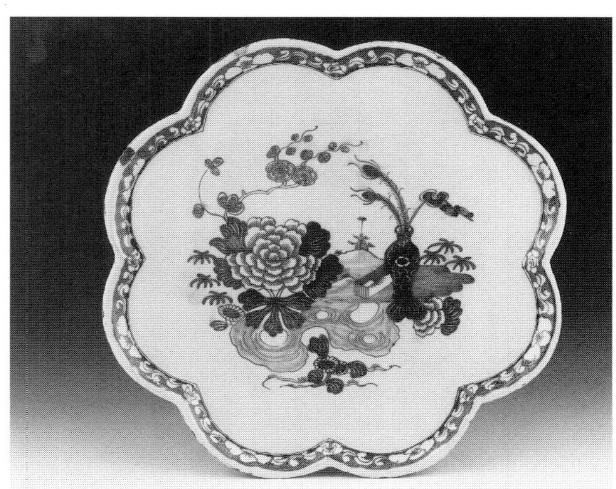

Top : Figure 166. *Dublin delftware table stands. Entirely flat upper surface, on tall circular footrims (see Fig. 64), each bearing a family crest and motto, possibly of the Wilson family. Diams. 280 and 270 mm. See also Colour Plate 22.*
Bottom : 167. *Dublin delftware eight-lobed tray, flat with raised edge and no footrim. 'Feathers in a Vase' pattern, painter's number '8' on glazed underside. Max. diam. 12$^{3}/_{8}$in., 314 mm.*

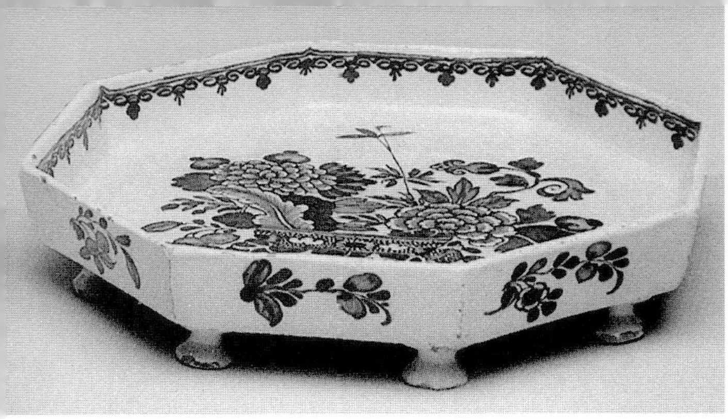

decoration and the highly uneven glaze characteristics on the reverse of these stands are strangely at odds with the exceptional quality of the painting of the front **(see Fig. 64)**.

Two different types of Dublin tray or salver are also recorded, one large and one small.

The first example, at Colonial Williamsburg, is a large, flat, eight-lobed tray with a slightly raised edge and <u>no</u> footrim.[59] **(Fig. 167)**. The central design is the *'Feathers in a Vase'* pattern - one of the most common of all Dublin designs, and the painter's number '8' is present on the glazed reverse.

The second example is a smaller tray or salver **(Fig. 168)**, which was only discovered by Garry Atkins in London within the last year or so.[60] It is octagonal in form, imitating a silver shape, with a pronounced, vertical edge, and with eight small feet around the edge at the points of the octagon. The central painted design in this case is the *'Chinese Flower-bowl'* pattern, perhaps the most common Dublin pattern of all, and the painter's number '7' is present in the centre of the glazed underside.

The range of painted patterns recorded on trays and stands suggest that they all formed part of larger dinner services originally.

TANKARDS

Only one small tankard, described previously with Armorial wares (p. 103, **Fig. 113**), is presently attributed to Dublin. The attribution is based both on the Irish armorial and on the style of painting, which compares well to other Dublin armorials.

The tankard is unexpectedly small, less than four inches in height. Its baluster-shaped body and 'broken-scroll' handle are identical in form to silver and pewter tankards of c.1740-60. A handle fragment of similar shape, in unglazed delftware biscuit, was recovered close to the site of the Little Patrick Street pottery in Belfast (p.155, **Fig.196 right**). There is thus a slight chance that this piece was made in Belfast, but on the basis of the painting style, the Dublin attribution is much more likely.

TILES

The only tile presently believed to have been made in Dublin is attributed very tentatively, and solely on stylistic grounds. **(Fig. 169)**. It is painted in blue and white with an unusual design of a squirrel nibbling a hazelnut, several features of which point to a Dublin origin. The most convincing is the style of foliage painting, which is strongly reminiscent of some Dublin floral-painting.

There are no references to tiles among the Dublin pottery's advertisements, but this does not exclude the possibility that some were made. (A few unglazed wall tile fragments were found on the site of the Belfast Potthouse, p. 32). One clue that suggests a small number of Dublin tiles might exist comes from the Westropp manuscripts in the National Library of Ireland.[61] In 1936, Dudley Westropp was contacted by Mrs. Florence Hodgkin of Reading, who, with her husband Stanley, had formed a once famous collection of *'over two thousand tiles'*.[62] Some of these tiles possessed numbers on the reverse - comparable to the painter's numbers on Dublin

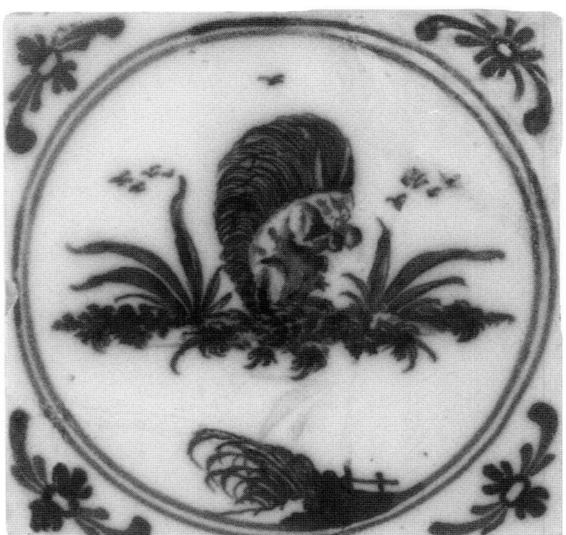

Top Left : Figure 168. *Dublin delftware octagonal salver, 'Chinese Flower-bowl' pattern, painter's number '7' on glazed underside. Width 10½ in., 265 mm.*
Above : Figure 169. *Delftware tile, tentatively attributed to Dublin on stylistic grounds. The top right corner is restored. No mark. 128 x 128 mm., 6 mm. thick.*

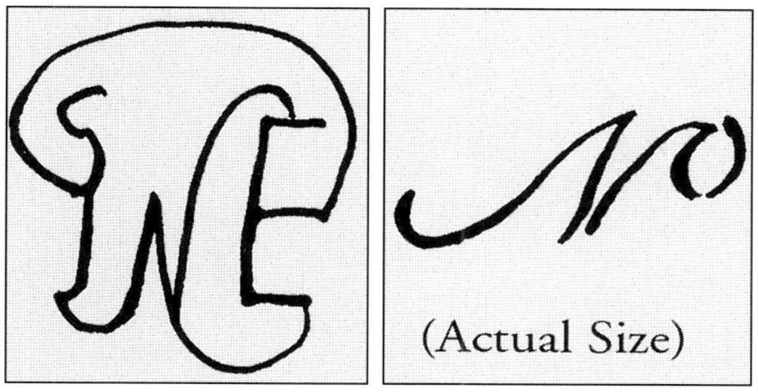

Figure 170. *Two marks recorded on the back of delftware tiles in the Hodgkin collection in 1936.*

delftware - leading Mrs. Hodgkin to conclude that such tiles might have been Irish. The vast majority of such numbers, *on tiles*, are different in character to the painter's numbers that occur on Dublin wares, and are believed to signify a Liverpool origin.

In the Hodgkin collection there were two further tiles with monogram marks, however, which seem especially intriguing. **(Fig. 170)**. One is comparable to a mark that occurs on a '*coarsely painted*' bowl **(Fig. 85b)**, or both may represent variations of the distinctive, Dublin '*NE*' painter's monogram. Unfortunately, the Hodgkin collection was dispersed at auction over a number of years from 1950 onwards. There is therefore no record of the design that appeared on the face of either of these tiles, and their present whereabouts are unknown. For now, we can simply record the existence of these two unusual marks, in the hope that the tiles will reappear at some future date.

The '*Radial Flower*' pattern that occurs on Dublin delftware plates, **(Colour Plate 14)**, is also recorded on tiles, in both cobalt-blue and manganese-purple. The pattern was undoubtedly a common one, however, and there are no features among the published tiles of this design to suggest they are anything other than English.[63]

Although a small number of tiles may have been produced in Dublin, the relative cheapness of Dutch tiles ensured their enduring popularity in Ireland. As early as 1667, a nobleman in County Antrim placed a single order for over 10,000 '*painted tiles*' costing £54 from Ostend for his gardens.[64] Their continuing, widespread use in Ireland is confirmed in 1774 by Charles Smith in his second edition of '*The Ancient & Present State of the County & City of Cork*', p. 245, where he notes that '*A remarkable branch of this* [earthenware] *trade, and one which we continue to import in considerable quantities from Holland, is the article of tiles, for roofing and flooring, as also chimney tiles, on many of which one meets with no unelegant designs, done by children in that country, and sold extremely cheap. In the Dutch work-houses, things are so managed, that a child of five years old may earn its livelihood; and the inuring child betimes to labour, seems to be a natural cause of the busy habit, which a stranger easily observes among the people of Holland*'.

TUREENS

In compiling this list of different Dublin forms, perhaps the most unexpected finding of all was that,

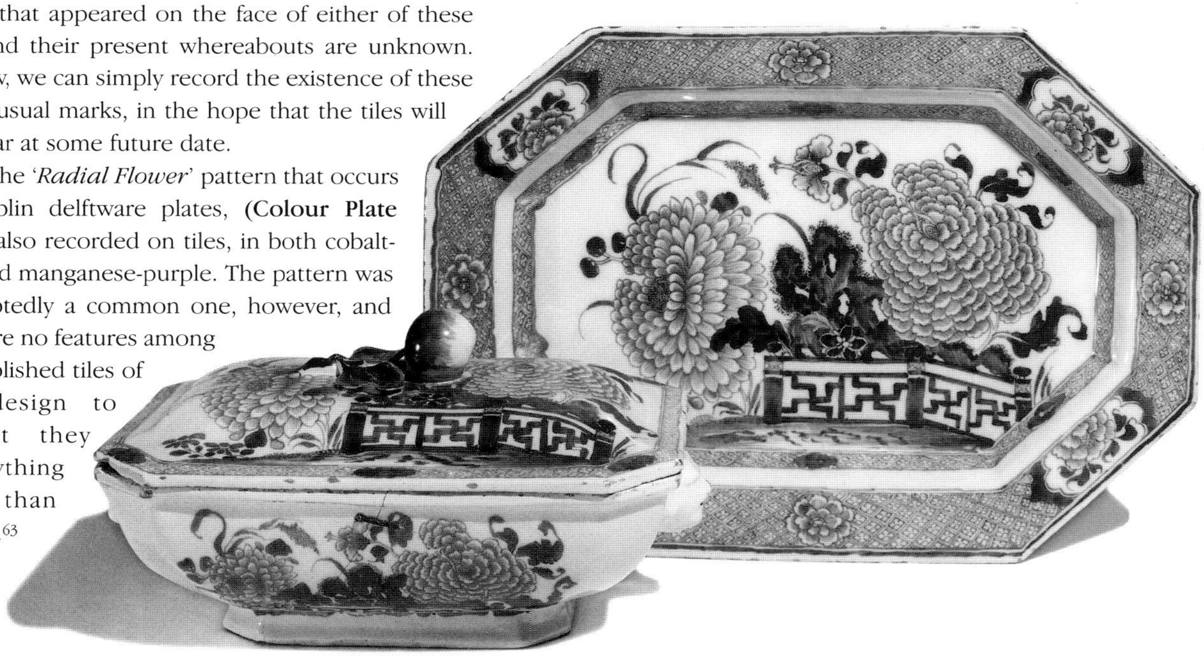

Figure 171. *Dublin delftware tureen and stand, painted with the particularly striking 'Peony and Fence' pattern, copied from Chinese porcelain. Painter's number '7' on underside of tureen, lid and stand. Tureen; Ht. 6 3/8 in., 162 mm., L. 12 3/8 in., 315 mm., W. 7 5/8 in., 193 mm. Lid; Ht. 2 15/16 in., 75 mm., L. 11 5/16 in., 288 mm., W. 7 9/16 in., 192 mm. Stand; L. 17 in., 431 mm., W. 11 15/16 in., 303 mm.*

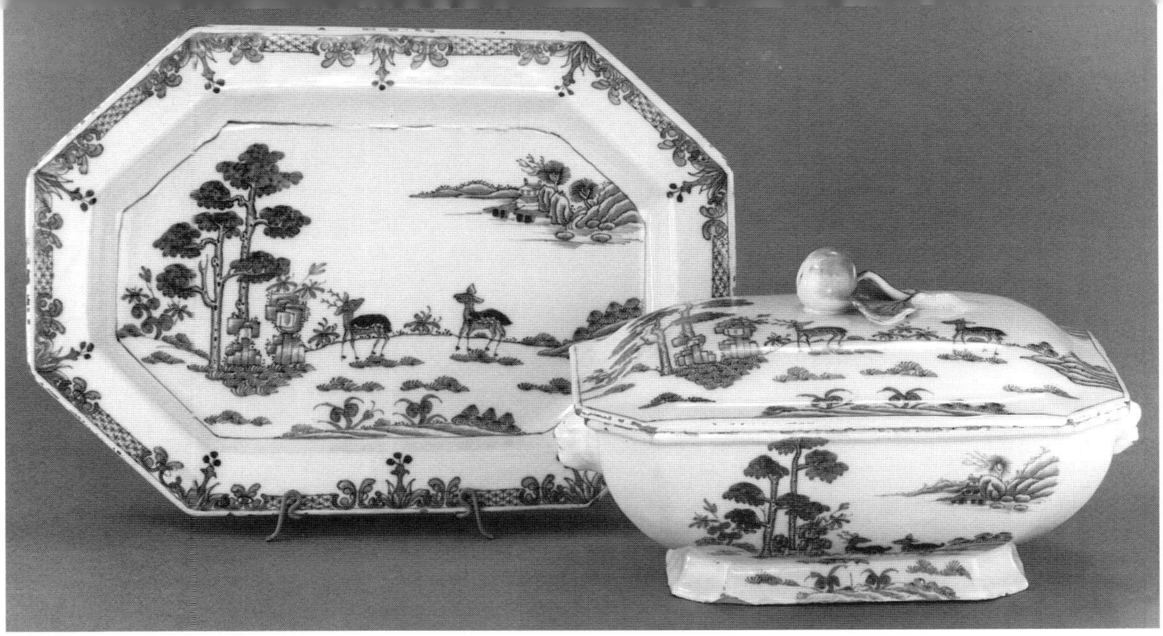

Figure 172*. Dublin delftware tureen and stand, 'Two Deer & Pagoda' pattern. Painter's number '8' on underside of tureen, lid and stand. Tureen; Ht. 8 in., 203 mm., L. 13⁵/₈ in., 346 mm., Stand; L. 17 in., 432 mm.*

so far, only one type of Dublin delftware tureen seems to have been recorded. There is a considerable discrepancy here with the documentary evidence, as the 1759 advertisement for Mary Delamain's delftware included *'round and long Terenes, scalloped and plain'*, (p.58), which suggests that four varieties existed, maybe more. Even when we examine the known range of Dublin objects, it is obvious that certain types of tureen are simply not represented. There are no fluted examples, for example, to accompany the recorded butter-tubs, **(Figs. 134-5)**, nor are there tureens to match the scalloped, oval platters imitating Chinese porcelains, **(Fig. 99)**.

The recorded Dublin tureens are octagonal, '*long*' tureens, two examples of which are illustrated with their matching stands. **(Figs. 171, 172)**. All three parts - tureen, lid and stand - have been press-moulded. There are considerable differences in size of up to 2-4 inches overall, but the two examples are nonetheless identical in form. Each sits on a flared foot and has a broad, flat, glaze-free footrim. The applied knops are modelled as hollow apples, pierced on the underside, and set on a short stalk with two leaves. The two applied handles on either end are also hollow, press-moulded in the form of open-mouthed, human faces. Each individual portion - tureen, lid and stand - is marked with a painter's number. (For further, detailed illustrations of **Fig. 171**, see Archer, G.21).

Ironically, although no other Dublin tureen forms are known, examples of this type seem to be comparatively common. All are decorated with patterns based on Chinese porcelains, suggesting that they probably date from the 1760s, and all are marked with painter's numbers. Known examples are painted with the *'Chinese Flower-bowl'*, *'Feathers in a Vase'*,

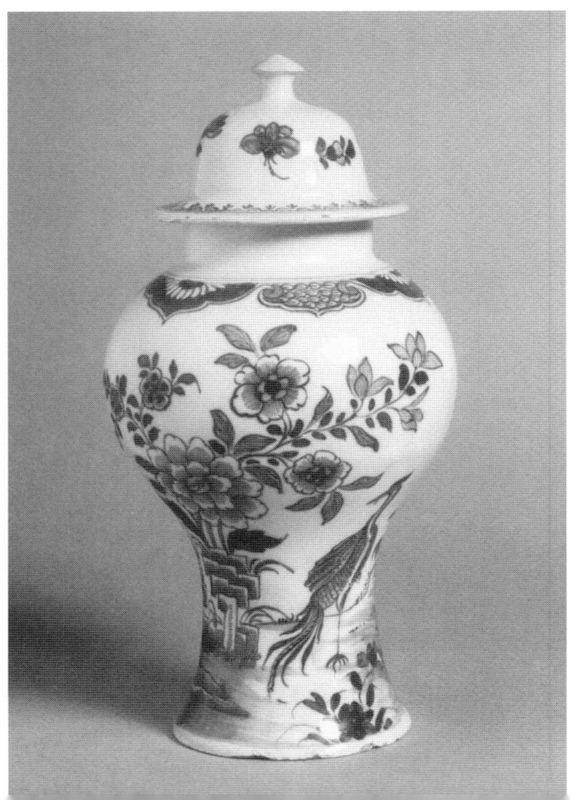

Right : Figure 173*. Dublin delftware, small baluster vase and cover, painted in blue with a design copying Chinese porcelain. One of three, identical vases, all marked on the base and inside the lid with painter's number '11'. The same pattern is recorded on a platter in the National Museum of Ireland that was almost certainly made in Dublin, c. 1760-70. Ht. 4⁷/₈ in., 124 mm., diam. 4⁹/₁₆ in., 116 mm.*

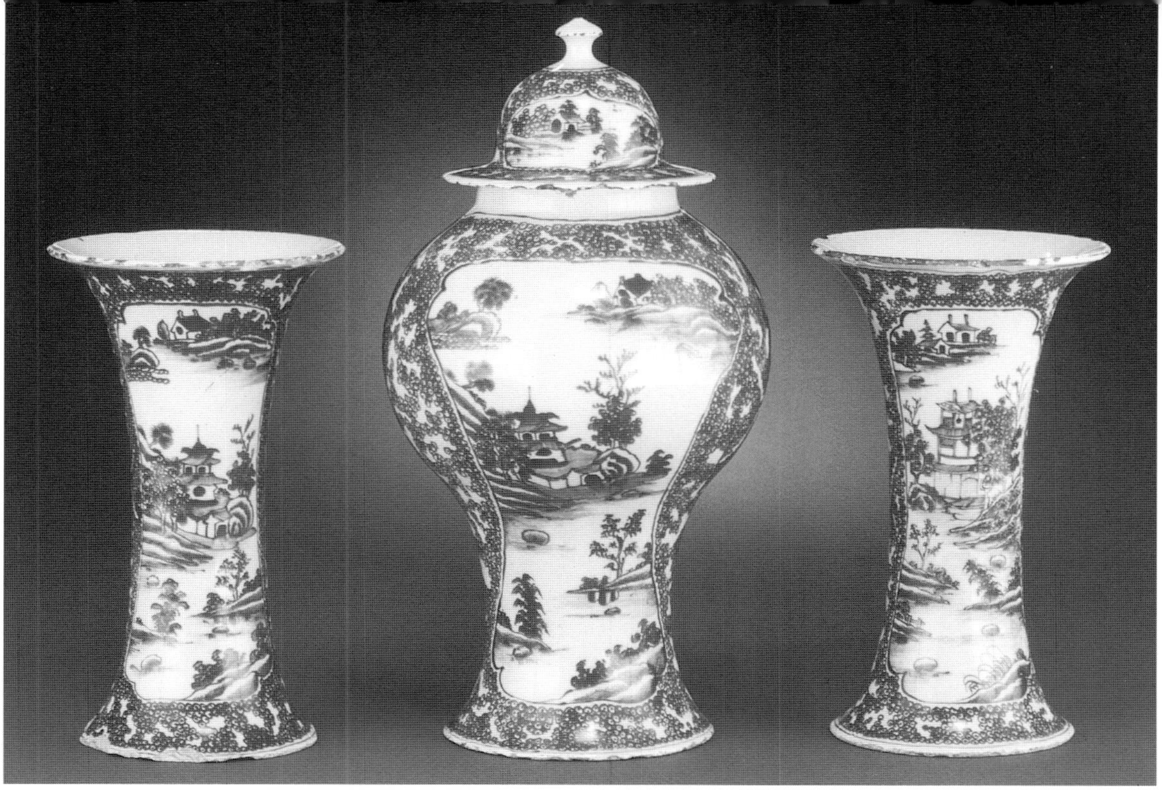

Figure 174. Dublin delftware, part-garniture consisting of baluster vase and cover, with two flared trumpet-vases, all painted in blue with a slightly compressed version of the 'Sampan Lake' pattern. (missing its 'Sampan'). (See Colour Plate 41). Painter's number '4' on base of all three pieces. Baluster vase and cover. Ht. 11½ in., 292 mm., Flared vases Ht. 8 in., 203 mm.

'*One Bird*' and '*Flower spray & Ribbon*' patterns.[65] Yet despite the variety in the painted decoration and size, the form appears to be entirely constant throughout, even in the details of the applied knops and handles.

Clearly, much remains to be discovered in this area. There appear, as yet, to be no examples marked with painters' monograms rather than numbers, and no '*round*' or '*scalloped*' tureens. There should also be greater variation in size, if the Dublin potters were attempting to imitate contemporary Chinese porcelain services. Most Chinese dinner services of this period usually include several small tureens, of about 6 to 8 inches in length. The author has to date handled only one example of a small, Dublin delftware, octagonal tureen stand, but this does at least confirm that small tureens do exist. This stand is painted with the '*Three Pagodas*' pattern, **(Fig. 158)** and is 7⅜ in., 186 mm. in length.[66]

VASES AND JARS

Dublin examples of vases and jars are among the most difficult objects to identify with any degree of certainty, for two main reasons. Firstly, only three examples are decorated with patterns that occur on more typical Dublin flatwares, and so there are few points of comparison with known pieces. Secondly, the majority of vases and jars are unmarked. Although painters' numbers do occur occasionally, none are marked with distinctive, Dublin monograms, to provide a safe point of reference. Michael Archer's remark that '*There is an Irish-Liverpool category* [of delftwares] *that will probably never be completely disentangled*' probably applies more to vases and jars than to any other group of wares.

Nonetheless, two groups of vases can be recognised as very probably Dublin. The first example is a small vase and lid, one of three from a single *garniture de cheminée*, formerly in the Lipski collection.[67] **(Fig. 173)**. The neatly painted number '11' appears on the base and lid of each of the three vases. The painted pattern represents a long-tailed bird in an oriental landscape, which precisely matches the design on a large, scalloped delftware platter in the National Museum of Ireland that was almost certainly made in Dublin.[68] The fact that these vases are decorated with a known Dublin pattern and are also marked with recognised Dublin painters' numbers provides some confidence in this particular attribution.

Another group of vases in Colonial Williamsburg are similarly marked with painters' numbers - in this case, the number '4' on the base of

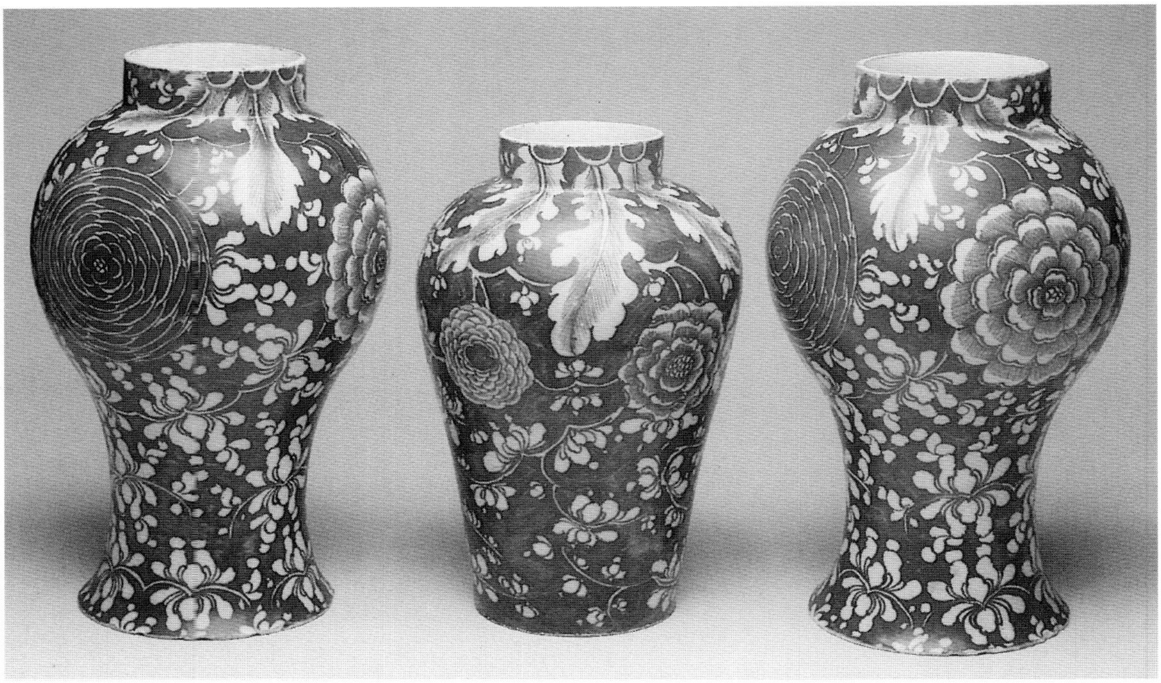

***Figure 175**. Delftware vases & jars, Dublin or Liverpool. The two baluster vases are marked on the base with painter's number '2'. Ht. of vases 6½ in., 165 mm.*

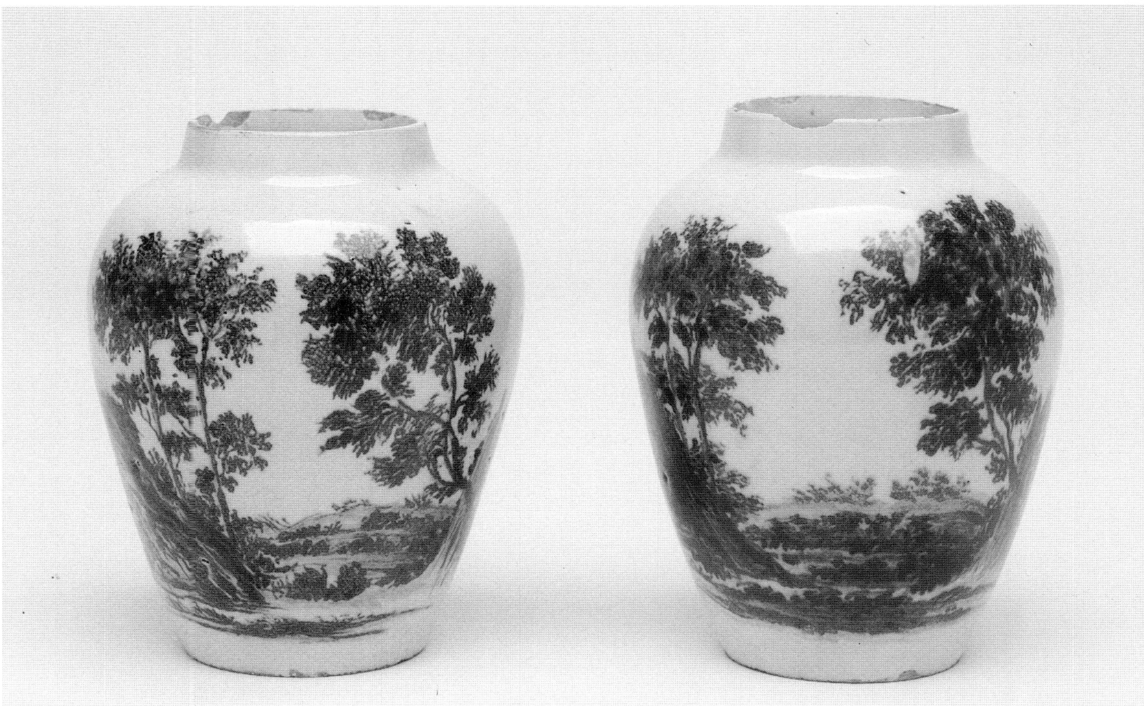

***Figure 176**. Dublin delftware, pair of small jars, finely painted in blue with European landscape scenes. (See Colour Plate 20). No marks. Ht. 4 in., 100 mm.*

all three pieces. **(Fig. 174, Colour Plate 41)**. A scan of the literature suggests that painters' numbers of this kind are not common on vases, so that the fact that the painted decoration on this trio also corresponds with a known Dublin pattern is highly significant. The main scene on the large vase, and on the left-hand beaker-shaped vase, represents a slightly compressed version of the '*Sampan-Lake*' pattern, (without its sampan). The original garniture probably contained five pieces, but we are fortunate that the two beaker-shaped vases have survived, as the form does not appear to be otherwise recorded in Irish delftware.

The fact that both of these sets bear painters' numbers and also feature recognised Dublin designs strengthens their Irish attribution. (Another point of coincidence is that the form of the knop is identical). Unfortunately, a painter's number is not as sure an indicator of a Dublin origin as a painter's monogram. In cases where there are no other points of comparison, an Irish attribution is more difficult to sustain. This is clearly demonstrated by an extremely unusual group of blue-ground floral vases and jars, six of which have come to light during the past few years.[69] The large baluster-vases illustrated are both marked with a painter's number '2' on the base. **(Fig. 175)**. The fact that other examples of baluster-vases with painters' numbers seem to have been made in Dublin does suggest that these vases and jars might also be Irish. On the other hand, their decoration does not seem to have any parallel among known Dublin delftwares, and so - without any other point of comparison - a '*Dublin or Liverpool*' attribution remains the safest conclusion.

As we have noted previously, many of the Dublin wares decorated with European landscapes were entirely unmarked. In some cases, the style of landscape painting is so distinctive that examples can be readily recognised, regardless of the form or the presence of a mark. This is the case with a unique pair of small jars in the Ulster Museum, which both feature very fine quality European landscapes. **(Fig.176, Colour Plate 20.)**. Not all Dublin landscape-painted vases are so easily distinguished.

The small polychrome jar illustrated in **Fig.177 and Colour Plate 32** is one of the most interesting pieces to have been discovered since the Castletown

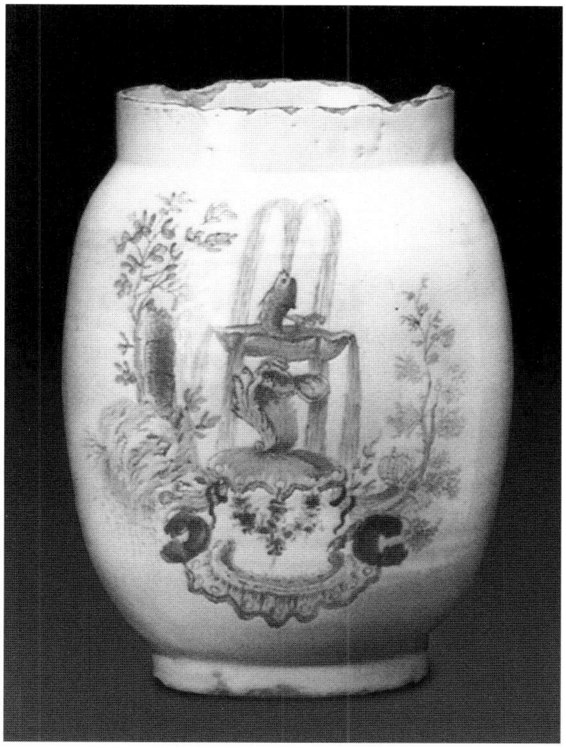

***Figure** 177. Dublin delftware, polychrome wide-mouthed jar. (See Colour Plate 32). No marks. Ht. 9⁵/₈ in., 245 mm., Base Diam. 4¹/₄ in., 108 mm., Lip Diam. 5¹/₈ in., 130 mm.*

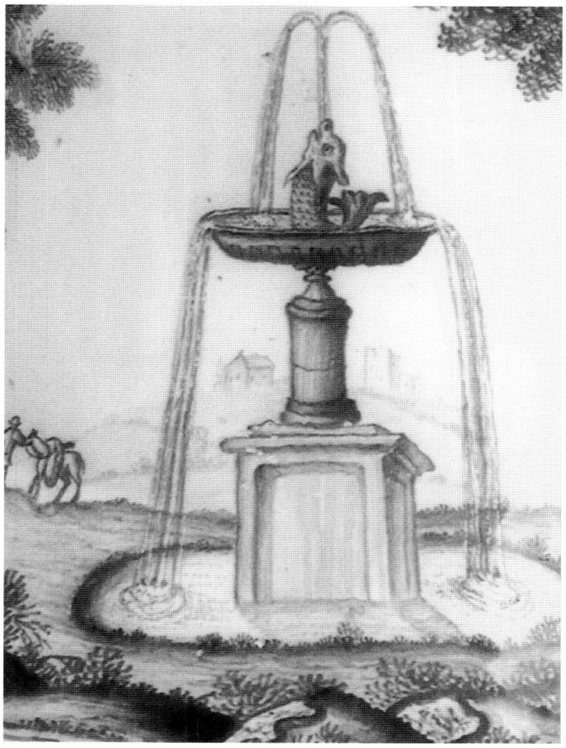

***Figure** 177a. Detail of the fountain illustrated on a Dublin delftware cistern, (See Fig.140). See also Fig.178 overleaf.*

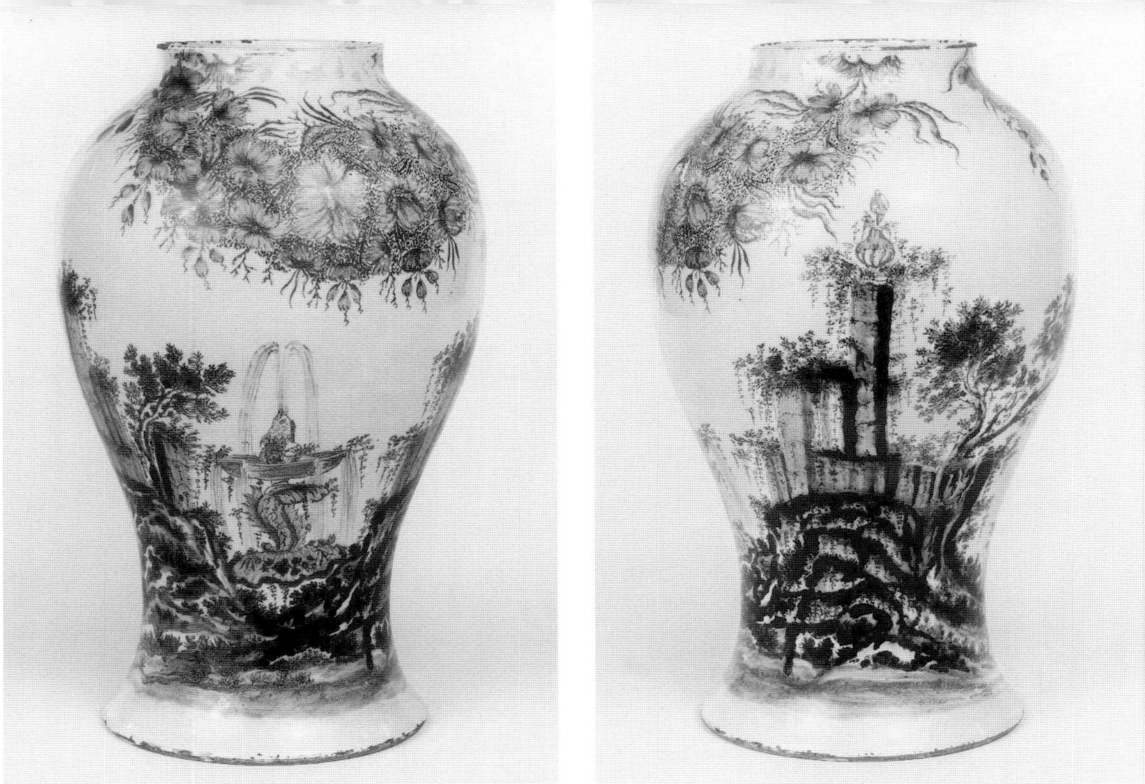

***Above* : Figures 178a & b.** *Dublin Delftware vase, painted in blue. No mark. Size not recorded.*
***Below* : Figures 179a & b.** *Delftware vase, probably Dublin. The unusual floral design appears to be a finely-painted version of the distinctive 'parasol-flower' pattern, (compare Fig. 156). No mark. Ht. 11⅝ in., 295 mm.*

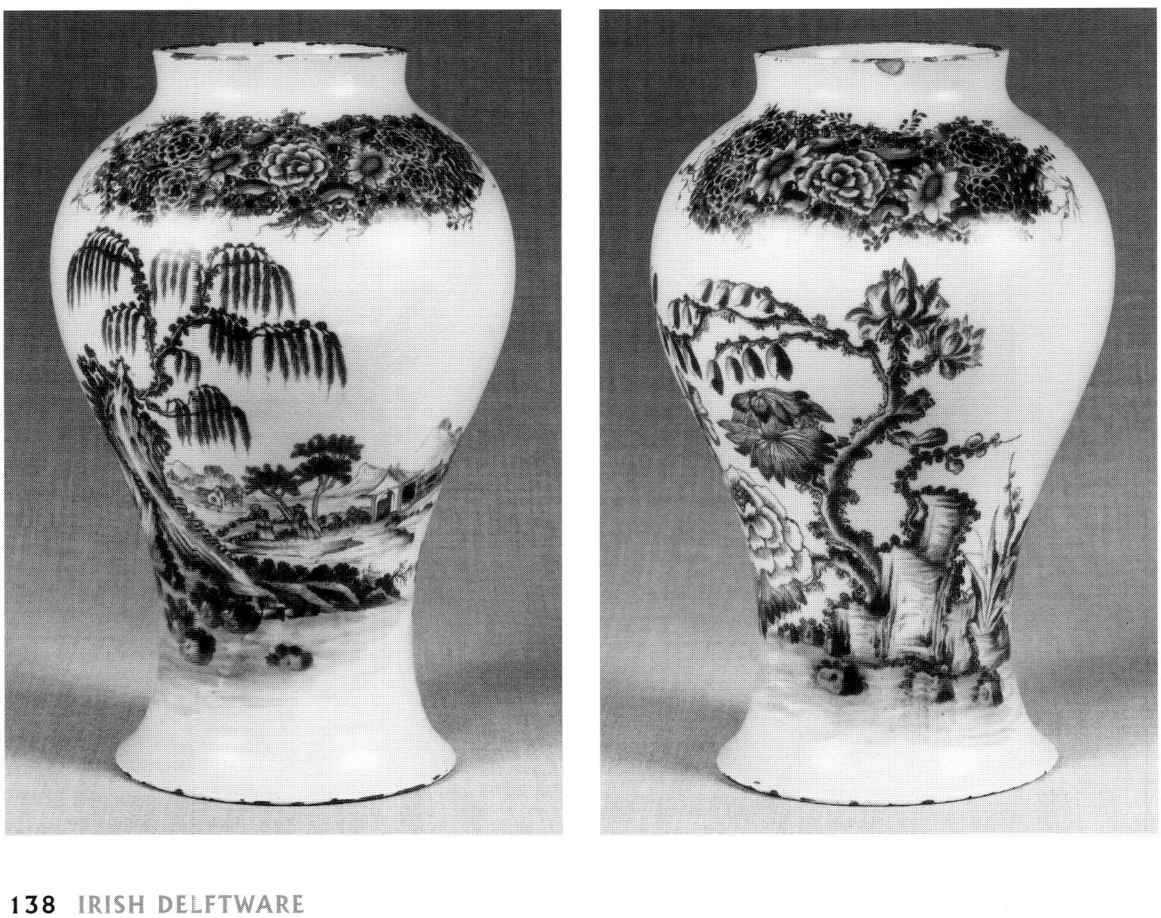

exhibition. As was noted on p.100, there are several features that clearly point to a Dublin attribution, most notably the unusual, soft colours and the design of a dolphin-like fountain, which is very similar to a fountain that appears on one of the Dublin cisterns **(Fig. 177a)**. Precisely the same fountain appears on an impressive, blue painted baluster-vase, which appeared at auction in 1985. **(Fig. 178)**.[70] Certain features of this vase are so unlike known Dublin wares that initially, the obvious presumption was that English and Irish potters copied the fountain design from a common print source. Looking more closely at the details of the painting, however, there are very good grounds for believing that this vase is also Irish. The feathery trees and segmented columns are painted in a style that is completely typical of Dublin's European landscapes, even though the overall effect is more intense than usual. Details of the painting in the peculiar swag of flowers on a dotted ground, which drapes over one shoulder of the vase, also have very close parallels in well recognised examples of Dublin delftware. (Some of the large flower-heads are similar to those that appear in **Fig. 143a**, for example, and the groups of three long, finger-like leaves near the rim are similar to some polychrome floral sprigs, for example, on the Verner bowl, **Colour plate 31a**).

One of the most distinctive features of the decoration on this vase - the tightly packed floral swag 'draped' onto the shoulder - occurs on other vases also.[71] Looking at the various examples recorded, it is tempting to believe that this 'shoulder swag' might have been a distinctive characteristic of Dublin vases, but this may not have been the case. Many of Dublin's designs closely copied Liverpool delftwares, and it is therefore possible that the 'shoulder swag' occurs on Liverpool wares also, copied from a common source. Nonetheless, the same feature appears on another fine vase, formerly in the Morgan collection, which also may have been produced in Dublin **(Fig. 179)**. This is beautifully painted with a Chinese landscape on one side and a distinctive group of pendant flowers and angular rocks on the other. As Archer and Morgan have observed, these flowers and rocks seem to represent a variant of the *'parasol flower'* design **(Fig. 156)**,

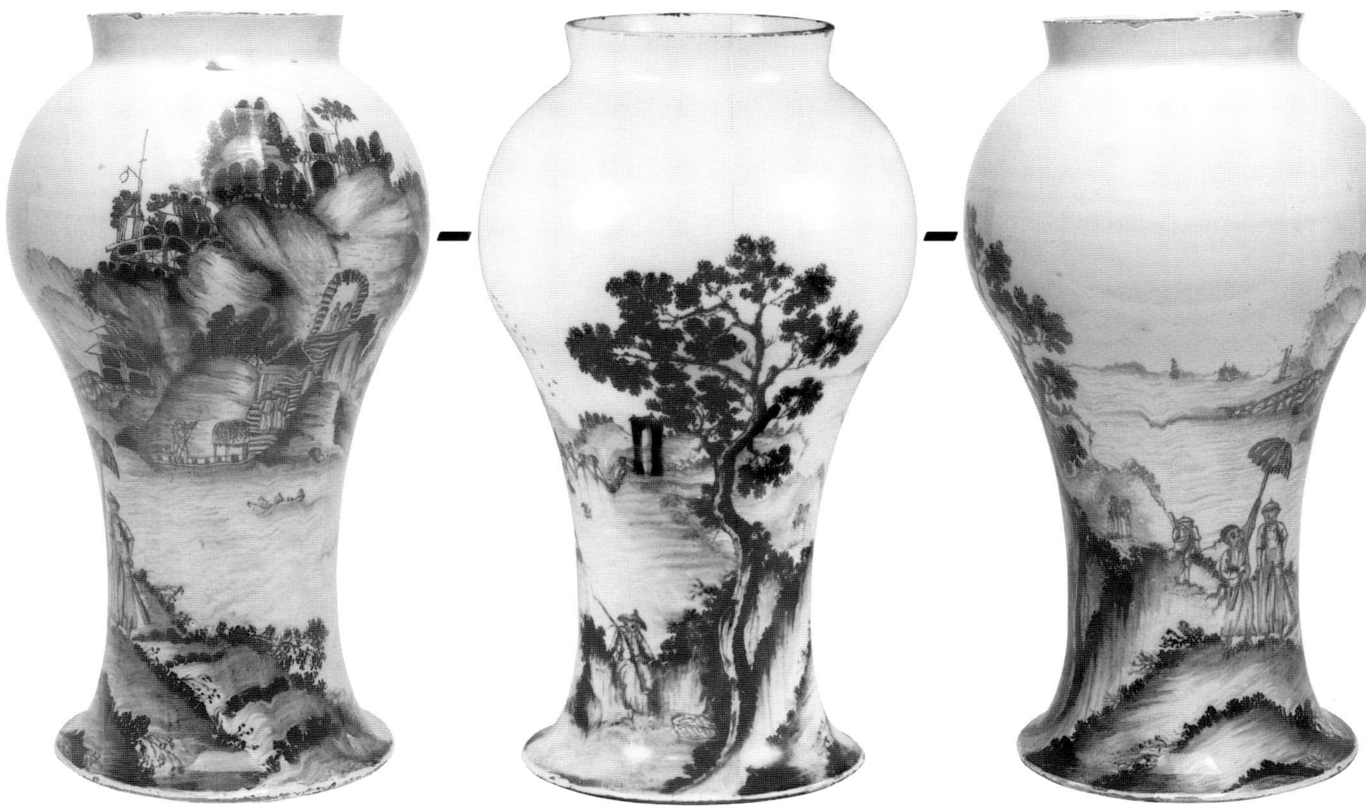

Figure 180 a - c. *Delftware baluster vase, painted in blue with Oriental landscape scenes. Probably Dublin, possibly Liverpool. No mark. Ht. 12½ in., 318 mm.*

although the quality of the painting is finer than any noted previously. There are certain elements in the decoration of this vase that suggest it might well have been made in Dublin, most notably the details in the painting of the floral swag. The willow tree is also similar to some that occur on known Dublin wares, such as the Drug Jars **(Fig. 144a)** and platters **(Fig. 92)**. On balance, there seems a strong possibility that this vase was made in Dublin, even though there is no sign of a painter's mark.

A final example, **(Fig. 180)**, originally a pair with an example in the Victoria and Albert Museum (or part of a garniture), is also worth considering in this context, as it clearly illustrates the dilemma faced in attempting to attribute such vases to either Liverpool or Dublin.[72] The Chinese scene is slightly at odds with other Dublin landscapes - some of the most similar comparable landscapes seem to occur on Liverpool porcelains.[73] Nonetheless, as we have seen in examining the previous vase **(Fig. 179)**, there are grounds for believing that this kind of Chinese landscape occurs on Dublin wares. Furthermore, Archer in 1979 also found that many characteristics in the painting of the present example were strongly suggestive of Dublin. In his words, '*Not only is the sensitive drawing of the trees and grass comparable to the best Irish work, but the method of building up the foreground with broad humps is the same, with the same dark shading to one side of lines ... close comparison with known Irish pieces shows no immediate differences*'.

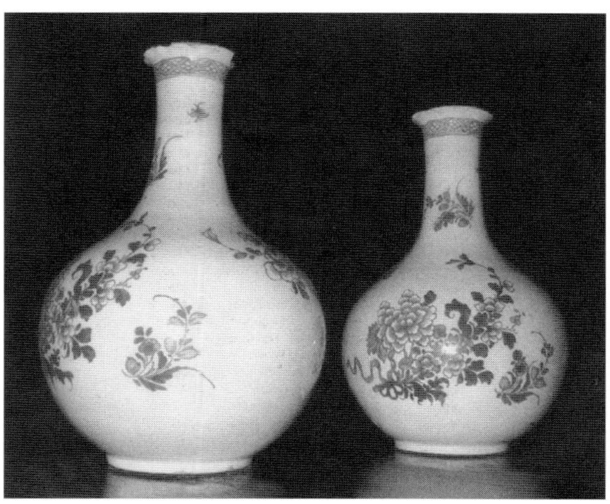

Figure 181. Dublin delftware, a pair of identical large water bottles, painted in blue with 'Floral Spray & Ribbon' pattern. Painter's marks '2' on bases. Ht. $11^{3}/_{4}$ in., 255 mm.

In summary therefore, until such times as a specific study is made of the various landscape painted vases that are known to exist, the only truly safe attribution for many of them will remain '*Liverpool or Dublin*'. (Most are simply described as '*probably Liverpool*' in the literature). But these are a particularly interesting and impressive group of wares, and even this fairly rudimentary evaluation suggests that, with further research, we might well find that more of these vases are Irish than has hitherto been recognised.

WATER BOTTLES AND BASINS

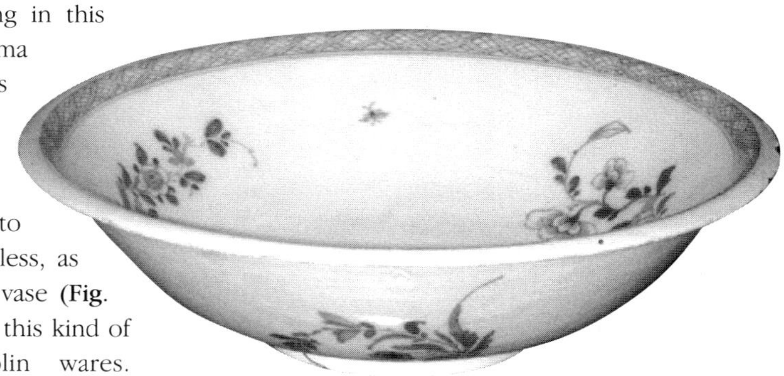

Figure 181a. Dublin delftware, large basin, en suite with the pair of bottles (Fig. 181), painter's mark '2' on base. Lip Diam $14^{3}/_{4}$ in., Footrim Diam. $4^{1}/_{2}$ in., Ht. $3^{1}/_{2}$ in.

Although often confused with vases, these thin-necked, round-bodied water bottles were originally sold with an accompanying hand-basin. These bottle (or 'gugglet') and basin sets, were usually used in the bedroom for washing, and they would originally have stood on a wooden wash stand. (An example of the complete arrangement is illustrated by Archer, Fig. 35, p. 274).

As with the vases and jars discussed previously, differentiating water bottles made in Dublin and Liverpool can be particularly difficult. Once again, a painter's number or a recognised Dublin pattern can help to sway the argument. As on vases, however, numbers are seldom present on some of the more interesting bottles, such as those painted with landscape scenes.

The safest place to begin is in identifying forms that can be attributed to Dublin with some degree of confidence. **Fig. 181** illustrates a very simple form of large bottle, with a straight, plain neck and flared lip. This pair has survived at Lonhydrock House in Cornwall with an accompanying basin of the same design. The basin is unusually large, and judging from the capacity of the bottles, it is possible that - in this case - these *two* bottles and one basin constitute the complete, original set. (More usually, a set consisted of a single bottle and basin). The painted design is the *'Floral Spray & Ribbon'* pattern noted elsewhere, **(e.g. Figs. 141 & 142)**, and all three pieces are marked with the painter's number '2' on the underside. On balance therefore, a Dublin origin seems highly likely.

Two further bottles of identical form are known, both from a private collection. (Not illustrated). One of these is painted with the common *'Chinese Flower-bowl'* pattern and bears the painter's number '1', the other is painted with the similarly common *'Feathers in a Vase'* pattern, and is inscribed '4'. A further example showing the *'Chinese Flower-bowl'* pattern is illustrated by Ray, Fig. 89, which bears the painter's number '15'.

Viewed together, these five bottles - all of identical form, painted with common Dublin patterns and each bearing painter's numbers - can readily be attributed to Dublin. When we attempt to progress beyond this point, however, to discover other forms, conclusive Dublin characteristics rapidly disappear.

Even a cursory scan of the delftware literature shows that water bottles were produced in a wide variety of forms. (See for example Austin, pp. 239-49, Britton *Bristol*, Cat. 6.25 - 6.36). These bottles are often decorated with common Dublin patterns, such as the *'Chinese Flower-bowl'* pattern, (e.g. Austin 587, 589), but without a confirming feature, such as diagnostic form or painter's number, it is impossible to tell whether these were made in Dublin or in Liverpool. On balance, without additional evidence to the contrary, the great majority are probably English.

A further example of a water bottle is illustrated as a possible example of Dublin delftware, to demonstrate that there is still scope for further discoveries in this area. **(Fig. 182)**. This bottle, attributed by Anthony Ray to *'Dublin or Liverpool'*, is entirely different in form to those illustrated in **Fig. 181**, and is more finely decorated with a landscape view of fisherman, boats and ruins. The style of painting is directly comparable to some of the problematic 'Liverpool or Dublin' vases described previously, **(Figs. 179 & 180)** but in this case there are two small features of particular note. As Ray observed, the segmented columns with bushy foliage are highly reminiscent of the single column in a landscape that occurs on the *'Primate's Coals'* bowl (and indeed, on several of the Dublin landscape wares, such as **Colour Plate 24**). Similarly, the trefoil border below the lip is similar to borders that appear on well-recognised examples of Dublin delftware, such as the cisterns and some landscape plates. **(Figs.139, 140 & 155)**. These features are certainly a strong indication that this bottle could indeed be Irish. However, much of this review of water bottles and vases has been based solely on photographs. Until such times as these landscape painted wares are studied in detail, and at first hand, the only safe conclusion remains, as Ray suggested, *'Dublin or Liverpool'*.

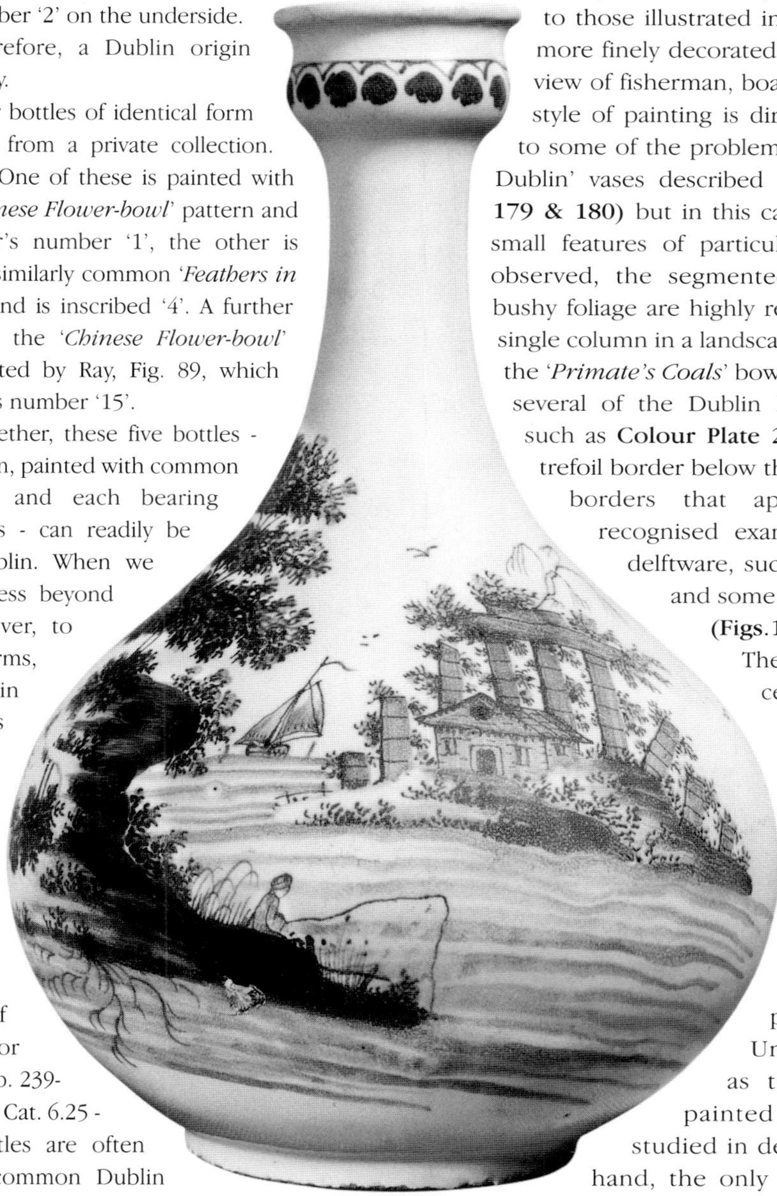

Figure 182. *Delftware water bottle, probably Dublin, possibly Liverpool. Painted in blue with a fisherman and classical ruins. Note the trefoil border around the lip. No mark. Ht. 9³/₄ in., 248 mm., diam. 6¹/₄ in., 159 mm.*

CHAPTER 3
MINOR POTTERIES

As we have seen, delftware was made in Ireland for almost seventy-five years, between c.1697 and late 1771. For most of that seventy-five year period, only one delftware pottery was active in the country at any given time, either in Dublin or in Belfast. There were, however, a number of other attempts to manufacture delftware in various parts of the country, but either because these ventures were short-lived, or because they were comparatively small in scale, much less is known of them. For a brief period during the early 1760s, it even appears that as many as four delftware potteries worked simultaneously throughout the length of the country, with one in Belfast, two in Dublin and a fourth in Limerick.

As far as possible, these smaller delftware ventures are described in chronological order, rather than ranked in terms of relative importance.

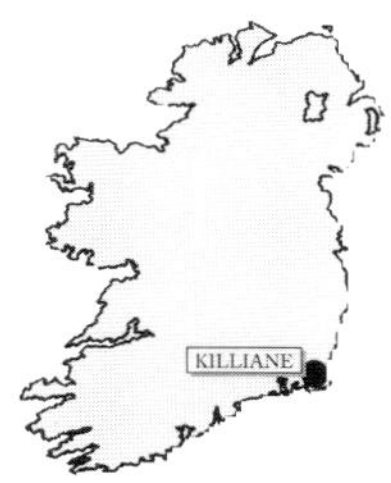

3 i : Killiane, Co. Wexford
Jonathan Chamberleyne (c.1719?)

There is no doubt that a pottery of some size worked in Killiane from the seventeenth-century onwards. Attempts were certainly made there to produce some kind of fine-quality, white ceramic during the early eighteenth-century, but the evidence for delftware manufacture is inconclusive.

Much of our knowledge of the Killiane venture derives from a highly inaccurate account in George Griffiths' *Chronicles of the Co. Wexford*, published in Enniscorthy in 1877, pp. 243-4.

'A POTTERY AT GREAT KILLIANE

Among the new settlers who came into the County Wexford after the "Revolution" was a Quaker of the name of Chamberleyne, and he settled at Great Killiane, close to the retired old Parish Church, and on the waters of Wexford Harbour. He was of a Staffordshire family, and had more or less knowledge of the Pottery Art. He had possession of the townlands of Great Killiane and Ballykelly, containing altogether over 410 acres. Being a Quaker, he married a young woman of the same creed, whose father had, by the Cromwellian Settlement, obtained possessions in the Glynn. As a speculation, and favoured with the convenience of water-carriage for either the import or export of material and wares, he commenced the manufacture, at first of the coarser kind of ware, for which he found a ready and remunerative demand. Succeeding so well, he was induced to embark in a more extensive and higher class of business, which encouraged him on by its success and sale. He imported material from England, and he increased his business concerns - substantial houses and stores. On the end of a well built store, immediately opposite the ruins of the Parish Church, the writer of this paper saw, in large well-formed letters, eighteen inches long, and made of white earthenware, the following line:

"JONATHAN CHAMBERLEYNE, 1719."

This remained until the wall was thrown down in 1831. The trade prospering, the enterprising manufacturer was induced to try his hand at China. The earliest efforts were successful - and the present writer remembers having seen in his young days, teacups and saucers semi-transparent, of small size, the fashion no doubt of the day, which were said to be equal any English make. Elated by success, he ventured on a much larger "batch" - five kilns, it is said - and the result was a total failure, or nearly so! in the baking! - and the consequent ruin of the enterprising manufacturer. The writer has seen some of the wares, and in the house of a dear kind friend he was first told that they were made at Killiane. As lately as March, 1876, he had the pleasure of seeing in what was once that friendly home, but the old owner is in the grave, and the name of the family changed, two articles of this pottery. One, a jug of about a quart capacity; but it had lost the handle - the body blue and what was called "frosted" - and a larger one, having the shape of a modern wash-stand water jug, with a handle formed of two coloured twisted cords, all ornamented with red and yellow flower leaves entwined round the body. The ware-kilns were standing grass-covered at Killiane until cleared away by the present occupant, Mr. John Pettit, who had then but recently become the tenant - and to the present day, shreds of Pottery and partially prepared clays are turned up.'.

In recent years, genealogical research by local historian Evelyne Miller has identified the individual who first started the pottery in the seventeenth-century as Jonas Chamberleyne, a *'potter of the town of Northampton, England'* (rather than Staffordshire).[1] Like many English settlers, Jonas arrived with Cromwell's army and subsequently received a grant of Irish land in lieu of pay. Jonas died in 1695, bequeathing his pottery and estate to his wife Alice (*née* Ivory) and eldest son, Jonas (II). The will confirms that the pottery was located in the townland of Killiane Little, rather than in Great Killiane as stated by Griffiths.[2]

John or Jonathan Chamberleyne, whose name and the date '*1719*' appeared on the white ceramic plaque on the pottery wall, was born at Killiane Little in 1688, the second son of Jonas (II).[3] As Jonathan presumably made the plaque, it seems reasonable to suspect that he was also the individual who conducted the experiments with fine-quality, white-firing wares, as described by Griffiths. There is no obvious significance in the date 1719 - it may signify the year in which Jonathan assumed ownership of the pottery, or it may correspond with the date at which the improvements were made. Other family documentation indicates that Jonathan was still alive some years afterwards, until after 1727 at least.[4] The pottery is believed to have continued working until about 1788, when John's successor, a Thomas Chamberleyne, is known to have died.

The present owner of the site, James Cullen, takes great personal interest in the pottery's history, and has collected large quantities of shards in the gardens and fields nearby. Both Mr. Cullen and Evelyne Miller were exceptionally hospitable and helpful during a visit to the site in 1994.[5] Although much of the main site is now cemented over, some of the features described by Griffiths in 1877 still stand. The most interesting of these is a large, early eighteenth-century stone-built shed, possibly one of the original pottery buildings, which once adjoined the wall that bore the dated plaque, and which still faces the church that Griffiths described. **(Fig. 183)**. The shed contains the remains of a small blacksmith's forge.

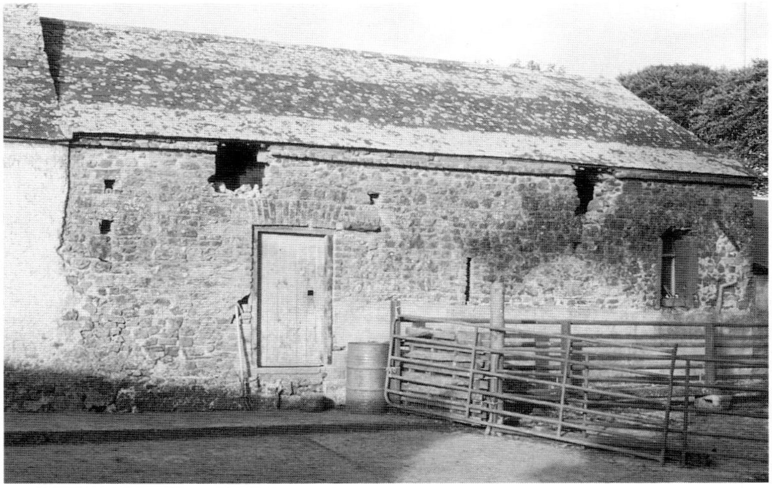

***Figure 183**. The oldest surviving building on the Little Killiane pottery site, 1994. The wall that bore the white ceramic plaque, inscribed 'Jonathan Chamberleyne 1719', formerly adjoined this building.*

The shards collected by Mr. Cullen are a diverse assemblage, certainly when viewed in an Irish context. (Examples are now in the National Museum of Ireland and in the Hunt Museum, Limerick). The majority of the fragments seen at the site in 1994 **(Fig. 184)** - like those in the museum collections - are simple, lead-glazed redwares, often with a combed or trailed, white clay-slip decoration. This at least indicates that the Killiane potters had ready access to a source of white clay. A number of more complex shards are decorated with patterns of deep, incised lines, and there are

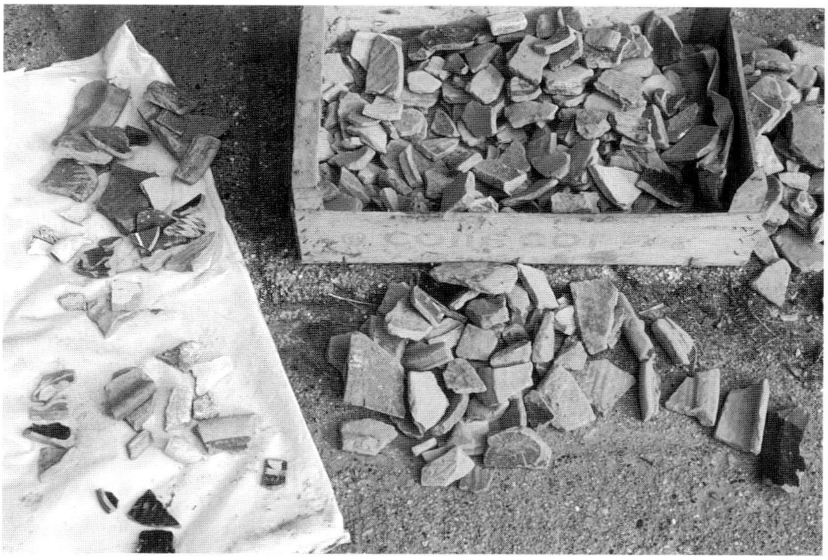

Figure 184. A mixed selection of pottery shards recorded at Little Killiane in 1994.

even some true sgraffito-wares (with patterns scraped through an overlying white slip). In short, the Killiane pottery was amongst the more sophisticated of Ireland's country potteries, producing wares that were similar to those being made in Staffordshire and Somerset at about the same time.[6] If the potters at Killiane had sought to produce a fine quality white-ware, then they certainly possessed the skills necessary to make a reasonable attempt.

There are comparatively few white-ware shards amongst the Killiane assemblage, which implies that such wares were never produced in quantity. Nonetheless, several fragments of an almost pure white, earthenware body were recorded, **(Fig. 185)**, some of which possess irregular patches of volatilised, blue-green glaze on one side, and one shard in the National Museum bears a '*crude, uneven, bluish-white glaze*'.[7] More obvious delftware shards were also found, but none seemed to represent wasters that had unquestionably been made at this site.[8] One of the more encouraging finds amongst Mr. Cullen's collection in 1994, however, was a portion of what appeared to be a small saggar, of about 4 inches internal diameter, which at least indicates that attempts were made to produce small, fine-quality items.

Unfortunately, recent research has shown that Griffiths' 1877 account is highly unreliable. Mairead Dunlevy of the National Museum has succeeded in locating a number of the pieces that he described in 1877, but these have turned out to be *nineteenth-century* English imports, not eighteenth-century Killiane wares as Griffiths believed.[9] Research by Evelyne Miller has similarly shown that much of Griffiths' documentary and genealogical information is deeply flawed. Nonetheless, some aspects of his account, such as the description of the white pottery plaque dated 1719, cannot be entirely dismissed. The shards that have been collected in recent years by Mr. Cullen also prove that some kind of white-bodied, lead-glazed earthenware was produced at Little Killiane. Faced with the conflicting documentary evidence, however, and in the absence of any intact examples of the wares made there, it is difficult, for now, to gauge the pottery's true significance.

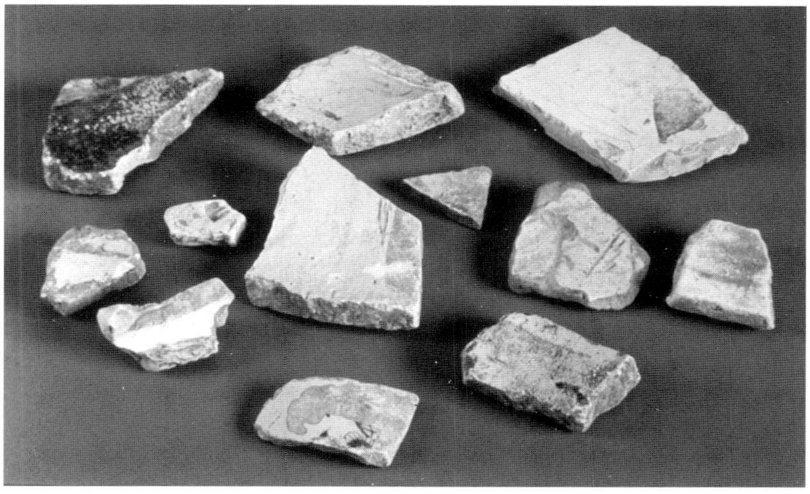

Figure 185. White-ware and delftware shards collected by James Cullen on the Little Killiane site, now in the Hunt Museum, Limerick.

3 *ii : Rostrevor*

William Bright & Alexander Owens (before 1739 - after 1744)

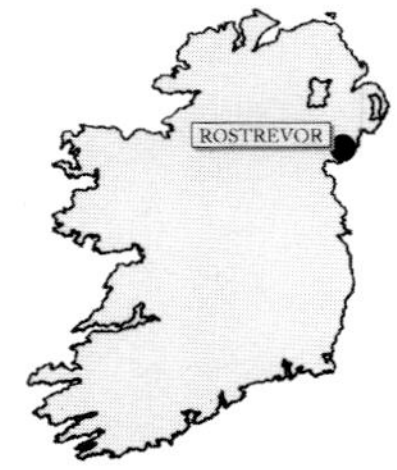

The pottery at Rostrevor lay in the most charming and picturesque setting of any delftware pottery in Ireland, **(Fig. 186)**, yet the commercial sense in this choice of location is not so immediately apparent. Rostrevor was, and still is, a very small port indeed. The workforce, the fuel, the clay and all of the other potting materials had to be imported from sources many miles distant, and the best marketplace in Ireland, Dublin, lay sixty miles away.

There was a time during the mid-eighteenth century, however, when Rostrevor was probably considered an excellent location for a new delftware pottery, because of its proximity to the Newry Canal, which opened in March 1742.[1] In its day, the Newry Canal represented Ireland's foremost engineering achievement. Having taken eleven years and vast sums of money to build, the canal ultimately connected Lough Neagh, in the heart of Ulster's interior, with the Irish Sea at Carlingford Lough, (near Rostrevor). This was one of the very first major canals to be built anywhere in the British Isles during the canal era; as one modern writer has observed, a '*comparable engineering feat in today's terms would be the digging of the Channel Tunnel*'.[2]

The principal objective in building the Newry canal was to supply Dublin with cheap coals from County Tyrone, but there would have been numerous side-benefits to attract delftware potters. The town of Newry, for example, had thrived on the public money spent in building the canal and therefore represented a substantial marketplace in its own right - as did the newly accessible Ulster hinterland. The Newry Canal also opened up new areas of deciduous forest around Lough Neagh for exploitation, promising sources of cheap wood with which to fuel the kiln. (Delftware was not fired with coal at this date, even in Dublin).[3] Some of the advantages of the location are summarised in a later newspaper advertisement, which offered land for sale in Rostrevor in 1758.[4]

'Rosstrevor is very well situated to carry on any branch of trade.., it is a seaport with a good quay, within six or eight hours sail of Dublin; it has a communication with the inland country by the Canal to Lough Neagh, it lies within 5 miles of Newry and Dundalk [&c.] *... all good markets, ... ashes, kelp, coals, turf and other materials.., to be had on very reasonable terms, wreck* [seaweed], *sea-sand* [and other materials to be had] *in abundance on the lands'*

The earliest known reference to either of the two owners of the Rostrevor pottery dates from 1737, when Alexander Owens, an '*earthenware and glass dealer*' at the Cheshire Cheese, Hammond Lane, Dublin, advertised that he imported English pottery and glass.[5] Like Henry Delamain ten years later, therefore, Owens began his career as a retailer of ceramics, before being drawn into manufacturing delftware in his own right.

The pottery itself is first mentioned in passing in Dr. Samuel Madden's pamphlet, printed in 1739, (see p.37), where he states, '*our Earthen Ware* [potteries are] *beginning to be set up to good purpose, and with large advantage, both at Rosstrevor, and near Dublin...*'. We learn more of the pottery's owners, however, from their first advertisement, which appeared three years later in the *Dublin Journal* of 30th March 1742. Their principal intention was probably to proclaim the Dublin Society premium they had recently been awarded, but coincidentally perhaps, the Newry Canal had also opened just five days earlier;

'William Bright of Charles Street, and Alexander Owens, of Hammond Lane, Dublin, proprietors of the Rostrevor Pot House in the County of Down, make and sell all sorts of the best blue and white earthenware. Such gentlemen as are pleased to bespeak sets of dishes and plates may have their coats of arms or any other pattern they please done on them in the best manner. As the whole work is performed by natives of this kingdom, only, they humbly hope to meet with proper encouragement, and propose to sell at the most reasonable rates.

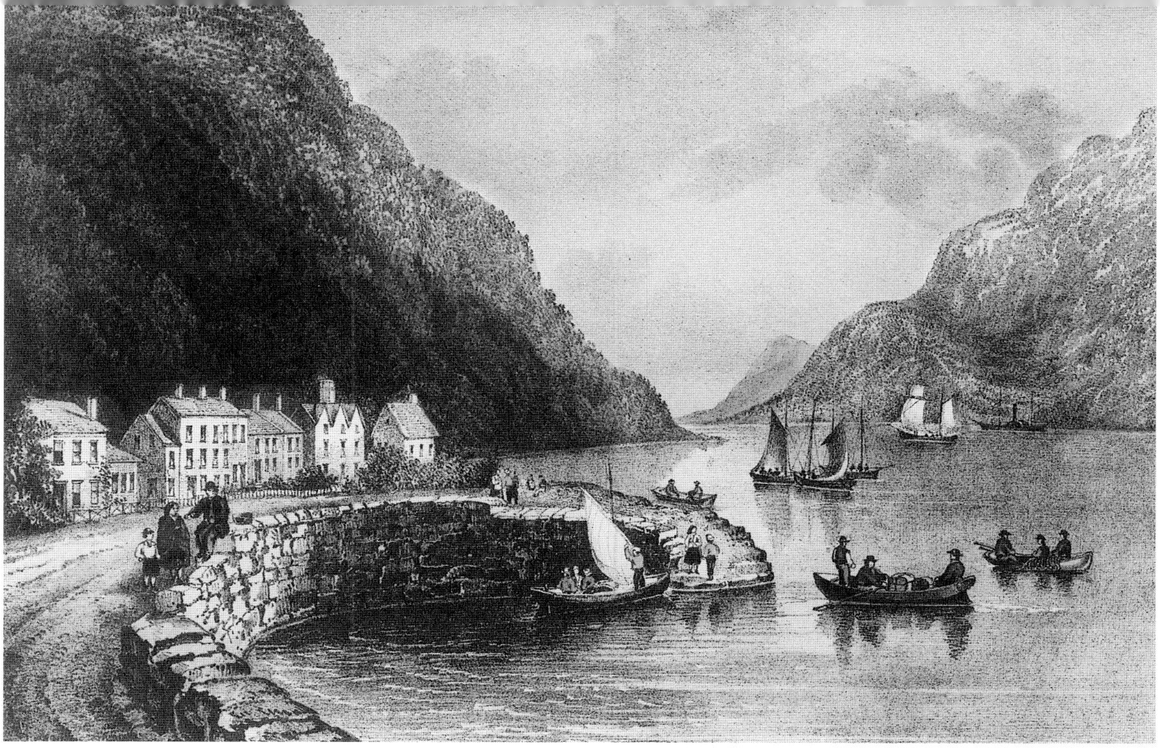

Figure 186. A romanticised view of the 'Old Quay' at Rostrevor, published by Currier and Ives, New York, probably during the 1840s. The eighteenth-century pottery was situated close to this quay.

N.B. - The said proprietors obtained the premium of £10 from the Dublin Society for exhibiting the best set of earthenware consisting of nine dishes and three dozen plates, which were immediately bought by his Excellency the Lord Chancellor [see footnote][6] *to encourage paid work*'.

Further details of the award are recorded in the Dublin Society's proceedings, which state that '*William Bright* [of Rostrevor] *produced two complete sets of earthenware for the premium and Mr. William Lake one; Mr. Lake's was allowed to have the advantage of colour, but Mr. Bright's being thought the better set on the whole the premium was adjudged to him.*'[7] (The location of William Lake's pottery is presently unknown. See p.163).

Whilst the successful Dublin Society application confirms that the Rostrevor pottery produced delftware of reasonable quality, perhaps the most significant phrase of all in this first advertisement is the remark that '*the whole work* [was] *performed by natives of this kingdom, only*'. This clearly indicates that Bright and Owens only employed *Irish* delftware potters at Rostrevor, but if this was the case, then where had their workforce come from? The most likely source seems to have been John Chambers' delftware pottery in Dublin, which is the only other delftware pottery known to have been working in Ireland at this time. Chambers stated that he had brought workmen from abroad to establish his pottery in Dublin (before 1735), but his apprentices were probably recruited locally. It is possible therefore that some of these Irish potters were keen to move by 1739, in order to work as skilled or freemen potters in their own right, rather than as apprentices. Seven years is traditionally regarded as the normal term of apprenticeship, but Henry Delamain in 1753 remarked that his '*Schoolboy apprentices... will be masters of the trade in three years.*'[8] Alternatively, Rostrevor may have been operated by Irish potters who had previously worked in England, or perhaps at the Potthouse in Belfast.

For unknown reasons, Bright and Owens' partnership did not survive for long, as we learn from a second advertisement just a year later;

'Whereas the partnership between Alexander Owens, at the Cheshire Cheese in Hammond Lane, Dublin, and William Bright of Charles Street, of the Pot House of Rostrevor near Newry Co. Down, is dissolved, now said Owens carries on said Pot House and will furnish any gentleman with any sorts of blue and white earthenware, such as dishes and plates of any pattern, or their coats of arms done on them. Said Owens makes all sizes of punch bowls, tea cups and saucers, basins of all sizes, chamber pots

and several other sorts of blue and white earthenware. Also apothecaries may be fitted out with any sort or kind of their pots. Likewise said Owens has imported all sorts of English earthenware. Country shopkeepers and dealers may be furnished at the Pot House of Rostrevor with all sorts of the blue and white ware made there, or English earthenware, where a Warehouse will be kept, and attendance given at all times, and sold there as cheap as in Dublin, being a seaport'.[9]

The range of delftware produced in Rostrevor, which included armorial services and apothecary wares, seems similar to that offered by John Chambers in Dublin at about the same time. The specific reference to delftware teacups and saucers is particularly noteworthy.

The later fortunes of the Rostrevor pottery are unclear - it may have closed immediately, or could perhaps have continued on for some years. On balance, the fact that Owens was already selling English wares at Rostrevor in 1743, alongside his own delftware, does tend to imply that the pottery was in decline even at that stage. Apart from one further, brief remark in 1744, (see below), there are no subsequent references to the Rostrevor pottery.

LOCATION

The pottery's location is plainly stated in *The Ancient and Present State of the County of Down*, published in 1744;

'At the lower end of the village is a small quay for ships, and here is also a salt house and a pottery for white earthenware made of the fine clay found near Carrickfergus, and frequently exported to foreign parts.'[10]

Clearly, the pottery was situated near the *'small quay'*, which exists to this day, but repeated searches in recent years have failed to locate either the kiln site or any signs of pottery waste. There are no kiln-like structures on the earliest Ordnance Survey map (1834), and much of the principal area of interest now lies under concrete, beneath the extensive forecourt and yard of a motor-garage. A large, old, mill-like building nestles behind the garage, but this appears to be late-eighteenth or early-nineteenth century in date. (A tall narrow chimney was added c. 1875). Local residents, in more modern houses next to the garage, do not recall encountering any evidence of pottery deposits in their gardens.

In 1977, in a short article entitled *'The Rostrevor Potworks'*, E.A.J. Byrne reported that the pottery site had been located by local historian, Dr. W. Haughton Crowe;

'*He* [Haughton Crowe] *tells me that he has located the site of the old Potworks "on the far side of the Kilbroney river as you walk up the Glen from the village, about 55 paces below the remains of a cottage destroyed in the recent troubles. A small portion of the wall of the pottery is still standing*".'[11]

Although the remains of the cottage described have since disappeared, these directions are fairly easily followed. The remains of the wall mentioned still stand, but there seems to be no evidence to suggest that this was once part of a pottery. The location appears unlikely for several reasons. For example, the 1744 reference clearly indicates that the pottery was at the lower end of the village, close to the quay, whereas the site described by Haughton Crowe was in the upper village, half a mile away. Similarly, why would potters have chosen to bring wood and clay to a site so far uphill from the quay, when many superior sites lay much closer to the shore? The site described by Dr. Haughton Crowe, by the river, was excellent for a business that required waterpower, but this was not a necessary prerequisite of delftware manufacture. Possibly the early building encountered was some form of workplace or habitation, with a scatter of discarded household pottery around. There certainly seems to be no obvious evidence of delftware waste at the site today.

A final, tantalising clue to the pottery's location may lie in the highly inaccurate and romanticised view of the quay, published in America during the mid-nineteenth century. **(Fig. 186)**. The layout of the houses by the quayside does not match the earliest Ordnance Survey map, perhaps suggesting that the print was based on an earlier view, drawn before 1834. Behind the row of houses near the quay stands an unusually broad and tall chimney, which an optimist might interpret as the top of a *'hovel'* or pottery kiln. **(Fig. 187)**. Whether this peculiar chimney really had anything to do with the delftware pottery of c.1740 remains to be seen, but for now, it appears to be one of the only clues we have.

WARES

There are no known examples of Rostrevor delftware. Within the past fifteen years, perhaps half a dozen pieces of delftware have been recorded in private collections in County Down that are believed, by family tradition, to have been made there. Some of these pieces, such as the drug jar shown in **Fig 145**, p.121, are rare and important examples of Irish delftware, but as yet there has been no reason to connect any of them with the pottery at Rostrevor.

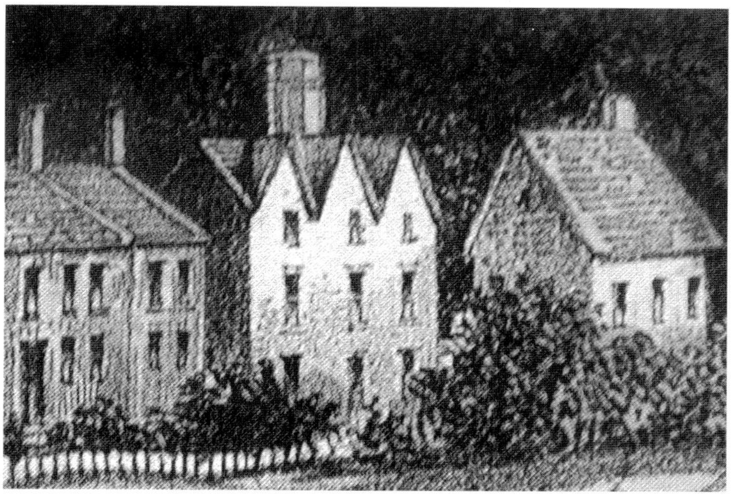

Figure 187. *Detail of the print illustrated in Fig. 186. The top of a large, tall chimney is evident behind the central house.*

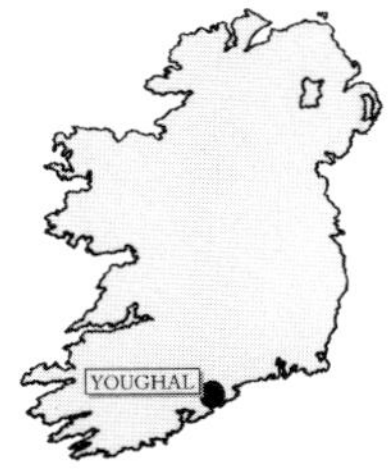

3 *iii : Youghal*

(c. 1751?)

A sizeable coarse-earthenware industry existed in the vicinity of Youghal in County Cork from about the middle of the seventeenth-century onwards. This gave rise to a handsome and distinctive range of country wares, but references to delftware manufacture there are more ambiguous.[1] Dudley Westropp, writing in 1935, found *'no mention.. of any fine earthenware ever having been made in Youghal'*, whereas Ada Longfield, writing thirty-six years later, concluded that *'a small amount* [of delftware] *was undoubtedly made there'*.[2] The simplest way to judge between these two opposing positions is to review the evidence.

The argument for the existence of a delftware pottery initially appears weakened by the fact that no fine-earthenware potteries are mentioned in any contemporary accounts of the town and county. Charles Smith wrote the only passing remark recorded on the subject in 1774, when he stated that *'earthenware ... is a manufacture of which we also import considerable quantities* [in County Cork]. *There is of late, a tolerable kind made at Youghal, but far from being brought to that perfection the manufacture requires'*.[3]

The best evidence for delftware manufacture dates from as late as 1889, when the celebrated Cork antiquarian Robert Day received a letter from Robert J. Lecky, a descendant of an old Youghal family then living in London.[4] As Lecky explains;

> *'The tradition re the Youghal 'delf' is that a vein of white clay was discovered in the neighbourhood, and some trials were made with it, but only in a very small way, that the place was covered up and the locality entirely forgotten. I have a doll's cup and saucer made of it, diamrs. 1 7/8 x 2 5/16 in.; a thick, white glaze; the clay, a light straw colour. This is a fac-simile of the saucer.* [Fig. 188]. *The cup has the initials and date inside, and the mock Chinese ornamentation outside; colour, light blue. These were part of a set given to my great-grandaunt, Hannah Poole née Lecky,* [born] *in 1741, when 10 years old (she died in Cork in 1820). I have the tradition from my father who was born in Youghal in 1764...'*.

Although family traditions can be unreliable, the provenance in this case seems straightforward. The child's saucer illustrated, **(Fig. 188)**, just 65mm. wide, is a highly unusual and charming object, especially if it is made of delftware, but unfortunately the present whereabouts of the set are unknown.

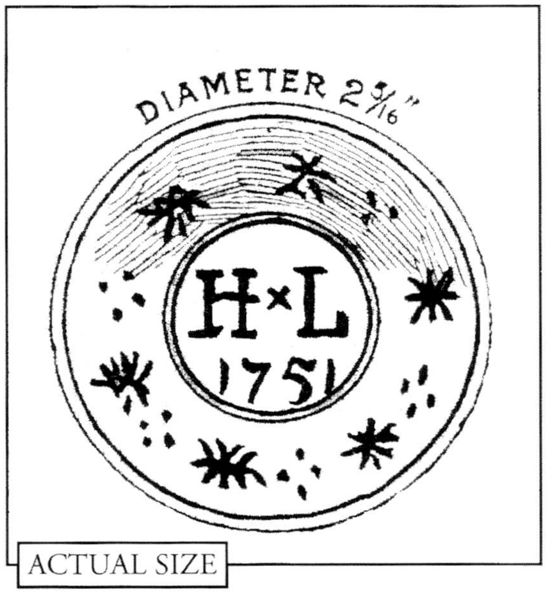

***Figure 188**. Detail of a miniature saucer, (Diam. 2 5/16 in., 65 mm.), said to have been made in Youghal, as illustrated by Robert Day in 1892.*

Lecky's reasonable-sounding attribution was unfortunately undermined by Robert Day himself, who in the same paper proceeded to attribute other, more spurious pieces of delftware to Youghal, either on the basis of broadly similar appearance, or because they had turned up locally. Several of these pieces are known to this day, and some are of considerable interest in their own right, (for example, **Fig. 52**). But with the benefit of a comparative literature that was not available in Day's time, it is clear that most, if not all of these pieces were imported from England.[5]

Nevertheless, independent evidence exists which seems to corroborate Mr. Lecky's assertion that *'delf'* was once made in Youghal. Samuel Lewis's

'*Topographical Dictionary of Ireland*', published in London in 1837, records the following brief statement in the description of Youghal town (Vol. 2, p. 727); '*The Manufacture...of porcelain and fine delf was* [formerly] *carried on for a time, but the only manufactures at present are those of bricks...* [and] *a coarse kind of pottery made for the use of the neighbourhood*'. In other words, the tradition that fine quality white-ware was produced in Youghal existed in the town more than 50 years before Mr. Lecky wrote his remarks in 1889. Furthermore, the pioneering geologist Sir Robert Kane, author of '*The Industrial Resources of Ireland*' (1844), remarked that '*Of a Quality much superior to the common sort* [of potter's clays] *are whitish clays found near Cloyne and at Youghal in the county of Cork...*'. This similarly bolsters Lecky's account of the discovery of '*a vein of white clay*'. (The Cloyne clays mentioned by Kane were later extracted on a large-scale, commercial basis).[6]

In conclusion, the available evidence does tend to suggest that a small quantity of a white-ware, comparable to delftware if not a true tin-glazed earthenware, was probably made in Youghal in the eighteenth century. (The references to the '*thick white glaze*' and '*straw-coloured*' body of the saucer dated 1751 certainly seem to describe a delftware). The most likely scenario, as Mr. Lecky suggested in 1889, is that some of the established country potters encountered a deposit of unusually fine white clay, with which they produced some fine-quality earthenwares on a limited scale. Perhaps, if a piece from Mr. Lecky's set of doll's cups and saucers could be located, the debate regarding the existence of Youghal delftware might be swiftly settled.

3 iv : Belfast

The Little Patrick Street Pottery (Pre-1754 to post-1763)

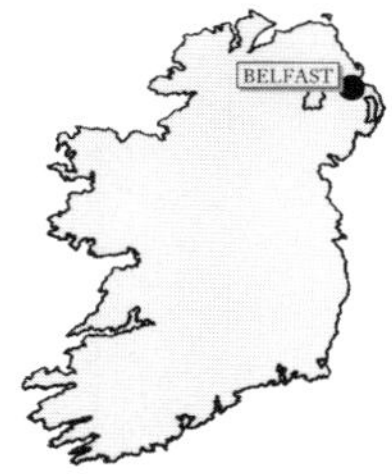

An unexpected bonus of the recent research in Belfast was the discovery that a second, previously unrecorded delftware pottery worked in the town during the middle years of the eighteenth-century, twenty years or more after the first Belfast Potthouse closed. The evidence for this second venture remains meagre, consisting of little more than two documentary references and a handful of pottery fragments, but the shards recovered on the site do at least confirm that the pottery existed and that delftware was made there. A particularly interesting feature of this venture is that it seems to have been owned by Thomas Greg, who later went on to manufacture creamware in Belfast on a very large scale.

Fortunately, one of the two known documentary references to the pottery also contains a map, so that determining its location is straightforward.[1] **(Fig. 189**, below). When the position is plotted onto the larger map of Belfast, we can see that it was situated some 400 metres to the north-east of the original *'Potthouse'*, on the very outskirts of mid-eighteenth century Belfast.**(Fig. 190**, above).[2] The pottery was certainly in existence before 1754, and was perhaps among the *'several houses and salt pans and other improvements* [that were] *lately made and erected'* in this area shortly before May 1743. (The area in which the pottery was situated lay in present-day Little Patrick Street, probably about 30 - 40 metres from the junction with Corporation Street).

It is not clear whether this second delftware pottery was connected with the original Potthouse in any way, but one dubious piece of evidence suggests that a direct family link *might* have existed. This was recorded by George Benn in his monumental *'History of the Town of Belfast'*, (1877), in which he stated that one *'Mr. John Galt Smith ...* [was] *associated with many projects and companies, including the*

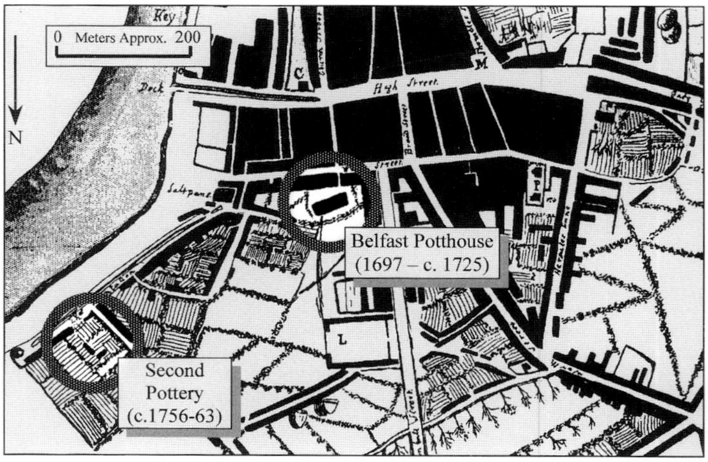

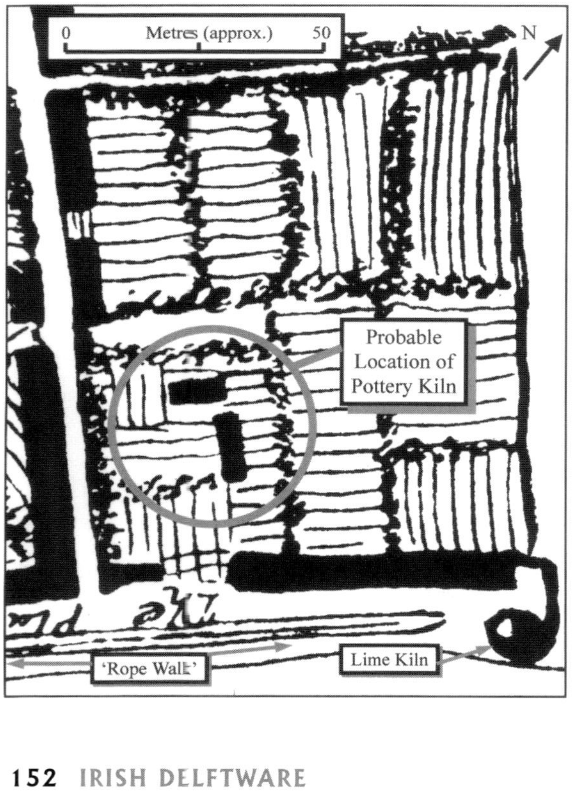

Left : Figure 189*. A detail of the 1757 map of Belfast (see Fig. 190), showing the parcel of ground in which the Little Patrick Street pottery was located. The two sheds indicated, which are set apart from neighbouring buildings, represent the most likely kiln site.*

Above : Figure 190*. A hand drawn map of Belfast, produced in 1757, showing the relative positions of the original 'Belfast Potthouse' and Thomas Greg's later 'Little Patrick Street' pottery.*

extensive Roperies extending from Waring Street to Lime Kiln Dock, the Pottery manufacture &c., &c.'. Benn's remark is entirely unsubstantiated, but it agrees so neatly with the known facts that it might contain a germ of truth. The '*Roperies*' and '*Lime Kiln Dock*' referred to both lay alongside the Little Patrick Street pottery, which implies that this was probably the '*Pottery manufacture*' to which Benn alluded. (See **Fig. 189**, bottom edge). John Galt Smith (1731-1802) was also related to the Smith family, the owners of the original Potthouse, although the precise nature of his relationship is not as clear as it appeared in Benn's day. (Benn believed him to be the nephew of Patrick Smith, co-founder of the Potthouse, but this is now known to be incorrect).[3] It would be unwise to speculate further on this possible connection until an accurate genealogy has been established.

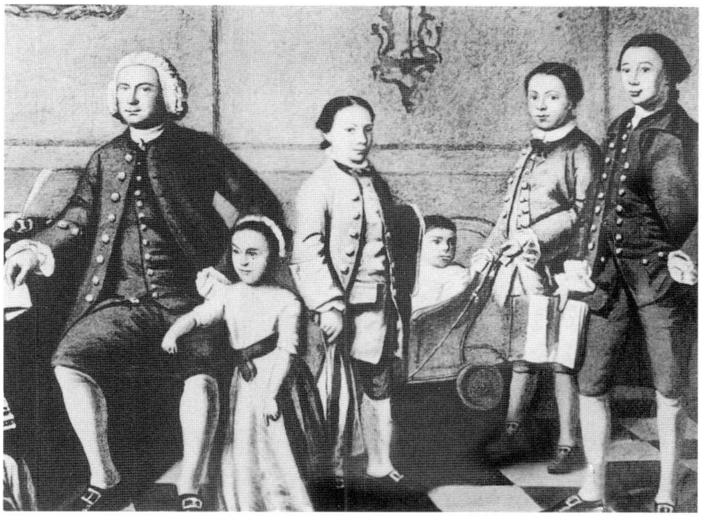

More reliable information comes from the Grand Lease for the entire area, which lists the pottery amongst its established fixtures in May 1754.[4] The Grand Lease was renewed at this time by the Donegall family for a fresh term of 41 years, and was let in its entirety to the Belfast merchant Daniel Mussenden for an annual rent of £6. A second document, dated 2nd November 1763, is a receipt from Mussenden's personal papers, which shows that he in turn sub-let the individual properties on the Grand Lease to no fewer than 16 undertenants, for a total rent of £45 per annum.[5] (Thus returning Mussenden a yearly profit of £39 on the £6 paid to the Donegalls). The most striking feature of this second document is that this very large Grand Lease, (not just a portion of it), was described by Mussenden as '*The Pothouse Lease*'.[6] This implies that the Little Patrick Street pottery was the most substantial business on the property - more substantial even than the extensive Saltworks and Ropeworks which, by 1763, had worked on the site for more than 20 years. (It also suggests that, despite the present paucity of documentary evidence, the pottery might well have been a very substantial commercial venture).

The founders of the Delftfield Pottery in Glasgow in 1748 (Appendix I, iii) specifically mentioned Daniel Mussenden, the landlord, in connection with the Carrickfergus clay trade. (See p.169). It is therefore tempting to believe that he might also have participated in the pottery venture in Belfast. Mussenden was one of the most important landowners in Belfast at the time, however, and so his ownership of the Grand Lease probably represents little more than coincidence. Of greater significance is the fact that the most expensive property on this '*Pothouse Lease*' - almost certainly the pottery itself - was let to a '*Mr. Greg*', at an annual rent of £10. This refers to another important Belfast merchant, Thomas Greg, **(Fig. 191)**, who in 1787 built the first purpose-built creamware pottery in Ireland - the '*Downshire China Manufactory*' **(Fig. 192)**.[7]

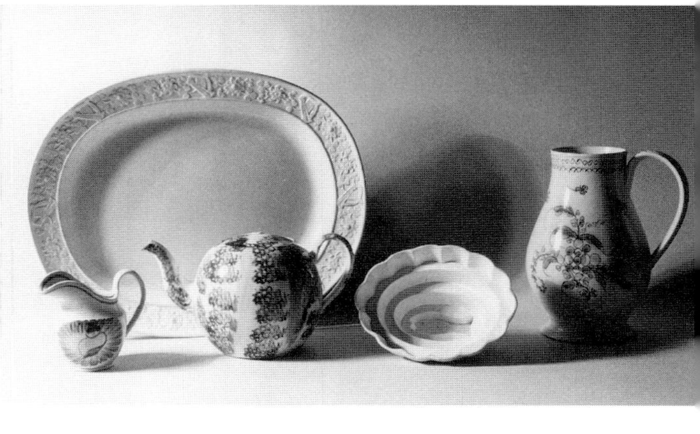

***Above** : **Figure 191**. Thomas Greg and his children, c.1765. Samuel Greg, who founded the Quarry Bank cotton mill at Styal in Cheshire, stands by Thomas's left side. (See footnote 9).*
***Right** : **Figure 192**. Creamwares manufactured with Irish clays at Thomas Greg's later 'Downshire Pottery' in Belfast, c. 1787-1806. Ht. of coffee-pot, 8 1/4 in., 210 mm.*

Greg was involved in many diverse activities at this time. Much of his wealth derived from the linen trade and the manufacture of vitriol, (sulphuric acid, used for bleaching linen). Like Mussenden, he was a major Belfast landlord, and the owner of a merchant fleet involved in transatlantic trade. At about the time the delftware pottery was working, he was also directing schemes for improving Belfast's docks, and was a prime mover in the project to construct the Lagan Canal, which later connected Belfast with Lough Neagh.[8] Clearly, Thomas Greg was not a potter, but throughout his life he was more involved in manufacturing ventures than most Belfast merchants.[9]

The Downshire Pottery that Thomas Greg went on to establish in another part of Belfast in 1787 was an exceptionally ambitious and expensive undertaking, built to employ a workforce of two hundred or more. Greg was 69 years of age in 1787, and so, in the past, it was difficult to understand why he should suddenly have decided to build such a very large pottery so late in life, with no prior experience of the ceramics industry. Import restrictions also meant that these creamwares had to be made with Irish, white-firing clays - a rare commodity. Without prior experience in producing ceramics, how could Greg have been certain that clays suitable for making creamware existed locally? (Carrickfergus delftware clay was entirely unsuited to creamware manufacture). The discovery that Greg owned this earlier pottery, during the middle years of the eighteenth-century, helps to explain some of his later activities.

The Little Patrick Street pottery certainly made delftware, to judge from the very few shards that were found near the kiln site. **(Figs. 194-6)**. In view of the fact that Greg later went on to manufacture creamware, however, it is quite possible that experiments were also conducted with other types of ceramics. The shards indicate that a utilitarian, lead glazed red-ware was certainly made at this site. This may have been the manufacturing site of a coarse-ware known locally by archaeologists as *'Brown Ware'*, which has been recorded on excavations as far north as Londonderry, and as far south as Dublin.[10] More intriguing, perhaps, is the single shard of an extremely unusual white-ware that was also recovered, which appears to be unlike any known delftware or creamware, but which may instead represent some form of experimental ceramic **(Fig. 196**, left).

Unfortunately, there is no further documentary evidence after 1763, which might imply that the Little Patrick Street pottery had little real significance. Considering Thomas Greg's subsequent investments in ceramic manufacture, however, and judging from the very few finds that have been recovered to date, this site might yet prove to be one of the more interesting pottery sites in Ireland.

THE POTTERY SITE

Many of the buildings on present-day Corporation Street in Belfast, close to Little Patrick Street, were demolished in the summer of 1992 to

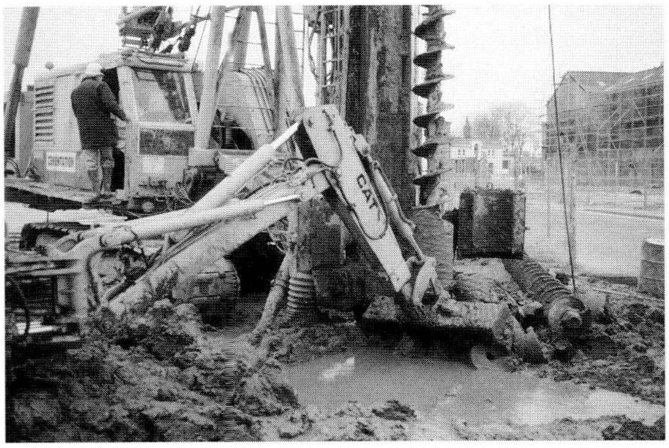

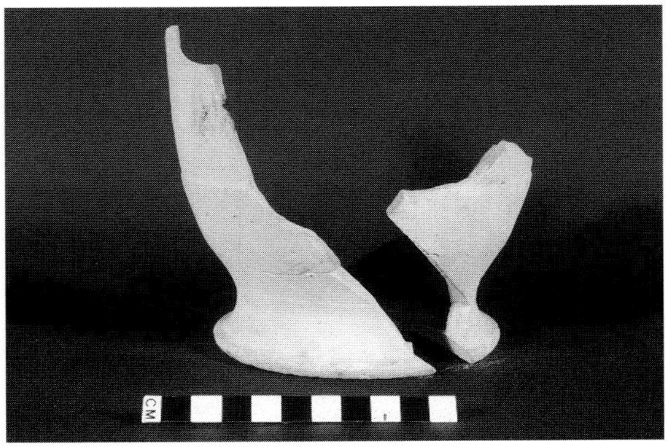

***Left** : **Figure 193**. The piling screw employed to dig bridge foundations near the 'Little Patrick Street' pottery site in 1992, which brought up the pottery fragments illustrated in Figs. 194-6.*
***Right** : **Figure 194**. Delftware biscuit fragment of a drug jar from the 'Little Patrick Street' pottery site.*
Max. Ht. 5 1/4 in., 134 mm., basal diam. 4 6/10 in. 117 mm.

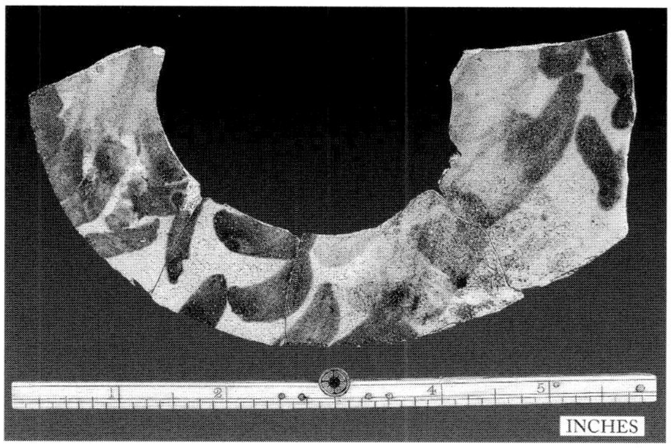

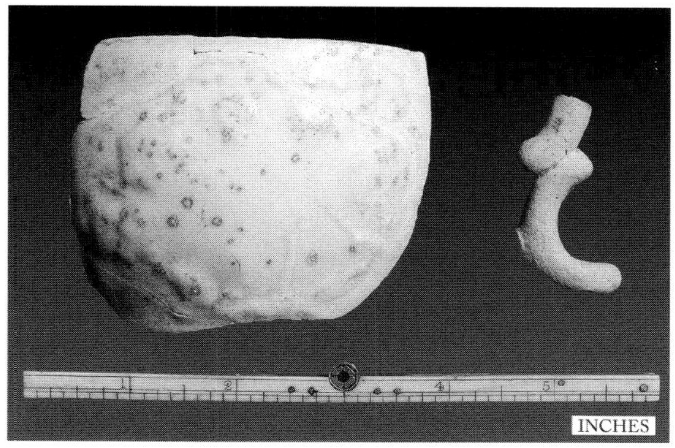

Left* : *Figure 195. *A portion of a glazed delftware bowl, employed to test the firing colour of the cobalt decoration.*
Right* : *Figure 196. *Right; Biscuit-ware fragment of a delftware tankard handle, of 'broken scroll' form, c.1740 - 60. (Compare Fig. 113). Left; Fragment of a small bowl with moulded floral decoration, made of an unidentified, white-bodied, lead glazed ceramic.*

make way for a new road-bridge, which now crosses the River Lagan nearby. This seemed a perfect opportunity to look for pottery waste, perhaps even to pinpoint the precise kiln site.[11] Unfortunately, it transpired that the floors of the demolished buildings were left undisturbed, so that any eighteenth-century occupation layers that might have been present remained hidden by concrete. The few shallow holes and trenches encountered around and about contained only disturbed, modern material.

Fortunately, a number of very large, deep holes were drilled with a piling-screw to accommodate the supports of the new bridge, spaced at c. 20 m. intervals along the northern side of Corporation Street, **(Fig. 193)**. It is difficult to imagine a less suitable tool for archaeological investigation, but the topmost soil and clay thrown up by the piling screw was occasionally found to contain pottery fragments. Once washed, these turned out to be more interesting than they initially appeared **(Figs. 194, 195, 196)**. Of the 46 shards collected in total, 24 were unglazed delftware biscuit (including some small saggar fragments), 7 were glazed delftware (not necessarily wasters), 1 consisted of an unusual, unidentified white-ware and the remainder included 4 *wasters* of a fine-bodied, lead-glazed red-ware (possibly '*Brown Ware*').

Three of the most interesting delftware shards are illustrated, each one an obvious waster and therefore likely to have been produced nearby. The largest fragment, **(Fig. 194)**, appears to be a portion of a drug jar, made of unglazed, typically straw-coloured, delftware biscuit. Although this originally seemed to be the most impressive fragment collected, it actually tells us little about Thomas Greg's pottery, as drug jars were amongst the most conservative and static of all delftware forms. Dated examples of this same form were made as early as the 1650s and continued through into the 1760s or even later.[12] A second, large waster is glazed. **(Fig. 195)**. This was originally part of a shallow bowl or saucer dish, but at some stage the delftware painters have used it as a test-piece, to experiment with the firing-colours of their cobalt.

Whilst it was encouraging to find two such obvious delftware wasters close to the suspected pottery site, neither of these large fragments is particularly informative. It is difficult to determine their date, even approximately, so that rather than originating at the second delftware pottery, it is possible that they could have been carried from the older '*Belfast Potthouse*', four hundred metres away. (See **Fig. 190**).

The third and smallest shard, which originally formed part of the handle of a delftware tankard, is therefore the most important delftware fragment found to date. **(Fig. 196**, right**)**. As it is made of unglazed delftware biscuit, it was obviously produced locally. This style of 'broken-scroll' handle did not develop until c.1740, (in silver or pewter), and so this piece could not have originated at the earlier Belfast Potthouse, which ceased during the 1720s.[13] Slim though the evidence may be, this one small fragment effectively confirms that a second delftware pottery existed in Belfast during the mid-eighteenth century, and probably lay in this vicinity.

The same style of 'broken-scroll' handle was probably being produced on delftware tankards in Dublin at about the same time, during the late 1750s or early 1760s, (See **Fig. 113**).

One of the most intriguing shards recovered from the Little Patrick Street area was a single fragment of a small, rounded bowl, about 5 inches in diameter and bearing moulded floral swags on the outside. **(Fig. 196**, left**)**. The piece appears to be lead glazed, but the extremely white, chalky fabric is entirely unlike any extant creamwares or delftwares. It is even possible that this fragment represents a misfired, experimental porcelain. The presence of this piece supports the possibility that the Little Patrick Street potters may have experimented with manufacturing a variety of fine-quality ceramics.

ATTRIBUTED WARES

Only one piece of delftware is tentatively attributed to the Little Patrick Street pottery, a unique, manganese-painted sundial tile, inscribed '*For James Reily of Carrickfergus 1765*'. **(Fig. 197, Colour Plate 42)**. This is one of only two dated English or Irish tiles presently known. It is also the only known example of a sundial tile. A number of clock faces have been recorded in English delftware, but these are finished to a much more professional standard.[14]

Given the quantity of clay that was traded between Liverpool and Carrickfergus, there will always be a possibility that this object is English. If so, however, then it prompts one to wonder why this example should be unique. (Transfer or block-printed sundials would be especially easy to produce). Similarly, the modest character of the sundial does not suggest that it was a specially commissioned piece from England.

Another factor to be considered is that the face of the sundial was only accurate at the latitude of Carrickfergus; 54 degrees and 45 minutes. If it was made at Liverpool, therefore, then the measurements on the face must have been copied from a template sent with the order, or else they were calculated by an individual who understood sundial manufacture. On balance, it seems more likely that the piece was produced locally, where small brass sundials of similar size were commonplace.[15] The individual for whom the sundial was made, James Reilly, was a well-known character in Carrickfergus, '*one of the eccentric figures of the Evangelical Revival*' mentioned in John Wesley's diaries. Reilly later moved to London, and was buried in Southwark.[16]

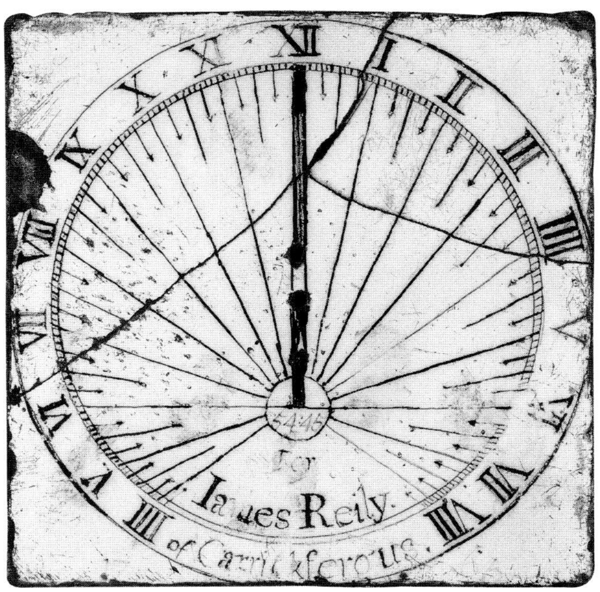

Figure 197. *A unique, manganese-painted sundial tile, attributed to the Little Patrick Street pottery, inscribed 'For James Reily of Carrickfergus 1765'. (The date, on the bottom edge, is faint). 4 3/4 in., 120 mm. square.*

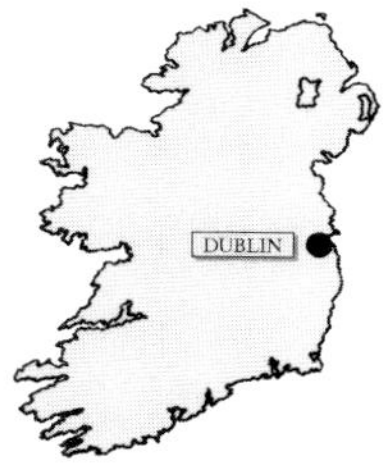

3 *v. Dublin II*
Stoneybatter
Ambrose Hanley and James Murphy (c.1760 - 1766)

For a brief period during the 1760s, there were two delftware potteries in Dublin. The first, as we have seen in Chapter 2, was situated at the World's End, on the eastern margin of the city's northern suburbs. Much less is known of the second pottery, which worked for six years or so at Stoneybatter, about 1$\frac{1}{2}$ - 2 miles from the World's End pottery, on the western edge of the city. John Rocque's 1756 map of Dublin pre-dates the documentary references to the Stoneybatter pottery by a few years, and shows no obvious indication of kilns or pottery buildings in this area.

The earliest reference to the Stoneybatter pottery comes from the Dublin Society minutes of the 10th December 1760, which record that '*a memorial of Ambrose Hanley was produced, relating to a Manufacture of White earthenware set up by him in Stony-batter*.' To evaluate the petition further, the Society's committee '*Ordered that the consideration of the said memorial may be put off to the first meeting of the Society in March - and that in the meantime the following Members of the Society;* [Messrs. Madden, Caire, Rutland & Philips] *do view & consider Mr. Hanly's Manufactory & at the same time give the Society their opinion what encouragement is proper to be given him*'.[1]

Presumably these members of the Dublin Society inspected the works a few months later. Consequently, Ambrose Hanley's memorial was finally '*read for the first time*' to the Dublin Society on April 23rd 1761, but there is no indication that he received an award in that year.[2] During the early 1760s, in cases where there was more than one applicant for a premium, the Dublin Society seems to have presented its award to the best quality manufacturer. It is possible, therefore, that Hanley lost out to Delamain's pottery in Dublin in 1761-2 and to Stritch's pottery in Limerick in 1762-3.[3] From 1765, however, the premium system was revised, so that all suitable applicants were subsequently awarded a flat rate payment equivalent to 15% of their annual production, (backdated to 1764). When this new scheme was introduced, Hanley received a premium of £45 from the Dublin Society, for producing delftware to the value of £300 between June 1764 and June 1765.[4] William Delamain's production was valued at £1,000 during the same interval, (see p.63).

Spurred on by this success, perhaps, Hanley seems then to have falsely reported the value of the following year's production, in order to gain a larger premium. At the end of the succeeding 12 months, he claimed that the value of his production had almost doubled, to £573, (even though the value of Delamain's output fell by 25% during the same period).[5] Accordingly, Hanley was awarded a premium of £70 by the Dublin Society in June 1766, based on the figures that he had submitted. Soon afterwards, however, the Dublin Society learned that this application had been deceitful, and they ordered that Hanley should receive no further premiums.[6] A few months later, in October 1766, a James Roach was paid a reward of £12 for '*discovering a fraud by which the Society were imposed upon in June last to give a premium of £70 to Ambrose Hanley and James Murphy, manufacturers of earthenware*'.[7]

The James Roach who discovered the fraud is probably the same James Roche who later held a senior position at the World's End pottery, in 1769-70, (see p.65). It is not clear, however, that he was working at the World's End when he exposed the deception - he might as easily have been working with Hanley at Stoneybatter at that time. The lack of subsequent references to the Stoneybatter pottery is also usually taken to imply that this pottery closed down shortly afterwards, but similarly, this is by no means proven.

No examples of the delftwares that were made at the Stoneybatter pottery are known. There was, at one stage, a view amongst some of the Dublin antiques trade that a particular design featured in the Castletown exhibition was produced at Stoneybatter (Cat. No. 52). The pattern portrays a rather naive, intensely painted Chinese pagoda amongst flowers, quite distinct in character from other Dublin wares. Excavated evidence now suggests, however, that delftwares of this design were probably made in London.[8]

3 vi : Limerick

John Stritch & Christopher Bridson (before June 1761 - c. late 1763)

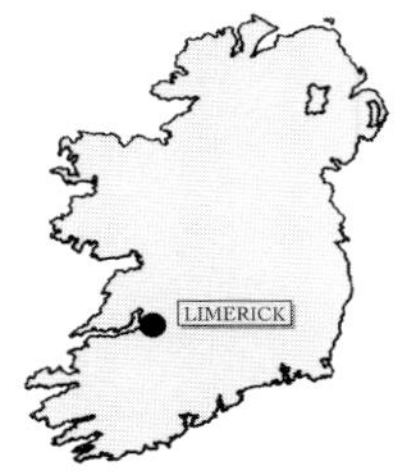

The last delftware pottery to be built in Ireland was established in Limerick during the early 1760s. As is so often the case, very little is known of the venture. Had our knowledge been based solely on the existing documentary evidence, then Limerick would merit a brief footnote indeed in Irish ceramic history, but by pure good fortune, a few pieces of delftware that were produced there have also survived. These amount to just five plates in total, (**Figs.198-9**. **Colour Plates 43-45**), but they are sufficiently interesting to entirely transform the status of the Limerick pottery.

The principal individual involved was John Stritch, whose name appears on each of the five attributed plates alongside the dates of their manufacture; 4 June and 6 July 1761. A native of Limerick, Stritch was probably a young man at the time these events took place, possibly in his late teens or early twenties. His father, Michael Stritch, was the owner of a well-established family business in the city, dealing in wine, provisions and general goods such as glass.[1] One particularly striking coincidence between the Stritch and Delamain families is that both were involved in the Irish/French brandy trade. (See **Colour Plates 9 & 10**). A Matthew Stritch owned one of the older brandy houses in Dublin, and another branch of the family settled in Nantes.[2]

A retrospective letter written in 1763 by John's father, Michael Stritch, to Sir Edward O'Brien, M.P. for Clare, was recently brought to light by the Knight of Glin. (Appendix IV, p.177). This indicates that his son had been the cause of some distress and '*disappointment*' to him, shortly before the pottery was established. During the late 1750s, John's father had invested 200 guineas in finding his son a suitable position as an apprentice to a wine merchant in Bordeaux, a trade more in keeping with the family business. John, however, had arrived home early from France, having served just three years of his apprenticeship and thus forfeiting the 200 guineas. His father '*forgave him*' and attempted to bring him into partnership in Limerick, but John refused '*to stick to ye shop*', even though his father offered to '*lay in a stock.. for him*', so that he might deal independently. Despite all his efforts, John's father was unable to '*smite his Element*' - his son seems to have been absolutely determined to make pottery.

Realising that this was the case, John's father then offered to find him a suitable property in which to build this new venture, acting through another local M.P., Edmond Sexton Pery, (for whom two of the transfer-printed plates were made - see **Colour Plate 44**). The intention seems to have been to invest in a building that could be converted to a dwelling or storehouse, in the event that John '*should faile in his Crockedie Ware*'. At about this time, John also declined Counsellor Lucius O'Brien's request for a dozen '*Crucebills: to be Made by him & Carried up to ye Society & that he'd forward them to ye* [Dublin] *Society & Get him a premium*'. This portion of the letter is open to interpretation, but it suggests that John's father would have been happier if his son had heeded Councillor O'Brien's advice to make crucibles, rather than delftware, and use these to seek a Dublin Society premium. At first reading, there might seem to be little difference between crucibles and delftware - they were both pottery, after all, but in reality the differences were great. Delftware was essentially a decorative household ware, whereas the crucibles referred to were probably intended for industrial use. (They were mainly employed in the glass-making and metal-smelting trades). Crucibles were also made from fireclays, which were capable of withstanding prolonged, intense heat, but on their own they were unsuitable for delftware manufacture.[3]

John's father's advice was probably sound, as crucibles were undoubtedly a sought after and saleable commodity in Ireland at this time - others were competing for Dublin Society premiums on precisely these lines at about the same time.[4] The reference might also suggest that John was aware of some of the different sorts of pottery clay that were available locally. It was recorded a few years later, in 1785, that Dutch potters went to exceptional lengths to obtain *delftware* clay from the Devil's Bit mountain in Co. Tipperary, some 20-25 miles to the north-east of Limerick.[5] Other extensive deposits of white-firing pottery clays occurred a similar distance to the south-east of Limerick, and these too were later exported in quantity to potters in England.[6] A major discovery of cobalt ore, the blue pigment employed in delftware decoration, was also reported in Killarney in 1794.[7]

One possible explanation for the very existence of the Limerick pottery, therefore, could be that John Stritch learned of these various local clay deposits, and sought to capitalise on them by establishing a pottery of his own. (It is difficult to imagine how the Dutch might have discovered these Tipperary clays without some prior, local experiments to point the way). A second possibility, suggested by the five surviving Limerick plates, is that Stritch sought to introduce the manufacture of transfer-printed wares to Ireland. Although Henry Delamain had claimed in 1753 that he had *'purchased the art of printing earthenware'*, there is no evidence to suggest that he ever succeeded in putting the art into practice. Where Stritch might have learned the techniques of transfer-printing remains a mystery, but knowledge of the method was becoming widespread by 1761. He could as easily have discovered the secret in France as in Ireland.

Whatever his motivation, and against his father's advice perhaps, John opted for making decorative delftwares rather than industrial ceramics. Like other Irish delftware potters before him, (John Chambers, for example), his first act was to produce wares specifically for local politicians in order to elicit parliamentary aid. On closer examination, however, the plates that Stritch produced for the two MPs were probably not typical of Limerick delftwares. Had transfer-printing become the standard method of decoration, then other examples of these transfer-printed delftwares would surely have come to light. Perhaps the most likely scenario, first suggested by Mairead Dunlevy, is that Stritch initially possessed only a small, enamelling kiln, with which he fired-on the transfer-printed and coloured enamel decoration of these early samples.[8] (Rather than *'made in Limerick'*, the plates might simply have been *'decorated in Limerick'*). There appears to be no evidence of a significant pottery building or kiln-like structure on any eighteenth-century map of Limerick, nor amongst contemporary documents, which has prompted Dunlevy and a second researcher in Limerick, Michelle Starr, to conclude that the pottery possessed only a small, experimental or enamelling kiln.[9] Stritch's kiln might well have been too small or short-lived to appear on a map, but subsequent documentation does suggest that the pottery went on to produce delftware in its own right, rather than simply decorating delftware blanks that had been made elsewhere.

John Stritch probably began the pottery on his own, as only his name appears on the plates. Soon afterwards, however, *'in a hurrie with oute* [his father's] *Consent Will or Ever leave or Abrobation he Goes & Joyns One Christopher* [Bridson] ... *Clark of oure Custom house'*. If the pottery had indeed commenced as a small enamelling kiln, then a kiln for making the delftware itself was probably built before 14th December 1762, when Stritch and Bridson received a Dublin Society premium specifically *'for erecting a manufactory of earthenware in imitation of Delft or White Ware'*.[10] The Dublin Society also proved to be more impressed with Limerick delftware than John's Stritch's father, for its members remarked that the specimens produced were *'well approved of'*, when they presented the award of £30.

The subsequent evidence concerning the pottery, scant though it is, could scarcely be more conflicting. On the 12th March 1763, John Stritch's father wrote that *"They Make But Course Mugs: Course Dishes or Course Crockedie Ware as yet from which noe Credit Can arise..."* (despite winning the Dublin Society premium). Yet six months later, the *Cork Evening Post*, in the section devoted to news from Limerick, recorded that on the 19th September 1763 *'was this day drawn, the most inimitable Pattern of Delft Ware ever seen in this Kingdom...'* [the fruits of the] *'unwearied endeavours of the Proprietors Messers Stritch and Bridson ...'*.[11] This latter, patently flattering remark is reminiscent of statements that appeared in the press when applications for Dublin Society premiums were in the offing, but no subsequent applications are recorded.

Apart from noting the death of Christopher Bridson in Limerick in 1768, there are no further references to the Limerick pottery.[12] In all probability, as no applications were made for the standard, *pro rata* premiums paid out by the Dublin Society from mid-1764 onwards, the pottery probably ceased in late 1763 or early 1764.

WARES

A total of five Limerick plates are known. Four are now in the National Museum of Ireland, the fifth is in the British Museum. Three were first recorded in 1942 at a sale of the property of Mrs. Wilson Fitzgerald of London, whose family seems to have had connections with County Clare.[13] The others were acquired at auction by the National Museum in 1952.

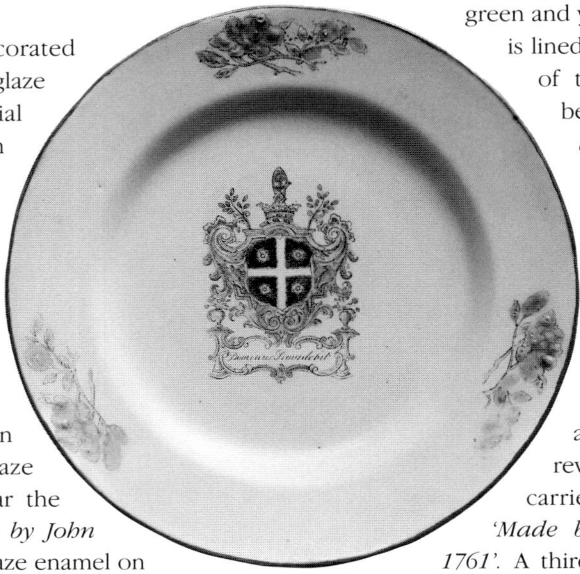

The plates are decorated with two different, overglaze transfer-printed armorial designs, highlighted with painted overglaze-enamel colours.[14] At least one example of each of the two types has a plain edge, the remainder bear additional transfer-printed flower sprays, repeated three times around the rim, and again highlighted in overglaze colour. All five plates bear the painted inscription *'Made by John Stritch Limerick'* in overglaze enamel on the reverse, but only those bearing the Burton coat of arms (see below) are inscribed with the precise dates of their manufacture; *'4 June 1761'* and *'6 July 1761'*. The five plates were therefore produced in at least two separate firings a month apart, despite the overall uniformity of their appearance.

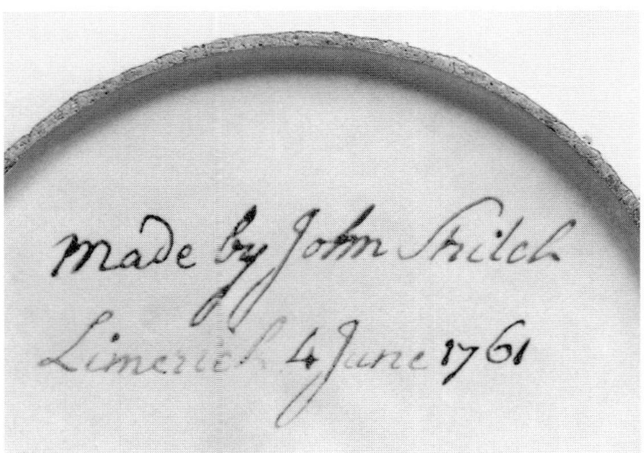

One example of each of the two armorial designs is illustrated here. The first example illustrated is one of three bearing a finely engraved coat of arms containing the motto *'Dominus Providebit'*, **(Fig. 198)**. The on-glaze (manganese?) transfer-printed decoration has been enhanced with painted, coloured enamels in blue, blue-green and yellow, and the plate's edge is lined in red-brown. The reverse of this example **(Fig. 198a)**, bears the inscription *'Made by John Stritch Limerick 4 June 1761'*, hand-written with an italic quill or brush in overglaze blue. A second example of this armorial design is illustrated in **Colour Plate 43**, which does not bear the three floral motifs around the border. Its reverse **(Colour Plate 45)** also carries a simpler inscription; *'Made by John Stritch Limerick 1761'.* A third example in the National Museum is dated *'6 July 1761'*.

The arms present on these plates are those of the Burton family. The Burton in question was identified by W.B. Honey as Francis Pierpoint Burton of Buncraggy, Co. Clare, who was elected to the Irish House of Commons in 1760 as member for County Clare. (Part of the city of Limerick lies within Co. Clare).[15]

There are two known examples of the second type of Limerick plate, one of which is illustrated **(Fig. 199, Colour Plate 44)**. These are similarly on-glaze transfer-printed with a finely engraved coat of arms, containing the name *'Edmond Sex. Pery'* (i.e. Edmond Sexton Pery), again enhanced with painted overglaze enamels in blue, blue-green and yellow, with a red-brown rim. As on the Burton plates, one example (in the British Museum) has a plain edge,

Above Top : Figure 198. *Transfer-printed and overglaze enamelled delftware plate made by John Stritch, Limerick, 1761, bearing the arms of Francis Pierpoint Burton, MP for Co. Clare. (See also Colour Plate 43). Diam. 8 11/16 in., 220 mm.*
Above : Figure 198a. *Reverse of Fig. 198.*
Opposite Page : Figure 199. *Transfer-printed delftware plate, bearing the arms of Edmond Sexton Pery, MP for Limerick. Diam. 8 11/16 in., 220 mm. (See also Colour Plate 44).*

another (illustrated), has three identical transfer-printed flower sprays spaced around the rim, highlighted in blue-green and yellow enamels. This second pair of plates bear identical inscriptions on the reverse, *'Made by John Stritch Limerick 1761'*, hand-written in similar fashion to the previous pair with an italic quill or brush in overglaze blue.

Edmond Sexton Pery, for whom this second pair of plates was made, later rose to prominence in the Irish House of Commons, to which he was elected as member for Limerick in 1760.[16]

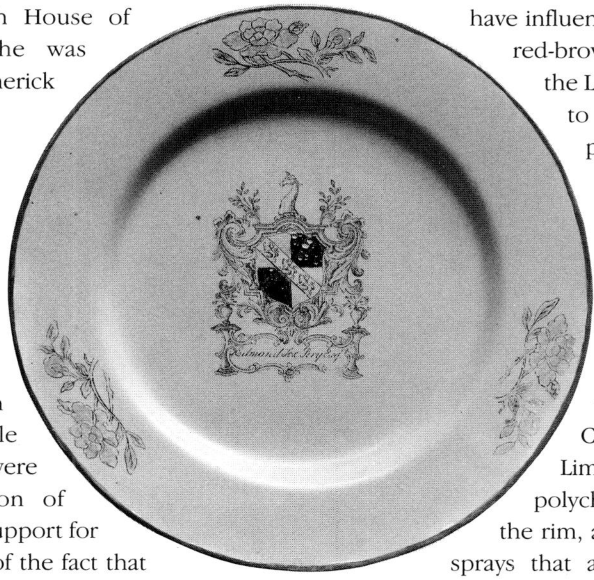

DISCUSSION

As the recipients, or at least, the *intended* recipients of these five plates were two of the MPs responsible for Limerick's interests in 1761, there can be little doubt that the plates were made with the intention of attracting parliamentary support for the new pottery. In view of the fact that the plates are over-fired and might have been considered imperfect, it is by no means certain that they were presented to the MPs concerned. (If they were, then why should plates made for two different families have turned up together in 1942?). Two years after the plates were made, in 1763, Edmond Sexton Pery presented a speech to the Irish House questioning the manner in which Dublin Society premiums were distributed, although his remarks probably had little direct association with Stritch's application.[17]

The plates are exceptional rarities. First and foremost, they are the only known examples of transfer-printed Irish delftware. (Henry Delamain claimed in 1753 that he had *'purchased the art of printing earthenware'*, but to date no examples of transfer-printed Dublin delftware have been identified). Transfer-printed delftware objects, other than tiles, are also extremely scarce. Apart from these five Limerick plates, only eight pieces are known, all of them transfer-printed from copper plates at Liverpool, perhaps a year or so later, (c.1762-3).[18] It is even rarer to find polychrome enamelling on transfer-printed delftwares, although a small number of John Sadler's printed tiles, which were produced at Liverpool in the late 1750s and 1760s, are also highlighted in overglaze enamel colours.[19]

The designs of the Limerick plates do not copy other delftwares, but instead seem to mimic a group of transfer-printed *porcelain* armorial plates, produced at Bow during the second half of the 1750s.[20] The clearest indication that Bow may have influenced Stritch lies in the dark red-brown edge which appears on the Limerick plates - Bow seems to have been the only English porcelain factory to routinely paint a dark red-brown or purple line around the very edge of its transfer-printed wares.[21] (At Worcester, for example, a blue line was usually painted *inside* the edge rather than on it). Certain details on the Limerick plates, such as the polychrome floral sprays around the rim, are strongly reminiscent of sprays that appear on other transfer-printed porcelains, particularly those produced at Vauxhall in c.1758-60, but the colour control demonstrated by the Vauxhall enamellers was greatly superior.[22]

Dunlevy's suggestion that these plates were simply decorated in Limerick, using plain delftwares produced elsewhere, seems to agree with the evidence of the plates themselves. As the plates have been re-fired it is difficult to be certain, but the character of the delftware does appear suspiciously 'Dublin-like' on the reverse. (There are splits in the body, pulled-back glaze, bare areas of biscuit and so on). The one negative observation in this regard is that the Limerick plates are a little smaller than standard Dublin plates (220 - 225 mm., compared to c.230 - 235 mm.), but Dublin plates of this smaller size certainly exist, decorated with the *'Broken Scroll'* pattern for example.[23]

The one unique feature of the reverse of the Limerick plates is the fact that they each bear *two* sets of support scars. The causes of these scars are obvious; one set was produced in the glost firing, when the delftware plate itself was glazed, the second set were produced when Stritch re-fired the plate to add his transfer-printed and enamelled decoration. The presence of this second set of scars indicates that Stritch operated his decorating kiln at a very high temperature - sufficient to soften and even re-melt the tin-glaze. This in turn indicates that Stritch had really only conquered one of the difficulties associated with transfer-printed decoration - that of producing the transfer-print itself. He does not seem to have mastered the chemistry involved, particularly with regard to 'fluxes' - the additives that controlled the firing temperature of the enamels.

Most enamelling kilns today, using modern fluxes such as boron, operate at comparatively low temperatures of c.600-750 degrees centigrade.[24] When the kiln temperature is too low, the enamels do not fire to their true colours, and they are easily rubbed off or scratched. The required firing temperature also varies according to colour - yellow (antimony) fires naturally at a lower temperature than blue (cobalt), for example.

The best flux available in Stritch's day was probably lead, which should have allowed most of the enamel colours to fire at around 650-750 degrees, but the fact that Stritch's kiln-supports left such prominent scars indicates that he operated his kiln at temperatures closer to the melting temperature of tin-glaze. (Probably around to 900 - 1100 degrees, or in other words, the highest temperature possible). This was an exceptionally high temperature for an enamelling kiln. Presumably, Stritch must have required these temperatures to ensure that the transfer-prints were properly fired-on, but the excessive heat in turn over-fired the low temperature enamel colours - the yellow and blue-green (copper). Evidence of his problems can be clearly seen on the transfer-printed flowers around the border **(Colour Plate. 44)**, where the yellows and greens have partly volatilised. The enamels that remain are patchy and bubbled, with a rather muddy appearance.

Two Irish names are usually mentioned in association with the Limerick plates, as individuals who might have taught Stritch the secret of transfer-printing.[25] The first is John Brooks, the Dublin engraver credited with inventing the transfer-printing process more than a decade earlier. (See p.48). As Brooks is now known to have remained in London throughout the 1760s, it is highly unlikely that he had any involvement with the Limerick venture.[26] The second individual commonly mentioned is Michael Hanbury, another Dublin engraver, who in 1758 was awarded a Dublin Society premium of 20 guineas for '*a new invention for ornamenting with great despatch, china and earthenware, etc, from copper plate engraving on the unburnt glaze*'.[27] The two sets of support scars prove, however, that Stitch's transfer-prints were applied onto *fired* rather than '*unburnt*' delftware. This does not rule out the possibility that Stritch learned some of the basic technique from Hanbury, but equally, there is no particular reason for believing that an Irish connection necessarily existed. By 1761, transfer-printing had been achieved on enamels at Battersea and Birmingham, on porcelain at Chelsea, Bow, Longton Hall, Vauxhall, Worcester and Liverpool, on white salt-glaze at Battersea or Staffordshire and on delftware in Liverpool. At least one of the several English methods known was published in France by 1755.[28] Given this range of potential sources, it is impossible to determine where Stritch might have gained his knowledge of transfer-printing - he might even have learned of the technique during his apprenticeship in France. Purely on stylistic grounds, an as yet unidentified contact in London - at Bow or perhaps Vauxhall - seems the most likely option.

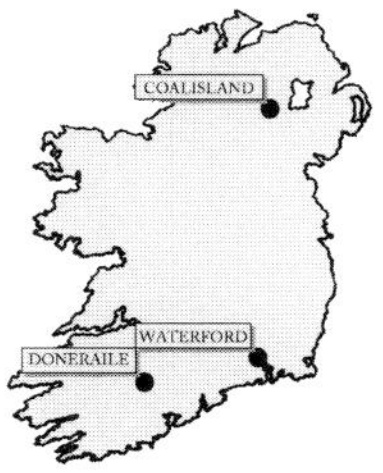

3 vii. Other Potteries

There are a number of more tenuous references to the manufacture of fine-quality white ceramics in Ireland. Some of these potteries may have made delftware, but in the absence of further evidence, we can do little except record their existence.

One of the earliest references, and a puzzle for anyone who has studied Irish delftware, lies in the Dublin Society's records of earthenware premiums paid on April 1st, 1742;

'*William Bright* [of the Rostrevor pottery] *produced two complete sets of earthenware for the premium and Mr. William Lake one; Mr. Lake's was allowed to have the advantage of colour, but Mr. Bright's being thought the better set on the whole the premium was adjudged to him*'.[1]

This reference indicates that there were at least two delftware potteries working in Ireland in 1742, but the location of Mr. Lake's venture is unrecorded and his name does not recur subsequently. (A paper-maker named William Lake is mentioned in Rathfarnam in Dublin in 1719, but apart from the fact that paper-makers and potters both used large quantities of timber there is nothing to link the two individuals).[2] The most likely answer to this particular mystery seems to be that William Lake had some association with the World's End pottery in Dublin in 1742, as to the best of present knowledge, only two delftware potteries were working in Ireland at that time - at Rostrevor, and at the World's End. (This was confirmed three years earlier by Dr. Samuel Madden of the Dublin Society - see p.37). If Lake was involved at the World's End pottery, however, then this obviously raises other questions concerning John Chambers' status at that time. (See p.38).

Another promising lead is a clear, contemporary statement, written by William Smith in his *History of Cork*, (1750), that '*a Pottery of white ware* [is] *carried on at Doneraile in the north of the county*'. Unfortunately, nothing further is known of this pottery. The area is within a few miles of '*an extensive district of Tipperary, between Cahir and Clonmel*' in which white-firing pipe-clays are recorded, and so there might well be more substance to this pottery reference than has hitherto been recognised. In 1844, the pipe clay of the area was '*considered equal in quality to the pipe clay of Bovey Tracey. It burns purely white, and large quantities of it have been exported to England*'.[3]

Much farther to the north, in County Tyrone, we have already seen that the '*Primate's Coals*' delftware bowl made by Henry Delamain in 1753 appears to have been produced using an experimental, white-firing fireclay from coal mines near Coalisland, (p.52). It seems that this discovery, and the presence of other, fine-quality ball and pipe-clays close by, led to the development of an extensive country pottery industry in the vicinity of Coalisland, which only ceased in the 1950s.[4] Shortly after the '*Primate's Coals*' bowl was made, however, in 1759, there appear to have been plans to establish a fine-quality pottery in this area, at Port Tallyhoa near Creenagh, just east of Coalisland and next to the new Tyrone canal. The works were established by three local men, Acheson Johnson, James Greer and Thomas Campbell, and by September 1759 their pottery was producing '*all kinds of black and brown ware*'.[5] They obviously had more ambitious plans, however, as they stated that '*the work ... will be extended into many other branches, when proper persons arrive from England for such purposes*'. By 1772, only James Greer seems to have been involved, but he fully intended '*to carry on his Earthenware Manufacture at his Pottery at Creenagh in as extensive a Manner as formerly*'.[6] Interestingly, Greer also manufactured soap in nearby Milton, which seems reminiscent of the references to the Belfast Potthouse in 1719 as a '*Potthouse and Soaphouse*', (p.20).

The Creenagh pottery has proven difficult to locate, as the area near the old canal is densely overgrown. Two days of field-walking in the area in 1995 turned up only coarse pottery shards and a nineteenth-century kiln site.[7] As late as 1960, however, the Coalisland fireclays were extracted from a nearby mine-shaft known as the '*Rectory Shaft*' and '*at one time* [they had also been] *dug from an open pit*'.[8] Between 1897 and 1900, a small number of potters from Belleek operated a pottery nearby on the site of the old '*Ulster Fireclay Works*' in Coalisland town.[9] This succeeded for a short time in producing a close imitation of Belleek porcelain, using these same, pure white fireclays. In view of the rich variety of clays in this area, it is quite possible that attempts were made to produce fine-quality ceramics there during the eighteenth-century, just as Creenagh's 1759 advertisement suggests.

A further reference concerning earthenware in 1759 seems to have been unrelated to the Tyrone pottery. In the Dublin Society's minutes for January 18th 1759, it was recorded that '*A petition of Messrs. Plunkett and Bourke* [was] *read, praying that, to enable them to make valuable earthenware etc., the Society be pleased to lend them Ten pounds. Ordered that the Treasurer do lend them ten pounds, taking their bond for twelve months without interest*'.[10] The location of Messrs. Plunkett & Bourke's pottery is unknown.

The only other mention of a fine-quality white ceramic pottery in Ireland at this time is the rather conflicting evidence relating to a porcelain experiment in Waterford in 1755. (See p.54-5).[11] In 1772, one William Browne, John Bowcock's predecessor as clerk of the Bow porcelain works, also applied personally to James Caulfield, the Earl of Charlemont, (a partner in the '*Primate's Pits*' consortium, p.52), offering to establish a porcelain manufactory in Ireland, but the matter does not appear to have been pursued.[12]

With the rise in popularity of creamware, the exports of Carrickfergus clay fell away dramatically from 1766 onwards and ceased entirely in 1778. (See **Fig. 200**, p.166). By the late 1770s, delftware manufacture had ceased almost everywhere in the British Isles, although remarkably, one or two potteries in London did manage to survive into the early-nineteenth century. There were certainly further attempts to produce fine-quality ceramics in Ireland during the closing years of the eighteenth-century. One of these ventures, Thomas Greg's '*Downshire Pottery*', which produced creamware in Belfast from 1787, seems to have been almost as ambitious as some of Henry Delamain's schemes, but there is no evidence to indicate that delftware was made anywhere in Ireland after 1771.

APPENDICES I - V

APPENDIX I : CARRICKFERGUS CLAY

The town of Carrickfergus is situated seven miles from Belfast, on the northern shore of Belfast Lough in County Antrim. With the possible exception of some potteries in Bristol, all of the delftware potteries that set up around the Irish Sea during the eighteenth-century seem to have obtained their delftware clay from Carrickfergus, yet mysteriously, there is virtually no record whatever of potters' clay in the town itself. One distinguished local historian, in compiling material for a detailed, documentary history of Carrickfergus, did not encounter even one reference to pottery clay amongst local papers, whilst the only indications of clay-workings on early maps seem to be the brick-pits that occur virtually everywhere in the north of Ireland.[1] At one stage, this complete lack of evidence suggested that the delftware clay must have been found elsewhere in County Antrim, and was simply brought to Carrickfergus for shipment.

In recent years it has become evident that Carrickfergus clay was, after all, extracted from a two-mile stretch of shore immediately adjacent to the town.[2] (The clay-pits were probably not indicated on contemporary maps because they lay below the high tide mark). So much clay seems to have been removed from the shore, in fact, that Carrickfergus was partly inundated by the sea on several occasions during the late-eighteenth and early-nineteenth centuries. Ironically, the coastal defences and sea walls that were subsequently built to protect the town from these marine incursions now help to disguise the traces of Carrickfergus clay that might remain.

Further details of the occurrence and geology of Carrickfergus clay are recorded elsewhere.[3] The following account simply attempts to briefly address the three main aspects of Carrickfergus clay that are of greatest relevance to Irish delftware history, namely, its character, the extent of the trade, and the connections with the Belfast Potthouse.

i. The character of the clay

Carrickfergus clay was described in early accounts as a '*bluish-white*' or '*light blue*' clay, which ideally was weathered for three years before use.[4] An account of some Bristol potters in 1767 suggests that Carrickfergus clay was not used alone, but was added to local clays to produce the ideal delftware clay mix;

'*The clay which is found here* [in Bristol] *is altogether too fat and no work could be done on it alone; they have therefore to mix it with the lean Irish clay. These clays are sieved, wetted and kneaded together*'.[5]

Some unrelated clay recipes recorded by John Dwight in 1697 suggest that Carrickfergus clays were probably mixed with local red clays in a ratio of 1:1.[6] This estimate is borne out by later exports to Liverpool, where the potters seem to have imported clay from Carrickfergus that was already prepared as a delftware clay.[7]

To better understand the special significance of Carrickfergus clay for the delftware potters, we must briefly consider the terms '*fat*' and '*lean*' clay, which are still widely used to this day. A '*fat*' clay is a typical, red-firing potters' clay, of the sort used for making flower-pots or country pots.[8] Such clays are rich in clay minerals and are therefore easy to throw and work, but their iron-red colour and comparatively low porosity make them unsuitable as a delftware body. (The viscous tin-glaze will not adhere unless the porosity is high). '*Lean*' clays on the other hand have a low clay content and are difficult to throw. In the case of Carrickfergus clay, this lower clay content was compensated by a much higher proportion of calcium carbonate or chalk (c. 30-40% by weight). When fired, the chalk was burned off with two main effects - firstly, the iron colour of the red, '*fat*' clay bleached out to a much lighter, straw colour, and secondly, the body became suffused with a minute honeycomb of bubbles, greatly increasing the porosity and permeability.[9] For delftware potters, the principal difficulty seems to have lain in judging the correct clay mixture, to arrive at a delftware clay that had sufficient porosity to receive a tin-glaze, yet remained manageable and easily thrown. Perhaps this was the skill that Thomas Molyneux was referring to in 1708, when he mentioned that Belfast delftware was *'very clean and pretty ... not so much owing to any peculiar happiness in the clay, but rather to the manner of beating and mixing it up'*. (See p.17).

Although chalk-rich clays are common around the south-east of England, in East Anglia and Kent especially, they are much rarer farther north. The unusually high chalk content of Carrickfergus clay was the result of a unique, highly localised, geological phenomenon, which seems to have been restricted to this two-mile stretch of Belfast Lough.[10] Visually, however, there is little to distinguish Carrickfergus clay from other types of estuarine clay found elsewhere in the British Isles, for example on the Liffey, Clyde, Mersey and Severn estuaries. This seems to have led some potters - in Liverpool and Glasgow - to believe that their local clays were adequate for delftware manufacture, but both of these potteries were ultimately forced to depend upon clay shipments from Carrickfergus.[11] A further measure of the rarity of Carrickfergus-type clays comes from the early delftware pottery in Burlington, New Jersey, which seems to have failed during the 1680s because the potters were unable to find a suitable delftware clay anywhere in that part of North America.[12] Ultimately, they imported a shipment of clay from East Anglia, to demonstrate that their failure was not due to deficiency in the skill of the potters.

ii. Carrickfergus Clay Exports

As long ago as 1934, Aubrey Toppin published details of the quantities of Carrickfergus clay that were imported into England during selected years of the eighteenth-century.[13] This work was pursued much more thoroughly in 1986 by Frank Britton, who extracted all of the entries for Carrickfergus clay from the customs records at Kew. These figures were published in the English Ceramic Circle Transactions in 1994.[14]

The graph below **(Fig. 200)** is based on Britton's published figures, **(Table App. Ia)**, which list the total tonnages imported in each year at English *'outports'*. (The term *'outports'* refers to English ports other than London, but as London potters did not use Carrickfergus clay, the figures are probably accurate for the country as a whole).

Figure 200.

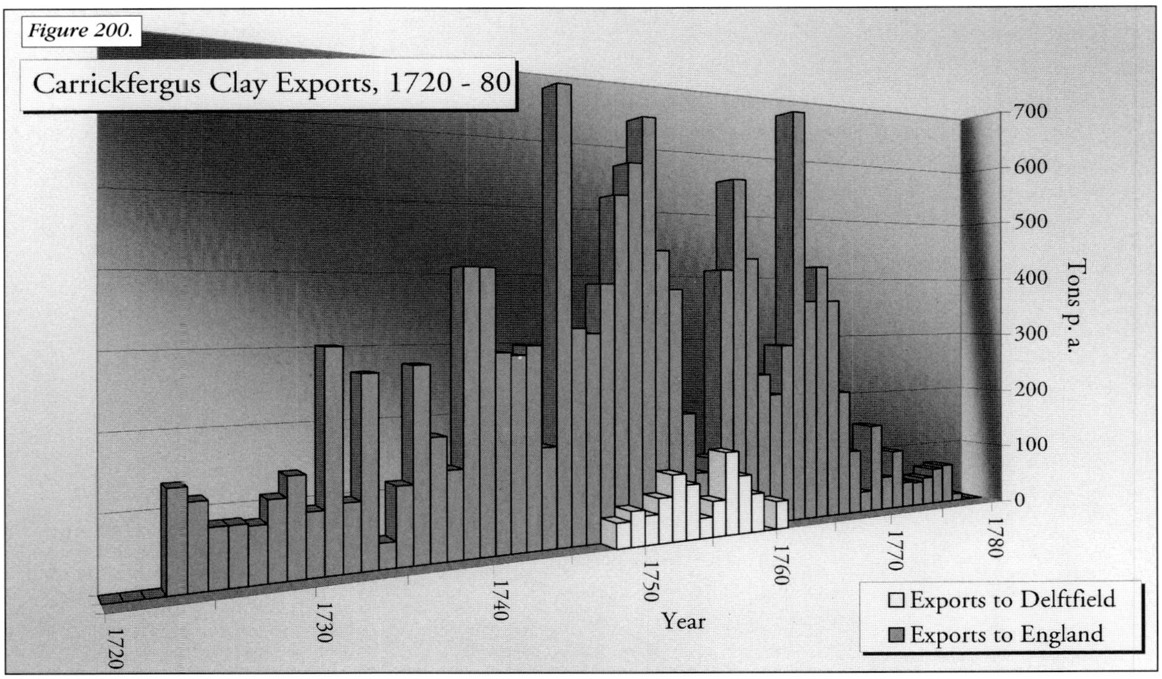

The second, smaller graph relates solely to the Delftfield pottery in Glasgow, the only delftware pottery known to have worked in Scotland. These figures were first published in 1979 by Peter Denholm, who extracted them from customs records relating specifically to the port of Glasgow.[15] To be strictly accurate, therefore, these figures should be added to the English outport figures to discover the gross exports of Carrickfergus clay from Ireland.[16] By plotting them alongside, however, we gain a much clearer impression of the volume of clay that was required by a single delftware pottery during the mid-eighteenth century. As a further measure of the quantities involved, it has been calculated that 300 tons of Carrickfergus clay was sufficient to make approximately one million items of delftware, of one pound weight apiece.[17] This in turn suggests that the 13,205 tons of Carrickfergus clay exported to England between 1723 and 1778 was sufficient to produce something in the order of 44 million pieces of delftware.

In addition to publishing gross figures for all English outports, Frank Britton also studied the individual port books of Bristol and Liverpool, where most Carrickfergus clay would have been used. Unfortunately, comparatively few of these port books have survived - Britton was only able to record the years 1723 and 1726 for Liverpool, and 1742 for Bristol, and so the results do not appear to have been published. Nonetheless, these books do provide useful information, listed here as **Table App. Ib**. The records describe details of individual shipments, and they include the names of the potters who ordered them, such as Thomas Pennington and Thomas & Richard Frank in Bristol, or Robert Fazackerly, Josia Poole and James Shaw in Liverpool.[18]

TABLES APP. Ia & Ib: ENGLISH IMPORTS OF CARRICKFERGUS CLAY

Table Ia : Total Imports of all English 'Outports', (Ports other than London).

Year	Tons	Value £.s.d	Delftfield (tons)	Year	Tons	Value £.s.d	Delftfield (tons)
1720	No Entry	Nil		1750	570	143.09.09	44
1721	No Entry	Nil		1751	641	175.13.01	68
1722	No Entry	Nil		1752	437.5	109.17.06	101
1723	132	43.16.00		1753	379	92.11.03	84
1724	113	23.08.05		1754	186	34.19.01	31
1725	79	18.06.00		1755	92	22.00.06	55
1726	79	19.15.00		1756	114	28.10.00	128
1727	76	15.04.00		1757	410	102.03.04	90
1728	107.5	34.03.06		1758	55	141.02.09	60
1729	136	33.11.01		1759	428	122.09.05	0
1730	87	30.04.06		1760	242	61.15.11	>44
1731	301.5	79.08.04		1761	209	45.17.00	
1732	94.5	17.19.03		1762	288	75.08.08	
1733	265	107.05.10		1763	672.5	171.15.03	
1734	36	12.16.09		1764	360.5	89.05.08	
1735	111	45.09.10		1765	417	104.08.03	
1736	274	136.02.00		1766	360.5	85.10.00	
1737	174	57.08.00		1767	207	48.02.03	
1738	127	39.00.05		1768	105	29.00.02	
1739	409	117.00.09		1769	34	8.10.00	
1740	408	129.03.00		1770	145.5	35.01.06	
1741	288	24.10.00		1771	55	295.07.09	
1742	283.5	79.13.03		1772	98	24.13.00	
1743	297	83.14.06		1773	42	7.14.04	
1744	149	39.17.03		1774	40	26.00.00	
1745	679	141.09.06		1775	46.5	232.14.02	
1746	321	74.07.00		1776	60	300.00.00	
1747	313	79.15.00		1777	65	16.13.09	
1748	387	97.05.00	38	1778	12	3.00.10	
1749	519.5	122.04.00	53	1779	No Entry	Nil	
				1780	No Entry	Nil	

Table Ib : Liverpool & Bristol Port Book Records of Clay Imports. [19]

Liverpool 1723

Date	Vessel	Ship's Master	Arriving from	Consignor	Clay (tons)	Value £.s.d
10 Apr.	*Industry*	Jno. Inglefield	Carrickfergus	Robert Fazackerly	22	£5.10.00
11 May	*Salamander*	Jno. Kirkham	Carrickfergus	Josia Poole	40	£5.00.00
14 May	*Diligence*	Thos. Jackson	Belfast	Thos. Jackson	12	£2.02.00
19 Jun.	*Industry*	Jno. Inglefield	Carrickfergus	James Shaw	20	£5.00.00
1 Jul.	*Ross*	Wm. Reacaske	Newry	Thos. Jackson	30	£5.05.00
26 Aug.	*Endeavour*	Josias Minis	Belfast	Arthur Hamilton	45	£9.00.00
31 Aug.	*Diligence*	Thos. Jackson	Belfast	Thos. Jackson	35	£7.00.00
9 Sep.	*Industry*	Jno. Inglefield	Carrickfergus	Robert Fazackerly	20	£5.00.00
9 Oct.	*Endeavour*	Josias Minis	Newry	Josias Minis	12	£3.00.00
29 Nov.	*Diligence*	Thos. Jackson	Belfast	Thos. Jackson	16	£3.03.00
19 Dec.	*Industry*	Jno. Inglefield	Carrickfergus	Jno. Inglefield	12	£3.00.00
				Total Annual Tonnage:	264	*See below

Liverpool 1726

Date	Vessel	Ship's Master	Arriving from	Consignor	Clay (tons)	Value £.s.d
25 May	*Industry*	Jno. Inglefield	Belfast	Jno. Inglefield	25	£5.00.00
10 Aug.	*Industry*	Jno. Inglefield	Belfast	Jno. Inglefield	24	£6.10.00
23 Aug.	*Francis*	Jno. McClarie	Strangford	Jno. McClarie	12	Not Listed
6 Dec.	*John & Thomas*	Jno. W'mson	Belfast	Jno. Murdoch	15	£4.02.06
				Total Annual Tonnage:	76	

Bristol 1742

Date	Vessel	Ship's Master	Arriving from	Consignor	Clay (tons)	Value £.s.d
27 Apr.	*Rotterdam Merchant*	Dan. Holdrick	C'fergus / Belfast	Th. Pennington & Co.	60	£19.10.00
4 May	*Rotterdam Merchant*	Dan. Holdrick	C'fergus / Belfast	Th. Pennington & Co.	25	£11.11.00
17 Jul.	*Charming Molly*	Peter Wright	Carrickfergus	Th. & Rich. Frank	20	£6.05.00
21 Jul.	*Charming Molly*	Peter Wright	Carrickfergus	Th. & Rich. Frank	6	£1.19.00
				Total Annual Tonnage:	111	

* Note that the total imports of 264 tons of clay at Liverpool in 1723 was precisely twice the figure of 132 tons of *Carrickfergus* clay, imported into England in that year. (Table App. Ia). This suggests that Carrickfergus clay was already mixed with an equal measure of standard potters' clay when it arrived in Liverpool. (Duty was only charged on Carrickfergus clay, not the potters' clay).

iii. The Carrickfergus Clay leases

When the delftware pottery was established at Delftfield in Glasgow in March or April 1748, the potters there intended using local clays to make their delftware.[20] As an added insurance, however, one of the owners, Robert Finlay, wrote to the distinguished Belfast merchant Daniel Mussenden to discover how Carrickfergus clay might be obtained. (See p.153). The attempt to produce delftware with Scottish clays failed, and so, in 1749, legal proceedings were initiated against the potters involved. Finlay's letter to Daniel Mussenden, and Mussenden's reply, were presented as evidence during the court case. It is from these two letters that almost all of our knowledge concerning the individuals involved in the Carrickfergus clay trade is derived.[21]

To: Daniel Mussenden, Merchant in Belfast
From: Robert Finlay, Glasgow, 18th April 1748

'Sir, As there are some. ..intending to try a small Project, for the Execution of which they may stand in Need of a Quantity, from Time to Time, of the very same Clay which those in Liverpool, who make the painted earthen Ware, get near to your Place, and I hear not only them, but others, may get what Quantities they want, in sundry Places where Vessels can go, I must therefore beg a very particular Favour, that, as soon as possible after Receipt of this, you will advise me if we can be served, and if we can learn the Price of the Ton-Weight laid down at the Ship-Side. If we can be served, ... we may be obliged to give you the Trouble of making the Contract for us, and to pay our Accompts from Time to Time...'

To: Robert Finlay, Glasgow
From Daniel Mussenden, Belfast, 28th April 1748

'Mr. Robert Finlay, Sir,

I am favoured with your's of the 18th instant... In Answer to which, Messieurs Kirk and Cobham of Carrick-Fergus are the Gentlemen who usually supply Liverpool and Bristol with that Kind of Clay, and I have been treating with them about it, and they propose to serve you with what Quantity you want, which they expect will not be less than one hundred Tons in a Year, delivered at the Key of Carrick-Fergus, being the only convenient Place for shipping it; they propose to deliver it you there at the Ship-Side for 5 s. 6 d. per Ton British Money, and 20 Hundred Weight to the Ton, and Sixscore to the Hundred, [i.e. 1 Ton = 2,400 lbs.], *you paying the Duty; Keyage, and Custom-House Charges of shipping it: The Duty is 2 d. per Ton, and Officers Fees about eight or ten Shillings upon each Vessel. Mr. Kirk says his Part is upon his own free-hold Estate, and Mr. Cobham is Agent for one Mris. Atkinson; and the former will agree to serve for what Term of Years you please, as long as his Pits last, and the latter during the life of Mris. Atkinson; for at her decease it falls to one Mr. Banks of this Town* [of Belfast]*: So that if these Terms are agreeable, and you go on with your Project, on your advising me* [I] *shall enter an Agreement with them on your Behalf..*

Daniel Mussenden'

Daniel Mussenden's letter provides clear details of the ownership of the Carrickfergus clay deposits in 1748. There appear to have been two leases. One was owned freehold by a '*Mr. Kirk*', the other was managed by '*Mr. Cobham*', an agent for a '*Mris. Atkinson*', whose land was to fall to '*Mr. Banks*' of Belfast upon her decease.

The interrelationships between these various individuals can be deduced from some rather complex land documents dating from the 1720s and 30s. The first lease is straightforward and is simply interpreted; '*Mr. Kirk*' was probably a James Kirk, '*Town Clerk*' who in 1723 leased land on the shore at Cronaghbane, in the very centre of Carrickfergus, close to the castle.[22] Prior to 1723, this lease had been in the possession of James' father, John Kirk, and a second individual, William Taylor.

The lease belonging to '*Mris. Atkinson*' was much larger and more valuable than James Kirk's, and contained a small '*castle*', several houses, and a stretch of shore to the east of Carrickfergus town.[23] Several individuals were named in Mussenden's letter in relation to this lease. The '*Mris. Atkinson*' concerned was a '*Mary Atkinson, alias Taylor*', who in 1731 had leased the property from her sister, '*Ann Smith of Carrickfergus, widow*'.[24] Her agent, '*Mr. Cobham*', was probably James Cobham, who also owned brick-pits in Belfast.[25] Upon Ann Smith or Mary Atkinson's decease, the leasehold of this second property was to fall to a '*Mr. Banks*', almost certainly a Stewart Banks of Belfast.[26]

Many of these names were also associated with the Belfast Potthouse, but the various family relationships have not been fully researched. For now, it is only possible to indicate some of the more obvious connections. William Taylor, the seventeenth-century individual whose surname seems to link the two Carrickfergus clay leases, arrived in Belfast from Glasgow at the very same time as William Smith, the father of David and Patrick Smith of the Belfast Potthouse.[27] Ann Smith *may* have been William Taylor's eldest daughter. Ann had obviously married into the Smith family, although she was not married to either David or Patrick.[28] (It is possible that Ann was David and Patrick's sister-in-law or aunt, married to one Samuel Smith).[29] In 1731-2, Ann Smith and her sister Mary Atkinson, *alias* Taylor, leased the Carrickfergus property containing the clay lease to David Crawford, a relation of Thomas Crawford (another partner in the Belfast Potthouse), but he appears to have died shortly afterwards.[30] Finally, as Daniel Mussenden's letter explains, the leasehold was to revert after Mary Atkinson's decease to Stewart Banks, eldest son of Thomas Banks of Belfast. The same Thomas Banks - the agent for the Donegall family - had managed the Belfast Potthouse during its closing years in the 1720s.[31] Clearly therefore, these Carrickfergus clay leases and the Belfast Potthouse were strongly tied by family connections, but precisely defining these links will require further work.

APPENDIX II : HENRY DELAMAIN'S LETTERS, *Dec. 1753 - Jan. 1754*

and his Petition to the English House of Commons, 21st Jan. 1754.[1]

---

i. Letter from Liverpool, 18th December, 1753

To Mrs Mary Delamain at the India Warehouse Abby Street Dublin

My Dr Poll,

Inclos'd I send you a letter to Mr Stringfellow the purport of it is to desire him by all means to answer some letters that will be wrote to him this night from Liverpoole to know how our large Kiln has turned out; send for him on the rect. of this & right or wrong beg of him to write it was burnt twice before I left Ireland, and once since, & that it succeeds so well that not a bit of ware was smoked & that it Glazes the Ware better than Turf & Wood & makes it harder, less subject to peel, and that about two Tun or 2 and a half of coals will burn it off; give him this letter for fear he s^d. forget writing them all the above particulars, let him write the night he receives mine, for as soon as his letter arrives at Liverpoole the Mayor Corporation & all the Potters will Joyne in a Petition for me to Parliament & they will give Mr. Stringfellow a handsome some of money to build them Kilns.

I go to London this day and shall call in my way at Worster to see the fine new China Manufactory.

I long to get to London to receive your letters, but long more to be with you, I thank God I am well, and shall make all the haste home I can, take Care of yourself & my D^r. Mary Love to all friends & believe me y^rs. for ever

Henry Delamain

---

ii. Letter from Liverpool, 19th December, 1753

To Mr William Stringfellow, at the Delft Manufactory on the Strand, Dublin.

Dr Sir,

I was obliged to go for England at an hours warning therefore had not time to bid you farewell, or settle any of my affaires; In my way to London I Called at Liverpoole, where I was advised to Petition the Parliament of England for a reward for having burnt & Glazed Delft Ware with Coals and at the same time to get the Magistrates and Corporation of Liverpoole to Back my Petition, and to get the Potters here to Joyne them, all which I have effected, but some of the Potters doubts the success of our Large Kiln, which I have assur'd them has answer'd as well as the Small one did, and that it was twice burnt before I left Dublin, as they are in correspondence with you, they say you gave them no such information, therefore they will write to you by this post to know whether it was twice burnt before I left Dublin and how it succeeds, therefore I beg you will answer them by return of post, that it was burnt before I left Dublin with perfect Ware which turn'd out as well as ever it was done with Turf & Wood and that you have burnt it since I left Ireland and that it answers to all our wishes & that not a bit of ware was Smoaked but all white and better Glazed than ever you saw it done with wood or Turf; Suppose it has hapned quite the reverse do you write what I desire you for your own advantage as well as my Credit, for I set them all on fire to burn their Ware with coals, and have come into this agreement with them that you are to come over to build their Kilns, for which they all promise to pay you handsomely, some offered me money I told them if they gave me £500 0 0 I would not touch a penny of it but that it should be all for you, but all that I desired of them was to back my Petition to Parliament with the Mayor & Corporation which they have promised to do provided the great Kiln turns out well which they doubt therefore by all means write to them in answer to theirs by return of the post, all you can say in Its favour and more if necessary for I know we shall make it do, as well as the little one, Its the opinion of most people here the Parliament of England won't do any thing for me, it being unusual, and this branch of trade thought nothing of by them let that be as it will, I have push'd on yr. Affairs here much better, than ever you Could do it yr. self; & hope you will receive a large sum from them.

I shall make what haste I can to Dublin and be assur'd I will settle all your affaires to your Satisfaction, and beg you will push on my business in the Interim, they dont want you here these two months before which time I hope to be in Dublin, dont let any one know in Liverpool, I wrote to you on this subject.

I beg to hear from you directed to me to George Fitzgerald Esq London let me know how everything goes on since I parted, my respects to Mr. Hornby Mr. Shee &c. Pray let me hear from you by return of the post, & let me know whats wanting for the Manufactory & whether the front of the house is finish'd.

I am, Dr. Sir, Yr. Assurd friend & most Obt. Servt.

Henry Delamain

Liverpoole Tuesday 19th Decr. 1753.
I go of to London in an hour.

---

iii. Letter from London, 9th January, 1754

To Mr William Stringfellow, (no address, probably in Liverpool)

Sir,

I am glad you're safe arrived in England, and am surpriz'd you did not receive my 2d. letter before you parted. The Gentlemen in Liverpool will assure you, if they do me Justice, that I beg'd nothing from them but to gratifye you for the trouble you may be at to build Kilns & to Sign a Petition for me to Parliament, which can by no means either prejudice you or them, I am informed this post that they refuse to Sign the Petition, which I think ungratefull for this Secret would never have been found out only for me, who contrary to yr. opinion and all others I persued the scheme to burn with Coal which several of the Workmen of my manufacturie made Oath of; before I left Ireland, & which is con firm'd here by the Votes of the house of Commons of Ireland as it has been always my intention to Serve you & settle you master of manufactorie, and that I have freed you from all yr. troubles, It will be the highest Ingratitude of you to do any thing to my disadvantage, therefore beg you will not enter in any agreement, with the Manufacturers at Liverpoole 'till my affair is decided in the house of Commons of England which will be done in a few days, for If you do it without my approbation, the Consequence may be yr. ruin, and perhaps wont hurt me, and theirs no money they can give you can recompense the loss it may be to me, and I am both able and willing, to pay you any sum they will give you, and even more, I now make it my request to you that you will not inform them any part of the secret, and declare to them you never will unless they sign my Petition and If they Parliament grants me a sum for this whatever they have agreed to give you, I will immediately pay you down in Cash that sum which I promise by these presents, and also you will be recompensed by one man in London more to build him a Kiln than all the People of Liverpoole together will give you. I have great friends here and a strong interest is making for me, therefore entreat you will not do any thing to hurt me, as soon as my affair is decided in Liverpool you must come up to London, Where we will Settle all our affairs, and as soon as they Kilns are built & properly burnt, we must go to France together on some extraordinary affairs to both our advantage, in the Interim I will continue y$^{r.}$ guinea a week to y$^{r.}$ Wife 'till our return to Dublin. Inclosed I send you a Draught for five pounds and beg you will get my petition signed with an absolute promise that as soon as my affair is settled in Parliament that you will build their Kilns & do them all the Service in y$^{r.}$ power, but 'till then you can't do anything, as soon as the Petn. Is Sign'd which must be done imediatly come up to me to London the next day, as fast as you Can, You will perhaps Get a horse at Liverpoole for London if not hire one to Warrington and come up in the Stage coach to London, You must leave Liverpoole a Sunday next to get to Warrington in the Monday's Stage, or you will be too late, If you can hire a good horse you will be in London sooner than in the Stage. If you can't dont miss the Mondays Warrington Stage coach, for I want you much here on several accts. And as soon as my affair in Parliament is over We can set people to work both here and at Liverpoole not to loose time, for we must go to Paris as soon as possible Write to me Saturday's post what is done & don't let any one in Liverpoole know y$^{r.}$ coming to London As soon as you arrive get a Porter or a Coach to Shew you the way to Mr. Chiltons a perriwig makers in porter Street near Newport Alley, just by Saint Martin's lane, or Newport market, If I am not at home theirs a Tavern next door to me where you may sup & I have had a bed for you this fortnight past at my own Lodgings, don't let y^{r}. wife know any thing of our going to Paris for fear she should inform mine which I dont chuse should know it. Be assured while we are Absent she shan't want for any thing. By all means get the Petition signed & send it me by Saturday's post. Apply to Mr. John Hardman who is my friend about it. I do assure you the manufacturers of Liverpoole as I am well informed have no other intention to serve you but to get the Secret out of you, & than to take you as a Journeyman painter, therefore take care what you do, or this affair may be y$^{r.}$ perdition, but agreeing to what I would have you do, you can't fail of making y$^{r.}$ advantage of it let things turn as they will.

Since I wrote the above I have consulted with one of y$^{r.}$ Members of Parliament of Liverpoole, who thinks its better you should not leave Liverpoole in So great a hurry after the Petition is Signed for they are Jealous people and may raise numbers of false conjectures to my prejudice therefore don't come up to London 'till you hear further from me unless you think y$^{r.}$ leaving the town will not hurt me, for I want you much and wish you was here this moment but w$^{d.}$ not chuse either of us shouled do any thing to disoblige the manufacturers at Liverpoole, therefore let us Act with prudence which will turn to both our advantage, I have wrote this post that y$^{r.}$ wife may receive a guinea every Saturday night till we return & that all Care may be taken of her and the Children if wanted.

As soon as you receive this go with the Inclosed Bill to Mr. Sandford, Mr. Gibson will shew you where he lives and he will pay you five pounds English on Sight, I will in a few days send you down a letter of Credit in case you want more money that you may take it up without writing to me or drawing for it. pray observe that I have wrote and dont do any thing with the people of Liverpoole without my Consent I shall write to you constantly how my affairs goes on in Parliament, push the Manufacturers to sign my Petition without delay, write to me every post what occurs. I believe I shall receive my money in Holland as soon as we get over. I am D$^{r.}$ Sir Your assurd friend & most ob$^{t.}$ Serv$^{t.}$

London 9th Jan. 1753 [1754 n.s.]

P.S. Direct for me to George FitzGeralds Esq$^{r.}$

Henry Delamain

iv. Petition, from the English House of Commons Journals.

[Less than two weeks after completing the personal letters above, Henry Delamain presented the following petition to the English Parliament].

21st January, 1754

A petition of Henry Delamain, Gentleman, being offered to be presented to the House.

Mr. Chancellor of the Exchequer, by his Majesty's Command, acquainted the House, That his Majesty having been informed of the Contents of the said petition; recommends it to the consideration of the House to do therein as they shall think fit.

Then the said petition was brought up and read; setting forth; That Porcelain and Earthen Wares, have always been, and now are burnt and glazed with Wood Fires; the Manufacturers not having been able to make use of Coal without discolouring, and consequently greatly depreciating the Value of their Goods; and that the Petitioner has discovered a Method of firing Kilns of a particular Construction (and which may be built for the same Expense as the Kilns now made use of) which perfectly burn and glaze all sorts of White Ware with Coal in less Time, and in larger Quantities, than the Method now practised by burning of Wood; and at One Third-part of the Expense; and alleging, That, as Coal is much Cheaper in this Kingdom, than any Sort of Fuel whatsoever is in any other Country, this Discovery, if made publick, would enable our Manufacturers to produce the said Wares at a much cheaper rate than they could be made abroad; and thereby this Branch of Trade, by reason of a more plentiful and cheaper supply of Fuel, would be always enjoyed by this Kingdom without a Rival; and further setting forth: That the Kilns invented by the Petitioner, having been proved before the Dublin Society, he was recommended by them to the House of Commons of Ireland, who granted him £1000, to be given to him for his Encouragement, and to enable him more effectually to carry on the said Manufacture; and that the Petitioner has expended in making Experiments and in perfecting his Discovery, a much larger sum than hath been granted by the Parliament of Ireland; and that as an Undertaking of this Kind cannot be carried on to so great an Extent, and with so much Advantage to both kingdoms, and particularly to this, as if the Invention was made publick, the Petitioner is willing to discover the same, upon such Compensation for his Expense, Trouble, and Loss of Time, as shall be thought proper, and as the Utility and Merit of his Discovery, upon Experiment and Trial, shall appear to deserve: And therefore praying the House to take the Premises into Consideration.

Referred to a Committee to examine the matter thereof and report the same with their opinion thereupon, to the House.

v. Letter

[The recipient of the following letter, which was accompanied by two of Delamain's personal letters (probably ii & iii above), was Lord Strange, MP, a member of the parliamentary committee formed to examine the petition. It would appear that Stringfellow testified in person before the committee, and he may have expressed some qualms concerning the petition, but he did not produce the letters as he feared that Delamain would not release him from his service. Shortly afterwards, Stringfellow was granted his release, (presumably in London), and was given two guineas by Delamain to bear him to his home town of Liverpool. He then presented the letters to John Hardman, whom Delamain refers to as '*my friend*' in Letter iii. He, in turn, forwarded them to Lord Strange with the following cover note].

From John Hardman, Liverpool, to Lord Strange, London.

Liverpool, February 12, 1754

My Lord, - I have only to enclose your Lordship the two letters of Delamain's own writing, and I have had Mr. Stringfellow with me, and said a good deal to him about keeping them from the Committee; he says the reason was that Delamain made him promise not to produce them, if possible to avoid it, or he would not sign his release, and when Delamain sent that order down here he knew Stringfellow had them. I shall also enclose you another of his letters to him.

I hope this may prevent Stringfellow's coming up again, and that the original letters may do; no doubt Delamain will own them his own. Stringfellow says he would not have come, but he waited on your Lordship first, and you advised him not to come without release, which he obtained from Delamain, and he gave him Two Guineas to bear his charges, and he had no money to support himself longer than that. I fancy you had as good close the Committee, and excuse his appearing; however, I show'd him Sir Ch. Mordaunt's order for his appearance there.

I am, my Lord,
Your Lordship's m't obd't Serv't,
John Hardman

To Lord Strange, M.P., London

[As Hardman's phrase '*I fancy you had as good close the Committee*' implies, the contents of the letters seem to have destroyed Delamain's chances of receiving an award. Nothing more is heard of the petition, although Delamain continued to exhibit a model of his coal-fired kiln at John Saunder's pottery in Vauxhall for a further month or more. See p.53].

APPENDIX III : CASTLETOWN HOUSE RE-ATTRIBUTIONS

The catalogue of the 1971 exhibition at Castletown House, Celbridge, near Dublin, is still widely circulated as a useful guide to the identification of Irish delftware. After an interval of almost thirty years, it is natural that some of the attributions should have changed. For example, the presence of '*Dublin*' marks on some open-work circular baskets once meant that all such baskets were considered Irish, but English examples of virtually identical form have since been recognised. A design that occurred on some of these baskets, the '*Chinese Lotus*' pattern, was correspondingly believed to be exclusively Irish, whereas today there appear to be no Irish examples of this pattern.

Despite such changes, more than 80% of the Castletown attributions remain accurate, and the catalogue continues to represent a valuable source of information on Irish delftware. (A number of patterns that it illustrates have not been re-published here). The following remarks, compiled with Michael Archer's kind assistance, bring the Castletown catalogue fully up to date.

Cat. No.	Object	Remarks (M. Archer)
5	Plate inscribed '$I^{C}E$ 1748'	Probably English
9	Armorial Plate, '*Fitzgerald*' arms*	English or Irish
10	Armorial Plate, '*O'Brien*' arms**	English or Irish (see Fig. 114)
21	Sugar Sifter	Moustiers (French)
23	Basket, open sides	Probably Liverpool
24	Basket, '*Chinese Lotus*' pattern	English
29	Open Dish, interlaced sides	Probably English
31	Barber's Bowl, '*Chinese Lotus*' pattern	English
32	Water Bottle	English or Irish
33	Water Bottle	English or Irish
34	Water Bottle	Liverpool
35	Water Bottle '*Chinese Lotus*' pattern	Probably English
38	Wall Pocket, '*Chinese Lotus*' pattern	English
50	Large Dish, arms of '*Order of St. Cuthbert*'	English or Irish (see Fig. 115)
52	Large Dish	Probably London
53	Large Dish '*Chinese Lotus*' pattern	Probably English
54	Large Dish	Probably London
55	Large Dish	English or Irish
56	Large Dish	Probably Liverpool
59	Large Dish '*Chinese Flower-bowl*' pattern	Liverpool
65	Small Tureen stand	Liverpool
68	Dish or Tureen stand	Liverpool
72	Dish or Tureen stand ('vertical' pattern)	English or Irish
73	Dish or Tureen stand ('vertical' pattern)	English or Irish
96	Bowl, frilly edge	English or Irish
123	Jug inscribed '*Mr White 1750*'	Very Probably English

* The arms are those of Fitzgerald, but not necessarily the Fitzgeralds of Desmond & the Knights of Glin.

** The arms are now interpreted as perhaps 'Ludlow of Shropshire/impaling Kynaston'. See p.103.

APPENDIX IV : LETTER FROM MICHAEL STRITCH

(father of John Stritch), to Sir Edward O'Brien, 12th March 1763.

Nat. Lib. Ire., ***Inchiquin Mss.***, Folder 2065.
Addressed externally to *'Sr Edwd O'Brien Baront &c., Dromoland'*
[2nd Baronet, MP for Clare, d. 1765]

Sr

Lim[k].. *ye 12 March* <u>*1763*</u>

I recd. youre Esteemed feavour for which I am as Ever before Obliged to you & yours. As to my sone I have it not in my power as yet to recomend him in regard to his now new undertaking as I would sooner suffer death than say an uncertainty or a word of unknowne truth for him I am to this Day an Intire stranger to his p.formance In his Ware, nor have I any opinion of his p.formance. If he had led me in to its nature I offerd him to goe to you properly in parliament time for youre Interest But to be sure for not to Impose on youre friendship or [Interes?] *or me for that for ye worlds wealth I would not Vouchsafe one word but what should be reale truth for him I have but him & would purchase all I could for him in an honourable way for him I first sent him to Bourdeaux where I bound him to a wine Merchant & it Cost me 200* [?] *Guineas he come hoame affter 3 years & it Cost him that sume tis true he was young I forgave him that I prayd him to stick to ye shop & that I would lay in a stock in it for him & my famely noe that would not smite his Element. I then offerd & Gave Mr. Pery my pro* [po] *sall by yr hands of Dochter Masten that I would lay onto 500 pds on an Acher ot two of his Ground In such houses as this Youth would Direct But Incase he should faile in his Crockidie Ware that such building would Answer for a dwelling house or Store houses. Counselor Lucious O'Brien's* Request Even: a doz*[n] *off Crucebills: to be Made by him & Carried up to ye Society & that he'd forward them to ye Society & Get him a premium I desird this youth to Make them & let me be able to testifie that he was ye Maker & That I would goe up to Dublin With him which he Declind Then in a hurrie with oute My Consent Will or Ever leave or Abrobation he Goes & Joyns One Christopher Britson Whoe you Might have hard off was Clark of oure Custom house - They Make But Course Mugs: Course Dishes or Course Crockedie Ware as yet from which noe Credit Can arise as yett I beg pardon for this long Screed & had you not put it In My Way I should not trouble you now nor neither Will I with oute Good Ground. I heard Mr. Pery tell Joseph Langton that he Imposed on him My verry Worthey friends shant have that to say of Me - as I am with reale Esteem Sr Your Ever Oblidg & Most hm Sert to Come Whilst*

Micl. Stritch esq.

* Lucius O'Brien, 3rd Baronet, Privy Councilor, M.P. for Clare (d.1795). Son of Edward O'Brien, to whom this letter was addressed.

APPENDIX V : EARTHENWARE IMPORTS TO IRELAND

Efforts were made to extract details of all earthenware imported into Ireland during the eighteenth-century from the series of Irish customs records preserved at Kew, (*Cust. 15*). Owing to time constraints it was not possible to extract information for each individual year, and so, as an interim measure, some decades (such as the 1740s) were sampled at five-yearly intervals. The information presented in the two graphs that appear as Figs. 5 and 57 was based on the following data.

EARTHENWARE IMPORTS TO BELFAST 1700 - 1725 (Fig. 5)

Year	Value £
1700	175
1701	136.71
1702	93.32
1703	33.55
1704	59.325
1705	34.63
1706	43.77
1707	49.35
1708	18.98
1709	53.45
1710	37.51
1715	39.45
1720	65.49
1721	38.65
1722	89.51
1723	118.44
1724	153.26
1725	100.72

EARTHENWARE IMPORTS TO IRELAND 1740 - 1770 (Fig. 57)

Year	England	Holland	France	
1740	£4036	£673	£55	
1745	£2820	£179	£144	
1750	£6470	£668	£942	
1751	£8337	£780	£1201	
1755	£7322	£636	£131	
1756	£6286	£378	£0	*Seven Years War* (1756–1762)
1757	£7591	£471	£0	
1758	£7037	£575	£0	
1759	£7196	£751	£0	
1760	£8107	£680	£0	
1761	£7964	£911	£0	
1762	£8797	£751	£0	
1763	£11317	£1051	£419	
1764	£11078	£1126	£291	
1769	£13205	£1315	£130	
1770	£10730	£1176	£121	

BIBLIOGRAPHY

Abbreviations

BNL	: *Belfast Newsletter*
Dub. Jour.	: *Faulkner's Dublin Journal*
ECC Trans.	: *English Ceramic Circle Transactions*
PRO Kew	: Public Record Office, Kew, London
PRONI	: Public Record Office of Northern Ireland
RoD	: Registry of Deeds, Dublin
Nat. Lib. Ire.	: National Library of Ireland

Adams & Redstone : E. Adams & D. Redstone, *Bow Porcelain*, Faber & Faber, London, (1981).

Agnew, *Belfast* : J. Agnew, *Belfast Merchant Families in the Seventeenth Century*, Four Courts Press, Dublin, (1996).

Archer : Michael Archer, *Delftware: The Tin-Glazed Earthenware of the British Isles, A Catalogue of the Collection in the Victoria & Albert Museum*, The Stationery Office, London, (1997).

Archer (1979) : Michael Archer, *Irish Pottery & Porcelain*, The Irish Heritage Series: 27, Eason & Sons Ltd., Dublin, (1979).

Archer & Morgan : Michael Archer & Brian Morgan, *Fair as China Dishes: English delftware from the collection of Mrs. Marion Morgan & Brian Morgan*, the catalogue of an exhibition circulated in America by the International Exhibitions Foundation, 1977-79, London, (1977).

Atkins : Garry Atkins, *An Exhibition of English Pottery*, 1990-2000. (Catalogues of annual exhibitions at Church Street, Kensington, London).

Austin : John C. Austin, *British Delft at Williamsburg*, Williamsburg, VA, (1994).

Britton *Bristol* : Frank Britton, *English Delftware in the Bristol Collection*, Sotheby's, (1982).

Britton *London* : Frank Britton, *London Delftware*, Horne, London, (1987).

Castletown : Michael Archer & Patrick Hickey, *Irish Delftware*, the catalogue of an exhibition held by ROSC at Castletown House, Celbridge, Co. Kildare, 21 Oct. -29 Dec., 1971, Dublin, (1971).

Francis (1992) : Peter Francis, *The Early Fine-Ceramic Potteries of Belfast & the Carrickfergus Clay Trade*, unpublished MA thesis, Archaeology Dept., The Queen's University of Belfast, (1992).

Francis (1994) : Peter Francis, 'The Belfast Potthouse, Carrickfergus Clay & the Spread of the Delftware Industry', *ECC Trans.*, Vol. 15, Pt. 2, (1994), pp. 267-82.

Fraser, *Dublin Potters* : Mrs. A.M. Fraser, 'Some Early Dublin Potters', *Dublin Historical Record*, Vol. XII, No. 2, (May 1951), pp. 47-58.

Gabszewicz & Freeman : Anton Gabszewicz & Geoffrey Freeman, *Bow Porcelain, The Collection formed by Geoffrey Freeman*, Lund Humphries, London, (1982).

Garner & Archer : F.H. Garner & M. Archer, *English Delftware*, Faber & Faber, London, (1972).

Horne : Jonathan Horne, *A Collection of Early English Pottery*, Parts I-XX, 1981-2000. (Annual catalogues of exhibitions at Church Street, Kensington, London).

Lipski and Archer : Louis L. Lipski & Michael Archer, *Dated English Delftware*, Sotheby's, London, (1984).

Longfield : Ada K. Longfield, (Leask),'Irish Delft', *Irish Georgian Soc. Quart. Bull.*, Vol. XIV, No. 3, (Jul-Sep. 1971), pp. 36-55.

Ray : Anthony Ray, *English Delftware Pottery in the Robert Hall Warren Collection, Oxford*, Faber & Faber, London, (1968).

Westropp (1913) : M.S. Dudley Westropp, 'Notes on the Pottery Manufacture in Ireland', *Proc. Royal Irish Academy*, Vol. XXXII, Section C, No. 1, Dublin, (1913).

Westropp (1935) : M.S. Dudley Westropp, *General Guide to the Art Collections, Pottery and Porcelain*, National Museum of Ireland, Dublin, (1935).

Young, *Town Book* : R. M. Young (ed.), *The Town Book of the Corporation of Belfast, 1613-1816*, Belfast, (1892).

Other Publications relevant to Eighteenth-Century Irish Fine-Ceramics.

Michael Archer 'Irish Delftware: an exhibition at Castletown House', *The Connoisseur*, (Oct. 1971), pp. 99-107.

Mairead Dunlevy 'Irish Fine-Ceramic Potteries, 1769-96', *Post-Mediaeval Archaeology*, Vol. 18, (1984), pp. 251-61.

Mairead Dunlevy *Ceramics in Ireland*, National Museum of Ireland, (1988).

Peter Francis 'Irish Creamware, The Downshire Pottery in Belfast', *ECC Trans.*, Vol. 15, Pt. 3, (1995), pp. 400 -25.

Peter Francis 'Recent Discoveries in Irish Ceramics', *Irish Arts Review Yearbook*, Vol. 13, (1997), pp. 88-101.

Peter Francis *A Pottery by the Lagan, The Downshire Pottery, Belfast*, Ulster Museum & Queen's University, Belfast, at press.

Illustration Credits

The author is indebted to the following institutions and collectors for kindly providing the following illustrations for this book.

ENDPAPERS : Author

FIGURES

Chapter 1. Belfast

1 Modified from Thomas Phillip's map of Belfast, 1685, Linenhall Library Belfast reprint
2 Young, *Town Book*, p.139
3 Author's photograph, courtesy Queen's University, Belfast and Environment and Heritage Service
4 National Library of Ireland
5-6 Author
7 National Museum of Ireland
8 Ulster Museum
9 Modified from G.Gamblin, *The Town in Ulster,* (1951), pl.31.
10 Private Collection
11 Author's photograph, courtesy National Museum of Ireland
12-30 Author's photographs, courtesy Queen's University, Belfast and Environment and Heritage Service
31 Modified from R.M.Young, *Belfast & the Province of Ulster,* Brighton, 1909, p.278
32-3 Author's photographs, courtesy Queen's University, Belfast and Environment and Heritage Service
34 Colonial Williamsburg
35 Author's photograph, courtesy Queen's University, Belfast and Environment and Heritage Service
36 Private Collection
37 Longridge Collection
37a F. Britton
38 Author's photograph, courtesy Queen's University, Belfast and Environment and Heritage Service
39-40 Longridge Collection
41-4 Author's photographs, courtesy Queen's University, Belfast and Environment and Heritage Service
45 Modified from C.H. de Jonge, *Delft Ceramics,* (1969), pl.110
46 Private Collection
47 Author's photograph, courtesy Queen's University, Belfast and Environment and Heritage Service

Chapter 2, 1, Dublin

48 Modified from John Rocque's 1756 map of Dublin, Irish Georgian Society reprint
49 Victoria & Albert Museum
50a M.Archer
50b Modified from Adams & Redstone, pl..103
51 Hunt Museum, Limerick
52 M.Archer
53 Modified from John Rocque's map of Dublin, Irish Georgian Society reprint
54 Author. Detail from John Taylor's *Map of Dublin & Its Environs,* n.d., c. 1810
55 Taylor B. Williams, Chicago
56 British Museum
57 Author

Chapter 2, 2, Dublin delftware

58 Author, compiled from a variety of sources. (See p.196).
59 Manchester City Art Gallery
60 Author, with the assistance of Garry Atkins
61 National Museum of Ireland
62 Author
63 Author, from marks recorded in Westropp Ms, Nat. Lib. Ire.
64 National Museum of Ireland
65 Author and Private Collection
66 Private Collection
67 Hunt Museum, Limerick
68 Knight of Glin
69-70 Author
71 John Austin, author
72-5 John Austin, Colonial Williamsburg
76 Author
77 John McCormack, Limerick
78-84 John Austin, Colonial Williamsburg
85 Private Collection, photographs courtesy Garry Atkins
86 John Austin, Colonial Williamsburg
87-9 Author
90 Private Collection
91 George Stacpoole, Limerick
91a Author
92 M.Archer
93 Author
94 Ulster Museum photograph, courtesy National Museum of Ireland
95 Private Collection
96 Author
97-9 Private Collection
100 Yvonne Healey, Dublin
101-3 Author
104 George Stacpoole, Limerick
105 Knight of Glin
106 Jonathan Horne
107 Courtesy Michael Baron, Sampson & Jellinek. with thanks also to M.Archer
108 Christie's, London, 13th March 1989, Lot 204
109 Crookshank, Glin Photographic Archive of Irish Painting, Dept. of History, Trinity College, Dublin
110 Christie's 12th March 1990, Lot. 258
111 National Library of Ireland
112-13 Colonial Williamsburg
114 Knight of Glin
115 Hunt Museum, Limerick
116 Anton Gabszewicz
117 Phillip's London 3-4th June 1998, Lot. 523.
118 Sothebys', London, 15th May 1979, Moor Wood coll., lot. 32
119 Sothebys', London, 18th June 1963, lot. 154
120 Hunt Museum, Limerick
121 Sothebys', London, 10th March 1981, Lipski coll.,lot 217
122-4 Private Collections
125 Colonial Williamsburg
126 Hampshire County Council Museums Service
127 Private Collection
128 Private Collection
129 Colonial Williamsburg
130 Garry Atkins, (now Private Collection)
131 Garry Atkins, Private Collection
132 Graham Walpole, London
133 Knight of Glin

134 Private Collection
135 M.Archer
136 The Minneapolis Institute of Arts, The Gift of Mr and Mrs George R. Steiner
137 Victoria & Albert Museum, Schreiber Coll.
138 Victoria & Albert Museum
139 National Museum of Ireland
140-3 Private Collections
144 M.Archer (now National Museum of Ireland)
145 From J.Lewis-Crosby, Sothebys', N. Ireland
146 Sotheby's, London, 10th March 1981, Lipski coll., lot 139
147 M.Archer
148 Fitzwilliam Museum, Cambridge
149 Ulster Museum photograph, courtesy National Museum of Ireland
150 M.Archer (now National Museum of Ireland)
151-2 Author
153 M.Archer (now National Museum of Ireland)
154 M.Archer, courtesy Dúchas, Dublin and Roseanne Meenan
155-6 Private Collections
157 Garry Atkins
158 Private Collection
159 Colonial Williamsburg
160 M.Archer (now National Museum of Ireland)
161-2 Private Collection
163 Hampshire County Council Museums Service
164 Ulster Museum
165 Hampshire County Council Museums Service
166 National Museum of Ireland
167 Colonial Williamsburg
168 Garry Atkins
169 Author
170 Author, modified from Westropp Ms. Notes, Nat. Lib. Ire.
171 Victoria & Albert Museum
172 Colonial Williamsburg
173 Victoria & Albert Museum
174 Colonial Williamsburg
175 Jonathan Horne
176 Ulster Museum
177 Private Collection (Two pieces)
178 Christies, London, 14th October 1985, Lot. 15. Courtesy M.Archer
179 M. Archer (formerly B. Morgan Collection)
180 Ulster Museum
181 Lonhydroch House, Cornwall, courtesy of the National Trust
182 Fitzwilliam Museum, Cambridge

Chapter 3, Minor Potteries

183-4 Author
185 Hunt Museum, Limerick
186-7 Author
188 Modified from *Jour. Cork Hist. & Arch. Soc.*, Vol.1, (1982), pt.III, p.69.
189-90 Modified from G. Gamblin, *The Town House in Ulster,* (1951), pl.31
191 Quarry Bank, Styal, Cheshire, courtesy the National Trust
192-6 Author
197 Ulster Museum
198-99 M.Archer (now National Museum of Ireland)
200 Author

Illustration Credits

COLOUR PLATES

1 Private Collection
2 Author's photograph, courtesy Queen's University and Environment and Heritage Service
3 Author's Collection
4 Longridge Collection
5 Longridge Collection
6 Private Collection
7 Victoria & Albert Museum, courtesy M.Archer
8 British Museum
9 Madame Noël Sauzey, with thanks also to Prof. L.Cullen and M. Alain Braastad
10 Madame Noël Sauzey, with thanks also to Prof. L.Cullen and M. Alain Braastad
11 National Museum of Ireland
12 Author's Collection
13 Author, Nicholas Mosse Collection
14 Author's Collection
15 Jonathan Horne
16-17 Crookshank, Glin Photographic Archive of Irish Painting, Dept. of History Trinity College, Dublin.
18 National Museum of Ireland
19 Manchester City Art Galleries & Museums
20 Ulster Museum
21 Ulster Museum
22 National Museum of Ireland
23 Private Collection
24 Private Collection
25 Ulster Museum
26 M.Archer (now National Museum of Ireland)
27 Hunt Museum Limerick
28 M.Archer (now National Museum of Ireland)
29 M.Archer, courtesy Dúchas, Dublin and Roseanne Meenan
30 National Museum of Ireland
31 Fitzwilliam Museum Cambridge
32 Private Collection
33 Knight of Glin
34 Private Collection
35 M.Archer, (now Victoria & Albert Museum)
36 Private Collection
37 Colonial Williamsburg
38 Private Collection
39 Private Collection
40 Private Collection
41 Colonial Williamsburg
42 Ulster Museum
43 National Museum of Ireland
44 National Museum of Ireland
45 National Museum of Ireland

FOOTNOTES

Preface & Introduction

1. J.Sproule, (ed.), *The Irish Industrial Exhibition of 1853: A Detailed Catalogue of its Contents,* Dublin, (1854), p. 406.
2. William Chaffers, *Marks & Monograms on Pottery & Porcelain,* London, 4th Revised Ed., (1874), p. 934.
3. Hugh Owen, *Two Centuries of Ceramic Art in Bristol,* London, (1873), pp. 393-97. George Benn, *A History of the Town of Belfast,* London, (1877), p. 355.
4. Westropp (1913) & (1935). See Bibliography.
5. Nat. Lib. Ire., MS 24938, (Westropp *Ms,* Pottery).
6. See Bibliography.
7. See p. 62. The Dublin Society questioned Mrs. Ann Day concerning the pottery's ability to make creamware, or *'flint ware'* at this early date.
8. Britton, *London,* pp. 18-29, provides many details that appear here concerning the early delftware industry in England.
9. An argument first presented by Rhoda Edwards in L. Weatherill & R. Edwards, 'Pottery Making in London and Whitehaven in the Late Seventeenth Century', *Post-Mediaeval Archaeology,* Vol. 5, (1971), pp. 160-81.
10. Frank Britton, 'Some Sources of Delftware Clay', *ECC Trans.,* Vol. 13, Pt., 1, (1987), pp. 24-32. Southwark potters also testified in 1674 that *'The Dutch could not make this ware without English earth'* (from East Anglia). See Ivor Noel Hume, 'Early English Delftware from London and Virginia', *Colonial Williamsburg Occasional Papers in Archaeology,* Vol. II, (1977), p. 12.
11. Francis, (1994), p. 276.
12. R. Edwards, 'London potters circa 1570-1710', *Journal of Ceramic History,* No. 6, (1974), p.107.
13. *Ibid.,* p. 180.
14. *London Gazette,* 11th - 14th Sept. 1693.
15. Edwards, *op. cit.* at n. 12, p. 107. Garner established his stoneware pottery with Luke Talbot at Gravel Lane, Southwark in 1694.
16. *Ibid.,* p. 78-9. Moses Johnston, also of Montague Close, set up his pottery at the Bear Garden, Southwark, but was sued by Dwight in 1695. The Elers brothers and others had established a red stoneware pottery at Vauxhall, and Dwight's litigation followed in June 1693. See D. Haselgrove & J. Murray (eds.), 'John Dwight's Fulham Pottery 1672-1978', *Journal of Ceramic History;* No. 11, (1979), pp. 9-12.
17. *Ibid.* Garner moved to Ireland in 1697, Elers to Dublin in 1701.
18. For an account of the *'Excise Act',* see F.H. Garner, 'Lambeth Earthenware', *ECC Trans,* No. 4, (1937).
19. Edwards, *op. cit.* at n. 12 above, p. 97.
20. Francis, (1994), p. 276.
21. For discussion of the Navigation Acts in the 17th-century, see Agnew, *Belfast,* pp. 110-26.
22. *Ibid.,* p. 120.
23. See p. 62.
24. The prices are listed in 1766. (See p. 62). Customs records at PRO Kew, (Cust. 15), contain virtually no references to indicate that Irish delftware was exported to England or Scotland at any time during the eighteenth-century, with the single exception of a shipment valued at £6 from Belfast in 1706.
25. Britton, *Bristol,* p. 12, lists the 13 potteries.
26. 'Reports of a Committee ... Relative to the Adjustment of Commercial Intercourse between Great Britain & Ireland', *House of Lords Sessional Papers, (1785),* p. 6. Testimony of John Blades, Cut Glass manufacturer. Some of the 9 glasshouses established by 1785 made bottle & window glass.
27. Possibly because of the small quantities involved, or because they were simply not declared, the Irish customs books contain virtually no records of any exports of Irish delftware during the eighteenth-century. (See p. 56).
28. See p. 56 and 62.
29. See p. 62.
30. See *'coarsely-painted wares',* pp. 83-8.
31. See p. 55.
32. See p. 53.
33. See Fig. 200, p.166, and p.146.
34. See p. 60.
35. See Castletown, p.25, for further discussion.
36. *BNL* 11th June 1756, p. 3 Col. 1, *'This is to inform the Publick that the Drumcondra Printed Linen-Ware House of Alexander McDonnell & Co., hitherto on George's Hill near Linenhall now Usher's Quay near Bridge Street now has a large Sortment of all the Patterns especially for Furniture. As the Manufactory is the First and Only one in the Universe, the Art of printing Linen from Metal Plates ingraved being never before Discovered'.*
37. Westropp, (1935), p. 14. No specific date is recorded, other than *'in 1758 ... Michael Hanbury of the City of Dublin, engraver, having exhibited several specimens of his performance before the Dublin Society of a new invention for ornamenting with great despatch, china and earthenware, etc., from copper plate engraving on the unburnt glaze, the Society ordered him twenty guineas towards carrying on the business'.* Westropp also notes that *'Hanbury is mentioned as a copper-plate printer and engraver in George's Lane and Skinner's Row, Dublin, between 1748 and 1755. He died in 1762'.*
38. The petitions of Mary Delamain in 1759 (p.57) and William Delamain in 1762 (p.59-60) both reiterate almost all of Henry's expenditure in improving the works, but make no mention of transfer-printing - which featured in Henry's 1753 petition to Parliament, (p.50).
39. See p. 162.
40. Chaffers, *op. cit.* at n. 2 above. The harp and *'Dublin'* mark illustrated was on a landscape basket *'in the possession of Mr. Stopford of Drayton House, Northamptonshire',* a descendant of Lionel Sackville, Lord Lieutenant of Ireland during the 1750s. The basket may have been that which appears as Colour Plate 19.

Chapter 1, The Belfast Potthouse

1. R. Edwards, 'London Potters circa 1570-1710', *Jour. Ceram. Hist.,* No. 6, Stafford (1974), p. 66. All of the details concerning Garner's early career in London are derived from this source.
2. *Ibid.* The causes of the bankruptcy were explained in a pamphlet written in 1718 by Thomas Oade, son of Nathaniel, entitled *'A Full REPLY To a late PAMPHLET, intituled, The Indulgent Parents* ...', p. 29. This also explains that Garner went to Ireland in 1697.
3. The family's surname is recorded in Belfast as Garner, Gurner and Garnett. No individuals bearing these names are recorded on any surviving Potthouse document.
4. Agnew *Belfast,* p. 16.
5. *Ibid.,* pp. 20-1. Also Young *Town Book, 'Belfast Freeman's Rolls',* pp. 239-300.
6. Agnew, *Belfast,* p. 115.
7. PRO, Kew, Cust 15, (1698-1700). See also Brit. Lib. Ms. 4759, (Irish imports-exports 1682-4), reprinted by William Pinkerton in *Ulster Journal of Archaeology;* Vol. III, p. 194.
8. A senior member of the family, Nicholas Garner, was a chandler in Belfast. His nephew, Matthew Garner, completed an apprenticeship with him on 9th Sept. 1669.

(Young, *Town Book, 'Freeman's Rolls',* p. 270). A relation, Rev. Matthew Garner was curate of Belfast and vicar of Carnmoney at about this time. See Agnew, *Belfast*, p.248. See also n. 9 below. It is worth noting that a merchant by the name of Thomas Harper was admitted a freeman of Belfast on 21st Jan. 1670. Matthew Garner was apprenticed to a Thomas Harper at the Montague Close pottery in London in 1680, but the occurrence of Harper's name in Belfast may simply represent coincidence.

9. Matthew Garner's position in the hierarchy of the Belfast Garners can only be assumed, but he may have been a brother or cousin of one James Garner, b. Belfast 1657, who became a successful merchant, a burgess in 1707 and sovereign in 1713 & 16. James Garner's wife (m. 1693) was also the stepmother of Francis Thetford, the owner of the Potthouse Grand Lease. Two further relations of James were clerics - the Rev. Nicholas Garner, and the Rev. Matthew Garner (see n. 8 above).

A second individual named James Garner was apprenticed on 25th May 1709 to the Montague Close pottery in London, where Matthew Garner had completed his apprenticeship in 1680, raising the possibility that this second James was Matthew's son. (See Edwards, *op. cit* at n. 1 above, p. 122). He was apprenticed to Samuel Wilkinson, a name that has special significance in Dublin later. (See p. 59).

10. George Benn, *A History of the Town of Belfast,* London, (1877), p. 318. Local forests were reserved for local needs by an Act prohibiting the export of timber to Scotland in 1695, and import figures suggest that these supplies remained adequate until the mid-1710s.

11. Lesley Simpson, Peter Bryan, Tom Delaney & Andy Dickson, 'An early thirteenth-century double-flued pottery kiln at Carrickfergus, Co. Antrim: an interim report', *Mediaeval Ceramics: Bulletin of the Mediaeval Pottery Research Group,* Vol. 3, (1979), pp. 41-52. The kiln was situated on the shore at Cronaghbane - the site of one of the two leases for Carrickfergus clay in 1748. (See p. 169).

12. Richard Dobbs, 'A Description of County Antrim in 1683', in Rev. George Hill, *An Historical Account of the MacDonnells of Antrim,* Belfast, (1873). *'Within the Liberties of* [Carrickfergus] *is good store of Freestone and Limestone: Likewise very good clay and marl for tobacco pipes, brick and tile'.* Tobacco-pipe clay was not suitable for delftware manufacture, but Dobbs was obviously aware of a variety of clays near Carrickfergus.

13. C. J. Robb in *Belfast Telegraph,* Nov. 30 1938. Robb quotes several seventeenth-century sources that are otherwise unrecorded, including a receipt from the builders of St. Paul's stating *'To Robert Douglas, brickmaker of Belfast, for 5,500 brick, £10',* consigned to London by ship. (The dome was completed in the first decade of the eighteenth-century). He also quotes a Dublin newspaper which stated that in 1706 *'300,000 brick from Belfast'* were discharged on the Liffey wharves in Dublin, and provides transcripts from an early seventeenth-century diary that has since been lost.

14. Anno 6 & 7 GUL.III. Cap. XVIII, 29th Sep. 1695. Rescinded Anno 9 & 10 GUL. III. Cap. XLV, 1st Aug. 1698. See also F.H. Garner, 'Lambeth Earthenware', *ECC Trans,* No. 4, (1937), for further details of the consequences of this act for potters.

15. F. Buckley, *The Taxation of English Glass in the Seventeenth Century;* Stevens & Sons Ltd., London, (1914), pp. 46-7, 54.

16. William Sacheverell, *'An Account of the Isle of Man ... With a Voyage to I-Columb-kill',* London, (1702), p. 125. (The voyage was erroneously dated *'In the Year 1688').* Manx Mus. Lib., Douglas, Cat. F64/9.

17. Agnew, *Belfast,* pp. 59-60, 228-29.

18. A copy of the original deed is not preserved, but the details were reiterated in 1719 when Francis Thetford, the landlord, used the Potthouse lease to secure a loan. (See n. 44 below).

19. Agnew, *Belfast,* p. 220, 246.

20. *Ibid.* Henry Chads the younger, merchant of Belfast, probably in Bruges c.1696. Admitted free commoner of Belfast 21st Jan. 1670 [n.s.], and thus probably in his late 40s when the Potthouse was founded. His close relation, Eleanor Joy (*née* Chads?), was related by marriage to the Garners and the Thetfords.

21. Young, *Town Book,* p. 187, 328.

22. Agnew *Belfast,* pp. 245-6, and Benn, *op. cit.* at n. 10 above, Vol. II, pp. 187-88, provide all biographical details concerning the Smith family quoted here.

23. *Ibid.* p. 43.

24. *Ibid.* See also Anon., *Historic Memorials of the First Presbyterian Church of Belfast,* Belfast, (1887), pp. 64-94. Records in this burial register indicate that John & William Smith were described as *'merchants',* and invariably associated with the *'Sugar House'.*

25. Douglas was granted sole permission to manufacture delftware in Scotland by Act of Parliament 17th July 1695. For further (not entirely accurate) information see J. Arnold Fleming, *Scottish Pottery,* Glasgow, (1923), p. 149.

26. Agnew, *Belfast,* p. 245. David presented a book dated *'1705'* to his church (now in the Ulster Museum), but he is also known to have died before 6th Aug. 1705.

27. George Linn, Merchant in Edinburgh and William Montgomerie of Mackbiehill were granted *'sole power of makeing ... Lame Purslane and Earthen ware'* in Scotland by Act of Parliament dated 16th September 1703. See Fleming, *op. cit.* at n. 25 above, p. 149.

28. PRONI, D/501, (Isaac Macartney Letterbook), pp. 321-22.

29. PRONI, D/501, (Macartney Letterbook), p. 353, 9 Sep. 1706, Macartney to Timothy Forbes, Dublin, 'Our *good friend Andrew Skeen remitted me a bill of £30, which with 8s is owed him. He ordered me to remit you out of said money. I have since, per his order, paid to a potter sent from hence to Edinburgh £2-4-8'.*

30. Benn, *op. cit.* at n. 10 above, p. 333.

31. See n. 24 above.

32. Dr. Thomas Molyneux, *A Journey to the North of Ireland,* (1708), Trinity College Dublin, MS 883/2, f.136).

33. PRO Kew, Cust. 15. This graph is based on imports recorded to Belfast, 1700-25, but is incomplete. The years 1711-14 and 1716-19 have not yet been recorded. See Appendix V.

34. Dr. Jean Agnew, *pers. comm.,* 1994. The Arthur Thetford who paid for the funeral of *'old Matthew Garner'* in *1725* (see n. 53 below), was the grandson of Eleanor Garnett or Garner. The Matthew Garner who trained as a candle-maker in 1669 (see n. 8 above) was Eleanor's cousin. Arthur Thetford's father, Nicholas, was therefore a son of Eleanor Garner, and a cousin of the Francis Thetford who owned the Potthouse Grand Lease. See also Agnew, *Belfast,* p. 247-48.

35. Edwards, *op. cit.* at n. 1 above, p. 123.

36. *Ibid.,* p. 84.

37. Reg & Philomena Jackson, and Roger Price, 'Bristol Potters and Potteries, 1600-1800', *Jour. Ceram Hist.,* No. 12, Stoke on Trent City Museum, (1982), p. 143.

38. Entwistle Papers, Liverpool Public Record Office, 942 ENT (Folder 2). The pottery's first advertisement, which contains the quoted text, appeared in *The Post Boy,* 23rd May 1710.

39. As the reference specifically mentions *'Belfast clay',* the Belfast Potthouse may have come to some form of mutual agreement with the Lord Street potters. A possibility is that the arrangement allowed the Belfast Potthouse to avoid some of the constraints imposed by the Navigation Acts. Without some sort of reciprocal benefit, it is difficult to understand why the Belfast potters should have relinquished control of their clay deposits.

40. Despite export restrictions imposed in 1695, (see n. 10 above), Belfast remained a net exporter of timber into the early 1700s. (see Agnew, *Belfast,* p. 107). The last local oak tree used in house-building was felled in 1716. (Prof. M.G.L. Baillie, Queen's University Palaeoecology Laboratory, *pers. comm.* 1992).

41. PRONI, Millin Ms, T 811/1, p.100, 109, 110 & 112 all relate to these two North St. tenements.

42. Anon., *Historic Memorials of the First Presbyterian Church of Belfast*, Belfast, (1887), pp. 64-94.

43. RoD 23.184.13041, 14th Mar. 1719, Henry Chads to Richard Hodgkinson and Robert Donaldson. (Donaldson was an attorney). For further details see Agnew, *Belfast*, p. 228. Chads was executor of the will of Sarah (*née* Stewart), the wife of Richard Hodgkinson, merchant of Belfast. Sarah's sister (Rose) was married to Abel Hadskis, who later owned an iron foundry that was built on the Belfast Potthouse site during the 1730s. Hodgkinson was also a nephew of Thomas Banks, who assumed management of the Potthouse following Hodgkinson's death c. 1722.

44. RoD 25.203.14741, memorial of assignment dated 20th Aug. 1719, Francis Thetford to Joseph Innis.

45. RoD 27.314.17107, memorial of assignment dated 10th Nov. 1720, Francis Thetford to Thomas Banks (for £40) and John Montgomery (for £9. 00.04).

46. RoD 36.170.21944, 6th Sept. 1722, Joseph Innis (executor of Francis Thetford) to John Potter of Killinchy, Co. Down, merchant. Transferred again by RoD 35.198.21946, 27th Oct. 1722, John Potter to William Legg of Malone, Belfast, and again by RoD 38.119.23577, 26th Apr. 1723, William Legg to Joseph Innis.

47. See Appendix I, p.170. Thomas Banks was a senior Belfast merchant - the successor to Robert Leathes as the agent for the Donegall family. He also seems to have owned the freehold to the clay lease at Carrickfergus that was granted to *'Ann Smith, widow'* until 1731, then to her sister, *'Mris. Atkinson'* until 1748 (or later). For biographical details of Thomas & a portrait of his son, Stewart Banks, see Shannon Millin, *Additional Sidelights on Belfast History*, Belfast, (1938), pp. 98-103.

48. See Appendix I, p. 168.

49. The Liverpool Port Books list the import of a total of 264 tons of clay. The Customs Records for the entire country, (written in London), show that only precisely half this amount - 132 tons - was liable for Customs Duty. This suggests that Carrickfergus clay was mixed with an equal measure of standard potters' clay, (which was not liable for duty), before it left Ireland. (See Appendix I, Tables App. Ia & Ib, pp. 167-8).

50. Britton, *Bristol*, p. 12, provides details of the thirteen Liverpool potteries.

51. See Francis, (1994), pp. 275-76 for further details. A John Smith was resident in Bristol by 28th July 1728, and later worked at two of Bristol's six delftware potteries - the Redcliff Back and Limekiln Lane potteries. The Bristol Port Book of 1742 shows that only two Bristol potteries used Carrickfergus clay - these were the same Redcliff Back and Limekiln Lane potteries that employed an individual named John Smith.

52. PRONI, Millin Ms., T811/1, p. 110. Memorial of lease dated 19th July, 1723, George Bigger to John Ferguson, apothecary, *'in perpetuity at Twenty shillings yearly, all that tenement situate in North Street of Belfast, late in the possession of John Smith, potter, deceased ... bounded on the east with the tenement let to James Smith junior'*.

53. Burial register, *op. cit.* at n. 24 above, p. 83. Buried by Arthur Thetford. (See n. 34 above).

54. *Ibid.*, p. 83. 15th August 1725. *'Mr. John Challmbrs, Marchant* [was buried by] *his Son James'*.

55. The 1719 transfer of the Potthouse lease from Chads to Hodgkinson (see n. 43 above) describes the property as *'Two Tenem^ts. On the North side of Broad* [Waring] *Street ... demised by Arthur Late Earl of Donegall to David Smith Esqr. As also all that Parcell of Ground part of Bullars Meddow and the Pott House And Soaphouse Together with all such goods, Utensils and Things as are Contained in a Schedule ... being in and about the Potthouse...'*. Sadly, the *'Schedule'* of the pottery's contents has not survived.

56. Francis Thetford's assignment offering the Potthouse lease as security on a loan in 1719 (see n. 44 above) described the property as *'All that parcell of Ground part of the Field called Bullars Meadow in front Six score and Thirteen Foot & the Potthouse & Sopehouse with the Backside & Garden bounded by a Former Demise to said David Smith...'*.

57. PRONI, Donegall Ms., T/1622. C. Brett's modern map attached to these lease tranfers, dated 1757, indicates that the Potthouse site was then an iron foundry in the possession of Abel Hadskis - a relation of Henry Chads successor, Richard Hodgkinson (see n. 43 above). A new foundry was built on the site soon after 1757, which in 1775 was *'believed to be the largest furnace ... in this kingdom'*. See Benn, *op. cit.* at n. 10 above, p. *354-55*.

58. Young, *Town Book*, p. 80. *'Pot House Lane'* appears on John Mulholland's map of Belfast, 1788.

59. Compare for example Montague Close, Britton, *London*, p. 42-43.

60. For further discussion see P. Francis, 'Delftware and Soap', *ECC Trans.*, Vol. *15*, Pt. 3, *(1995)*, pp. 426-31.

61. Britton, *London*, Fig. 5, p. 42, item 8. See also Edwards, *op. cit.* at n. 1 above, p. 71. This was described in 1692/3 as *'one shed employed for sope making and ... being in length twenty foote and in depth twenty & four foote'*.

62. Benn, *op. cit.* at n. 10 above, p. 355. The illustration was reprinted in Llewellyn Jewitt, *The Ceramic Art of Great Britain*, 2nd. Ed., London, (1883), p. 598, Figs. 1719 & 1720.

63. Nat. Mus. Ireland, Acc. No. 23.1925.

64. Discovered 17th Feb. 1995 by Shirley Tumelty of Bangor, Co. Down.

65. Young, *Town Book*, p. 326. '*...a shoe in blue and white is at Nettlefield* [where] *is still preserved the Oak Punchbowl presented to Robert Leathes ... another* [shoe] *is dated 1724*'. Nettlefield House was the home of the Lewis family of Belfast, who were possibly descended from the Leathes family, but the pedigree provided by Young is highly flawed.

66. A square-toed shoe inscribed *'ER 1707'*, in the National Museum of Ireland, was also regarded as an example of Belfast delftware by Dudley Westropp (1935), p. 6. The possibility that this is so should certainly not be excluded, but without further evidence the attribution is unsupportable - it might as easily have been made in England. The same applies to a similar, square-toed shoe in the Ulster Museum's collection, more simply dated *'1707'*. Both examples are illustrated in Lipski & Archer, p. 411, nos. 1717 & 1718, where they are seen to share many features in common with English shoes. A third shoe in the Ashmolean Museum in Oxford, (Lipski & Archer, no. 1719), inscribed *'AR 1707'*, is obviously related to this group.

67. R. M. Young, *Notes and Queries*, Vol. II, Ser. III, June 17 1911, pp. 472-73.

68. R. M. Young, *Belfast and the Province of Ulster in the 20th Century*, Brighton, (1909). The shard is part of a group photograph on p. 278.

69. T.E. McNeill & M.G.L. Baillie, 'An Early Eighteenth Century Pottery Assemblage from Dunbar Street, Belfast', in G. MacNiocaill & P. F. Wallace, (eds.), *Keimelia*, Galway Univ. Press, (1988), pp. 349-64. Also T.E. McNeill in A. Hamlin & C. Lynn, (eds.), *Pieces of the Past*, Belfast, (1988), pp. 79-81.

70. The shards were collected from the site on the corner of Hill Street and Commercial Court in May 1990, and were subsequently washed and sorted by Maura Mulholland. The shards now reside in the Archaeology Dept., Queen's University, Belfast. Sections and other data were recorded but are not yet published.

71. Collected during re-cobbling work in Hill Street, 14-16th Sept. 1993. Sections were also drawn, but these are not yet published.

72. Collected 7th-9th Sep. 1994, with the help of Tom McErlean and others. The author

is indebted to the Historic Monuments Service, Hill Street, Belfast, for their help in recovering these shards.

73. For example, a large saucer dish, Sotheby's New York, Oct. 20 1993, Lot 24; a porringer, Rous Lench Coll. Vol I, Sotheby's, 1st Jul. 1986, Lot 11.

74. Frank Britton, *pers. comm.*, 23rd April 1994.

75. An intact example is shown in the Lipski Collection., Pt. III, Sotheby's, London, 1st Mar. 1983, Lot 422.

76. Britton, *London,* p. 70, Fig. 11 I, p. 142, Fig. 119.

77. Lipski & Archer, Nos. 312, p. 79, & 440, p. 101.

78. John Philip Kassebaum Collection, Sotheby's London, 7th Oct. 1992, Lot 42, illustrated p. 24.

79. Archer, Cat. H. *2,* p. 349, further discusses the term *capuchine*.

80. *Ibid.*

81. Philip Kassebaum Collection, Sotheby's London, 7th Oct. 1992, Lot 85, illustrated p. 35. Now Longridge Collection. A different style of barrel-shaped tankard dated 1724 is illustrated by Lipski & Archer, No. 808, p. 180. The form imitates contemporary silver shapes. Examples are also recorded in Chinese porcelain, some of which possessed matching porcelain lids. For example, see Solveig & Anita Gray, *A Catalogue of Oriental Ceramics & Works of Art,* No. 2, London, (n.d., c.1992), Fig. 47c., p. 38.

82. Phillips', London, 13th June 2000, Lot 167.

83. Solveig & Anita Gray, *A Catalogue of Oriental Ceramics & Works of Art,* No. 1, London, (n.d., c.1988), Fig. 22a., p. 26. This is a K'ang Hsi blue and white flask of identical form, but with a cylindrical rather than flared spout. The top and bottom borders are also ribbed, but the style of painting is dissimilar. Ht. 5½in., 140 mm.

84. Illustrated in Francis, (1994), Fig. 4, p. 269. This fragment is in very fine, deep red biscuit, and may represent an 'Eler's-type' red stoneware.

85. For example, a long-spouted ewer in olive-green from Delft is illustrated in C.H. de Jonge, *Delft Ceramics,* Praeger, New York & London, (1970), p. 89, *Ill.* 85. A pair of Dutch oil and vinegar bottles with similar spouts, in an *imari* palette, are illustrated by Jacob Stodel, *The Splendour of Dutch Delftware,* exhib. cat., London, (1993), Fig. 38, p. 53.

86. Lipski & Archer, Nos. 869-76, pp. 195-97.

87. Sotheby's New York, Oct. 20 1993, Lot 25.

88. This Dutch example is polychrome, finely painted in an *imari* palette, with the mark PAK (Pieter Adriaenson Kocks) of the *'Griekshe A'* pottery in Delft, c. 1701-22. It is illustrated by de Jonge, *op. cit.* at n. 85 above, *Ill.* 110, p. 111.

Chap. 2, DUBLIN, Part 1; The World's End Pottery

2,1 i: John Chambers

1. The *'World's End'* pottery was situated on the north side of present-day Beresford Place near the Custom House, in the immediate vicinity of Frenchman's Lane & Store Street.

2. Charles Brooking's 1728 map of Dublin, (Nat. Lib. Ire. reprint, n.d., c. 1990), clearly shows that the World's End site was fully built up by this date.

3. Nat. Lib. Ire., MS 24938, (Westropp *Ms,* Pottery). Westropp's annotated copy of his 1935 *Guide,* p.10, contains the additional reference to *'the Strand'*. Westropp further records that a *'John Grizold, Potter, of Lazar's Hill'* (directly across the River Liffey from the Strand), died in Dublin c. 1734. Another Dublin potter, *'John Bell',* died in 1722 - see Fraser, *Dublin Potters,* p. 47.

4. Edwards, *op. cit.* at Chap. 1, n. 1 above, pp. 60-62. Francis Place, another individual who experimented with stoneware manufacture, was also in Ireland during the late 1690s. For further information, see R. Loeber, 'An Unpublished View of Dublin in 1698 by Francis Place', *Bull. Irish Georgian Soc.,* Vol. XXI, Nos. 1 & 2, (Jan. - Jun. 1978), pp. 7-15.

5. RoD, 56. 505. 38946, memorial of indenture dated 4th June 1728, from Mary Vernon of Holborn, Middlesex, (heir of Edward Vernon of North Aston, Oxfordshire), to Paul Elers of Middle Temple, London, Edward Webb & John Fortescue of Gray's Inn, and William Harrison and Richard Warburton of Dublin. The document recorded the sale of the title deeds to the town and country surrounding Clontarf, on Dublin's northern outskirts. See also RoD 57.293.38536 and 58.107.38738.

6. The names *'Chambers', 'Challmbrs', 'Chalmers'* were used by various members of the same family in Belfast. 'De *la Chambre'* was adopted by the branch that went with Patrick Smith to Waterford in 1746. (See n. 9 below).

7. Agnew, *Belfast,* pp. 217-18, p. 246.

8. *Ibid.,* p. 218. For further information concerning Patrick Smith and his family in Waterford see Rev. Thomas Gimlette, 'The French Settlers in Ireland - No. 7. The Settlement in Waterford', *Ulster Journal of Archaeology,* Series I, Vol. 4, (1856), pp. 207-11.

9. Agnew, *pers. comm.*, May 2000. The relationship with another Belfast Smith, Samuel Smith, who appears in Belfast records during the late-seventeenth and early eighteenth centuries, has not been established. Samuel was possibly a brother of William, (David and Patrick's father). He is also recorded as the father of the Patrick Smith *junior* who was acquainted with John Chambers. (Patrick *junior* received £450 from the division of Samuel's estate in 1726 - see RoD 73.14.49514; 73.165.50340 & 88.405.63078). See also Compton Reade, *The Smith Family,* London, (1904), pp. 192-93, pedigree of the *'Smiths of Waterford',* which confirms that Patrick *(junior's)* wife was Mary Chambers, *(De la Chambre).*

10. Henry R. Wagner, *Irish Economics,* London, (1907), p.11, no. 22. This pamphlet proposed the formation of a bank in Dublin, with around 200 subscribers throughout the country investing a minimum of £500 of personal funds. The list included *'Mrs. Ann Smith, Widdow'* (who owned the larger of the two Carrickfergus clay leases - see Appendix I, p. 170), and *'Mr. Patrick Smith, Merchant, Belfast'*. (Patrick Smith *senior*, of the Potthouse, had died before 1718).

11. RoD, 54.366.36082, 14th October 1727, Chalmers (Chambers) to Smith.

12. Agnew, *Belfast,* p. 218. PRONI, Dobbs Papers, D162/24, John Chalmers, Antigua, to Arthur Dobbs, 21st June 1731. For further information concerning Dobbs at this time see Desmond Clarke, *Arthur Dobbs Esq., 1689-1725,* Chapel Hill, North Carolina, *(1957),* pp. 26-33.

13. Anon., *Historic Memorials of the First Presbyterian Church of Belfast,* Belfast, (1887), p. 90. 15th January 1733 (n.s.), *'mr James Challmbrs, marioner'* was buried. See also 12th May 1733, which shows that James Chambers lived in Waring Street, in which the Potthouse was situated ('Wern St', Fig. 9).

14. PRONI, T722, pp. 99-100. Lord Lieut. & Privy Council of Ireland to Duke of Newcastle, *'An Act for granting to his Majesty a further Additional Duty on Wine, Silk, Hops, China, Earthen, Japanned or lacquered Ware...* '. The additional duty amounted to a further 2½% (six pence to the pound).

15. RoD 36. 170.21944, 6th Sept. 1722, Innis to Potter.

16. RoD 73.14.49514. This confirms that Robert Leathes had formed a partnership with Samuel Smith and Patrick Smith *junior* to make linen before 1726. (Leathes' will was proved in 1723).

17. Castletown, p. 10.

18. For further information see Mairead Dunlevy, 'Samuel Madden and the Scheme for the Encouragement of Useful Manufactures', in Agnes Bernelle, (ed.), *Decantations: A Tribute in Honour of Maurice Craig,* Dublin, (1992), and Terence de Vere White, *The Story of The Royal Dublin Society,* Tralee, (1955), Chaps. 1-5.

19. Anon. (S. Madden), *A Letter to the Dublin Society, on the Improving their Fund; and the Manufactures, Tillage, &c. in Ireland',* Dublin, (1739), p. 29. I am grateful to the Knight of Glin for bringing this reference to my attention.
20. Longfield, p. 39. The petition was submitted 21st February 1739.
21. *Ibid.*
22. Dunlevy, *op. cit.* at n. 18 above, p.6.
23. *Ibid.,* and Minute Book of the Dublin Society, Jan. 14th 1741; *'The petition of John Brooks for an encouragement for having introduced the Art of Graving into this Kingdom was read & referred to further consideration',* and Feb. 4th 1741; John Brooks' petition *'for introducing & improving the* Art *of Graving & Mezzotint.., could not come into competition for a Premium for invention given by Dr. Madden'.* I am indebted to Mairead Dunlevy and Mary Kelleher, librarian of the Royal Dublin Society, for their help in obtaining this reference.

John Brooks moved to London *'early in 1746 to establish himself as an engraver in the Strand',* taking with him two of his ablest pupils, James McArdell and Robert Houston, (two of the most talented Irish *'Scrapers',* a group that included Thomas Frye of Bow). See David Alexander, 'The Dublin Group; Irish Mezzotint Engravers in London, 1750-1775', *Irish Georgian Soc. Quart. Bull.,* Vol. XVI, No. 3, (Jul-Sep. 1973), pp. 73-93.
24. Longfield, p. 39.
25. Westropp (1935), p. 11. The coincidental timing of John Chambers' death and Henry Delamain's arrival (c. April 1752), raises the possibility that Chambers worked at the pottery throughout, even though he is not recorded as the proprietor after Jan. 1740.
26. Lipski & Archer, p. 94, No. 399, (V&A, c.155-1929) and No. 400 (Metropolitan, 47.132).
27. I am extremely grateful to Michael Archer for his help in studying this plate at first hand.
28. Britton, *Bristol,* pp. 309-17.
29. *Ibid.,* p. 310. The five examples are Cat. Nos. 12.45 - 12.48 and No. 15.35. For a further example of the *'Eight Horses'* design see Austin, No. 244, p. 155
30. See, for example, Lipski & Archer, No. 415. With further research, plates with under-rim markings other than concentric circles can also be tied to this group, such as Lipski & Archer Nos. 429 and 490. Another dated example, inscribed *'IHM 1742',* is illustrated by Austin, Cat. No. 251, p. 158.
31. C. J. Holdaway, 'Tin-glazed earthenware from Liverpool', *Antique Dealer & Collector's Guide,* Dec. 1981, (No page nos.), Fig. 4. The shard matches the *'Emperor Yao'* design illustrated by Britton, *Bristol,* Cat. Nos. 12, 47 and 48.
32. Another example, with unusual under-rim markings of *'three scrolls and a central cross',* is in the Long Collection, Castle Museum, York, acc. no. 1300.1976, Cat. No. 56.
33. Adams & Redstone, Plate 21, p. 103. The example illustrated is in the Fitzwilliam Museum, Cambridge, acc. no. c.16-1992.

2, 1 ii: John Crisp & Co.

1. Westropp, (1935), p. 11.
2. Longfield, p. 39, n.4.
3. Westropp, (1935), p. 11. Dated precisely by Longfield, *ibid.*
4. Britton, *London,* pp. 61-2, p. 193. Crisp & Saunders owned a delftware pottery at Glasshouse Street, Lambeth in the 1740s & 50s. They also owned a windmill (for grinding glaze ingredients) at Battersea in 1753, when Delamain was involved in the Battersea enamel works. Delamain himself was also on sufficiently good terms with Crisp & Saunders to exhibit a model of his new, coal-fired kiln in their Lambeth pottery in 1754. See p. 53).
5. For example, Bernard Watney, 'The Vauxhall China Works', *ECC Trans,* Vol. 13, Pt. 3.
6. Britton, *London,* p. 44.
7. Castletown, cat. no. 3. The six examples are noted in Lipski & Archer, p. 119, Nos. 521 - 521 E. For further discussion see Archer, No. B.128, p. 179.
8. See Archer, *ibid.* The theory that the plates relate to John & Elizabeth Crisp seems to have originated with W. J. Pountney and Dudley Westropp.
9. Archer, *ibid.*
10. Hunt Museum Limerick, acc. no. HCL. 30. For further illustration see Lipski & Archer, No. 1506, p. 339.
11. Ross E. Taggart, *The Burnap Collection of English Pottery,* Kansas City Missouri (1967), Cat. 156, p. 56. See also Lipski & Archer, No. 510, p. 116.
12. R. Day, 'Historical Notes', *Journal of the Cork Historical & Archaeological Society,* Vol. 1, (1892), pp. 69-71. Illus., p. 70.
13. Day's paper label, on the reverse of this plate, is illustrated in Ross E. Taggart, *op. cit.* at n. 11 above, p.205.

2, 1 iii: David Davis & Co.

1. Fraser, Dublin Potters, p. 48.
2. Westropp, (1935), p. 11. The same advertisement seems to have been run in the *Dublin Courant* in 1748 & 49.
3. Longfield, p. 40.
4. Compare the wages offered to apprentices by Henry Delamain in his advertisement in Sept. 1754, (p. 53).
5. Westropp, (1935) pp.11-12. The only pottery outside Dublin's immediate environs that was awarded a premium at this time was in Arklow, a seaport 30 miles to the south of the city. Other mid-eighteenth century potteries, such as those in Coalisland, Co. Tyrone and near Enniscorthy, Co. Wexford, do not seem to have made applications.
6. Delamain's petition to the Irish House of Commons, Nov. 1st 1753. (See p. 50).
7. Westropp, (1935), p.12.
8. See n.6 above.
9. Reprinted in A. Day (ed.), *Letters from Georgian Ireland, the correspondence of Mary Delany 1731-68,* Friar's Bush, Belfast (1991), p. 163.
10. Longfield, p. 40.

2, 1 iv: Henry Delamain

1. Danny Parkinson, 'The Delamain Family in Ireland', and Olive Keane, 'The Pedigree of the Delamain Family from 1625'. Unpublished manuscripts, National Museum of Ireland. I am indebted to Mairead Dunlevy for forwarding copies of these valuable notes.
2. Aubrey J. Toppin, 'The Will of Henry Delamain, the Dublin Potter', *ECC Trans.,* No. 8, (1942), pp. 158-59. On July 24th 1745, *'appeared personally Henry Delamain of the Parish of St. Paul, Covent Garden, Middlesex with Ziphorah Maitland...'* The marriage took place on 26th July 1745 at St. Marylebone. Ziphorah's previous husband was John Maitland of St. Andrew's Holborn, bachelor, whom she married as Ziphorah Alvares, spinster, February 12th 1726 (n.s) in London.
3. I am deeply indebted to Dr. Nessa Roche for bringing this previously unrecorded advertisement to my attention.
4. These details were provided by Peter Shee, in his testimony to the Irish parliamentary committee, 10th Nov. 1761, (p.61).
5. S. Benjamin, *English Enamel Boxes,* Orbis, London, (1978), pp. 40-47.
6. E. Veale, 'Sir Theodore Janssen, Huguenot and merchant of London c.1658—1748', *Proc. Huguenot Soc.,* Vol. XXVI, No. 2, (1995), pp. 282-3.
7. A. Toppin, 'Battersea: Ceramic and Kindred Associations', *ECC Trans.,* No. 9, Vol. 2, (1946), p. 172. Lorenzo Moore's wife, Henrietta Janssen, was the principal legatee of her father's estate. Moore was also a Ranger for the Curragh, MP for Dungannon in 1783, and for Ardfert in 1799 in the Irish House of Commons.
8. Minute Book of The Dublin Society, 14th January and 4th February 1741. See M.

Dunlevy, 'Samuel Madden and the Scheme for the Encouragement of Useful Manufactures', in *Decantations; a tribute in honour of Maurice Craig*, Dublin, (1992).

9. B. Watney, 'Brooks and Janssen as Antigallicans', *ECC Trans.*, Vol. 11, Pt. 1, (1981), pp. 33-4.

10. C. Cook, 'James Gwin and his Designs on Battersea Enamels', *Apollo*, March 1952, pp. 66-69.

11. C. Cook, *ECC Trans.*, Vol. 3, Pts. 4 & 5, (1955), p. 191. Quoted from *Anthologia Hibernica*, May 1793.

12. For further details see Veale, *op. cit.* at n. 6 above, pp. 43-4.

13. The central illustration portrays *'Richard de Quinzica disembarking with the ransom offered for his wife to the Corsair Pagamin'*. For further details see C. Cook, *The Life and Work of Robert Hancock*, London, (1948).

14. See Toppin, *op. cit.* at n. 7, p. 173. Formerly in the coll. of E.C. Dykes.

15. The Sackville box is illustrated by E. Mew, *Battersea Enamels*, Medici Society, London, (1926), Fig. 15. The Maria Gunning box, in the Victoria and Albert Museum, (Ac. No. C.129-1963), is illustrated in *'Rococo; Art and Design in Hogarth's England*, V & A Mus. Cat., (1984), p. 269.

16. RoD 161.399.109152, memorial of 31-year lease dated 24th June 1753, Jolly to Delamain. First recorded in Mairead Dunlevy, 'Irish Fine-Ceramic Potteries, 1769-96', *Post-Mediaeval Archaeology*, Vol. 18, (1984), pp. 251-61. I am deeply indebted to Mairead Dunlevy for bringing this lease to my attention.

17. Castletown, p. 12.

18. Longfield, p. 40. The premium was paid in April 1754.

19. Westropp, (1935), p 14.

20. *Ibid.*, pp. 12-13.

21. Castletown, p. 26.

22. For details of coal exploration and improvements made to the Newry Canal in the late 1740s/early 1750s, see W. A. McCutcheon, *The Industrial Archaeology of Northern Ireland*, Fairleigh Dickinson Univ. Press, (1984), pp. 330-34.

23. Mairead Dunlevy, 'Samuel Madden and the Scheme for the Encouragement of Useful Manufactures', in Agnes Bernelle, (ed.), *Decantations: A Tribute in Honour of Maurice Craig*, Dublin, (1992), p. 4.

24. McCutcheon, *op. cit.* at n. 22 above, p. 329.

25. *Ibid.*, p. 341. See also Chap. 3, vii; Minor Potteries, p. 163.

26. George Minty, an English glass-maker resident in Ireland from 1746-57, possessed a knowledge of fireclays, and he later submitted his own application to the Dublin Society for fireclay crucibles in 1758. In 1757 he wrote *'In the County of Wicklow, I found two Sorts of Earth, not far apart; one Sort is extraordinary for taking Grease out of Cloth or Silk,* [i.e. Fuller's Earth]; *and of the other I made some Crucibles,* [i.e. Fireclay], *which proved as good as ever were used. I produced them to the Dublin Society. It was by Means of this Stuff* [Fireclay] *that the Delf Ware was brought to stand boiling Water, which got £1000 Premium. But Mr. Stringfellow, to whom I made known the Secret, has left Dublin, and the Work is much altered'.* Minty's account therefore seems to confirm that the *'Primate's Coals'* bowl (which earned Delamain the *'£1000 Premium'),* was probably made using a fireclay/delftware-clay mixture. For further details of Minty's work on Irish fireclays, see P. Francis, 'The Glass-Maker's Memoirs: George Minty's "Crusonian" Adventures in Ireland, 1746-1757', *Journal of Glass Studies*, Corning Museum New York, Vol. 42, (2000), p. 127.

27. Toppin, *op. cit.* at n. 2 above, p. 158.

28. Nat. Lib. Ire., MS 24938, (Westropp *Ms*, Pottery). Correspondence from E.S. Price, West Kirby, Cheshire, 14th April 1953. *'William Stringfellow... served his time at Liverpool from about 1733-40 with Thomas Seel & Co.* [Lord St. Pothouse] *as a delft painter, and was married at St. Nicholas' Church in Liverpool in 1746. After returning from Ireland* [in February 1754] *he settled in Park Lane Liverpool, and later became a copper enameller of clock and watch faces* [suggesting a] *connection with the enamelling business at Battersea'* Correspondence from Peter Entwistle, Liverpool, 21st Sep. 1936 states; *'William Stringfellow (married 1747 at St. Nich. Church) is described as an enameller, Park Lane in Liverpool in 1756, his will was proved 1791. Sometimes described as Watch Enameller.'* Entwistle's correspondence also suggests that another William Stringfellow, (the son?), served his apprenticeship at the same pottery, Thomas Seel & Co., on 13th Nov. 1760, and was made a Freeman on 14th Mar. 1761.

29. *BNL*, 5th February 1754.

30. It is clear from Hardman's letter to Lord Strange, (Appendix II, v) that Stringfellow obtained his release from Delamain shortly before arriving in Liverpool. Information in n. 28 above suggests that he remained in Liverpool afterwards.

31. Britton, *op. cit.* in Chap. 2, 1 ii; John Crisp & Co., n. 4 above.

32. Longfield, p. 43. The advertisement appeared in the *London Gazette* of 19th March 1754.

33. Toppin, *op. cit.* at n. 7 above. Delamain was recorded as partner in the first two quarters of 1754, but was not mentioned subsequently.

34. Lorna Weatherill & Rhoda Edwards, 'Pottery Making in London and Whitehaven in the Late Seventeenth Century', Post Mediaeval Archaeology, Vol. 5, (1971), p, 174, 'As [John Dwight's answer in 1697] *says, because tin-glaze ware "will not endure a stronge fire", it was fired by wood only, coal being suitable for ordinary earthenware only'.* Henry Delamain's letters, (e.g. Appendix II, letter ii) indicates that the Liverpool potters expected his coal-fired wares to be *'Smoaked'.*

35. Reg & Philomena Jackson, and Roger Price, 'Bristol Potters and Potteries, 1600-1800', *Jour. Ceram Hist.*, No. 12, Stoke on Trent City Museum, (1982), p. 19. A description of Richard Frank's pottery in 1767 stated *'Great quantities of wood are expended* [here]. *Coal is unserviceable* [as a kiln fuel]'.

36. For further discussion see Castletown, p. 26.

37. *Ibid.*, pp 13-14.

38. Peter Francis, 'Irish Creamware, The Downshire Pottery in Belfast', *ECC Trans.*, Vol. 15, Pt. 3, (1995), pp. 412.

39. Westropp (1935), pp. 37-40.

40. Adams & Redstone, Appendix VI, p. 215.

41. Rodney Hampson, 'Longton Potters 1700-1865', *Journal of Ceramic History*, Stoke on Trent Museum, Vol. 14, (1990), No. 271, p. 175, lists William Wright as an earthenware potter in Longton in 1733. No Proctors are listed in Longton before 1790, nor Simpsons before 1776, but both became common names in the nineteenth century. R.G. Cooper, *English Slipware Dishes, 1650-1850*, London, (1968), p. 75, 97 & 114 lists John Simpson (1685-74, of Newcastle under Lyme), and an earlier William Wright (fl. 1709). Westropp, (1935), p. 40 records that the potters listed here accused Allen with stealing from Joseph Warburton near Burslem shortly before he came to Ireland, and then he *'run away to Ireland with some money Mr. Samuel Proctor of Lesne Delft in Staffordshire entrusted him'.* Warburton might well have been associated with the Pomona works, having worked previously at Bow. See Adams & Redstone, p. 72.

42. The *Dublin Journal* advertisement of 1st - 5th November 1743 stated *'All sorts of old and new china, all kinds of glasses, japann'd way, great variety of China toys & ornamented China to be sold by Catherine Davey at the corner of Jervis Street in Abbey Street.'* The author is indebted to Dr. Nessa Roche for this reference.

43. Westropp, (1935), p. 19.

44. PRONI, Downshire Ms., D607/E/41. Benjamin Edwards of Belfast, fine-

glassmaker, to 2nd Marquess of Downshire.
45. PRO, Kew, CUST 15. The only exports of Irish earthenware recorded during the entire eighteenth century were two shipments from Belfast in 1705-6, consisting of wares valued at £4.10.00 to England, and £1.10.00 to Scotland. (CUST 15-8).
46. Prof. Louis M. Cullen, *pers. comm.*, 28th April 2000.
47. Longfield, p. 43-44.
48. *BNL,* 16th March 1756.
49. Nancy Valpy, 'Extracts from 18th Century London Newspapers', *ECC Trans.,* Vol. 12, Pt. 2, (1985), p. 181, from *Read's Weekly Journal,* 27th March, 1756.
50. Westropp, (1935), p. 20.

2, 1 v. Mary Delamain

1. Aubrey J. Toppin, 'The Will of Henry Delamain, the Dublin Potter', *ECC Trans.,* No. 8, (1942), pp. *158-59.*
2. *Ibid.,* p. 159. Buried as Ziphorah Delamain at St. Margaret's Westminster, 17th June 1757. Administration of her goods and chattels was granted to her *'niece'* and next of kin, Deborah Minshull.
3. RoD 289.253.190687, 18th April 1772, contains the reference *'11th June 1751 Thomas Shanly of Dublin Gent did demise and set to Mary Bijar of Abby Street Dublin all that house or Tenement then late in the possession of Robt. Bijar dec'd and then in the possession of sd. Mary Bijar for 31 years from 29th September 1749'.* I am very grateful to Mairead Dunlevy for bringing this reference to my attention.
4. Toppin, *op. cit.* at n. 1 above, p. 158. Robert Bijar's premises in 1807 were at No. 12 Little Mary Street.
5. Adams & Redstone, pp. 36-41. See also Michael Wynne, 'A Note on Thomas Frye', *Quar. Bull. Irish Georgian Soc.,* Vol. XIII, Nos. *2 & 3*, April-Sept. 1970, pp. 38-44.
6. *Ibid.,* p. 88. The first auction recorded was 20th February 1755.
7. Elizabeth Adams, *Chelsea Porcelain*, London, (1987), p. 145.
8. Adams & Redstone, p. 44. Bowcock was married to Ann Wilkinson, possibly the daughter of Samuel Wilkinson.
9. Westropp, (1935), pp. 20-1.
10. Longfield, p. 45.
11. *Ibid.* Henry Delamain mentions his daughter Mary in his letter to Mary Senior in Dec. 1753. See Appendix II, i.
12. Westropp, (1935), p. 21.

2, 1 vi. William Delamain and Samuel Wilkinson

1. See Section 2, 1 iv, note 1. *BNL* 27th July 1753, p. 3, col. 3 records that William was Marshall of Dublin by that date. ('.. *the late Worthy Grand Jury of the Tholsel, Alderman Robert Donovan, Foreman, instead of Dineing together as usual, unanimously agreed to apply their Money to Charity, and accordingly lent to William Delamain, Esq., City Marshal, ten Pounds to release confined Debtors, who added five pounds to the above Charity, and released ten poor Debtors.'*).
2. L. M. Cullen, *The Irish Brandy Houses of Eighteenth-Century France,* Lilliput, Dublin, (2000), p. 43.
3. *Faulkner's Dublin Journal*, 14-17 Feb. 1761. '*William Delamain At the new Tea Ware-house in Little Strand Street near Caple-Street begs to inform his friends and the Public that he has laid in a large Sortment of the very best Tea from the East India tea sale in London*'. Danny Parkinson. *op. cit.* at 2, I, iv, n.1 above, p. 107, also indicates that Henry Delamain had offices at 15-16 Essex Street.
4. Britton, *London*, p. 43-4.
5. *Ibid.*, p.44. Richard Day & Son who succeeded Wilkinson at Montague Close were not potters originally, but third generation members of the *Cooper's* Company in London. Mary Bijar's family, including Richard Bijar, were *coopers* in Dublin. (See section 2, I, v, n.4 above). As Richard Bijar, Catherine Bijar and Ann Day were listed together as witnesses to Henry Delamain's will in 1753, this raises the possibility that Mrs. Ann Day may have been Mary Bijar's sister.

Although there initially appear to be no connections between coopering and delftware manufacture, this was not the case - both required large quantities of either soft soap (to make barrels) or soaper's waste (for delftware glaze). Coopers' records in the Guildhall Mss. show that in the eighteenth century only two trades on London's South Bank employed qualified coopers, other than cooperages. These were soaphouses and delftware potteries. (Frank Britton, *pers. comm.*, 31st Jan. & 10th Oct. 1994).
6. Longfield, pp. 45-6.
7. The first record of the Stoneybatter pottery is on 10th Dec. 1760. (See p.157).
8. The disruption caused by the war may have improved Ireland's trading situation in some way, but at present, it is not clear why the number of potteries should have increased at this time.
9. Westropp, (1935), p. 21-22.
10. The maximum value of French earthenware imported was £1201 in 1751, falling to £131 by 1755. During the same years the value of imported English earthenware was £8337 and £7322 respectively.
11. Westropp, (1935), p. 22. and following. All the testimonies which appear in this section are transcribed from this source, supplemented with additional lines of text from Longfield, pp.47-8.
12. W. G. Strickland, *A Dictionary of Irish Artists,* Dublin & London, 1913, pp. 347-48. See p.97. Shee's remarks here are often taken to indicate that he left the pottery when Delamain died in 1757, but it is obvious that the committee was questioning him about the pottery's accounts during Henry Delamain's period of ownership (1752-7). The fact that Shee was called to present these figures to the committee in November 1761 suggests that he was still one of the pottery's accountants at that time.
13. Westropp, (1935), p. 23.
14. Possibly James Hamilton, 8th Earl of Abercorn.
15. Nat. Lib. Ire., *Castletown* Ms, TCD Ms 3974-84 [61], contains a billhead of George Newton, Essex Bridge, dated 1748. In Dublin trade directories he is also listed at this address in 1752, then (as Newton and Darragh) as china merchants on Lower Ormond Quay in 1760.
16. See p. 66.
17. Longfield, p. 48., n. 17.
18. For further quotations from these debates, see Castletown, pp. 15-16.
19. Mairead Dunlevy, 'Irish Fine-Ceramic Potteries, 1769-96', *Post-Mediaeval Archaeology,* Vol. 18, (1984), p. 251.
20. Entwistle Papers, Liverpool Public Record Office, 942 ENT (Folder 1). John & James Roscoe were recorded as potters in 1761. The family had been potters there since the early seventeeth-century.
21. The fraud was exposed by one James Roach or Roche, who received a £12 reward from the Dublin Society in October 1766. Where Roche worked at this time is unclear, but it was probably at one of the two potteries, at Stoneybatter or the World's End.
22. Nat. Lib. Ire., MS 24938, (Westropp *Ms,* Pottery).
23. Estimated very approximately from Ann Day's testimony in March 1762, of about £1,000 in the previous 12-18 months, *'but that was only the cash account'.* Other figures are from Westropp, (1935), p. 24.
24. The second advertisement on 9th-12th Aug. is an abbreviated version.
25. Danny Parkinson, *Ms.*, *op. cit.* at Chap. 2, 1, iv, n. 1 above, p. 1.
26. M. Alain Braastad, Jarnac, *pers. comm.* 8th May 2000.

2, 1 vii. Stacey, Roche & partners.

1. Mairead Dunlevy, 'Irish Fine-Ceramic Potteries, 1769-96', *Post-Mediaeval Archaeology* Vol. 18, (1984), pp. 251-61. See p. 251.
2. *Ibid.,* p. 259, n. 7. RoD 289.253.290687. The properties included the 50 x 90 ft.

'garden' adjoining the Strand, next to the pottery, originally demised by John Jolly to Henry Delamain in 1753. (See p. 49).

3. Westropp, (1935), p. 24.

4. *Ibid.,* p. 29.

5. Dunlevy, *op. cit.* at n. 1 above, p. 251. From the Proc. Dub. Soc., 5th April 1770.

6. *Ibid* From the Proc. Dub. Soc., 12th April 1770.

7. *Ibid.*

8. *Ibid.* Proc. Dub. Soc. 12th July 1770.

9. *Ibid.,* and Longfield, p. 49. From the Proc. Dub. Soc., 12th Dec. 1771.

10. Nat. Lib. Ire., MS 24938, (Westropp *Ms,* Pottery). Correspondence from E.S. Price, 14th Apr. 1953. Edward Ackers, trained in Liverpool as a delftware potter, but upon gaining his freedom in 1761 went to live and work in Staffs. (where no delftware was made). See also Rodney Hampson, Longton Potters 1700-1865, *Jour, Ceramic History,* Vol. 14, (1990), p. 145. Thomas Shelley, master potter, b. Longton Staffs 1746. Returned to Staffs in 1774 and opened Park Works pottery, Longton Staffs. in that year.

11. Westropp, (1935), p. 29. (The presence of Edward Stacey's name on these post-1771 documents confirms that he had probably been the principal owner since 1768, when he purchased a lease for part of the pottery, at least. See n. 2 above).

12. Dunlevy, op. *cit.* at n. 1 above, p. 252. From Proc. Dub. Soc., 1st April 1773. The payment was for Mar. 1772-Mar. 1773.

13. *Ibid.*

14. See n. 10 above.

15. Dunlevy, *op. cit.* n. 1 above, p. 253.

Chapter 2, DUBLIN, Part 2: DUBLIN DELFTWARE

2, 2 i. Dublin Delftware Characteristics

1. Michael Archer, 'Irish Delftware: an exhibition at Castletown House', *The Connoisseur,* (Oct. 1971), p. 104.

2. Austin, pp. 20-23.

3. Castletown, 'Notes on Marks', p. 32.

4. Westropp (1913), p. 18, pl. 1, 2, 3.

5. L. M. Cullen, *The Irish Brandy Houses of Eighteenth-Century France,* Lilliput, Dublin, (2000), p. 43. The contract was dated 1st Nov. 1762, the ceremony took place on 24th November.

6. George Haggarty, 'The Tin-Glaze Pottery of Delftfield - Some New Marked Finds', *Scottish Kiln Club Newsletter,* No. 7, Edinburgh, (1997), p. 6. The *'ED'* marked dish mentioned by Garry Atkins was recorded in the Drawing Room of a National Trust property, Calke Abbey, at Ticknall, Derby in 1989.

7. Nat. Lib. Ire., MS 24938, (Westropp *Ms,* Pottery). Westropp and Toppin also gained considerable help from the London dealer Louis Gautier.

8. *Ibid.*

9. Gabszewicz & Freeman. A *'Broken Scroll'* plate is illustrated and dated, pl. 67. The date of the *'Sampan Lake'* plate is taken from an example in the Victoria & Albert Museum, Schreiber Coll., acc. no. C.593-1924.

10. Lipski & Archer, No. 490, 490a, p. 111.

11. The *'Primate's Coals'* Bowl (Colour Plate 8) and an excavated bowl fragment (Fig. 80).

12. Henry Sandon, *Worcester Porcelain,* London, (3rd Ed., 1980), p. 30 & Pl. 1. Elizabeth Adams & David Redstone, *Bow Porcelain,* London, (1981), pp. 225-6.

13. Maurice Hillis & Roderick Jellicoe, *The Liverpool Porcelain of William Reid,* Ex. Cat., (Mar.-Apr. 2000). See for example painter's mark '7', plate S, p. 42.

14. Painters' monograms were still in use in Dublin until 1762 at least, by which time Reid's factory had already closed (in 1761).

15. Compare Adams & Redstone, *op. cit.* at n. 12, p. 226, marks *'in blue'.*

16. The English mark illus. in Fig. 65 is taken from a poor quality Liverpool octagonal platter, painted with the *'Chinese Flower-bowl'* pattern, formerly in the author's collection.

17. For example, personal inscriptions interpreted by Frank Britton in *London Delftware,* p. 110, 111, 131 and elsewhere.

18. Petra Coffey, 'Huguenot Freemen of the City of Dublin, *Proc. Huguenot Soc.,* Vol. XXVI, No. 5, (1997), pp. 635-49. See p. 641.

19. *Proc. Huguenot Soc.,* Vol. XVIII, (1947-52), p. 289. ('Settlements & Churches in the West of England').

20. A plate inscribed for *'Charles and Jane Megee 1756',* (a common surname in the north of Ireland), is recorded by Lipski and Archer (No. 590), but this is more likely to have been made in Liverpool, which also had a large Irish community.

21. *Irish Industrial Exhibition Expositor and Advertiser,* No. XIX, 1853, p. 4, Col. 4.

22. Now that the Delamain/Ranson service (Fig. 61) is known to date from 1762, no examples bearing painters' numbers or monograms are recorded that were made during Henry Delamain's lifetime. (Apr. 1752 - Jan. 1757).

23. See Chap. 2, 1, iv, n. 28

24. See Chap. 2, 1, vii, n. 10

25. See Chap. 2, 1, vi, n. 20

26. Castletown, p. 31.

27. For further comments on these characteristics, see also Michael Archer's remarks in Castletown, p. 31.

28. The *'sunken blue'* characteristic was first described by Westropp (1935), p. 26; *'A peculiarity noticeable about a good deal of what is practically certainly Irish delft is that the blue, where it is heavy; has decidedly sunk into the glaze'.*

2, 2 ii; Dublin Delftware, Decorative Styles

1. Austin, pp. 20-23. I am also very deeply indebted to John Austin for providing me with his detailed files concerning these finds at Chesterfield Courthouse.

2. For example, Castletown, p. 33, mark 95a.

3. Austin, *op. cit.* at n.1. One bowl was excavated in New York State in a privy at Johnson Hall, the home of Sir William Johnson. The two further bowls were excavated at Wetherburn's Tavern (9NA. 1532) and William Finnie House (2BA.0864), both in Williamsburg.

4. T. Holdaway collection, London.

5. Austin, p. 20. The second example of painter's number '14' was excavated at the Orlando Jones House, (1OCA.0079).

6. M. Archer, pers. comm., 17th Apr. 1998.

7. Austin. (Detailed unpublished notes). Shards # 30, 31, 38. The two bowls fragments decorated in blue and manganese feature floral sprays and insects, similar in style to the *'trumpet flower'* bowl illustrated (Fig. 86). The copper green and manganese decorated fragment (#38) is part of a floral motif on a bowl interior - the design is not recognisable.

8. 7 Geo. I. c. 26 (Brit.).

9. 12 Geo II. c. 22 (Brit.).

10. David S. Howard, 'Chinese Armorial Porcelain for Ireland', *Irish Georgian Soc. Bull.,* Vol. XXIX, Nos. 3 & 4, (Jul. - Dec. 1986), pp. 3 - 24

11. Neville John Iröns, 'Chinese Blue and White', *Irish Arts Review,* Vol. 2, No. 3, (Autumn 1985), p. 44

12. A similar 'honeysuckle' border feature is evident on some rare Liverpool porcelain plates, attributed to Brownlow Hill, c. 1755-67. See B. Watney, *Liverpool Porcelain of the Eighteenth Century,* R. Dennis, Somerset, (1997), p. 73, Fig. 286.

13. The author has seen no Chinese example of either pattern during the past ten or fifteen years, although hearsay evidence suggests that Chinese porcelain originals for the *'Chinese Flower-bowl'* pattern do exist. A similar pattern was produced in Derby porcelain of the 1770s. A transfer-printed version also occurs on English ironstones of the 1830s, which is identical to that of Dublin delftwares, (including the border motifs).

14. Geoffrey Godden, *Oriental Export Market Porcelain,* London, (1979), p. 131. The plate was sold at Christie's, London, 5th December 1766.

15. Michael Archer, 'Irish Delftware: an exhibition at Castletown House', *The*

Connoisseur, (Oct. 1971), p. 104.
16. Marks recorded on landscape-decorated wares in the literature and private collections are;
1. Mock-Chinese script, crowned harp and/or 'Dublin'
2. 'NE', 'JB', 'K', 'KB', 'IS' monograms. (All under-rim).
3. Painter's numbers 2, 3, 5, 6 and 7, usually under-rim, but not invariably. The dated manganese plate (Fig. 68), produced during the 1760s, was probably part of a service that also bears under-rim numbers. (See Austin, No. 290, p. 168).

Many landscape-decorated wares are also unmarked, irrespective of their 'quality'.
17. The 'harp' marked landscapes are obviously of a finer quality than most manganese-painted landscapes, but there is a large area of overlap. The finest quality landscapes are often painted with extremely pure, refined cobalt, and have often been dipped in a final lead glaze, to give them a higher 'gloss' than most Dublin wares.
18. For example, J. O'Brien & D. Guinness, *Great Irish Houses & Castles,* London, (1992), p. 252, *'The artist chiefly responsible* was *Peter Shee...'.*
19. See Chap. 2, 1, iv, n. 16 above.
20. *Ibid.*
21. William Laffan (ed.), *Masterpieces by Irish Artists 1660-1860,* ex. cat., Pyms Gallery, London, (n.d., c. 1999), pp. 26-29. This source contains all biographical details provided here concerning Robert Carver. I am indebted to the Knight of Glin for his help in finding this information.
22. Sotheby's, London, Irish Sale, 21st May 1998, Lot 221, (Shee landscape). Catalogue entry notes.
23. Shee's address is recorded in Nat. Lib. Ire., MS 24938, (Westropp Ms, Pottery). The correction appears in Westropp's personal copy of his 1935 guide, p. 23.
24. Butterfield's auctions, San Francisco, 19 Nov. 1997. Subsequently Sotheby's London, *(op. cit.* n. 22 above).
25. Westropp (1935), pp. 37-8.
26. Nat. Lib. Ire., MS 24938, (Westropp Ms, Pottery).
27. See Chap. 2, 1, iv, n. 28.
28. Anne Crookshank & the Knight of Glin, *The Watercolours of Ireland,* London, (1994), pp. 61-2.
29. Archer (1979), pl. 13.
30. *Ibid.,* pl. 14.
31. The Fitzwilliam Museum's notes record *'that an Irish dealer..* [had indicated] *that it was made for Thomas Verner of Verner's Bridge, Co. Armagh and that he had bought it from there and sold it to the Earl of Gosford'.* The bowl was purchased by a London dealer, Frank Stoner, at Christie's *'Gosford Castle Sale'* on 21st April 1921, and sold to Dr. J.W.L. Glaisher the following year.
32. *Ibid.* The quotation from this song was noted by Glaisher. The first verse reads;
'Here's a health to the Queen, and a lasting peace
To faction an end, [and] *wealth increase,*
Come let's drink it while we have breath
For there's no drinking after death
And he that will his health deny
Down among the dead men let him lie'.
33. Lipski & Archer, no. 1162, p. 276.
34. Christies, London, 12th March 1990, Lot. *258,* cat. notes; *'perhaps Bassano'.*
35. Compare, for example, C. Dauget & D. Guilleme-Brulon, *'reconnaître les origines des faïences',* Ch. Massin, Paris, n.d. (c. 1990), particularly wares decorated with 'naturalistic' flowers in 'grande feu' colours, pp. 32-42. (e.g. pl. 77 Moustiers, Lyons, pl.81 Marseille, pl. 96 Toulouse).
36. Roseanne Meenan, 'Delamain Pottery Excavated from Dublin Castle', *Irish* Arts *Review,* Yearbook 1991-2, p. 154.
37. The marks recorded are a 'B' monogram on a manganese *'epergne on stand'*, and painters' number '4' on a blue and white *'epergne without stand'*. (See Figs. 147-8).
38. It is very odd to find that the footrim diameter (108 mm.) is considerably less than the lip diameter (130 mm.).
39. The coat of arms is clearly identified as Richards. Four families are listed in the 1899 edition of Burke's *Landed Gentry of Ireland* (pp. 384 - 7), three of whom share common ancestry in Co. Wexford. The motto *Vincet vel mori, ('He shall conquer or die'),* which could be changed from generation to generation without reference to heraldic authority, is attributed in printed sources to families of McDowall. I am grateful to Jonathan Horne and Thomas Woodcock, Norroy and Ulster King of Arms for their research of this armorial.
40. Austin, Cat. 257, p. 159.
41. *Ibid.,* Cat. 100, p. 110.
42. Notes to Lot 35, the Moor Wood collection, Sotheby's, London, 15 May 1979.
43. The arms were identified by researchers at the Hunt Museum, Limerick.
44. Sarah Foster, 'Going Shopping in 18th-century Dublin', *things,* Vol. 4, (summer 1996), p. 43.
45. Tony Stevenson, 'Some Bow Inkstands', *ECC Trans.,* Vol. 14, Pt. 3, (1992), p. 276.
46. L.M.Cullen, *The Irish Brandy Houses of Eighteenth-Century France,* Lilliput Press, Dublin, 2000, pp. 42-3.
47. Solange de Plas, *Les Faïences de Nevers et du centre de la France,* Ch. Massin, Paris, (n.d., c. 1990), pp. 73-4. A plate is illustrated from the Musée du Château de Saumur.
48. Adams & Redstone, p. 44. Ann Wilkinson died during a plague in 1760 - the year in which Samuel Wilkinson came to Dublin.
49. *Ibid.,* pl. 19, for example.
50. For example, the platter illustrated Fig. 117. (Phillip's London, 3-4th June, 1998, Lot 523). A Bow example that is even closer to the Dublin *'Sampan Lake'* is in the Victoria & Albert Museum, C.593-1924.
51. In reality, the Dublin epergnes are not copied precisely from any of the English porcelain epergnes, but some of the shell-moulded dishes and encrusted bases are most similar to those that were made at Bow. It is possible that moulds for the individual shell dishes were lifted directly from Bow examples.
52. Only monogram marks are recorded on the Dublin versions, suggesting they were all made during the 1750s or early 1760s.
53. BNL 8th & 11th July 1760, *'Mrs Hamilton ... in Belfast, hath just imported a good assortment of Indian and Wor'ster China, consisting of Tea-Table China, Dishes and Plates, Bowls, Racking Juggs, Quart and Pint Muggs, Sauce-boats and many other articles...'.*
54. Horne, Part 4, (1984), no. 86. See also notes to Austin, No. 721, p. 289.

2, 2 iii; Dublin Delftware Forms

1. For example, Austin, Archer.
2. Archer, notes to Cat. E. 22, p. 278.
3. *Ibid.* Average size is c. 5 inches (127 mm.) length. They are robust, neatly potted, and usually decorated in monochrome blue or manganese, often applied as a powder ground. The character of their potting and glaze bears little resemblance to known Irish wares. The group may date from the closing decades of the eighteenth-century, in which case they post-date delftware manufacture in Dublin.
4. The first baronet of the Molyneux family, of Castle Dillon near Armagh, was created in 1730. The pair to this barrel, similarly decorated but with different scenes, is in the National Museum of Ireland, Dublin. It is illustrated by Longfield, (1971), Plates 9, 9a.
5. Formerly Lipski collection, (Pt. I), Sotheby's 10th March 1981, Lot 217.
6. Sold Sotheby's 27th July, 1982, Lot. 194. Now private collection.
7. For further discussion, see Archer, p. 278.
8. Nat. Lib. Ire., MS 24938, (Westropp *Ms,* Pottery). Westropp corrected his own copy of Westropp (1935), p. 28.
9. Archer, p. 278.
10. Archer, p. 335. Notes to Cat. No. G.15.
11. Some creamware baskets originally possessed covers. No covers have yet been recorded on delftware examples.
12. Austin, notes to Cat. 292, p. 169.
13. Wolf Mankowitz, *Wedgwood,* London,

(1953), Plate 8, shapes 43, 44.
14. Sold at Phillips', 10th Sep. 1986. See also Dennis Cockell, 'Some Delftware Baskets', *ECC Trans.,* Vol. 13, Pt. 2, (1988), pp. 121-3, pl. 81.
15. Margaret Macfarlane, in unpublished Hampshire County Council Museums Service notes on this item, endorses the *'probably Dublin'* attribution.
16. The flowers are identified as *'plum tree'* flowers from comparison with Chinese originals. See T. Misugi, *Chinese Porcelain Collections in the Near East, Topkapi and Ardebil,* Hong Kong, (1981), Vol. 1, p. 208, Fig. A.93.
17. For a Worcester example, c. 1768, see S. Spero, *Worcester Porcelain, The Klepser Collection,* London, (1984), pl. 121, p. 112.
18. Nicholas Mosse, *pers. comm.,* June 2000.
19. D. Cockell, 'A Piece of delftware at Hardwick Hall', *ECC Trans.,* Vol. 12, Pt. 2, (1985), pp. 112-19. See also Cockell, *op. cit.* at n. 14 above.
20. Garry Atkins, *pers. comm.,* April 1998.
21. The National Trust, Calke Abbey, Ticknall, Derby. The *'ED'* marked dish was recorded in the Drawing Room in 1989. I am indebted to Garry Atkins for bringing this dish to my attention.
22. Archer, notes to Cat. G.17, p. 336.
23. A pair of blue and white Liverpool bough-pots, c. 1765, are illustrated in Horne (141), and a possible London example c. 1785 by Archer (I.27). A Worcester example is illustrated by S. Spero, *Worcester Porcelain in the Klepser Collection,* London and Minneapolis, (1984), p. 89, Cat. No. 91 and Colour Plate 24.
24. E. Adams, *Chelsea Porcelain,* London, (1985), p. 115, Fig. 95.
25. Formerly Horne, Part II, No. 40. The piece illustrated is now in a private collection, the other is at Colonial Williamsburg.
26. J. Kinghorn & G. Quail, *Delftfield, A Glasgow Pottery 1748-1823,* Glasgow, (1986), pp. 34-5, illustrates further examples.
27. These glass candlesticks were long attributed to Michael Edkins, a Bristol manufacturer, but the style of flower painting suggests that a source in the English Midlands is more likely. See R. J. Charleston, 'Michael Edkins and the Problem of English Enameled Glass', *Trans. Soc. Glass Technology,* (1954). Other examples are illustrated in W. A. Thorpe, *English and Irish Glass,* (1927), Fig. 26, Sotheby's 4th Dec. 1967 Lot 294, and 6th Mar. 1978, Lot 163.
28. I am deeply indebted to Nicole Gibbs and Christopher Monkhouse of The Minneapolis Institute of Arts, for their help in studying the pair of candlesticks in their collection.
29. Horne, Part IV, No. 86, illustrates an extremely rare pair of delftware 'shell-base' candlesticks in Fazackerly colours, attributed to Liverpool c. 1760. A pair of blue and white candlesticks dated 1753, recorded by Lipski and Archer, p. 354 Cat. No. 1563 & 1563a, is similarly based on a metal original. Other eighteenth-century blue and white forms are recorded by Britton, p. 128 (Cat. No. 9.4) and Austin, p. 289 (Cat. No. 721),
30. Many continental cisterns were accompanied by a matching wash-hand basin, fixed to the wall below the faucet. Cf. H.P. Fourest, *Delfter Fayencen,* Fribourg, (1981), P1. 139, p. 143.
31. Geoffrey Godden, *Oriental Export Market Porcelain,* London, (1979), p. 216. Fig. 132 illustrates an example among a large Chinese dinner-service, albeit of later date, c. 1798.
32. G.E.Howard, *Early English Drug Jars,* London, (1931), p. 16, Fig. Nos. 20-22.
33. Mairead Dunlevy, (Reynolds), 'The Boileau and Boyd Apothecary Jars', *Irish Pharmacy Journal,* Vol. 60, No. 9, (Sept. 1982), pp. 300-302.
34. Abstract of Wills, Vol. 2, 1785-1832. See entry for John Westlake. I am extremely grateful to Dr. Nessa Roche for her assistance in checking the Dublin Directories.
35. For further discussion, see Archer, p. 332.
36. Sotheby's, London, 10th Mar. 1981, Lot 139.
37. Victoria & Albert Museum, C.21-1980, and Glasgow Museum, E.1978-24.
38. Horne, Catalogue 1, (1981), No. 14.
39. Fitzwilliam Museum, Cambridge, Glaisher coll., G. 1549, acc. no. 1549-1928.
40. Compare, for example, the shell-form Bow salt illustrated by Gabszewicz & Freeman, pl. 42., p. 43.
41. Archer, p. 360.
42. One example of this pair is in the National Museum of Ireland, (Acc. No. 1909 - 667), the other is on permanent loan to the Ulster Museum, (Nat. Mus. Acc. No. 1909-668).
43. Another pair of blue-painted flower-bricks attributed to Dublin, with a wavy basal edge, was illustrated by Longfield in 1971, (pl. 8). The arrangement of the pierced holes matches the Dublin examples described here, and the style of flower painting also supports the attribution, but without examining the pieces it is difficult to be certain. The dimensions and painter's marks were unrecorded.
44. Cf. Austin, pp. 266 - 70.
45. Britton, *Bristol,* p. 105, Cat. Nos. 7.30, 7.31, 17.17. The forms are identical to some Dublin examples (e.g. Fig. 151), but the styles of painting are unlike any yet recorded on Dublin delftware.
46. Sotheby's New York, Oct. 19th 1994, Lot 171. (L. 5⅞ in., 150 mm.). I am indebted to Garry Atkins for spotting this example.
47. Reading Museum and Art Gallery, Acc. Nos. 1961.240.26 & 33. (L. 5½ in., 140 mm., W. 2½ in., 64 mm., Ht. 2¾ in., 70 mm.). Illustrated in J. Kinghorn and G. Quail, *Delftfield, A Glasgow Pottery, 1748-1823,* Glasgow Museum & Art Galleries, (1981), p. 34.
48. Rosanne Meenan, 'Delamain Pottery Excavated From Dublin Castle', *Irish Arts Review Yearbook,* (1991-2), p. 154.
49. Even a cursory examination of the available literature indicates that continental tin-glaze plates more commonly possessed this type of wavy-edged or shaped margin than English delftwares. In one book on French faience, for example, more than 90% of the 18th-century plates illustrated possess shaped rims. See C. Dauguet & D. Guilleme-Brulon, *reconnaître les origines des faïences françaises,* Paris, (n.d., c.1985).
50. Jonathan Kinghorn and Gerard Quail, *op. cit.* at n. 47 above, p. 34.
51. Austin, p. 167. Notes to Cat. 288.
52. Michael Archer, 'Irish Delftware: an exhibition at Castletown House', *The Connoisseur,* (Oct. 1971), p. 103.
53. Gabszewicz and Freeman, pl. 22, p.33. This is a circular plate of similar size to the Dublin plates, painted with a polychrome flower-spray. (Diam. 9 in., 229 mm.). Plates with trellis-moulded margins were produced at Derby, c.1760, but the moulding is quite unlike the Dublin pieces. (See Phillips, Watney Sale Pt.1, 22 Sep 1999, Lot 373).
54. For example, the *'Pine Cone Group',* c.1770-85, and the *'Wispy Chrysanthemum Sprays',* c. 1770. See L. Branyan, N. French & J. Sandon, *Worcester Blue & White Porcelain, 1751-1790,* (1981), pp. 332-337.
55. *Ibid.,* pp. 217-220. Gabscewicz & Freeman, pl. 95, p. 70, illustrate a moulded Bow coffee-pot, c. 1760-62, with a painted flower spray that is particularly similar to that which appears on the Dublin plates.
56. The second set marked with a '2', painted with the *'Floral Spray & Ribbon'* pattern, is in the Hunt Museum Limerick, acc. no. HCL. 37. The incomplete sets with painters' numbers '3' and '4', both painted with floral sprigs, are in private collections. The example marked 'S' or '8', painted with the *'Chinese Flower-bowl'* pattern, is illustrated in the Castletown exhibition, (No. 36).
57. Lipski & Archer, Nos. *1552-1557,* pp. 352-3.
58. Jonathan Horne postulated a link with Lionel Sackville, Duke of Dorset, (Lord Lieutenant of Ireland 1751-55), in a letter to the National Museum in April 1989. Research conducted since by Mairead Dunlevy suggests that the crest and motto relate to the Wilson family, *(pers. comm. 15th* Aug. 2000).

As can be seen by comparing Colour Plates 21 and 22, these stands were not produced with the same, fine-quality cobalt as the Sackville plates, nor were they dipped in a final, clear lead glaze, (which gives the Sackville plates an unusually 'glossy' surface).

59. Austin, Cat. 132, p. 120.
60. Garry Atkins, March 2000, cat. no. 68.
61. Nat. Lib. Ire., *Westropp Papers,* Ms. 24938. There are seven letters from Mrs. Hodgkin of Old Southcote Lodge, Reading, written to Westropp between the 5th and 21st January 1936.
62. For further details concerning the Hodgkin collection of tiles, see Archer, p. 582-83.
63. Two examples are shown in Archer, p. 478, Cat. Nos. N. 241 & N. 242.
64. R. P. Pentland, (Ed.), *Calendar of State Papers; Ireland, 1666-69,* London, (1908), pp. 354 & 392, letters dated 30st April and 5th July 1667. The painted tiles were purchased for Viscount Conway and Killulta at Lisburn Castle by his agent, Sir George Rawdon, who remarked, *'The gardener says he cannot use half of these and they have been very costly'.*
65. Various private collections. The tureens possess painters' numbers 3, 2, 7 and 12 respectively.
66. Kassebaum Collection, Pt. 1, Sotheby's London, 1st Oct. 1991, Lot 73.
67. Archer Cat. I.20, p. 373.
68. The National Museum platter is painted with two birds, only one of which appears on the vase. Details of the foliage are also identical, and this is certainly the same pattern. The platter possesses no painter's mark, but otherwise conforms to Dublin delftware in every respect.
69. Horne, Pt. XVI, (1996), No. 460 - a pair marked '2' and an unmarked jar (as illustrated). Garry Atkins, (1998), Nos. 38 & 39, showed a pair of lidless 'Ginger Jar' shaped vases and a taller example ($8^{1}/_{2}$ and $13^{1}/_{4}$ in. high respectively).
70. Christies 14th October 1985, Lot 15.
71. For example, a narrow baluster vase with classical ruins, private collection, no mark, Ht. $7^{3}/_{4}$ in. 195 mm.
72. Archer, Cat. I.21, p. 373-4.
73. *Ibid.*

CHAPTER 3: Minor Potteries

3, i. Killiane, Co. Wexford

1. Evelyne Miller, 'The Pottery at Killiane', in *By Bishop's Rath and Norman Fort,* (n.d., c. 1995), p. 51.
2. Society of Friends in Ireland, Swanbrook House, Morehampton Road, Dublin 4. *Quaker Records,* No. 48, Ms. F.6.25, Will of Jonas Chamberlin, 10 Oct. 1695. Ref. courtesy Evelyne Miller.
3. Evelyne Miller, *pers. comm.,* 18th May 2000.
4. *Ibid.* The genealogy is based on the Poole family papers, which appear in Quaker Records, *(op. cit.* at n. 2 above). Thomas Chamberleyne was married to a Dorothy Poole in 1775. (There appears to have been no connection with the Pooles of Liverpool - a distinguished family of delftware potters).
5. The visit took place 28th August 1994.
6. Comparable slipware and sgraffito wares are recorded in J. H. Kelly, 'The Hill Top Site Burslem', *City of Stoke on Trent Mus. Arch. Soc.,* Report No. 3, Hanley, (1969), and R. Coleman-Smith & T. Pearson, *Excavations in the Donyatt Potteries',* Chichester, (1988).
7. M. Dunlevy, *pers. comm.*, 20th April 2000.
8. The straw colour of the delftware body is distinctly different from the white-ware shards.
9. Dunlevy, *pers. comm.* 15th May 1998. *'Cups, jugs etc. held locally and in Youghal or Enniscorthy museums are attributed to Chamberlains, but* [appear to be] *early 19th century Staffordshire'.*

3, ii. Rostrevor

1. W. A. McCutcheon, *The Industrial Archaeology of Northern Ireland,* Fairleigh Dickinson University Press, Cranbury N. J., (1984), p. 54.
2. Tony Canavan, *Frontier Town, An Illustrated History of Newry,* Blackstaff Press, Belfast, (1989), p. 82.
3. Eileen McCracken, *The Irish Woods Since Tudor Times,* Queen's University Belfast, (1971), pp. 55-6.
4. *BNL,* Feb. 10th 1758, p. 3. Advertisement offering 3000 acres of land for sale by *'Robert Ross of Rosstrevor'.*
5. Westropp (1935), p. 34.
6. Robert Jocelyn, successively Solicitor-General, Attorney-General, Lord High Chancellor of Ireland, and twelve times a Lord Justice in the absence of the Viceroy, created Baron Newport of Newport [Ireland] in 1743, and Viscount Jocelyn [Ireland] in 1755.
7. Westropp (1935), pp. 34-5.
8. *Dub. Jour.,* Oct. 16th 1753. See p.49.
9. *Dub. Jour.,* Mar, 29th 1743.
10. Westropp (1935), p. 35. The wording of this text is ambiguous. It might indicate that Rostrevor delftware, rather than Carrickfergus clay, was *'frequently exported to foreign parts'.*
11. *Northern Ceramic Soc. Newsletter,* No. 28, (1977), item 19. I am grateful to Michael Archer for this reference.

3, iii. Youghal

1. For coarse-earthenware manufacturers, see Westropp, p. 35. A Youghal jug is illustrated by Tenison Little, 'The Ceramic Art of Ireland', *The Antique Collector,* Feb. 1966, p. 28.
2. *Ibid.,* Longfield, p. 53.
3. Charles Smith, *The Ancient & Present State of the County & City of Cork,* Vol. II, 2nd Ed., Dublin, (1774), p. 245.
4. Robert Day, 'Historical Notes ... Book II, Chapter I, Town of Youghal', *Jour. of Cork Hist. & Arch. Soc.,* Vol. I, (1892), Pt. III, pp. 69-71. See also Robert Day, *Jour. Royal Soc. Antiquaries of Ire.*, Vol. 33, (1903), pp. 321-2.
5. The armorial plate illustrated by Day in 1892 appears here as Fig. 52. A second plate, inscribed *'EH 1738'* is listed in Lipski & Archer, (No. 423, p. 98), and is similar to a plate inscribed *'MH 1738'* which they illustrate, (No. 422).
6. Patricia Lyons, 'The Cloyne Mineral Company', in Pádraig Óloingsigh (ed.), *The Book of Cloyne,* No. 47, pp. 286-296.

3, iv. Belfast II, The Little Patrick Street Pottery

1. PRONI, Donegall Ms., D509/91. For further information on locating this pottery site, see Francis, (1992), pp. 124-8.
2. Detail of the 1757 map of Belfast showing relative positions of the Little Patrick Street pottery and the Belfast Potthouse. The original map is illustrated in G. Gamblin, *The Town in Ulster,* (1951), pl. 31.
3. Agnew, *Belfast,* pp. 245-6 & pp. 253-4. Improved understanding of the genealogy of the Galt and Smith families clearly indicates that John Galt Smith was not Patrick Smith's nephew, but a family relationship probably existed nonetheless.
4. PRONI, Donegall Ms., D509/91.
5. PRONI, Mussenden Ms., D354/351. *'Rents of Pothouse Lease, 2nd Nov. 1763'.*
6. The lease ran along present day Corporation Street, close to the eighteenth-century shore, and hence was set some distance from the original *'Belfast Potthouse'.* The earlier *'Belfast Potthouse'* could not, therefore, have been the pottery referred to in the name *'Pothouse Lease',* (n. 5 above).
7. For further information on Greg's creamware pottery, see P. Francis, *A Pottery by the Lagan; The Downshire Pottery in Belfast, 1787-c.1806,* Queen's University/Ulster Museum Belfast, *(at press).*
8. *BNL* 9 Sep. 1763. Thomas Greg made the first voyage on the Lagan Canal to Lisburn, with much celebration.
9. Thomas Greg's name is actually better known in England in the context of pottery than it is in Ireland, thanks to the *'Thomas Greg Collection'* of early ceramics, which now resides in Manchester City Art Gallery & Museum. This collection was formed by Thomas *Tylston* Greg, a great-great grandson of the Thomas Greg who lived in Belfast. Thomas's son, Samuel, (see Fig. 191), left Belfast to establish the Quarry Bank cotton mill at Styal in Cheshire in 1784. It was from this branch of the family that Thomas Tylston Greg was descended.
10. M. Mulholland, *Brown Ware: A Post-Mediaeval Pottery Assemblage in Ireland,*

unpublished B.A. Thesis, Dept. of Archaeology, Queen's University of Belfast, (1988).
11. The area was visited on several occasions between late July and mid-September 1992.
12. Lipski & Archer, pp. 386-90, nos. 1595-1673.
13. H.H. Cotterell, *Old Pewter, Its Makers* & Marks, London, (1929), Plate VII. The trade card of pewterer John Alderson of London, *(fl.1764-82)*, shows that tankards and handles of this form remained in fashion during the 1760s C. A. Peal, *British Pewter & Britannia Metal,* New York/London, (1971), p. 135, indicates that the *'broken scroll'* handle form was introduced in pewter c.1750.
14. For example, see Horne, XVI, No. 454.
15. I am indebted to Robert Heslip of the Ulster Museum, Belfast, for his help with this interpretation, and for finding examples of comparable, locally made, brass sundials.
16. N. Cumnock (ed.), *The Journal of the Rev. John Wesley, A.M.,* London, (1909), Vol. IV, pp. 178-9.

3, v. Dublin II, Stoneybatter

1. Nat. Lib. Ire., Westropp Papers, MS 24938. Transcribed from the Minutes of the Royal Dublin Society.
2. *Ibid.*
3. Longfield, p. 49.
4. *Ibid.*
5. Westropp, (1935), p. 30.
6. *Ibid.*
7. *Ibid.*. The additional name of James Murphy is mentioned in the Nat. Lib. Ire., Westropp Papers, MS 24938. Westropp seems to have located this extra information in the Minutes of the Royal Dublin Society, after 1935.

An advertisement relating to the event also appeared in George Faulkner's *Dublin Journal* of 9th - 12th August 1766; *'Whereas it appeared this day to the Dublin Society, that Ambrose Henly, Manufacturer of Earthen-ware, did on the 19th of June last, impose upon the Society, by producing false evidence concerning the Quantity of Earthen-ware manufactured by him as was alledged and for which he fraudulently obtained a Premium of £70. The Society came to the following resolution, That the said Ambrose Henly and James Murphy shall be incapable hereafter of receiving any Premium, bounty or mark of favour whatsoever from this Society.'.*

8. Archer, *pers. comm.* March 2000.

3, vi. Limerick

1. 'J. Ainsworth, (ed.), *Baron Inchiquin, The Inchiquin Manuscripts,* Dublin, (1961). Notes to entry No. 614 (the Michael Stritch letter) provide details of further receipts from Stritch for glass, provisions &c.
2. L. M. Cullen, *The Irish Brandy Houses of Eighteenth-Century France,* Lilliput, Dublin, (2000), p. 46, 48, 51, and *pers. comm.* 28th Apr. 2000.
3. The *'Primate's Coals'* bowl probably *incorporated* fireclay in its manufacture to improve heat resitance, but neat fireclay, on its own, had insufficient porosity for a satisfactory delftware biscuit.
4. George Minty received a premium of £20 in 1758 for fireclay crucibles, made of clays from coal mines in Co. Kilkenny. See P. Francis, 'The Glass-Maker's Memoirs: George Minty's "Crusonian" Adventures in Ireland, 1746-1757', *Journal of Glass Studies,* Corning Museum New York, Vol. 42, (2000), pp. 113-131. See also Section 2,1 iv above, n. 26.
5. Westropp, (1935), p. 31, from The *Dublin Evening Post,* 22nd Nov. 1785; *'The English take away our clay from Carrickfergus for Liverpool earthenware, and the Dutch procure it from Waterford for the manufacture of their delft and Rouen ware. So valuable is this article to them, which is brought on horses from the Devil's Bit mountain in Co. Tipperary to Clonmel, and from thence transported in small boats to Waterford, that our correspondent has known a Dutch vessel of 200 tons remain nine months in the river for cargo. If this were not exported, it would be the means of keeping at home £15,000, which is annually remitted to England for earthenware'.*
6. Robert Kane, *The Industrial Resources of Ireland,* Dublin, 2nd ed., (1845), p. 231 *'Mr. Griffith describes an extensive district ... in Tipperary, between Cahir & Clonmel, which he considers equal to the pipe clay of Bovey. It burns purely white, and in the extreme heat of a porcelain furnace only acquired a very slight buff tinge. Large quantities of this clay have been exported to England, but no use has ever been made of it at home'.*
7. *Gentleman's Magazine,* Vol. 64, Pt. 2, (1794), p. 1045, *'Cork, Oct. 22. Mr. Raspe the celebrated Mineralogist has been lately in this city, after having explored the mines in the vicinity of Killarney. His researches have been crowned with the greatest success; among many others, he has discovered the richest cobalt mine in Europe, a ton of ore of which is computed, at a moderate calculation, to be worth £250 sterling; and what renders this ore more precious is, that it is in great demand in China, where the India Company export annually to the amount of £180,000 worth, which they principally draw from Saxony at very heavy expense'.*
8. Mairead Dunlevy, *pers. comm.,* c. 1995 and 15th May 2000.
9. Dunlevy and Starr, *pers. comm.,* c. 1995. The results of Michelle Starr's researches do not appear to have been written up.
10. Westropp, (1935), p. 35 and Longfield, p. 51.
11. Longfield, p. 51.
12. Westropp, (1935), p. 35.
13. W. B. Honey, 'Limerick Delftware', *ECC Trans.,* Vol. 2, No. 8, (1942), pp. 155-57.
14. The original engravings were probably produced on copperplates, and transferred onto the delftware surface by the *'glue bat'* method. For further information on the methods employed see D. Drakard, 'Early On-glaze Transfer Printing', *ECC Trans.,* Vol. 15, Pt. 3, (1995), pp. 331-40.
15. Honey, *op. cit.* at n. 13 above, p. 156.
16. *Ibid.*
17. Archer, notes to Cat. F.40, p. 306-7.
18. *Ibid.*
19. David Drakard in, *Made in Liverpool,* ex. cat. Nat. Mus. & Gall. on Merseyside, (1993), Cat. No. 198, p. 127.
20. Compare for example, Gabszewicz & Freeman, pl. 121, p. 83, with the arms of the *'Anti - Gallican Society'.* See also S. Spero, *18th Century English Transfer-Printed Porcelain and Enamels, The Joseph M. Handley Collection,* Carmel, California, (1991), p. 196, pl. 7.9, a Bow plate with mimic *'Arms of the Moderns'.* A Worcester plate, with a blue line *inside* the edge, is illustrated as pl. 7.1.
21. Gabszewicz & Freeman, Plates 119-120, p. 83-4.
22. See Drakard, *op. cit.* at n. 14 above.
23. A Dublin *'Broken-Scroll'* plate, in a private collection, with painter's number 13 on the reverse, is 222 mm. in diameter.
24. Nicholas Mosse, *pers. comm.,* 28th July 2000. See also Susan Benjamin, *English Enamel Boxes,* London, (1978), pp. 30-35 for further details of the manufacturing processes.
25. See Castletown, Appendix B, pp. 25-6, for further discussion. See also notes 36 and 37 to the introduction of the present work.
26. Cyril Cook, 'James Gwin and his Designs on Battersea Enamels', *Apollo,* (March 1952), pp. 66-69. Brooks is recorded living with Gwin at *'Mr. Rose's in Broad Sanctuary, Westminster'* in 1761 and 1763. He resided with Gwin subsequently at *'The Buffalo'* in Bloomsbury, probably also with Charles Spooner, another Irish mezzotinter. Gwin died there on 26th April 1769, but there is no further mention of Brooks.
27. Westropp, (1935), p. 14.
28. Colin Wyman, 'A Review of Early Transfer Printing Techniques', *ECC Trans,* Vol. 16, Pt. 3, (1998), pp. 307-316. The transfer-printing method appeared in Jean Andre Rouquet's *L'Etat des Arts en Angleterre,* Paris, (1755).

3, vii. Other Potteries

1. Westropp, (1935), p. 34.
2. *Ibid.*, p. 35.
3. See Kane, *op. cit.* at Section 3, vi., n. 6 above.
4. For further information on the country potteries of Coalisland, see M. McManus, The Potteries of Coalisland, Co. Tyrone; some preliminary notes', *Ulster Folklife,* Vol. 30, (1984), pp. 67-77.
5. *BNL*, Sept. 4th 1759 p. 3.
6. *BNL*, Fri. July 24th 1772, p. 1.
7. Fieldwork conducted by the author, 18th & 19th July 1995. The eighteenth-century pottery site is not evident on the first O.S. map. (1833).
8. W. A. McCutcheon, *The Industrial Archaeology of Northern Ireland,* Fairleigh Dickinson Univ. Press, (1984), p. 341.
9. Information concerning the 'The *Ulster Pottery Co.'*, as it was called, is based on the author's unpublished research. Examples bearing red or black transfer-printed marks and the text *'Coalisland Ireland'* are in the Ulster and Armagh Museums. Mr. J. Walsh of Annaghmore found wasters of these wares in the 1980s during building work on the site of the Ulster Fireclay Works.
10. Westropp, (1935), p. 29.
11. *Ibid.*, pp. 37-40.
12. Dr. Bernard Watney, 'A China Painter Writes to an Earl', *ECC Trans.*, Vol. 11, Pt. 1, (1981), pp. 48-9.

Appendix I, Carrickfergus Clay

1. Sheila Speers, Ulster Museum, *pers. comm.* 1991. The research extended over a period of fifteen years.
2. Francis, (1992), Section 3, and Appendices 1-4.
3. *Ibid.*, Appendix 1.
4. Described as *'bluish white'* by John Angel, *A General History of Ireland,* Dublin, (1781), and as *'light blue'* by Samuel McSkimmin, *The History and Antiquities of the County of the Town of Carrickfergus from the Earliest Records',* Belfast, (1811), p. 225. The remark that *'The clay should be three years old before it is used'* was made by William Delamain in 1762, (see p.62).
5. R. J. Charleston, 'Bristol and Sweden: Some Delftware Connections', *ECC Trans., Vol. 5,* Pt. 4, (1963), pp. 222-234.
6. Quoted by L. Weatherill & R. Edwards. 'Pottery Making in London and Whitehaven in the late seventeenth-century', *Post. Med. Arch.,* Vol. *5,* (1971), p. 164. Dwight prepared his delftware clays with a mixture of 3 parts *'Red Clay', 5* parts *'Blue Clay'* and 7 or 8 of *'White Clay'.* Carrickfergus clay was the almost certainly the equivalent of Dwight's *'White Clay'.*
7. See notes to Table App. Ib, p. 168.
8. I am grateful to potter Nicholas Mosse of Bennettsbridge for his help in understanding some of this terminology, and in describing the possible implications for delftware potters.
9. It is important to note that the calcium carbonate was not present as nodules or fragments, (which would simply explode in the firing). Rather, it was present in ionic form, within the clay lattice. When fired, the calcium carbonate liberated carbon dioxide, increasing the porosity. The calcium oxide that remained formed complex calcium-iron silicates with the iron-rich clays, diluting the intensity of their red colour.
10. During the last glaciation, Carrickfergus lay next to the outlet of a major ice-bound lake or 'outwash channel', which cut a deep gorge in limestone cliffs behind the town (the 'Woodburn Glen'). These river waters were therefore rich in dissolved calcium bicarbonate, which precipitated as calcium carbonate in coastal clays, as the freshwaters met seawater at the river mouth.
11. Initial attempts to produce delftware tiles at Liverpool's Lord Street pottery in 1701 relied on a *'blue slutchy clay'* from the shore, but Carrickfergus clay was later used. (The local name in Belfast for a Carrickfergus-type clay is a blue, estuarine *'sleech').* See PRO Liverpool, *Entwistle Ms,* 2, p.6 for further details. Glasgow's failed attempts to use local, estuarine clays are described in J. Kinghorn & G. Quail, *Delftfeld, A Glasgow Pottery 1748-1823,* Glasgow, (1986), pp. 18-9.
12. I. Noel Hume, 'Early English Delftware from London and Virginia', *Colonial Williamsburg Occasional Papers in Archaeology,* Vol. II, (1977), p. 12.
13. A Toppin, 'The China Trade & Some London Chinamen', *ECC Trans.,* Vol. 1, No. 3, (1934), p. 37.
14. F. Britton, 'Carrickfergus Clay', *ECC Trans.,* Vol. 15, Pt. 2, (1994), pp. 308-9.
15. P. Denholm, 'Pottery Exports from Port Glasgow to the Americas', *Scottish Pottery Archive News,* No. 4, (1979).
16. Scottish & English customs records seem to have been separately kept. The lack of agreement in some years confirms this, (e.g in 1756, more clay was sent to Glasgow alone than to all of England).
17. The figure is based on four assumptions.
1. Each ton was 2400 lbs wt. (As stated by Daniel Mussenden, 1748).
2. Carrickfergus clay was mixed with local clays in a 1:1 ratio. (See n. 6 above).
3. A weight loss of 30% occurred on firing, (described by potter Alan Caiger-Smith as a good *'rule of thumb'* estimate).
4. That an average piece of delftware weighed one pound. (An estimate suggested by P. Denholm, *op. cit.* at n. 15 above).
300 tons of clay therefore equates to 1,008,000 lbs. or pieces of delftware.
18. For further notes on these records, see Francis (1992), Appendices 2-4.
19. From Port Books, Chancery Lane. (No ref. given). See Francis, (1992), App. 2, pp. 178-80 for further notes from F. Britton.
20. Kinghorn & Quail, *op. cit.* at n. 11 above.
21. No author, *'State of the Mutual Process Betwixt John Bird, late of London, Potter, and Robert Dinwiddie, Merchant in London, Laurence Dinwiddie and Patrick Nisbet, Merchants in Glasgow and Robert Finlay Tanner there'*, published Nov. 1st, 1750. Royal Faculty of Procurators' Library, Glasgow.
22. RoD 44.89.27695, 1st August 1723, James Savage of Annacloy to James Kirk, Town Clerk, (late in the possession of John Kirk deceased and William Taylor).
23. RoD 66.413.47180, 29th & 30th Sept. 1731, Ann Smith of Carrickfergus Widow to her sister Mary Atkinson *alias* Taylor.
24. *Ibid.*
25. PRONI, Millin Mss, T811/2, p. 209. Assignment 20th May 1727 included brick pits owned by James Cobham.
26. For further information on Thomas and Stewart Banks see Shannon Millin, *Additional Sidelights on Belfast History,* Belfast (1938), pp. 98-103. Thomas Banks of the Potthouse had died in 1746.
27. Young, *Town Book,* p. 255-6. William Smith was made a Freeman 13th Nov. 1656, William Taylor was made Free on the 20th November. Both paid an unusually large sum of money for their freedom. (Smith £2, Taylor £2.10.00).
28. Agnew, *Belfast,* pp. 245-6. David & Patrick Smith's wives are known to have been Grissell Clugston and Margaret Bennet.
29. The relationship of a Samuel Smith, *tanner*, who was an important Belfast merchant at this time, has not been established. He may have been a brother of William Smith. He was certainly the father of Patrick Smith *junior* (see Section *2,* 1 i, *'John Chambers',* n. 9), who also appears to have been a relative of *'Ann Smith, widow'.*
30. RoD 70.20.47181, 22nd & 23rd Oct. 1731, Mary Atkinson to David Crawford. For mention of David Crawford see Agnew, *Belfast,* p. 220.
31. See Chap.1, n.47 above.

Appendix II

1. The versions of Delamain's letters that appear here are transcribed from Castletown, Appendix B, pp. 26-29. The originals now reside in the National Museum of Ireland.

Key to Marks illustrated in Figure 58, p.68 and Inside Back Cover.

Note : Marks indicated below by the prefix (UR) are painted *under the rim* of flatwares. All other marks on flatwares appear *within the footrim*.

Where possible, every attempt has been made to reproduce these marks at actual size, and to maintain their correct relative proportions. However, as many of the marks illustrated were taken from photographs without scale, or were copied form secondary documents, there are likely to be inaccuracies.

The numbers recorded on Dublin delftwares are often small and relatively neat compared to those that occasionally occur on English wares, but as Fig.58 shows, large-sized numbers are not uncommon. The number '5', for example, (No.25), is c.11 mm. high when recorded on standard sized plates of 'Chinese Flower-bowl' pattern, but is recorded up to 24 mm. high on large-sized circular platters of the same design.

Abbreviations : C'town = Castletown Exhibition Catalogue, *cf.* = comparable to

No.	*Illustration*	*Source*
1.	Fig. 124	Pierced oval dish, *'Feathers in a Vase'* pattern, private collection.
2.	Fig. 151	Flower-brick, floral decoration, author's collection.
3.	--	Saucer-dish, *Peony/Willow/Fence* design copying Chinese porcelain, private collection, Ireland.
4.	(*cf. Col. Pl. 13*)	Circular plate, *'Chinese Flower Bowl'* pattern, Nicholas Mosse collection.
5.	~~(*cf.* Fig. 124)~~	Pierced oval dish, *'One Bird'* pattern, private collection.
6.	(*cf. Col. Pl. 13*)	Circular plate, *'Chinese Flower Bowl'* pattern, Nicholas Mosse collection.
7.	--	Large circular plate, floral painting copying Chinese porcelain, George Stacpoole collection.
8.	--	Circular soup-dish, *'Flower Spray & Butterfly'* pattern, author's collection.
9.	*Col. Pl. 25*	(UR) Wavy-edge manganese European landscape platter, Ulster Museum.
10.a.	(*cf.* Fig. 157)	Wavy-edged plate, *'Floral Spray & Butterfly'* pattern, Garry Atkins collection.
10.b.	(*cf.* Fig. 157)	Wavy-edged plate, *'Floral Spray & Butterfly'* pattern, Garry Atkins collection.
11.a.	--	Circular soup-dish, *'Floral Spray & Butterfly'* pattern, Jonathan Horne collection.
11.b.	(Col. Pl. 15)	Punch-bowl, *'Three-window House'* pattern, Jonathan Horne collection.
12.	--	Large circular plate, *'Flower Spray & Ribbon'* pattern, Nicholas Mosse collection.
13.	(*cf.* Fig. 88 left)	Large circular platter, *'Feathers in a Vase'* pattern, formerly author's collection.
14.	(*cf. Col. Pl. 13*)	Circular plate, *'Chinese Flower Bowl'* pattern, Nicholas Mosse collection.
15.	(*cf. Col. Pl. 13*)	Circular plate, *'Chinese Flower Bowl'* pattern, Nicholas Mosse collection.
16.	(*cf.*. Austin, 379)	Long, octagonal tureen, *'Chinese Flower-bowl'* pattern, underside of base, private collection.
17.	(*cf. Col. Pl. 24*)	(UR) Wavy-edge circular plate, manganese European landscape, private collection.
18.	Fig. 60	Octagonal plate/soup dish, *'Chinese Flower Bowl'* pattern, Garry Atkins collection.
19.	--	Large saucer dish, *'Feathers in a Vase'* pattern, author's collection.
20.	Fig. 133	Butter tub, *'parasol flower'* pattern, mark at centre of glazed base, private collection.
21.	Fig. 60	Octagonal plate/soup dish, *'Chinese Flower Bowl'* pattern, Garry Atkins collection.
22.	(*cf. Col. Pl. 24*)	(UR) Wavy-edge circular plate, manganese European landscape, private collection.
23	(*cf. Col. Pl. 25*)	Wavy-edged oval platter, manganese European landscape, National Museum of Ireland, (C'town 48).
24.	(*cf.* Fig. 90)	Large octagonal platter, *'Sampan Lake'* pattern, author's collection.
25.	Fig. 88 left	Circular plate, *'Feathers in a Vase'* pattern, author's collection.
26.	(*cf.* C'town 49)	(UR) Wavy-edged oval platter, blue European landscape, private collection.
27.	Fig. 94	Octagonal soup dish, *'Peony & Bamboo'* pattern, Ulster Museum.
28.	Fig. 95	Large octagonal platter, *'Peony & Bamboo'* pattern, private collection.
29.	(*cf.* Fig. 60)	Large octagonal platter, *'Chinese Flower Bowl'* pattern, private collection.
30.	Fig. 171	Tureen, lid & stand, *'Peony & Fence'* pattern, Victoria & Albert Museum.
31.	Fig. 149	Flower brick, floral decoration, Ulster Museum.
32.	C'town 97	Tureen & lid, *'Feathers in a Vase'* pattern, private collection.
33.	Fig. 150	Flower brick, floral decoration, National Museum of Ireland.
34.	Fig. 100	Circular plate, *'Two Deer & Pagoda'* pattern, Yvonne Healey collection.
35.	C'town 36	(UR) Sweetmeat Set, *'Chinese Flower-bowl'* pattern, National Museum of Ireland.
36.	C'town 74	Large octagonal dish, *floral/vase/table* design copying Chinese porcealin, formerly Corcoran collection.
37.	Fig. 167	Eight-lobed tray, *'Feathers in a Vase'* pattern, Colonial Williamsburg.
38.	Fig. 125	Pierced oval dish, *'Two Deer & Pagoda'* pattern, Colonial Williamsburg.
39.	Fig. 60	Octagonal plate / soup dish, *'Chinese Flower Bowl'* pattern, Garry Atkins collection.
40.	Fig. 60	Octagonal plate / soup dish, *'Chinese Flower Bowl'* pattern, Garry Atkins collection.
41.	--	Large circular platter, *'Flower Spray & Butterfly'* pattern, formerly Corcoran collection.
42.	Fig. 106	Octagonal platter, *'Two Birds & Bulrush'* pattern, Jonathan Horne collection.

No.	*Illustration*	*Source*
43.	Fig. 134	Oval flat dish, scalloped edge. *'parasol flower'* pattern butter-tub stand, private collection.
44.	Fig. 60	Octagonal plate/soup dish, *'Chinese Flower Bowl'* pattern, Garry Atkins collection.
45.	(*cf.* Fig. 104)	Circular plate, *'Two Birds & Fence'* pattern, Jonathan Horne collection.
46.	(*cf.* Fig. 91a)	Octagonal platter, *'Small Pagoda & Large Flower'* pattern, National Museum of Ireland.
47.	Fig. 88 right	Circular plate, *'Feathers in a Vase'* pattern, author's collection.
48.	(*cf. Col. Pl. 13*)	Circular plate, *'Chinese Flower Bowl'* pattern, Nicholas Mosse collection.
49.	Fig. 91	Large octagonal platter, *'Large Pagoda & Tree'* pattern, George Stacpoole collection.
50.	Fig. 91a, left	Large circular dish, *'Small Pagoda & large Flower'* pattern, author's collection.
51.	*Col. Pl. 14 right*	Large circular dish, *'Radial Flower'* pattern, author's collection.
52.	(*cf.* Fig. 97)	Circular plate, *'Two Deer & Pagoda'* pattern, butterfly border, formerly Corcoran collection.
53.	Fig. 97	Small octagonal dish, *'Two Deer & Pagoda'* pattern, yellow edge, private collection.
54.	Fig. 60	Octagonal plate/soup dish, *'Chinese Flower Bowl'* pattern, Garry Atkins collection.
55.	Fig. 76	Large circular platter, *'Bamboo Fence'* pattern, author's collection.
56.	(*cf. Col. Pl. 13*)	Circular plate, *'Chinese Flower Bowl'* pattern, author's collection.
57.	--	Circular plate, (slightly small - 222mm.), *'Broken Scroll'* pattern, private collection.
58.	Fig. 102	Circular plate, *'One Bird & Insect'* pattern, author's collection.
59.	--	Circular plate, *'Two Birds & Fence'* pattern, Jonathan Horne collection.
60.	(*cf.* Fig. 100)	Circular plate, *'Two Deer and Fence'* pattern, yellow-edge, formerly author's collection.
61.	(*cf. Col. Pl. 13*)	Circular plate, *'Chinese Flower Bowl'* pattern, author's collection.
62.	--	Large circular saucer-dish, *'Chinese Flower-bowl'* pattern, private collection.
63.	*Col. Pl. 13, left*	Circular plate, *'Chinese Flower Bowl'* pattern, author's collection.
64.	(*cf. Col. Pl. 13*)	Circular plate, *'Chinese Flower Bowl'* pattern, Nicholas Mosse collection.
65.	C'town 95a	Small side-plate, *'Chinese Flower-bowl'* pattern, private collection.
66.	Fig. 62	(UR) Octagonal soup dish, *'Flower-lady'* pattern, author's collection.
67.	(*cf.* Fig. 155)	(UR) Wavy-edge circular plate, manganese European landscape. *'trefoil'* border, private collection.
68.	C'town 104	(UR) Octagonal dish, *'Broken Scroll'* pattern, (Revelstoke service). Whereabouts unknown.
69.	(*cf.* Fig. 90)	(UR) Octagonal soup-dish, *'Sampan Lake'* pattern, private collection, Ireland.
70.	Archer, G.24	Large octagonal meat-dish or tureen stand, no footrim, *'parasol flower'* pattern, Victoria & Albert Museum. Mark on centre of reverse.
71.	(*cf.* Fig. 90)	(UR) Octagonal soup-dish, *'Sampan Lake'* pattern, (C'town 81), National Museum of Ireland.
72.	(*cf.* Fig. 90)	(UR) Octagonal soup-dish, *'Sampan Lake'* pattern, private collection.
73.	C'town 110	(UR) Octagonal dish, *'Broken Scroll'* pattern, (Revelstoke service), private collection.
74.	Fig. 92	(UR) Wavy-edged large platter. *'hybrid'* Chinese landscape, National Museum of Ireland.
75.	(*cf.* Fig. 62)	(UR) Octagonal soup dish, *'Broken Scroll'* pattern, private collection.
76.	(*cf.* Fig. 62 top)	(UR) Octagonal soup-dish, *'Flower-lady'* pattern, private collection.
77.	--	Recorded by M.S.D. Westropp on *'Broken Scroll'* pattern service. Whereabouts unknown.
78.	C'town 109	(UR) Octagonal dish, *'Broken Scroll'* pattern, (Revelstoke service), private collection.
79.	Fig. 62	(UR) Octagonal soup dish, *'Broken Scroll'* pattern, author's collection.
80.	Fig. 62	(UR) Octagonal soup dish, *'Broken Scroll'* pattern, author's collection.
81.	C'town 40	(UR) Wavy-edge plate, manganese European landscape, National Museum of Ireland.
82.	Fig.153 & Col.Pl.26	*'Armstrong'* Jug - manganese European landscape, National Museum of Ireland.
83.	(*cf.* Fig. 62 lower)	(UR) Octagonal soup dish, *'Broken Scroll'* pattern, private collection.
84.	(*cf.*Fig. 62 top)	(UR) Octagonal soup-dish, *'Flower-lady'* pattern, private collection.
85.	(*cf.* Fig. 62 top)	Octagonal soup-dish, *'Flower-lady'* pattern, private collection.
86.	Fig. 123 right	Pierced basket dish, *'Flower-lady'* pattern, private collection.
87.	--	(UR) Large Octagonal Platter, *'Broken Scroll'* pattern, Nicholas Mosse collection.
88.	C'town 107	(UR) Octagonal dish, *'Broken Scroll'* pattern, (Revelstoke service). Whereabouts unknown.
89.	--	Recorded by M.S.D. Westropp on *'Broken Scroll'* pattern service. Whereabouts unknown.
90.	Fig. 123 left	Pierced basket dish, floral painting, private collection.
91.	--	Pierced basket dish, recorded by M.S.D. Westropp. Whereabouts unknown.
92.	(*cf.* Fig. 123 right)	Pierced basket dish, *'Flower-lady'* pattern, National Museum of Ireland.
93.	C'town 103	(UR) Octagonal dish, *'Broken Scroll'* pattern, (Revelstoke service), private collection.
94.	C'town 57	(UR) Large octagonal platter, *'Sampan Lake'* pattern, private collection.
95.	(*cf.* Fig. 144)	Large Drug Jar, inscribed *'George Wilson Druggist'*, National Museum of Ireland.
96.	Fig. 144b	Large Drug Jar, inscribed *'George Wilson Druggist'*, National Museum of Ireland.
97.	C'town 42	(UR) Wavy-edge plate, manganese European landscape, private collection.

presumably Sybil Connolly

where is oct. soupdish cf

where is Sampan Lake from NMI?

C'town 81 is shown as private collection John Corcoran

No pic (refers to C'town 81 which is a diff version of Sampan Lake than PF. fig 90. & mark 57 (C'town) = mark 94 - PF

Nb. 57 C'town is also shown as in pve collection - Sybil Connolly

INDEX

C

D

G

H

I

J

K

N I = not illustrated

Nb - marks are not to scale & should not be compared to eachother

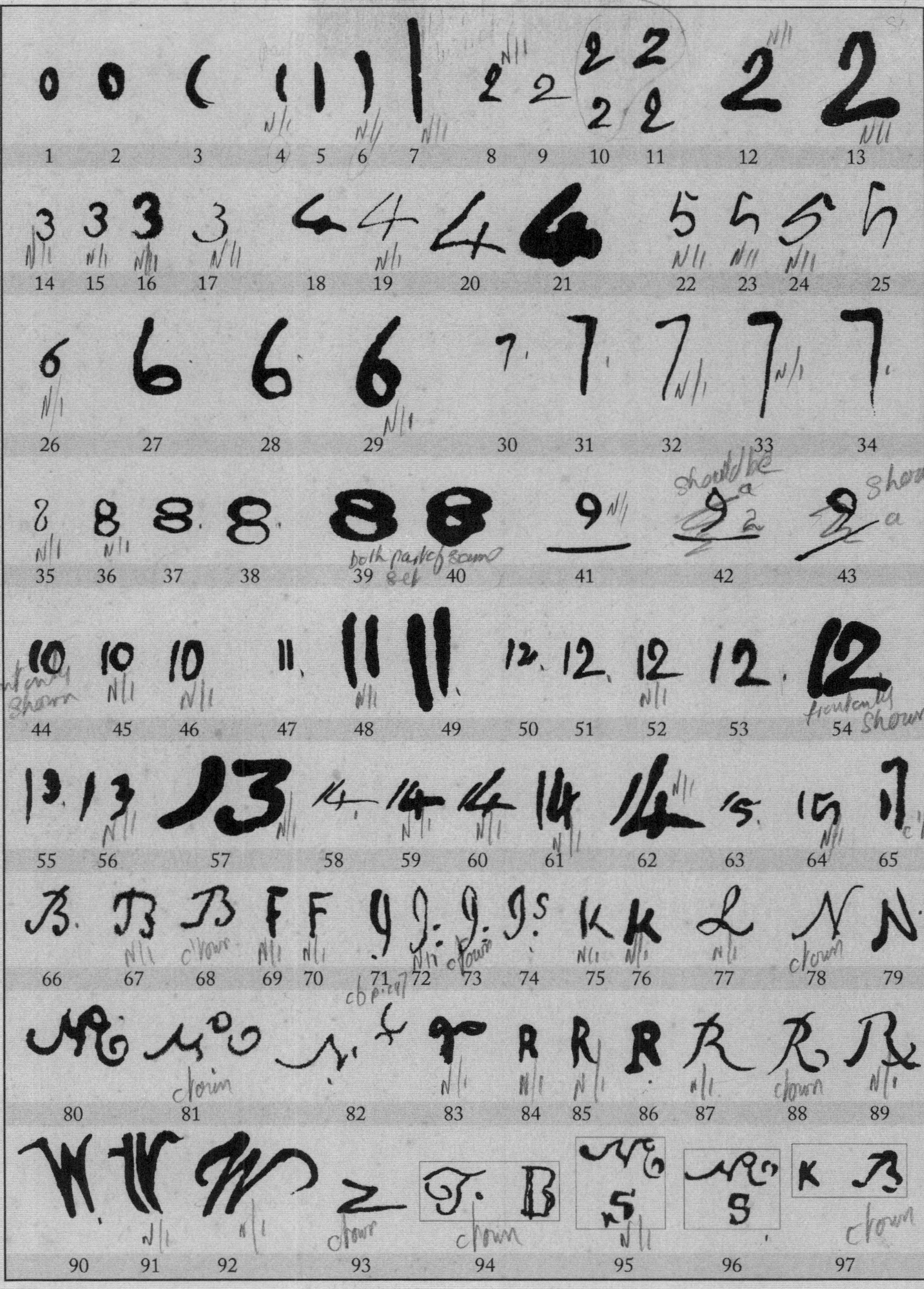